THE THIN JUSTICE OF INTERNATIONAL LAW

The Thin Justice of International Law

A Moral Reckoning of the Law of Nations

STEVEN R. RATNER

OXFORD
UNIVERSITY PRESS

OXFORD
UNIVERSITY PRESS

Great Clarendon Street, Oxford, OX2 6DP,
United Kingdom

Oxford University Press is a department of the University of Oxford.
It furthers the University's objective of excellence in research, scholarship,
and education by publishing worldwide. Oxford is a registered trade mark of
Oxford University Press in the UK and in certain other countries

First Edition published in 2015
Impression: 1

Published in the United States of America by Oxford University Press
198 Madison Avenue, New York, NY 10016, United States of America

British Library Cataloguing in Publication Data
Data available

Library of Congress Control Number: 2014949430

ISBN 978–0–19–870404–1

Printed and bound by
CPI Group (UK) Ltd, Croydon, CR0 4YY

To Nancy, Ben, and Isabel,
With love and appreciation

Peace

WHEN will you ever, Peace, wild wooddove, shy wings shut,
Your round me roaming end, and under be my boughs?
When, when, Peace, will you, Peace? I'll not play hypocrite
To own my heart: I yield you do come sometimes; but
That piecemeal peace is poor peace. What pure peace allows
Alarms of wars, the daunting wars, the death of it?

O surely, reaving Peace, my Lord should leave in lieu
Some good! And so he does leave Patience exquisite,
That plumes to Peace thereafter. And when Peace here does house
He comes with work to do, he does not come to coo,
He comes to brood and sit.

Gerard Manley Hopkins

Acknowledgments

This book has been percolating inside me for many years. As I have grappled with issues of war, peace, and human rights from the perspective of international law, I have been nagged by the sense that the truly paramount questions and answers on these matters were beyond law, in the realm of ethics and morality. As I have discovered and navigated my path through international law and philosophy, many people have helped guide me.

I begin by expressing my appreciation to a group of philosophers who helped me navigate the bridge from international law to ethics and global justice. Robert Kane and John Deigh initiated me into key contemporary philosophical debates while I taught at the University of Texas School of Law. In more recent years, Elizabeth Anderson, Allen Buchanan, and Robert Goodin have shared countless conversations and exchanges with me, simultaneously pointing out the shortcomings of my arguments and encouraging me to dig deeper as well as share my work with philosophers. Other scholars steeped in ethics have provided enormously useful commentary on various chapters of this book—Rainer Forst, Kristen Hessler, David Lefkowitz, Daniel Philpott, and Mathias Risse.

On the law side of the house, many colleagues at the University of Michigan Law School have pored over parts of this book and given me ample and helpful feedback: Kristina Daugirdas, Monica Hakimi, Scott Hershovitz, Don Herzog, Christopher McCrudden, Julian Mortenson, Don Regan, and Mathias Reimann. Robert Axelrod of Michigan's Ford School of Public Policy also provided important suggestions. Beyond Michigan, I thank Eyal Benvenisti, Daniel Bodansky, Peter Cane, Jeffrey Dunoff, David Gartner, Ryan Goodman, Benedict Kingsbury, Dino Kritsiotis, Anne Peters, Brad Roth, Greg Shaffer, and Chantal Thomas for their willingness to read and comment on parts of the manuscript.

This volume benefitted as well from reactions of students and colleagues at presentations I have made over more than a decade at numerous law schools, philosophy departments, and interdisciplinary conferences. In chronological order, they include the University of Georgia School of Law, University of Bern, UCLA Law School, Georgetown Law School, the Institut de Hautes Etudes Internationales et du Développement, Yale Law School, John Marshall Law School, Arizona State University College of Law, New York University School of Law, Università Commerciale Luigi Bocconi, Australian National University's College of Asia and the Pacific Regulatory Institutions Network, Goethe Universität's Normative Orders Cluster, Universiteit Leiden Law School, and the University of Richmond, as well as the University of Michigan Law School and Philosophy Department. In March 2013, Arizona State convened an author's workshop composed of scholars in both ethics and international law whose input proved to be a turning point in my work. I greatly appreciate the hard work of Daniel Bodansky, Daniel Rothenberg, and Emoline Fox in putting together that sunny weekend.

As with the rest of my scholarship, I owe a major intellectual debt to my two greatest teachers of international relations and law, Leon Gordenker and Michael Reisman.

Most of the research on this volume has been conducted since I arrived at the University of Michigan Law School in 2004. I have been most fortunate to have received generous funding for summer research and travel, as well as for a 2010 Roundtable on Interdisciplinary Research on Global Justice, from Deans Evan Caminker and Mark West. Barbara Glipsin provided first-rate logistical support for the 2010 Roundtable. The staff of the Law Library, led by Barbara Garavaglia, was enormously helpful in all aspects of my research. I cannot think of a source the librarians could not provide to me quickly. My faculty assistant, Karen Pritula, has provided immense assistance on all the administrative matters associated with the project. I have been fortunate to have a group of superlative research assistants over the years—Raphaelle Monty, Peter Borock, Betsy Fisher, Sarah Manley, Lara Wagner, and Valian Afshar.

Lastly, at Oxford University Press, John Louth has supported my scholarship within the Press for many years, and Merel Alstein and Emma Endean helped see the parts fall in place seamlessly. Alison Floyd provided exemplary copy-editing of the manuscript.

Although the vast majority of this volume represents material not published before, parts of Chapter 1 appeared in the 2013 volume of *International Theory*, in Ulrich Fastenrath et al. (eds.), *From Bilateralism to Community Interest: Essays in Honor of Bruno Simma* (Oxford: Oxford University Press, 2011), and in Mahnoush Arsanjani et al. (eds.), *Looking to the Future: Essays on International Law in Honor of W. Michael Reisman* (Leiden: Brill, 2010). Parts of Chapter 2 appeared in the 2005 volume of *Legal Theory*, and one part of Chapter 5 appeared in the 1996 volume of the *American Journal of International Law*. An earlier version of Chapter 7 was published in Lukas Meyer (ed.), *Legitimacy, Justice, and Public International Law* (Cambridge: Cambridge University Press, 2009).

Long before I had any inkling of what global justice or human rights were, my parents, Anne and Milton Ratner, encouraged me to learn and think about social justice as well as the fate of those beyond our borders. In the years during which I have made those concerns central to my professional life, I have always been able to count on my wife Nancy and my children, Ben and Isabel, to keep everything in perspective. I cannot offer enough thanks to them for their support in this and all my other endeavors.

Steven Ratner
Ann Arbor

Michigan
September 2014

Contents

List of Shorthand References used in Footnotes xiii

Introduction: Looking for Justice in International Law 1

I. THE FRAMEWORK OF THIN JUSTICE

1. Legal and Ethical Approaches to Global Justice: The Dialogue of the (Near-)Deaf 19
2. Conceptual Groundwork for a Standard of Global Justice 42
3. A Standard of Global Justice 64

II. THE JUSTICE OF CORE NORMS ON STATEHOOD

4. Norms of Territorial Integrity and Political Independence: The Ban on the Use of Force and Non-Intervention 103
5. The Claims of Peoples: Self-Determination and State Borders 143
6. Norms of Participation: Sovereign Equality of States 184
7. Sovereign Equality's Limits: Membership and Decisionmaking Rules in International Organizations 220

III. THE JUSTICE OF TERRITORIALLY-BASED PROTECTIONS OF HUMAN RIGHTS

8. Human Rights for Whom?: Territoriality, Extraterritoriality, and Universal Jurisdiction 267
9. Extraterritorial Protection of Human Rights through Force: From Humanitarian Intervention to the Responsibility to Protect 292

IV. THE JUSTICE OF CORE NORMS ON THE GLOBAL ECONOMY

10. Regulating Global Trade 315
11. The International Investment Regime 349

V. LIMITATIONS AND ASPIRATIONS

12. The Limits of Thin Justice: International Humanitarian, Criminal, and Environmental Law 383
13. Beyond Thin Justice 408

Bibliography 435
Index 463

List of Shorthand References used in Footnotes

Friendly Relations Declaration: Declaration on Principles of International Law concerning Friendly Relations and Cooperation among States in accordance with the Charter of the United Nations, UNGA Res. 2625 (XXV), 24 October 1970

GATT: General Agreement on Tariffs and Trade, 15 April 1994, 1867 UNTS 187

Geneva Conventions I–IV: Geneva Convention (I) for the Amelioration of the Condition of the Wounded and Sick in Armed Forces in the Field, Geneva Convention (II) for the Amelioration of the Condition of Wounded, Sick and Shipwrecked Members of Armed Forces at Sea, Geneva Convention (III) Relative to the Treatment of Prisoners of War, Geneva Convention (IV) Relative to the Protection of Civilian Persons in Time of War, 12 August 1949, 75 UNTS 31

ICC Statute: Rome Statute of the International Criminal Court, 17 July 1998, 2187 UNTS 3

ICCPR: International Covenant on Civil and Political Rights, 16 December 1966, 999 UNTS 171

ICESCR: International Covenant on Economic, Social and Cultural Rights, 16 December 1966, 993 UNTS 3

ILC Articles on State Responsibility: International Law Commission, Responsibility of States for Internationally Wrongful Acts, 2001, UNGA Res. 56/83, Annex, 12 December 2001

UNCLOS: United Nations Convention on the Law of the Sea, 10 December 1982, 1833 UNTS 3

UN Convention Against Torture: Convention against Torture and Other Cruel, Inhuman or Degrading Treatment or Punishment, 10 December 1984, 1465 UNTS 85

VCLT: Vienna Convention on the Law of Treaties, May 23, 1969, 1155 UNTS 331

Note: All abbreviations used in the text (other than UN, EU, UK, and US) are spelled out in full the first time they appear in a chapter. Journal abbreviations used in the footnotes are spelled out in full in the Bibliography.

Introduction: Looking for Justice in International Law

In a world suffused with war and human misery, global justice remains one of the most compelling missions of our time. Philosophers, political scientists, historians, international legal scholars, and others have all sought to make their mark on global justice debates, whether through abstract theorizing, qualitative and quantitative empirical examination, or the development of norms and institutions for effecting justice. Each discipline must eventually put its faith in real-world decisionmakers—states, international organizations, NGOs, corporations, citizens, and others—to carry out its particular visions.

To date, much of the intellectual effort on theorizing global justice has been within political and moral philosophy. Ethical theory from these disciplines has asked the fundamental questions about what individuals or states owe one another and, in some cases, how such relationships can be imagined through domestic and international structures. Scholarship over the last generation or two is quite advanced, moving beyond issues of global distributive justice that dominated in the wake of Rawls' *A Theory of Justice* to address manifold questions of war and peace, self-determination, environmental degradation, global poverty, and others.

Yet philosophical accounts of global justice have more often than not stayed clear of international law, refraining from discussing both its actual workings and the scholarship about it. International law represents a system of norms and processes for resolving competing claims, moral, political, and otherwise, among international actors in a manner both legitimate to them and effective among them. It includes institutions, whether viewed as the conceptual building blocks of world order (for example statehood, global commons, or human rights) or as formal international organizations in which those actors have rights and responsibilities.

International law is critical to global justice in three senses. First, international law transforms moral prescriptions into legally binding rules with implementation mechanisms and processes. Law and legal institutions both constrain and expand opportunities for carrying out visions to advance the cause of global justice. Without some sort of legal form, the ethics of global justice remains academic, or at least incompletely realized. Second, international law tells us something about what morality and justice at the international level mean in the first place. The law is intrinsic to the normative universe of practices, institutions, and expectations that form our understandings about global justice. And third, the rules and structures of international law turn out to have their own morality and represent a real-world, albeit far from ideal, incarnation of a vision of global justice. We can learn a great deal about the current state, as well as future promise and limitations, of global justice by examining the legal regimes to which states have already agreed. Much philosophical work seems to assume the law to be irrelevant for the derivation of theory or has mischaracterized it to suggest fundamental incompatibilities between global justice and international law.

The disconnect is not one-way. International lawyers, for their part, especially academic ones, either ignore global justice as something belonging to morality and thus outside the law; construe it narrowly as international criminal justice or perhaps the decisions of international courts; or equate it, in an undertheorized way, with a greater concern for populations that have been marginalized in the international legal system. The discipline refuses to see the obvious—that so many choices confronting international actors involved in prescribing, interpreting, and enforcing international law are *ethical choices*. Without ethics, the law of global justice is ad hoc or at best a matrix of bargains.

The Argument and its Aims

This book offers a new approach to global justice that integrates the work and insights of international law and ethics. It offers an analysis of the international legal order for its contribution to global justice. My specific thesis is three-fold.

First, I argue that the core norms of international law, even if they came about as a result of political compromises, power politics, and historical contingencies, conform in major respects to a standard of global justice deserving of the name. Under that standard, one that I term 'thin' justice, the justice of international law norms is assessed in terms of two principles or 'pillars'—their advancement of international and intrastate peace and their respect for basic human rights. *Second*, in some important areas, those core norms do not, or might not, meet that standard because they do not reflect the right considerations under those two pillars. Those norms are therefore currently or, if interpreted a certain way by decisionmakers, potentially, unjust. *Third*, reform of the rules and institutions of international law must take account of the justice reflected in the norms to date and, more broadly, the ethical ramifications of choices for new norms. Whether in changing an existing rule to meet the standard of thin justice or aspiring to a higher standard of global justice, we must remain aware of the risks to peace or human rights of alternative rules and not endanger what has been achieved to date.

In making these arguments, my goal is to demonstrate that to build a more just world order, we must understand what has been achieved in international law and institutions, including both the shortcomings of those rules and the risks inherent in some proposals for alternative rules. As Rawls wrote, 'political philosophy may try to calm our frustration and rage against our society and its history by showing us the way in which its institutions, when properly understood from a philosophical point of view, are rational, and developed over time as they did to attain their present, rational form'.[1] In the case of philosophers of global justice, it will, for instance, turn out that some of their calls for major restructuring of international law rely on misunderstandings of key global institutions and thus risk undermining critical normative foundations of the world order. Only this sort of sober appraisal of what has been achieved can pave the way for a path to more just rules. In a word, we must understand the moral character of the existing legal order before we propose changes to it.

But this project will also offer a framework for lawyers and legal scholars who may be designing the rules and institutions of the future. For even those who identify themselves as purely positivist, in the sense of seeing the law's moral content as irrelevant to its status as law, should appreciate that law should reflect certain moral principles. Certainly, international lawyers understand the importance of rules that advance peace and human rights, the values at the heart of the two pillars of justice. But the right balance between those goals is a moral question requiring moral reflection. This study represents one way to move beyond legal analysis centered on the internal coherence of the international legal system to one that can contribute directly to a just international legal order.

An evaluation of the justice of international law is not, however, merely a project for scholars or lawyers. This study thus has a deeper purpose. Because international law is central to constructing a more just world order, we need to give international actors—from presidents and prime ministers to ordinary citizens, from business tycoons to leaders of rebel movements—*good reasons* to respect it and develop it, or good reasons to change it or supplement it. When governments, citizens, or scholars question the justice of international law, a sometimes easy task because some of its features seem a priori unjust, the result is reduced respect for it. This challenge cannot be dismissed on the ground that 'the law is the law' or by reference to the law's formal characteristics (the response of many international lawyers), nor on the ground that the law is irrelevant to global affairs or justice (the response of some political realists). Rather, it needs to be taken on its own terms.

Thus, when it turns out that a set of norms is morally defensible under a considered moral viewpoint, we have provided those actors additional reasons for respecting it beyond just the fear of adverse consequences for ignoring the rules, or an appeal to some inner respect for the law as law, and a good reason to appreciate the consequences of altering the law and its institutions in one direction or another. Where, on the other hand, the critics are right, this study will have given us good reasons to change some rules, as well as guideposts for that change. With greater awareness of the values underlying a just international law, we can move to create new rules that will earn our respect as just. Such an evaluation of the justice

[1] John Rawls, *Justice as Fairness: A Restatement* (Cambridge, MA: Harvard University Press, 2001) 3. As the reader will discover, I am not suggesting that all of international law is rational.

of international law's norms does not overlook the possibility that there may be reasons for us to follow or tolerate even unjust rules—perhaps out of a respect for the rule of law generally or stability—but it gives us the ability at least to discern better exactly what we are doing and why.

So my aim here is to provide those good reasons for stasis or change, as well as a set of guiding principles for the latter. For in the end, we want actors to follow the rules of international law not simply because they are law, but because they are just. To use another term frequently found in legal and political discourse, one might say that a just international law is also a legitimate one insofar as it gives us good reasons to comply with it.[2]

A Project of Non-Ideal Theory

The appraisal of the law and legal institutions in this volume is a project of non-ideal theory in the philosophical sense. While non-ideal theory has a number of meanings, in this case I mean that my approach develops and applies a standard of justice in a way that takes account of core realities of international politics and the global system.[3] It does so in three key ways. First, it assumes the existence and durability of the state system as the dominant organizing political structure for the globe. The system of independent and sovereign states can be justified normatively in a number of ways, which I will discuss, but regardless of one's views about its desirability, it has been around for centuries and seems unlikely to disappear any time soon. Most philosophers long ago abandoned theorizing about a world state not merely because of its impossibility but because, as Kant pointed out even longer ago, of the many dangers it poses to individual liberty (as well as communal autonomy).[4] Although many other clusters of power and authority, public and private, are competing with the state at the internal, transnational, or supranational level, the state system is still absolutely central to global politics.

Second, and relatedly, this foray into non-ideal theory accepts that states will continue to possess different amounts of power, broadly conceived, and that those differences cannot be assumed away. We might hope for a world in which these capacities of states are somehow evened out, but that is not a realistic prospect. We must derive principles of global justice that work within a structure in which such power differentials are likely to persevere in the long term. These heterogenous capacities include the power of some states to refuse to comply with rules

[2] Indeed, as Raz points out, it is often too much to ask any actor to follow the rules solely because they are rules. Joseph Raz, *Practical Reasons and Norms* (Oxford: Oxford University Press, 1999) 178–82.

[3] See Laura Valentini, 'Ideal vs. Non-ideal Theory: A Conceptual Map', *Philosophy Compass* 7 (2012): 654, 658–60.

[4] Immanuel Kant, 'Perpetual Peace: A Philosophical Sketch', in Hans Reiss (ed.) and H.B. Nisbet (trans.), *Kant: Political Writings*, 2nd ed. (New York: Cambridge University Press, 1991) 93, 113–14.

that make heavy demands on them. Non-ideal theory accepts and adjusts to the possibility or reality of non-compliance.

Third, my approach appreciates and takes strong account of the role of institutions in administering law. General visions of and specific proposals for global justice are carried out significantly through institutions, whether the law itself or the organizations and structures that make, interpret, and enforce it. We must understand the institutions we have because they inform both the meaning of and possibilities for justice—even as we may push them to do more or argue for additional institutions. Most importantly, we must remain vigilant to the limited capacities of institutions at the global level compared to those at the domestic level. For instance, once we know more about the International Court of Justice or the UN Human Rights Council, we will have a better sense of their weaknesses as vehicles to carry out a vision of global justice. Taking account of institutions means more than wishing for new institutions to carry out an ideal theory of justice.

The advantages and disadvantages of non-ideal theory are the subject of seemingly endless philosophical debates. I come down squarely in favor of non-ideal theory for the simple reason that I think it is the better route for imagining and achieving a more just world. It sees the world as it is and finds a way to make it better rather than assuming away the most difficult obstacles to the better path. With respect to institutions in particular, as Allen Buchanan has noted, they matter not only because they affect the feasibility of proposals for ethical conduct, but also because they affect the underlying moral justification for the principles in the first place. Failure to consider them results in prescription that ignores the moral costs of changing existing institutions.[5] Ideal theory thus has its place, but it must be complemented by institutionally grounded or referenced theory.

None of these three starting points associated with non-ideal theory equates with an acceptance of the status quo. My approach certainly does not accept all the realities of the international system as fixed—indeed, its project is to improve the prospects for global justice—but it prescribes justice and evaluates international law rules for their justice from certain initial positions, certain core constructs of the international system as it exists today.[6] These choices I make thus rest on my sense that we *must* work from a realistic foundation to propose a better world order, and that we *can* improve the world order with such a starting point. An acceptance of these core constructs is no more inconsistent with an improved status quo than is a doctor's recognition that a broken arm is better healed with a cast than replaced with a new arm. While I recognize the intense disagreements throughout philosophical discourse surrounding decisions on what aspects of the world we must accept before we offer our own views, at a certain point some

[5] Allen Buchanan, *Justice, Legitimacy, and Self-Determination: Moral Foundations for International Law* (Oxford: Oxford University Press, 2004) 22–3.

[6] It could be argued that my project is one of ideal theory insofar as such theory can take account of realities, and that, rather than offering a set of second-best principles, I am offering a vision of justice tailored to its subject, international law. I nonetheless see my approach as distinctive in its integration and acceptance of the three realities so as to be closer to the non-ideal end of theory.

choices must be made. Though I am not seeking Rawls' 'realistic utopia' for the world, I underline his own recognition that we must 'proceed[ ] from the international political world as we see it'.[7]

A Project Grounded in Law

While non-ideal theories of global justice are not new (though they are still the exception rather than the rule), my non-ideal theory is particular in one important sense: it is grounded in international law. By grounded I mean three things. First, the *subject* of my inquiry is international law itself, because I see that law as central to the construction of a just world order. If we have a set of just or unjust core international law norms, namely those that regulate the major claims of global actors, then we are that much closer to or further from, respectively, a more just world order. A just international law cannot be sufficient for a just world order for the same reasons that a just domestic law is not sufficient for a just domestic order—law can only regulate certain aspects of behavior.

But philosophers, even in ideal theory, can theorize about the justice or injustice of international law rules, and some have done so. Thus, second, I see legal concepts and practice as informing, though certainly not determining fully, our understanding as to *what is just*. We can, without being circular, find justice in international law by applying a philosophical conception to legal norms, but also see the corpus of international law as saying something about what is just in the first place. Law is where many of the key claims about what a just world should look like are contested and ultimately resolved through rules. As part of the social context, it is one of many sources that helps generate morality. If we believe that 'ought implies can', that what is morally required must be in some sense feasible, international law tells us much about the 'can' and thus a great deal about the 'ought'. As Peter Cane writes, 'it is a philosophical mistake to think that morality can be properly and fully understood without reference to law. [L]aw has institutional resources that enable it to make a distinctive contribution to answering practical questions about what one ought to do or what sort of person one should aim to be'.[8] This does not mean that we throw out moral concepts and look to the law as the alpha and omega for a standard of justice. Rather, philosophical conceptions of justice, which permeate this book, will be informed by principles, choices, constraints, and opportunities at the heart of a functioning legal system.

Thus, in this study, I will identify and extract certain normative commitments from international law. This strategy does not mean that any values pursued through or by international law are just, but it does claim that those values central

[7] John Rawls, *The Law of Peoples* (Cambridge, MA: Harvard University Press, 1999) 83; see also David Miller, *National Responsibility and Global Justice* (Oxford: Oxford University Press, 2007) 20 (theory of distributional responsibilities designed 'to fit the world in roughly its present condition').

[8] Peter Cane, 'Morality, Law and Conflicting Reasons for Action', *CLJ* 71 (2012): 59, 83–4.

to justice are present, broadly speaking, within international law. Based on these commitments, I then develop a standard of justice that is philosophically defensible as one of justice but also one that reflects its subject—international law—and apply that standard to that law's core norms. My work takes as given Andrew Hurrell's important insight that 'the ethical claims of international law rest on the contention that it is the *only* set of globally institutionalized processes by which norms can be negotiated on the basis of dialogue and consent, rather than being simply imposed by the powerful',[9] a point that offers a cogent rebuttal to skeptics of the law by virtue of its origins in political compromise. As will be seen, I will go beyond that claim by arguing that those ethical claims are not solely a function of the inclusive *process* by which international law emerges and evolves, but also by virtue of the law's *content*. For we will see that much of its content is just when measured against a bona fide standard of justice, even as significant areas fall short.

Third, my study is grounded in law insofar as I believe that it reflects the lawyer's perspective as one of intimate familiarity with *institutions of governance*. Although institutions are central to much non-ideal theory, the lawyer or legal scholar has a special competence and appreciation when it comes to institutions. For lawyers help design such institutions and advance claims—of governments, individuals, NGOs, businesses, and others—through institutions that make, apply, and interpret the law. They focus on the constraints such institutions face; in particular, at the international level, legal scholarship and legal practice is—or at least ought to be—attuned to the capacities of such institutions in a world of independent states with unequal power.

Clearly my choice to look for global justice in international law, and the standard of justice that I will develop, is based on my own professional identity as an international lawyer and legal scholar. As one who has practiced and observed that law, I see Cane's observation as not merely academic or theoretical, but one that I have experienced in looking at legal rules in the process of development and in action. My way of thinking about justice is one that comes, at least in part, from thinking like a lawyer. Political and moral philosophers need not have a monopoly on theorizing about global justice, in particular of the non-ideal variety where one has decided up front to design a system that takes account of important realities—realities which the lawyer has a professionally imposed predisposition to appreciate.

Non-ideal theory grounded in law will offer not just a different approach to global justice; it will, I believe, offer a better one. Theorizing about global justice by examining international law, and with an understanding of law's normative implications, will be a significant improvement in our way of both examining and advancing global justice. For that project is about constructing a better world, not just imagining it. And at least in the case of global justice, we should seek out

[9] Andrew Hurrell, 'International Law and the Making and Unmaking of Boundaries', in Allen Buchanan and Margaret Moore (eds.), *States, Nations, and Borders: The Ethics of Making Boundaries* (Cambridge: Cambridge University Press, 2003) 275, 277 (emphasis in original).

a theory that will actually make the world a better place. Ideal theory, and even non-ideal theory without an appreciation of legal institutions, seems fundamentally deficient in that regard.

The result, then, is that a study looks at the world as it is, including the international law in it, rather than deriving the most morally attractive idea of justice for international law.[10] Rather than a blueprint for a perfectly just world order, it will measure international law against a standard that is most definitely not ideal. The project reflects the need to conduct what Michael Walzer has called 'connected criticism'—'criticism from within the cave, written by critics who [are] committed to the well-being of the society they criticize[]', rather than 'critics who climb the mountain in order to look down on the rest of us and tell us what we are doing wrong'.[11]

Yet the approach is far from a mere description of international law, nor is it an apology for it. First, my vision of justice expresses a normative commitment, one that I will defend in moral terms in Chapter 3. I am not merely matching the law to some idea of justice or, put differently, developing a standard of justice based on some lowest common denominator of the legal system. Second, as will become clear in the appraisals of the individual norms, certain norms or aspects of them will not pass the test of justice that I develop. Third, throughout this volume, I will offer thoughts for the best directions for international law to conform to that standard of justice. And lastly, at the end of this volume, I will offer ideas for how international law should conform to a thicker notion of justice.

These points regarding the value of my approach to global justice can be synthesized in a slightly different manner, based on two connections I see between law and morality generally. These connections build upon H.L.A. Hart's distinction between morality as a quality of certain societal norms of conduct as ethically good (so-called critical morality) and morality as simply the universe of those societal norms of conduct (so-called positive morality).[12] First, the morality—in the first sense of its ethical defensibility—of legal rules can offer us a good (though not conclusive) reason for respecting those rules. International law is important for governing international affairs; the extent to which its norms are moral or just will affect our respect for these rules governing international affairs, and so it is important to explore that justice. And second, the legalized nature of some aspects of morality—in the second sense of the landscape of moral rules—can offer us a good (though not conclusive) reason for respecting that part of morality. International law's status as law and its institutionalized setting should influence, though hardly determine, our views as to what is moral or just in international affairs.

[10] I appreciate clarification on this point from Robert Goodin.

[11] Michael Walzer, 'The Political Theory License', *Annual Review of Political Science* 16 (2013): 1, 5.

[12] H.L.A. Hart, *The Concept of Law*, 3rd ed. (Oxford: Oxford University Press, 2012) 172, 180–3.

The Structure of this Book

I lay out my thesis as follows: Part I devotes three chapters to presenting the analytical framework for this volume. Chapter 1 sets the stage for, and ultimately explains the need for, this study by critically examining the state of scholarly debates on global justice. When we consider the approaches of both international law and ethics, as well as international relations theory, we discover a set of serious shortcomings of each discipline's approach to constructing a just world order and its incapacity in many cases to consider the insights of cognate fields.

Chapter 2 situates my approach by framing and justifying it as one of justice, rather than morality writ large, even if its subject is quite different from that in Rawls' *A Theory of Justice*. It then offers a structural overview of the international legal system, conceptualizing it in terms of participants, claims, and outputs, the last of which are largely, though not exclusively, best seen as duties. It will also lay the groundwork for the standard of justice by discussing the morally acceptable method by which such a standard can be derived. We must start from a position of impartiality, but a standard of global justice will also reflect the distinction between the subject of domestic justice and of global justice. This will lead me to a largely consequentialist framework that sees justice principally in terms of its contribution to a specific state of affairs in the world.

Chapter 3 presents the standard of justice that will be used to appraise international law. That standard is based on two core principles, or what I call pillars—the promotion of international and intrastate peace, on the one hand, and respect for the basic human rights of all individuals, on the other. The justice of international norms will be determined by the extent to which they lead to a state of affairs involving peace and human rights, with some room for deontological considerations in limited situations. The chapter will defend the choice of these two pillars, offer my understandings of peace and basic human rights, and explain their operation in evaluating the justice of individual rules of international law. That form of justice is not as thick as the justice we might minimally demand for domestic polities, nor is it the limit of justice for which we should strive in the international realm, but it is justice deserving of the name—one justifiable from an impartial perspective and, indeed, broadly consistent with a cosmopolitan vision of the world. Like a sheet of titanium, it is thin but strong in its inner structure.

That chapter also builds on the non-ideal theory and grounding in law in two additional ways. First, I introduce two core assumptions regarding the state system that will apply in my analysis. And second, I introduce two conceptual overlays necessary to a project that appraises *legal* norms: one requires us to consider the implications of norms or proposed norms for the rule of law generally and procedural fairness in particular. Although this is not a book on the procedural aspects of international law, which would fill another volume, I will at points highlight the need to be aware of the implications for fairness to participants of certain rules or their alternatives. The second overlay requires us to take cognizance of the prospects for the compliance of key actors with norms or proposed norms. This means that we will have to be cautious in endorsing norms that clusters of important states will not accept, although this does not entail tolerating the status quo simply because some states are reluctant to change it.

In Parts II to IV of the book, I examine the core norms of the international legal system that respond to the claims of the global actors in order to gauge the justice in them. In each case, I offer an attempted crystallization of the law as it currently stands, taking into account areas of disagreement or flux, and then proceed to evaluate the justice of those norms. I also explore claims by international actors and scholars to change the existing norms in one direction or another. In some cases, the law will prove just under my test; in others the law will not. But the arguments of those seeking to change the law will merit as much scrutiny as the status quo. Consistent with my focus on non-ideal theory, I will not explore every conceivable objection to the existing norms, but only those that have been made in diplomatic or scholarly intercourse.

Part II comprises four chapters that appraise the justice of the core norms created in response to the claims of states and peoples. Chapter 4 concerns what I call sovereignty norms, those absolutely critical rules that ban the use of force by states and intervention by one state in another's internal affairs. I will first (ap)praise the UN Charter's prohibition on the use of force and the exception to it for a state's self-defense in response to an armed attack (while reserving the role of the Security Council in repelling aggression and humanitarian intervention for Chapters 8 and 10, respectively). Claims by actors to expand or contract the norm of self-defense, by allowing states to respond to attacks by non-state actors such as transnational terrorists or to respond before an armed attack, will then be scrutinized—some favorably and others less so. As for non-intervention, that norm will prove more limited than some have argued insofar as it does allow for many non-coercive transborder actions by states to influence other states. The chapter will explore the justice of those limits, evaluate proposals for greater or fewer limits, and address some important ways in which the law has changed over time in a way that shows a greater concern for human rights.

Chapter 5 turns to the claims of peoples for self-government, and in particular the law on self-determination that has evolved to address those claims. The law's endorsement of full statehood for colonial peoples seeking independence—one that came on the heels of the wave of decolonization after World War II—will be contrasted with the very limited acceptance of secession as an option for groups dissatisfied with their own state, whether Bosnians or Quebecers. I will also consider and critique alternative rules, proposed by states and scholars alike, either to constrain secessions even more or to allow them more liberally. Along with the rules on self-determination are corresponding rules on the determination of borders. Here I will contrast the merits of the *uti possidetis* rule that turned the imperial boundaries of colonies into the international boundaries of new states with the costs of a rule that would turn the administrative boundaries of seceding provinces into the international borders of states.

Chapter 6 is the first of two chapters on the norms governing the participation of states in the international legal process. It focuses on the sovereign equality of states, the somewhat mystical legal construct that makes states juridically equal, one said by many scholars to be either illegitimate morally or belied by reality. After a brief foray into the rules on the recognition of new states, I will examine and generally endorse three of sovereign equality's key features—the right of states to participate in lawmaking on an equal legal footing, the duty of all states to comply with legal obligations on an equal legal basis, and the immunity of states from the jurisdiction of other states for certain official acts of the state. I will also cast a skeptical eye toward proposals for the law to treat states even more as legal equals as well as critiques of state equality as anti-cosmopolitan or anti-democratic. With respect to the immunity of states and officials, an issue made famous in the saga of Augusto Pinochet in London, full immunity has negative consequences for victims of human rights abuses seeking justice, and I will consider proposals to reduce immunity for international crimes.

Chapter 7 turns to one particularly important aspect of participation based on sovereign equality, namely the practices of international institutions. Those entities and the states in them seem to have interpreted sovereign equality as not preventing them from treating states very differently in terms of organizational membership and decisionmaking. Because international organizations are key venues for the making, interpretation, and enforcement of international law, in this chapter I will emphasize procedural fairness as a central feature, alongside substantive justice. I will first look at the admissions policies of several key organizations, including the UN, the World Trade Organization (WTO), and major European regional institutions, to see if they are just and fair. Turning to internal decisionmaking, I will focus on two institutions whose unequal treatment of states, combined with their massive influence on all states, has elicited great criticism: the United Nations Security Council, including the veto power of the five permanent members (and its contrast with the egalitarian General Assembly), and the International Monetary Fund, with its weighted voting based on member states' financial contributions.

Part III turns to the norms developed to address the claims of individuals. Human rights law raises a nearly infinite variety of fascinating normative questions, but I focus on what I regard as the most fundamental justice-related issue associated with human rights, namely whether states should uphold or defend the rights of people beyond their own boundaries. The starting point of international law is that a state's duties with respect to human rights extend only to those on its territory or otherwise under its control. I examine the justice of this presumption and then turn to the three critical exceptions to it that international law has recognized (even though these three areas are not typically considered doctrinally linked): the extraterritorial effect of human rights law, i.e. the extent of a state's duty to apply human rights law when its acts abroad; universal jurisdiction, namely the rules governing a state's ability to try persons for crimes with no obvious connection to the state; and humanitarian intervention, or the possibility of a state to use force to save lives threatened in foreign countries.

The first two of these are considered in Chapter 8. A norm requiring states to apply some human rights protections extraterritorially helps protect those under the power of a state when it acts abroad, for example by kidnaping them. A norm permitting a state to exercise universal jurisdiction over certain gross violations of human rights offers states the chance to vindicate human rights, although it raises questions about its impact on interstate peace. The third norm, governing humanitarian intervention, will be considered in Chapter 9. Here we will discover a significant disconnect between the black-letter rule of international law prohibiting such acts without Security Council approval and justice, although far less of a gap between what I see as the actual expectations of states and justice. I will also explore an important normative development in this regard, the UN's endorsement of a responsibility to protect those facing rights abuses abroad.

Part IV turns to the justice of international economic law. Because of the large number of potential issues, I focus on the two most relevant and rich bodies of law, those regulating global trade and foreign investment. These two chapters provide an opportunity to address the concerns of many within ethics regarding the distributional aspect of international law's rules. They are structured to address a series of critiques of the law for violating human rights—that the rules deny states 'policy space' to protect the economic rights of their residents, that the rules are applied by institutions skewed toward downplaying human rights, and that the entire body of rules reflects a deep hostility to economic rights and the alleviation of poverty. Chapter 10 will look at the responses of states and the WTO to potential conflicts between trade law and human rights, including issues such as conflict diamonds, intellectual property rules, and health and safety regulations. Chapter 11 will focus principally on the decisions of international tribunals interpreting the rules of investment law for their effect on basic human rights. In both cases, I find some merit in the criticism while revealing a much more complex, and in the end, uncertain picture as to the justice of the rules.

Part V wraps up the study. In Chapter 12, I turn to three important core areas of law where the framework of thin justice reaches some analytical and conceptual limits—international humanitarian law, international criminal law, and international environmental law. In the case of international humanitarian law or the law of war, the effect of norms governing the conduct of war on the prospects for war itself is very hard to discern; and the effect of the norms on human rights turns on ancillary, foundational questions about what it means to enjoy human rights during wartime compared to peacetime. For international criminal law, the decision by states to provide for individual criminal responsibility for only a relatively small number of international law violations is difficult to appraise under either pillar. And in the case of international environmental law, we need to reckon with intergenerational concerns before considering the law's effects on human rights; even then, the framework of thin justice does not consider the effect of the law on non-human species.

Chapter 13 concludes the book by reviewing the bidding regarding the justice of international law norms. It then offers a standard of thicker global justice to which I believe international law can aspire while still working within some of the tough realities of the international system. Rather than a switch to ideal theory, the final chapter offers a move to a different kind of non-ideal theory. The key to achieving more just rules will involve expanding existing duties under international law so that they do more to actively protect human rights, while also ensuring that the new rules do not sacrifice the justice achieved to date. It then considers what the core norms in the study would look like if they achieved this higher standard of global justice, as well as certain procedural requirements for this transition to happen in a fair way that respects the rule of law.

The Boundaries of the Inquiry

Given the potentially vast nature of the task of evaluating the justice of international law, it is important to state some clear boundaries to the present study.

First, my project is to appraise the justice of *norms* of international law rules on certain subjects, not to examine individually whether a particular *action* by an international actor is just. To take one example discussed in Chapter 4, with respect to economic sanctions, my inquiry will not be 'Are the EU's sanctions against this or that repressive government just?' but rather 'Is the norm of international law that permits the EU to impose economic sanctions against that regime just?' This will require that I (a) identify what the rule actually requires, permits, or prohibits of states (a task that may be difficult when rules are in flux); and (b) assess the justice of the rule, not merely with respect to the EU's policies vis-à-vis that state, but with respect to all other conduct either permitted, prohibited, or required under the rule.

An additional project beyond this study's scope would evaluate the morality or justice of individual acts of states or other global actors taken in conformity with those rules. We might presume that all acts taken in accordance with the rule are just, although that is not the only possible conclusion.[13] It might well be the case that in some situations following a just rule of international law leads to an unjust outcome. And many just actions are not mandated by international law, which is, after all, not some sort of comprehensive moral code of global behavior. Like all law, international law has limits as a guide to institutional decisionmaking. But my goal is not to ask what international actors need to do in order to act justly in particular situations, but rather whether the rules they have developed to govern their relations are just.

Second, this book does not focus on the nature of law in general or of international law in particular. I sidestep these enormous jurisprudential and ontological questions and instead assume that treaties, custom, and the other modalities

[13] For one approach deriving from rule-consequentialism, see Brad Hooker, *Ideal Code, Real World* (Oxford: Oxford University Press, 2000) 32–3 (acts would be unjust or immoral if and only if they violate the rules we have determined are just based on the rule's consequences). Hooker's approach is appealing for those rules of international law conceived in terms of duties but less so for rules of international law that are only permissions.

accepted as a matter of practice for prescribing international law do, in fact, have as their output something that we can call law. Questions about the philosophical justification for the norm of *pacta sunt servanda* (the duty to carry out treaties in good faith) or the nature of legal responsibility are also not part of this volume. Despite their interest to philosophers of law and international law, in the end I avoid them for the same reason that I assume a state system—the basic ways of making international law represent a highly settled practice of states, who see it in their self-interest to make law this way, and one that has been accepted in its broadest sense by other actors in the international system. Similarly, I make no claim at all about the formal *validity* of a rule (or norm, terms I will use interchangeably) of international law that turns out to be unjust. I generally assume that unjust rules are still valid, but this too raises hugely complex questions about positivism and natural law that have been central to the debates among H.L.A. Hart, Lon Fuller, Ronald Dworkin, and other legal theorists.

Third, and relatedly, this volume is also not the place for a comprehensive theory of the morality of the processes of lawmaking, which would also occupy another volume. I will thus not ask whether the international legal system, to the extent that we have one, is a just one, even as I recognize that our tolerance for unjust norms may or should depend on the justice of the system as a whole. Nonetheless, in appraising the justice of certain core rules, I will discuss some of the normative difficulties associated with lawmaking by states possessing unequal powers. The chapter on sovereign equality addresses concerns about so-called unequal treaty partners and the dominance of certain states in the formation of custom; and the chapter on international organizations assesses the decisionmaking processes of the UN, the World Bank, and the WTO, that privilege some states over others.

Fourth, and also relatedly, this volume is not concerned with the duties of states or individuals to obey the law. Although I believe that, as a descriptive matter, the justness of particular rules will influence the proclivity of international actors to follow those rules and other rules of a legal system, I refrain from addressing whether we do or should have content-independent reasons to respect international law (or law generally). Certainly, content-independent reasons are important for compliance, in that actors' constant questioning of the morality of rules before following them is highly disruptive to the rule of law domestically or globally. (To that extent, a volume appraising the justice of individual norms may be seen to some as threatening to the rule of law.) But an inquiry into the necessity of such content-independent reasons raises manifold jurisprudential issues about obedience to law that are best left to others.[14] In other words, in claiming that the justice of any norm gives us a good reason to respect or obey it, I do not opine on whether that reason is a necessary one for following any rule. Indeed, I do not even wish to opine whether that reason is a sufficient one, as there may even be reasons to disobey just rules.

[14] See Leslie Green, 'Law and Obligations', in Jules Coleman and Scott Shapiro (eds.), *The Oxford Handbook of Jurisprudence and Philosophy of Law* (Oxford: Oxford University Press, 2002) 514.

Fifth, my choice of norms to evaluate in this volume is based on my own sense of the fundamental norms of international law that respond to the most important claims of the key global actors. This selectivity reflects my own views as an international lawyer, with which some readers may disagree. We might call these core norms constitutive norms, though I make no claims that international law has a constitution or constitutional law. The substantive body of international law is far broader than the ones I analyze. It includes many rules within the general subject matters I address (for example hundreds of rules of trade law not discussed here). And it extends to many other subject areas, not only to familiar ones like the law of the sea but to technical areas ranging from telecommunications to antitrust to global health to international labor.

Many of the rules cannot be appraised from the vantage point of my theory any more than one might ask whether an arcane provision of the tax code or the customs duties can be defended under Rawls' difference principle—they are too divorced from the goals of international justice as I see them for us to have a meaningful appraisal. Indeed, as will be seen in Chapter 12, the framework is not even comprehensive for appraising the justice of even the core rules. Other rules of international law are fundamentally rules of coordination, where justice or morality are strangers, for example rules to avoid collisions at sea or avoidance of radio interference. Others might take this framework to these dark and quiet corners of the international legal landscape, but I will focus on the dominant features of the global legal system.

Sixth, this study is not focused on distributive justice in the sense of the proper distribution of economic benefits and burdens in society. As discussed in detail in Chapter 2, I adopt a broad understanding of justice that extends well beyond distributive justice. And, as the rest of the book demonstrates, I apply my standard of justice to areas of law that, with the exception of those in Part IV, are not principally concerned with economic distributions. Although distributive justice has until recently dominated the philosophical literature on global justice, it is clear to me that treatment of global justice must reach further.

Lastly, I will largely stay clear of the current debates in international law circles about international law's relationship to other legal orders, whether domestic or, potentially, something supranational like the European Union. Many of these issues arise in scholarship under the rubric of global constitutionalism and global pluralism as well. Though these studies address important questions about the supremacy of international law compared to other legal norms, the subject is really quite different from that of justice in the sense of this study.

PART I

THE FRAMEWORK OF THIN JUSTICE

1

Legal and Ethical Approaches to Global Justice: The Dialogue of the (Near-)Deaf

The project of examining the justice of core international law norms proceeds against a background of mutual ignorance and suspicion between the two academic disciplines with the most to contribute to our understanding of global justice—international law and philosophical ethics. The gaps between the distinct approaches of the two fields have resulted in significant shortcomings to theory on global justice, and any interdisciplinary approach to global justice needs to take account of the nuances of that separation. To provide the context and underlying rationale for the concept of thin justice and its application to international law, this chapter elaborates on the forms, causes, and consequences of the gaps between the disciplines. I will also consider briefly the contributions of international relations theory, which, while generally descriptive in orientation, has nonetheless waded into debates on global justice. Once that tri-disciplinary landscape is carefully mapped, we can see both the imperative of and challenges to the project of thin justice.

A few caveats before beginning are needed. First, law and philosophical ethics do and should ask different questions about global justice. Neither the critique in this chapter nor my own independent approach seeks to blunt those inquiries or merge them into one giant field of 'global justice'. Second, each field is characterized by diverse perspectives, and so it is important not to overgeneralize across and within fields. Third, and relatedly, this chapter is necessarily selective, focusing on contemporary work in the field, leaving aside ancient, classical, and indeed many recognizably modern scholars, and even then does not purport to be comprehensive.

I. International Legal Scholarship and its Distance from Ethics

Even as international law is by its nature normative, most international law scholarship is empty or thin on questions of moral reasoning or ethical theory. It is descriptive or doctrinal, seeking to accurately portray the state of the law, advocate an interpretation of the law, or bring coherence to an area of law characterized by competing interpretations. This starting point is hardly surprising given the dominance of the positivist method within international law, but it nonetheless has so far limited possibilities of collaboration with ethics. To international lawyers, positivism is a two-pronged conception, to wit: (a) as with legal positivism generally, what we consider as law is a matter of social fact, making *lex lata* (the law as it is) and *lex ferenda* (the law as it should be) distinct issues; and (b) the fundamental formal criterion for law to be valid is the consent of states, particularly through the prescriptive processes of treaty and custom—though many scholars who call themselves positivists accept the importance of other sources, such as decisions of international organizations and courts. Positivism remains the lingua franca of international law and even its detractors know how to play the good positivist when the situation warrants it.[1]

As a consequence, many scholars write for an imagined audience, in particular a judicial one, that would consider moral arguments *ultra vires*.[2] They often move beyond description—what is the content of the law—to prescribe and advocate legal norms and institutions that we should support, but they generally do the latter within a methodology that relies on accepted practices regarding sources and interpretation, with perhaps the occasional nod to political realities, or efficiency, to guide among competing choices.[3] My sense is that, as much as scholars may have strongly held views on morality or justice, many or even most take it as a point of pride to divorce these concerns from their scholarship, or at least hide them well. For many positivists, the emphasis on these formal sources is a way of accommodating the diversity of national systems across the planet (avoiding the one-size-fits-all approach of natural law), as a result of which they may well see discussions of global justice as simply beside the point. Jean d'Aspremont voices this strain in insisting that international law is about accommodating national interests, not furthering global values, a project he regards as antithetical to legal scholarship.[4] From a more practical perspective, lawyers see themselves as problem-solvers for clients, so at times issues of morality or justice may seem too far from their everyday work.

Yet the lawyer's imperative to identify norms through formal sources does not make appraisal of those norms ethically beyond his or her writ, let alone threatening to it. And even if norms come about as a result of overlapping national interests, they can still correspond to global values. One can still endorse—or criticize—certain norms as reflecting certain values without conceding a degree of moral consciousness to states that they may well not deserve.

[1] Steven R. Ratner and Anne-Marie Slaughter, 'Appraising the Methods of International Law: A Prospectus for Readers', in Steven R. Ratner and Anne-Marie Slaughter (eds.), *The Methods of International Law* (Washington DC: American Society of International Law, 2004) 1, 5.

[2] Cf. Daniel Bodansky, *The Art and Craft of International Environmental Law* (Cambridge, MA: Harvard University Press, 2011).

[3] See Martti Koskenniemi, 'Methodology of International Law', in Rüdiger Wolfrum (ed.), *The Max Planck Encyclopedia of Public International Law*, online edition (Oxford: Oxford University Press, 2008–) <http://opil.ouplaw.com/home/EPIL>.

[4] Jean d'Aspremont, 'The Foundations of the International Legal Order', *Finn YBIL* 18 (2007): 219.

As for the broader question of whether scholars can engage in interpretive techniques and recommendations for future decisions that do not entail moral or ethical choices, this remains a great methodological question for all of law.[5] But the point is not whether legal scholars and decisionmakers can avoid moral reasoning, but whether they actually do so, and here I believe international law must accept that they do. In the end, many scholars are simply missing an opportunity to consider the ethical underpinnings of their positions as well as to contribute their expertise on legal structures to debates on a more just world order.

Yet even within the positivist tradition, issues of morality can never be completely avoided, as doctrine itself seems to find a place for it. In particular, scholarly treatment of *jus cogens* norms—peremptory norms that override even treaties—and some obligations *erga omnes*—duties extending to the community of states as a whole and not merely to individual states—generally assumes that part of the rationale for the distinctiveness of these norms is that states have recognized that some rules are, in a sense, more fundamental than others because they reflect important moral positions.[6] Scholars will argue about which norms fall into one category, or both, as well as the consequences of a breach of them. In determining the state of the law, the actual moral views of states become a relevant consideration.[7] Moreover, proposals for new norms could take into account moral views held by states and individuals.[8] And when states violate these norms, legal scholars should think more broadly about which states should take corrective measures and why.[9] Such an inquiry resonates with, but would also benefit from more engagement with, the work of philosophers regarding the division of global duties into national responsibilities.[10]

Looking beyond *jus cogens* and *erga omnes* duties, legal scholarship evinces three encounters with ethics, even as it remains at a distance from philosophical debates on global justice.

A. Mainstream methodologies and the back door of morality

Two prominent contemporary methodologies have found a place for ethics, even while skirting many key issues of global justice.

[5] See Scott J. Shapiro, 'The "Hart-Dworkin" Debate: A Short Guide for the Perplexed', in Arthur Ripstein (ed.), *Ronald Dworkin* (Cambridge: Cambridge University Press, 2007) 22.

[6] See, e.g., *Application of the Convention on the Prevention and Punishment of the Crime of Genocide* [2007] ICJ Rep 43, paras. 161–162 (26 February).

[7] Cf. H.L.A. Hart, *The Concept of Law*, 3rd ed. (Oxford: Oxford University Press, 2012) 203–4.

[8] Robert E. Goodin and Steven R. Ratner, 'Democratizing International Law', *Global Policy* 2 (2011): 241.

[9] See, e.g., Christian J. Tams, 'Individual States as Guardians of Community Interests', in Ulrich Fasternath et al. (eds), *From Bilateralism to Community Interest: Essays in Honour of Judge Bruno Simma* (Oxford: Oxford University Press, 2011) 379 (in responding to breaches of obligations *erga omnes*, states should consider a division of responsibilities so those in the best position to act take a leadership role).

[10] See, e.g., David Miller, 'Distributing Responsibilities' *J Pol Phil* 9 (2001): 453.

1. *'Enlightened' positivism and community interests*

First, a strand of positivist thinking that calls itself enlightened, highly influential in continental scholarship, seeks to soften positivism's formalistic light through subtle recourse to moral argumentation. Bruno Simma, one of its leading proponents, is eager to see the positivist lawyer engage with morality, as long as this does not threaten positivism's reliance upon formal sources to determine the validity of a claimed norm. His scholarship suggests that international law should serve certain ends of justice, in particular the advancement of human rights; and that the lawyer has a responsibility to recognize which rules do or do not further those goals.[11] His position on the role of morality thus resembles that of Neil MacCormick, for whom 'laws we judge unjust or detrimental to the public good are... deficient examples of that genus to which they belong, even though we may also judge them to belong validly to that genus'.[12] This position extends to the recognition that it may be morally required to disobey international law.[13]

Yet, as a good positivist, Simma emphasizes less the ideal goals of international law than the norms on which there is state consent. Indeed, he offers up a sociological observation in asserting that states and other actors are, in fact, acting as if they had some agreement on these moral ends.[14] He posits that international law has moved from a set of bilateral relations among states, each advancing its own interest, to one of community interest.[15] The idea of community interests has become conventional wisdom among international lawyers, although it is precisely the positivists' need to ground community interests in state consent that represents the great limitation of their methodology, however enlightened. Yet this notion is also an opportunity for input from philosophers who develop notions of justice with reference to some kind of political community.[16]

2. *Policy-oriented jurisprudence, base values, and public order goals*

On the other side of the Atlantic, one strand of scholarship, the policy-oriented approach to international law, developed its own approach to morality within the law. The New Haven School conceptualizes law as a process for advancing policy goals in an authoritative and controlling manner; so once lawyers and other participants can identify the relevant goals of the community, we can begin a process

[11] See, e.g., Bruno Simma, 'From Bilateralism to Community Interest in International Law', *Recueil des Cours* 250 (1994): 217, 229, 292.

[12] Neil MacCormick, 'Natural Law and the Separation of Law and Morals', in Robert P. George (ed.), *Natural Law Theory: Contemporary Essays* (Oxford: Oxford University Press, 1992) 105, 113.

[13] Bruno Simma, 'NATO, the UN, and the Use of Force: Legal Aspects', *EJIL* 10 (1999): 1, 22.

[14] Simma, 'Bilateralism', *supra* note 11, at 233–4 ('worldwide social consciousness').

[15] Ibid.

[16] One scholar in the European tradition who has managed to move beyond the community concept is Anne Peters. See Anne Peters, 'Humanity as the A and Ω of Sovereignty', *EJIL* 20 (2009): 513.

of prescribing legal norms to accomplish these goals.[17] Minimum and optimum public orders are the chief policy goals of the international legal process.[18] The basic content of these two concepts was grounded in sociology (Harold Lasswell's contribution to the endeavor) and instantiated in law. Minimum public order refers to the global state of affairs with limited recourse to unauthorized violence to solve disputes and authoritative procedures for deploying force in exceptional situations.[19] Optimum public order is synonymous with a world in which human dignity is maximally protected. It was said to be the state of affairs allowing for maximal enjoyment by individuals of eight 'base values'.[20]

The move from elaborating the processes for promoting minimum public order to elaborating those for advancing optimum public order entailed a great focus on the importance of those base values; how they had been used or abused by governments and non-state actors to deprive individuals of their enjoyment; and how international law could be a vehicle for their deployment and their fulfillment. The result was a fountain of scholarship on a range of international law issues, including topics of great interest to philosophers such as humanitarian intervention, secession, and human rights, each considered in a highly fact-dependent methodology.

The identification of minimum and optimum public order—based on preservation of peace and protection of human rights—is highly significant, yet the New Haven School's engagement with ethics has always been constrained. Although never denying the role of morality in international law—certainly human dignity is a moral concept—it sees morality through an anthropological lens. International law reflects morality because it reflects the demands of the community as determined by their base values. Any other theorizing was defective because it lacked social context. Thus, McDougal and his associates attacked Rawls in particular for his lack of empiricism.[21] Yet philosophers would find this position equally frustrating for its failure to recognize that the content of these base values is often contested by different communities and that moral argumentation is inherent in the process of evaluating claims and ultimately identifying base values.[22]

As a result, the New Haven School's emphasis on context in gauging the expectations of international actors and projecting future policies leaves us wondering

[17] Myres S. McDougal and W. Michael Reisman, 'The Prescribing Function in the World Constitutive Process: How International Law is Made', in Myres S. McDougal and W. Michael Reisman (eds.), *International Law Essays* (Mineola, N.Y.: Foundation Press, 1981) 355, 368–9.

[18] Siegfried Wiessner and Andrew R. Willard, 'Policy-Oriented Jurisprudence and Human Rights Abuses in Internal Conflict: Toward a World Public Order of Human Dignity', in Steven R. Ratner and Anne-Marie Slaughter (eds.), *The Methods of International Law* (Washington D.C.: American Society of International Law, 2004) 47, 61.

[19] See UN Charter, Arts. 2(4), 42, and 51.

[20] These are respect, power, wealth, skill, enlightenment, rectitude, affection, and well-being.

[21] See, e.g., Myres S. McDougal, Harold D. Lasswell, and Lung-chu Chen, *Human Rights and World Public Order: The Basic Policies of an International Law of Human Dignity* (New Haven, CT: Yale University Press, 1980) 454 n.9, 459–60 n.23.

[22] See W.B. Gallie, 'Essentially Contested Concepts', *Proc Aris Soc* 56 (1956): 167.

whether more general recommendations can be made. For example, in the work of its leading scholar, Michael Reisman, the emphasis on human rights translated into support for humanitarian intervention to protect the Ibos in Nigeria, but not for secession in Bosnia.[23] The inherently sociological approach of the New Haven School—one might call it 'fact-based international law'—that is its great strength can be a shortcoming for finding generalized guidance on the tradeoff between minimum and optimum public order. The standard of justice based on two pillars that I develop in this book takes the observations and public order goals of the New Haven School to heart, but it goes beyond them by situating peace and human rights within the framework of theories of ethics and justice so that we can assess the balance between those goals.

B. Critical approaches: giving a voice to the marginalized

For the past two to three decades, various critical methodologies have not merely engaged with morality, but in many ways have put it at the center of their agenda. These approaches seek to identify hidden agendas and biases within international law—including its norms, institutions, practitioners, and methodologies—and reform it. Critical legal scholars, who now prefer the appellation 'New Stream', built their methodology of deconstruction from literary theory and linguistics to identify myriad tensions within international law. Where positivists saw consent and acceptance, critical legal scholars saw power and hegemony;[24] where positivists saw international law as a language of communication, critical scholars saw lawyers seeking to preserve their own relevance in a changing world.[25] Feminist scholars saw international law as dominated by male views of society and individuals. Looking to the building blocks of the international system, they found certain assumptions made by positivism to reflect the biases of male statesmen and scholars who developed and promoted them.[26] And Third World Approaches to International Law (TWAIL) took a similar path with regard to the legacy of colonialism within international law.[27] Some works not self-identified as within the critical legal methodology place concern about international law as benefiting the powerful at the center of their concern.[28]

[23] Compare W. Michael Reisman, 'Humanitarian Intervention to Protect the Ibos', in Richard B. Lillich, *Humanitarian Intervention and the United Nations* (Charlottesville, VA: University of Virginia Press, 1973) 167, with Remarks by W. Michael Reisman, *ASIL Proc* 87 (1993), 258–9.

[24] See generally Martti Koskenniemi, *From Apology to Utopia: The Structure of International Legal Argument* (Helsinki: Finnish Lawyers Publishing Co., 1989).

[25] David Kennedy, 'When Renewal Repeats: Thinking Against the Box', *NYU JIL & Pol* 32 (2000): 355.

[26] Hilary Charlesworth and Christine Chinkin, *The Boundaries of International Law: A Feminist Analysis* (Huntington, NY: Juris Publishing, 2000).

[27] See, e.g., James Thuo Gathii, 'TWAIL: A Brief History of its Origins, its Decentralized Network, and a Tentative Bibliography', *Trade, Law, and Development* 3 (2011): 26. For a 'post-colonial' approach that both builds on and challenges TWAIL, see Sundhya Pahuja, *Decolonising International Law: Development, Economic Growth and the Politics of Universality* (Cambridge: Cambridge University Press, 2011).

[28] See, e.g., Benedict Kingsbury, 'Sovereignty and Inequality', *EJIL* 9 (1998): 599; Gerry Simpson, *Great Powers and Outlaw States: Unequal Sovereigns in the International Legal Order*

In one sense, ethics and global justice is *the* agenda of these critical methodologies. Each sees power as having both constituted and corrupted international law and argues for reform that takes into account voices marginalized for centuries. Critical legal studies is more catholic in its identifications of the defects of international law. The solution for Martti Koskenniemi, the most influential of the critical scholars, is a return to formalism; for international legal scholarship that has incorporated approaches from other disciplines—whether sociology (the New Haven School) or international relations—has yielded descriptions and prescriptions that serve the interests of the most powerful voices (typically American). He fears that calls for global governance subject to a standard of legitimacy will simply erode the standards within law into mere interest-balancing that benefits the powerful.[29] So in their view, their goal is surely a more just world order, one where international law is made through a process in which all voices are given their due weight.

Yet the ethics seems to end with this agenda. Critical scholars generally do not make a significant effort to engage with contemporary ethical theory by philosophers. Some scholarship is based mainly on the fear that too much power in the hands of one state in the no-longer-bipolar world will be damaging to everyone, using the record of the Bush years as Exhibit 1. Critical legal studies, in particular, often vacillates between a skepticism, even cynicism, of ethical inquiry as somehow hegemonic at worst, or at least a subterfuge for advancing each side's power, on the one hand, and a generally unarticulated commitment to egalitarianism, on the other.[30] It is not that these works lack theory—on the contrary. It is just typically not theory about justice or ethics. They are all far better at identifying what is wrong with international law than at providing a theoretical grounding for the way forward; and ethics offers such a foundation that would also make their criticisms far more powerful—as well as more nuanced.

C. Direct engagement with ethics

A final approach among legal scholarship is to integrate philosophical ethics directly into its work—the generally rare receptivity by legal scholars to cross-disciplinary dialogue.[31] The most influential work in this genre has been

(Cambridge: Cambridge University Press, 2004); José E. Alvarez, 'Hegemonic International Law Revisited', *AJIL* 97 (2003): 873. See also Michael Byers and Georg Nolte (eds.), *United States Hegemony and the Foundations of International Law* (Cambridge: Cambridge University Press, 2003).

[29] Martti Koskenniemi, 'Carl Schmitt, Hans Morgenthau, and the Image of Law in International Relations', in Michael Byers (ed.), *The Role of Law in International Politics* (Oxford: Oxford University Press, 2000) 17; Martti Koskenniemi, 'Global Governance and Public International Law', *Kritische Justiz* 37 (2004): 241. See also David Kennedy, *The Dark Sides of Virtue: Reassessing International Humanitarianism* (Princeton, NJ: Princeton University Press, 2004). These scholars are interdisciplinary in embracing history, anthropology, and other perspectives.

[30] See, e.g., Martti Koskenniemi, *The Gentle Civilizer of Nations: The Rise and Fall of International Law 1870–1960* (Cambridge: Cambridge University Press, 2001) 489–94.

[31] I am excluding scholars of an earlier generation who grappled with international law's ability to promote justice, for example Julius Stone, 'Approaches to the Notion of International Justice'

Thomas Franck's *Fairness in International Law and Institutions*, a comprehensive attempt by an international lawyer to measure international law against a standard of justice. Franck posited that 'fairness' encompassed two notions—legitimacy, i.e. a procedural fairness based on a norm's development through a right process, and distributive justice, which he equated with a norm's substantive justice. Distributive justice meant compliance with Rawls' difference principle of maximin. Franck then worked through key norms and institutions to see if they met these two criteria.[32]

Yet the ambition of Franck's reach was severely compromised by the narrowness of his criteria for *substantive* justice. As John Tasioulas wrote, 'a distributive principle cannot be the sole substantive principle in a theory of international law', noting that Rawls' more fundamental principle was equal rights.[33] This flawed starting point not only limited Franck's inquiry into the justice of institutions, but it forced him to squeeze odd topics—such as humanitarian intervention or self-determination—into the box of distributive justice when they should instead be evaluated according to other elements of substantive justice, for example respect for individual rights or the importance of peace. The result was an expansive scope of topics coupled with a highly undertheorized and incomplete notion of justice.[34] At the same time, the difference principle does matter with respect to some aspects of the international legal order, in particular the distribution of wealth and the role of international trade and investment law, issues discussed further in Chapters 10 and 11.[35]

Other legal scholars have offered less comprehensive, and sometimes idiosyncratic, visions of justice. In his 1990 book *Eunomia*, Philip Allot offered a highly original, but also frustratingly abstract, attack on international law for failing to take into account the interests of humanity as a whole.[36] Yet the work remains mostly isolated from debates among philosophers as to the makeup of that new international society. Fernando Tesón offers a critique of the legal order grounded in Kantian justice, in which democratic legitimacy should

in Cyril E. Black and Richard A. Falk (eds.), *The Future of the International Legal Order*, Vol. 1 (Princeton, NJ: Princeton University Press, 1969) 372.

[32] Thomas M. Franck, *Fairness in International Law and Institutions* (Oxford: Oxford University Press, 1995). In an earlier important book, *The Power of Legitimacy Among Nations* (New York: Oxford University Press, 1990), Franck (at 208–46) set forth a theory that states comply with international rules because of certain traits internal to those norms; but he bypassed matters of global justice, arguing that justice is done to persons alone and is a concept confined to the nation-state.

[33] John Tasioulas, 'International Law and the Limits of Fairness', *EJIL* 13 (2002): 993, 1008.

[34] See Gerry J. Simpson, 'Is International Law Fair?', *Mich JIL* 17 (1996): 615.

[35] See, e.g., Frank J. Garcia, 'Global Justice and the Bretton Woods Institutions', *JIEL* 10 (2007): 461; and the essays in Chios Carmody, Frank J. Garcia, and John Linarelli (eds.), *Global Justice and International Economic Law: Opportunities and Prospects* (Cambridge: Cambridge University Press, 2012).

[36] Philip Allott, *Eunomia: A New Order for a New World* (New York: Oxford University Press, 1990).

be the lodestar of international legitimacy.[37] Tesón deserves credit for bringing Kant back into the scholarship of international law, though his later work claimed that states that do not meet Kantian standards of legitimacy are proper targets of unilateral intervention, a view quite at odds with the justice of some of the law's core norms on the use of force.[38] Partly in response to Tesón and other cosmopolitans, Brad Roth offers a robust defense of interstate diversity, arguing that, in a world of deep moral disagreement, law must remain tolerant of different moral visions. This makes him skeptical about the project of global justice (as well as about US-based ideas of refashioning the world according to American democracy).[39]

Lastly, certain topics of international law have been more open to ethical inquiry even in the absence of some general engagement with morality, as seen in the works just mentioned. Human rights scholarship is replete with discussions of utilitarian versus deontological justifications for international norms and the translation of rights into duties, although even much of that scholarship is still fairly divorced from contemporary ethical scholarship about global justice.[40] International environmental law has done a better job of reckoning with moral concepts such as intergenerational equity and the proper distribution of burdens to prevent and remediate environmental harm.[41]

D. A missing link: distributive justice

A more glaring gap between international lawyers' engagement with global justice and that of philosophers is on the importance of global distributive justice. Philosophers' fascination with this issue is seen in the four decades-long debates over extending Rawls' difference principle to the international realm. International lawyers far less frequently directly engage with distributive justice. Although lawyers talk and write about aspects of distributive justice, for example the place of economic rights within the pantheon of human rights, or the

[37] Fernando R. Tesón, 'The Kantian Theory of International Law', *Colum L Rev* 92 (1992): 53; Fernando R. Tesón, *A Philosophy of International Law* (Boulder, CO: Westview Press, 1998).

[38] Fernando R. Tesón, *Humanitarian Intervention: An Inquiry into Law and Morality* (Ardsley, NY: Transnational Publishers, 2005) 144–67; Fernando R. Tesón, 'Ending Tyranny in Iraq', *Ethics & Intl Aff* 19 (2005): 1, 1.

[39] Brad R. Roth, *Sovereign Equality and Moral Disagreement: Premises of a Plurality International Legal Order* (New York: Oxford University Press, 2011). For an approach that (despite its title) relies solely on domestic legal analogies to appraise certain aspects of the justice of international law, see Lea Brilmayer, 'International Justice and International Law', *W Va L Rev* 98 (1996): 611.

[40] See, e.g., Jack Donnelly, *Universal Human Rights in Theory and Practice*, 2nd ed. (Ithaca, NY: Cornell University Press, 2003); Abdullahi An-Na'im, *Islam and Human Rights: Selected Essays of Abdullahi An-Na'im*, Mashood Baderin (ed.) (Burlington, VT: Ashgate Publishing, 2010).

[41] See the excellent review in Christopher Stone, 'Ethics and International Environmental Law', in Daniel Bodansky, Jutta Brunnée, and Ellen Hey (eds.), *The Oxford Handbook of International Environmental Law* (Oxford: Oxford University Press, 2007) 291.

balance between the rights of the foreign investor and those of the host-state international investment law, most shy away from scholarship or concrete proposals to alter radically the global distribution of wealth. The notable exceptions here are some scholars in international economic and environmental law and scholars associated with TWAIL.[42]

Why this reluctance by legal scholarship? First, for positivists, even of the enlightened variety, distributive justice is a risky subject because the gap between the expectations of states as determined through recourse to formal sources and the demands of distributive justice is enormous. An examination of UN documents simply does not suggest that states have generally recognized distributive justice in the sense of wealth transfer between North and South as a goal, let alone an obligation (even of conduct). The International Court of Justice (ICJ) has rejected it as a rationale for determining maritime boundaries.[43] At the same time, for those seeking to make new law, particularly in the environmental area where burden-sharing is so central, ethical ideas of distributive justice may provide an important source of ideas and arguments to convince states to endorse a new consensus.

Second, international law is still dominated by Northern governments and scholars, who see wealth inequities as one of many global issues to be addressed, but not morally or politically more imperative than the others, such as the improvement of basic human rights, the resolution of festering conflicts, and nuclear non-proliferation. As this volume makes clear, these other issues are, in my view, all morally compelling, and some more so than certain claims for distributive justice.

Third, international law and lawyers value solving problems through existing structures and institutions. During the heyday of international attention to distributive justice in the 1970s and 1980s—including the Brandt and Palme Commissions and various North–South conferences—it seemed that such institutions were developing. But the end of the Cold War halted that process, as developing countries that had benefited from the largesse of the other superpower now vied for Northern investment. As they have sought to play in the institutions established by the North—in a word, to switch, rather than fight—the focus of attention has shifted to the WTO, the World Bank, and the IMF. As a result, as long as international law lacks a single mechanism or institution for addressing global economic inequities comprehensively, international lawyers will think about distributive justice in only a piecemeal manner. The practical focus of lawyers makes sense at a certain level, but it strikes me as giving up too soon on the lessons of the ideal theory, and some interaction with philosophers handling global justice questions would improve the work of both.

[42] See sources cited in notes 35 and 41 and the works cited in Antony Anghie and B.S. Chimni, 'Third World Approaches to International Law and Individual Responsibility in Internal Conflicts' in Steven R. Ratner and Anne-Marie Slaughter (eds.), *The Methods of International Law* (Washington DC: American Society of International Law, 2004) 185, 187.

[43] *Continental Shelf (Libya v Malta) (Judgment)* [1985] ICJ Rep 13, para. 46 (3 June).

II. Moral and Political Philosophy: Global Justice and the Suspicion of Law

Contemporary moral and political philosophy has left a vast imprint on questions of global justice. Much of it falls within debates between communitarians and cosmopolitans over the territorial scope of individual and state duties and, relatedly, the permissible limits of diversity among territorial units globally. These works all ask, as Brian Barry put it, 'given a world that is made up of states, what is the morally permissible range of diversity among them?'[44] Some of these debates originate in questions of interpersonal ethics and then extend in many directions, from the justice of existing interstate borders, to the distribution of economic wealth, to the design of international institutions. Philosophical engagement with international law has varied significantly, and in reviewing the landscape, it is useful to adopt a broad understanding of philosophy here to include political theorists who have engaged with global justice.[45]

A. Ethical scholarship about international norms

One strand of moral and political philosophy makes its subject, or at least a central part of it, the morality of the rules of international law. That is, the inquiry itself, and any theory resulting from it, seems in significant part to be generated by a need to understand, justify, or challenge the existing law. Thus, Michael Walzer's *Just and Unjust Wars* sees as a significant part of its project the holding up of legal norms of *jus ad bellum* and *jus in bello* to ethical scrutiny.[46] Others continue to examine the rules of war.[47] And human rights norms have received

[44] Brian Barry, 'International Society from a Cosmopolitan Perspective', in David R. Mapel and Terry Nardin (eds.), *International Society: Diverse Ethical Perspectives* (Princeton, NJ: Princeton University Press, 1998) 144, 154.

[45] See, e.g., Terry Nardin, 'International Ethics', in Christian Reus-Smit and Duncan Snidal (eds.), *The Oxford Handbook of International Relations* (Oxford: Oxford University Press, 2009) 594, section 1 (the need to preserve international ethics as a part of international politics). As noted in the Introduction, I do not address jurisprudential approaches. For some of the recent scholarship see, e.g., John Tasioulas, 'Customary International Law and the Quest for Global Justice', in Amanda Perreau-Saussine and James Bernard Murphy (eds.), *The Nature of Customary Law: Legal, Historical and Philosophical Perspectives* (Cambridge: Cambridge University Press, 2007) 307; Jeremy Waldron, 'Are Sovereigns Entitled to the Benefit of the International Rule of Law?', *EJIL* 22 (2011): 315; Ronald Dworkin, 'A New Philosophy for International Law', *Phil & Pub Aff* 41 (2013): 2. See generally Samantha Besson and John Tasioulas (eds.), *The Philosophy of International Law* (Oxford: Oxford University Press, 2010) (containing ethical and jurisprudential works).

[46] Michael Walzer, *Just and Unjust Wars: A Moral Argument with Historical Illustrations*, 4th ed. (New York: Basic Books, 2006) 45–6.

[47] David Luban, 'A Theory of Crimes Against Humanity', *Yale JIL* 29 (2004): 85; Jeff McMahan, *Killing in War* (Oxford: Clarendon Press, 2009); Larry May, *Aggression and Crimes Against Peace* (Cambridge: Cambridge University Press, 2008); David Rodin, *War and Self-Defense* (Oxford: Clarendon Press, 2002); Henry Shue and David Wippman, 'Limiting Attacks on Dual-Use Facilities Performing Indispensable Civilian Functions', *Corn ILJ* 35 (2002): 559.

significant attention to determine their ethical grounding.[48] Thus, some within ethics regard these norms as mattering enough in international relations, or the ways that we think about international relations, to merit serious appraisal. At the same time, this scholarship is not typically connected with the literature on global justice because the latter derives mostly from Rawls' seminal works, including *A Theory of Justice*, which gave little consideration to human rights.

B. General theory first, application to norms second

A more common practice within ethics is to hold international law up to scrutiny, but only after presenting a more general argument about some aspect of global justice. Charles Beitz's *Political Theory and International Relations* offered a normative account of the international order that called for a morality of states based on a link between state autonomy and just domestic institutions, as well as a deep form of distributive justice. After presenting his vision, he provided an ethical appraisal of certain international law norms, for example defending the right of colonial self-determination by conceptualizing it as a claim to rectify social injustice.[49] From a very different standpoint, Mervyn Frost argued that the system of sovereign states itself helps constitute the individual and promote his or her flourishing, thereby justifying many of the basic rules of international law.[50]

A great deal of the communitarian/cosmopolitan debate falls into this category, with theories that provide blueprints for key aspects of a just world order and then some testing of extant legal norms and institutions. David Held and others sharing his outlook present a comprehensive conception of a cosmopolitan world order, emphasizing its legal components, assessing, for example, the structure of the EU and the UN.[51] Jürgen Habermas has stepped into these debates by arguing that international law is now becoming a constitution for Kantian-based international community, even though certain improvements will still need to be made. Although preferring constitutionalization to cosmopolitanism as the goal, he, like Held, sees positive trends from the trajectory of international law since 1945.[52] In the course of this work, they propose radical reorganization of the UN organs, based on a need to dilute the influence of powerful states, ensuring

[48] See, e.g., James W. Nickel, *Making Sense of Human Rights*, 2nd ed. (Malden, MA: Blackwell Publishing, 2006); Charles R. Beitz, *The Idea of Human Rights* (Oxford: Oxford University Press, 2009); Henry Shue, *Basic Rights: Subsistence, Affluence, and U.S. Foreign Policy*, 2nd ed. (Princeton, NJ: Princeton University Press, 1996); William J. Talbot, *Which Rights Should be Universal?* (Oxford: Oxford University Press, 2005).

[49] Charles R. Beitz, *Political Theory and International Relations* (Princeton, NJ: Princeton University Press, 1979) 92–105.

[50] Mervyn Frost, *Ethics in International Relations: A Constitutive Theory* (Cambridge: Cambridge University Press, 1996) chs. 4–5.

[51] See, e.g., David Held, *Democracy and the Global Order: From the Modern State to Cosmopolitan Governance* (Stanford, CA: Stanford University Press, 1995) 267–83; David Held, 'Law of States, Law of Peoples: Three Models of Sovereignty', *Legal Theory* 8 (2002): 1; Daniele Archibugi, David Held, and Martin Köhler (eds.), *Re-imagining Political Community: Studies in Cosmopolitan Democracy* (Cambridge: Polity Press, 1998).

[52] Jürgen Habermas, *The Divided West* (Cambridge: Polity Press, 2006) 115–93.

a greater role for individual voices and relying on judicial mechanisms for resolving disputes (including, for example, advocating for the compulsory jurisdiction of the International Court of Justice (ICJ)).[53] Although the project helps us see the big picture of the global order, its utopianism as well as skepticism about the morality of international law invites the response I offer in this book.[54]

These general theories can, to their credit, give prominence to institutions. As noted in the Introduction, Allen Buchanan persuasively argues that moral questions about the duties of individuals or states can be answered only with careful consideration of the institutions currently capable of allowing those duties to be carried out. Substantively, he argues that a state's legitimacy turns fundamentally on its observance of human rights and democratic participation, and institutional legitimacy turns on similar factors.[55] For Thomas Pogge, the focus is on institutions that should mete out distributive justice. At first arguing for the globalization of Rawls' difference principle and later asserting a more robust view of equality, Pogge claims not only that the rules of international trade and intellectual property are unjust, but also that individuals in the North are violating duties not to harm those in the South by participating in that system.[56] This view will be considered in Chapter 10. On the other hand, Rawls derived his theory of global justice with virtually no consideration of the role of global or regional organizations.[57]

C. Ethical arguments built on law

Ethical claims can incorporate the law in a further respect, by building an argument on international norms themselves. Terry Nardin took an early significant

[53] Held, *Democracy, supra*, note 51, at 279; Daniele Archibugi, 'Principles of Cosmopolitan Democracy', in Daniele Archibugi, David Held, and Martin Köhler (eds.), *Re-imagining Political Community: Studies in Cosmopolitan Democracy* (Cambridge: Polity Press, 1998) 198, 221.

[54] For applications of cosmopolitan thinking to international norms, see, e.g., David Beetham, 'Human Rights and Cosmopolitan Democracy', in Daniele Archibugi, David Held, and Martin Köhler (eds.), *Re-imagining Political Community: Studies in Cosmopolitan Democracy* (Cambridge: Polity Press, 1998) 58; Pierre Hassner, 'Refugees: a Special Case for Cosmopolitan Citizenship?' in *Re-imagining Political Community* (*supra*) 273; Edward A. Page, 'Cosmopolitanism, Climate Change, and Greenhouse Emissions Trading', *International Theory* 3 (2011): 37. See also Roland Pierek and Wouter Werner (eds.), *Cosmopolitanism in Context: Perspectives from International Law and Political Theory* (Cambridge: Cambridge University Press, 2010); Christian Barry and Thomas W. Pogge (eds.), *Global Institutions and Responsibilities: Achieving Global Justice* (Malden, MA: Blackwell Publishing, 2005).

[55] Allen Buchanan, *Justice, Legitimacy, and Self-Determination: Moral Foundations for International Law* (Oxford: Oxford University Press, 2004) 331–400.

[56] See, e.g., Thomas W. Pogge, *Realizing Rawls* (Ithaca, NY: Cornell University Press, 1989); Thomas W. Pogge, *World Poverty and Human Rights: Cosmopolitan Responsibilities and Reforms*, 2nd ed. (Cambridge: Polity Press, 2008); Thomas W. Pogge, 'Recognized and Violated by International Law: The Human Rights of the Global Poor', *LJIL* 18 (2005): 717.

[57] John Rawls, *The Law of Peoples* (Cambridge, MA: Harvard University Press, 1999).

step with his call for a limited vision of interstate justice based on a traditional positivistic notion of international law.[58]

Held constructs his model of cosmopolitan democracy (and Habermas his idea of constitutionalization) in part on the significant changes within the international legal order, notably the development of human rights, limitations on state immunity, the notion of common economic heritage, and the increased powers of international organizations.[59] Thomas Mertens supports Rawls against cosmopolitan criticism in part by noting that Rawls is closer to the view of toleration expressed in the United Nations' universal membership.[60] And Peter Singer has relied upon the UN Charter and actions of the Security Council to endorse limits on a state's domestic jurisdiction regarding human rights abuses.[61]

International law can also be used defensively in ethical reasoning. Robert Goodin, in his pioneering article justifying a state's special duties to its own nationals on utilitarian grounds, pointed out situations where, under international law, a state's duties to foreigners are actually greater than its duties to its citizens (for example with respect to the protection of private property and the ability to draft people into an army).[62] He uses these examples to rebut the strong nationalist claim that states should always owe greater duties to their own citizens than to foreigners, thereby assuming that these rules count as ethical arguments for rebutting the strong nationalist position. Kok-Chor Tan uses the presence of institutional coercion at the level of international law as one argument against the view that reciprocity limits duties of justice to the domestic level.[63] And arguing against much ethical theorizing about human rights, Beitz and Cohen effectively take human rights as they appear in legal instruments and generate arguments against a top-down derivation of such rights.[64]

D. Getting the law wrong

Despite the prior examples, philosophers mentioning international law sometimes get it wrong. Most notably, in *The Law of Peoples*, Rawls cites as support,

[58] Terry Nardin, 'Legal Positivism as a Theory of International Society', in David R. Mapel and Terry Nardin (eds.), *International Society: Diverse Ethical Perspectives* (Princeton, NJ: Princeton University Press, 1998) 17.

[59] Held, *Democracy, supra* note 51, at 101–11.

[60] Thomas Mertens, 'Defending the Rawlsian League of Peoples: A Critical Comment on Tan', *LJIL* 18 (2005): 711, 713–14.

[61] Peter Singer, *One World: The Ethics of Globalization* (New Haven, CT: Yale University Press, 2002) 127–35.

[62] Robert E. Goodin, 'What is So Special About Our Fellow Countrymen?', *Ethics* 98 (1988): 663.

[63] Kok-Chor Tan, *Justice Without Borders: Cosmopolitanism, Nationalism, and Patriotism* (Cambridge: Cambridge University Press, 2004) 175–7. See also Joshua Cohen and Charles Sabel, 'Extra Rempublicam Nulla Justitia?', *Phil & Pub Aff* 34(2) (2006): 147 (making a similar argument to reject Thomas Nagel's view about the territorial limitations of justice).

[64] Joshua Cohen, 'Minimalism About Human Rights: The Most We Can Hope For?', *J Pol Phil* 12 (2004): 190, 194–9; Charles R. Beitz, *The Idea of Human Rights* (Oxford: Oxford University Press, 2009); see also Joseph Raz, 'Human Rights Without Foundations', in Samantha Besson and John Tasioulas (eds.), *The Philosophy of International Law* (Oxford: Oxford University Press, 2010) 321.

or perhaps recognition, of his basic principles of mutual respect between peoples James L Brierly's 1963 treatise *The Law of Nations*.[65] On the positive side, Rawls seems to have accepted that international law already embodies certain ethical principles. For Rawls, those principles are defensible from a contractarian perspective, as he claims—though does not really prove—that they would be agreed to by democratic peoples in an original position and then supported by so-called decent peoples.[66] But Rawls cited and endorses an outdated restatement of international law that, most glaringly, does not reflect the developments in human rights law that limit a state's freedom to govern itself however it chooses (as well as its immunity from external, non-military interference).[67]

From a different perspective, we witness philosophers challenging the notion of cosmopolitan justice in part by arguing that there is no global basic structure because no international power can assign rights and duties equally to all agents.[68] Setting aside whether a basic structure indeed requires such an authority, and whether that authority must be able to assign individual duties and rights as opposed to states' duties and rights, it is highly formalistic, if not simply wrong, to say that no international institution has such authority. In the most obvious cases, the Security Council may effectively assign duties to individuals (for example not to export certain items to a target state); and the International Criminal Court can throw (or order a state to throw) someone in jail.[69] At the other extreme, the optimism of some cosmopolitans for compulsory ICJ jurisdiction seems based on a misunderstanding of that Court's actual functioning. The ICJ is actually a highly conservative tribunal, whether in avoiding politically contentious cases, as it did concerning France's nuclear testing in the 1970s, NATO's bombing of Serbia in 1999, and Kosovo's 2008 declaration of independence; or in its overt disdain for distributive justice.[70] As discussed in the following chapters, the nature of these institutions needs to play a significant role in one's moral appraisal of the existing international law on numerous issues.

[65] J.L. Brierly, *The Law of Nations: An Introduction to the International Law of Peace*, 6th ed. (Oxford: Oxford University Press, 1963).

[66] Rawls, *Law of Peoples, supra* note 57, at 37 (identifying Brierly's principles as 'familiar and traditional principles of justice among free and democratic peoples').

[67] See, e.g., Allen Buchanan, 'Rawls's Law of Peoples: Rules for a Vanished Westphalian World', *Ethics* 110 (2000): 697.

[68] Saladin Meckled-Garcia, 'On the Very Idea of Cosmopolitan Justice: Constructivism and International Agency', *J Pol Phil* 16 (2008): 245, 261; see also Michael Blake, 'Distributive Justice, State Coercion, and Autonomy', *Phil & Pub Aff* 30 (2001): 257, 280.

[69] For a philosophical argument showing this effect, see Cohen and Sabel, 'Extra Rempublicam Nulla Justitia?', *supra* note 63.

[70] See, e.g., *Legality of the Use of Force (Serbia v Belgium)* [2004] ICJ Rep 279 (15 December); *Accordance with International Law of the Unilateral Declaration of Independence in Respect of Kosovo* [2010] ICJ Rep 403 (Advisory Opinion of 22 July); *Continental Shelf, supra* note 43, para 46.

E. Law as the passing stranger: causes and consequences

Notwithstanding some examples cited earlier, most ethical scholarship regarding global justice operates parallel to, rather than with a serious understanding of, international norms and scholarship about them.

1. *An attempted explanation for philosophical distance from international law*

Several factors seem to account for the disconnect. First, some theory in global justice addresses foundational questions where the state of international law seems beside the point. Some scholarship is about interpersonal ethics, for example what each of us owes individually to those within and outside national borders. As Pogge has noted, this sort of interactional morality is quite distinct from institutional morality.[71] Thus, a line of scholarship has focused on the identities, roles, and responsibilities of individuals, not institutions.[72] In this case, the lack of engagement with law can be justified on the ground that the content of norms that, at least in the first instance, regulate the activities of states is not relevant to the duties of individuals. But this reason cannot shield scholarship on global *institutional* ethics that shies away from international law and institutions. Much scholarship argues for duties states should have at the global level, yet with little regard to the rules that states *have in fact* derived and enforced.

This omission suggests a second explanation, namely that the practical arrangements that humans have derived for their global interactions—including legal norms—should not get in the way of good theorizing about ideal arrangements.[73] Ideal theory surely has its place in ethics, and indeed there is nothing wrong with postponing the 'ought implies can' questions until certain basic principles are derived. Yet the avoidance of international law by philosophers seems to go much deeper. Much of it seems based on the notion that: (a) because much or most law emerges from a political process, it can neither ground nor undercut an ethical argument; and (b) that because law inevitably involves compromises, either in its creation or enforcement, its content is marginal to principled ethical argumentation. Either way, law becomes simply an instrument for delivering, institutionalizing, or enforcing a previously derived ethical position.[74] It is not that the law is morally wrong, but simply that it is irrelevant. But the first of these confuses the

[71] Thomas W. Pogge, 'Cosmopolitanism and Sovereignty', *Ethics* 103 (1992): 48, 50–2.

[72] See, e.g., Peter Singer, 'Famine, Affluence, and Morality', *Phil & Pub Aff* 1 (1972): 229; most of the essays in Robert McKim and Jeff McMahan (eds.), *The Morality of Nationalism* (New York: Oxford University Press, 1997); Samuel Scheffler, *Boundaries and Allegiances: Problems of Justice and Responsibility in Liberal Thought* (New York: Oxford University Press, 2001).

[73] This position has many nuances. One extreme might be G.A. Cohen's view that ethical principles cannot be grounded in facts at all. G.A. Cohen, *Rescuing Justice and Equality* (Cambridge, MA: Harvard University Press, 2008) 229–73.

[74] For one of many examples, see David Copp, 'International Law and Morality in the Theory of Secession', *J Ethics* 2 (1998): 219, 222 ('the question whether there is a moral right of secession is *morally prior* to the question about international law').

origin of a claim with its moral validity; and the second suggests that ethical reasoning does not involve compromise, whereas it typically includes the weighing of competing considerations, maybe not at first but at some stage.[75]

A further nuance is the possibility that philosophers see law and institutions as irrelevant to global justice because they regard them as making no difference to how global actors will ultimately behave, a skepticism invented by some political realists.[76] Under this view, ethical theory should devise solutions, but those solutions will be realized through non-legal avenues. Yet if philosophers have this view, it is simply wrong descriptively. As a generation of international relations and legal scholarship and the lived experiences of international actors—states, non-governmental organizations (NGOs), corporations, international organizations, and even criminal syndicates—has demonstrated, international law and institutions both constrain the behaviour of international actors and channel and frame discussions for international cooperation.[77] International law is a fundamental institution for the advancement of moral claims beyond borders.

A third potential justification might explain the distance between international law and one area of global justice scholarship, distributive justice—namely, that international law has generally had little to say about that topic. Yet this argument fails for two reasons. First, although distributive justice has certainly dominated the field of global justice, that would seem to be a shortcoming in the ethical scholarship, not a reason to ignore international law. As other philosophers have recognized, global justice involves manifold other issues, from the use of force, to self-determination and statehood, to human rights. Just as Tasioulas criticized Franck for using the distributive justice lens for examining all of international law, one can criticize philosophers for focusing on distributive justice to the exclusion of other components of global justice. It is, at times, as if some philosophers have neglected Rawls' first principle of justice, namely, the equality of individuals, attention to which could push global justice discussions in a different direction.

Second, even if one wishes to focus on distributive justice, the legal landscape is not so barren. Although, as noted, international law lacks strong norms in favor of the global distribution of wealth, it does have norms worthy of ethical inquiry—in international environmental law (through the core principle of common but differentiated responsibilities); economic and social human rights (weakly in favor of distributive justice); the law of the sea (weakly in favor with respect to exploitation of the continental shelf); and international trade and intellectual property

[75] I appreciate this point from Robert Goodin at a 2010 workshop at the University of Michigan Law School as well as James Nickel's paper 'On Ideal Normative Theory' presented at that workshop.

[76] See Allen Buchanan and David Golove, 'Philosophy of International Law', in Jules Coleman and Scott Shapiro (eds.), *The Oxford Handbook of Jurisprudence and Philosophy of Law* (Oxford: Oxford University Press, 2002).

[77] For a review of different perspectives on effectiveness, see Steven Ratner, 'Persuading to Comply: On the Deployment and Avoidance of Legal Argumentation' in Jeffrey L. Dunoff and Mark A. Pollack (eds.), *Interdisciplinary Perspectives on International Law and International Relations* (Cambridge: Cambridge University Press, 2013) 568.

law (probably weakly against it). More importantly, it has institutions that could, or already do, implement some form of distributive justice.[78]

2. *Consequences of ethical suspicion*

Avoidance of engagement with rules and institutions results in distinct gaps in ethical scholarship:

- First and most generally, is a general impoverishment of ethical theory for producing prescriptions that do not contribute to the project of a more just world order. As Buchanan writes, failure to understand global institutions means that philosophers derive 'principles... not suitable for institutionalization because they are inconsistent with existing institutional arrangements whose abandonment would be morally prohibitive... or because institutionalizing them would generate incentives that undermine the realization of other important principles'.[79]
- Second, is a dismissive attitude to the moral justification of key norms of international law. Although this point will be reinforced throughout this volume as I examine individual norms, at this stage one might cite a particularly flagrant case. In a pioneering essay, Brian Barry found, with little argument, that the principle of national sovereignty over natural resources, a core norm of international law, 'is without any rational foundation'.[80] Such a position would strike a lawyer as astonishing, if only because of the notion of ownership to avoid the tragedy of the commons seems like such a basic idea, one easily justified on utilitarian grounds, a point I will explore in Chapter 10.[81] (Perhaps Barry was just being hyperbolic and meant that other ways of dividing up national resources are also valid.) Ethical scrutiny of international law will not and should not result in uniformly upholding its morality, but it explores a certain set of arguments not sufficiently discussed in philosophical circles. More generally, international law shows that these issues are not as simple as philosophers may conceive by highlighting contrary positions widely accepted by states that philosophers may have ignored.

[78] Pogge and Held appraise these institutions (and generally find them woefully lacking); and others invoke them in arguments over whether the international order of today includes the basic structure necessary to the application of Rawls' principles of justice. See, e.g., Charles R. Beitz, 'Cosmopolitan Ideals and National Sentiment', *J Phil* 80 (1983): 591; Cohen and Sabel, 'Extra Rempublicam Nulla Justitia?', *supra* note 63; Andrea Sangiovanni, 'Global Justice, Reciprocity, and the State', *Phil & Pub Aff* 35 (2007): 3.

[79] Buchanan and Golove, 'Philosophy of International Law', *supra* note 76, at 868, 870; see also Andrew Hurrell, 'Norms and Ethics in International Relations', in Walter Carlsnaes, Thomas Risse, and Beth A. Simmons (eds.), *Handbook of International Relations* (New York: Sage Publications, 2002) 137, 139–41.

[80] Brian Barry, 'Do Countries Have Moral Obligations? The Case of World Poverty', in *The Tanner Lectures on Human Values*, Vol. 2 (Salt Lake City, UT: University of Utah Press, 1981) 25, 36.

[81] Permanent Sovereignty over Natural Resources, GA Res. 1803 (XVII), 14 December 1962; UNCLOS, Pts. V, VI (regimes on exclusive economic zone and continental shelf); Garrett Hardin, 'The Tragedy of the Commons', *Science* 162 (1968): 243.

• Third, much philosophy zeroes in on issues and develops proposals that seem unconcerned with rather clear strictures of international law. For example, as discussed in Chapters 5 and 9, two remedies for oppressed people abroad—secession and humanitarian intervention—have elicited significant philosophical attention, particularly among cosmopolitan scholars, despite international law's overall stance against them. Philosophers' response to this lack of concern with international law's limits on these two remedies might simply be: 'So what? Change the law. We are in the business of ideal theory.' But that is only a partial answer. Philosophers should recognize that international law's aversion to these remedies still leaves open numerous possibilities for influencing the way a state treats its people. If philosophers are concerned with responses to a state's abuse of its own people, then they should not leave out of the discussion the main methods that other states actually deploy in these situations—dialogue, capacity-building, diplomatic protest, naming and shaming, linkage of foreign assistance, and sanctions. Yet they receive less attention precisely because the more drastic remedy is left on the table.[82]

Philosophers might reply that they recognize these other options and are trying to focus on the hardest question—when has a state so lost its legitimacy that it can be dismembered or invaded?[83] This is a valid project. But this disproportionate attention ignores two points: first, the other options, including diplomatic repercussions or sanctions, raise difficult moral issues as well, for example whether sanctions should be used given uncertainties over their efficacy; and second, careful institutional scholarship on global justice should consider methods actually attempted by states. Otherwise, the scholar shortchanges the opportunities for progressive change toward global justice.

• A final consequence is the derivation of prescriptions for aspects of global justice that are close to that recognized in international law, without any acknowledgment of the similarity. As discussed in Chapter 5, a number of philosophical proposals regarding self-determination resemble that of international law, though the connection goes unrecognized by their proponents.

Again, one might ask why this omission of the coincidence with law matters to the philosopher's task. Perhaps the question should be reversed: Is a philosopher deriving principles of justice ready to assert that it is *irrelevant* to her argument that her seemingly original vision is one that states have already accepted through international law? On the positive side, the existence of these rules suggests that the philosopher's position is indeed feasible, lending support to that position from those who believe that ought implies can. On the other hand, it could also suggest that the philosopher's position may not be quite as original as he or she thought, as statesmen and women devising these rules indeed have been thinking along the same lines. All these consequences, then, suggest that global justice scholarship would benefit from closer attention to law and legal structures.

[82] For a recognition of these options among philosophers, see Kok-Chor Tan, 'International Toleration: Rawlsian versus Cosmopolitan', *LJIL* 18 (2005): 685, 703–4.

[83] See, e.g., Rawls, *The Law of Peoples, supra* note 57, at 79–81.

III. International Relations Theory and the Role of Descriptive Scholarship

A discussion of the landscape of global justice would be incomplete without consideration of the work of international relations theory. As an initial matter, within the international relations box of political science, realist scholars, who have dominated much thinking in the field, have been generally dismissive of law and ethics, even though two of realism's founders, Hans Morgenthau (an international lawyer) and E.H. Carr, engaged with morality and justice and recognized that both of them, as well as international law, do and should matter to some extent to international politics.[84] As an alternative to the realists, rationalist institutional scholarship, constructivist scholarship, and the English School have delved directly into questions concerning international norms.

Yet the line between description and prescription nonetheless remains thick.[85] The rational institutionalists have for the most part sacrificed consideration of morality for the sake of a positive description of the effect of law and legalization on international politics. The most recent stage of work has been a burgeoning of quantitative studies that seek to predict the design of law and institutions as the outputs of political processes and the impact of legal norms and institutions on state behavior.[86] Some have turned their attention to a concept related to international justice, namely legitimacy in the international order. [87] Yet for political scientists concerned with legitimacy, legitimacy is about a belief by actors that a norm or institution should be obeyed, not about some actual trait of the norm or institution.[88] Although a focus on this form of legitimacy is an improvement over realist conceptions that states obey rules only out of immediate self-interest or coercion, it is not a substitute for an overt examination of objective notions of legitimacy.[89] As a result, the justice of existing rules and institutions is often considered only implicitly.[90]

[84] See, e.g., Hans J. Morgenthau, *Politics Among Nations: The Struggle for Power and Peace*, 7th ed., Kenneth W. Thompson and W. David Clinton (eds.) (Boston, MA: McGraw-Hill Higher Education, 2006) 240–69, 283–92; Edward H. Carr, *The Twenty Years Crisis, 1919–1939: An Introduction to the Study of International Relations*, rev. ed. (Houndmills: Palgrave Macmillan, 2001) 135–55.

[85] For a fuller account of the ethical approaches within international relations, see Christian Reus-Smit and Duncan Snidal (eds.), *The Oxford Handbook of International Relations* (Oxford: Oxford University Press, 2008).

[86] For one example among hundreds, see Beth A. Simmons, *Mobilizing for Human Rights: International Law in Domestic Politics* (Cambridge: Cambridge University Press, 2009). For a review of the state of play, see Jeffrey L. Dunoff and Mark A. Pollack (eds.), *Interdisciplinary Perspectives on International Law and International Relations* (Cambridge: Cambridge University Press, 2013).

[87] See Ian Hurd, 'Legitimacy and Authority in International Politics', *Intl Org* 53 (1999): 379.

[88] Ibid., at 381.

[89] Cf. Daniel Bodansky, 'The Legitimacy of International Governance: A Coming Challenge for International Environmental Law?', *AJIL* 93 (1999): 596 (sociological versus normative dimensions of legitimacy).

[90] A key exception is Robert Keohane, who, in work with Buchanan, has offered criteria for legitimate international institutions. See Allen Buchanan and Robert O. Keohane, 'The Legitimacy

Constructivists are intensely interested in norms, which they see as helping to form the identity of states rather than merely emanating from the interactions of states expressing predetermined interests. They have traced how international norms spread—'cascade'—through networks of norm entrepreneurs, for example in the case of the proliferation and development of international human rights norms.[91] Their inquiry indirectly contributes to discussions of global justice, as they have demonstrated the possibility of diffusion of norms independent of power politics to create an international consciousness about global justice. Yet their work is mostly limited to specific norms, a tactic that seems methodologically driven, and their research agenda seems tilted toward examples where the cosmopolitan prevails over the statist. They have not made the move to demonstrating the possibilities for and consequences of those identities to build a more just world. More fundamentally, although their work highlights the possibilities of a global moral consensus, they remain unwilling to engage in a deep normative appraisal of the developments they study.[92]

Lastly, the English School has overtly embraced questions of global justice. From its origins in the work of Hedley Bull and Martin Wight, it conceives of the world in terms of an international society,[93] a sort of mid-point between a Hobbesian state of nature and a Kantian federation of states. Bull described that society as Grotian in that international law reflects certain notions of the right, just as Grotius saw international law as incorporating natural law. Wight usefully developed the idea of a political morality, in which states owe duties not only to their own people, but to other states as well.[94] The school's adherents have long been divided between those who see the current world order as corresponding to or tolerating a pluralist society and others who see a liberal solidarism of states.[95] The English School's vision is not a theory of a future world, but a thick description of the world as it exists. Its adherents make a link between ethics and international law in seeing states as having expressed, *through the law that they have prescribed*, a certain ethical vision of a society of states. Thus, the pluralist group sees a communitarian morality in the practices of current society, while the

of Global Governance Institutions', *Ethics & Intl Aff* 10 (2006): 405; Allen Buchanan and Robert O. Keohane, 'Precommitment Regimes for Intervention: Supplementing the Security Council', *Ethics & Intl Aff* 25 (2011): 41.

91 See, e.g., Ellen L. Lutz and Kathryn Sikkink, 'International Human Rights Law in Practice: The Justice Cascade: The Evolution and Impact of Foreign Human Rights Trials in Latin America', *Chicago JIL* 2 (2001): 1.

92 Richard Price, 'The Ethics of Constructivism', in Christian Reus-Smit and Duncan Snidal (eds.), *The Oxford Handbook of International Relations* (Oxford: Oxford University Press, 2009) 317.

93 Among Bull's key works, see Hedley Bull, *The Anarchical Society: A Study of Order in World Politics*, 3rd ed. (New York: Columbia University Press, 2002).

94 Martin Wight, 'Western values in international relations', in Herbert Butterfield and Martin Wight (eds.), *Diplomatic Investigations: Essays in the Theory of International Politics* (Cambridge, MA: Harvard University Press, 1966) 89, 127–8.

95 Compare Robert Jackson, *The Global Covenant: Human Conduct in a World of States* (Oxford: Oxford University Press, 2000), with Andrew Hurrell, *On Global Order* (Oxford: Oxford University Press, 2007) 57–94; see also R.J. Vincent, *Human Rights and International Relations* (Cambridge: Cambridge University Press, 1986).

solidarist camp sees a cosmopolitan morality in certain respects, with more on the horizon. The law is thus not only an expression of policy and shared interests, but has its own morality.[96]

Yet the School has still fallen short on offering a true ethical appraisal of the international legal order. It recognizes the relevance of ethical theory to constructing an international society and indeed emphasizes the critical role of international law in promoting communication among international actors.[97] But thus far, while embracing the concept that the challenge for the international society is justice, it fails to offer a view as to how just the current international order is and whether and how it can become more so. It maintains a type of moral skepticism that prevents it from appraising the order's morality not only in terms of practices (including law), but in terms of moral theory. Although recognizing that ethics and interests are not mutually exclusive, it still focuses on 'the monitoring of international consensus and what it can support', thereby analyzing the international moral community in terms of 'measurement rather than judgment'.[98]

The result, then, for the English School, is that international law is the independent variable to determine the extent to which society is pluralist or solidarist. Although this approach has it advantages, it is still quite a different inquiry from asking whether international law itself corresponds to a view of morality based on moral theory. Nonetheless, unlike the rest of international relations theory, its adherents remain aware of moral debates about global justice and have an empirical interest in gauging how international law actually matters.[99]

IV. Conclusion

The project of holding international law up for its contribution to global justice thus works from a scholarly landscape of missed opportunities by two core disciplines that should be giving us the greatest insights into how to construct a more just world order. We have seen how legal scholarship fails to consider the extent to which our judgments of existing law and our proposals for future law turn on ethical choices. If agreement among the parties is the only concern of international law, it will isolate itself from debates about what a just world under law will look like. And we have seen how philosophical work on global justice gives short shrift to both the moral underpinnings of existing international law and the

[96] See Andrew Hurrell, 'International Law and the Making and Unmaking of Boundaries', in Margaret Moore and Allen Buchanan (eds.), *States, Nations, and Borders: The Ethics of Making Boundaries* (Cambridge: Cambridge University Press, 2003) 275.

[97] Hurrell, *On Global Order, supra* note 95, at 84–6, 312–14; Jackson, *Global Covenant, supra* note 95, at 16–22, 416–19.

[98] Molly Cochrane, 'The Ethics of the English School', in Christian Reus-Smit and Duncan Snidal (eds.), *The Oxford Handbook of International Relations* (Oxford: Oxford University Press, 2008) 286, 293.

[99] See Christian Reus-Smit, 'Imagining society: constructivism and the English School', *BJPIR* 4 (2002): 487.

extent to which institutional constraints and opportunities are integral to sound moral evaluation and prescription.

In the case of the latter field, existing work can undermine the project of global justice in two opposite ways. First, it can offer ideas for a more just world order that neglect or even imperil some of the significant accomplishments that international lawmaking has achieved over the past century—a trait seen in much cosmopolitan thinking. Second, it can assume that justice has only a small role to play in the international order because of the state of international law and institutions, an attribute evidenced by Rawls and others who draw the wrong conclusions form the differences between the domestic and global spheres. International relations scholarship helps to give us a sense of the possibilities for law to make a difference in the behaviour of states, which is a crucial part of seeing the role for that law in making for a more just world, but it has not itself seen offering a moral compass as being part of its mission.

The following chapters will offer an approach to global justice and international law that directly responds to these shortcomings. In the remainder of this part of the book, I will develop, propose, and defend a standard of global justice, that of thin justice. In the subsequent parts, I will evaluate the content of the core norms of international law against that standard. In so doing, I hope to move beyond legal scholarship by showing that such an inquiry is hardly *ultra vires* and simultaneously challenge much philosophical scholarship by demonstrating that international law, and certain institutions as well, are neither fatally flawed nor irrelevant in moral terms. In appraising the law's core norms, we will find out that many are just or mostly just, even though some are unjust and require reform. We will also see how international law can build on its existing body of norms to attain a higher standard of global justice. It is now time to turn to that inquiry.

2

Conceptual Groundwork for a Standard of Global Justice

This chapter lays the foundations for the standard of global justice that will be developed and deployed to appraise the core norms of international law. I begin with an explanation of the concept of global justice and contrast it with other types of justice, in particular the Rawlsian idea of distributive justice for a domestic society. This analysis thus delimits the overall scope of the inquiry into the justice of international law that I will undertake in the chapters that follow. I continue with a short primer on the ambit of international law. I see international law as a process for responding to the claims of various global actors through the derivation of norms. The identification of the claimants, their claims, and the kinds of norms that result frames my choice of norms for appraisal. Lastly, I set forth the methodology used for identifying and defending thin justice as a standard by which to evaluate international law. For a standard of justice, composed of principles of justice, to be deserving of that name, it must first be derived in a certain way that fits the idea of justice. In particular, I will ask whether the Rawlsian social contract model using a basic structure of society should be used to derive principles of justice for the international sphere, and ultimately opt for an alternative, predominantly consequentialist framework.

I. The Realm of Global Justice

'Justice', Rawls writes at the start of *A Theory of Justice*, is 'the first virtue of social institutions, as truth is of systems of thought.... [L]aws and institutions no matter how efficient and well-arranged must be reformed or abolished if they are unjust'.[1] By just institutions, Rawls spoke, in terms that still ring true today, of those where 'no arbitrary distinctions are made between persons in the assigning of basic rights and duties and when the rules determine a proper balance between competing claims to the advantages of social life'.[2] This broad view of justice is merely the opening act for Rawls' theory of what he calls 'social justice', and more

[1] John Rawls, *A Theory of Justice*, rev. ed. (Cambridge, MA: Harvard University Press, 1999) 3.
[2] Ibid., at 5.

specifically for social justice that addresses the 'distributive aspects of the basic structure of society'—a theory of distributive justice for domestic societies.[3]

Yet it is equally clear that Rawls' social justice (a) is merely one *form* of justice against which the basic structure of a society is to measured; and (b) has only one *subject* insofar as it applies only to states and their basic structure, and not to localities or global institutions.[4] The implications of these points are critical to explaining why the standard of justice against which I evaluate international law is one of justice (and not something else).

A. What form of justice? Beyond distributive justice

First, much of justice, even at the level of domestic societies, is not about distributive justice of the sort about which he writes, namely 'underwriting an agreement on the proper distributive shares'.[5] Justice had many meanings and understandings before *A Theory of Justice* and it continues to have them after it. Those meanings are not confined to the three simple branches of distributive, corrective, and retributive justice.[6]

So how broad is justice? As an initial matter, it differs from morality in that justice in a commonsense understanding is a *relational* concept—not just about personal decisions about the right way to act but about who gets to do what, or who gets to have what, vis-à-vis other actors' claims. As Brian Barry writes: '[J]ustice as impartiality is not designed to tell us how to live. It addresses itself to a different but equally important question: how are we to live *together*, given that we have different ideas about how to live?'[7] And H.L.A. Hart wrote that 'justice is traditionally thought of as maintaining or restoring a *balance* or *proportion*', so that the leading precepts of justice are: '"Treat like cases alike"... "and treat different cases differently"'.[8] It is in this sense that Hare defines 'formal justice' and declares that: 'We are being formally unjust if we make different moral judgments about identical cases, and act on them.'[9]

In thinking about justice as relational, it seems like we cannot escape the idea of distributions, or more precisely of allocations—an idea of the relative shares of some core social constructs (more on this later) to be granted to individuals.[10]

[3] Ibid., at 8.

[4] John Rawls, *Justice as Fairness: A Restatement* (Cambridge, MA: Harvard University Press, 2001) 11 (three levels of justice: local justice, domestic justice, and global justice).

[5] Rawls, *A Theory of Justice*, *supra* note 1, at 4.

[6] Compare Joel Feinberg, 'Noncomparative Justice', *Phil Rev* 83 (1974): 297, 297 ('the inference from three general kinds of human activity to three distinct and theoretically interesting forms of justice would be a *non sequitur*'), with Lea Brilmayer, 'International Justice and International Law', *W Va L Rev* 98 (1996): 611 (endorsing these three forms alone).

[7] Brian Barry, *Justice as Impartiality* (New York: Oxford University Press, 1995) 77.

[8] H.L.A. Hart, *The Concept of Law*, 3rd ed. (Oxford: Oxford University Press, 2012), 159.

[9] R.M. Hare, *Moral Thinking: Its Levels, Method, and Point* (Oxford: Clarendon Press, 1981) 157.

[10] For examples of this view, see Michael J. Sandel, *Justice* (New York: Farrar, Straus and Giroux, 2009) 19 ('how [society] distributes the things we prize'); John Gardner, 'What is Tort Law For? Part I. The Place of Corrective Justice', *Law & Phil* 30 (2011): 1, 6 ('Norms of justice... are norms for tackling... questions about who is to get how much of what'). See also Rawls, *A Theory of Justice*,

Yet even as justice is relational, it is not limited to a focus on comparisons, but has non-comparative elements as well. Thus, as Joel Feinberg pointed out, we can speak about the injustices involved in the punishment of the innocent, or the violation of a contract, or the indignity of slavery.[11] If Feinberg is right that justice must include these non-comparative principles, then it is about more than distribution or relative allocations. Barry's definition recognizes something beyond comparative notions when he sees rules of justice as norms that 'assign rights and duties to people...in such a way that...it is clear what each person is entitled or required to do'.[12]

When I ask about whether norms of international law conform to a certain standard of justice, the justice I have in mind fits within either the comparativist/relativist concept or the broader one. On the one hand, for some norms, we will ask questions about allocations and comparisons: for instance, is it just for international law to grant some people but not others a right to secede? Is it just that some states seem to get more privileges than others? Is it just that a state must protect some people's human rights but cannot protect others'? On the other hand, for other norms, we will ask questions that are harder to conceive in comparative terms, although they certainly are relational: is it just for international law to require a state to await an armed attack to respond in self-defense? Is it just that international law allows a state to prosecute war criminals for acts abroad? Readers who insist only on justice as about allocations will perhaps see me as barking up the wrong tree. And, a fortiori, those who insist that the distributional concept is limited to the distribution of goods will be in for even more of a disappointment, as this matter is addressed with respect to international economic law but not other subjects.[13] But the questions that I will ask about, and the standard that I will apply to, international law, are those of justice and not just morality in that they are focused on relations and institutions and not merely personal choices.

B. What subject for justice? Justice beyond the state

The second implication of Rawls' distinctions is that other kinds of justice besides Rawls' social justice can provide standards for institutions that are *not* part of the domestic basic structure of a society. Global justice has as its subject institutions

supra note 1, at 7 ('justice applies whenever there is an allotment of something rationally regarded as advantageous or disadvantageous').

[11] Feinberg, 'Noncomparative Justice', *supra* note 6, at 299–302.

[12] Barry, *Justice as Impartiality, supra* note 7, at 72, 77. But see Brian Barry, *Theories of Justice* (Berkeley, CA: University of California Press, 1989) 3 ('the central issue in any theory of justice is the defensibility of unequal relations between people'). Barry's notion resembles the broad definition from Roman law: 'Justice is the set and constant purpose which gives to every man his due'. J.B. Moyle, *The Institutes of Justinian*, 5th ed. (Oxford: Clarendon Press, 1913) bk I, title 1, available at <http://droitromain.upmf-grenoble.fr/Anglica/just1_Moyle.htm>.

[13] In this sense, my understanding of justice covers political justice and economic justice, both of which are central to an understanding of global justice. See Kok-Chor Tan, *Justice Without Borders: Cosmopolitanism, Nationalism, and Patriotism* (Cambridge: Cambridge University Press, 2004) 4.

beyond those in domestic societies, at the international level. Those institutions include at their very core international law, which is the subject of the justice in this study.

For some scholars, the principles of global justice are no different from the principles of domestic justice because the international realm is already characterized by a basic structure—or perhaps because neither the principles of domestic justice nor global justice require a basic structure in the first place. But if we do not believe that to be the case, or do not wish to prove the existence of a global basic structure, then we need to be open to the possibility that the principles of global justice will be quite distinct from the principles that apply to the domestic basic structure. Theorists of global justice recognize that we are applying justice to a distinct set of institutions compared to domestic justice, even as they define the project or principles of global (or international) justice in their own terms. Global justice gives particular attention to the role of states and the relations between them.[14]

Just as at the domestic level, however, global justice is very much about more than distributive justice. Thus, following Feinberg's and Barry's views about the breadth of justice, I see global justice as *process or outcome that assigns rights and duties to global actors so that it is clear what each such actor is entitled or required to do or have.* Norms of international law are just if they assign those rights and duties in a way that meets a substantive standard of justice. In Chapter 3, I will identify a standard comprising two principles or pillars—promotion of peace and respect for basic human rights.

This broad definition does not mean that all international law norms can be appraised as just or unjust or something in the middle. Like domestic law, much of international law is about coordination, in the sense of rules of the road that lack any obvious moral grounding. This includes much of the specialized and technical law that comes out of UN agencies, including that on telecommunications, aviation, food safety, aspects of the law of the sea (some of which are indeed tied up with notions of justice), and aviation. Nonetheless, these rules remain relevant to the project of creating a just world order. At a minimum, we may say that it is just to have such rules compared to the absence of them.[15] Moreover, the presence of multiple coordination norms may itself be evidence of a global order that is becoming more just. All these rules seem to be part of what Jeremy Waldron has called a 'dense thicket of rules that sustain our life together, a life shared by people and peoples, [that] includes some of the most mundane things imaginable...the ordinary as well as the extraordinary,

[14] Terry Nardin, 'International Ethics', in Christian Reus-Smit and Duncan Snidal (eds.), *The Oxford Handbook of International Relations* (New York: Oxford University Press, 2008) 594, 596, 603 (project of 'investigating the moral basis of international order as requiring states to coexist within a common framework of international law'); Charles R. Beitz, 'International Liberalism and Distributive Justice', *World Politics* 51 (1999): 269, 270 (international political justice includes 'the prerogatives of the state, the authority of international law and institutions, and the minimum requirements of fair participation in international governance').

[15] I appreciate this insight from Paola Carozza.

the tedious as well as the exciting, the commercial as well as the ideological'.[16] As such norms proliferate, we are closer to forming the sort of relationships across the planet from which new norms, grounded in justice, can sprout.

II. The Realm of International Law

Before we can examine the justice of the international legal order, we must first understand its basic contours. International law comprises an enormously complex set of norms and legal relationships among a large group of international actors. These norms and relationships are the product of a process of claim and counterclaim among those actors, a process that may lead to treaties, customary international law, resolutions of international organizations, soft law, and other forms of law. Although some of the following exposition might seem somewhat basic to some international legal scholars, I nonetheless wish to frame my approach to the field that will be deployed in later chapters.

A. Actors and claims

It is critical first to identify clearly the players in the system. As a general matter, six major actors participate in the international legal process: states, individuals, peoples, international organizations, non-governmental organizations (NGOs), and business entities. By participate, I mean that they make claims against each other for the advancement of various goals, where those claims have led to the creation of norms of international law characterized by legal relationships. Some traditional international legal scholars prefer to label these participants, or at least some of them, as international 'persons' based on the old concept of 'legal personality', i.e. the capacity to be subject to legal rights and duties.[17] My listing does not rely on this notion because it is both circular in its usage and unhelpful in contributing to any understanding of whether an entity has rights and duties.[18]

It is not necessary here to delve into international law doctrine or disagreements over the legal definition of each claimant. Obviously, some of the terms are hard to define without wrongly excluding or including some entities. Taiwan, for

[16] Jeremy Waldron, 'Cosmopolitan Norms', in Seyla Benhabib (ed.), *Another Cosmopolitanism* (New York: Oxford University Press, 2006) 83, 97. In a similar move, Robert Wai has characterized the array of norms of international economic law as reflecting a cosmopolitan vision of economic relations. See Robert Wai, 'The Cosmopolitanism of Transnational Economic Law', in Cecilia M. Bailliet and Katja Franko Aas (eds.), *Cosmopolitan Justice and its Discontents* (Milton Park: Routledge, 2011) 153.

[17] See, e.g., Nkambo Mugerwa, 'Subjects of International Law', in Max Sørenson (ed.), *Manual of Public International Law* (New York: St. Martin's Press, 1968) 247, 249.

[18] In a similar vein, Brent Fisse and John Braithwaite, as well as Peter Cane, have rejected the notion that an actor can only be blameworthy if it is previously determined to have 'philosophical personality'. Brent Fisse and John Braithwaite, 'The Allocation of Responsibility for Corporate Crime: Individualism, Collectivism and Accountability', *Syd L Rev* 11 (1988): 468, 483–8; Peter Cane, *Responsibility in Law and Morality* (Oxford: Hart Publishing, 2002) 143–50.

instance, is not quite a state, though it typically acts like one. And international organizations range from those created by treaty to much looser arrangements, after which point they are so loose as to be mere gatherings of governmental officials. Others overlap at the margins, for example a business-initiated NGO (or BINGO) is as much an NGO as it is a business. Moreover, the legal process includes other participants—organized religions, sports entities, and transnational criminal or terrorist groups. To the average person, at least some of these may play a greater role in their personal lives. But with the possible exception of the transnational terrorist group, they are not major participants in the claims process.

I now sketch the principal claims of the six actors and identify upon whom they are making them. The key norms discussed in this volume are organized based on these claims because they respond to the major lawmaking endeavors that take place among relevant actors. The rather stale doctrinal categories of traditional international law do not capture this dynamic.

1. The state

The state's fundamental claim in the international order is to its *sovereignty*, a mystical term encompassing several key concepts. Rather than ascribing any legal meaning to the term, I view sovereignty as a shorthand for a series of claims made by states. First among these is *territorial integrity*, the claim not to be invaded and conquered. The state may also include within the concept of territorial integrity the idea of unity, which is a claim not to be broken up from within. Second is the idea of *political independence*, the claim not to be subservient to or controlled by another state. Governments within states realize that they may need to make compromises in order to gain outside supporters, but they generally insist upon the freedom to make certain essential choices and not have them made for them. This claim is fundamentally one of non-interference. Third is a claim to *participation*. This claim extends from negotiating and signing treaties as an equal partner to joining and contributing to international organizations. These three claims are explored principally in Chapters 4 to 7. The sovereignty claim has extended to the claim to be left alone in a broad sense of opting out of emerging international norms or, more insidiously for international lawyers, of seeking to opt out of binding international norms.[19] These are claims that international law does not accept, though states continue to make them.

Against whom does the state make these sovereignty claims?: principally against other states—states seeking to dominate it through political or economic strong-arming, intervention, non-recognition, or, rarely, aggression. But the state can make the claim against other participants as well. Russia and China are making sovereignty claims against peoples—Chechen and Tibetans, respectively—and

[19] See Louis Henkin, *International Law: Politics and Values* (Boston: Martinus Nijhoff Publishers, 1995) 8–9; see also Stephen D. Krasner, *Sovereignty: Organized Hypocrisy* (Princeton, NJ: Princeton University Press, 1999) 65–7.

Israel against Palestinians. Those states are also making claims against NGOs that oppose their actions. Many poor states also make a sovereignty claim against the International Monetary Fund (IMF), an organization of states seen to be controlling the way a state can make fiscal and monetary policy. And the attempts by the developing world to regain control of their natural resources after decolonization were sovereignty claims in part against transnational business entities.[20]

The sovereignty claim is surely the principal claim of states, but it is not the only one. A broad second category of claims are claims of *economic security*. One group, which is an analogue of the political independence claim noted previously, is the idea of *economic control*, in the sense of control over the exploitation of natural resources on its territory or adjoining seas, but also the freedom to choose its economic policy free from foreign pressure and to distribute the material benefits of commerce as its chooses. But a broader claim is to *access to economic benefits*, in the sense of participation in the international economic system to achieve material improvement of its residents. Poor states may seek global intellectual property rules that allow them to make products without compensating patent holders; rich states may seek investment rules that protect their investors from local governments who want to renege on contracts. These claims are explored in Chapters 10 and 11.

2. *Peoples*

Although many groups within and across states call themselves a people, my own sense is that international law generally views peoples as having something beyond ethnic kinship—some sort of territorial claim, affiliation, or attachment (for example the Finnish, Corsican, or Sioux people).[21] Despite these definitional difficulties, the central claim of peoples is to *self-government*. This includes a claim to *recognition* as a distinct actor and not merely a loose group of individuals and, most significantly, claims to *control its future* through political arrangements ranging from self-administration within states up to creation of its own state. (Minority groups not usually regarded as peoples, such as territorially dispersed religious groups, typically make more modest claims, for example to assert and perpetuate to future generations their identity through linguistic, educational, cultural, and other practices.) This claim resonates with Iris Young's interpretation that self-determination concerns non-domination rather than simply non-interference.[22] The primary target of these claims is the state or, in some cases (like secession) a community of states, as they generally have the power to act on these claims. Such claims are addressed in Chapter 6. Peoples also make

[20] See generally Steven R. Ratner, 'Corporations and Human Rights: A Theory of Legal Responsibility', *Yale LJ* 111 (2001): 443, 452–9.

[21] See generally Thomas D. Musgrave, *Self-Determination and National Minorities* (Oxford: Clarendon Press, 1997) 148–79.

[22] Iris Marion Young, *Global Challenges: War, Self-Determination and Responsibility for Justice* (Malden, MA: Polity Press, 2007) 50–1.

claims against their members, in seeking to constrain their behavior, including by preventing exit.

3. *The individual*

The individual's rise as a participant in the international legal process gained momentum in the nineteenth century in the anti-slavery movement; it stood on its own after World War I as states agreed to protect ethnic minorities in the new states created after the war and to protect some workers through international labor law. The era after World War II saw the rise of individual human rights and the codification of numerous treaties to advance them.[23] As David Held has noted, through these developments, 'a bridge is created between morality and law where, at best, only stepping stones existed before'.[24] The individual's fundamental claims are of *personal freedom* and *governmental protection*. The claims of personal freedom (or autonomy) arise from an interest in being immune from governmental abuse, being left alone by those who have the power to interfere negatively with the person's welfare. She might make this claim in seeking the freedom to worship without interference as well as not to be tortured following an arrest. The claim of governmental protection is, effectively, about not being left alone, in the sense of being left alone to suffer. An individual makes such a claim when she wants to attain a certain standard of living for herself and her family; but she also makes it when she wants the state to conduct a fair trial if she is accused of a crime. These claims are addressed throughout this volume in the emphasis on human rights.

The individual principally makes these claims on the state, usually his or her own, for it generally has the readiest capacity to grant that which the claimant seeks. But at times an individual may make a claim on another state to protect him or her in some way. International law's recognition of some of these claims is the subject of Chapter 9. An individual can assert a claim against a people, as when a member of an indigenous group seeks to opt out of a practice that the group mandates; or against business entities, as when an individual accuses such entities of not providing proper conditions of labor.

4. *International organizations*

International organizations, consisting mostly but not exclusively of states, in many ways reflect the interests of their members. Their claims will thus be dictated to a large degree by what their members want to emphasize. Yet international

[23] As stated by the UN's International Criminal Tribunal for the Former Yugoslavia (ICTY), 'A State-sovereignty-oriented approach has been gradually supplanted by a human-being-oriented approach.... [T]he maxim of Roman law *hominum causa omne jus constitutum est*...has gained a firm foothold in the international community'. *Prosecutor v Tadić*, Case No. IT-94-1-T, *Decision on the Defence Motion for Interlocutory Appeal on Jurisdiction* (2 October 1995), para. 97, <http://www.icty.org>.

[24] David Held, 'Law of States, Law of Peoples: Three Models of Sovereignty', *Legal Theory* 8 (2002): 1, 13.

organizations also generate claims from their own secretariat officials. While those claims can never be in opposition to the views of most of the members, they need not be in accordance with the views of all of them. Thus, for instance, even as the UN is dedicated to international peace and security, with a significant focus on advancing the sovereignty claims of its members—for example through strategies to prevent and respond to violence—it advances in many ways the claims of individuals and peoples. At a more general level, international organizations also make a claim for *relevance.* That is, even as states create international organizations, whether global or regional, they remain ambivalent as to how much authority to delegate to them.[25] Leading states and the officials of these institutions want them to be key fora for decisionmaking. They make these claims against states—often their own members—as well as against other organizations. International organizations are considered throughout this volume, with a special treatment of their membership and decisionmaking in Chapter 8.

5. *Non-governmental organizations*

NGOs share the same general claim as international organizations—*relevance.* With their resources devoted to skilled staff, they must influence those who have the power or resources to advance their substantive agenda. In the two most significant areas for international NGOs, namely human rights and the environment, they must persuade, through the power of their research and argumentation, those with decisionmaking authority and influence of the rightness of their cause. They make these claims against all the other actors in the international legal process, because all of them can help the NGO advance its goals.

6. *Business entities*

From the large multinational corporation to the small family enterprise, the pre-eminent claim of business is for *economic wealth.* Businesses may frame these claims in terms of consumer benefit, environmental protection, or even national security, and they may indeed donate their some of their profits to charitable causes, but, in the end, they are making claims for a greater share of economic wealth. They make this claim against all of the other participants. Their claims are central in Chapters 10 and 11 on international economic law.

B. From claims to norms

Like all law, international law is about the resolution of competing claims. When we say that international law resolves claims, we mean that the law encompasses multiple rules and processes that assign to different persons, entities, and

[25] See Andrew Guzman, 'International Organizations and the Frankenstein Problem', *EJIL* 24 (2013): 999.

institutions various rights, duties, and powers, including the power to make the rules. In a pithy description of the 1982 United Nations Convention the Law of the Sea, Philip Allott wrote:

> It is comprehensive in dealing with the whole nonland area of the world. . . . It has a rule for everything. The rule may be a permissive rule. It may be an obligation. It may confer an explicit freedom or leave a residual liberty by not specifying a right or a duty. But a Flying Dutchman wandering the sea areas of the world, carrying his copy of the Convention, would [find that] [t]he Convention would never fail him.[26]

First and foremost among these legal relationships are duties. Duties remain the defining legal relationship for our understanding of international law for three reasons:

- First is a conceptual reason grounded in jurisprudence. Law, to deserve that moniker, must, at a minimum, be authoritative. Joseph Raz has identified a common understanding of authority as expressing first and foremost the 'right to impose duties'.[27] Law can do many other things besides impose duties but, Raz adds: 'In every case the explanation of the normative effect of the exercise of authority leads back, sometimes through very circuitous routes, to the imposition of duties either by the authority itself or by some other persons.'[28]
- Second is a reason grounded in sociology—about how international law works. For while international law recognizes many rights—and rights of all the Hohfeldian variety held by all sorts of participants making claims—we care particularly about what international law requires and of whom it requires it. Duty-holders are the actors who must adopt a specific course of conduct in order for the law's ends to be achieved. Even if a person or a state has a right to a specific state of affairs (for example territorial integrity or freedom of the high seas), it is to the duty-holder we turn to ensure that that the right is realized. As Onora O'Neill writes: 'The perspective of obligations is simply more directly connected to action. . . . obligations provide the more coherent and more comprehensive starting point for thinking about ethical requirements, including the requirements of justice.'[29]
- Third, as a matter of international law doctrine, much of the evaluation of lawful conduct is through the lens of state responsibility for wrongful acts, by which we ask whether a state has acted in breach of its international obligations.[30] Indeed, under a very traditionalist understanding of international law, as reflected in the decision of the Permanent Court of International Justice in the *S.S. Lotus* case, international law itself consists only of duties on states, with

[26] Philip Allott, 'Power Sharing in the Law of the Sea', *AJIL* 77 (1983): 1, 8.

[27] Joseph Raz, *The Morality of Freedom* (Oxford: Clarendon Press, 1986) 28–9; see also at 37: 'Orders and commands are among the expressions typical of practical authority. Only those who claim authority can command . . . [A] valid command (i.e. one issued by a person in authority) is a peremptory reason. We express this thought by saying that valid commands or other valid authoritative requirements impose obligations.'

[28] Ibid., at 44–5.

[29] Onora O'Neill, *Bounds of Justice* (New York: Cambridge University Press, 2000) 199.

[30] See generally ILC Articles on Responsibility, Art. 2(b).

rights unnecessary because all behavior not prohibited by those duties is perfectly permissible.[31] From human rights to trade and investment, we are interested in determining whether a state has failed to live up to its duties.

The centrality of the state to the international political and legal order for most of the past 350 years has meant that the law recognizes the most elaborate set of duties as those of *states* toward other *states*, although states also have important duties in the area of human rights and self-determination toward individuals and peoples, respectively. The other five actors may also have duties, though the law has not developed them in nearly as much detail.[32]

Nonetheless, some core norms are best viewed outside the framework of duties, for example the rights of self-determination, the principle of sovereign equality, and the special privileges of the permanent members of the UN Security Council. In those cases, we are most interested in rights or privileges. Yet these other relationships may require consideration of duties, either because they themselves involve duties by other actors or because we might wish to ask why certain duties are not recognized. The absence of a duty to do something or not to do something can be as significant morally as the presence of a duty. There is no formula for determining whether a norm of international law will be best evaluated in terms of its duties or in terms of other legal relationships. It depends on how the prescription process for resolving the competing claims turns out. In the end, this book will focus on the core norms, rather than all norms resulting from the claims of the six actors.

C. General and special duties

The norms and duties in international law will vary along multiple dimensions. Norms may be more or less central to the international legal order; and only those in the former group will be addressed in this book. They may also be more or less 'hard' or 'soft' in terms of their specificity, source of authority, and associated mechanisms for achieving compliance with them.[33] Or they may take shape in treaty, customary law, or other forms.

One further dimension that bears a brief explanation at this stage is a norm's generality, and the resultant distinction between general and special duties. These last two terms owe much of their staying power to H.L.A. Hart's *Are There Any Natural Rights?*, which introduced the notion of special and general *rights*.[34] Special rights 'arise out of special transactions between individuals or out of some

[31] *S.S. 'Lotus'*, 1927 PCIJ Series A No. 10, 18 (7 September) ('Restrictions upon the independence of States cannot therefore be presumed').

[32] For a summary of the law's basic list of duties on the three main actors, see Steven R. Ratner, 'Is International Law Impartial?', *Legal Theory* 11 (2005): 39, 47–53.

[33] For more on this idea, see W. Michael Reisman, 'The Concept and Functions of Soft Law in International Politics', in Emmanuel G. Bello and Bola A. Ajibola (eds.), *Essays in Honour of Judge Taslim Olawale Elias*, Vol. 1 (Boston, MA: Martinus Nijhoff Publishers, 1992) 135, 136.

[34] H.L.A. Hart, 'Are There Any Natural Rights?', *Phil Rev* 64 (1955): 175.

special relationship in which they stand to each other'; thus 'the persons who have the right and those who have the corresponding obligation are limited to the parties to the special transaction or relationship'; general rights 'are rights which all men capable of choice have in the absence of those special conditions which give rise to special rights [and] have as correlative obligations not to interfere to which everyone else is subject and not merely the parties to some special relationship or transaction'.[35]

Hart's distinction led to the conceptualization of special and general *duties*. As Robert Goodin writes:

> In contrast to the universality of the general moral law, some people have special duties that other people do not. In contrast to the impartiality of the general moral law, we all have special duties to some people that we do not have to others. Special duties, in short, bind particular people to particular other people.[36]

These constructs, developed to describe the rights and duties of individuals, are equally relevant to the legal relationships of states and non-state actors. Most of international law's core state-to-state duties are general.[37] And the core duties upon states to individuals and businesses are also in one sense general duties: these include the ban on torture, slavery, genocide, and other serious human rights abuses; the non-return of refugees to their place of persecution (non-*refoulement*); and fair treatment to all business entities that set up in one's territory. To say that someone has a human right not to be so mistreated means that all states have a duty not to engage in such conduct against anyone. Two categories of general duties are particularly important. First, when a state has an obligation *erga omnes*, not only does the state have a duty to all other states, but all states may invoke the obligation in the event of a breach, not merely those specially affected by it.[38] A related category are *jus cogens* norms, so-called peremptory norms in that no treaty between states may override them.

But many other duties are not general. When two or more states agree to a treaty, they create a set of special duties, explicitly agreeing to treat each other differently from the way they treat other states. Hart recognized promises as 'the most obvious cases of special rights'.[39] International law generally permits such disparate treatment provided (a) any general duties under customary international law regarding the subject of the treaty are default rules rather than *jus cogens* rules; (b) the treaty does not contravene the UN Charter; and

[35] Ibid., at 183, 188.

[36] Robert E. Goodin, 'What is So Special about Our Fellow Countrymen?', *Ethics* (1988): 663, 665. As Philip Pettit and Goodin note, these special duties can arise by virtue of agents' 'identities, relationships or histories'. Philip Pettit and Robert Goodin, 'The Possibility of Special Duties', *Can J Phil* 16 (1986): 651, 651.

[37] Many of these norms resemble what Thomas Franck has called the 'ultimate canon', obligations which 'attach to all states by virtue of their status as validated members of the international community'. See Thomas M. Franck, *Fairness in International Law and Institutions* (Oxford: Clarendon Press, 1995) 45.

[38] See, e.g., *Barcelona Traction, Light and Power Company, Ltd (Belgium v Spain)* [1970] ICJ 3, 32 (5 February).

[39] Hart, 'Are There Any Natural Rights?', *supra* note 34, at 183–4.

(c) the states are not violating any earlier treaties on the subject (unless the parties to the earlier and later treaties are the same).[40] Thus, two states could divide a river to give one state most of it as long as no rule of customary law mandated division down the middle (there is, in fact, no such rule) and as long as those states had not previously signed a treaty with other states mandating such a division.[41]

Some special duties of states arise independently of contractual ties per se. States owe some duties to their neighbors based on physical proximity. For example, even before the UN Convention on the Law of the Sea, international law recognized duties on neighbors sharing waters and submerged offshore areas. Today, states opposite each other (for example Spain and Morocco across the Straits of Gibraltar) are to divide any overlapping areas of their territorial sea—the waters within twelve miles of shore—equally, with only a weaker obligation to negotiate over how to divide up the continental shelf off their shores.[42] In this case, the physical accident of geography creates a relationship between the states giving rise to special duties.[43]

The clarification of these two types of norms is important insofar as distinct questions of justice arise with respect to special duties because they involve disparate treatment by dutyholders of different states or of different individuals; special rights for states vis-à-vis other states raise such questions as well. Much of the analysis of the justice of international law will concern only general duties of states, but we will see a new layer of issues related to special duties and rights.

III. Foundations for a Standard of Global Justice

Having clarified my understanding of both justice and international law, I now provide the groundwork for deriving my standard of global justice. For any standard of justice of the domestic or global variety to be worthy of its name, its underlying principles must be derived through a certain form of reasoning, i.e. they must be grounded in concepts that are necessary and sufficient for any theory or standard of justice. In this final Section, I will consider the basic frameworks for developing principles of justice and the possibilities of building on them for deriving principles of global justice.

[40] VCLT, Arts. 30, 53; UN Charter, Art. 103.

[41] As the number of states to any treaty increases, it becomes difficult to label the duties under it special. Indeed, widespread acceptance of a treaty is evidence that its duties are customary international law, binding even non-ratifying states.

[42] UNCLOS, Art. 15.

[43] These special duties can also become general duties. As science has demonstrated that one state's pollution may travel to the other side of the planet, the targets of the state's duties not to pollute have expanded beyond neighbors to all states. The contemporary embodiment of that understanding is Principle 21 of the 1972 UN Environmental Conference in Stockholm, which says that states have 'the responsibility to ensure that activities within their jurisdiction or control do not cause damage to the environment of other States'. Declaration of the United Nations Conference on the Human Environment (Stockholm Declaration), 16 June 1972, principle 21, UN Doc. A/CONF.48/14.

A. Justice as impartiality, not mutual advantage

Certain basic fault lines divide the groundings of theories of justice. In one camp lies Thomas Hobbes' idea of justice as mutual advantage, where justice is the performance of a covenant, in particular a covenant whereby men agree, for their own self-interest, to transfer certain of the rights that they enjoy in the state of nature to a sovereign or commonwealth. Assuming there is a civil power that can force compliance with that covenant, justice demands compliance with any such contract, regardless of the bargaining power of the sides that agreed upon it and the contents of the bargain.[44] With few exceptions, whatever the parties believed was to their mutual advantage and have put into their covenant—and thus authorized the state to enforce—is obligatory as a matter of justice.[45] If that bargain perpetuates inequalities, or creates significant harm to particular individuals, the parties must still follow it.

Rawls termed such a bargain a mere *modus vivendi*, lacking the overlapping consensus necessary for a political conception of justice; indeed, he considered a treaty between two belligerents ending a war as a paradigmatic *modus vivendi*.[46] The underlying relationship was based on mere mutual advantage and not reciprocity, which was required for a society to which principles of justice could apply.[47] Barry went even further to say that any theory of justice that brought in mutual advantage was not really about justice at all.[48] Even if one conceded that a bargain based on mutual advantage might improve the situation of the parties compared to pure anarchy, or limit the extent to which they pursue their self-interest, it still 'fails egregiously to . . . provide some moral basis for the claims of the relatively powerless'.[49]

Accepting the Hobbesian position would make the inquiry at the heart of this book a very simple one. For since most international law is the product of agreement, whether through treaty or custom, the justice of international law would depend entirely on the extent to which there is a coercive power behind the agreement. Treaties with real sanctions for non-compliance, regardless of their content, would be just. That group would include the 1938 Munich Agreement dividing up Czechoslovakia (for which non-compliance by France might have meant earlier invasion by Germany) or the Warsaw Pact treaty (for which non-compliance by the Eastern bloc would have meant invasion by the Soviet Union). Treaties with little or no coercive force behind them, such as the UN Charter or human rights treaties, would not themselves be unjust, but there would certainly be no duty based on justice to follow them. Such an inquiry would fail to do what Neil MacCormick has noted is essential to the task of inquiries regarding justice: to

44 Thomas Hobbes, *Leviathan* (New York: Penguin Books, 1985) chs. XIV–XV, 189–217.

45 Ibid., at ch. XIV, 198, 202 ('When a Covenant is made, then to break it is Unjust').

46 John Rawls, *Political Liberalism*, expanded ed. (New York: Columbia University Press, 2005) 144–9.

47 Ibid., at 15–18.

48 Barry, *Justice as Impartiality*, *supra* note 7, at 39–46.

49 Ibid., at 46. See also Will Kymlicka, 'The Social Contract Tradition', in Peter Singer (ed.), *A Companion to Ethics* (Malden, MA: Blackwell Publishing, 1993) 186, 189–95.

'ask about the justice of the law, not only about justice in its administration and its observance by citizens'.[50]

Rejecting a Hobbesian conception of justice does not require the rejection of all his premises. Indeed, agreements among persons—or states—that create some stability of expectations have a significant value for the actors concerned, even if the actors are ready to break them when circumstances change. The state of nature is awful, and stability has many advantages for improving the lives of human (and non-human) beings.

Of the alternatives to Hobbes as a grounding for justice, including the Rawlsian idea of reciprocity, I will adopt Barry's idea of *justice as impartiality*.[51] At its most fundamental level, impartiality describes a way that individuals and institutions decide and act, one based on disinterestedness, consistency, and fairness and not merely personal motives.[52] It is appealing as the essence of justice as described earlier insofar as it is, at its most fundamental, about *not playing favorites*. In deriving duties of justice, impartial reasoning requires a commitment to the equal treatment of individuals. Equal treatment does not mean equal outcomes. But any unequal outcomes, including special duties to certain people or states, must be justifiable from an impartial perspective.[53] As Thomas Hill wrote: 'All the impartiality thesis says is that, if and when one raises questions regarding fundamental moral standards, the court of appeal that one addresses is a court in which no particular individual, group, or country has *special* standing.'[54] In earlier work, I asked whether some of the basic duties that international law recognizes as special could be justified as impartial.[55] Any standard of global justice, including my own, must see justice as grounded in impartiality.[56] Rainer Forst adopts a related concept when he argues that the criteria of justification of all norms, institutions, and practices to which an individual is subjected must be that of 'reciprocity and generality'.[57]

[50] Neil MacCormick, *Practical Reason in Law and Morality* (New York: Oxford University Press, 2008) 135.

[51] See Barry, *Justice as Impartiality, supra* note 7; Allen Gibbard, 'Constructing Justice', *Phil & Pub Aff* 20 (1991): 264 (reviewing Brian Barry, *Theories of Justice* (1989)).

[52] It is in this sense that Barry and Terry Nardin define justice as impartiality. See Barry, *Justice as Impartiality, supra* note 7, at 20–7; Terry Nardin, *Law, Morality, and the Relations of States* (Princeton, NJ: Princeton University Press, 1983) 258–9, 265.

[53] Barry, John Deigh, and Marcia Baron have deployed the notion of 'second-order impartiality' to describe this approach. See, e.g., Barry, *Justice as Impartiality, supra* note 7, at 191–5; Marcia Baron, 'Impartiality and Friendship', *Ethics* 101 (1991): 836; see also Susan Mendus, *Impartiality in Moral and Political Philosophy* (Oxford: Oxford University Press, 2002).

[54] Quoted in Barry, *Justice as Impartiality, supra* note 7, at 226.

[55] Ratner, 'Is International Law Impartial?', *supra* note 32.

[56] David Held endorses the same idea—what he calls the 'metaprinciple of impartialist reasoning'—as one of two core starting points (along with a 'metaprinciple of autonomy') for his derivation of cosmopolitan principles. David Held, *Cosmopolitanism: Ideals and Realities* (Malden, MA: Polity Press, 2010) 85–91. See also Tan, *Justice Without Borders, supra* note 13, at 190.

[57] Rainer Forst, 'Towards a Critical Theory of Transnational Justice', *Metaphilosophy* 32 (2001): 160, 169.

B. Choosing among impartialist frameworks

Yet impartiality (in both moral and legal reasoning) still demands an underlying theory for deciding which differences count and which ones do not.[58] Impartial moral reasoning about global justice may be undertaken under the terms of any one of the major approaches of ethics. Thus, utilitarianism works from the impartial standpoint to derive principles of justice based on the idea of maximizing total individual welfare. Hare's two-level approach sees our most intimate relationships as guided by intuition but views most big questions, including presumably those concerning global justice, as best answered by asking which schemes will maximize overall utility.[59] From the deontological starting point of Kant's vision of international society, practical reason compels people to act according to the categorical imperative; the result is states based on freedom and individual equality and, eventually, relations among states that will pursue perpetual peace.[60] Finally, a contractarian position would seek to ground global justice on what an actual or hypothetical group of equal individuals would agree upon. As Barry writes, 'just rules are those that can be freely endorsed by people on a footing of equality'.[61]

The choice of which of these three impartialist perspectives to adopt in proposing a standard of global justice is a great challenge, and each scholar's perspective is informed by certain pre-theoretical intuitions as to the sorts of considerations that should go into moral thinking. As noted in Section I, Rawls' contractarian approach, the dominant model for domestic distributive justice, is limited on its own terms in two respects: it is a theory of social justice (focused on distributive issues), and its subject is the basic structure of a domestic society.[62] Yet the appeal of this dominant model, even as its author noted its limitations, requires that we consider its suitability to grounding a standard of justice at the global level.

[58] David Miller, *On Nationality* (Oxford: Clarendon Press, 1995) 53–5.

[59] Hare, *Moral Thinking, supra* note 9, at 25–8; Peter Singer, *One World: The Ethics of Globalization*, 2nd ed. (New Haven, CT: Yale University Press, 2002) 159–67.

[60] Immanuel Kant, 'On the Common Saying: "This May be True in Theory, but it does not Apply in Practice"', in Hans Reiss (ed.) and H.B. Nisbet (trans.), *Kant: Political Writings*, 2nd ed. (New York: Cambridge University Press, 1991) 61, 74–77; Immanuel Kant, 'Perpetual Peace: A Philosophical Sketch', in *Kant: Political Writings* (*supra*) 93, 108–14. Allen Buchanan has grounded his own impartial deontological view in what he calls a 'Natural Duty of Justice', which requires individuals to 'help create structures that provide all persons with access to just institutions'. Allen Buchanan, *Justice, Legitimacy, and Self-Determination: Moral Foundations for International Law* (Oxford: Oxford University Press, 2004) 86–8.

[61] Barry, *Justice as Impartiality, supra* note 7, 52. Thomas Pogge took a Rawlsian contractarian approach and derived a vision of global justice characterized by universalization of the difference principle. Thomas W. Pogge, *Realizing Rawls* (Ithaca, NY: Cornell University Press, 1989).

[62] Rawls, *Political Liberalism, supra* note 46, at 11 ('By the basic structure I mean a society's main political, social, and economic institutions, and how they fit together into one unified system of social cooperation from one generation to the next'). Although Rawls talked about 'mutual respect among peoples' in connection with a global basic structure in *The Law of Peoples*, it seems clear that he did not see the global order as having a basic structure in the sense he originally saw it. John Rawls, *The Law of Peoples* (Cambridge, MA: Harvard University Press, 1999) 62.

1. Philosophical responses: a global basic structure

In philosophical terms, the suitability of the Rawlsian model turns on whether international society has a basic structure, and here we discover significant disagreement. Much of that debate originates in the implications for distributive justice of the existence of a global basic structure. In general, cosmopolitans urge strong forms of global distributive justice and nationalists seek to confine such justice to the state.[63] Some cosmopolitans insist that the *interactions* across boundaries characterized by the world today are sufficient to create the sort of cooperation inherent in a basic structure, and that that structure is composed of individuals at the global level.[64] On the other side, one nationalist perspective has emphasized the necessity of *coercion* for a basic structure, with Thomas Nagel finding that the absence of significant coercion at the global level makes global justice, at least of the distributive variety, simply impossible.[65]

Yet Nagel's view is simplistic as a description of the international system and wrong in its emphasis on coercion; the international system has indeed many features that resemble enough of a global structure so as to apply principles of justice to it.[66] As Joshua Cohen and Charles Sabel write, the world currently has 'a mix of precisely the conditions of interdependence, cooperation, and institutions that have justice-generating implications'.[67] As they note, these conditions include the implications of the decisions of international institutions, such as the World Trade Organization or the International Labor Organization, for ordinary citizens. International law is not merely the output of these relationships, but constitutive of them. That is, as states have constructed their international relations, they have created something resembling a realm in which principles of justice (including distributive justice) should apply.[68] Some cosmopolitan scholars abjure concepts of interactions or coercion to argue, in non-relational terms, for strong distributive justice at the global level.[69]

[63] See the discussion of the positions in Thomas Risse, *On Global Justice* (Princeton, NJ: Princeton University Press, 2012) 7–10; Forst, 'Towards a Critical Theory', *supra* note 57, at 161–5.

[64] Charles R. Beitz, 'Social and Cosmopolitan Liberalism', *International Affairs* 75 (1999): 515, 521–4; Pogge, *Realizing Rawls*, *supra* note 61, at 236–41.

[65] Thomas Nagel, 'The Problem of Global Justice', *Phil & Pub Aff* 33 (2005): 113; see also Andrea Sangiovanni, 'Global Justice, Reciprocity, and the State', *Phil & Pub Aff* 35 (2007): 3.

[66] Joshua Cohen and Charles Sabel, 'Extra Rempublicam Nulla Justitia?', *Phil & Pub Aff* 34 (2006): 147; A.J. Julius, 'Nagel's Atlas', *Phil & Pub Aff* 34 (2006): 176. For an argument for distributive justice taking Nagel at his word, see Lea Ypi, Robert E. Goodin, and Christian Barry, 'Associative Duties, Global Justice, and the Colonies', *Phil & Pub Aff* 37 (2009): 103.

[67] Cohen and Sabel, 'Extra Rempublicam Nulla Justitia?', *supra* note 66, at 166.

[68] See Andreas Follesdal, 'The Distributive Justice of a Global Basic Structure: A Category Mistake?', *PPE* 10 (2011): 46.

[69] See, e.g., Simon Caney, *Justice Beyond Borders: A Global Political Theory* (Oxford: Oxford University Press, 2005) 112–25.

2. *Responses from international law: the international community*

The community concept that shadows the idea of the basic structure resonates particularly strongly among international lawyers. But legal scholarship cannot help us too much with figuring out the suitability for deriving standards of global justice based on the domestic analogy. In at least two ways, the international community is the pre-eminent example of a *faux ami*[70] between ethics and international law.

First, the community concept that most international lawyers accept is a community of states.[71] Without doubt, scholars take increasing account of non-state entities—NGOs, civil society, armed groups, and others—and informal networks of actors in the making of international law,[72] yet such participation is not quite the same as envisioning them as part of a community. Even accepting that role for those actors, if one believes in a contractualist understanding of global justice, those making the contract—states and non-state entities—are quite different from individuals involved in the more typical contract.

Second, and more fundamentally, international lawyers do not generally regard it as part of their mandate to argue systematically for (or against) the existence of an international community, even if they may use the term in their work.[73] Bruno Simma, for instance, accepts the idea of a 'sense of community' as a key criterion for an international community, but it is frankly hard to know what this idea means—how, for instance, should it relate to the many national senses of community?—or how we should determine its presence.[74] Thomas Franck found 'emergent sense of global community' characterized as one of states and of individuals.[75] For the most part, international lawyers *assume* the existence of an

[70] A word whose cognate in another language means something different.

[71] Bruno Simma, 'From Bilateralism to Community Interest in International Law', *Recueil des Cours* 250 (1994): 217, 246 ('the international legal community [is] a community which is—and will for a long time in the future be—composed of (sovereign) States').

[72] See, e.g., Alan Boyle and Christine Chinkin, *The Making of International Law* (Oxford: Oxford University Press, 2007) 47–97; Anne-Marie Slaughter, *A New World Order* (Princeton, NJ: Princeton University Press, 2004).

[73] A small number of such scholars have looked in depth at the criteria for a community. See, e.g., Hersch Lauterpacht, 'Professor Carr on International Morality', in Elihu Lauterpacht (ed.), *International Law: Being the Collected Papers of Hersch Lauterpacht* (New York: Cambridge University Press, 1975) 67, 84–92; Rene-Jean Dupuy, 'Communauté internationale et disparités de développement', *Recueil des Cours* 165 (1979): 9; James Leslie Brierly, 'The Rule of Law in International Society', in Hersch Lauterpacht and C.H.M. Waldock (eds.), *The Basis of Obligation in International Law and Other Papers by the Late James Leslie Brierly*, (Oxford: Clarendon Press, 1958) 250; Charles de Visscher, *Théories et réalités en droit international public*, 2nd ed. (Paris: A. Pedone, 1955) 117–31.

[74] See Bruno Simma and Andreas Paulus, 'The "International Community": Facing the Challenge of Globalization', *EJIL* 9 (1998): 266, 276. See also Antonio Cassese, 'Soliloquy', in Paola Gaeta and Salvatore Zappalà (eds.), *The Human Dimension of International Law: Selected Papers* (New York: Oxford University Press, 2008) lix, lxxvi–lxxx (discussing the current state of a world community and whether a true international community can exist).

[75] Franck, *Fairness in International Law, supra* note 37, at 13. In a trenchant critique, Dino Kritsiotis questions whether such a community exists except in the rhetorical sense and whether international law needs an idea of community to accomplish its ends. Dino Kritsiotis, 'Imagining the International Community', *EJIL* 12 (2002): 961.

international community of states that needs to, and is competent to, make rules to govern itself. They seem satisfied that either the juridical equality of states, the universality of membership of the UN, or the need for or presence of global cooperation on certain issues itself means that states now form an international community.[76]

For international lawyers, then, the international community is at worst a rhetorical shorthand for a group of powerful states; or at best a tool for solving common problems among states that all agree must be handled jointly, whether concerning the environment, human rights, or the prevention of armed conflict. To them, the tension between a global community and diversity across states is less troublesome. In Rawlsian terms, this community is completely consistent with interstate relations based on a mere *modus vivendi*, without much of an overlapping consensus on a political conception of justice. As a result of the need to cooperate, states and other actors accept duties toward each other, enter into agreements, and prescribe law.[77] Such an assumption (or at best a meager understanding of the term community) will not work for our purposes. We need an *argument* for an international community if a community-based basic structure is our starting point for deriving a standard of global justice.

A more nuanced perspective appreciates that there is something distinct about the subject of global justice—the structure of the international order—compared to the basic structure of the state. The English School of international relations has termed the international system a 'society', but its adherents have also remarked on that society's differences from domestic societies. Robert Jackson has aptly said that the 'universal *societas* of states . . . centered on the UN and . . . defined by operative standards of conduct specified by the charter . . . is a noticeably thin community'; as for a 'community of humankind', it is 'contingent on the prior existence of sovereign states that agree to recognize human rights'. [78] Even a strong cosmopolitan like David Held refers not to one global community, but to 'overlapping communities of fate, where the trajectories of countries are heavily enmeshed with each other'.[79] Yet even while we recognize multiple communities of different densities and characteristics—one need only look at the EU compared to the UN to make such a claim—it does not help to identify such communities if one wishes to apply a contractarian view of global justice based on the idea of a single global community or basic structure.

[76] See, e.g., Georges Abi-Saab, 'Cours général de droit international public', *Recueil des Cours* 207 (1987): 9, 91–100; Manfred Lachs, 'Quelques réflexions sur la communauté internationale', in *Le droit international au service de la paix, de la justice et du développement* (Paris: A. Pedone, 1991) 349.

[77] See Rawls, *Justice as Fairness, supra* note 4, at 192–5.

[78] Robert Jackson, *The Global Covenant: Human Conduct in a World of States* (Oxford: Oxford University Press, 2000) 344.

[79] Held, *Cosmopolitanism, supra* note 56, 118–19.

3. Shifting the ground of argument

To adopt the Rawlsian approach, then, it seems one must endorse a firm position regarding the existence of the basic structure or community at the global level. As for me, given the possibility of describing the international system as one community, no community, or multiple or layered communities, I would choose all three.

Indeed, I would argue that at the global level we have *one community, no community, and multiple communities at the same time*.[80] In terms of both cooperation and coercion, in some ways we interact closely, feeling the influence of each other's lives and the global institutions we have created to enforce rules. Think of all of us at a large international airport, mixing as we pass and board flights, all subject to rules set by the International Civil Aviation Organization, the EU, or other international bodies. But at times we are very much nationally oriented, and the community almost seems to dissipate. Again, think of many of us on our national holiday, or thinking about an upcoming national election. And at times we are each members of multiple global communities, whether as co-religionists or environmentalists, workers or consumers. Just as Peter Singer has criticized the notion of an imagined community as a basis for special obligations to the nation-state, one cannot simply imagine an international community for purposes of applying a contractarian model.[81] So for certain purposes (international travel regulations) we are a community, whereas for other purposes (rooting for national teams at the Olympics or caring about our co-religionists' fate abroad) we are not.

The difference between the international community and the domestic community may not be a sufficient reason to discard completely the contractarian view of justice, even in its distributive form. But the project of identifying the principles of justice that a global community would or would not endorse given the complexities of interactions, exclusive and overlapping jurisdictions of states, expectations, and world views, is, in my mind, extraordinarily difficult; and it will always elicit a counter-claim that it is based on a vision of community that does not conform to reality.[82] It thus seems far more promising to sidestep these debates, especially given this project's orientation as a study in non-ideal theory. Allen Buchanan has made a similar move when he grounds his obligations of global justice in both a basic structure and a deontological natural duty of justice, but ultimately prefers the second.[83]

[80] The international community—the basic structure for a concept of global justice—is thus analogous to the concept in quantum physics that light is both a particle and wave simultaneously.

[81] Singer, *One World, supra* note 59, at 170–1. Singer does urge us to imagine an international community, but he says we should do that based on consequentialist grounds because it will improve the lives of people everywhere.

[82] It is certainly possible to use a contractualist framework to think about how states would solve specific problems of cooperation or coordination. In that sense, one might apply, as an alternative to the approach here, a set of contractualist understandings to each core norm of international law. However, such an approach would not suggest any unifying idea of justice other than that the norms do or do not reflect what rational actors should do under conditions of uncertainty. I appreciate this idea from Elizabeth Andersen.

[83] Buchanan, *Justice, supra* note 60, at 83–98. See also Noah Feldman, 'Cosmopolitan Law?', *Yale LJ* 116 (2007): 1022, 1056–61 (grounding cosmopolitan legal duties in natural duties and duties based on association).

In light of the evanescence of the global community or basic structure—related to its 'thinness', as Jackson points out—I will ground the principles of global justice against which international law should be assessed primarily in consequentialist terms, with deontological concepts superimposed at points on that model, without relying on a contractarian model that would require the construct of a basic structure or international community. Consequentialism does not demand (although it does not preclude) that we limit justice to certain spheres; it is by its nature a global approach to ethics, even if individual philosophers might choose to consider only the utility of those within a particular jurisdiction.[84] And deontological forms of argument can also be indifferent to such spheres; they are principles of right for all relevantly similar situations, universally.[85] I will have more to say in Chapter 3 about the forms of consequentialist and deontological reasoning I will deploy, and offer responses to possible criticisms of them, but for now the key point is that both frameworks treat individuals impartially and as being of equal worth.[86]

Consequentialist reasoning also meshes with my own intuitions as an international lawyer. From the orientation of one who seeks to solve problems, the best rule to devise is, at a very general level, the one with the best consequences, even as we may seek to justify some rules based on Kantian reasoning or duties. In evaluating the justice of individual legal norms, we should similarly be concerned with the extent to which compliance with the rule will contribute to a state of affairs associated with a just world. The connection between consequentialism and international law is as old as Jeremy Bentham, who not only first introduced the term 'international law', but argued that its content must be based on 'the greatest happiness of all nations taken together'.[87]

Grounding a standard of global justice without relying on the idea of a global community or basic structure does not make the concept of community irrelevant for international law. Indeed, in many ways, the norms and institutions of international law help constitute a global community—one united by shared rules, expectations, forms of acceptable argumentation, institutions, and practices.[88] Particular rules and institutions within a subfield might constitute more confined global communities, as with those who focus on international trade or human

[84] See Stephen L. Darwall, 'Theories of Ethics', in R.G. Frey and Christopher Heath Wellman (eds.), *A Companion to Applied Ethics* (Malden, MA: Blackwell Publishing, 2005) 17, 29 ('there is nothing in the consequentialist conception of morality that ties it specially to the condition of other members of the moral community').

[85] Immanuel Kant, *Groundwork of the Metaphysics of Morals*, Mary Gregor and Jens Timmermann (ed. and trans.) rev. ed. (Cambridge: Cambridge University Press, 2012) 46.

[86] Rawls nonetheless argued that the latter takes more seriously what is known as the separateness of persons. Rawls, *A Theory of Justice, supra* note 1, at 23–4. For a response, see Robert E. Goodin, *Utilitarianism as a Public Philosophy* (New York: Cambridge University Press, 1995) 23.

[87] Jeremy Bentham, 'Principles of International Law', in John Bowring (ed.), *The Works of Jeremy Bentham* (Edinburgh: William Tait, 1843) 537, 538.

[88] For one argument to this effect within law, see Adeno Addis, 'Imagining the International Community: The Constitutive Dimension of Universal Jurisdiction', *HRQ* 31 (2009): 129.

rights.[89] Yet that community is *formed* by the rules; it cannot be used to *justify* the rules.

IV. Conclusion

This chapter has laid some key groundwork for the scope of this study. The justice that will be our concern is a broad construct, more than distributive justice, and it is one whose subject is not a domestic basic structure, but international law. International law, for its part, will be viewed as comprising norms of diverse characters that respond to claims by key global actors, with my focus on those most central to the international system. Most of its norms are best examined in terms of the duties on states, but in some cases other relationships are more useful to examine. And lastly, I have explained my first premises for deriving principles of global justice. That process begins with the idea of impartiality, but I do not proceed from that starting point in the contractualist direction used by Rawls because of the important differences between the domestic basic structure and the international realm. Rather, I will follow a consequentialist framework, one that will justify a standard of global justice that assesses international norms for their contribution to a state of affairs defined in terms of two critical values—peace and human rights.

[89] See, e.g., Andrew Lang and Joanne Scott, 'The Hidden World of WTO Governance', *EJIL* 20 (2009): 575.

3

A Standard of Global Justice

The standard of global justice that I offer here and that will be the basis for appraising the core norms of international law comprises two principles or, as I prefer to call them, pillars: one about peace and one about human rights. Under this standard, *international law rules will be deemed just if and only if they (a) advance international and intrastate peace, and (b) respect, in the sense of not interfering with, basic human rights.* Justice conceived in such terms does what justice is supposed to do—to serve as 'the first virtue of social institutions'.[1] This chapter will introduce and defend the two-pillar standard in some detail. I will elaborate on the notions of peace and human rights that form the test of the justice of international law and explain the broadly consequentialist way in which these pillars will operate in practice as we assess individual norms. I will complete the framework with some additional assumptions about the state system that flow from my orientation in non-ideal theory, as well as two important conceptual overlays necessary and unique to a project aimed at evaluating legal (as opposed to social) norms. Once the standard of justice and modus operandi are explained, the chapter will propose a modifier—'thin'—to accompany this standard of global justice, defend this standard against other standards, and situate it within debates about cosmopolitan justice.

I. The Two Pillars of Global Justice

The choice of principles for a standard of justice involves both observation and justification, both the logic of discovery and the logic of appropriateness. Rawls captured the importance of the observation component when he stated that, to arrive at any coherent political conception of justice, '[w]e start, then, by looking to the public culture itself as the shared fund of implicitly recognized basic ideas and principles'; he emphasized the necessity for justification when he argued that those principles must eventually 'accord with our considered convictions'.[2] If such a 'look' at public culture—an educated hunch based on observation and

[1] John Rawls, *A Theory of Justice*, rev. ed (Cambridge, MA: Harvard University Press, 1999) 3.

[2] John Rawls, *Political Liberalism*, expanded ed. (New York: Columbia University Press, 2005) 8; see also John Rawls, *Justice as Fairness: A Restatement* (Cambridge, MA: Harvard University Press: 2001), 5 note 5 ('common sense of every day life').

intuition—is justified to identify principles of justice in ideal theory such as that of Rawls, it is, a fortiori, justified as the first step for identifying principles of justice in non-ideal theory like mine.

In terms of the initial identification of principles of justice with which to evaluate international law, I rely on my own set of observations about fundamental ideas permeating the normative structure of international affairs that includes international law. From that perspective, it seems clear to me, as I believe it would to any international lawyer, that the two basic values in that normative structure are peace and human rights, or more precisely the preservation of peace and the protection of human rights. These are the first two principles mentioned in the UN Charter, the most important document of contemporary international law.[3] They are the subject, explicit and implicit, of numerous treaties and areas of customary international law; and they guide decisionmakers in most of the great questions facing global governance today. They are at the core of the public culture when it comes to international law in particular and the normative structure more broadly. Although some may regard economic welfare as a third pillar, and indeed it is mentioned in the Charter's preamble,[4] my sense is still that the other two are of a qualitatively higher level of importance.

The challenge, and the purpose of this Section, is to show how these two very general *ideas or values* already in the public culture can be distilled into more concrete *principles* of justice that are justified through the logic of appropriateness. Once this is done, the principles can then be deployed in the form of a critical appraisal of the justice of rules of international law.

A. Peace

1. *Peace as a demand of global justice*

A common starting point for all conceptions of global justice is the centrality of international peace. Hobbes regarded man's search for peace as grounded in nature, whereas Kant saw it as grounded in a duty, but both agreed on the advantages of peace among nations for human welfare and flourishing. Peace is thus a particularly critical value for the global order. But it is more than that. In terms of the Rawlsian 'first virtue' concept, the centrality of the value of peace makes its preservation a justifiable demand for global justice and thus a component of a standard of global justice. In the terms put forth in Chapter 2, the extent to which a norm of international law promotes peace is a valid criterion for assigning rights

[3] UN Charter, preamble:

WE THE PEOPLES OF THE UNITED NATIONS DETERMINED

- to save succeeding generations from the scourge of war, which twice in our lifetime has brought untold sorrow to mankind, and
- to reaffirm faith in fundamental human rights, in the dignity and worth of the human person, in the equal rights of men and women and of nations large and small...

[4] Ibid., preamble ('to promote social progress and better standards of life in larger freedom').

and duties to global actors so that it is clear what each such actor is entitled or required to do or have. Under this pillar, the relationship of international law to justice is seen in consequentialist terms; we judge the justice of international law norms by their consequences in terms of their contribution to international and interstate peace.

This pillar is broad in one sense yet narrow in another. It is broad in encompassing not merely peace between states, but peace *within* them. A just world is one where states, peoples, and individuals settle their differences with minimal recourse to physical coercion—although certainly a just world permits coercion, at least by the state, in response to certain violations of law.[5] At the same time, it is narrow in that it does not regard peace as the absence of conflict, where the lion lies down with the lamb. A fortiori it is not the robust notion of 'positive peace' advanced by Johan Galtung and followed by many cosmopolitan scholars—the absence not merely of personal violence, but of structural violence as well, a concept that effectively incorporates social justice within the notion of peace.[6] International law must ideally advance this goal, but a conception of justice that insists upon an end to tensions between states, communities, and individuals over money, territory, or other resources is far too demanding. Rather, as the visionary international lawyer Hersch Lauterpacht wrote in a seminal volume on international law from the inter-war period: 'The first function of the legal organization of the community is the preservation of peace. Its fundamental precept is, "there shall be no violence".'[7]

Setting the advancement of peace as a first principle for a standard of global justice does not imply preservation of the status quo, for three reasons. First, to the extent that international law rules undermine peace, they will require adjustment. Second, when individual welfare can be improved through peaceful change, consequentialism demands nothing less. Indeed, much of the international lawmaking over the last century has been to create institutions that advance individual welfare in a way that does not upset the peace.[8] Those who assume a conflict between peace and progress often neglect the possibility of global change through those processes. Third, as the other pillar of my standard of global justice makes clear, international legal norms designed to preserve peace will require change if human rights considerations demand it. Thus, this pillar does not demand peace at all costs or regard all wars as anathema to justice. It does not insist on rules that would tolerate what might be called an unjust peace or forbid a just war.

[5] When I say that norms must advance interstate and intrastate piece, I am being somewhat loose with the word 'and'. As will be seen, many norms concern only one or the other. But for any norm that concerns both aspects of peace, we must examine whether it advances both aspects.

[6] See Johan Galtung, 'Violence, Peace, and Peace Research', *Journal of Peace Research* 6 (1969): 167, 183; see also Iain Atack, *The Ethics of Peace and War: From State Security to Human Community* (New York: Palgrave Macmillan, 2005) 116–17.

[7] Hersch Lauterpacht, *The Function of Law in the International Community* (Oxford: Clarendon Press, 1933) 64.

[8] See generally Hisashi Owada, 'Peaceful Change', in Rüdiger Wolfrum (ed.), *The Max Planck Encyclopedia of Public International Law*, online edition (Oxford: Oxford University Press, 2008–) <http://opil.ouplaw.com/home/EPIL>.

2. *Justifying peace as a pillar of global justice*

The principal normative appeal of this pillar of global justice comes from contemporary world history, and in particular the events of the twentieth century. War has unparalleled catastrophic consequences for overall human welfare. More than any other activity over which humans have control, war undermines the possibility of people to live decent lives. As an initial matter, its death toll is staggering. Jonathan Glover's estimate is 86 million people killed in twentieth century wars between 1900 and 1989; although this is a fraction of those killed by hunger, it still amounts to one hundred people per hour for nearly all of that century.[9] Niall Ferguson puts the death toll of twentieth-century organized violence (which would include 'peacetime' purges of political opponents or manmade famines, for instance) at 167 to 188 million.[10] As Willy Brandt said: 'Peace is not all, but without peace all is nothing.'[11] It is thus essential to human flourishing.

War also creates an atmosphere of havoc, fear, irrationality, and aggressive human behavior that facilitates the commission of horrible acts against individuals. Once armies and militias begin fighting, it does not take long for forcible displacements of populations, sexual assaults, and other actions against the innocent to begin—actions that many governments and their opponents would not commit in peacetime. As Tony Judt wrote: 'The thin veneer of civilization rests upon what may well be an illusory faith in our common humanity.... [I]t is that faith—and the constraints it places upon human misbehavior—that is the first to go in times of war or civil unrest.'[12]

In his remarkable book *Bloodlands*, Timothy Snyder catalogues the destruction wrought upon those parts of Europe that shifted between Nazi and Soviet control in the years from 1939 to 1945. Even as he emphasizes how Stalin's policy of mass murder began long before the war, he writes:

> During the Second World War, the bloodlands were subjected not to one invasion but to two or three, not to one occupation regime but to two or three. The mass murder of Jews began as the Germans crossed into lands that the Soviets had just annexed for themselves a matter of months before [from Poland], from which they had deported tens of thousands of people just weeks before, and in which they had shot thousands of prisoners just days before.... This sort of accumulation could also affect, and indeed end, the lives of millions of people who were thousands of miles away from the bloodlands.[13]

[9] Jonathan Glover, *Humanity: A Moral History of the Twentieth Century* (London: Jonathan Cape, 1999) 47.

[10] Niall Ferguson, *The War of the World: Twentieth-Century Conflict and the Descent of the West* (London: Allen Lane, 2006) 649.

[11] Willy Brandt, Speech on the occasion of the 100th anniversary of the J.H.W. Dietz Publishers, 3 November 1981, in Karl Rudolf (ed.), *Willy Brandt: Berliner Ausgabe, vol. 5: Die Partei der Freiheit. Willy Brandt und die SPD 1972–1992* (Bonn: Verlag J.H.W. Dietz Nachf. 2002) 363, 369.

[12] Tony Judt, 'Edge People', *New York Review of Books*, 25 March 2010.

[13] Timothy Snyder, *Bloodlands: Europe between Hitler and Stalin* (New York: Basic Books, 2010) 392–3.

In more recent times, Israel's war of independence included its expulsion of Arabs who had lived alongside Jews for generations, just as the breakup of Yugoslavia led Serbs, Croats, and Muslims to oust their friends and neighbors of different ethnicity from their homes and communities.[14] Beyond these physical and psychological traumas, war leads to the collapse of public health infrastructures, leading to needless deaths from curable diseases. Educational facilities close with long-term consequences for students. Refugee flows are a direct consequence of interstate and civil war. And it devastates property, damages the environment, and destroys cultural heritage.

War's consequences are long lasting, not merely in physical terms but in psychological ones. (Natural disasters do not engender the same long-term mistrust of neighbor against neighbor as wars; indeed they quite likely do the opposite.) Even though some former combatants quickly reconcile (for example Germany and Japan with the Allies after World War II), far more common is extended animosity that takes generations to conquer. The resultant mistrust makes the everyday negotiation of human conflicts, large and small, that much harder, and drives societies and individuals into despair. Chris Hedges, one of the most perceptive commentators on modern warfare, writes:

> The cost of war is often measured in the physical destruction of a country's infrastructure, in the blasted buildings, factories, and bridges, and in the number of dead. But probably worse is the psychological and spiritual toll. This cost takes generations to heal. It cripples and perverts whole societies.... In the beginning war looks and feels like love. But unlike love it gives nothing in return but an ever-depressing dependence... on the road to self-destruction.... The world we once understood and longed to return to stands before us as alien, strange, and beyond our grasp.[15]

Or, as Elizabeth Neuffer quotes a Rwandan survivor whose family was murdered in the 1994 genocide: 'We have all lost something. We even have an expression for it: *bapfuye buhagazi*. It means the walking dead. This is the land of the walking dead.'[16]

These claims are increasingly backed by quantitative measures as well. War is not the chief cause of poverty, but there is now rich empirical evidence showing the malicious and even devastating consequences of war.[17] Mitigation of armed conflict is supremely important to alleviating poverty. Indeed, to the extent that efforts to eradicate poverty in certain situations will reduce prospects for armed conflict, then advancing those efforts is also imperative.

Among states and national groups, the differences between those who tolerate (or even settle) their disputes—even deep-seated ones—without warfare and those

[14] See Ari Shavit, *My Promised Land: The Triumph and Tragedy of Israel* (New York: Spiegel and Grau, 2013) 99–132 (describing events in Lydda in 1948).

[15] Chris Hedges, *War is a Force that Gives Us Meaning* (New York: Public Affairs, 2002) 162.

[16] Elizabeth Neuffer, *The Key to My Neighbor's House: Seeking Justice in Bosnia and Rwanda* (New York: Picador, 2001) 251. Neuffer was killed in 2003 while covering the war in Iraq.

[17] For a useful literature review, see Patricia Justino, *War and Poverty*, Microcon Research Paper No. 32, 2010, <http://papers.ssrn.com/sol3/papers.cfm?abstract_id=1666787>.

that choose to fight, even where there is an obvious winner, is significant. Once ethnic groups or states cross the Rubicon to armed conflict, there is simply no going back to the status quo. Mistrust is frequently (though not always—witness Germany's reconciliation with the West) seeded for generations. Economic and political development generally suffers as pre-war cooperation between groups or states dissipates and rebuilds only slowly. Even private interpersonal violence is directly related to ongoing conflict or the legacy thereof as individuals settle private scores through the worst means. This realization is what has prompted some far-sighted leaders of both states and civil society to emphasize prevention of conflict above all. Thus, the Organization for Security and Co-operation in Europe drew from the disaster of the war in Yugoslavia to create a High Commissioner on National Minorities, a mechanism to negotiate differences between governments and ethnic minorities before they become violent;[18] and leading members of civil society formed institutions like the International Crisis Group to draw attention to international conflicts before they turn bloody.[19] Once 'the fragile edifice of civilization', in Ferguson's words, collapses due to armed conflict, it is very difficult to reconstruct it.[20]

A standard of global justice that morally validates rules and institutions in terms of the extent to which they promote international peace is thus strongly grounded in consequentialist morality. Indeed, it is somewhat remarkable that most cosmopolitan scholars who emphasize human rights as a central tenet of their view of global justice seem to place so little weight on the importance of avoidance of armed conflict.[21]

At the same time, the consequentialist reasoning I deploy here regarding the consequences of norms for peace is not meant to overstate the relationship between international law rules and either peace or war. Clearly, the causes of both interstate and civil conflict are multifarious and often hard to identify in a particular situation.[22] Without doubt, numerous other factors play a greater role in why war breaks out than do international law rules, just as many factors besides the legal framework of a country affect whether a business set up there will succeed or not.

[18] See Steven R. Ratner, 'Does International Law Matter in Preventing Ethnic Conflict?', *NYU JIL & Pol* 32 (2000): 591.

[19] See <http://www.crisisgroup.org>.

[20] Ferguson, *The War of the World, supra* note 10, at 645. Recall also the words of James Madison:

> Of all the enemies to public liberty war is, perhaps, the most to be dreaded, because it comprises and develops the germ of every other. War is the parent of armies; from these proceed debts and taxes; and armies, and debts, and taxes are the known instruments for bringing the many under the domination of the few. In war, too, the discretionary power of the Executive is extended;...and all the means of seducing the minds, are added to those of subduing the force, of the people.

James Madison, 'Political Observations', 20 April 1795, in *Letters and Other Writings of James Madison*, Vol. 4 (Philadelphia, PA: J.B. Lippincott, 1867) 491–2, <https://openlibrary.org>.

[21] A rare exception is Singer, who argues that 'a consequentialist should support the rule of international law because of its potential to reduce the likelihood of war'. Peter Singer, *One World* (New Haven, CT: Yale University Press, 2002) 132.

[22] For a summary of the voluminous literature, see Greg Cashman and Leonard C. Robinson, *An Introduction to the Causes of War: Patterns of Interstate Conflict from World War I to Iraq* (Lanham, MD: Rowman & Littlefield Publishers, 2007) 3–25.

Indeed, international law has probably played little part in preventing truly major wars.[23] Yet it is also clear that states bind themselves through international law rules in part in order to prevent war and solidify peace.[24] We can draw at least tentative conclusions about the connections between individual norms and peace based on past experiences and a careful consideration of how the normative background can affect the behavior of global actors.

Although my argument for the importance of peace is framed in terms of the history and consequences of war, we might go so far as to say that people *deserve* peace in the sense of living in an environment free of the violence, terrors, and traumas of armed conflict. If one of the points of justice is to overcome the bad luck of one's place of birth (an idea certainly associated with distributive justice), then we can say that people ought to be able, at a minimum, to live in an environment of interstate and internal peace. I would not, however, go as far as some to extend this justification to say that there exists a human right to peace, for my notion of human rights is based on the actual practice of human rights, which does not yet accept such a right.[25]

This consequentialist argument is completely impartial in the sense required for all standards of justice as discussed in Chapter 2. It treats all persons equally and is oblivious to personal ties and circumstances. It is a simple claim that the preservation of peace advances overall human welfare. At the same time, consequentialism has, as it were, consequences that rattle its critics. In the claim I am making here, it means that international rules under which some individuals suffer but whose overall consequences are to reduce the prospect of war, so that overall welfare is maximized, are just—up to the point where they run into the second principle discussed later. Certain key norms, such as the stability of international borders, or the near-ban on humanitarian intervention, will prove justifiable on this ground.

3. *Why not peace as a precondition to justice?*

Some might view peace's place as a principle of, or demand for, global justice as an odd connection between the two. Is peace not better seen as a *precondition* for global justice rather than a component of it? Such a view arguably follows from two strands of political theory. The first sees justice in the distributive terms discussed in Chapter 2, such that it focuses on distributing things, and maybe even

[23] Michael Howard, 'The Causes of War', in Øyvind Østerud (ed.), *Studies of War and Peace* (Oslo: Norwegian University Press, 1986) 17, 26–7.

[24] See, e.g., Charles A. Kupchan, *How Enemies Become Friends: The Sources of Stable Peace* (Princeton, NJ: Princeton University Press, 2010) 42–5.

[25] I appreciate this idea from Alex Sinha. On efforts in the UN to codify such a right, see Report of the Human Rights Council Advisory Committee on the right of peoples to peace, 16 April 2012, UN Doc. A/HRC/20/31; see also ASEAN Human Rights Declaration, 19 November 2012, Art. 38 ('Every person and the peoples of ASEAN have the right to enjoy peace within an ASEAN framework of security and stability, neutrality and freedom').

rights or duties, rather than a value like peace.[26] The other, greatly influenced by Rawls, assumes or proposes that humans can and should discuss and agree upon matters of justice only once they have exited the state of nature and achieved some basic stability. One might go further, as have some critical approaches to international law, to suggest that global order is in fact opposed to global justice.[27]

Several responses are in order. First, as a preliminary matter, philosophical debates on justice should not assume *any* a priori relationship between justice and peace. Each concept can be elaborated in different terms, with various possible relationships between them depending upon the type of peace that concerns us and the type of justice that concerns us.[28] There is nothing inherently threatening to the idea of justice in making peace a component of justice, just as there is nothing inherently threatening to the idea of peace in making justice a component of peace.[29] Thus, we can evaluate how just a norm is by the extent to which it achieves a certain kind of peace just as we can evaluate how peace-promoting a norm is by the extent to which it achieves a certain standard of justice—although each of those evaluations will entail different conceptions of peace and justice. Essentialism does not help us understand the possible links between these two values.[30]

Second, even if justice is fundamentally about allocation (a position I rejected in Chapter 2), that allocation must still reflect certain values, and the allocative conception does not preclude a proposal in which peace is a value or demand of justice. Third, we might also think of peace not merely as a value to be reflected in allocative justice, but as a value which itself needs to be allocated. Justice is not just about allocating rights or goods, but about deciding how much peace we wish to advance—or how much we wish to sacrifice—as part of the allocative mix. The result of my analysis might well be an endorsement of rules that some would call unjust in one allocative sense, but that are just insofar as they take peace into account.

Fourth, as for the argument that justice requires—and cannot be envisioned without—the peace that comes from leaving the state of nature, this response certainly makes some sense if justice is seen in distributive terms or seen as dealing with the bad luck of one's birth—the social justice of which Rawls wrote. But,

[26] See John Gardner, 'What is Tort Law For? Part 1. The Place of Corrective Justice', *Law & Phil* 30 (2011) 1, 6 ('liv[ing] in a peaceful world' is 'not assignable', and so not part of questions of justice).

[27] Martti Koskenniemi, 'The Police in the Temple: Order, Justice, and the UN: A Dialectical View', *EJIL* 6 (1995): 325. I leave aside Galtung's equation of peace with justice because, as noted, it relies on a notion of peace that cannot bear that weight.

[28] Daniel Philpott demonstrates a variety of possible relationships between justice and national reconciliation, each of which turns on a different idea of justice. See Daniel Philpott, *Just and Unjust Peace: An Ethic of Political Reconciliation* (Oxford: Oxford University Press, 2012) 23–6, 48–54, 82–8.

[29] See, e.g., SC Res. 242 (22 November 1967), para. 1 ('just and lasting peace in the Middle East').

[30] See Gunther Hellman, 'Introduction—Justice and/or Peace?', in Gunther Hellman (ed.), *Justice and Peace: Interdisciplinary Perspectives on a Contested Relationship* (Frankfurt: Campus Verlag, 2013) 7.

as noted both earlier in this chapter and in Chapter 2, that sort of justice does not exhaust the concepts of justice. Most significantly, we must return to, and recognize, the difference between domestic societies and the international realm. It may be possible to isolate peace as a precondition for discussing justice in the case of domestic societies (Rawls' basic structure), but in the international sphere, we do not have that luxury if we want to offer a content for justice—the 'supreme virtue' of institutions—that is *relevant* for today's challenges.

In particular, the persistence of, or potential for, interstate and intrastate war are such a constant feature of the landscape, with such serious consequences, that a standard of global justice that neglects the necessity of ending war seems quite impoverished. It *assumes away* some of the hardest questions and defines justice based on an ideal peaceful world that remains very elusive.[31] I realize that theories of domestic justice have flourished despite domestic strife within states, and I am not arguing that such theories are irrelevant because they assume a peaceful setting—indeed they may offer useful ideas for the post-conflict situation. But for a standard of *global* justice—for what it means to have a just order *on the planet as a whole*—peace between and within states deserves to be part of and not merely antecedent to the vision of justice. Indeed, unless we enter the world of ideal theory, peace seems central to *any* standard or concept of *global* justice, not merely the one that I offer and against which I will appraise international law. It need not be where I place it, but it deserves to be a component of and not merely a precondition to justice. As the interaction between the two pillars will show, the choice between the two places for peace vis-à-vis justice—outside/precondition versus inside/component is not merely a semantic one; rather, it deeply affects the analysis of the international law rules.

Lastly, my argument should not be confused with discussions among policy-makers and commentators about 'peace versus justice'. Those debates concern whether a society emerging from a national trauma like a civil war or a brutal regime should focus on domestic tranquility or criminal justice against the perpetrators. The positions often boil down to the arguments that (a) peace is often incompatible with, and ultimately more important than, criminal justice versus (b) criminal justice is necessary (or at least very important) to secure peace.[32] My argument does not take a position in this debate, which involves different notions

[31] I accept Steven Pinker's valuable point that the twentieth century was not the bloodiest century in world history and that the trajectory of both interstate and civil wars is in a long historical decline (in frequency and casualties), even more so since the end of the Cold War. Steven Pinker, *The Better Angels of Our Nature: Why Violence Has Declined* (New York: Viking Press, 2011) 193–200. Yet however better things might be now than they were fifty or five hundred years ago, serious interstate or intrastate violence should be not seen as relegated to the past. The historical comparison does not, then, support neglecting peace as a pillar of global justice.

[32] See, e.g., Steven R. Ratner, Jason S. Abrams, and James L. Bischoff, *Accountability for Human Rights Atrocities in International Law: Beyond the Nuremberg Legacy*, 3rd ed. (Oxford: Oxford University Press, 2009) 167–76; Jon Elster, *Closing the Books: Transitional Justice in Historical Perspective* (Cambridge: Cambridge University Press, 2004); Philpott, *Just and Unjust Peace, supra* note 28.

of peace and justice. Rather, it asserts that with, respect to global justice writ large, as opposed to merely criminal justice, peace is the first purpose of justice.

B. Respect for Basic Human Rights

Justice cannot, however, be grounded solely on the priority of eliminating war. First, as a consequentialist matter, justice also needs to be concerned with the welfare of individuals. On a consequentialist account, if peace comes at the cost of significant loss of life—or if, contrariwise, many lives can be saved but only at the cost of peace—a rule that only advances peace is morally defective. Second, consequentialist reasoning seems insufficient to ground a standard of global justice. Consequentialism tolerates some very serious harms to certain individuals as long as they can be justified for the greater good. A just outcome must also be one that respects certain fundamental values regarding the way we treat people—that we, and thus the law, must treat individuals the right way, with a certain degree of basic respect. Such a pillar is necessary not only as a matter of ideal theory.[33] The increased global consciousness about human rights means, quite simply, that human rights today are a core component of what we understand it means to have a just world. At the same time, the contours of this pillar raise several important issues.

1. A meaning for basic human rights

When we talk about a norm not interfering with basic human rights, which ones do we mean? Before offering my view, two preliminary points should be made. First, this study is not the place to offer a full theory of human rights any more than it is to offer one of global justice writ large. Compelling theoretical accounts have already been developed by James Nickel, James Griffin, Amartya Sen, and Charles Beitz. Instead, I seek to give a sense of the contours of basic human rights that are—or should be—respected by a just international law. Second, the meaning of basic human rights leaves open the question of the full extent of human rights. I am not suggesting that those rights that are not basic are not human rights properly understood.

(a) A practice-based concept

My starting point for defining a basic human right is that of Charles Beitz and James Nickel, both of whom focus on the actual practice of states in invoking and enforcing human rights. This approach stands in contrast to theories based either

[33] Thus, for instance, Rainer Forst conceptualizes justice as a 'principle' and peace a mere 'value' that is 'qualified by justice'. As he writes, 'not every social order of peace is an order of justice'. Rainer Forst, 'The Normative Orders of Justice and Peace', in Gunther Hellman (ed.), *Justice and Peace: Interdisciplinary Perspectives on a Contested Relationship* (Frankfurt: Campus Verlag, 2013) 69, 71, 74. Though Forst and I might differ on whether the advancement of peace is a criterion for just international law norms (or whether peace can be a component of global justice), I share his view that peace is only one value associated with a just world order and a just international law.

on what it means to be human (what Beitz calls naturalistic theories) or on what reasonable people can agree upon (what he calls agreement theories).[34] To decide what a human right is means looking at how states and other key actors think about human rights and what they do with them. It is a fundamentally political and practical concept:

> [W]e might frame our understanding of the idea of a human right by identifying the roles this idea plays within a discursive practice. We attend to the practical inferences that would be drawn by competent participants in the practice from what they regard as valid claims of human rights. An inventory of these inferences generates a view of the discursive functions of human rights and this informs an account of the meaning of the concept.[35]

Beitz himself attributes this approach to Rawls' *The Law of Peoples*, though he elaborates and clarifies it to give it more theoretical punch.[36]

This practical conception is not some simple equation between human rights and the list of rights in international legal instruments like the International Covenant on Civil and Political Rights (ICCPR) and the International Covenant on Economic, Social and Cultural Rights (ICESCR), for the codification of some claimed rights into legal form is neither necessary nor sufficient for something to be a human right—although it certainly is relevant.[37] I thus take human rights to be a *moral* concept even as we give that concept some content by reference to its political role and legal codification in the world.

What, then, is the content of human rights? I begin (as do Beitz and Nickel) with the most pathbreaking account in this area, Henry Shue's *Basic Rights*. Human rights are individual entitlements, creating requirements on other actors, for protection from a set of 'standard threats', which are 'predictable dangers... to which [individuals] are vulnerable under typical circumstances of life in a modern world order composed of states'.[38] In terms of judging the justice of international law, this concept captures the imperative of law and institutions to respond to the greatest vulnerabilities of people, whether caused by states, non-state actors, or even natural disasters. Indeed, this focus on the vulnerable can itself form the basis for a set of individual and institutional moral responsibilities.[39]

[34] See Charles R. Beitz, *The Idea of Human Rights* (Oxford: Oxford University Press, 2009) 48–95.

[35] Ibid., at 102. For a theory that seems to focus on the role of human rights in political discourse but nonetheless is derived from first principles, see Joshua Cohen, 'Minimalism About Human Rights: The Most We Can Hope For?', *J Pol Phil* 12 (2004): 190.

[36] Joseph Raz offers up a practical (although I believe unduly narrow) vision when he rejects human rights 'foundations' in favor of a 'political conception' that sees human rights as 'limits to the sovereignty of states, in that their actual or anticipated violation is a (defeasible) reason for taking action against the violator', Joseph Raz, 'Human Rights without Foundations', in Samantha Besson and John Tasioulas (eds.), *The Philosophy of International Law* (Oxford: Oxford University Press, 2010) 321, 328, 336–7.

[37] See James W. Nickel, *Making Sense of Human Rights*, 2nd ed. (Malden, MA: Blackwell, 2007) 32–3 (criticizing the 'legal entitlement' approach to human rights).

[38] Beitz, *The Idea of Human Rights*, *supra* note 34, at 109; Henry Shue, *Basic Rights: Subsistence, Affluence and U.S. Foreign Policy*, 2nd ed. (Princeton, NJ: Princeton University Press, 1996) 17.

[39] See, e.g., Robert E. Goodin, *Protecting the Vulnerable* (Chicago, IL: University of Chicago Press, 1985); Peter Singer, 'Famine, Affluence, and Morality', *Phil & Pub Aff* 1 (1972): 229.

(b) Basic human rights versus other human rights

But if all human rights respond to these standard threats, what do I mean by basic human rights? Shue's conception of basic rights is one that can be called a moral minimum—'the line beneath which no one is to be allowed to sink... everyone's minimum reasonable demands upon the rest of humanity... the rational basis for justified demands the denial of which no self-respecting person can reasonably be expected to accept'.[40] He then identifies two broad categories of basic rights—rights to physical security—against arbitrary killing, inhuman treatment, or arbitration deprivation of liberty—as well as to minimal economic security—adequate food, clothing, shelter, and health. Though I do not question Shue's concept of basic moral rights generally, I believe a concept of basic *human* rights must take greater account of the practices used by global actors in their understanding of such rights.

Rawls notably attempted such an account regarding human rights generally (not just basic human rights) in *The Law of Peoples*. There he claimed that the role of human rights in society means that human rights—not just basic ones—are 'a special class of urgent rights'—a concept that seems even more limited than Shue's concept of basic rights.[41] But Rawls' political conception does not correspond to the practices of states in defining even basic human rights (and, even more glaringly, the practice of states in human rights generally). Rawls sees human rights solely in terms of ground for military intervention—'they restrict the justifying reason for war and its conduct, and they specify limits to a regime's internal autonomy'[42]—whereas the practice of states in identifying both human rights and basic human rights is far more diverse. Thus, a *basic human right* involves an entitlement to more than what Shue calls a basic moral right or what Rawls calls a human right, but to less than the full panoply of internationally recognized human rights.

The practices of states seem to me to permit the identification of some rights as basic insofar as they demonstrate an acceptance of some hierarchy of human rights. For instance, the ICCPR essentially creates three categories of rights: those that may be limited or balanced against certain state or other private interests (for example the right to expression or assembly); those that may not be limited for those purposes (for example the rights of due process or fair elections); and those that may not be breached even in the event of a national emergency threatening the life of the nation (for example the rights against arbitrary killing or torture).[43] In

[40] Shue, *Basic Rights, supra* note 38, at 18–19. For an approach to global justice that sets as its linchpin basic human needs, rather than human rights, see Gillian Brock, *Global Justice: A Cosmopolitan Account* (Oxford: Oxford University Press, 2009) 48–72. I nonetheless differ with that approach in that, along with Shue, I do not see needs as capturing all that is important in basic rights; moreover, I see human rights as a fundamentally practice-based concept.

[41] John Rawls, *The Law of Peoples* (Cambridge, MA: Harvard University Press, 1999) 79. Rawls' examples are 'freedom from slavery and serfdom, liberty (but not equal liberty) of conscience, and security of ethnic groups from mass murder and genocide'. See also Raz, 'Human Rights', *supra* note 36.

[42] Rawls, *The Law of Peoples, supra* note 41; see the criticism by Beitz, *The Idea of Human Rights, supra* note 34, at 101–2.

[43] ICCPR, Arts. 2, 3,6(1), 7, 9, 21, 25.

addition, international law has recognized some human rights as *jus cogens* insofar as no treaty or norm of customary international law can override them. This list probably includes the bans on torture, slavery, genocide, and crimes against humanity.[44] At the same time, states have repeatedly emphasized that all human rights are linked, thus rejecting some priority ab initio between civil and political rights, on the one hand, and economic, social, and cultural rights, on the other.[45]

Although the categories of the ICCPR do not map directly onto a hierarchy of rights nor would I argue that one covenant (or category of rights) is supreme to the other, the existence of categories accepted in treaties and *jus cogens* still reflects the acceptance of some rights as more important than others. This hierarchy is also reflected in the attention that states, international organizations, and NGOs give to some rights violations compared to others, whether in terms of decisions to criticize them, punish states or individuals for them, or fund programs to remedy them. I admit such attention is difficult to quantify, as some states and international organizations are concerned about a variety of rights violations and NGOs exist to address quite specialized issues. But, on the whole, certain rights seem to be of greater global concern than others, and this, I think, allows us to consider them as 'basic'.[46] Whether this stems from a sense that they are less culturally contingent (though there may still be differences across cultures as to what is basic), that they are somehow more important to individuals, or that we can see no legitimate reason for the state to interfere with them is not as important as the outcome in terms of greater concern.[47]

The rights that garner greater concern certainly begin with Shue's basic rights to physical and economic security as described previously. But this extends to other core protections recognized in the two covenants, including the ban on discrimination based on certain traits, including race, gender, ethnicity, and religion; freedom to form (or not form) a family; freedom to believe and practice one's religion or culture or abstain from doing so; some freedom of political expression; freedom from alien rule, linked with ideas of self-determination; some type of representative government; primary education; and a safe workplace. Thus, when I speak of basic human rights, I refer to these rights and others that receive a similar range of international attention. In my mind, the rights commanding that attention are generally those that guarantee a life free of external intrusion on the

[44] ILC Articles on State Responsibility, Art. 40, Commentary; see also Robert E. Goodin and Steven R. Ratner, 'Democratizing International Law', *Global Policy* 2 (2011): 247.

[45] World Conference on Human Rights, Vienna Declaration and Program of Action, 25 June 1993, para. 5, <http://www.ohchr.org/Documents/ProfessionalInterest/vienna.pdf>. Legal scholars have argued over whether the law recognizes a hierarchy of rights or all human rights as of equal weight. Compare, e.g., Theo van Boven, 'Distinguishing Criteria of Human Rights', in Karel Vasak and Philip Alston (eds.), *The International Dimensions of Human Rights*, Vol. 1, rev. ed. (Portsmouth, Va.: Greenwood Press, 1982) 43, with Theodor Meron, 'On a Hierarchy of International Human Rights', *AJIL* 80 (1986): 1, 21–2.

[46] See Beitz, *The Idea of Human Rights, supra* note 34, at 109 ('Human rights are matters of international concern').

[47] I thus disagree with Miller that it is impossible to identify basic rights from the practice of states. David Miller, *National Responsibility and Global Justice* (Oxford: Oxford University Press, 2007) 168–72.

fundamental freedom of the individual vis-à-vis the state and other powerful actors that threaten him or her, coupled with the *basic material goods and conditions* necessary to a minimally flourishing life and thus addressing each individual's most important vulnerabilities.[48]

(c) Alternative conceptions for a second pillar

My choice of respect for basic human rights as the second pillar means that I am not choosing three related values for the second pillar. First, why not all human rights? Clearly, as a matter of ideal theory, one can develop a standard of justice such that international law is just only if it respects the full range of human rights. A limitation to basic human rights reflects the orientation of this project in non-ideal theory insofar as I do not think that all of international law can be expected to re-orient itself toward protecting all of human rights at this point; it is more weight than international law writ large can bear.

Equally important, international law as a whole *need not* be the vehicle for the advancement of all human rights—for international law now includes a branch of norms and institutions of immense depth and complexity precisely for that purpose—namely, the law of international human rights. That body of law does not exist, and cannot be justified, merely as a check on the advancement of peace; rather it developed and is independently justified on more basic grounds—as providing a large range of protections of the individual from the threats of the state or other powerful actors. That law exists, and it is a fact that non-ideal theory must take into account. So we already have a vast array of law whose goal is the protection of all human rights.

Even if we see all of international human rights law as somehow morally required to address the human vulnerabilities from the 'standard threats', that does not mean that *other* core norms of international law are unjust if they do not respect the non-basic human rights, or that they can be defended only if we can show that they respect each and every non-basic human right. For example, we can defend as just the near-ban on unilateral secession of territory from an existing state because it preserves interstate and intrastate peace overall while allowing for secession at the point at which a full ban would impinge on basic human rights. But we need not reject that norm as unjust simply because a frustrated group of citizens believes that the state in which it lives is not respecting its right to a minimum wage—even if we know that that right would be guaranteed in the new state. In that sense, the existing norm does indeed interfere with the non-basic human rights of individuals to a minimum wage. But that means that the advancement of that right must work within the framework of other norms of international law that are just. It does not require that the advancement of those rights commandeer those other norms. Granted, this calculation ends up making

[48] Despite the differences between my approach and Miller's, my idea of a minimally flourishing life resembles his standard for human rights as those that guarantee a 'decent life'. Miller, *National Responsibility*, *supra* note 47, 180–4.

the non-basic rights less important or foundational than the basic rights, but it does not mean that a system that recognizes this difference is unjust.

Second, why not human dignity as a second pillar? Dignity certainly captures some attribute of humanity distinct from the rights of an individual and has been the subject of judicial interpretation.[49] Scholars have attempted to move beyond the plasticity of the term to see dignity's relationship to rights,[50] but in the end the concept seems too slippery for purposes of appraising the justice of international law. International law, like domestic law, can serve to protect human dignity in a variety of senses,[51] but dignity itself is too unstable a pillar for a standard of justice. Rather, with basic human rights we have a clear sense of the practice of states that can be used in our second pillar.

Lastly, why not human security? As authoritatively defined in the 2003 report of the UN Commission on Human Security, this term refers to the protection of 'the vital core of all human lives in ways that enhance human freedoms and human fulfilment'.[52] In particular: 'It means protecting people from critical (severe) and pervasive (widespread) threats and situations... [by] creating political, social, environmental, economic, military and cultural systems that together give people the building blocks of survival, livelihood and dignity.'[53] It is thus a huge concept, encompassing many ways to improve human welfare, and is seen by its advocates as a new paradigm to stand alongside the idea of national security. Human security captures the idea of threats and vulnerability, but it, like dignity, is too open-ended for a second pillar. Moreover, it faces the same obstacle as human rights writ large in that it places too much of a demand on international law to insist that all its norms affirmatively respect human security. The concept may be useful to another standard of justice, but it is not one that serves my purposes here.

2. *Respect as non-interference*

My notion of respect is also quite specific. In the doctrine of international human rights law, respect is one of the three duties of states (and perhaps other international actors too) originally developed by Shue but now endorsed by bodies interpreting human rights instruments.[54] When a state *respects* human rights, it avoids violating those rights directly by its own actors. The other two duties on states are to *protect* rights, by which the state must take reasonable measures to prevent their violations by other actors, notably private parties; and to *provide* for the achievement of certain rights, by which the state must spend material resources

[49] Christopher McCrudden, 'Human Dignity and Judicial Interpretation of Human Rights', *EJIL* 19 (2008): 655.

[50] See Christopher McCrudden (ed.), *Understanding Human Dignity* (Oxford: Oxford University Press, 2013).

[51] See, e.g., Jeremy Waldron, 'How Law Protects Dignity', *CLJ* 71 (2012): 200.

[52] Commission on Human Security, *Human Security Now* (2003) 4, <http://www.unocha.org/humansecurity/chs/finalreport/English/FinalReport.pdf>.

[53] Ibid., at 4.

[54] Shue, *Basic Rights*, *supra* note 38, at 52.

to achieve those rights (such as economic, social, and cultural rights).[55] Another action associated with human rights, though not typically in terms of a duty, is to *promote* human rights, for example by the education of relevant constituencies.

The second pillar of global justice, however, concerns not duties of states but the *link* between rules of international law and basic human rights. Thus, in stating that a just *norm* must respect rights, I mean that the norm does not interfere with the enjoyment of those rights by individuals.[56] This notion of non-interference applies to both so-called negative rights (against governmental abuse like arbitrary arrest) and so-called positive rights (such as the right to food or education). Respect or non-interference is minimalist in that the second pillar does not demand that international law norms promote observance by states and non-state actors of basic human rights (and certainly not of rights beyond the basic rights); it is sufficient that they do not interfere with the enjoyment of those basic rights. Yet it has a real 'bite' in the sense that the second pillar would not tolerate a norm that either threatens an individual's enjoyment of the basic rights or perpetuates a status quo of violation of basic human rights. It would thus not tolerate a norm that renders illegal actions by states necessary to ensure the enjoyment of those rights. Respecting rights may also include some notion of *vindicating* rights, by which the individual receives some expression from society about—a sort of practical affirmation of—her rights following a violation.[57]

At the same time, when I appraise a norm of international law for its non-interference with basic human rights, I am not insisting that the norm advance or improve human rights. (This move will be made in Chapter 13, when I offer a higher standard of global justice.) I do not do so for precisely the same reasons that the second pillar is limited to basic human rights and not all human rights. As a matter of non-ideal theory, a demand that all norms of international law positively promote human rights seems too much to expect now. And, as pointed out earlier, we can take the existence of international human rights law, with precisely that purpose, as a given and thus need not insist that all norms of international law achieve its very ambitious goals in order to regard those norms as just.

3. *What kind of pillar?*

Lastly, we are left with at least two possibilities for the *function* of human rights in the second pillar of global justice. One would be that the rules of international

[55] Economic, Social and Cultural Rights Committee, General Comment 12: The right to adequate food, 12 May 1999, para. 15, UN Doc. E/C.12/1999/5; Report of the Special Representative of the Secretary-General on the issue of human rights and transnational and other business enterprises, John Ruggie: Guiding Principles on Business and Human Rights: Implementing the United Nations 'Protect, Respect and Remedy' Framework, 21 March 2011, Annex, para. 2, UN Doc. A/HRC/17/31.

[56] I will generally use the shorthand 'interfere with basic human rights'. I avoid the term 'violate' because it seems odd to say that a rule, as opposed to an actor, can violate anyone's rights.

[57] I appreciate this insight from Elizabeth Andersen.

law are just if and only if they do not interfere with the enjoyment by individuals generally of their basic human rights. This position reflects a concern with human rights in consequentialist terms. We seek to evaluate rules by the extent to which they advance a state of affairs characterized by such non-interference vis-à-vis individuals as a whole. A second idea is to treat non-interference with basic human rights as a deontological trump on the consequentialist goal of advancing peace. Although these two positions gloss over many nuances for the ways of conceiving of rights, they correspond to the choice in ethics between respect for rights as a *moral goal* and respect for rights as a moral *side-constraint*. These two positions can have serious implications for the interactions between the two pillars.

Under the first view, we attempt to appraise the consequences of a rule for the overall or aggregate enjoyment of basic human rights. Along these lines, Shue writes: 'One's goal is for everyone to enjoy everything they have a right to enjoy.'[58] Yet in so doing, we face difficult questions about both the utility to be assigned to certain horrendous violations that may only be against one person (for example torture) and the utility of a state of affairs characterized by respect for rights compared to the state of affairs characterized by peace. Under the second view, advanced by Robert Nozick as central to his theory of justice,[59] efforts to advance the first pillar must be constrained by a moral duty on human institutions, including law and its implementation processes and structures, to respect basic human rights. But that view has two opposite potential flaws—that it does not give human rights enough of an impact on justice (compared to the consequentialist idea that looks at aggregate levels of respect); and that it gives it too much impact by simply ruling out any possible rules that interfere with one person's rights. This may be too demanding and is contrary to commonsense morality that actually balances the costs and benefits of rights violations.[60]

In the end, I opt for the most part for the consequentialist view of the role for human rights; thus, when my second pillar asserts that international law rules must respect basic human rights, I mean it in terms of producing a state of affairs characterized by the respect of the basic rights of individuals as a whole. My choice is grounded in the reasons that Robert Goodin offered for his defense of utilitarianism as a mode of moral reasoning with respect to public policy. Consequentialist morality is adaptable to multiple situations, in particular the uncertainties inherent in policymaking, without forcing us to engage in difficult and highly personal debates about our moral duties.[61] In that sense, it is suited for guiding and evaluating the rules for governance of a society better than morality based on deontology.

[58] Shue, *Basic Rights*, *supra* note 38, at 161.

[59] Robert Nozick, *Anarchy, State, and Utopia* (New York: Basic Books, 1974) 30–4. This resembles Dworkin's idea of rights as trumps.

[60] See, e.g., Peter Singer, 'Ethics and Institutions', *J Ethics* 9 (2005): 331; Theresa Lopez, Jennifer Zamzow, Michael Gill, and Shaun Nichols, 'Side Constraints and the Structure of Commonsense Ethics', *Philosophical Perspectives* 23 (2009): 305.

[61] Robert E. Goodin, *Utilitarianism as a Public Philosophy* (Cambridge: Cambridge University Press, 1995) 3–8.

The same holds true a fortiori in the international arena, given cultural differences concerning our duties to one another. Such a choice means, as noted, that difficult balancing must be done in applying the two pillars to a rule or suggested rule of international law if the pillars 'pull' in different directions—but this is not itself an argument against consequentialism. Moreover, as Goodin observed, the difference between the rules that result from a utilitarian reasoning focused on responsibilities (for better outcomes) as opposed to duties (regardless of outcome) may well turn out to be quite small.[62]

Yet I am not quite willing to be wholly consequentialist in thinking about human rights. For I believe that each of us, and the institutions that we create, has certain duties regarding human rights that should prevent us from labeling a legal norm as just even if it advances peace and even if it otherwise promotes a state of affairs characterized by overall respect for basic human rights. The bans on torture, slavery, or arbitrary killing are moral prohibitions of sufficient force such that legal rules that violate them or tolerate their violation, even when the potential victims are only a few people, might fall into this category. In some situations, to take rights seriously demands going beyond balancing the state of affairs characterized by their respect with the harms to peace, or balancing the state of affairs characterized by their violation with the benefits to peace.

Moreover, side-constraints need not be the absolute trumps that upset our commonsense morality (though international law treats *jus cogens* norms as trumps). Rather, they can serve as a set of alarm bells that bring human rights considerations to the fore more than they would be through consequentialist reasoning. Some of this notion is captured in Joseph Raz's ideas of mandatory norms as exclusionary reasons—concepts that keep off the table certain arguments that might be used to justify a certain conduct, even if those norms do not themselves always ban the particular conduct.[63] Goodin calls these 'input filters'—filters on what is part of the consequentialist conversation—as opposed to 'output filters' that simply take certain policy options off the table after the consequentialist calculations are completed.[64] As Richard Pildes has further developed Raz's ideas, rights are 'better understood as channeling the *kinds of reasons* government can invoke when it acts in certain arenas'.[65] The point of rights is not individual self-interest but a 'means of realizing certain collective interests', what he called a 'structural conception of rights'.[66] This understanding of rights is generally deontological in that it is grounded in a concept of morality stemming from acting out of a duty and not balancing certain consequences (although it is certainly not

[62] Ibid., at 81–7.

[63] Joseph Raz, *Practical Reasons and Norms* (Oxford: Oxford University Press, 1999) 39–40, 71–80 ('exclusionary reasons...may exclude all or only some of the reasons which apply to certain practical problems....Only undefeated exclusionary reasons succeed in excluding.' ibid., at 40). Regarding human rights, he states: 'Individual rights are human rights if they disable a certain argument against interference by outsiders in the affairs of a state.' Raz, 'Human Rights', *supra* note 36, at 332.

[64] Goodin, *Utilitarianism as a Public Philosophy*, *supra* note 61, at 133–4.

[65] Richard H. Pildes, 'Why Rights are not Trumps: Social Meanings, Expressive Harms, and Constitutionalism', *Journal of Legal Studies* 27 (1998): 725, 729 (emphasis in original).

[66] Ibid., at 730–1.

anti-consequentialist insofar as it sees rights as serving certain purposes), but it is not as inflexible as the trump. In a separate move, Michael Ignatieff has argued for a mixed consequentialist-deontological approach to address state responses to terror and evil. His judgment of state policy for its contribution to the 'lesser evil' rejects rights as trumps or 'table-clearing justifications' in favor of a more realistic ethic based on minimizing rights infringements and insisting on a good reason to do so.[67]

This idea is reflected in human rights law itself, as many treaties simultaneously provide for certain rights and list particular interests (for example the rights or reputation of others, public safety and health) that the state may consider in limiting the enjoyment of those rights.[68] The state may not justify any limitations for reasons beyond those listed, so in that sense the rights instantiate exclusionary reasons for state conduct.[69] In the case of the European Convention on Human Rights, the state must also demonstrate that the limitations taken for the listed reasons are 'necessary in a democratic society'.[70] As a result, the European Court of Human Rights searches into the importance of the right with which the state interferes, the weight of the government's interest, and the proportionality between the two.[71]

With respect to the second pillar of global justice, the idea of exclusionary reasons means that when we see that a norm of international law potentially does not respect the basic human rights of some people, even if it does respect the basic rights of others, we will have to come up with particularly strong reasons for saying it is nonetheless just, and those reasons cannot simply be about balancing utility. We may discover that no such reasons exist, in which case a norm will be deemed unjust even if it passes an overall consequentialist balancing formula. For now, I do not need to say more about how this will work for specific norms, but I would suggest that at times, when the two pillars pull in different directions, we will need to do more than just balance.

When the two concepts of 'respect' and 'basic human rights' are combined and understood, we have constructed the second principle or pillar for my standard of global justice. It means that a norm that does not respect basic human rights—or more precisely, the operation of which leads to a state of affairs in which basic human rights are not respected, either writ large in the consequentialist sense or, at times, even in individual cases in a deontological sense—will be prima facie unjust, even if it advances peace. Like the first pillar, the second pillar is also impartialist in the sense outlined earlier. It sees all individuals as possessed of a certain inherent worth, or needing certain freedoms or material

[67] Michael Ignatieff, *The Lesser Evil: Political Ethics in an Age of Terror* (Princeton, NJ: Princeton University Press, 2004) 7–9.

[68] See, e.g., ICCPR, Art. 19.

[69] See, e.g., UN Human Rights Committee, General Comment No. 27: Freedom of Movement, 2 November 1999, para. 12, UN Doc. CCPR/C/21/Rev.1/Add.9.

[70] European Convention on Human Rights and Fundamental Freedoms, 4 November 1950, Art. 8(2), 213 UNTS 222.

[71] See generally David Harris, Michael O'Boyle, Ed Bates, and Carla Buckley, *Law of the European Convention on Human Rights*, 2nd ed. (Oxford: Oxford University Press, 2009) 348–60.

goods, regardless of any special ties between the maker or applier of law and the object of the law, and the latter's station in life (for example wealth, education, intelligence, or power).

C. Consequentialism, Rules, and Predictions

My choice to opt for a consequentialist approach to appraising the justice of international law, even with its partially deontological overlay, means that, for the most part, I am following an approach of rule consequentialism. I am asking whether various rules or alternatives to them, if followed by the actors to whom they are directed, would be reasonably expected to lead to certain states of affairs defined in terms of peace and human rights.[72] We are not asking whether particular acts by global actors are just, but whether particular rules are just.[73]

Because the appraisal is largely consequentialist, the justice of international law rules will depend on facts—what Goodin, in his defense of utilitarianism, has called 'utterly contingent and baldly empirical facts'.[74] Each step of the way in this study, I will make claims about the state of affairs to which a particular rule or alternative to it would lead. As mentioned in Chapter 2, this choice for consequentialism also flows from my orientation as a lawyer—lawyers are problem-solvers, and so consequences are, if not everything, certainly critical to the choice of the best rules.

This approach opens up my appraisal to the huge debate between the criticisms and defenses of consequentialist morality, much of which focuses on the possibility of determining other people's utility.[75] This volume is not the place to review these debates. Suffice it to say that I recognize the imperfection of prediction in any context but do not see the alternative to it (whatever one's overall approach to moral reasoning). Moreover, as noted earlier, I am not claiming that international law rules are the primary drivers of state behavior. International law is but one of many factors that affect how states will act regarding both peace and the protection of human rights. But I do not need to make that strong a claim about the rules in order to assess whether they are just (although I do have to assume that their observance has some consequences). Some readers may disagree with the conclusions I reach based on the precedents I cite or my honestly held

[72] Cf. Brad Hooker, *Ideal Code, Real World* (Oxford: Oxford University Press, 2000) 2–3, 32, 72–5. Hooker's definition is somewhat different from mine in that, as an exercise in ideal theory, he is searching for the code with the greatest expected value and evaluating consequences based on internalization and not merely compliance with a proposed rule. Ibid., at 75–80.

[73] As an epistemological matter, what counts is the consequences of the rules in terms of likely outcomes, not the subjective viewpoints of those who make the rules as to those outcomes. Peter Railton, 'Alienation, Consequentialism, and the Demands of Morality', *Phil & Pub Aff* 13 (1984): 134, 152.

[74] Robert E. Goodin, 'Utility and the Good', in Peter Singer (ed.), *A Companion to Ethics* (Oxford: Blackwell, 1991) 241, 247.

[75] For strong defenses, see R.M. Hare, *Moral Thinking: Its Levels, Method and Point* (Oxford: Oxford University Press, 1981) 87–129; Goodin, *Utilitarianism as a Public Philosophy, supra* note 61, at 18–23; Hooker, *Ideal Code, supra* note 72, 113–17.

'seat-of-the-pants' views as an international lawyer about the reactions of global actors to the rules or alternatives to them. Such disagreements are not, however, an argument against consequentialism, for we have already accomplished a great deal in our understanding of the justice of international law if we confine our disagreements to these contingencies.[76]

D. The interaction of the two pillars

The interaction between the two pillars will be demonstrated throughout this study. We can sketch out the general methodology as follows, though I do not mean to suggest a precise flowchart:

(1) If a norm or proposed norm survives scrutiny under the first pillar by advancing peace, it is presumptively just under my standard of global justice. At that point, the second pillar is then considered as we ask whether the norm interferes with basic human rights. The norm or proposed norm will survive scrutiny if it passes that test, but will be considered unjust if it does not.

(2) If the latter, it will be necessary to explore alternatives that satisfy the second pillar but do so in a way that causes minimal disruption to the first pillar.

(3) If, on the other hand, a norm fails under the first pillar by undermining peace, it is presumptively unjust; it can only be defensible if the norm is needed to create a state of affairs characterized by respect for human rights and even in that case must do so with minimal disruption to peace.

In some situations, we will discover that the norm passes the first pillar in a more minimal sense by not undermining peace, though it cannot be said to advance it. In that situation, the thin justice of the norm is harder to evaluate. The diversity of norms means that not every one even triggers both tests. This feature of the norms will be considered later in this study.

These two pillars leave open many possibilities for the content of international law. For most norms or proposed norms, I will argue one of two positions: (a) that my standard of global justice *permits* a particular norm, i.e. that it passes scrutiny under the two pillars; or (b) that my standard of global justice *prohibits* a particular norm, i.e. that it does not pass the tests of the two pillars. I will not generally seek to, nor need I, argue a third position, namely (c) that my standard *requires* a particular norm, i.e. that it passes scrutiny under the two pillars and no other rule would do so, although at times I will make such a claim. Certainly those engaged in ideal theory might wish to make such claims exclusively, endorsing only those rules would do the best job of advancing peace without interfering with human rights. But as the

[76] See Goodin, *Utilitarianism as a Public Philosophy*, *supra* note 61, at 21 ('Even where utilitarianism proves indeterminate, it sets off the terms of that public debate').

goal of this project is to appraise the norms we have, I need not show that they are the only ones that meet the standard of justice, even as I will need to identify those that do not meet the standard and suggest alternatives that do.

Moreover, these pillars do not represent a rigid formula, where we identify exactly ab initio what constitutes peace or respect for human rights and then reach a binary conclusion that a particular norm is either just or unjust. Rather, these two pillars are general principles. As I approach each fundamental norm and institution of international law, it will become necessary to provide some greater specificity to the notions of both peace and basic human rights. We will also see that certain norms may be just only under certain conditions of their operation. We will also discover that many of the key interpretive differences among states and scholars about what the law is or what it should be map onto different perspectives on how much the norm should advance peace as opposed to ensure respect for human rights. But in the end, the claim of a norm to be just will involve a balancing of the values represented by the two pillars, and norms may require reform until they reach a point in which they pass muster under both pillars.

II. Completing the Framework: Additional Considerations in Applying the Two Pillars

The standard of justice based on two pillars is not the alpha and omega of the appraisal of the norms that will follow. To complete the framework of analysis, I will address two overarching issues related to the justice of international law, one more philosophical and one more legal: the implications for justice of the relation between states and individuals, and the implications for justice of international law's situation within a legal system. The first issue leads me to clarify a few assumptions for the analysis that follows, while the second demands that I supplement the two-pillared analysis in two important ways.

A. States and Individuals

Although my standard of international justice is impartialist by treating individuals as of equal worth, and thus grounded in an idea necessary for all standards of justice, it does not evaluate rules solely by reference to their effect upon individuals. Rather, it works from the following starting point: *In determining whether particular legal arrangements meet the standard of justice, the interests and claims of states (and, to a certain extent, other political communities at a substate level) deserve serious consideration alongside the interests and claims of individuals.*

This position can be justified on numerous grounds. The strongest grounds would argue that states possess moral standing, though not the same sort of moral standing as individuals. States possess that standing under different rationales, including because (a) they somehow legitimately express the interests or will of their population,[77] (b) they are vessels in which individual identity is created,[78] or (c) the state system is in fact the best available structure to advance individual welfare. Each position offers a defense of the state, the first more or less Kantian (a position that cannot be used to defend all states, but only some), the second communitarian, and the third more consequentialist. I happen to endorse the last of these—what Liam Murphy has called the instrumentalist justification for the state system, a view that Goodin has invoked as a justification for special duties toward compatriots.[79] Under this view, the state system may not be the best system in all conceivable worlds, but it is probably the best we can have given humankind's history and the alternatives we have seen, whether empires or failed states riven by anarchy.

But for purposes of defending the need to consider state interests, I do not need to adopt any of those three arguments. Indeed, that position can be defended on more economical grounds, such as Mathias Risse's position—namely, that given the impossibility of imagining how alternatives to the state (for example a world state or no states) would work or of feasibly getting to them, theories of global justice need to accept states both morally and pragmatically.[80] The state system appears to be a fixed attribute of the international order, so that we limit the role of moral reasoning if we ignore the interests of states. As a practical matter, states remain the primary and indispensable agents of individuals, and so we must work with a system of international law that gives states rights and duties.[81] Such a view does not mean that states alone suffice to prevent anarchy, for we need international institutions as well.[82]

Second, whatever our justification for considering state interests, even if it is Murphy's, *the claims of states cannot all be conceived as simply the sum of the claims of the individuals in them*. Some very important state interests are not by their nature additive in the sense that the claims of states with larger populations automatically outweigh the claims of states with smaller populations. If preservation of the state system is important, then, for some state interests, population is irrelevant. For example, the interest of the state in not being invaded, or in having the immunity

[77] Immanuel Kant, 'On the Common Saying: "This May be True in Theory, but it does not Apply in Practice"', in Hans Reiss (ed.) and H.B. Nisbet (trans.), *Kant: Political Writings*, 2nd ed. (New York: Cambridge University Press, 1991) 61, 73–74; Allen Buchanan, *Justice, Legitimacy, and Self-Determination* (Oxford: Oxford University Press, 2004) 233–49.

[78] See the argument in Kok-Chor Tan, *Justice Without Borders: Cosmopolitanism, Nationalism, and Patriotism* (Cambridge: Cambridge University Press, 2004) 90–3.

[79] Liam Murphy, 'International Responsibility', in Samantha Besson and John Tasioulas (eds.), *The Philosophy of International Law* (Oxford: Oxford University Press, 2010) 299, 304; Robert E. Goodin, 'What is So Special about Our Fellow Countrymen?', *Ethics* 98 (1998): 663. See also the discussion in Chapter 6 on sovereign equality.

[80] Mathias Risse, *On Global Justice* (Princeton, NJ: Princeton University Press, 2012) 315–18.

[81] See Toni Erskine, 'Locating Responsibility: The Problem of Moral Agency in International Relations', in Christian Reus-Smit and Duncan Snidal (eds.), *Oxford Handbook of International Relations* (Oxford: Oxford University Press, 2008) 699, 705 ('A moral agent can only reasonably be assigned a duty, or blamed for its evasion, if it enjoys the conditions that would make discharging the duty possible').

[82] Onora O'Neill, *Bounds of Justice* (Cambridge: Cambridge University Press, 2004) 181–5. The choice is not, however, as Simon Caney puts it, between states and supra-state institutions. Simon Caney, *Justice Beyond Borders: A Global Political Theory* (Oxford: Oxford University Press, 2005) 156–82.

of its diplomatic agents protected, is not a function of the size of its population (even if we think the state is simply an instrument of individual interests). Some state interests might, however, be additive of individual interests, for example the claims of states for a certain share of global economic wealth.

B. International law as part of a legal system

My analysis will also need to take account of the project's focus on the justice of *legal* norms. International law seeks and must seek not merely to advance peace and respect human rights, but to do so *by way of the law*. Legal norms originate and function differently from social norms, and the law's normative requirements need to inform our assessment of those rules and alternatives to them. Two such characteristics of international law as law are most important for the analysis.

1. *The rule of law and fairness*

First, societies have a particular set of expectations about the appropriate processes for the promulgation, interpretation, and enforcement of legal norms; their faith in and general acceptance of (and perhaps even their legal duties to respect) legal rules, turn on these expectations. Lon Fuller, for instance, identified criteria for what he called the internal morality of the law—factors that in his view make a rule a legal rule (as opposed to a social or other rule) and a system of governance a legal system. His eight criteria are generality, publicity, non-retroactivity, comprehensibility, non-contradiction, feasibility of compliance, stability over time, and congruence between rules and their administration.[83] Fuller's larger point is that the fidelity of the governed to the law turns on certain attributes of the law and the way that it operates.[84] Waldron has usefully built on Fuller's insights to speak about the notion of the rule of law as including both the need for legal certainty and predictability (central to Fuller's internal morality), as well as procedural fairness in the administration of the rules—a sort of due process for the participants.[85]

As a result, the appraisal of the justice of norms needs to be supplemented at points with considerations of the rule of law regarding both the content of the law and its procedures for implementation.[86] I think of the rule of law as fundamentally about the *fairness* of the law and its administration, as distinct from its substantive justice. Fairness-related shortcomings will arise, for instance, if an existing rule diverges too much from its actual application, or if a proposed rule would upset the stability of expectations too much. Fairness in procedural terms is particularly important with regard to international organizations because they are

[83] Lon Fuller, *The Morality of Law* (New Haven, CT: Yale University Press, 1964) 38–94.
[84] Ibid., at 41.
[85] Jeremy Waldron, 'The Concept and the Rule of Law', *Georgia Law Review* 43 (2008): 1, 6–9.
[86] My notion of fairness thus resembles Waldron's notion of the rule of law in its concern for both the form of rules and the procedures for their implementation.

key venues for making and applying law. I will call this set of important considerations the *fairness corollary.*

At the same time, my approach to fairness is admittedly somewhat selective. Application of the Fullerian criteria to the core rules of international law or full consideration of the fairness of the procedural aspects of international law would divert me from the primary project of assessing the justice of the core norms. Thus, for instance, I will not ask whether the existing norms came about as a result of a fair process, though as noted I will ask if certain institutions that interpret them have done so in a fair, in addition to a just, manner. Justice remains the 'first virtue' as expressed by Rawls, and fairness (of rules or procedures), though part of the overall discussion of the justice of international law, is not my main focus here.

2. *The existence of a legal system and compliance*

Second, and consistent with my starting point in non-ideal theory, we must take into account the basic positive criteria of any legal system. As Hart wrote, the minimum criteria for such a system are general obedience to—in the sense of compliance with, for whatever motivation—valid rules by private citizens and acceptance of the basic rules of recognition by public officials.[87] A legal system deserving of the name must elicit actual compliance by those said to be bound by the rules (which, in international law, includes states more than private citizens). However much we might have legal rules validated by rules of recognition, the existence of a legal system turns upon certain realities about society's response to those rules.[88] Compliance is central to a legal system.

Hart's idea is reflected across numerous disciplines beyond jurisprudence, and I need not go into all its elaborations here. Long before Hart, Kant recognized that the law might need to refrain, at least in the short term, from the normal punishment of certain conduct if society finds that conduct virtuous.[89] And long after Hart, modern jurisprudence continues to recognize the centrality of effectiveness to a legal system.[90] Within international law, Michael Reisman pointed out that 'lawful acts, to be such, will require a minimum degree of effectiveness'.[91] Full conformity is neither required nor realistic, and indeed many legal systems are characterized by what he calls 'operational codes' governing conduct in a way that may be at odds with the 'myth system' of formal legislation.[92]

[87] H.L.A. Hart, *The Concept of Law*, 3rd ed. (Oxford: Oxford University Press, 2012) 116–17. On the reasons for compliance, see Raz, *Practical Reasons, supra* note 63, at 178–82.

[88] Hart, *The Concept of Law, supra* note 87, at 103–4.

[89] See Immanuel Kant, 'The Metaphysical Elements of the Theory of Right', in *Kant: Political Writings*, Hans Reiss (ed.) and H.B. Nesbit (trans.) (Cambridge: Cambridge University Press, 1991) 158–9 (exempting honor killings—duels and infanticide—from the death penalty).

[90] See Waldron, 'The Concept and the Rule of Law', *supra* note 85, at 43.

[91] W. Michael Reisman, 'Law from the Policy Perspective', in Myres S. McDougal and W. Michael Reisman (eds.), *International Law Essays*, (Mineola, NY: The Foundation Press, 1981) 1, 7; see also Carlo Focarelli, *International Law as Social Construct: The Struggle for Global Justice* (Oxford: Oxford University Press, 2012) 55.

[92] W. Michael Reisman, *Folded Lies: Bribery, Crusades, and Reforms* (New York: The Free Press, 1979) 15–29.

This reality has an important implication for this study. For we might discover that some proposed alternatives to existing rules, even if those alternatives pass scrutiny under the two pillars—and indeed even if they are just alternatives to an existing unjust rule—place such demands on the law that they would not garner such general acceptance. In evaluating those alternatives, we must take into account prospects for compliance by global actors. For example, an appraisal that simply ignores the lessened chances of compliance when powerful states do not accept certain proposed rules would be highly unrealistic. Those states do not merely refrain from complying with rules they regard as placing excessive demands on them, but they have the power to block the compliance of others by obstruction. I will call this important concern the *compliance corollary*.

The compliance corollary is more of an alarm bell about, than it is a barrier to, some proposed changes to international law. But in some situations it could suggest we rule out certain proposed rules permitted (or even demanded) by the two pillars of justice. That eventuality could occur with proposed changes in the law so at odds with the motivations and claims of key international actors that their adoption, followed by their inevitable violation, would put the existence of the legal system in doubt. The reach of the compliance corollary is, in the end, a judgment call—perhaps even a pretheoretical hunch. But this process seems to me quite similar to the need for care in deploying the axiom that 'ought' implies 'can' in non-legal moral theory.

Yet taking compliance seriously in a theory of global justice does not mean that we must simply accept international law as just based on fears of reactions to changes to it by powerful states or non-state actors. Nor can it provide a sort of moral cover to actors who oppose rules more morally appealing than the status quo and thereby make them less likely to be obeyed. Even as prospects for obedience must be part of our theorizing about law, ideas for morally better rules should not be abandoned simply because they will not command *immediate* acceptance *by all*. As David Estlund writes: 'A requirement of general acceptability cannot plausibly count just any objection as decisive'.[93] Many areas of progress in international law, such as those of human rights and the environment, overcame arguments by opponents that the underlying ideas would never be accepted by states.

III. The Result: Thin Justice

The standard of justice explained here that will be used for appraising international law is thus one deserving of the name in the three senses discussed in this chapter and in Chapter 2: (a) its scope—a set of principles to assign rights

[93] David M. Estlund, *Democratic Authority: A Philosophical Framework* (Princeton, NJ: Princeton University Press, 2008) 39; see also at 40–52.

and duties in the relational scheme of the international arena; (b) the means by which it is derived—impartialist reasoning; and (c) its content—reflecting two core values the combination of which fairly describe the first virtue of a social institution at the international level, namely international law. Yet, as I have emphasized, this standard of justice differs from other standards, and it does so in two senses: first, it is not the sort of standard of justice we would use to appraise domestic institutions—the basic structure of society; and second, it is not the only standard for appraising international institutions—and certainly does not demand as much as would a standard of global justice that tracked a standard of domestic justice.

In light of these differences, I prefer to assign to my standard a modifier, and the qualification I have chosen is 'thin'. I take that idea from Walzer's distinction between thick and thin morality.[94] Walzer argues that the former, 'maximalist' morality governs relations within a community, where duties of individuals and institutions are multifarious—covering many aspects of human conduct—and strong out of a sense of special concern by the community for its members. Principles of distributive justice are part of the moral maximum. Thin morality, on the other hand, is a 'moral minimum'—universal in scope, reflecting values shared across cultures that are a baseline from which thicker, community-based morality may be developed.[95] 'Thinness' appears too in Jackson's description of the global community, one that is less dense in terms of the relationships of key actors than a domestic community.[96]

The justice that I posit is thin, in the sense that it is less dense, and certainly less demanding on individuals, than the justice needed for the governance of domestic societies. It is quite obviously thin compared to the Rawlsian conception of distributive justice within a state. And it is thin compared to standards, like Thomas Pogge's, that evaluate global institutions according to an international version of Rawls' theory.[97] Formally, the standard I have elaborated is not allocating rights, duties, or resources among individuals alone, and it recognizes the interests of states. And substantively, it is not mandating a robust set of human rights protections and certainly not requiring the distributive justice that Rawls develops. It is a justice that reflects the thinness of the community in which it operates. In Chapter 13, I will offer a thicker version of justice which international law can set as a realistic goal without undermining its thin justice.

[94] See Michael Walzer, *Thick and Thin: Moral Argument at Home and Abroad* (Notre Dame, IN: University of Notre Dame Press, 1994).

[95] Ibid., at 4–19. I do not accept Walzer's exact definition of thin morality, nor the normative argument that follows. Global justice is and should be about more than a 'minimal' set of understandings among global actors.

[96] See Robert Jackson, *The Global Covenant: Human Conduct in a World of States* (Oxford: Oxford University Press, 2000) 336–44.

[97] See Thomas W. Pogge, *Realizing Rawls* (Ithaca, NY: Cornell University Press, 1989) 241–6.

IV. Alternative Visions of Global Justice

The standard of justice offered previously faces challenges from a number of directions; I now defend it against four alternatives.

A. A pillar of human rights alone?

The choice to defend a standard of justice whose first principle is the advancement of peace may seem odd for those scholars, principally cosmopolitan, who make individual rights or dignity the core construct of global justice. Thus, Simon Caney sees global justice in terms of principles of civil and political justice, on the one hand, and of distributive justice, on the other, both of which place individual rights front and center.[98] That position might argue that (a) justice should be grounded solely in advancing human rights (either as a matter of consequences or duties) because peace is merely instrumental to respect for human rights, or, more appealingly (b) justice should be grounded solely in respect for human rights because the latter's fulfillment is necessary and sufficient (or, in a weaker version, simply the best way) to advance peace.

As for argument (a), I reject the idea that the sole function of peace is the protection of human rights, basic or otherwise. Peace is not merely an instrument for the enjoyment of human rights. Peace has numerous other ramifications and advantages for the flourishing of the planet, in terms of human, animal, and planetary welfare. Most significantly, peace gives individuals the *space* they need for *flourishing in all ways*—not only in achieving their basic or even non-basic rights. If we set a standard for justice merely in terms of the extent to which it promoted basic human rights, we would actually be left with a thinner notion of justice than I have proposed. And if we expand human rights to include all these other advantages that flow from peace, we end up with a rather loose theory to the effect that rules are just if they promote everyone's welfare.

Argument (b) accepts the importance of peace to justice, but it assumes that the best—indeed, the only moral—way to achieve that goal is through unmitigated advancement of individual human rights. Certainly some norms of international law both advance peace and respect human rights. In these situations, the second pillar is not acting as a constraint on the first. Yet it is clearly not the case that the advancement of human rights necessarily promotes peace. Human rights law itself recognizes the tension between human rights protection and internal peace in numerous ways, for example by granting states the ability to derogate from most human rights in the event of a 'public emergency that threatens the life of the nation', such as a civil war or natural calamity, as well as allowing the state to restrict the exercise of numerous rights for the sake of *ordre publique*.[99]

[98] Caney, *Justice Beyond Borders, supra* note 82, at 63–147.
[99] ICCPR, Art. 4; see also ICCPR, Arts. 18, 19, 21, 22.

So a single pillar of justice demanding respect for human rights would neglect a core construct of human rights law. Such a single standard does not do enough work to evaluate the justice of international law; for norms and institutions could respect those rights and still detract from or fail to advance the fundamental goal of peace.[100]

We can also look beyond human rights law to international practice and history. Although a glance at the map of the globe shows that, as a general matter today, states with the best practices for the protection of human rights are also at peace internally and with their neighbors,[101] the direction of causation is not obviously one-way. Did those states operationalize a robust version of human rights first, and then achieve peace internally or with their neighbors, or did civil and interstate peace form the linchpin that enabled them to protect individual rights? Whether in Europe or the United States, securing internal peace has historically involved a tradeoff with some human rights. Philip Bobbitt has described the period between 1776 and 1914 as one of transformation in the role of a state, in which 'states-nations', a state that commandeers a nation and is responsible for it, were transformed, through external and internal conflict and constitutional reform, into nation-states, where the state's legitimacy derives from the judgment of the people.[102] As he writes: 'The State is born in violence; only when it has achieved a legitimate monopoly on violence can it promulgate law'.[103]

To pick one small example of the lack of any necessary causal relationship between human rights and peace, after World War I, the Swedish community of the Finnish Åland Islands sought to advance their human rights to practice their language and culture through either independence or union with Sweden. This option was fiercely resisted by Finland, newly independent from Russia, and ultimately rejected by the League of Nations, all in the name of creating a united Finland and avoiding precedents for future secessions.[104] In sacrificing the maximal claims of the islanders for respect of their human rights, the League managed to advance peace between Sweden and Finland and within Finland. Indeed, the causation from that episode seems to flow in the opposite direction suggested by argument (b) earlier; for today, the high standard of human rights within both Sweden and Finland seems to be a beneficiary of the avoidance of war (and indeed most tensions at all) between those two states.[105]

More recently, it seems highly unlikely that respect for human rights would alone have ended the conflict in Northern Ireland or Bosnia. Rather, a solution had to include governance structures in which all sides felt some certainty that

[100] As for those rights the corresponding obligations of which may not be derogated even during such emergencies, they do act like trumps upon the state's ability even to secure internal peace.

[101] This is the general case. Some states with strong domestic records engage in wars for different reasons (e.g. the U.S. and Israel).

[102] Philip Bobbitt, *The Shield of Achilles: War, Peace, and the Course of History* (New York: Knopf, 2002) 144–209.

[103] Ibid., at 336.

[104] See, e.g., The Aaland Islands Question: Report Presented to the Council of the League of Nations by the Commission of Rapporteurs, League of Nations Doc. B7/21/68/106 (1921).

[105] Yet, as discussed later, I am not willing to shed the second pillar on the assumption that respect for human rights always flows from peace.

they would be involved in the state's future. As a result, mediators devised institutions to guarantee the participation of certain ethnic groups, a result that does not simply emerge from a starting point of the need to protect individual human rights. Indeed, on their face, they were discriminatory as concerns individual rights,[106] but they were clearly justifiable in these circumstances (even if they have proved more successful in the former case than in the latter). The same can be said of the 2004 unratified UN peace plan for Cyprus, which provides for representation for specific ethnic communities.[107] One might argue that the community rights recognized in Northern Ireland, Bosnia, or the Cyprus settlement proposal are simply derivative of individual human rights, but it is not so simple, as those communal rights often conflict with individual rights.[108] A focus on one pillar thus skews our vision as to what is just and underplays the benefits of peace for humankind.

B. A pillar of peace alone?

An alternative argument would suggest that the first pillar of justice is sufficient, either because (a) peace is more important than respect for basic human rights; or, more appealingly, (b) the achievement of peace will result in respect for basic human rights.[109] Nico Krisch, for example, in endorsing a complete ban on humanitarian intervention, has written 'it is arguable that the protection of peace is more precious to individuals than the preservation of their human rights *in all circumstances*'.[110] But these arguments fail too. As for (a), even under a consequentialist view, it is far too broad a generalization to say, as Krisch suggests, that situations of gross violations of human rights must *always* be tolerated for the sake of peace. As for (b), the evidence from world history does not suggest that peace necessarily leads to the achievement of basic human rights. The peace of the empire, the conquest, the occupation, or the brutally effective regime is common and obviously highly deleterious to human rights—and indeed is rarely peaceful anyway due to the persistence of armed resistance to occupation and armed responses to it. Even if, in some cases, pacification of territory may pave the way for the government eventually to respect human rights, the corpses and shattered

106 For the European Court of Human Rights' finding that certain aspects of the Bosnian constitution are discriminatory, see *Sejdić and Finci v Bosnia and Herzegovina*, ECHR (2009), Apps. 27996/06 and 34836/06.

107 See, e.g., The Comprehensive Settlement of the Cyprus Problem, 31 March 2004, <http://www.zypern.cc/extras/annan-plan-for-cyprus-2004.pdf>.

108 For a study of the hazards of court-applied human rights law to power-sharing, see Christopher McCrudden and Brendan O'Leary, *Courts and Consociations: Human Rights versus Power-Sharing* (Oxford: Oxford University Press, 2013).

109 A third argument might be that peace necessarily includes the enjoyment of basic human rights. But my notion of peace set forth earlier, in Part III.A.1, is far more limited, and I argue there that the promotion of peace tout court is itself a value for global justice.

110 Nico Krisch, 'Legality, Morality and the Dilemma of Humanitarian Intervention after Kosovo', *EJIL* 13 (2002): 323, 332 (emphasis added).

lives along the way suggest that human rights can easily suffer significantly in the short and medium term, and even the long term.

C. Reversing the pillars

A third alternative is the reverse of my standard—namely, that international law norms are just if they respect basic human rights, subject to their not disrupting peace. Three comments are in order. First, if both pillars are deployed in a consequentialist manner, it is not obvious that reversing the order in which they are utilized to appraise norms of international law will make any difference in the appraisal of international legal norms. Second, if the second pillar is to be deployed more as a trump or exclusionary reason, it might well affect our appraisal to say that norms are just to the extent they respect human rights, subject to a duty not to disrupt peace. But it is hard to know which way that cuts—toward finding more norms just (because peace is not balanced against them in consequentialist terms) or fewer norms just (because peace becomes a trump that strikes down more norms).

Third, whatever the effect of applying that alternative standard, such a position is not an argument against my standard; it is simply another standard, one that seems ethically defensible, unlike the first two alternatives of simply abandoning one pillar. As stated earlier, my standard, unlike the reversal of the pillars, is one that I believe is both ethically rigorous and better captures the goals and capacities of international law writ large. As I will explain in the last chapter of the book, I very much favor the transformation of the law to conform to what is best seen as a thicker standard insofar as it places more emphasis on human rights. But my advocacy for such a thicker standard over time is not an argument against the thin standard.

D. What about equality?

Another challenge would ask where the equality of individuals, particularly regarding access to global resources, fits in this framework. As noted, my starting point is indeed one of equality of inputs, insofar as each person's individual worth is the same under an impartialist conception of justice. I think this matches up with Ronald Dworkin's notion of 'equal concern for the fate of every person' that he regards as the first requirement of every legitimate government.[111] But my standard does not include equality of resources (or even of access to resources) as a test for the thin justice of international law. I make this choice for three reasons.

First, such equality, even though perhaps a laudable standard under ideal theory, seems oblivious to some core realities of the international arena, notably a state system that begins with an infinite number of inequalities (size, population,

[111] Ronald Dworkin, *Justice for Hedgehogs* (Cambridge, MA: Harvard University Press, 2011) 2; see also at 352.

GDP per capita, exploitable natural resources, educational level, infrastructure, etc.). We can hope to eliminate some of these inequalities, but it is unreasonable to expect *international law* to eliminate them and thus demanding too much to judge international law by its ability to do so.

Second, the second pillar incorporates core notions of equality, even if it does not call for equality regarding resources. The ban on invidious discrimination is very much about equality. Recognition of other basic human rights seeks to eliminate the greatest threats to individuals and therefore improve the condition of those suffering under the power of the state or the market. Non-interference with human rights incorporates many of the core ideas of what Elizabeth Anderson has termed the 'democratic conception of equality', a relational (as opposed to distributional) concept oriented toward the abolition of oppression and equal respect and consideration. Her concept goes beyond non-interference with basic human rights, but not that much further.[112]

Third, and relatedly, by guaranteeing the basic human rights that are outlined earlier, we make a great deal of progress on addressing some of the derivative reasons for caring about global inequality. Beitz points out that whatever one's views on the morality of inequality per se, global economic and political inequality matter because they cause material deprivation, humiliation of individuals and groups, denial to groups of control over their future, and procedural unfairness.[113] Although the pillar of respect for human rights does not catch these harms to the same extent as would a pillar based on equality, it goes a long way. If international law norms pass the second pillar, they have placed a significant limit on the harms caused by global inequality.

V. Thin Justice as Cosmopolitan Justice

Before concluding this chapter, it is useful to place the standard of thin justice within debates on global justice, and in particular about justice based on cosmopolitanism.[114] Cosmopolitan ideas of justice start from idea that the individual, wherever situated, is the ultimate unit of moral concern, and each individual—qua individual and not as a member of a community—is equal as the object of moral concern. Kant captured the idea in prophesizing a 'universal community...where a violation of rights in *one* part of the world is felt *everywhere*'.[115] As Scheffler writes, it means that 'norms of justice must be seen as governing the

[112] Elizabeth Anderson, 'What is the Point of Equality?', *Ethics* 109 (1999): 287, 312–15. For example, her description of the oppressive relationships that equality is supposed to terminate captures many of the harms that protection of basic human rights seeks to eliminate. Ibid., at 315.

[113] Charles R. Beitz, 'Does Global Inequality Matter?', *Metaphilosophy* 32 (2001): 95.

[114] Samuel Scheffler, 'Conceptions of Cosmopolitanism', in *Boundaries and Allegiances: Problems of Justice and Responsibility in Liberal Thought* (Oxford: Oxford University Press, 2001) 111. Scheffler distinguishes this form of cosmopolitanism from one about culture, which addresses (and rejects) group identity as relevant for conceptions of individual identity.

[115] Kant, 'Perpetual Peace: A Philosophical Sketch', in *Kant: Political Writings*, Hans Reiss (ed.) and H.B. Nesbit (trans.) (Cambridge: Cambridge University Press, 1991) 93, 107–8.

relations of all human beings to each other, and not merely as applying within individual societies or bounded groups of other kinds'.[116] In addition, we can distinguish between cosmopolitanism (or other theories of global justice) as prescribing a set of relations among individuals—an interactional conception—and cosmopolitanism as describing structures for and relations among institutions—an institutional conception.[117] The project here is concerned with cosmopolitanism in the latter sense, in that it tells us how we should construct institutions and how they should relate to each other.[118]

In these terms, the standard of thin justice is a cosmopolitan standard. It embraces the notion of the individual, wherever situated, as the ultimate unit of moral concern. The consequentialist reasoning places the preservation of interstate and internal peace as the first principle of global justice precisely because peace is the linchpin to advancing the welfare and overall flourishing of individuals, wherever situated. And the second pillar is based upon putting the individual's basic rights first in situations where the advancement of peace may conflict with those rights. It thus stands in sharp contrast to a 'statist' or 'morality of states' position in which states alone are the moral actors and order among them is the only value.[119]

The two pillars do not, I believe, require me to take a position in the longstanding debates between so-called strong cosmopolitans and moderate or weak ones. Strong cosmopolitans believe in equal regard for all persons in determining all duties; any special treatment we give to those in special relationships with us (for example co-nationals) is derivative of that equal worth. Weak or moderate cosmopolitans argue that we have both general duties to all persons on the planet and special duties to those in certain relationships to us that are of independent moral significance; the latter, toward families or co-nationals, need not be derivative of general duties.[120] My standard endorses the idea of global justice and duties across borders based on the equal worth of all people; it is agnostic on whether special duties within states—either by individuals or by the state—must be derivable from considerations of the interests of people based on their equal worth.

At the same time, my standard differs from some strong cosmopolitan accounts of global justice in at least two respects: (a) its emphasis on peace as a pillar of

[116] Scheffler, 'Conceptions of Cosmopolitanism', *supra* note 114, at 14.

[117] Thomas Pogge, 'Cosmopolitanism and Sovereignty', *Ethics* 103 (1992): 48, 50–2; Brian Barry, 'International Society from a Cosmopolitan Perspective', in David R. Mapel and Terry Nardin (eds.), *International Society: Diverse Ethical Perspectives* (Princeton, NJ: Princeton University Press, 1999) 144; Charles Beitz, 'Cosmopolitanism and Global Justice', *J Ethics* 9 (2005): 11, 17–19.

[118] Beitz, Barry, and Tan define institutional cosmopolitanism somewhat differently from me, as a moral view that dictates a certain institutional structure, i.e. a global state (a view that Pogge calls legal cosmopolitanism and Miller calls political cosmopolitanism). My cosmopolitan vision is open to a variety of governance structures.

[119] For an excellent review of this position, as well as others, see R.J. Vincent, *Human Rights and International Relations* (Cambridge: Cambridge University Press, 1986) 113–19.

[120] Scheffler, 'Conceptions of Cosmopolitanism', *supra* note 114, at 111, 114–16. For a somewhat different definition of strong versus weak cosmopolitanism, see Miller, *National Responsibility*, *supra* note 47, at 27–31 (distinguishing between insistence on equal treatment of all persons and equal value to all persons).

justice; and (b) its assumption that the claims of states should be considered alongside those of individuals. Both of these ideas cut against what Caney has called a key feature of (strong) cosmopolitanism—'that the moral values that inform our account of global politics must be cut from the same cloth as the moral values that inform our account of domestic politics'.[121] Certainly, with respect to (a), peace is taken for granted in the account of domestic justice but is a separate moral value in our accounts of global justice, so if strong cosmopolitans insist on the same moral values, they might find my standard of global justice unacceptable.

As for (b), my consideration of the interests of the state, this need not conflict with strong cosmopolitanism if we saw the state purely in instrumental terms—that its sole justification is to serve as a guardian of cosmopolitan values.[122] Yet if we do not insist on the instrumental justification, but simply see the state system as a fixed feature that does as well as possible in the world as we know it, then we have essentially conferred on the state some kind of separate moral standing. Jean Cohen has criticized strong cosmopolitanism (what she labels 'cosmopolitan liberalism') for its move from seeing the individual as the ultimate unit of moral concern to the idea that 'respect for the "fundamental" human rights of persons [should be] the *sole* criterion for assessing the legitimacy [of] states and supranational institutions'.[123]

But in the end I hope that strong cosmopolitans do not see my standard of global justice as working at odds with their project. My standard works from the position that it is more important for evaluating the justice of legal rules to see that the state *in fact functions* as a guardian of individual welfare in the world that we have, than to insist that the state or state system *can only be justified ab initio* based on such a guardian function. Weak or failed states—just look at Congo, Afghanistan, and other places—are today far more of a threat to cosmopolitan values than are strong states.[124] As Nigel Dower writes: 'The last thing a cosmopolitan wants in the world as it is now are weak or failed states.'[125] But that does not mean that we must justify the state solely on instrumental grounds.

My standard remains far from statism, which looks at international justice solely through the prism of state interests and cooperation. In evaluating the rules of international law, we are still considering individuals' welfare through the first pillar's emphasis on the preservation of peace and the second pillar's emphasis on human rights.[126]

[121] Caney, *Justice Beyond Borders*, *supra* note 82, at 267. [122] Ibid., at 274.

[123] Jean L. Cohen, 'Sovereign Equality vs. Imperial Right: The Battle over the "New World Order"', *Constellations* 13 (2006): 485, 488 (emphasis in original; '[of]' replaces the original 'for', which I assume is an error).

[124] See Steven R. Ratner and Gerald Helman, 'Saving Failed States', *Foreign Policy* 89 (1992): 3.

[125] Nigel Dower, *The Ethics of War and Peace* (Cambridge: Polity Press, 2009) 171.

[126] This position resembles Vincent's account of the role of human rights in international relations:

> From the morality of states we keep the cautious awareness that political power is concentrated at the level of the state, and that any scheme for moral improvement has to find its way in this world of states. From [strong] cosmopolitan morality we keep the sense

The standard of thin global justice does not insist that every rule of international law be justifiable in terms of its advancement of equal human rights along the lines of moral or interactional cosmopolitanism. Rather, it embraces a utilitarian logic that includes the Hobbesian search for peace—and the order that comes from it—in global relations, a logic that may well give prominence to borders and special duties and rights that may not always be justifiable from a strong moral cosmopolitan starting point. Proper respect for Hobbes' emphasis on order, when combined with a respect for basic human rights, can justify robust international law and institutions.[127]

VI. Conclusion

This chapter has provided the core theoretical framework for the rest of this volume. I have identified two ideas as inherent in the public culture of international law and distilled them into a standard of global justice. Under it, the core norms of international law will be appraised for their justice in terms of their proclivity to advance international or internal peace while respecting basic human rights. Peace is principally about the absence of armed conflict, whereas basic human rights are a subset of human rights derived from examining the practice of states. International law as a whole need not advance human rights—that is the job for human rights law—but it must not interfere with the basic ones. That standard reflects a largely consequentialist approach to justice, though we will at times give human rights their due through more than just balancing. Consistent with the approach in non-ideal theory, I will, in applying the standard, take the state system for granted. And because this is a project to assess legal rules—rules that operate within an institutionalized legal system and not just as freestanding moral precepts—I emphasized the importance of the rule of law, and procedural fairness in particular, as well as overall compliance with the rules, as considerations that will affect the appraisal of both existing and contemplated norms.

This standard of global justice—thin justice—that I propose is a bona fide standard in terms of its scope, its method of derivation, and its content. This standard also proved more convincing than a number of alternatives that we can imagine, either because those alternatives were normatively unappealing or because they glossed over key realities of the international system that must be taken into account in a project of non-ideal theory. Yet it contrasts with standards of justice appropriate for the basic structure of a domestic society as well as thicker standards for global justice that might be part of ideal theory.

> of direction [i.e. toward realizing a global community]. And from Realism we keep the suspicion of any purportedly universalist doctrine.

Vincent, *Human Rights, supra* note 119, at 124.

[127] See Barry, 'International Society', *supra* note 117, at 145.

Lastly, I sought to show the basic compatibility of thin justice with cosmopolitan justice. In both cases, we start with a fundamental concern about the individual. We may disagree on the role for states in protecting individuals or on the extent to which certain aspects of the international system are fixed or changeable. But I believe we are dedicated to a morality based on the individual rather than merely the state. Like a sheet of titanium or other similarly strong elements, even thin justice possesses much inner strength.

I now turn to the core norms of international law. The following eight chapters appraise norms on a range of subjects organized from the vantage point of the claimants and claims identified in Chapter 2: the use of force and intervention; self-determination and borders; sovereign equality; membership and decisionmaking in international organizations; the territorial scope of human rights protection (with a separate chapter on humanitarian intervention); international trade; and international investment.

In the case of each norm, my goal will be threefold: first, to explain in general the state of the law based on the existing normative expectations of global actors as gleaned from a variety of accepted sources; second, to clarify the correlative duties or rights involved in the norm, including the relevant duty-holders and rights-holders; and third, and most important, to examine the ethical justification for the norm under the framework of thin justice. In each case I will also examine a number of challenges to the law that either global actors or scholars claim would make for a more just norm.

PART II

THE JUSTICE OF CORE NORMS ON STATEHOOD

4

Norms of Territorial Integrity and Political Independence: The Ban on the Use of Force and Non-Intervention

I now begin the appraisal of the core norms of international law under the two-pillar standard of thin justice. As stated in Chapter 3, states first and foremost make what I call claims about sovereignty—about territorial integrity, political independence, and participation. Peoples, on the other hand, essentially make claims for self-government, including recognition as a distinct actor (and not merely a group of individuals) and some form of control over their own future. In the next four chapters, I will examine a set of norms that have developed in response to these claims—norms that we might call *norms on statehood*. These norms are four-fold—(1) the ban on the use of force in international relations, subject to a handful of exceptions; (2) the ban on intervention in the affairs of others states through extraterritorial conduct; (3) the norm of self-determination of peoples; and (4) the sovereign equality of states, including its operation in international organizations. These are, in my view, the most basic building blocks of the existing system of states insofar as they define the most important terms of cooperation between them as well as setting the parameters for the creation of new states.

I. International Law's Ban on the Use of Force

The most significant moral achievement within the current body of international law is the ban on the threat or use of force by states in their international relations.

A. Basic contours of the norm

Under both the UN Charter and customary international law, states may not use force against the territorial integrity or political independence of any other state, subject only to two exceptions: the use of force in self-defense in the event of an armed attack against the state, and use of force in accordance with an authorization (or, theoretically, a requirement) by the UN Security Council.[1] I will leave

[1] UN Charter, Arts. 2(4), 42, 51.

until Chapter 9 claims by both states and scholars for a third exception to the ban on the use of force, namely to rescue a population facing human rights abuses from its own government, and simply note that such a claim is both controversial and, at the very least, not overtly accepted by most states.

Although conditional or limited bans on force preceded the UN Charter—notably the 1907 Hague Convention Respecting the Limitation of the Employment of Force for the Recovery of Contract Debts, the Covenant of the League of Nations, and the 1928 Kellogg-Briand Pact—the Charter's prohibition is, subject to the two exceptions noted, complete.[2] It does not simply forbid states from waging war on each other, as the Kellogg-Briand Pact did;[3] nor does it simply ban those uses of force aimed at conquest and occupation of foreign territory. In 1974, the United Nations General Assembly adopted the Definition of Aggression that offered a useful illustrative list of acts of aggression. That list gives one a feel for the contours of Article 2(4), even as aggression as a legal matter probably requires a higher threshold of force than does a violation of Article 2(4). These acts include invasion, bombardment, blockade of ports, attacks on naval forces, and the use of force by foreign armies based in a state with its consent to commit acts against the state in violation of basing agreements.[4] In recent years, some states and scholars have come to regard certain cyber-attacks as uses of force.[5] Nor is the motivation for such force important. As made clear in the General Assembly's 1970 Friendly Relations Declaration, a unanimously endorsed key interpretation of the Charter, even a bona fide border dispute between two states, in which one claims that part of the other's territory belongs to it, does not justify force by one side. Thus, Iraq's pre-1991 claim to all or part of Kuwait did not justify its 1990 invasion to (re-) control it.[6]

At the same time, the ban has limits. Notably, it is focused on physical (and by implication cyber-related) force, thereby excluding economic 'force', in the sense of economic pressure that states exert on other states through embargoes, sanctions, unfair trade practices, or the extraction of economic concessions during political negotiations.[7] Even an internationally condemned boycott, such as

[2] Art. 2(4) also bans the threat of the use of force. Though an important provision of the Charter, it is less central than the ban on the use of force and so will not be explored here.

[3] General Treaty for the Renunciation of War (Kellogg-Briand Pact) Art. 1, 28 August 1928, 94 LNTS 57 ('The High Contracting Parties solemnly declare in the names of their respective peoples that they condemn recourse to war for the solution of international controversies, and renounce it, as an instrument of national policy in their relations with one another.').

[4] GA Res. 3314 (XXIX) (Definition of Aggression), Art. 3 (17 December 1974).

[5] See, e.g., Harold H. Koh, Legal Advisor, U.S. Department of State, Remarks at USCYBERCOM Inter-Agency Legal Conference: International Law in Cyberspace (18 September 2012), prepared remarks available at <http://www.state.gov/s/l/releases/remarks/197924.htm> ('Cyber activities that proximately result in death, injury, or significant destruction would likely be viewed as a use of force'); Michael N. Schmitt (ed.), *The Tallinn Manual on the International Law Applicable to Cyber Warfare* (Cambridge: Cambridge University Press, 2013) Rule 11.

[6] Friendly Relations Declaration, principle 1, para. 4.

[7] Albrecht Randelzhofer, 'Article 2(4)', in Bruno Simma, Daniel-Erasmus Khan, Georg Nolte, and Andreas Paulus (eds.), *The Charter of the United Nations: A Commentary*, 3rd ed., Vol. I (Oxford: Oxford University Press, 2012) 200, 209. If those negotiations included an explicit threat of force, they would cross the line to violating Art. 2(4).

the U.S. embargo on Cuba, is not a use of force. Moreover, the ban is focused on international uses of force—between states and, as discussed further later, between states and certain foreign transnational actors. It does not ban the use of force by a state against an insurgency or by an insurgency against the state—issues which are addressed by the norms of self-determination discussed in the next chapter.

Within these contours, the ban on the use of force is a very special norm of international law. It is one of the handful that the International Court of Justice (ICJ) has identified as *erga omnes*, owed to the international community as a whole.[8] The Eritrea-Ethiopia Claims Commission, set up to adjudicate legal claims arising from those two states' border war, called Article 2(4) a 'fundamental rule of international law'.[9] And scholars repeatedly refer to it as a rule of *jus cogens*, namely a rule that overrides any treaties to the contrary.[10] In addition, aggression was recognized as an international crime—for which individuals can be tried—in the 1945 Charter of the International Military Tribunal at Nuremberg, and is now within the jurisdiction of the International Criminal Court.[11]

Indeed, the ban on the use of force suffuses other areas of law. Most notably, the modern law of treaties, codified in the 1969 Vienna Convention on the Law of Treaties, declares void ab initio all treaties procured through the threat or use of force in violation of the UN Charter.[12] Although this rule may not affect the validity of many treaties in practice—threats of force are rarely as overt as that underlying the 1938 Munich Agreement in which Czechoslovakia was forced to cede the Sudetenland to Germany, and agreements between two states following a war may not be easily traced to the use of force by one against the other—it is a very important statement of principle that extends the consequences of the ban on the use of force and the remedies for the victims of it.

The ban on the use of force creates a duty on all states not to use force; it also implies a Hohfeldian correlative right on all states as well—the right not to be the object of force by other states. In international law terms, this is the essence of the right of a state to its territorial integrity.[13] In the terms used earlier, it is a general norm, one that does not play favorites among states. States may not use arguments about spheres of influence, special relationships with other states, or other ties to justify uses of force. At the same time, such special relationships permit a state to

[8] *Case Concerning Barcelona Traction, Light, and Power Co. (Belgium v Spain), Second Phase* [1970] ICJ Rep 3, para. 34 (5 February).

[9] *Jus Ad Bellum (Ethiopia v Eritrea)*, Ethiopia's Claims 1–8, Partial Award, para. 10 (Eritrea Ethiopia Claims Communication, 19 December 2005), <http://www.pca-cpa.org>.

[10] Robert E. Goodin and Steven R. Ratner, 'Democratizing International Law', *Global Policy* 2 (2011): 241. See also Andrea Bianchi, 'Human Rights and the Magic of Jus Cogens', *EJIL* 19 (2008): 491.

[11] See Charter of the International Military Tribunal, 8 August 1945, Art. 6, 82 UNTS 280; Statute of the International Criminal Court, Art. 5(1)(d). The crime of aggression is defined in an amendment to the Statute, which also specifies preconditions before the Court will be able to hear cases of aggression. See Amendments to the Rome Statute of the International Criminal Court on the Crime of Aggression, Art. 8*bis*, <http://www.icc-cpi.int>.

[12] VCLT, Art 52.

[13] Steven R. Ratner, 'Drawing a Better Line: *Uti Possidetis* and the Borders of New States', *AJIL* 90 (1993): 590, 601.

receive the consent of another state for military involvement in its affairs, which is as a general matter not covered by Article 2(4) of the UN Charter.[14]

What about the two exceptions? As a formal matter, as David Rodin has pointed out, self-defense is best viewed as a justification for force that gives rise to a liberty on the attacked state to respond with force against the aggressor. At that point, the attacking state has a Hohfeldian no-right to its territorial integrity, assuming the responding state acts in accordance with secondary norms concerning the proportionality of the response.[15] Moreover, because the Charter recognizes the concept of collective self-defense, the victim state also has the liberty to call upon its friends to assist it in self-defense.

The liberty of self-defense can give rise to a new set of special duties, as states can agree by treaty to come to the aid of an attacked state. The network of mutual defense treaties created by the United States during the Cold War is a testament to this liberty; thus the centerpiece of the North Atlantic Treaty of 1949 is the commitment by NATO's members that if one of them is attacked, 'each of them, in exercise of the right of individual or collective self-defense recognized by Article 51 of the Charter of the United Nations, will assist the Party or Parties so attacked by taking forthwith . . . such action as it deems necessary, including the use of armed force, to restore and maintain the security of the North Atlantic area'.[16] Thus, the general duty of states not to use force may be coupled with a series of special duties of states to one another. Such duties are not, however, part of customary international law—without such treaties, states may legally ignore the pleas of attacked states.

The right of a state to respond in self-defense is treated in the UN Charter as an 'inherent' right, one that pre-dates that Charter. At the same time, under the Charter, the state may invoke self-defense 'if an armed attack occurs'. The phrase is generally interpreted to mean 'only if' an armed attack occurs, even though this interpretation creates a potential asymmetry between Article 2(4) (which bans all uses of force and not just armed attacks) and Article 51 (which gives the right of self-defense only in the event of an armed attack).[17] Some states and scholars have sought to avoid the asymmetry by qualifying all uses of force as armed attacks or extending the right of self-defense to all uses of force, but the more prevalent view seems to be that there are still some uses of force against a state that do not trigger the right of self-defense.[18] Even setting aside this issue, this phrase has given rise

[14] David Wippman, 'Treaty-Based Intervention: Who Can Say No?', *Chicago L Rev* 62 (1995): 607.

[15] David Rodin, *War and Self-Defense* (Oxford: Oxford University Press, 2002) 29–33.

[16] North Atlantic Treaty, 4 April 1949, Art. 5, 34 UNTS 243.

[17] *Military and Paramilitary Activities In and Against Nicaragua (Nicaragua v United States)* [1986] ICJ Rep 14, paras. 195, 211 (27 June); Randelzhofer, 'Article 2(4)', *supra* note 7, at 667. According to the ICJ, victims of uses of force short of armed attacks may still take 'proportionate countermeasures', *Nicaragua*, para. 249, although the Court has never made clear exactly what those might be.

[18] Steven R. Ratner, 'Self-Defense Against Terrorists: The Meaning of Armed Attack', in Larissa van den Herik and Nico Schrijver (eds.), *Counter-Terrorism Strategies in a Fragmented International Legal Order: Meeting the Challenges* (Cambridge: Cambridge University Press, 2013) 334, 340–2.

to the interpretive disputes discussed later; indeed, they are the nub of the ethical controversy over Article 2(4).

As for the other exception, the Security Council has great flexibility as a legal matter to interpret its powers to authorize or require force to maintain international peace and security.[19] Its first two authorizations for military force were a form of collective self-defense and security after aggression—North Korea's invasion of South Korea in 1950 and, many years later, Iraq's invasion of Kuwait in 1990. But since that time, it has authorized force for explicitly humanitarian and human rights reasons following internal disorder or civil war—including to deliver food to Somalia in 1992, restore Haiti's deposed president to power in 1994, and prevent civilian casualties (and, effectively, aid the opposition forces) during Libya's 2011 civil war.[20]

B. The ethics of the ban: a starting point of consensus

Article 2(4) itself faces no serious ethical criticism from either states or scholars as a starting point for the relationship between states on the planet.[21] Whether from the perspective of pure realism or from an ethical perspective grounded in consequentialism or deontology, the ban on the use of force is generally agreed upon as a profound contribution to both order and morality on the international stage. From the perspective of my vision of global justice, Article 2(4) is a critical manifestation of the justice of international law insofar as it removes from the policy option of states—subject to the two exceptions noted earlier—those very courses of action most disruptive to international peace. Moreover, Article 2(4) also promotes domestic peace. Breaches of the ban that result in the conquest of one state by another—even one that is swift and poorly resisted—typically lay the seeds for internal instability and suffering in the victim state. Occupiers are unable to manage conflicts within the society as well as indigenous institutions, and, ultimately, domestic forces will resist the occupier, however powerful it might be. In recent times, this has been the lesson of the illegal invasions of Afghanistan by the Soviet Union, Kuwait by Iraq, and Iraq by the United States (and, indeed a lesson even from lawful interventions such as those approved by the UN in Somalia, Haiti, and other places).[22]

As a result of this basic consensus, the differences of opinion about the lawfulness or ethics of utilizing military force are framed in terms of exceptions to the

[19] See *Questions of Interpretation and Application of the 1971 Montreal Convention arising from the Aerial Incident at Lockerbie* (*Libya v United States*) [1992] ICJ Rep 114, paras. 43–44 (Order of 14 April); Thomas M. Franck, 'The "Powers of Appreciation": Who Is the Ultimate Guardian of UN Legality?', *AJIL* 86 (1992): 519.

[20] The Council invoked Chapter VII once during the Cold War to address a human rights issue, in Rhodesia in 1966, but it did not authorize force. See SC Res. 232 (16 December 1966).

[21] For a very different view about bans on force, see John Maynard Keynes, *The Economic Consequences of the Peace* (London: Macmillan and Co., 1920) 243 (League Covenant's guarantee of territorial integrity 'destroy[s] the conception of the League as an instrument of progress [and] equip[s] it from the outset with an almost fatal bias towards the *status quo*').

[22] Cf. Benedict Kingsbury, 'Sovereignty and Inequality', *EJIL* 9 (1999): 599, 620.

ban, not abandonment of it. This distinction may sound too fine, but it is not. All serious claims for allowing more force in international relations work from the premise that they do not entail any reversal of the presumption that states may not use force against one another. (And those proposals for fewer exceptions want to strengthen Article 2(4).) These ideas continue to place the burden of proof for use of force on those states that are using it. In the following, I will focus primarily on the exception for self-defense, as I believe it raises the most important questions of justice, though I will have a bit to say here about Security Council responses, an issue also covered in Chapter 8.

The exception to Article 2(4) for self-defense is well grounded in the consequentialist priority for peace and, in my view, satisfies the first pillar. Self-defense, individual and collective, in response to aggression furthers peace through its deterrent effect. The right of a state to respond in self-defense prima facie has a large deterrent effect on potential attackers compared to the absence of such a norm. Aggression also becomes far more costly when the aggressor can expect significant political support from other states for the victim state's exercise of self-defense (though it would probably defend itself even if the norm did not exist), including, most critically, the possibility of collective self-defense. Such deterrence need not drive the foreign or military policy of potential aggressors, who probably have manifold other reasons not to invade their neighbors—including the effect of the norm itself and the reputational consequences for violation of it, as well as the practical costs of taking over another state.[23] Collective self-defense has its dangers in terms of the possibilities for escalation. These worries probably led the ICJ to suggest, in its judgment on Nicaragua's suit against the United States for aiding the contras in the 1980s, a set of procedural conditions to collective self-defense, including a public invitation by the victim state (in that case, El Salvador).[24] But a denial of collective self-defense would put the victim of the armed attack in an untenable position.

This defense of Article 51 does not mean that the framers of the UN Charter specifically rationalized Article 51 in these consequentialist terms. They may well have believed—and states may still believe—in something like Walzer's 'legalist paradigm' that analogizes states to individuals and sees self-defense as the inherent right of a state or the community in response to the crime of aggression by one of its members.[25] But given my concerns about the existence of an international community stated in Chapter 2, the consequentialist rationale offers a better justification of the right of self-defense.

[23] See Thomas M. Franck, *The Power of Legitimacy Among Nations* (New York: Oxford University Press, 1990) (power of norms over behavior); Andrew Guzman, *How International Law Works: A Rational Choice Theory* (Oxford: Oxford University Press, 2008) (power of reputational effects).

[24] See *Nicaragua, supra* note 17, paras. 195, 199. See also Dino Kritsiotis, 'International Law and the Relativities of Enforcement', in James Crawford and Martti Koskenniemi (eds.), *The Cambridge Companion to International Law* (Cambridge: Cambridge University Press, 2012) 245, 249–50.

[25] Michael Walzer, *Just and Unjust Wars: A Moral Argument with Historical Illustrations*, 4th ed. (New York: Basic Books, 2006) 58–63.

The second pillar of thin justice requires that we ask whether allowing states to defend themselves—and seek military aid from other states—in the event of an armed attack somehow interferes with basic human rights. As an initial matter, there is no tension between self-defense and respect for human rights. If the deterrent associated with the consequentialist reasoning is successful, the residents of a state will enjoy protection from foreign conquest and occupation, which historically has been quite inimical to basic human rights. Whether one looks at World War II or occupations since then in Afghanistan, Western Sahara, or the West Bank, residents typically suffer in terms of physical harm from the occupying power, denial of basic economic rights (especially health), and an inability to exert minimal control over their political future.

Yet if deterrence fails and an aggressor attacks anyway, then self-defensive action by the victim state and its allies increases the likelihood that people on both sides will be killed and injured. Even if *jus ad bellum* norms of necessity and proportionality, which require the victim state to use only as much force as is needed to terminate the armed attack, are respected, human rights are severely harmed during wartime. In that sense, self-defense could be said to interfere with the basic human right to life by inviting high casualty figures.

This critique of the extant rule for purposes of the second pillar seems simplistic. Self-defense preserves respect for the basic human rights of the population of the attacked state against the predations of the aggressor state—although it might (at worst) just shift the harms to human rights from the population of the victim state to that of the aggressor state. We thus cannot say that allowing self-defense interferes with human rights if we think in terms of the consequences for overall respect of basic human rights from allowing it. Indeed, only if we know or can be reasonably confident that deterrence will typically fail and that conquerors will be benevolent—the latter against all we know historically—could a right of self-defense undercut respect for basic human rights.[26]

This consequentialist defense of the rule highlights the near-absurdity of seeing all basic human rights as trumps under the second pillar of thin justice, such that violations of those rights enjoyed by the members of the aggressor state would render the norm of self-defense unjust, regardless of the consequences for the victim state's population. If we choose to see rights as exclusionary reasons, we can say that, although we must reject many excuses for one state to harm the basic human rights of the members of another state (certainly a mere disagreement between them would not allow such action), when one state takes the initiative of invading another, with its likely effects upon the latter and harm to peace, we have found a

[26] We could imagine how the basic human rights of the citizens of the aggressor state could be so vastly improved by invasion of another state so as conceivably to outweigh the loss in rights of the latter. This scenario might occur if a state whose population was starving invaded a super-rich neighbor and plundered its resources, but not to the point of leaving the population of the victim state starving. Yet even then, the improvement in the economic rights of the population of the aggressor state would be counteracted by the significant loss in civil and political rights to the population of the victim state.

good reason for the victim to respond militarily to the aggressor, even if it interferes with the basic human rights of the latter's population.

In addition to these ways in which Article 51 passes muster under the second pillar of thin justice, further support is offered by the *jus in bello*, or international humanitarian law, developed over many centuries in an attempt to limit suffering to individuals during armed conflict, with a now-extensive body of law and even some judicial enforcement of it.[27] One of the core norms of the *jus in bello*—the principle of distinction that prohibits direct, indiscriminate, or disproportionate attacks on civilians—offers a decent approximation of a norm protecting the basic human rights of people on both sides of a war.[28] If those rules are respected, the rule allowing individual and collective self-defense will have fewer negative impacts on respect for the basic rights of the population of all states involved.

As for the other major exception to Article 2(4), Council-authorized force, the UN Charter's grant of authority to the Security Council to respond to aggression passes the threshold of the first pillar for the same reason as individual self-defense—for its deterrent effect on aggressors and contribution to interstate peace. The Council's infrequent authorization of force in the case of aggression is certainly a problem in operationalizing this justice, but the possibility of such action by the Council makes the norm just.

Yet it is also clear that, since the end of the Cold War, the members of the Security Council have significantly altered their interpretation of Chapter VII's authority to the Council to respond to threats and breaches of the peace. They have moved from authorizing force in response to aggression to authorizing it to protect human rights—even as some of the Council's members have insisted that their real concern is spillover effects and regional instability rather than human rights protection per se. This shift by the Council's members in their interpretation of the Chapter VII exception to Article 2(4) is significant as a matter of thin justice. For an interpretation of Chapter VII that took off the table Council action in defense of human rights would not pass the second pillar of thin justice, even as it would pass the first pillar. That is, the Council's current interpretation of Chapter VII is required as a matter of thin justice.

Yet perhaps the current interpretation of Chapter VII's exception to Article 2(4) still does not pass muster under the second pillar insofar as the Security Council has never interpreted Chapter VII to *require* it to respond militarily to ensure respect for basic human rights—even where it might be assumed that such action would be effective at terminating such violations. Rather, as witnessed by its inaction in response to genocide in Rwanda and war crimes in Sri Lanka, Syria, Congo, and Darfur, the Council's members, in particular the permanent ones, have been quite reluctant to approve of force. This potential injustice in the

[27] Chapter 12 will examine in more detail the core norms of *jus in bello* under the standard of thin justice.

[28] See generally International Committee of the Red Cross, *Customary International Humanitarian Law: Volume 1: Rules*, Jean-Marie Henckaerts and Louise Doswald-Beck (eds.) (Cambridge: Cambridge University Press, 2005).

Council's interpretation of the law raises two larger questions that will be considered later. One is the implication for justice of the inconsistency in the Council's decisionmaking, in particular in light of its membership, an issue explored in Chapter 8. The other is whether a norm that merely allows for force, but does not require it, in response to gross violations of human rights meets the standard of thin justice, an issue explored in Chapter 9.

This basic defense of international law's rules on interstate force must not obscure important differences of opinion by global actors (and scholars) on the scope of Article 2(4). Indeed, we witness pressures on the norm in two directions—to shrink the ban in key respects and to enlarge it. For now, I will consider these pressures insofar as they seek, respectively, to enlarge the permissibility of self-defense or to reduce it. There are other pressures on the ban on force as well—for a broad new carve-out for humanitarian intervention and for greater action by the Security Council under its authority, both of which will be considered in later chapters.

C. Pressures for a Broad Right of Self-Defense

Claims for a broad right of self-defense have come primarily from states—although some have been endorsed by scholars. In essence, these claims are primarily about an expansion in two dimensions—*personally*, insofar as they seek to extend self-defense to attacks by non-state entities; and *temporally*, insofar as they seek to extend self-defense to permit a response by a state prior to an actual armed attack.[29]

1. Expansion in personal terms—the problem of independent non-state actors

States have long employed and deployed independent actors to conduct hostile operations in other states—actions, which would, if conducted by the state, amount to a use of force or aggression. During the Cold War, the United States and Soviet Union armed and even dispatched guerrillas to fight governments each perceived as hostile, whether in Cuba, Angola, Nicaragua, El Salvador, Afghanistan, or Vietnam. States have long understood the prohibition on the use of force to ban such actions (even as the superpowers continued to flout the rules). Thus, in the Friendly Relations Declaration, states agreed that Article 2(4) of the UN Charter encompasses 'the duty to refrain from organizing or encouraging the organization of irregular forces or armed bands, including mercenaries, for incursion into the territory of another State'.[30] And the Definition of Aggression

[29] I leave aside here an additional claim. The United States, France, Israel, and other states have invoked self-defense in narrow circumstances to rescue nationals in imminent danger from a hostile government. See Oscar Schachter, 'In Defense of International Rules on the Use of Force', *Chicago L Rev* 53 (1986): 113, 138–9. Such operations have been overtly and tacitly accepted by other states, even if some scholars refuse to recognize such a right. See Randelzhofer, 'Article 2(4)', *supra* note 7. This expansion of Article 51 seems to pass muster under both pillars if the operations are truly limited to rescue.

[30] Friendly Relations Declaration, principle 1, para. 8.

includes 'the sending by or on behalf of a State of armed bands, groups, irregulars or mercenaries, which carry out acts of armed force against another State of such gravity as to amount to the acts listed above, or its substantial involvement therein'.[31] When Nicaragua sued the United States in the ICJ in 1984 for aiding the *contras* seeking to overthrow the former, the United States argued that the action was in lawful self-defense of El Salvador, then facing a guerrilla movement aided by Nicaragua. The Court ruled that if the United States could show that Nicaragua sent those forces into El Salvador, then El Salvador would have a right of self-defense against Nicaragua.[32] At this point, nobody seriously contests the extension of Article 2(4) to the sending of armed bands by one state against another, nor the right of the victim state to respond in self-defense in these situations. Effectively, in these situations, the armed groups are acting as agents of the sending state. The move also finds itself justifiable in the consequentialist rationale for the basic rule of self-defense.

But after this point, the controversy over the personal application of Article 51 begins, for armed bands may have relationships with states short of direct deployment that make it harder to say whether the state has really committed an armed attack. States may prefer to send money or weapons to groups already fighting abroad, as witnessed in the significant external support to opposition forces in Syria's civil war; they may tolerate or welcome them on their territory but play no role in their operations, as appears to have been the Taliban government's approach to Al Qaeda in the years before 2001; or they may be so weak that, although they would prefer that such groups not operate from their territory, they cannot do much about it, as may be the case for non-state armed groups operating in Somalia or Yemen today.

In these situations, the consensus on self-defense becomes far more difficult to sustain. Along with holding that El Salvador could assert self-defense if Nicaragua had sent guerrillas to fight in El Salvador, the ICJ said that El Salvador could not do so—that there was no armed attack against it—if Nicaragua were only sending weapons to guerrillas in El Salvador, a move strongly rejected at the time by some scholars.[33] Since 11 September 2001, and even before, a small number of states, led by the United States, have asserted a right to respond in self-defense to states that in some way harbor terrorists, even if the ties between the terrorists and the state fall well short of making them agents of that state. Thus, in its notification to the Security Council when it began operations in Afghanistan in October 2001, the U.S. government justified its actions based on self-defense on the grounds that the September 11 attacks 'have been made possible by the decision of the Taliban regime to allow the parts of Afghanistan that it controls to be used by [Al Qaeda]

[31] Definition of Aggression, *supra* note 4, Art. 3(g).

[32] *Nicaragua, supra* note 17, para. 195. The ICJ found that no such proof had been presented.

[33] See, e.g., Thomas M. Franck, 'Some Observations on the ICJ's Procedural and Substantive Innovations', *AJIL* 81 (1987): 116; John Lawrence Hargrove, 'The *Nicaragua* Judgment and the Future of the Law of Force and Self-Defense', *AJIL* 81 (1987): 135.

as a base of operation'.[34] Since that time, scholars have argued as to whether the notion of self-defense now lawfully encompasses such situations.[35]

My own view is that states' expectations have changed such that (a) armed attacks need not be attributable to states in order to trigger the right of self-defense (indeed, the Charter does not so limit armed attacks); and (b) in limited circumstances, victim states may take self-defensive action against states that are wholly unwilling or unable to take action themselves against such groups based on their territory.[36] But the matter is not free from doubt as a statement of the current state of the law. The Obama Administration has endorsed this view regarding its anti-terrorist military operations,[37] as have two ICJ judges in a case concerning non-state actors on the territory of the Congo,[38] and two sets of principles prepared by panels of academic experts (including this author).[39] On the other hand, the ICJ has not departed from its view expressed in 2004 that armed attacks triggering the right to self-defense can only come from states. In that case, it rejected Israel's claim of self-defense as a justification for the separation barrier it built in the West Bank, noting that suspected terrorists seeking to enter Israel from the occupied territories were not acting on behalf of any state.[40]

Whatever the scope of international endorsement, the parameters of each prong of the 'unwilling or unable' test raise numerous interpretive questions. At what point is a state truly unable to stop terrorists from using it as a base for operations? This may seem like an easy question for so-called failed states, but many states with fully functioning governments have not succeeded in preventing their territories from being used by terrorists despite bona fide criminal law enforcement and prevention efforts. Certainly Germany and Malaysia were unable to stop the September 11 hijackers from carrying out key planning activities there. Nobody has seriously suggested that such states meet the 'unable' test, yet if one chooses to adopt such a test it becomes incumbent to identify the criteria for the inability

[34] Letter from John Negroponte, Permanent Representative of the U.S. to the President of the Security Council (7 October 2001), UN Doc. S/2001/946.

[35] Among the many treatments, compare Christian J. Tams, 'The Use of Force Against Terrorists', *EJIL* 20 (2009): 359, 378–81, with Tom Ruys, *'Armed Attack' and Article 51 of the UN Charter: Evolutions in Customary Law and Practice* (New York: Cambridge University Press, 2010) 486–9; see also Marko Milanovic, 'Self-Defense and Non-State Actors: Indeterminacy and the Jus Ad Bellum', *EJILTalk! Blog* (21 February 2010), <http://www.ejiltalk.org> (on difficulty in determining state views on attribution).

[36] See Leiden Policy Recommendations on Counter-terrorism and International Law, in Larissa van den Herik and Nico Schrijver (eds.), *Counter-Terrorism Strategies in a Fragmented International Legal Order: Meeting the Challenges* (Cambridge: Cambridge University Press, 2013) paras. 38–44, at 706, 715–17.

[37] Harold H. Koh, Speech to the Annual Meeting of the American Society of International Law, 25 March 2010, <http://www.state.gov/s/l/releases/remarks/139119.htm>.

[38] *Armed Activities on the Territory of the Congo (Dem. Rep. Congo v Uganda)* [2005] ICJ Rep 168 (19 December), sep. op. Kooijmans, § 30, sep. op. Simma, § 12.

[39] Elizabeth Wilmshurst, 'The Chatham House Principles of International Law on the Use of Force in Self-Defence', *ICLQ* 55 (2006): 963, 969; Leiden Recommendations, *supra* note 36. For an excellent doctrinal approach, see Noam Lubell, *Extraterritorial Use of Force Against Non-State Actors* (Oxford: Oxford University Press, 2010) 29–42.

[40] *Legal Consequences of the Construction of a Wall in the Occupied Palestinian Territory, Advisory Opinion* [2004] ICJ Rep 136, para. 139 (9 July).

of a state to prevent terrorists from using its soil for attacks. If states chose to act on this theory in situations where governments are merely weak or poor, it would clearly exacerbate interstate tensions. Similarly, the standard of a state's 'unwillingness' to act is also prone to interpretive disputes and ultimately abuse. States have numerous domestic priorities and financial limitations, so at what point can another state reasonably conclude that the state is unwilling to prevent terrorists from using it?

In the end, states will probably see it as being in their interest to limit the scope of the concepts of harboring, inability, and unwillingness. The notions of necessity and proportionality, a key part of *jus ad bellum*, might provide guidance to them. The United States, which has served as the chief claimant of these ideas, has limited the argument to a very small number of states; and indeed in the case of Pakistan, it seems likely that the use of Predators for targeted killings has the acquiescence of the Pakistani government.[41]

Notwithstanding the uncertainty as to the *lex lata*, the move toward such a new position is, in my view, justifiable under the pillars of thin justice, subject to important conditions. The extension of self-defense is grounded in the reality that violence by non-state actors who are not agents of states can create as significant a harm to individual victims as a war conducted by a state. That is not to say that such acts always will; in such situations, they have not really committed an armed attack at all.[42] But where they do, then self-defense serves the same deterrent function as it does in the case of attacks by states. It therefore seems to pass muster under the first pillar and would not seem to raise new threats to the protection of basic human rights compared to self-defense against armed attacks by states. This defense does not mean that self-defense is equally *effective* as a deterrent against non-state actors. Members of groups such as Al Qaeda may have a martyr streak that renders deterrence useless, or they may simply be harder to locate to make self-defense a credible deterrent.

But the matter is not quite so simple. Self-defensive action against non-state actors and so-called harboring states can harm peace and human rights more than responses against aggressor states. It could threaten expansion of the conflict between the victim state and the non-state actors to the harboring state and its allies. And it could inflict significant harm to the basic human rights of residents of the harboring state. (Later, in Section D, I will discuss the argument that the costs of self-defense against even aggressor states argue against self-defense on consequentialist terms.) These are serious concerns. And they are not hypothetical. As Theresa Reinold has noted, the result in practice is that 'states are making indiscriminate use of the unwillingness and inability scenarios'.[43] States with the capacity to inflict significant damage on non-state groups abroad can claim that

[41] See Jane Mayer, 'The Predator War', *The New Yorker*, 26 October 2009, <http://www.newyorker.com/reporting/2009/10/26/091026fa_fact_mayer>.

[42] Leiden Recommendations, *supra* note 36, para. 39.

[43] Theresa Reinold, 'State Weakness, Irregular Warfare, and the Right of Self-Defense Post-9/11', *AJIL* 105 (2011): 244, 285.

target states are unwilling to prevent terrorism when they are actually unable to do so. Thus, for instance, Israel suggested during its 2006 war with Lebanon that Lebanon was unwilling to stop Hezbollah and indeed complicit in its attacks (though later stating that it had no gripe with Lebanon at all).[44] Or powerful states may argue that a state can be the target of self-defense if it is unable to prevent attacks, even though the state would be able to prevent attacks with assistance, which might explain the U.S. position regarding drone strikes in Pakistan or Yemen.

In order for an extension of self-defense to non-state actors to pass muster under the pillars of thin justice, then, we need a rule that addresses these abuses. One direction would be a rule whereby the victim state will need to exhaust all possible peaceful means to deal with the terrorist bases abroad and make genuine attempts to use the mechanisms of the criminal law—extradition, trial, and imprisonment—before attempting any sort of military response. This prerequisite would reduce the risk of war significantly. In addition, both pillars suggest that any military reply will have to be strictly tailored to eliminating the capability of the non-state actor to conduct armed attacks, with military force extending to the infrastructure of the so-called harboring state only to the extent absolutely needed to prevent future attacks.[45] Other details will need to be fleshed out as well, but the point is that these choices are not simply matters of policy, but moral choices about how best to advance peace while respecting human rights through the development of legal norms. At this point, most states seem to be avoiding military force to respond to foreign terrorist threats. As for those who do, it is frankly difficult to know whether they have acted according to a version of self-defense that meets the standard of thin justice, whether they have acted according to a version that does not, or whether they simply have not acted in a principled manner at all.

2. *Expansion in temporal terms: self-defense before an armed attack*

The other significant claim made by some states for expanding self-defense is to permit it, seemingly in contrast to the language of the UN Charter, in situations where an attack has not yet taken place.[46] These claims range from a claim of a right to *anticipatory* self-defense, which would permit states facing demonstrably imminent attacks to strike first, where toleration of a first strike from the aggressor would eliminate any chance of self-defense later; all the way through to broader claims of *preventive* self-defense, where a handful of states have argued

[44] See Milanovic, 'Self-Defense and Non-State Actors', *supra* note 35.

[45] For an endorsement of this position, see the Leiden Recommendations, *supra* note 36.

[46] I will not address here debates about how long a state is permitted to act in self-defense *after* an armed attack. Many international law scholars say that the U.S. use of force in Afghanistan many years after the 9/11 attacks has crossed the line from justifiable self-defense to a forcible reprisal, which international law prohibits.

that military action is permitted against ripening threats long before an armed attack is imminent.

Support in international law for anticipatory self-defense has typically been traced back to the *Caroline* Doctrine, enunciated by U.S. Secretary of State Daniel Webster after Canadian forces crossed into the United States to destroy a ship aiding rebels in Canada. Under his test, anticipatory attacks are allowed only if the 'necessity [is] instant, overwhelming, leaving no choice of means and no moment for deliberation', which the Canadian action was not.[47] The classic modern case invoked by many scholars and states in support of the legality of anticipatory self-defense is the Israeli attack on Egypt in June 1967, in which key global actors appeared to have endorsed Israel's move as a legitimate response to an imminent Egyptian invasion, though many states also opposed it and there remain disagreements about Egypt's plans at the time.[48] Anticipatory defense was for many years the source of great controversy among legal scholars, in part because it seemed to allow for nuclear retaliation by a target state before it had absorbed a first strike—or even before weapons were fired at it—which it seemed increased the risk of global conflagration. In what I regard as a decent reflection of international attitudes, the normally cautious UN Secretary-General endorsed anticipatory self-defense in a highly important report, following input from former world leaders, in 2005.[49] However, another group of experts, evaluating the legality of Russia's and Georgia's actions at the beginning of their 2008 war, said that there is no consensus on whether imminent self-defense is permitted.[50] And certainly not all scholars are convinced.[51]

To the extent that states accept anticipatory self-defense, much of the reason seems to be the effort by some states to push the more extreme notion of preventive self-defense, shifting the terms of the debate over one notch. Israel made the latter claim to justify its attack on Iraq's nuclear reactor in 1981, only to be

[47] Correspondence between Great Britain and the United States, respecting the Arrest and Imprisonment of Mr McLeod, for the Destruction of the Steamboat Caroline (March, April 1841) (1840–41) 29 BFSP 1126; R.Y. Jennings, 'The Caroline and McLeod Cases', *AJIL* 32 (1938): 82.

[48] See, e.g., Thomas M. Franck, *Recourse to Force: State Action Against Threats and Armed Attacks* (New York: Cambridge University Press, 2002) 101–5; Walzer, *Just and Unjust Wars, supra* note 25, 82–5. For a critique of the view that Israel faced an armed attack from Egypt, see John Quigley, *The Six-Day War and Israeli Self-Defense: Questioning the Legal Basis for Preventive War* (New York: Cambridge University Press, 2013).

[49] UN Secretary–General, 'In Larger Freedom: Towards Security, Development, and Human Rights for All: Report of the Secretary-General', 21 March 2005, para. 124, UN Doc. A/59/2005 ('Imminent threats are fully covered by Article 51, which safeguards the inherent right of sovereign States to defend themselves against armed attack. Lawyers have long recognized that this covers an imminent attack as well as one that has already happened.').

[50] Report of the Independent International Fact-Finding Mission on the Conflict in Georgia, Vol. II, 255 (2009), <http://www.ceiig.ch>.

[51] See, e.g., Olivier Corten, *The Law Against War: The Prohibition on the Use of Force in Contemporary International Law*, Christopher Sutcliffe (trans.) (Portland, OR: Hart Publishing, 2010) 406–43; see also Olivier Corten, 'Regulating Resort to Force: A Response to Matthew Waxman from a "Bright-Liner"', *EJIL* 24 (2013): 191.

condemned (unanimously) by the Security Council.[52] The Bush Administration supported this position in its 2002 National Security Strategy, announcing:

> For centuries, international law recognized that nations need not suffer an attack before they can lawfully take action to defend themselves against forces that present an imminent danger of attack.... We must adapt the concept of imminent threat to the capabilities and objectives of today's adversaries. Rogue states and terrorists do not seek to attack us using conventional means. [They] rely on acts of terror and, potentially, the use of weapons of mass destruction....
>
> The United States has long maintained the option of preemptive actions to counter a sufficient threat to our national security. The greater the threat, the greater is the risk of inaction—and the more compelling the case for taking anticipatory action to defend ourselves, even if uncertainty remains as to the time and place of the enemy's attack. To forestall or prevent such hostile acts by our adversaries, the United States will, if necessary, act preemptively.[53]

It used similar rhetoric during the run-up to the Iraq invasion of 2003, even while it formally stated that its use of force was authorized under prior Security Council resolutions.[54]

At this stage, preventive self-defense is still a highly suspect concept among international decisionmakers, and the catastrophe of the Iraq war—waged in the name of preventing the acquisition of weapons that it turns out Iraq was not even pursuing—has further entrenched the opposition to such claims.[55] Both the Annan report and the EU report on Georgia unequivocally rejected the position, as has the ICJ.[56] Nevertheless, such claims continue to be made, notably in Israeli and U.S. statements regarding a 'red line' that will be crossed if Iran develops a nuclear weapons capacity.

As with debates about the targets of self-defensive action, debates over the timing of such action are fundamentally about the best way to preserve peace. From this perspective, the current rules of international law, at least as I interpret them, satisfy the first pillar of thin justice. Anticipatory self-defense, in the highly limited circumstances in which it is tolerated, serves the deterrent function, for if the

[52] SC Res. 487 (19 June 1981).

[53] The U.S. National Security Strategy: Prevent Our Enemies From Threatening Us, Our Allies, and Our Friends with Weapons of Mass Destruction, September 2002, <http://georgewbush-whitehouse.archives.gov/nsc/nss/2002>. For the more ambiguous position of the Obama Administration, see National Security Strategy, May 2010, at 22, <http://www.whitehouse.gov/sites/default/files/rss_viewer/national_security_strategy.pdf> ('The United States must reserve the right to act unilaterally if necessary to defend our nation and our interests, yet we will also seek to adhere to standards that govern the use of force').

[54] Compare ibid.; and Interview by Wolf Blitzer with Dr Condoleezza Rice, Assistant to the President for National Security Affairs (7 September 2002), <http://www.cnn.com/2003/US/01/10/wbr.smoking.gun/> ('We don't want the smoking gun to be a mushroom cloud'), with UN Doc. S/PV.4726 (resumption 1), 25 (27 March 2003) (statement of U.S. delegate justifying action based on prior Security Council resolutions).

[55] See the useful discussion in Alex J. Bellamy, *Just Wars: From Cicero to Iraq* (Cambridge: Polity Books, 2006) 163–79.

[56] 'In Larger Freedom', *supra* note 49, para. 125; Report of the Fact-Finding Mission, *supra* note 50, 254–5; *Armed Activities*, *supra* note 38, para. 148.

aggressor state knew that self-defense following an armed attack would be impossible for the victim state, it would have little hesitation to attack. However, in order for the rule not to become an invitation to states perceiving a threat from another state to strike first, thereby increasing the risk of war, the target state will need to demonstrate that it had met the *Caroline* standard and really had no other choice in the situation. International reactions to Israel's first strike in 1967 suggest it had made that case (or at least that states did not wish to question its case), whereas the reactions to its 1981 actions against Iraq suggested otherwise. I recognize that others may judge these matter differently. Legal scholars opposed to anticipatory self-defense seem to reflect a moral position that any opening at all for a state to strike first will harm both peace and human rights, presumably on the assumption that such a rule will not only *not* deter aggression, but will increase it (by the threatened state).

As for the second pillar, the invocation of anticipatory self-defense in the very narrow circumstances in which international law accepts it does not undermine basic human rights, and indeed actually helps fill a gap in the protection of such rights created by a rule that requires a victim state to absorb a first strike. Thus, anticipatory self-defense is as justifiable under that pillar in the same way as is self-defense after an armed attack. Moreover, as with post-attack self-defense, rules of proportionality (in *jus ad bellum*) and of *jus in bello* reinforce the lack of interference of the rule with human rights.

The risks of anticipatory self-defense serve to highlight the dangers to interstate peace of preventive self-defense. Although the extension of the deterrence rationale to this scenario is not impossible—the broadened right could deter aggression by giving a potential victim a lawful right to strike well in advance of evidence of any attack—that possibility depends upon a number of conjectures about the potential aggressor's capacity and intentions that are extremely difficult to judge in situations short of imminent attack. The Iraq war was only the most obvious example of the costs of waging a preventive war. More generally, maintenance of such options can have a ratcheting-up effect, as the domestic pressure on each side toward war increases. As Neta Crawford has written: 'If all states reacted to potential adversaries as if they faced a clear and present danger of imminent attack, security would be destabilized as tensions escalated along already tense borders and regions.... [A] preemptive-preventive doctrine moves us closer to a state of nature than a state of international law.'[57] The issue is not free from doubt, but the course that international law has taken, endorsing only a narrow right of anticipatory self-defense, allowing force only in the face of a demonstrably (both ex ante and ex post) imminent armed attack against the state, seems far better able to promote global peace than the proposed alternative.[58]

[57] Neta C. Crawford, 'The Slippery Slope to Preventive War', *Ethics & Intl Aff* 17 (2003): 1. For an argument against rule-based decisionmaking regarding preventive war, see Chris Brown, 'After '*Caroline*': NSS 2002, Practical Judgment, and the Politics and Ethics of Preemption', in Deen K. Chatterjee (ed.), *The Ethics of Preventive War* (Cambridge: Cambridge University Press, 2013) 27. Though Brown rightly emphasizes political judgment, it is not clear how we are better off without international law rules than with them.

[58] Buchanan and Keohane have endorsed a right of preventive use of force when it is known that a terrorist group has plans to release a weapon causing massive casualties, but their assumption of

Proponents of preventive self-defense might argue that the second pillar of global justice justifies their view. Certainly, any norm concerning the use of force that does not permit a state to protect individuals from the possibility of violent death or other grave harms is unjust, even if it promotes peace. The procedure for deriving just norms, however, as explained in Chapter 3, requires that the second pillar be satisfied in a way that does the least damage to interstate or intrastate peace. In the case of anticipatory versus preventive self-defense, the balance seems to me to be struck with the former but not the latter. Although one might seek to defend preventive self-defense as some sort of extraordinary defense of human rights—allowing self-defense in the name of preserving rights well before an attack has occurred—the risks to the peace are too grave to justify it.

D. Pressures for a narrow right of self-defense

In contrast to the foregoing claims, which originate with states, arguments to reduce the scope of self-defense emanate principally from scholars and also reflect views held by some religious and other civil society groups. These arguments suggest that the current regime of self-defense either allows for more violence than it should or fails to protect human rights sufficiently. These claims do not favor eliminating self-defense, but conditioning it in new ways.

1. *Too many deaths: the pacifist challenge*

A number of challenges to Article 51 of the UN Charter are based on the idea that it causes more deaths than it avoids. E.H. Carr long ago offered gentle praise for the Munich Accords of 1938 for their ability to accomplish peaceful change in central Europe, effectively suggesting that world order would be improved at times if a state simply surrendered rather than defended itself.[59] Here I want to focus on two of the more significant recent challenges to Article 51, those by David Rodin and Larry May, who both question the consequentialist justification for Article 51 as promoting peace.

Rodin finds such a rationale unfounded because one can never be sure if self-defense will promote or undermine peace.[60] His response is to argue that national self-defense can only be viewed morally as an analogue to personal self-defense. Because 'not all acts of international aggression . . . violate the rights of citizens [or] involve imminent threats to the central rights of persons', and 'there is no general right to resist conditional threats against the central rights of persons with lethal force', a state should not have an inherent right of self-defense against

knowledge assumes away the most troublesome aspect of a rule permitting such force. Moreover, they would permit such force only by a group of states and subject to the approval or later ratification of an impartial international body, which takes the proposal outside the realm of self-defense. Allen Buchanan and Robert O. Keohane, 'The Preventive Use of Force: A Cosmopolitan Institutional Proposal', *Ethics & Intl Aff* 18 (2004): 1.

[59] E.H. Carr, *The Twenty Years' Crisis, 1919–1939* (New York: Palgrave, 1981; Michael Cox (ed.), 2001) 197–202.

[60] Rodin, *War and Self-Defense, supra* note 15, at 117–18.

all armed attacks.[61] Instead, the only authority for allowing such self-defense would be that of an impartial international body with the ability to determine the actual risks to individuals of the aggression, a body that he admits does not yet exist.[62]

May, for his part, argues that the UN Charter is based on a view of 'contingent pacifism'.[63] As a result, a state is not justified in responding in self-defense, and the killing of the innocent that it will cause, merely to defend territory. Instead, force is justified only if the threat is sufficiently grave as to justify the loss of life from war. In what appears to be a utilitarian calculation based on saving innocent life, he thus favors a narrowing of self-defense, limiting it to violations of territorial integrity 'that involve threats to the lives, or basic human rights, of the members of a State' and, at the same time, denying it to a state unless it 'is protecting the human rights of its members and can no longer do so [because of the aggression] or when the [aggression] jeopardizes human rights in some other significant way'.[64]

These positions are fundamentally concerned that an unfettered right of self-defense as stated in the UN Charter will (or, in the case of Rodin, at least may) disrupt public order or cost more lives than it will preserve peace or save lives. A consequentialist defense, under either pillar of thin justice, seems to be placed in a bind insofar as I cannot prove the deterrent effect in every instance of a right of self-defense. Nor can I show that in situations where a state's self-defense was denied by outside powers that the resulting interference with basic human rights was greater than would have been the case if it had been allowed to defend itself.[65] One possible example might be the Security Council's arms embargo on the former Yugoslavia as it was disintegrating in the early 1990s, which seems to have affected Bosnia's ability to defend itself against forces aided by Serbia (although whether Serbia's actions amounted to an armed attack on Bosnia under the Charter is still contested both legally and factually).[66] Bosnia might have been able to defend itself better without the embargo, but it might have made no difference, or the casualties might have been higher. Walzer's response in *Just and Unjust Wars* to defenses of the Munich Accord and other examples is to eschew utilitarianism for a communitarian justification of self-defense based on the value of multiple communities in the world and the right of those communities to flourish as they choose.[67]

[61] Ibid., at 137. [62] Ibid., at 180–8.

[63] Larry May, *Aggression and Crimes Against Peace* (New York: Cambridge University Press, 2008) 40–5.

[64] Ibid., at 104. The second formulation adds a condition—namely, pre-existing protection of human rights by the state—that brings his theory closer to the cosmopolitan notions discussed later. May also favors shrinking Article 2(4) by endorsing the idea that wars may be committed to prevent abuses. See also Anthony Burke, 'Just War or Ethical Peace? Moral Discourses of Strategic Violence after 9/11', *Intl Aff* 80 (2004): 329 (concern that self-defense will be abused by powerful states and that the *jus in bello* will not serve to protect innocent lives once war starts).

[65] There appears to be no quantitative research by political scientists on either of these points.

[66] SC Res. 713 (25 September 1991).

[67] Walzer, *Just and Unjust Wars, supra* note 25, at 72–3.

I do not disagree with Walzer's rationale, which is ultimately quite similar to international law's core principle of self-determination, but I believe that the consequentialist argument still rebuts these objections better. A consequentialist defense of (or attack on) a rule must be based on real-life situations, not just hypothetical cases designed to show that consequentialism results in the morally wrong act or rule. We have to evaluate, based on our intuitions and experiences, the expected real-world consequences of following one rule or another rule.[68] Nor does rule-consequentialism demand that conformity to the rule in every situation be moral.[69] In the case of self-defense, it seems reasonable to conclude, based on what we know about states and their historic behavior, that depriving states of a right of self-defense would invite aggression, and that aggression is historically bad for the respect of basic human rights. Wars of aggression, even if they lead to quick victories, are highly costly in terms of human lives and welfare. That may not be the case with every actual war, and certainly not with every conceivable war, but that is not the point for deriving a rule through consequentialist reasoning.

Moreover, Rodin's denunciation of self-defense leads to a morally compelled alternative rule that is impossible institutionally—a system where a state needs to seek a green light from some kind of international court before it can respond in self-defense. The point he makes—that one cannot prove that self-defense saves lives—is true, but the alternative in the real world is to deny self-defense until it may well be too late. A group of experts or judges would never be given this responsibility by states, as is clear from the limited jurisdiction of the existing international courts, and more importantly would lack the institutional capacity to make informed judgments in real time. One need only point to the response of the ICJ when Serbia sued the NATO states for attacking it after refusing to accept NATO's demands for the autonomy of Kosovo. Serbia sued in April 1999; six weeks later, the ICJ refused to issue any so-called provisional measures, i.e. an injunction to halt the war, and completely dismissed the case against the United States—the leading NATO power—for lack of jurisdiction.[70] Five and a half years later, it dismissed the entire case on jurisdictional grounds in what was widely perceived as an awkward attempt to avoid ruling on the merits.[71] Similarly, a group of states cannot be trusted with this responsibility because their political

[68] See R.M. Hare, *Moral Thinking: Its Levels, Methods, and Point* (New York: Oxford University Press, 1981) 134 ('If we are talking about intuitive thinking in a real-life sort of situation, the example needs to be a real-life sort of example'); Robert E. Goodin, *Utilitarianism as a Public Philosophy* (Cambridge, Cambridge University Press, 1995) 22 ('utilitarianism as a public philosophy spares us the burdens associated with maximizing at the margins in each and every case').

[69] Ibid., at 18.

[70] *Case Concerning the Legality of the Use of Force* (*Yugoslavia v Belgium), Request for the Indication of Provisional Measures* [1999] ICJ Rep 124 (Order of 2 June 1999); *Case Concerning the Legality of the Use of Force* (*Yugoslavia v United States), Request for the Indication of Provisional Measures* [1999] ICJ Rep 916 (Order of 2 June 1999).

[71] *Case Concerning the Legality of the Use of Force* (*Serbia and Montenegro v Belgium), Preliminary Objections* [2004] ICJ Rep 279 (15 December 2004).

relationships with the parties will often dictate their decisions. And we cannot realistically have a committee composed of Switzerland and Costa Rica.

Rodin accepts the view, which he attributes to realists, that 'the current mechanisms of international politics are irremediably devoid of morality'.[72] Certainly he is correct in arguing that states and institutions enforce the rules on self-defense inconsistently, that great powers can abuse the right of self-defense through brinkmanship leading to pre-emptive strikes (although this is exceedingly rare in practice), and that in some individual cases the victim of aggression may be in a morally inferior position. (It was morally good that the Khmer Rouge-dominated government was invaded and ousted by Vietnam in 1978 and that Idi Amin's Uganda was invaded and his administration ousted by Tanzania in 1978–79.) But the norm of self-defense most certainly has a morality in its concerns for peace. That his alternative may be more just as a matter of ideal theory—one that starts with a very different view of the state from the one I assumed in Chapter 3 and is ultimately untethered from the realities of the international system—does not serve to show the injustice of the existing rule under the conditions we have.

As for May, his proposal to deny self-defense when a state will lose only territory, or perhaps where the aggressor will not treat its newly absorbed population any worse than did the old sovereign, seems to grossly understate the costs of aggression in such situations. First, it is questionable whether an aggressor can ever invade and conquer truly empty land or *terra nullius* (even deserts and forests have inhabitants) or in any other way that does not harm the basic human rights of the residents. Thus his proposed norm faces serious doubts under the second pillar. Certainly the human right to political control over one's future (not necessarily democracy) is completely undercut.

Second, even accepting the possibility of those scenarios, the two-pillar approach of thin justice demands that any alternative to a norm that is thinly just also take account of the two pillars. In the end, whatever conceivable benefit may inure to human rights by May's constraints on the right of self-defense seems significantly outweighed by the costs to peace—costs not fully considered by May—in his alternative. Beyond the disruptions to trade and free movement of peoples, tensions arise within a region as states are concerned whether the aggressor will stop where it did or threaten other territories; military build-ups can begin; and the risk of warfare increases. One typical example is Libya's 1980 invasion of the Aouzou Strip, a desolate piece of land in northern Chad sparsely inhabited by a few thousand people. The conflict greatly inflamed tensions in West Africa and was only resolved through mediation by the Organization of African Unity, a decision of the ICJ, and the deployment of a UN force to monitor Libya's withdrawal.[73]

And as for advancing human rights, May's theory would even have denied Czechoslovakia its right of self-defense in 1938, for, after all, the Sudeten Germans were probably happier within the Reich than within Czechoslovakia,

[72] Rodin, *War and Self-Defense, supra* note 15, at 197.

[73] See *Case Concerning the Territorial Dispute* (*Libya v Chad)* [1994] ICJ Rep 6 (3 February).

and the ultimate plan of Hitler to conquer Europe and commit genocide would not yet have been evident. This example may demonstrate only that his rule will not always produce the most just outcome, but it is hard to see how the risks to human rights from his proposed rule are less—or the benefits to human rights greater—in the real world than those under Article 51 of the UN Charter. Carr's view, which is more extreme than May's, fails for the same reason. It also contains an internal contradiction in that it seems to favor peaceful change through the threat of force (as with Munich), but it does not explain how we can countenance threats of force without also countenancing their actual use.

Finally, even if May's view is somehow more just in an ideal world, it is difficult to imagine how May's proposed norm would work institutionally. How would states that have to decide whether they can aid the victim state, or even just condemn the attack, decide in real time whether the aggression is justified under May's test? To develop a doctrine of self-defense that depends upon institutions that are not even on the horizon of international relations does not seem to be an advance over the status quo norm.

2. *Unfit to be defended: the cosmopolitan challenge*

A more fundamental challenge to Article 51 comes from a cosmopolitan perspective that seems deontologically grounded, although May hints at the same idea in his more consequentialist view. Under this position, states that abuse the human rights of their citizens are simply not entitled to claim self-defense—and outsiders should perforce welcome the aggression for the sake of the human rights of the residents. This proposed rule would turn self-defense, a general norm in the terms used in Chapter 2, into a special norm, creating duties only to certain kinds of states.

The first major contemporary philosophical shot in this direction was David Luban's 1980 response to *Just and Unjust Wars*, in which he argued that only legitimate states are immune from intervention by others, including military intervention.[74] State legitimacy turns on its respect for the 'socially basic human rights' of its citizens, a term he takes from Henry Shue. As a result, states enjoy a right of self-defense only against unjust wars—those not in defense of socially basic human rights and also harmful to all other human rights. And a state thus lacks a right of self-defense against any war that is not an unjust war, i.e. a war that does not harm human rights or which defends socially basic human rights.[75] More recently, Simon Caney, like Luban, starts with skepticism about the state system as a whole and from that starting point eventually posits that unjust states have no right to defend themselves unless the invasion, if undefended, would

[74] David Luban, 'Just War and Human Rights', *Phil & Pub Aff* 9 (1980): 160, 175–6.

[75] Ibid., at 175. It is hard to see how Luban would view a war by a state to gain territory alone in an adjacent state. Under his definitions, it would not be a just war, but it also need not be an unjust war.

result in an even more unjust state.[76] Similar to Rodin, he seeks to rely on international institutions to make judgments as to whether a state can defend itself. Rawls takes a slightly more conservative view in *The Law of Peoples*, where his view is that 'any society that is nonaggressive and that honors human rights has the right of self-defense'.[77] He excludes from the protection of Article 51 so-called outlaw states, states that do not comply with the law of peoples; they may be attacked because they are aggressive, although he is not clear on whether they may be attacked simply for violating the human rights of their residents.[78]

Each of these critiques is based on a starkly different view of the state system from my own, a chasm with which I will not engage here. They are also part of a larger debate about the morality of humanitarian intervention, which is discussed in Chapter 9. For now, I will confine my discussion to the implications of their rejection of Article 51. At first, these critiques seem to represent a full assault on any sort of consequentialist grounding for Article 51, and so arguing in consequentialist terms is not likely to be very convincing. Yet Luban and Caney are not fully anti-consequentialist. Luban relies on the principle of proportionality to ensure that the violation of basic human rights caused by the violence of a war in which the target state lacks the right of self-defense is no worse than the severity of the rights violations before the war.[79] This calculation is essentially a consequentialist version of the second pillar—rights are not trumps here—in which the justice of the proposed, limited right of self-defense depends on its creating a situation where overall respect for basic human rights is increased.

But if we can take into account the costs of a war in defense of human rights compared to the ongoing costs of the human rights situation that the war seeks to eliminate—in other words, vis-à-vis the second pillar—then why can we not introduce all the costs associated with ignoring the first pillar by allowing any sort of war at all? Luban criticizes the status quo for giving 'absolute primacy to the world community's interest in peace' and thereby 'simply refus[ing] to consider' whether a war is just.[80] But this is not true if we see peace as part of justice; moreover, Luban's justice equally refuses to consider the costs to world peace of a norm that balances only two sets of human rights violations.

As for Caney, though deploying the notion of justice as the metric by which to appraise self-defense (i.e. we should deny self-defense when the result would be more just), he also admits that the determination of a just state of affairs domestically could involve a utilitarian calculation (as in the view of Singer, for example).[81] If we are open to a consequentialist framework, the burden is on him to claim why a more just state of affairs domestically will *ever* result from denying a state the right of self-defense. Moreover, even on these terms, why should a just state of

[76] Simon Caney, *Justice Beyond Borders: A Global Political Theory* (Oxford: Oxford University Press, 2005) 203–5. Caney adds that, in situations where self-defense is just, other states have a duty, not merely permission (as under Article 51), to aid the victim state.

[77] John Rawls, *The Law of Peoples* (Cambridge, MA: Harvard University Press, 1999) 92.

[78] Ibid., at 81 and n.26.

[79] Luban, 'Just War and Human Rights', *supra* note 74, at 175–6.

[80] Ibid., at 165.

[81] Caney, *Justice Beyond Borders, supra* note 76, at 203.

affairs be limited to the target state? If we want to consider the justice of limiting a state's right of self-defense, we should consider its implications for all affected people.

Rawls' removal of the right of self-defense for outlaw states is equally flawed. It is difficult to see why the world would be more just under either prong if states such as North Korea or Iran (presumably what Rawls would consider 'outlaw states') could simply be invaded *for whatever reason* and not be allowed to defend themselves. Why assume that an invasion will make the victims of non-decent governments per se better off or make the world more peaceful?

Finally, all these positions suffer from the institutional flaws noted with respect to the peace-based critiques. As part of ideal theory (even though Rawls says it is not ideal theory), the result is that a certain vision of justice commands certain rules of international law that are impossible institutionally. In the case of Caney, it is a 'supra-state political institution',[82] which might include a global parliament or an empowered ICJ to make determinations about aggression. Given the institutions we have now, it is hard to see how some sort of ex ante calculation regarding just outcomes is possible. And even if such a body magically appeared, why should we assume—indeed, trust—that it will do a good job at distinguishing just from unjust wars even under Luban's or Caney's tests? Neither the lack of immediate feasibility nor these doubts about the judgment of such a body make the extant rule per se just, but they certainly call into question why we should put any efforts as global citizens to moving to the alternative norm hinged to such institutions. That is, the simplicity of the current rule does not per se make it just, but it is hard to embrace a rule as just if it is so complex that it cannot be implemented.

It is worth putting to rest one other claim of those advocating diminution of the right of self-defense—that it is needed to ensure that an unjust status quo will be changed. Ironically, this position undergirded Carr's defense of Munich—that Czechoslovakia's right of self-defense needed to be sacrificed to rectify some of the injustices of the Versailles Treaty that naturally caused Germany to adopt a bellicose attitude toward its neighbors.[83] Peace should not be achieved at any cost; the founders of the UN were justifiably concerned that the Security Council might somehow force a peaceful but unjust settlement on a state as had happened at Munich.[84] But respecting the right of self-defense simply does not equate with an obligation or even preference for outside states to respect an unjust status quo. Other tools are at the disposal of states acting alone or through the UN or other groupings for the peaceful adjustment of unjust international situations, including the replacement of illegitimate regimes; and the Security Council has the power to order forcible adjustments of unjust situations. Indeed, it has claimed to have done so in the cases mentioned earlier—in Somalia in 1992, Haiti in 1994, Libya in 2011, and others.[85] In that sense, it might be said that self-defense

[82] Ibid., at 159; see also 156–62, 205.

[83] Carr, *The Twenty Years' Crisis, supra* note 59, at lxxvi–lxxvii (quoting earlier editions).

[84] Franck, *Recourse to Force, supra* note 48, at 15–16.

[85] SC Res. 794 (3 December 1992); SC Res. 940 (31 July 1994); SC Res. 1973 (17 March 2011).

perpetuates injustices, but only in the limited sense that it gives an immunity to a state responsible for an unjust situation when faced with *one* effort by another state to rectify that injustice—unauthorized use of force against it.[86] It otherwise affords no perpetuation of injustice.

II. International Law's Ban on Intervention

A state's sovereignty-based claims encompass more than protection of its territorial integrity. States, and the people in them, are also interested in maintaining independence, and not merely independence in the most formal of terms, but a more robust idea in which a state is not controlled by or subservient to another state. The norm that international law has developed to address this claim is that of non-intervention. Historically, efforts by states to develop a norm of non-intervention are quite old, indeed older than the UN Charter, although the notion gained its greatest acceptance, and a meaning beyond military interference, only after 1945.[87]

A. The contrast with the ban on force

The UN Charter's chief purpose is to promote peace through the creation of a collective security mechanism to respond to aggression. But outside—and before—the Charter, states agreed on an additional core norm of customary international law to ban actions short of the threat or use of military force. The ban on intervention by one state in the internal affairs of another state seeks to address and forbid instances of forcible and non-forcible measures by one state vis-à-vis another. Yet this norm has been rhetorically invoked by states to mean many different things, with colonial, Western, communist, and developing states all using the term to advance their political agendas.[88]

Today, in my view the norm is as significant for that which it excludes as it is for that which it covers, in a number of senses. First, the content of matters within the internal affairs of a state has adjusted over time. Even the conservative Permanent Court of International Justice (PCIJ) acknowledged long ago that: 'The question whether a certain matter is or is not solely within the jurisdiction of a State is an essentially relative question; it depends on the development of international relations.'[89] Thus, in the case of the ban on the intervention of the UN in the

[86] Cf. Michael Howard, 'The Causes of War', in Øyvind Østerud (ed.), *Studies of War and Peace* (Oslo: Norwegian University Press, 1986) 17, 26 ('one of the conditions of peace may unavoidably be the acceptance of situations widely perceived as unjust').

[87] Philip Kunig, 'Intervention, Prohibition of', in Rüdiger Wolfrum (ed.), *The Max Planck Encyclopedia of Public International Law*, online edition (Oxford: Oxford University Press, 2008–) <http://opil.ouplaw.com/home/EPIL>.

[88] John R. Vincent, *Nonintervention and International Order* (Princeton, NJ: Princeton University Press, 1974) 64–277, 385–7.

[89] *Nationality Decrees Issues in Tunis and Morocco (Advisory Opinion)* [1923] PCIJ Rep Series B No 4, 24 (7 February).

internal affairs of states expressed in Article 2(7) of the UN Charter, one sees that as early as 1946, the General Assembly condemned human right situations in Spain, and then South Africa, suggesting that even in its youth, its members were prepared to interpret the ban quite narrowly when it came to criticism of a state's human rights practices.[90] Indeed, in the long term, as Ulrich Preuss has put it, the integration of states into organs of international society means that Article 2(7) 'is doomed to erode'.[91]

Second, and most significantly, the norm precludes only action that is *coercive*, which certainly includes the use of force, though it is not clear just how much more it includes beyond that. On the one hand, the 1970 Friendly Relations Declaration elaborates a fairly broad view of the norm of non-intervention—in addition to 'armed intervention' and other acts against the 'personality' of the state, it encompasses 'economic, political or any other type of measures to coerce another State in order to obtain from it the subordination of the exercise of its sovereign rights and to secure from it advantages of any kind'.[92] The ICJ, for its part, emphasized the element of coercion as the 'very essence of, prohibited intervention', singling out interventions using force as 'particularly obvious'.[93] Concomitantly, the norm does not prohibit the state, through its lawful government, from inviting foreign involvement if this is needed to address a domestic insurgency.[94]

On the other hand, state practice suggests that coercion is not meant to describe many common foreign policy tools. Thus, for instance, verbal and written criticism by one state of another is routine and clearly accepted as lawful; and diplomatic intercourse on behalf of a state's nationals to persuade a state to treat them properly (even accompanied by not so subtle threats of diplomatic or economic consequences) is commonplace.[95] A state's decision to pass and apply legislation that covers acts that take place abroad—for example the taxing of worldwide income of nationals of a state, or the application of antitrust laws against companies for activities overseas that have an effect on the state—also does not violate the principle.[96] The funding of human rights, business, or environmental NGOs—even political parties—by outside states is also accepted as within the bounds of lawful state behavior, although it might cross the line if the state's law precluded such outside assistance. Certainly Russia seems to view it as crossing the line, given its anti-NGO laws.[97]

[90] GA Res. 39(I), 1946; GA Res. 44(I), 1946.

[91] Ulrich K. Preuss, 'Equality of States—Its Meaning in a Constitutionalized Global Order', *Chicago JIL* 9 (2008): 17, 48.

[92] Friendly Relations Declaration, principle 3, para. 2.

[93] *Nicaragua, supra* note 17, para. 205.

[94] Ibid., para. 246.

[95] See Robert Jennings and Arthur Watts (eds.), *Oppenheim's International Law*, 9th ed. (Oxford: Oxford University Press, 1992) 432–4.

[96] At the same time, an attempt to enforce a judgment within the state without the consent of the relevant state (usually through proceedings in its courts) would be a violation of international law. See, e.g., *Re Wood Pulp Cartel* [1988] ECR 5193; *Case of the S.S. 'Lotus' (France v Turkey)* [1927] PCIJ Rep Series A No. 10, 4 (7 September).

[97] See 'We view US statement on NGO's inspections as interference in Russian internal affairs—Foreign Ministry', Voice of Russia Radio, 30 March 2013, <http://english.ruvr.ru/2013_03_30/We-view-US-statement-on-NGOs-inspections-as-interference-in-Russian-internal-

Even economic sanctions, which certainly place pressure on a state to change its domestic or foreign policy, are a generally lawful tool of international relations by both states and international organizations to uphold international norms and do not typically cross the line to coercion.[98] Among the most pronounced developments are the decisions of the African Union to take strong action in the event of unconstitutional changes of government, which demonstrate an acceptance by a part of the world previously known for endorsing a strong version of the non-intervention norm and of the changing realities of acceptable conduct.[99] States have also deployed sanctions that freeze state or personal assets in order to advance human rights, though the legal standards governing such actions are still under debate.[100]

So what remains within the bounds of the ban on unlawful intervention? Among the clear cases, beyond those already barred by Article 2(4) would be: (a) intelligence operations aimed at overthrowing the government of a foreign state;[101] (b) financial assistance to an armed group in another state (perhaps subject to exceptions discussed later);[102] and (c) sabotage of a state's computer network through dispatch of a virus (which, in certain circumstances, might even violate Article 2(4)).[103] A state's motivation in undertaking such activities, even if it is expressed in terms of advancing the human rights of a state's residents, is not relevant.[104]

This norm, like the ban on the use of force, is a general norm that places a duty on all states. At the same time, it is clearly a different sort of norm from Article 2(4) in a number of respects. Its contours are a bit fuzzier, for it is more difficult to find an international acceptance of the definition of intervention or coercion than it is

affairs-Foreign-Ministry-207> (Foreign Ministry spokesman states that U.S. financing of NGOs through third parties is 'undisguised interference in our internal affairs').

[98] See, e.g., European Union, Sanctions or restrictive measures (2008), <http://eeas.europa.eu/cfsp/sanctions/docs/index_en.pdf>; see also Marcelo Kohen, 'The Principle of Non-Intervention 25 Years after the *Nicaragua* Judgment', *LJIL* 25 (2012): 157, 161.

[99] African Union Assembly Decision 269 (XIV), 2 February 2010, <http://www.au.int/en/decisions/assembly>; Paul D. Williams, 'From Non-intervention to Non-indifference: the Origins and Development of the African Union's Security Culture', *African Affairs* 106 (2007): 253.

[100] See Evan J. Criddle, 'Humanitarian Financial Intervention', *EJIL* 24 (2013): 583. Though not a violation of the ban on intervention, international law regards so-called secondary boycotts, where one state extends sanctions against a state to parties from third states, as suspect or unlawful. One prominent example is the U.S. sanctions against companies holding formerly American-owned assets expropriated by Cuba. See, e.g., Opinion of the Inter-American Juridical Committee on Resolution AG/DOC3375/96 of the General Assembly of the Organization Entitled 'Freedom of Trade and Investment in the Hemisphere' 35 ILM 1329 (1996).

[101] The prevalence of these operations, combined with the unwillingness of states to accept responsibility for them, puts such operations in somewhat of a legal limbo. See generally W. Michael Reisman and James E. Baker, *Regulating Covert Action* (New Haven, CT: Yale University Press, 1992).

[102] *Armed Activities, supra* note 38, paras. 163–165.

[103] Department of Defense, Office of General Counsel, 'An Assessment of International Legal Issues in Information Operations' (1999), <http://www.au.af.mil/au/awc/awcgate/dod-io-legal/dod-io-legal.pdf>; Todd C. Huntley, 'Controlling the Use of Force in Cyberspace: The Application of the Law of Armed Conflict During a Time of Fundamental Change in the Nature of Warfare', *Naval L Rev* 60 (2010): 167.

[104] See Brad R. Roth, *Sovereign Equality and Moral Disagreement* (Oxford: Oxford University Press, 2010) 77–80.

of force. Although many states regard it as foundational to the international legal order as the ban on the use of force, the absence of an explicit ban on intervention by states in the Charter has always rendered it slightly less important.[105] It is not generally considered a norm of *jus cogens* nor does its violation incur individual criminal responsibility. Moreover, the consequences for breach of the norm are quite different. Although the UN Charter provides for the liberty of states to respond in self-defense in the event of an armed attack, violations of the norm of non-intervention do not give a state a right to use force.[106] Indeed, the victim state is liable to have recourse to the same remedies as for any other violation of international law—diplomatic protest, sanctions (perhaps with the endorsement of an international organization), perhaps suit in an international or regional court, eventually leading to a negotiated end to the conduct.

From the perspective of thin justice, non-intervention, like its more robust counterpart, the ban on the use of force, furthers global peace. As a basic starting point, coercive measures by one state against another, though not per disrupting the peace the way that aggression does, raise tensions between states and frustrate relations between them.[107] Whether one considers the many attempts by the Soviet Union or the United States during the Cold War to use covert agents to topple a regime that had seemingly become hostile (for example Czechoslovakia or Afghanistan for the former and Guatemala or Iran for the latter), or the disruptions of computer systems in Latvia that appear to have emanated from Russia, interventions as a general matter heighten the risk of armed conflict and create new barriers between states. (It is, however, more difficult to assess whether such intervention fuels internal conflict.) At the same time, one cannot carry these risks too far, and indeed it is precisely the more speculative nature of the risks to peace caused by intervention that makes this norm—however fundamental on paper—far weaker in practice. State toleration of actions that seem as if they interfere in the other's affairs is thus inversely proportional to the amount of coercion deployed and directly proportional to the distinction between those actions and actual military force.

B. The push to a more robust norm

But if the norm prohibits only coercive interventions, then is it not unjust from the opposite standpoint, for not doing enough to preserve peace? If there is any risk of war at all from interventions, would not the first pillar demand a more robust norm than the one we have? In fact, a number of states have sought to push international law in this direction. The sentiment in the second quotation

[105] On ways of differentiating international norms, see Steven R. Ratner, 'Law Promotion Beyond Law Talk: The Red Cross, Persuasion, and the Laws of War', *EJIL* 22 (2011): 459; see also W. Michael Reisman, 'The Concept and Functions of Soft Law in International Politics', in Emmanuel G. Bello and Bola A. Ajibola (eds.), *Essays in Honour of Judge Taslim Olawale Elias*, Vol. 1 (Leiden: Martinus Nijhoff Publishers, 1992) 135, 135–6 (on dimensions of hardness and softness).

[106] *Nicaragua, supra* note 17, para. 195.

[107] See Anne Peters, 'Humanity as the A and Ω of Sovereignty', *EJIL* 20 (2009): 513, 534.

from the Friendly Relations Declaration set out earlier as well as other statements from, and ongoing debates within the UN—whether the General Assembly or the Human Rights Council—suggest that many states, particularly in the global South, would prefer a more demanding understanding of intervention and coercion. Under this view, Northern states would be precluded from trying to influence many of the domestic institutions of developing states, in particular their human rights practices. China has taken a particularly active role in this debate, ever sensitive to Western criticism of its human rights policies, but it reflects the views of many states.[108] Under this interpretation of non-intervention, the financial leverage that the North uses to pressure for compliance with human rights norms, including sanctions, would be illegal. The funding of NGOs and other acts now regarded as lawful would be suspect. The General Assembly has at times put these positions into resolutions, over a strongly divided vote.[109]

Certainly an ethical case can be made for a very robust view of non-intervention. Vincent argued for such a view in the 1970s, asserting that, in today's world, a strong principle would help preserve the 'islands of order' that states represented. Such a norm is thus critical for the respect that each state needs to give others so that individuals within those states could secure life, conclude contracts, and enjoy property.[110] Southern scholars, particularly those endorsing Third World approaches to international law, have seen non-intervention as a bulwark against Northern and neo-colonial influences.[111] More recently, Rawls said that liberal states must tolerate and accept certain non-liberal peoples—what he called 'decent peoples' who are not aggressive and respect a minimum of human rights, a view that would presumably prohibit sanctions and perhaps even protest against such states' human rights practices.[112] And Roth has linked non-intervention with sovereign equality to make an argument that calls for a strong norm as a defense of a plurality of political viewpoints in the global system.[113]

Yet such claims must be approached with significant caution under the pillars of thin justice. First, it seems wrong to assume that most or even many of the permitted interventions do realistically increase international tensions or the risk of war. Certainly, target states, most of them autocratic, wish to avoid international

[108] For details on China's position, see Sonya Sceats with Shaun Breslin, 'China and the International Human Rights System', Chatham House paper (2012), 6–9, 45–54.

[109] See, e.g., GA Res. 67/170 'Human rights and unilateral coercive measures' (20 March 2013) (urging states 'To cease adopting or implementing any unilateral measures not in accordance with international law…in particular those of a coercive nature…which create obstacles to trade relations among States.') (passed by 128 to 54 with 4 abstentions, with nearly all Northern states voting no). For earlier important resolutions, see Declaration on the Inadmissibility of Intervention in the Domestic Affairs of States and the Protection of their Independence and Sovereignty, GA Res. 2131 (XX) (21 December 1965); Declaration on the Inadmissibility of Intervention and Interference in the Internal Affairs of States, GA Res. 36/103 (9 December 1981) (broad definition passed by divided vote).

[110] Vincent, *Nonintervention, supra* note 88, at 328–33.

[111] Antony Anghie and B.S. Chimni, 'Third World Approaches to International Law and Individual Responsibility in International Conflict', in Steven R. Ratner and Anne-Marie Slaughter (eds.), *The Methods of International Law* (Washington DC: American Society of International Law, 2004) 185, 189.

[112] Rawls, *The Law of Peoples, supra* note 77, at 59–62.

[113] Roth, *Sovereign Equality, supra* note 104, at 77–80.

criticism of their actions and control domestic opposition when they call for a robust norm of non-intervention. But that does not mean they should be taken at their word regarding the risks of intervention. Such interference irritates the relationship between the two states—witness prolonged Chinese sensitivities to U.S. criticism of China's human rights record—but mild irritation does not equate with a threat to peace.

The case may be somewhat stronger that lawful interferences could foment domestic strife, insofar as outside assistance to NGOs, or pressure on the government, could embolden opposition forces to seek to overthrow the government; and such efforts could eventually lead to violence and even civil war. Critics of the status quo might see, then, a connection between weak norms of non-intervention and the civil conflicts in Libya, Syria, and Egypt, as authoritarian regimes were challenged by popular movements aided from governments—as well as foundations, NGOs, and individuals—abroad. Yet the causation between lawful outside assistance and violence becomes hard to determine. The funding of NGOs by outside states, for instance, can permit the participation of alternative viewpoints in a state's internal deliberations and lead to peaceful domestic change, as witnessed through the fall of military, racist, and communist regimes in Latin America, Eastern Europe, South Africa, and many other states over the last thirty years. Each of these transitions was aided by outside actors showing their support to opposition figures or their disapproval of governmental conduct. Diplomatic protest is an alternative to more drastic measures. To foreclose these measures would preclude many of the permitted interactions that actually promote international and internal peace, with perverse side-effects.

Second, at a certain point, the second pillar places a limit on the norm of non-intervention. If diplomatic protest or even the funding of NGOs makes a significant contribution to eliminating violations of basic human rights—including the right to life, to basic economic survival, to practice one's beliefs, and to attain some form of representative government—in the target country, the very marginal costs of increased tensions between the two states are outweighed. And if an alternative norm increases a state's ability to violate such rights with no significant benefit to peace, it is unjust.

Lastly, the compliance corollary introduced in Chapter 3 casts doubt on a stricter norm of non-intervention. A norm that would preclude routine and common interactions between states would not command their general assent in two senses. First, such a view would require a complete change in the attitude of most governments regarding appropriate transborder activity. To return to a mythical pre-modern era in which sovereigns stayed out of each other's business would be to fight the tide of globalization that has characterized interstate intercourse. States have grown accustomed to persuading other states to change their policies on domestic matters through a toolbox of foreign policy implements. Second, to the extent that multiple influences are simply beyond the control of governments, even a robust norm of non-intervention by states would be unable to grapple with transnational interactions by independent actors, such as corporations, NGOs, and individuals.[114] Even without

[114] See, e.g., Susan Strange, *The Retreat of the State: The Diffusion of Power in the World Economy*

external assistance, the internet-connected world allows for peoples under oppressed governments to learn and act against those regimes. These considerations do not per se make the extant, limited norm just, nor would they argue for rejecting a norm clearly more just than the status quo, but in this case, they represent a further argument against the alternative.

C. The push to a weaker norm

The push from ethics to a weaker ban on the use of force is replicated, a fortiori, in calls for a weaker ban on the norm of non-intervention, so I will not rehearse the arguments here again. What is different about the pressures on the latter norm are that they are rather, first and foremost, emanating from states, international organizations, and NGOs—the key actors within the international system.

The pressure has been at play for many years. As noted earlier, even the PCIJ noted long ago that the concept of domestic jurisdiction would change over time. When the League of Nations had to decide in 1920 whether it would make recommendations in the simmering dispute between Finland and Sweden over the claims of the Swedish-speaking Åland Islanders to separate from Finland and join Sweden, a panel of eminent jurists decided that the League Covenant's ban on involvement in matters within the domestic jurisdiction of states would not stand in the way. The Covenant's ban might foreclose League involvement in most attempted secessions, but it would not cover the unique case of the Islands. Part of the reason was that Finland was in a state of transition, having itself just emerged from another state (Russia), but the League also added that a ban on intervention would also not apply in the case of a manifest violation of the rights of a segment of the population of a state by the government.[115] And this continued into the UN Charter era with respect to human rights questions. Today, three attempts by states to contract the norms are particularly notable.

1. Aid to rebel movements

As noted earlier, one of the generally agreed components of the non-intervention norm is the ban on outside assistance to groups fighting governments. As stated by the ICJ, 'the principle of non-intervention prohibits a State "to intervene, directly or indirectly, with or without armed force, in support of an internal opposition in another State"'.[116] This ban includes all assistance, whether food, equipment,

(Cambridge: Cambridge University Press, 1996); for an intermediate position emphasizing governmental networks rather than centrally controlled foreign policy, see Anne-Marie Slaughter, *A New World Order* (Princeton, NJ: Princeton University Press, 2004).

[115] Covenant of the League of Nations, Art. 15; Report of the International Committee of Jurists Entrusted by the Council of the League of Nations with the Task of Giving an Advisory Opinion upon the Legal Aspects of the Aaland Islands Question, LNOJ, Special Supplement No. 3 (1920) 5–10. The report was speaking hypothetically as there was no accusation of such conduct by Finland.

[116] *Armed Activities Case, supra* note 38, para. 164 (quoting *Nicaragua Case*, para. 206).

training, or weapons. As a result, international law, whether Article 2(4) or the rule of non-intervention, generally permits (in the sense of not banning) external aid to the government but none to opposition forces within a state.[117] The Security Council has repeatedly reinforced this view in resolutions condemning aid to rebel movements in other states.[118]

Over the years, in particular during the Cold War, when the United States and the Soviet Union frequently channeled aid to groups in proxy wars, states have tried to ignore, evade, or change this norm. Arguments about the norm are directly relevant to the outside assistance that has been given to the Syrian opposition, although one can question whether many of the states providing such assistance have thought about the legality of their actions. To simplify the claims a bit, at least two possible alternative norms—which have been asserted by states or scholars already to be the *lex lata*—are possible:

- The first would claim that once a state enters a civil war, other states are prohibited from aiding either the government or the opposition *ab initio* on the theory that the state must be allowed to work out its own civil war free of foreign involvement. This position actually strengthens the norm of non-intervention, at least provisionally. But then if one side nonetheless received external aid, the rule would then allow (or perhaps excuse) aid to the other side—counter-intervention, if you will—on the theory that it would represent a lawful response or counter-measure.[119]
- The second alternative proposed norm would allow assistance to rebels in situations of human rights catastrophes, where a government is killing its own people, without specifying a specific threshold. It can be seen as a proposal to extend the exception to the ban on intervention in the case of aid to anti-colonial movements. Just as colonialism denies a people the right of self-determination, so does governmental repression of the population, thereby justifying an equal remedy—foreign military aid—for the victims.[120] (Self-determination is addressed in detail in the next chapter.) A version of this idea was expressed by the UK Foreign Secretary William Hague, when he announced in the spring of 2013 the UK's readiness to arm the Syrian opposition by stating:

> [W]e and our allies must always be prepared to respond to situations of extreme humanitarian distress. Our foreign policy is inseparable from upholding human rights, protecting

[117] The norm does not apply to aid to groups fighting colonialism, where such aid is, in fact, specifically allowed. See Friendly Relations Declaration, principle 4, para. 5 (colonial peoples 'are entitled to seek and to receive support').

[118] See Christine Gray, *International Law and the Use of Force*, 3rd ed. (Oxford: Oxford University Press, 2008) 68–75.

[119] See, e.g., *Oppenheim's International Law, supra* note 95, 438; Krzysztof J. Skubiszewski, 'Use of Force by States. Collective Security. Law of War and Neutrality', in Max Sørenson (ed.), *Manual of Public International Law* (New York: St Martin's Press, 1968) 739, 749–50; cf. Gray, *International Law, supra* note 118, at 80–1, 92–8 (right of counter-intervention only on behalf of the government); see generally Eliav Lieblich, *International Law and Civil Wars: Intervention and Consent* (New York: Routledge, 2013) 122–72.

[120] This proposed legal rule would seem to imply a prohibition on aid to the government committing such atrocities, although that position is not typically expressed.

lives, and supporting international law. We must assist the genuine moderate and democratic forces in Syria who are in dire need of help and who feel abandoned by the international community.[121]

Regardless of whether a state accepts the traditional rule or one of the alternatives, one way that states have effectively aided opposition groups is to recognize one as the government of the state. With such recognition, the external states can argue that the regime can then request and accept assistance on behalf of the state. Many states offering military aid to the Libyan opposition in 2011 recognized the so-called Transitional National Council as Libya's government at about the same time.[122] This tactic presents a convenient way for states to aid opposition groups while professing that they are not really interfering in the internal affairs of the state.

Under the two pillars of thin justice, the proposed relaxation of the norm against aid to rebel groups is quite problematic. As for the first pillar, a formal grant of permission to assist rebels once the conflict has reached a certain stage is likely to increase the bloodshed associated with the war. The violence in Syria, Congo, and other civil wars fueled by outside assistance suggests the dangers of allowing such aid. A version of this norm that banned assistance to both sides would be better under the first pillar in this respect, in that it would cut off the fuel to *both sides* in a civil war. But if it then allowed assistance to one or the other side once one external actor—such as Russia and Iran vis-à-vis Syria—violates the norm, then it still results in putting more fuel on the fire.

Yet under the second pillar, the current ban on aid to rebels is unjust if it bans assistance that can mitigate or terminate governmental actions against basic human rights—it effectively denies a group the right to defend itself with foreign-supplied arms against a government-sponsored slaughter. This seems to be a strong enough flaw in the status quo. Yet this injustice does not support the first alternative to a ban on aid to the rebels, for it is not tailored to the specific problem of protecting basic human rights. Instead, that alternative would allow or tolerate aid to rebels based on a threshold of armed conflict, aid by other states to the government side, or some combination thereof. Thus this alternative does little to protect human rights while aggravating the internal conflict. Indeed, it would seem that some states, such as Qatar and Saudi Arabia, are acting precisely according to that flawed theory, for their goal seems to be to replace the Assad regime and reduce Iran's influence in the region, not protect human rights.[123]

[121] See 'Foreign Secretary Statement to Parliament on Syria', 6 March 2013, <https://www.gov.uk/government/speeches/foreign-secretary-statement-to-parliament-on-syria>.

[122] See Stefan Talmon, 'Recognition of the Libyan National Transitional Council', *ASIL Insight*, 16 June 2011; see generally Gray, *International Law, supra* note 118, at 98–105.

[123] See Mark Mazzetti, C.J. Chivers, and Eric Schmitt, 'Taking Outsize Role in Syria, Qatar Funnels Arms to Rebels', *New York Times*, 29 June 2013, A1.

Only the second alternative, tailoring the aid to insurgents so as to protect human rights, passes the second pillar insofar as it would allow for aid for the purpose of terminating violations of those rights. The hardest question remains whether a norm can be developed that passes the second pillar while doing little harm to peace under the first pillar. Such a norm would give guidance to states in situations like that of Syria as to what is permissible. At this stage, the practice and *opinio juris* of states has given few clues as to what such a norm might look like. As noted, many states have provided aid to the rebels in Syria without regard to legality. Although the United States has pledged to aid the Syrian rebels, it conspicuously avoided offering a legal justification for this position.[124]

To pass the second pillar, such a norm will have to limit a state's assistance to those forces that will respect basic human rights themselves, whether during the conflict by respecting the rules of war or after the conflict in terms of their governance of the state.[125] Yet even describing such a norm highlights its perhaps insurmountable complexities. How can external actors ensure that aid will end up in the right hands—both in terms of avoiding transfer to groups not seeking to protect basic human rights (except perhaps their own), as well as ensuring that the recipients remain focused on protecting basic rights? From a consequentialist reading of the second pillar, shaping a norm that improves overall respect for basic human rights will require multiple conditions that may not be feasible in practice. As for the first pillar, it would seem that, if the violations of basic rights are pervasive and severe, respect for the second pillar may require toleration of significant violence under the first pillar. If we choose to see human rights as trumps or even as exclusionary reasons, a norm that tolerates additional violence resulting from aid to the rebels might be just in order to end pervasive violations of basic rights, such as those in Syria. But the calibration is extraordinarily difficult, and I do not claim to be able to describe in detail a norm that meets both pillars.[126]

These difficulties may, to some, simply show the need not to change the law. But I think decisionmakers need to be ready to respond to an unjust norm by proposing alternatives, even if we may not be actually ready to act on them in a particular case. In the case of aid to rebel movements facing such horrors from their government, international law needs to adjust to the imperative of protecting human rights. Yet, at the same time, I would also end on a note of caution, namely, that even if we could devise a norm that would respect the two pillars of thin justice, and even if we could act on that norm by ensuring that aid reaches the right people, it might still be very unwise as a policy matter to act according to the norm's permission (for we are talking about a permissive rather than mandatory

124 See Adam Entous, 'U.S. Legal Grounds for Backing Syrian Rebels', *Wall Street Journal*, 14 July 2013 (offering no justification under international law).

125 As for the exception for aid to anti-colonial movements, the arguments that it passes both pillars track those regarding the permissibility of separation of colonial territories from the metropole in the first place, which are considered in detail in Chapter 5.

126 For an endorsement of a proposed ban on aid to governments and rebel movements that slaughter civilians in civil wars, see Tom Ruys, 'Of Arms, Funding and "Non-lethal Assistance"—Issues Surrounding Third-State Intervention in the Syrian Civil War', *Chinese JIL* 13 (2014): 13.

norm here). In the case of Syria, for instance, the huge uncertainties for overall regional stability, including the receipt of weapons by transnational groups committing mass atrocities themselves, are strong arguments against aiding the rebels, even if advocates for it could devise a norm to make it legal.

2. *The changing norms on economic sanctions*

As noted earlier, economic sanctions on states with poor human rights records, though resisted by many Southern states, do not seem to violate the ban on intervention. The UN itself approved such sanctions on both Rhodesia and South Africa during their years of minority white rule, and they are now part of the foreign policy of many states.[127] In this case, we see the contours of the norm as reflecting the work of the second pillar by excluding from the norm's ambit measures meant to ensure the protection of human rights that do not otherwise increase risks to peace.

Yet even as many international decisionmakers now agree that a state's poor human rights record may, at least in some circumstances, justify diplomatic and economic sanctions upon it—thus seemingly weakening the norm of non-intervention—that very regard for human rights has ironically resulted in a strengthening of the norm in an important way. Ever since the Security Council imposed crippling sanctions on Iraq following its invasion of Kuwait in 1990, states seem to have accepted that economic sanctions must contain an exception for humanitarian supplies.[128] The UN expert committee that interprets the International Covenant on Economic, Social and Cultural Rights has similarly found food embargoes to violate that treaty.[129] Over time, many institutions have switched to targeted or so-called smart sanctions that are aimed at specific industries within states, or to individuals rather than states. Yet as these sanctions have been deployed, they have raised a host of new questions about whether they provide inadequate procedural protections to their targets and thus violate their human rights. Both the European Court of Justice and the European Court of Human Rights have found Security Council-mandated sanctions against individuals suspected of supporting terrorists to violate human rights, leading the Council to add procedural protections to the process of listing individuals subject to the sanctions.[130] The second pillar is thus doing more work than in the past, as states have

[127] See SC Res. 181 (7 August 1963) (non-binding arms embargo on South Africa); SC Res. 232 (16 December 1966) (embargo on Rhodesia); GA Res. 1761 (XVII) (5 November 1962) (non-binding embargo on South Africa); SC Res. 418 (4 November 1977) (arms embargo on South Africa).

[128] See, e.g., SC Res. 661, para. 4 (6 August 1990) (Iraq); SC Res. 1267, para. 4(b) (15 October 1999) (Afghanistan); SC Res. 1929, para. 10 (9 June 2010) (Iran).

[129] See Committee on Economic, Social and Cultural Rights, General Comment 12: Right to adequate food, para. 37, UN Doc. E/C.12/1999/5 (12 May 1999) ('Food should never be used as an instrument of political and economic pressure').

[130] See Erika de Wet, 'From *Kadi* to *Nada*: Judicial Techniques Favouring Human Rights over United Nations Security Council Sanctions', *Chinese JIL* 12 (2013): 787; Carlo Focarelli, *International Law as Social Construct: The Struggle for Global Justice* (Oxford: Oxford University Press, 2012) 483–6.

realized that certain sanctions, even if justifiable to end aggression or promote basic human rights, could actually undermine those rights.

As a result, we see the second pillar at work both to *constrain* the norm of non-intervention by permitting sanctions based on human rights *reasons* and to *expand* the norm by placing limits on the acceptable *means* of carrying out such sanctions. Here the basic rights act as trumps, for no matter what benefits the sanctions might have in pushing the government to change its policies, states may not impose sanctions that deny people basic rights to food and health. This is a laudable example of how the second pillar can work in a deontological manner. However, this trend has not been uniform. If we view the structural adjustments that the International Monetary Fund (IMF) demands of borrower states in exchange for their access to resources as a form of lawful intervention (as opposed to simply a condition of membership in the Fund), there remain serious questions as to whether those policies harm the human rights of the citizens of the affected state.[131] If they do and the IMF does not address this problem, the rules of international monetary law are not in accordance with thin justice.[132]

3. Arrest of war criminals abroad

The interpretation of the non-intervention norm to allow actions that defend human rights has even had remarkable, and multifaceted, consequences for the norms governing a state's arrest of individuals abroad. Though the rule is doctrinally distinct from the ban on intervention, states are generally banned from conducting such operations without the consent of the host state (i.e. the state where the suspect is located). It is part of the prohibition on physical intrusions by other states short of military force—a rule that the PCIJ described as 'the first and foremost restriction imposed by international law'.[133] Although the ban benefits individuals because these actions can amount to arbitrary arrest and deprive the arrested person of the protection of the host state, international law viewed it principally in terms of protection of the host state's interests.

As a result, traditionally when states violated the prohibition through extraterritorial arrest without the host state's consent, those arrested could not obtain any remedy from the violation through dismissal of the case in front of the court to which they were sent, and international law gave them no remedy.[134] Thus, for instance, after Israeli agents kidnapped Adolf Eichmann from Argentina and

[131] From the legal perspective, see Jason Morgan-Foster, 'The Relationship of IMF Structural Adjustment Programs to Economic, Social, and Cultural Rights: The Argentine Case Revisited, *Mich JIL* 24 (2003): 577; from the economic perspective, see M. Rodwan Abouharb and David L. Cingranelli, 'IMF programs and human rights, 1981–2003', *Rev Intl Orgs* 4 (2009): 47.

[132] Similar concerns have been raised within the World Bank, which has created an internal inspection panel to monitor the human rights effects of projects the Bank finances, though one criticized for its limited effectiveness. For a review of criticisms, see Enrique R. Carrasco and Alison K. Guernsey, 'The World Bank's Inspection Panel: Promoting True Accountability Through Arbitration', *Corn ILJ* 41 (2008): 577.

[133] *'Lotus', supra* note 96, at 18.

[134] *Ker v Illinois*, 119 U.S. 436 (1886); *United States v Noriega*, 746 F. Supp. 1506, 1533–4 (S.D. Fla. 1990).

brought him to Israel, the Israeli district court responded to his claim that Israel's violation of the rule deprived the Israeli courts of jurisdiction over him by stating that 'a person being tried for an offense against the laws of a State may not oppose his trial by reason of the illegality of his arrest'.[135]

Yet state views about extraterritorial arrest and kidnapping have evolved, in a way that suggests a new attitude to the norms of non-intervention and non-exercise of extraterritorial jurisdiction. On the one hand, states have been willing to look the other way regarding such actions when the defendant is accused of particularly horrendous acts, such as crimes against humanity. Thus, even in the Eichmann case, the UN Security Council's response to Argentina's complaint was neither an overt condemnation of Israel nor a demand for Eichmann's return to Argentina (which would have been the appropriate remedy under international law for a breach of the rule).[136] Rather, it only declared that such acts, 'may, if repeated, endanger international peace and security' and made a request to Israel to 'make appropriate reparation'.[137] Argentina and Israel agreed to restore relations less than three months after the event.

A generation later, in 1997, after NATO forces lured a Croatian Serb suspected war criminal, Slavko Dokmanović, out of Serbia into a UN-controlled area[138] without the knowledge of the Serbian government, the International Criminal Tribunal for the Former Yugoslavia (ICTY) rejected the suspect's claim that his removal deprived the court of jurisdiction.[139] More significantly, when NATO forces in Bosnia arranged for the abduction of another suspect, Dragan Nikolić, from Serbia to Bosnia, the suspect's motion for dismissal was also rejected. In a candid opinion of consequentialist reasoning, the Appeals Chamber wrote:

> 25. Universally Condemned Offences are a matter of concern to the international community as a whole. There is a legitimate expectation that those accused of those crimes will be brought to justice swiftly. Accountability for these crimes is a necessary condition to the achievement of international justice, which plays a critical role in the reconciliation and rebuilding based on the rule of law of countries and societies torn apart by international and internecine conflicts.
>
> 26. In the opinion of the Appeals Chamber, the damage caused to international justice by not apprehending fugitives accused of serious violations of international humanitarian law is comparatively higher than the injury, if any, caused to the sovereignty of a State by a limited intrusion in its territory. Therefore, the Appeals Chamber does not consider that in cases of universally condemned offences, jurisdiction should be set aside on the ground

[135] *Attorney-General of the Government of Israel v Eichmann*, 36 ILR 5, paras. 41–44 (1961) (Dist. Ct. Jerusalem).

[136] ILC Articles on State Responsibility, Art. 35 (on duty of restitution).

[137] SC Res. 138 (23 June 1960). Hannah Arendt seems to have captured the sense of members of the Council when she justified the kidnaping based on the 'unprecedentedness of the crime' and Argentina's record of hiding Nazis, concluding that 'the realm of legality offered no alternative to kidnaping'. Hannah Arendt, *Eichmann in Jerusalem: A Report on the Banality of Evil* (New York: The Viking Press, 1963) 264.

[138] The UN had control of Eastern Slavonia pending its transfer from Croatian control (gained during the Serb-Croat conflict) back to Serbia.

[139] *Prosecutor v Mrškić*, Case No. IT-95-13a-PT (1997).

that there was a violation of the sovereignty of a State, when the violation is brought about by the apprehension of fugitives from international justice.[140]

The result is, then, a shrinking of the ban on extraterritorial enforcement of criminal law because of concerns for the protection of basic human rights of victims. Thus, the same currents that led the UN to reject long ago the notion that it could not criticize a state for human rights violations are witnessed in the willingness of the law to tolerate even extraterritorial kidnapping to advance accountability for human rights atrocities. (At the same time, it is probably important that the kidnaping was connected with proceedings at an international court; state attitudes to kidnaping by one state to bring a defendant to trial there may well be unchanged, even for war criminals.) I am not arguing that this outcome is required by the two pillars, for there is a legitimate question as to whether preventing impunity is part of protecting the basic human rights of victims such that any rule that allows for impunity is unjust (an issue I turn to in Chapter 8 in discussing universal jurisdiction). Rather, the point is that norms can change in a direction that takes greater account of human rights without sacrificing peace.

At the same time, these same trends in favor of human rights vis-à-vis *victims* have done something else to the ban on kidnaping—transformed it from one aimed solely at protecting *states* to one aimed at protecting *defendants*. Thus, in a series of domestic court decisions, defendants who were seized from other states outside normal extradition channels—even with the consent of, or lack of subsequent protest, by the latter states—have challenged their incarceration, and courts have acknowledged that such circumvention of procedures alone can justify a dismissal of charges.[141] The ICTY also endorsed the importance of protecting the rights of defendants in its ruling in *Nikolić*, stating that if Nikolić had been mistreated during the abduction, the court might well lack jurisdiction.[142] Either way, the courts are recognizing that the defendant has interests to be protected independent of the interests of the states involved. The trends are not, however, uniform. The European Court of Human Rights, in ruling against Abdullah Ocalan, the leader of the Kurdish Worker's Party who was seized by Turkish police in Kenya and returned to Turkey for trial, insisted that any challenge to incarceration based on an extraterritorial abduction must first demonstrate that the seizure was done without the consent of the other state.[143]

[140] *Prosecutor v Nikolić, Decision on Interlocutory Appeal Concerning Legality of Arrest*, Case No. IT-94-AR73 (2003).

[141] See, e.g., *Levinge v Director of Custodial Services*, 9 NSWLR 546 (1987); *State v Ebrahim*, 1991 (2) SALR 553. Even the U.S. Supreme Court, in bizarrely holding that the kidnaping by U.S. agents of a suspect from Mexico without that state's consent did not violate the U.S.-Mexico extradition treaty, seemed to concede that a violation of that treaty would deprive the United States of jurisdiction. *United States v Alvarez-Machain*, 504 U.S. 655 (1992).

[142] *Nikolić, supra* note 140, paras. 28–30 (endorsing other courts); see also *Bozano v France*, ECHR Series A, No. 111 (1986), where the European Court of Human Rights found France's mistreatment of a defendant while in custody during his transportation to Italy in contravention of French law contributed to France's violation of the European Convention on Human Rights (though no state acted extraterritorially here).

[143] *Ocalan v Turkey*, ECHR 2005-IV, 12 May 2005, paras. 89–99. On the other hand, this case did not involve an allegation of any physical or mental abuses of the defendant during the transfer.

These debates also assumed great prominence during the controversy surrounding the seizure by the United States during the George W. Bush administration of individuals in Europe suspected by the United States of terrorism in order to send them to third countries for interrogation (not trial). The United States defended the practice of so-called irregular renditions based on the consent of the states with which it was working—a defense squarely grounded in the old rationale for the ban on extraterritorial arrests. European officials, legal advisers, and commentators condemned the practice for its violation of the basic human rights of the detainee—for both the brutal treatment during the renditions as well as the prospect of torture once the person was handed over to a third state (as well as several cases of mistaken identity).[144]

The outcome of this somewhat complex story is a change in state understandings of the norm against extraterritorial law enforcement that resembles that described earlier regarding economic sanctions. The basic norm remains well accepted, but it has *contracted* in the sense that the vindication of human rights can itself lead to a toleration of extraterritorial acts when they serve international criminal justice. At the same time, the norm has *expanded* insofar as its legal grounding is no longer confined to the protection of state interests but has shifted to protecting individual rights. The norm has resulted in new set of rights-holders associated with the duty—individuals and not merely states—as well as an exception to that duty—a liberty to kidnap, as it were—in exceptional situations.

Beneath this normative transformation—the simultaneous contraction and expansion of the ban on extraterritorial law enforcement—is a shift in the moral justification of the rule. We witness a *thickening* in the vision of justice associated with this norm—one beyond the standard by which I measure the rules of international law. (Indeed, a rule such as that stated by the Eichmann court, which seems to see no role for a court to consider mistreatment of the defendant in deciding whether it has jurisdiction, would not pass the second pillar of thin justice.) It is now increasingly tolerable to engage in such acts to achieve accountability for gross human rights violations, even as it is increasingly intolerable to do so in a way that physically or mentally harms the suspect in the process. Indeed, with respect to the latter, the second pillar is again operating, and for good reasons, as a trump: under the rule, if the defendant is tortured, no countervailing benefits to the protection of basic human rights from the arrest of the person, whether to his actual or his potential victims, will be accepted to make the arrest lawful.

We will see that this is not the only example where such thickening has taken place. International law demonstrates numerous openings where states, often prodded by civil society, have accepted rules that can withstand a more demanding

[144] Compare Condoleezza Rice, Remarks Upon Her Departure for Europe, 5 December 2005, <http://merln.ndu.edu/archivepdf/terrorism/state/57602.pdf> ('In those cases the local government can make the sovereign choice to cooperate in a rendition. Such renditions are permissible under international law'), with European Commission for Democracy Through Law, Opinion on the International Legal Obligations of Council of Europe Member States in Respect of Secret Detention Facilities and Inter-State Transport of Prisoners, 17 March 2006, <http://www.venice.coe.int/webforms/documents/CDL-AD(2006)009.aspx>.

form of justice—not demanding in the sense that it discounts the pillar of peace, but demanding in that it protects individual human rights even more than is required by thin justice. Strong cosmopolitans will certainly seize on these developments as a vindication of the role of individual human rights in international law. (The arrest of Augusto Pinochet, though it did not involve extraterritorial conduct by Spain, was similarly hailed as a transformative moment.) Whether they dominate the legal landscape will require greater inquiry.

III. Conclusion

The bans on the use of force and on intervention in the internal affairs of states stand at the apex of the matrix of duties that states owe one another in response to their sovereignty-based claims. We have seen how, in overall terms, both norms are just under the framework of thin justice; yet simultaneously, disagreements among global decisionmakers about the precise prohibitions under each norm reveal different preferences about acceptable risks to peace and about the balance between promoting peace and respecting basic human rights, the two pillars of thin global justice. In the case of the ban on the use of force, the arguments for expanding self-defense were grounded in both maintaining the deterrent effect of Article 51 and in protecting human rights; and my conclusion was that it was just that self-defense covered both attacks by non-state actors and demonstrably imminent attacks but not looming threats. The arguments for contracting self-defense were based on conjectures about advancing peace or protecting human rights, and in each case these arguments were found to grossly underestimate the costs to peace and assume too much about the potential improvements to human rights. In the end, thin justice did not tolerate, let alone demand, such new norms.

With respect to non-intervention, I also defended what I regard as the generally limited scope of the norm against claims that it should be expanded in the name of promoting peace. As for claims that the norm should be contracted further, we witnessed both the dilemmas inherent in proposing new norms (or new interpretations of existing norms) as well as the possibilities for new norms that are clearly better than the old ones. In the case of allowing aid to rebel movements, we are frankly caught between the injustice of a norm that could deprive people facing great human rights abuses of external assistance in ending them and the dangers to both peace and human rights from allowing aid to rebels during a civil war. Yet with both economic sanctions and extraterritorial arrests, the norms have moved from thinly just (at best) to representing a thicker version of justice. Economic sanctions are allowed to pressure states to improve their respect for basic human rights, but the sanctions themselves must not undercut those rights. The extraterritorial arrest of those who commit mass human rights violations is tolerated at least to some extent, but those suspects must be treated in a way that respects their basic human rights as well.

These conclusions underline both the moral content of the existing law but also the ways in which the law should and can change. It is critical that exceptions to the ban on the use of force, notably self-defense, and new interpretations of non-intervention not endanger the interstate and internal peace that is the chief goal of these norms and the first pillar of thin global justice. But, on the other hand, it is equally imperative that norms should change if they fail to respect basic human rights, certainly if an alternative norm does not interfere with peace and even, up to a point, if it does.

This first examination of core international law norms has also highlighted an objection to alternative norms that I will return to in later chapters—the complete inseparability of proposals for such norms and institutions that do not exist and frankly cannot reasonably be said to have a prospect of being created in the foreseeable future. Scholars proposing these alternatives recognize that their very complexity requires new institutions to implement them, but they just leave it at that without pondering either the feasibility or the dangers of such institutions compared to the status quo.

The shortcomings of these approaches are particularly relevant in the context of the use of force and non-intervention, for these are among the situations where existing international institutions are very weak in terms of getting states to act as they should. If it is uncommon for the UN to pressure one state into ceasing a use of force or stopping its intervention in the internal affairs of another state when those violations are fairly obvious, then how can we possibly expect such institutions to make decisions in real time about the legality of an attack on a state from abroad? Of course, the existing system that gives states an inherent power of self-defense is subject to abuse by states who may not have been attacked at all—this may well describe both the Brezhnev and the Reagan Doctrines during the Cold War—but the alternative is, frankly, far worse. As noted throughout this chapter, such institutional considerations cannot make an unjust norm just, but they are strong arguments against embracing an alternative norm when that norm relies on decisions by mythical institutions.

The foregoing appraisal has only been able to touch upon the principal norms and the principal challenges to them. Self-defense and UN-approved force raise other moral questions as well in terms of the appropriate amount of force that should be used, the acceptable goals of using force, the accountability of the actors using force, and the challenges to the existing law from cyber-attacks. International law has developed rules for some of these questions but certainly not all; but the framework of thin justice offers a heuristic for ensuring that new norms be as just, or more so, than those we currently have. But we still have more core norms to appraise, and we now turn to those that govern whether a group of people has a right to statehood and all the rights and duties that flow from it.

5

The Claims of Peoples: Self-Determination and State Borders

For all the importance of territorial integrity and political independence to states, international law must also address another set of claims critical to statehood—the demands of peoples for self-government. International law's response to those claims is the core norm of self-determination. That norm of statehood defines the basic terms under which peoples may participate as actors in the international legal system, and in particular the extent to which they may achieve self-government through statehood. Self-determination is a somewhat complex norm whose rights and corresponding duties depend on the sorts of people to which it applies. Its coverage extends from peoples living in colonies to those in existing states, including national minorities and indigenous peoples. After explaining the essential contours of the norm, I will appraise it according to the two pillars of thin justice. As with the earlier two norms, the norms of self-determination have been challenged from two different directions, each of which will be compared to the position of international law in terms of thin justice.

Before explaining and appraising the justice of this norm, it is worth noting that self-determination opens up for discussion numerous questions concerning the morality of the state system as a whole. As noted in Chapter 3, I make certain assumptions about that system and will avoid asking whether as a matter of ideal theory, given a planet composed of individuals and communities (however we might link such communities with 'peoples'), a system of states is morally justified. I will, however, ask whether, given the unique and substantial way in which the population of the planet is, and is likely to remain, divided into states (notwithstanding many other ways in which populations and territory are divided), the norms of self-determination that address the claims of peoples are ethically justifiable.

I. Self-Determination as a Multifaceted Norm

The self-determination of peoples appears in various legal incarnations within the corpus of international law. The UN Charter refers to it prominently as a 'principle'.[1] In 1960, as European states were in the midst of letting go of their

[1] UN Charter, Art. 1(2).

colonies—some quite reluctantly—the states in the General Assembly, many the products of decolonization, framed that principle as a right of all peoples, equating it with a right to 'freely determine their political status and freely pursue their economic, social and cultural development'.[2] This same language appeared in the UN's two major human rights covenants, so that that particular right of peoples is now linked to the body of human rights law; those treaties also oblige all parties to 'promote the realization' of the right.[3] The 1970 Friendly Relations Declaration, the unanimously passed General Assembly resolution that reflects states' interpretation of the principles in the Charter, expands on the scope of the right with a list of corresponding duties for states, including the duty to promote the principle, assist the UN in carrying it out, promote human rights, and refrain from forcible action to deny people the right; it also adds a right of peoples to 'seek and to receive support' in response to any forcible action to deny them their right of self-determination.[4]

The duties and rights emanating from the principle of self-determination are diverse. On the one hand, we see a set of general rights and duties—all peoples have the right to self-determination; all states have the duties specified in the Friendly Relations Declaration, including the duty not forcibly to deny peoples the right; and all peoples have the right to receive the support of states against those states that violate that last duty. On the other hand, the rights and duties associated with self-determination do not quite match up as Hohfeldian duties and claim-rights. The general duties on states are not, in fact, duties to *grant* self-determination to all peoples; and the right of all peoples to self-determination does not create a claim-right of all peoples against all states. Rather, what we discover is a set of special rights and duties. The substantive content of those duties, as well as the rights-holders and duty-holders, turn on a distinction that international law makes among different sorts of peoples.

The law as it developed identifies four different peoples, each of whose right of self-determination creates a set of more detailed rights that trigger certain duties:

(1) The people of an *existing state*—essentially its population as a whole—has (I speak in the singular of a unit) a right to maintain the status of statehood against external and internal coercion. External coercion would include the sorts covered by the ban on the use of force and the norm of non-intervention; internal coercion would include attempts from within to divide the state. That people may also have a right to a certain kind of government—although it is quite indirectly stated in the Friendly Relations Declaration:

> Nothing in the foregoing paragraphs shall be construed as authorizing or encouraging any action which would dismember or impair, totally or in part, the territorial integrity or political unity of sovereign and independent States conducting themselves in compliance

[2] GA Res. 1514 (XV) (14 December 1960), para. 2.

[3] ICCPR, Art. 1(1); ICESCR, Art. 1(3); see also Human Rights Committee, General Comment No. 12: The Right to Self-determination of Peoples, 13 March 1984, para. 6, UN Doc. A/39/40 (1984).

[4] Friendly Relations Declaration, principle 5, para. 5.

> with the principle of equal rights and self-determination of peoples as described above and thus possessed of a government representing the whole people belonging to the territory without distinction as to race, creed or colour.[5]

This paragraph suggests, albeit backhandedly, that states must have governments that are minimally representative—'representing the whole people... without distinction as to race, creed or colour'—but says nothing about a democratically elected government.

Indeed, the practice of states until recently has been to downplay minimal representativeness, as well as, a fortiori, the more maximal representativeness inherent in democracy. For most of the UN's history, the representativeness of governments went unchallenged as a matter of self-determination, with the most notable exception being the consensus since the 1940s that South Africa was clearly failing in the former regard.[6] The expert body that supervises the implementation of the International Convention on the Elimination of All Forms of Racial Discrimination (CERD) has pushed the more maximal version somewhat, interpreting the right of self-determination as being linked to the right of citizens under that treaty to participate in the political process at any level.[7] However, that body does not reflect governmental positions. Whatever the precise scope of the right, the state comprising that people has a duty to provide that sort of government to the people; and other states have a duty not to impede those rights through external coercion (which raises all the issues discussed earlier concerning the norm of non-intervention).

(2) The people of a *non-self-governing territory* has a different set of rights. Non-self-governing territories are essentially defined areas that a state administers, typically following some kind of conquest or acquisition from another state, that are not fully part of the state. In most respects, it is a legal shorthand for a colony. The people of a non-self-governing territory is its inhabitants, regardless of ethnic or other differences among them. That people has a right to determine the territory's own future political status, whether as an independent state (as happened with most European colonies in Africa, Asia, and Latin America), a freely associated state (a status that Micronesia enjoys with the United States), integration into the state that administers it, or any other status, including remaining non-self-governing (like some Caribbean islands with France and the Netherlands).[8] The state that administers such a territory must allow its people a choice of status and desist from any coercion of the people in that choice; if the group chooses independence, the state must grant it without delay.[9] A related category is peoples subject to foreign occupation following a use of force against

[5] Ibid.; see *Reference re Secession of Quebec* [1998] 2 SCR 217, paras. 126–130.

[6] See, e.g., GA Res. 44(I) (8 December 1946).

[7] Committee on the Elimination of Racial Discrimination, General Recommendation No. 21: Right to Self-Determination, 23 August 1996, para. 4, UN Doc. A/51/18 (1996).

[8] Friendly Relations Declaration, principle 4, para. 4. On state practice, see James Crawford, *The Creation of States in International Law*, 2nd ed. (Oxford: Oxford University Press, 2006) 621–47.

[9] GA Res 1514, *supra* note 2, para. 5.

their state; its right to self-determination generally translates into a right to be free of foreign control.[10]

(3) Peoples *within*—as contrasted with the people *of—a state* also have rights, although international law has stayed clear, not always helpfully, of defining what constitutes such a people.[11] Peoples within a state enjoy essentially two sorts of rights.

First, each such people has the same right to a representative government that the *people of* a state as a whole have. And the state in which they live has the duty to provide it to them. When the Supreme Court of Canada issued an advisory opinion regarding the legal permissibility of Quebec's potential secession from Canada, the Court interpreted the rights of the people of Quebec as follows (although the Court deftly avoided saying who exactly were the people of Quebec):

> A state whose government represents the whole of the people or peoples resident within its territory, on a basis of equality and without discrimination, and respects the principles of self-determination in its internal arrangements, is entitled to maintain its territorial integrity under international law and to have that territorial integrity recognized by other states.[12]

The Court went on to rule that Canada fulfills its duty to the people of Quebec through numerous formal and informal arrangements that ensure their full participation in the government of Canada; as a result, that people currently enjoys its right of self-determination.

Second, and the subject of more disagreement, there is a sense that peoples who qualify as *national minorities*—or at least the individuals who make up such peoples—have the right to enjoy their own culture, religion, or language within a state.[13] As with the definition of a people, international law has afforded limited guidance on the definition of a national minority, although some basic parameters regarding ethnic, religious, or linguistic kinship seem well accepted.[14] These two basic rights create corresponding duties on behalf of the states where the peoples live; but a state has those duties only to its own peoples (or minorities).

[10] See Antonio Cassese, *Self-Determination of Peoples: A Legal Reappraisal* (Cambridge: Cambridge University Press, 1995) 90–9.

[11] See, e.g., Thomas D. Musgrave, *Self Determination and National Minorities* (Oxford: Clarendon Press, 1997) 148–79.

[12] *Reference re Secession of Quebec*, *supra* note 5, para. 130.

[13] See ICCPR, Art. 27.

[14] See Special Rapporteur of the Sub-Commission on Prevention of Discrimination and Protection of Minorities, Study on the Rights of Persons Belonging to Ethnic, Religious and Linguistic Minorities, para. 568, UN Doc. E/CN.4/Sub.2/384/Rev. (1979) (by Francesco Capotorti) ('A group numerically inferior to the rest of the population of a State, in a non-dominant position, whose members—being nationals of the State—possess ethnic, religious or linguistic characteristics differing from those of the rest of the population and show, if only implicitly, a sense of solidarity, directed towards preserving their culture, traditions, religion or language'); Office of the United Nations High Commissioner for Human Rights (OHCHR), 'Minority Rights: International Standards and Guidance for Implementation', 2–3, UN Doc. HR/PUB/10/3 (2010).

Most European states have endorsed a broad set of rights for members of national minorities, even while leaving the term undefined.[15]

(4) *Indigenous peoples*, one special category of peoples within a state, have been recognized as a distinct group legally, having additional rights above other peoples within states. Though trends have moved slowly, the 2007 United Nations Declaration on the Rights of Indigenous Peoples recognized key rights that other peoples do not enjoy, including the right to autonomy and self-government, rights to practice and protect their culture in robust ways, the right to set up their own educational systems, and the right against forced removal from their land.[16] The state of nationality of the indigenous peoples assumes the duties in this regard.

Several general propositions follow from this very brief encapsulation of the state of the law. First, self-determination is not a one-size-fits-all-peoples sort of norm. On the contrary, the rights and duties vary directly with each sort of people. Second, the only people with a clear right to a state of their own are people who already have one (for example the people of the United States) and people under colonial domination. Even people under foreign occupation generally have only the right to liberation, not to their own state.[17]

Third, all other peoples must generally achieve their self-determination within the states where they currently reside; thus, their governments have a duty to provide them with certain participatory means to make for a fully representative state, but they have no duty to respect wishes for separation. Indeed, international law does not even give peoples, other than indigenous peoples, a right to autonomy in terms of the creation of separate governance structures.[18] Individuals are always legally free to leave their state,[19] but a people may not, as a general matter, separate from the state in the sense of forming a new state or merging with a neighbor.[20]

The only possible exception is when the state clearly fails in its responsibilities, as the Friendly Relations Declaration says, to provide 'a government representing

[15] See Framework Convention on the Protection of National Minorities, 1 February 1995, 2151 UNTS 243. The notable non-signatories to the treaty are France (which as a matter of constitutional law does not accept the concept of national minorities) and Turkey (which is concerned that its Kurdish minority would make new claims under the treaty).

[16] GA Res. 61/295, Annex (13 September 2007). Although the United States, Canada, Australia, and New Zealand voted against the text, all four—the United States in 2010—eventually endorsed it.

[17] The Palestinians are unusual in this regard because of changes in the treatment of their status since the beginning of Israel's occupation in 1967. See Orna Ben-Naftali, Aeyal M. Gross, and Keren Michaeli, 'Illegal Occupation: Framing the Occupied Palestinian Territory', *Berk JIL* 23 (2005): 551.

[18] Steven R. Ratner, 'Does International Law Matter in Preventing Ethnic Conflict?', 32 *NYU JIL & Pol* 32 (2000): 591; cf. *Gorzelik v Poland*, App. 44158/09, 17 February 2004, para. 67 (giving states flexibility as to official recognition of minorities).

[19] ICCPR, Art. 12.

[20] The CERD Committee stated the position somewhat awkwardly in writing that 'international law has not recognized a general right of peoples unilaterally to declare secession from a state', CERD General Recommendation 21, *supra* note 7, para. 6. But the ICJ later stated, with respect to Kosovo, that mere declarations of independence do not violate international law. *Accordance with International Law of the Unilateral Declaration of Independence in Respect of Kosovo* [2010] ICJ Rep 403 (Advisory Opinion of 22 July).

the whole people belonging to the territory without distinction as to race, creed or colour'. That exception is not ironclad in law because (a) states have not through their practice recognized a right of secession even in those cases; (b) no international instrument specifically recognizes that right—as noted, the Declaration's formulation offers only a very backhand endorsement; and (c) international courts have refrained from accepting it.[21] Certainly, some peoples have managed to separate from a state under other circumstances. The key secessions since World War II—Bangladesh, Eritrea, states of the former Yugoslavia (which was also a case of the dissolution of a federal state), and South Sudan—resulted from decisions by the people of (or at least one group of people within) part of a state to secede that garnered the prior or later endorsement of other states but did not necessarily meet the legal standard for self-determination that might justify secession.

One can get a sense of these different meanings of self-determination—and the possibilities of confusions among them—from the response of the special commission of judges appointed by the European Community to opine on legal issues that arose during the disintegration of Yugoslavia. In one opinion, the panel held in late 1991 that Yugoslavia was 'in the process of dissolution' due to the lack of power of the federal government over the republics—a clear admission of the reality of the situation on the ground, without any views as to whether the individual republics were legally entitled to separate from the state.[22] Yet one month later, when it considered whether Serbs living in Bosnia and Croatia enjoyed the right to self-determination, the Commission held that they enjoyed merely 'the right to recognition of their identity under international law' as well as 'every right accorded to minorities' under international law.[23] It appears that the commission sensed that the word 'self-determination' would be misconstrued as tantamount to independence so that, in an effort to prevent secessions by groups within Bosnia, it recognized only a different right. The continued attempts by Serbs and Croats in Bosnia to carve out ethnically unified territories in the hopes of independence (or unification with Serbia) also highlights the failure of states to enforce the norm against secession in a meaningful way, although they paid lip service to it in keeping Bosnia a formally unified state in the 1995 peace accord.

Another complication from the existing position is that, though it contemplates the possibility of secession in the event that a people is denied its right of internal self-determination, the operationalization of the position through the remedy of secession seems virtually impossible if the group is not also territorially concentrated.[24] So even though the Friendly Relations Declaration says nothing

[21] The ICJ turned down a chance to opine on this question in the Kosovo Advisory Opinion, *supra* note 20.

[22] Opinion No. 1 of the Arbitration Commission of the Peace Conference on Yugoslavia (1992), para. 3, 31 ILM 1494.

[23] Opinion No. 2 of the Arbitration Commission of the Peace Conference on Yugoslavia (1992), para. 2, 31 ILM 1497, 1498.

[24] Cassese suggests that the three bases of discrimination—race, creed, and color—may have been chosen because of the difficulties of secession taking place along these lines (as opposed to ethnic or national lines). Cassese, *Self-Determination of Peoples, supra* note 10, at 112–14.

about 'territorially concentrated peoples', it would seem to be an implicit requirement of a remedial right of secession for the group to have such a characteristic. Whether the group might be concentrated in two places, such that the result of secession would be two geographically separated parts of a new state, is not really something the law has addressed.

The result is admittedly a somewhat dissatisfying position, in that, formally international law clearly does not affirmatively authorize secession by the people of an existing state (in contrast to its position concerning peoples in non-self-governing territories), but it does not quite affirmatively prohibit it either. Rather, we see a strong bias against secession.[25] My own view is that the lack of affirmative authorization is not dispositive of the issue, and that the lack of affirmative prohibition, and indeed the explicit contemplation of secession in the Friendly Relations Declaration, means that the law accepts the possibility of secession under limited circumstances.

II. Appraising the Thin Justice of the Norm(s) of Self-Determination

The preceding review shows that in international law's response to the claims of peoples for control over their own future, the answer is skewed toward preservation of the state system, and even more, toward the state system *with the states that are in it*. The people of a state are generally seen as having their rights fulfilled by the existence of that state, although they may well have a right to a minimally representative government; and as long as the peoples (plural) within a state are somehow represented in that system, their rights are also being fulfilled. Disruption to the status quo from peoples who want to form their own state is only minimally tolerated in formal opinions of governments, even if states often eventually accept secessions as a matter of fact. The only clear acceptance of change emerges from the right of the people of a non-self-governing territory to whatever status it wishes, regardless of the wishes of the government of the state that administers it.

Such an attachment to the state system as a whole is hardly surprising for a system of international law, but the preference for the status quo within that system raises serious questions of even the thin justice of the underlying rules. In the discussion that follows, I will focus on the near-ban on secession, though in the course of the discussion I will also assess the permissive norm regarding colonial peoples.

[25] See Report of the Independent International Fact-Finding Mission on the Conflict in Georgia, Vol. II, 138–41 (2009), <http://www.ceiig.ch> (prevailing scholarly opinion against remedial right to secession); Daniel Thürer and Thomas Burri, 'Secession', in Rüdiger Wolfrum (ed.), *The Max Planck Encyclopedia of Public International Law*, online edition (Oxford: Oxford University Press, 2008–) paras. 13–19, <http://opil.ouplaw.com/home/EPIL> (reviewing debate and concluding secession is 'not explicitly forbidden'); Crawford, *Creation of States, supra* note 8, at 416–17. I share the view of the Georgia Report, 136–7, that it is wrong to say that international law does not regulate the question of secession from existing states.

A. The peace pillar

1. The consequences of secessions

The basic rules as they have developed prima facie meet the pillar of advancing interstate and internal peace. The support for this view is ultimately the same as that for the bans on the use of force and nonintervention discussed earlier—the violence and accompanying catastrophes that have come with most separationist struggles. As an empirical matter, many, though certainly not all, attempts at separation lead to violent struggles as the state authorities resist. A review of the secessions since 1945 shows violence during the successful secessions of Bangladesh, the states of the former Yugoslavia, and Eritrea; and violence during the unsuccessful secessions of Tibet (China), Katanga (Congo), Biafra (Nigeria), Kashmir (India), northern Cyprus, northern Sri Lanka, South Sudan, Bougainville (Papua New Guinea), Kurdistan (Iraq and Turkey), Chechnya (Russia), Abkhazia (Georgia), South Ossetia (Georgia), Nagorno-Karabakh (Azerbaijan), and parts of eastern Ukraine.[26]

This violence was not limited to the territory of the state of the secessionist movement. Rather, secessionist movements sought and received aid from abroad, were often manipulated by foreign governments, and in some cases their struggles led to interstate wars, as, for instance, in the cases of Katanga (Belgian intervention), Bangladesh (Indian intervention), northern Cyprus (Turkish intervention), Sri Lanka (Indian intervention), Abkhazia and South Ossetia (Russian intervention). Certainly, some successful secessions have been peaceful—Singapore's separation from Malaysia, Montenegro's separation from Serbia, the peaceful breakups of both the USSR and Czechoslovakia; and the departure of Crimea for Russia (a de facto annexation); and some failed secessions have also been peaceful, notably that of Quebec, where secessionists lost a referendum. Yet the track record regarding interstate and internal peace is overall poor when it comes to secessions, justifying a starting point of not recognizing their legality.

Though beyond the ambit of the peace pillar, we also see significant diminution of welfare from a loss of economies of scale, new borders and resultant regulations, increased suspicions of neighbors, and duplication of effort through the creation of new ministries. These post-secession costs are harder to measure than the lives lost or injuries during a secession, but they are nonetheless significant. The beneficiaries of keeping states intact are not, then, simply the ruling elite, but the entire population as a whole.

2. Responding to objections

Two objections to the consistency of the near-ban on secession with the first pillar can be made. First, it might be argued that this justification for the existing rule

[26] For a thorough listing, see Crawford, *Creation of States*, *supra* note 8, at 392–415; see also Bridget L. Coggins, 'The History of Secession: An Overview', in Aleksandar Pavković and Peter Radan (eds.), *The Ashgate Research Companion to Secession* (Surrey: Ashgate, 2011) 23, 32–9.

would also apply to the colonial context, insofar as decolonization also resulted in significant violence. Or, to put the matter somewhat differently, does not international law's grant of an unfettered right of colonial peoples to separate and receive aid from outside for that purpose also undermine peace? For example, whereas many decolonization episodes were peaceful, many important ones were violent, either internally or vis-à-vis the colonial power—for example in India, Indochina, Indonesia, Algeria, and Zimbabwe. And even those that seemed to transpire peacefully, without a full-fledged war between the colonial power and local elites, were characterized by ample violence between colonial powers and local resistance, for example in Kenya, Burma, and Palestine. We know that the violence inherent in colonialism led to violent reactions.[27]

This concern does not seem valid for two reasons. First, notwithstanding significant rebellions and wars in some colonies, the vast majority of efforts at decolonization did not lead to major wars between the colonial powers and their colonies nor major civil conflicts within the colonies. For the most part European powers generally saw the writing on the wall by the 1950s, and their populations simply lacked the resources and interest in resisting the tide too strongly. As a result, by the time international law recognized such a right—around 1960, with General Assembly Resolution 1514—states had seen that decolonization per se was not a threat to peace. Just as a norm against secessions can and does reflect the experiences of states in terms of the actual and anticipated consequences of past and future secessions, so a norm in favor of decolonization can and does reflect the experiences of states about the consequences of past and future acts of decolonization. Second, even if we prefer to view the decolonization period as violent overall, and thus a norm of international law that permits decolonization as one that detracts from interstate and internal peace, in that case the norm is only prima facie unjust for failing to pass the first pillar; as will be seen later, the second pillar does significant work in enabling us to consider that norm just.

A second objection would question the propriety of counting in a consequentialist calculation the violent reactions of states to what might well be legitimate claims by secessionist groups on their territory. Such a calculation seems to reward the wrongdoer (the oppositionist state) by banning legitimate conduct (justified secessions) simply because there is illegitimate resistance. As Thürer and Burri describe this position: 'The stigma attributed to secessions would...be a *cause*, and not a *consequence* of the instabilities following secession. If the stigma were removed...[secessions] would possibly not cause instability.'[28] This critique extends well beyond this issue to one of consequentialist and utilitarian morality generally.[29] It is an important criticism, though if it is true then it could well

[27] On the tensions within European states between maintaining empires and the nascent human rights movement, see A.W. Brian Simpson, *Human Rights and the End of Empire: Britain and the Genesis of the European Convention* (Oxford: Oxford University Press, 2001) 276–322.

[28] Thürer and Burri, 'Secession', *supra* note 25, para. 11.

[29] I appreciate this point from David Lefkowitz. See also Bernard Williams, 'Consequentialism and Integrity', in Samuel Scheffler (ed.), *Consequentialism and its Critics* (Oxford: Oxford University Press, 1988) 20; Robert E. Goodin, *Utilitarianism as a Public Philosophy* (Cambridge: Cambridge University Press, 1995) 132–48.

suggest that, in evaluating the justice of the norm, the actual or anticipated reactions of states should simply not be relevant at all.

Two responses are in order. First, in justifying rules for the real world, it does not seem a priori off limits to consider in a consequentialist calculation how states react under those rules or under alternative rules. In particular, in a non-ideal world where institutions to constrain states from opposing secessions are highly limited in power, to ignore those state reactions seems almost irresponsible, even if the result is to somehow capture within the ban some secessions that some would regard as legitimate. Even if this criticism of consequentialist reasoning is valid in individual morality, where it may not seem right to accept a consequentialist position that an act is immoral simply because it will face resistance from other individuals, it is not obvious that such considerations are equally inappropriate in the justifying international rules under non-ideal theory.

Second, counting for consequentialist purposes the negative reactions of states to secessionist movement, including the possibility of violence, is not the same as treating those reactions as dispositive. The second pillar will introduce human rights considerations that will compete with, and even exclude consideration of, certain consequences. Accordingly, it will become clear that, to be just, a rule will need to tolerate secessions in some limited circumstances.[30]

B. The human rights pillar

1. Group rights and individual rights

The operation of the second pillar is more complex. As an initial matter, in applying this pillar, we are asking how a norm that gives certain rights to certain *peoples* affects the basic human rights of *individuals*. In so doing, we may discover that granting a people a right (like the right of colonial peoples to independence) actually harms basic human rights of individuals—and not merely those outside the defined people, but those within it. We may also discover that denying a people a right (like the right of peoples within states to secede) harms basic human rights.

But the simultaneous consideration of group rights and individual rights is something that both international law and moral philosophy accept. In law, for instance, we can consider an important case concerning both rights in front of the UN Human Rights Committee, the body of experts that monitors state compliance with the International Covenant on Civil and Political Rights (ICCPR). The Committee had to consider the claim of a Canadian Maliseet Indian who lost her status as a Maliseet, and the right to live in Maliseet lands, by virtue of a Canadian law that removed such a status for women who married non-Maliseets

[30] I recognize that there is a contrast—perhaps a contradiction—between the way resistance is treated in the colonial versus secession context. In the former, the intensely felt needs of the colonial peoples are regarded as justifying a norm of decolonization for its promotion of long-term peace, but the equally intensely felt needs of the colonizers are not; in the latter, it is the intensely felt needs of the state to maintain its unity that count, while the equally intensely felt needs of the secessionist group are discounted.

(but not for men in that position), even though she later divorced her husband. Although the Canadian law was passed to respect the rights of Maliseet to control who lives in their lands, the Human Rights Committee found that the law nonetheless violated her *individual* right under the ICCPR to persons belonging to minority groups, i.e. 'the right, in community with the other members of their group, to enjoy their own culture, to profess and practise their own religion'.[31] The case shows the possibility of accepting individual human rights while appreciating the rights of groups, even if it does not mean that we need to accept the idea of group *human* rights.[32] Philosophical approaches similarly accept the possibility of group rights (even human rights), but such rights may be conceptually more difficult in terms of the proper identification of the rights-bearers or have different practical consequences compared to individual rights.[33]

2. *Protecting the human rights of new minorities*

Does the near-ban on secession, creating a highly constrained right for peoples within states, respect—in the sense of not interfere with—the basic human rights of individuals? One argument that it does concerns the effects of the creation of a new state on the basic human rights of individuals who are in a minority in that state. When new states are formed from secessions, they always take along individuals or groups who did not favor the secession, both groups who were part of the majority of the old state (those who neither fled nor were forced out) and groups who received special protection from the former state. In the hypothetical Quebec secession, these two groups would be English-speaking Canadians and indigenous peoples, respectively.

In those new states, the new majority, in an effort to assert its dominance, has often, perhaps even overwhelmingly, taken action that deleteriously affects the new minority. As Donald Horowitz has written:

> Secession or partition usually makes ethnic relations worse, because it simplifies intergroup confrontations. Simplification by secession reverses the benign complexity of states such as India or Tanzania that are fortunate enough to contain a multitude of dispersed groups, none with the power to control the others or to take possession of the state for its own ends.[34]

The result, for him, is 'lower-level ethnic tyrann[y]'.[35]

[31] ICCPR, Art. 27; Human Rights Committee, *Lovelace v Canada*, Comm. No. R.6/24, 166, UN Doc. A/36/40 (1979). The committee did not rule on the broader discrimination claim. For another case that upheld a law meant to protect group rights, see Human Rights Committee, *Kitok v Sweden*, Comm. No. 197/1985, 207, UN Doc. A/43/40 (1998).

[32] See, e.g., Jack Donnelly, *Universal Human Rights in Theory and Practice*, 2nd ed. (Ithaca, NY: Cornell University Press, 2002) 209–11, 217–18.

[33] See, e.g., Allen Buchanan, 'Liberalism and Group Rights', in Jules L. Coleman and Allen Buchanan (eds.), *In Harm's Way: Essays in Honor of Joel Feinberg* (Cambridge: Cambridge University Press, 1994) 1; Jeremy Waldron, 'Taking Group Rights Carefully', in Grant Huscroft and Paul Rishworth (eds.), *Litigating Rights: Perspectives from Domestic and International Law* (Oxford: Hart Publishing, 2002) 203.

[34] Donald L. Horowitz, 'Self-Determination: Politics, Philosophy, and Law', in Ian Shapiro and Will Kymlicka (eds.), *Ethnicity and Group Rights* (New York: New York University Press, 1997) 421, 433.

[35] Ibid., at 437.

These consequences have been recognized for centuries. During the debates over the ratification of the U.S. Constitution, James Madison wrote in the Federalist Papers: 'Extend the sphere [of a republic and] . . . you make it less probable that a majority of the whole will have a common motive to invade the rights of other citizens'.[36] The twentieth century has witnessed interference with the basic human rights of members of minorities as a result of successful secessions. Serbs in Kosovo continue to face systematic discrimination years after its separation from Serbia.[37] Hindus continue to face discrimination in Pakistan.[38] Even in the cases of the seemingly most justifiable secessions, that of Latvia from the USSR—the separation of a previously independent state from a state that was itself dissolving—some governments have enacted or tolerated a variety of legislation and other measures that discriminate against ethnic Russians.[39] It is, of course, impossible to know whether these violations of human rights are actually caused by secessions, given the many other human rights problems of some of these states. But particular discrimination seems reserved for those not in the new majority (or part of the old majority). And insofar as the near-ban on secession protects these groups, it passes the second pillar.

3. Harming the human rights of peoples facing discrimination?

But it is equally clear that the second pillar can cut the other way and is in tension with self-determination's strong aversion to secessions. For certainly we need to look at the basic human rights of those harmed *by the state from which they seek to secede*. A rule that absolutely prohibited secession and left them at the mercy of governments committed to violations of those rights would be unjust under the second pillar. Otherwise peoples must put up with the most oppressive states in the name of some strange notion of internal peace—that the peace of the oppressor is better than the disharmony of vindicating basic rights, a position that ought to be rejected just as is the peace of the conquest in an interstate conquest.

As the law now stands, the second pillar is taken into account in two places, one better than the other.

- First, international law respects the second pillar insofar as it reflects a decision that peace will need to give way to the claims of the peoples of *non-self-governing*

[36] James Madison, 'Number X', in James Madison, Alexander Hamilton, and John Jay, *The Federalist Papers*, Isaac Kramnick (ed.) (Hardmondsworth: Penguin, 1987) 127.

[37] US Department of State, Bureau of Democracy, Human Rights and Labor, 'Country Reports on Human Rights Practices for 2013: Kosovo' (2014) 30–2.

[38] US Department of State, Bureau of Democracy, Human Rights and Labor, 'Pakistan 2013 International Religious Freedom Report' (2014).

[39] See, e.g., Rights of National Minorities in Latvia, Parliamentary Assembly of the Council of Europe, Res. 1527 (2006); European Commission Against Racism and Intolerance, ECRI Report on Latvia (fourth monitoring cycle), 21 February 2012, paras. 94–99, <http://www.coe.int/t/dghl/monitoring/ecri/country-by-country/latvia/LVA-CbC-IV-2012-003-ENG.pdf>.

territories. Effectively, the law reflects a moral vision that colonialism in all its forms is such an affront to basic (and other) human rights that it must be abolished, such that the only non-self-governing peoples will be those who have chosen to be that way.[40] Colonialism fundamentally denies individuals in colonies their basic human rights insofar as it forces them to be ruled, indeed subjugated, by a state with which they have no meaningful links. In terms of the construct of basic human rights in Chapter 3, there is not even the possibility of minimal participation in governance. In creating a clear right of peoples of such territories to create their own state immediately, the second prong is indeed a trump, for even concerns about harms to peace have not been accepted as a justification for colonialism.[41]

Certainly, some individuals within states may suffer a similar fate, to which I will turn later. But in terms of granting an absolute right to independence, the line drawn between colonial peoples—nearly all of whom lived in so-called blue water colonies acquired and maintained through methods of conquest—and peoples within states is a justifiable attempt to single out the most pernicious denial of a people's right to choose its own future. The law needs to draw lines, and the line-drawing that gives these peoples the right of independence does a decent job of matching an egregious form of denial of human rights with a remedy. Yet it is decent but not perfect. One shortcoming is that the colonial peoples and indigenous peoples both suffered from conquest by settlers from far away, and yet the line gives only the former a right of independence, simply by virtue of their physical separation from the colonizing state.[42]

- Second, the law does a decent job of respecting the second pillar through a decision that the protection of human rights will outweigh the peace reflected in the territorial unity of an existing state in exceptional circumstances. Just how exceptional those circumstances must be remains subject to disagreement. As stated earlier, my reading of the law is that it effectively, albeit not explicitly, allows for secession in the event of systematic denial of representative government. In that case, it represents a just priority of respect for human rights over the dangers to peace. The rights that it respects are basic—some control over one's future—in the same sense as those at issue in the anti-colonial exception referred to previously.

With secession, the law is not operating, nor do I believe it should operate, as a trump in the same way as in the decolonization context. Rather, the practice of

[40] The motivations for Resolution 1514 are beside the point—they might well have been a political bargain between the elites in the North, sensing their loss of control over the colonies, and those in the South to transfer authority from one set of unaccountable leaders to another.

[41] These concerns also support the justice of the norm discussed in Chapter 4 under which aid to colonial movements seeking independence, unlike aid to rebel movements within a state, does not violate the ban on intervention in the internal affairs of other states.

[42] See Karen Knop, 'Statehood: Territory, People, Government', in James Crawford and Martti Koskenniemi (eds.), *The Cambridge Companion to International Law* (Cambridge: Cambridge University Press, 2012) 95, 102–4.

states in refusing to support most secessions (even if they recognize some of the resulting states afterwards) seems to reflect a consequentialist calculation of the costs of secession and the harms to basic human rights of the status quo. In other words, colonialism is analogous to intrastate violations of basic human rights in the sense that we will allow a remedy of independence in both cases, but it is unlike it in that we *automatically* grant the remedy in one case and only *conditionally* grant it in the other.

The basic human rights may, however, be doing a bit more work insofar as they provide exclusionary reasons in favor of the people seeking secession—namely, that we will not accept as a legitimate reason for the territorial unity of the state the *mere preference of the government* to keep the state together; that is a factor that will *not* be balanced against the harm to human rights from the status quo or the cost in terms of the disruption of peace. Rather, once the state has crossed the line to violating the basic human rights of its people, we will regard it as having in a sense forfeited unquestioned control of the territory and opened up a genuine conversation about the costs and benefits of secession.

But even as the norm respects the second pillar by leaving secession on the table and rejecting certain reasons to take it off the table, international law has two shortcomings. First, it does not offer the sort of definitive guidance that it provides for decolonization. In real-world situations where we need to evaluate the lawfulness of a particular attempted secession, the law may not give us a clear answer. For instance, in my view, the violations of basic human rights by the Belgrade government of the Socialist Federal Republic of Yugoslavia against individuals in the entities that became the SFRY's successor states did not rise to that level; others would insist, particularly in the case of Kosovo, that it clearly had a right to separate from Serbia.

Second, the law limits the types of human rights violations that might justify secession. If the law tolerates secession as a remedy only for discrimination based on, in the words of the Friendly Relations Declaration, 'race, creed, or color', then it might not allow for secession based on violations of the basic human rights of individuals who belong to peoples not defined along those lines—for example those defined based on ethnicity or national origin. And if international law closes off a remedy for those groups facing violations of their basic human rights, it would not pass the second pillar. Unfortunately, the ambiguous phrasing of the Declaration does not help us on this issue, and the emphasis in state attitudes against secession has not shed light on this question. In this sense, for the law to meet the test of thin justice, it needs to leave open the possibility of secessions for violations of any of the basic human rights of the group contemplating it.

Yet this modest suggestion for improvement is not meant to eliminate other constraints that the current law puts on secession. Notably, to the extent that international law tolerates secession as a residual remedy, it seems to do so only for violations of the rights of specific peoples and, in my view, of territorially concentrated peoples. Thus, if a government (a) violates the basic rights of everyone in the state, or (b) violates those rights against particular peoples who are not territorially concentrated, then secession is not tolerated. Do these effective exclusions—which I would not alter—violate the second pillar—in other words, is international law unjust as interfering with basic human rights by not permitting secessions whenever the state violates the basic human rights of its citizens? I would argue no, for the simple reason that a situation of generalized human rights violations or the violations of a non-territorially concentrated group does not lend itself to a *territorial remedy* through secession. In such situations, we have no group that is both systematically discriminated against and territorially concentrated such as to make secession feasible. To forbid secessions even in the face of gross violations of human rights not targeted at a territorially concentrated people does not violate the second pillar because the proposed solution (secession) does not address or solve the proposed problem (generalized violations of basic human rights). To hold otherwise would be like saying that it is unjust to forbid race-based affirmative action to address the imbalance between men and women entering public education.[43]

C. Other rationales for the position of international law

It is possible to endorse the position of international law by starting from very different principles. Anna Stilz has asked about the conditions under which a state has a right to territory. She develops four—the existence of a system of law on the territory, a legitimate claim for citizens to occupy the land, a legal system that rules in the name of the people, and a lack of usurpation of others' rights.[44] In describing the third criterion, she emphasizes the need for the state to protect the interests of citizens, which she equates with its providing 'minimal consideration to each member's interests by delineating a basic set of rights as a standard for state legitimacy'.[45] She does not insist on a standard of democracy to satisfy this test, but rather accepts the possibility of other, nondemocratic regimes having legitimacy if they meet 'minimal standards of political consultation and contestation'.[46] Although Stilz does not frame her theory in terms of self-determination, she ends up adopting a position quite similar to the thin notion of representative government that is the extent of the right of a people within a state to self-determination.

Daniel Philpott offers a robust defense of the idea of self-determination as a 'unique kind of democratic institution...that promotes participation and representation, the political activities of an autonomous person'.[47] He offers a series of principles that seem to lean in favor of secession for disaffected groups, allowing them the right to live with those whom they choose. He admits limitations to his

[43] It is possible to imagine situations where secession might be feasible for groups spread in several concentrated areas or even where those located outside those areas are willing to move to the new state. If the law were to foreclose such options in the event of human rights violations of those groups, it would seem to fail the second pillar.

[44] Anna Stilz, 'Nations, States, and Territory', *Ethics* 121 (2011): 572.

[45] Ibid., at 588.

[46] Ibid., at 589 n.28.

[47] Daniel Philpott, 'In Defense of Self-Determination', *Ethics* 105 (1995): 352, 358; see also Daniel Philpott, 'Should Self-Determination be Legalized?', *Terrorism and Political Violence* 12 (2000): 106, 118–19.

proposals, including the possibility that secessionist groups will prove illiberal. Yet in the end, Philpott discovers the consequentialist reasoning that grounds my defense of international law. His ultimate balancing test demands that 'the prospects for war and chaos must be weighed proportionally against the justice of self-determination and any injustice that the group has suffered. Secession . . . truly becomes a last resort; it should be endorsed only when a people would remain exposed to great cruelty if left with a weaker form of self-determination [for example autonomy within the state]', appealing to international law to endorse and institutionalize such a view.[48] Philpott's view is not identical to that of international law—notably, international law would not consider autonomy or integration a 'weaker' form of self-determination at all—but it is certainly close in its reluctance to countenance secession.

Finally, Charles Beitz has grounded self-determination in its ability to protect individual interests, promote self-government, and promote group identity (what he calls its constitutive significance). He rejects a 'maximalist view' that requires a state to be fully democratic as insufficiently deferential to diverse political cultures, as well as a 'minimalist' one, that he associates with Walzer, that leaves governance up to a people's own traditions. Instead, echoing Rawls' idea of a decent hierarchical society, Beitz favors an intermediate interpretation: 'the institutions of a self-determining state should place its members in a position to influence their own collective destiny [where] the members of the community can participate in directing the community's future in ways that do not require them to risk their lives'.[49] Although Beitz does not argue in consequentialist terms about the dangers of the more maximalist position or in terms of human rights, his ultimate stance again resembles that of international law.[50]

III. Dual Pressures on the Norm of Self-Determination

Like the ban on the use of force, the norm of self-determination faces a set of pressures for both contraction and expansion of the accompanying rights and duties. It is important to consider these alternatives a matter of thin justice.

A. Self-determination, once and only once

The negotiations among states at the UN over the wording of the Friendly Relations Declaration, though now decades old, is symptomatic of ongoing

[48] Ibid., at 382, 385.

[49] Charles R. Beitz, 'The Moral Standing of States Revisited', *Ethics & Intl Aff* 23 (2009): 325, 336–40.

[50] For a vision of self-determination based on Kantian concepts, see Jeremy Waldron, 'Two Conceptions of Self-Determination', in Samantha Besson and John Tasioulas (eds.), *The Philosophy of International Law* (Oxford: Oxford University Press, 2010) 397. Waldron sees the state 'in the first instance as a response to territorially local contestation', resulting in 'a pragmatic and generally respectful stance towards existing territorial demarcations'. Ibid., at 412.

disagreements between the developing world and Western states over the meaning of self-determination. For the former group of states, self-determination was more or less equivalent to decolonization. The result for them was a simple, binary way of looking at the claims of peoples—the peoples of independent states were enjoying the right; the people in colonies were not. For the latter set of states, self-determination of peoples did not end once they had become free of European control; it gave them ongoing participatory rights within the new state. The awkward compromise of the Declaration's paragraph on self-determination quoted earlier, in Section I, did little to end the disagreement. Thus, developing states are still far more reluctant to link the right of self-determination of peoples to a particular form of government. The organic instruments of both the African Union and its predecessor, the Organization of African Unity (OAU), as well as of the Organization of American States, do not even mention self-determination as a governing principle.[51] Many, perhaps even most, would regard the Friendly Relations Declaration's famous phrase about a government representing the whole of the people as simply a bone thrown to the North to achieve consensus—a loose caveat rather than any kind of affirmative grant of a remedy.

One small window into this perspective is the UN General Assembly's annual resolution entitled 'Universal realization of the rights of peoples to self-determination'. The resolution's text has singled out military intervention and occupation as barriers to self-determination and made no mention of the requirement of a state to adopt any sort of representative government.[52] Although the resolution has been adopted by consensus, at the 2011 General Assembly meeting where it was adopted, the EU representative distanced the EU from the content, noting that self-determination required states to hold free and fair elections and that, contrary to the resolution, self-determination was not a precondition for the enjoyment of human rights.[53] The Human Rights Council, in which the developing world has a majority of votes, has created only one so-called thematic mechanism (experts who study an issue) explicitly linked to self-determination, concerning mercenaries, refraining from linking its mechanisms on minority rights or indigenous peoples to self-determination.[54] So their emphasis continues to remain on foreign interference rather than governmental responsibilities for representative government.

At the same time, I do not wish to overstate the distinction between North and South. Northern states have certainly tolerated, through diplomatic and military support, numerous regimes in the South with unrepresentative governments. These include in particular ex-colonies (think of France's in Africa), but also military

[51] Charter of the Organization of African Unity, 13 September 1963, Art. III, 479 UNTS 39; Constitutive Act of the African Union, 1 July 2000, Art. 4, OAU Doc. CAB/LEG/23.15; Charter of the Organization of American States, 13 December 1951, Art. 3, 119 UNTS 3.

[52] See, e.g., GA Res. 68/153 (15 January 2014), paras. 1–3.

[53] Press Release, General Assembly, 'Draft Text Approved by Third Committee Recognizes Youth as "Key Agents for Social Change"', UN Press Release GA/SHC/4027 (8 November 2011).

[54] Compare HRC Res. 7/21 (28 March 2008) (mercenaries), with HRC Res. 16/6 (8 April 2011) (minority rights) and HRC Res. 6/12 (28 September 2007) (indigenous people's rights).

allies from both the Cold War period and beyond. And the EU's Fact-Finding Mission to Georgia, which examined the secessionist conflicts and Russian intervention there, has come quite close to saying that secession, even in response to human rights violations, is simply illegal.[55] Moreover, Southern states have moved away, in both rhetoric and action, from a refusal to peer into the representative nature of a state's governments. Notably, both the Organization of American States and the African Union have authoritatively denounced extra-constitutional governmental change;[56] and indeed they have strongly condemned specific coups or endorsed constitutionally elected leaders facing threats to their rule, including in Haiti (1991), Honduras (2009), Guinea (2008), Niger (2010), Côte d'Ivoire (2010), and Guinea-Bissau (2012).[57] Regardless of the size of the gap between the North and South over their willingness to challenge governments for lacking a representative or participatory form of government, they might well jointly agree that, as a matter of a remedy for unrepresentative governments, secession remains illegal. In other words, my interpretation of the ambit of the Friendly Relations Declaration that leaves open the possibility of some legal secessions may still be too generous toward secessions.[58]

This alternative interpretation of the norm—as a flat-out ban on secessions—passes the first pillar as a sort of a fortiori case compared to the interpretation of the norm I have offered previously. But of course it raises significant difficulties under the second pillar. One might argue that international law does not necessarily fail the tests of justice by subverting the claims of basic human rights of oppressed peoples because international law is not just composed of norms of self-determination—it includes manifold other norms that protect the basic human rights of oppressed peoples—most notably human rights law. So a narrow view of self-determination is not a recipe for ignoring the rights of peoples within states.

Yet the better argument would focus on the absolute ban as denying one remedy to those peoples facing violations of their basic human rights—the creation of their own state. And the denial of this remedy is significant—for in my view, a just international law, even a thinly just one, needs to preserve exceptional policy options for exceptional threats to one of the pillars of global justice. And if human rights law fails and secession is the only way to protect a people from flagrant

[55] EU Fact-Finding Mission Report, *supra* note 25, at 141 ('self-determination is basically limited to internal self-determination. A right to external self-determination in form of a secession is not accepted in state practice').

[56] See, e.g., Representative Democracy, OAS AG/Res. 1080 (XXI-O/91) (5 June 1991); Constitutive Act of the African Union, Arts. 4(p), 30, *supra* note 51. For a recent action in the Americas, see Suspension of the Right of Honduras to Participate in the Organization of American States, OAS AG/RES. 2 (XXXVII-E/09) (4 July 2009) (suspending Honduras' membership after ouster of elected president).

[57] See, e.g, Ernest Harsch, 'Africa Defends Democratic rule: "Zero Tolerance" for Coups, Constitutional Violations', *Africa Renewal Online*, <http://www.un.org/africarenewal/magazine/april-2010/africa-defends-democratic-rule>.

[58] For an endorsement of the more conservative view, see Report of the Fact-Finding Mission, *supra* note 25, at 138–41.

abuses, the absolutist position, advocated most strongly by states in the global South, becomes morally indefensible under the second pillar of thin justice. It fails whether that second pillar is viewed in terms of consequences, trumps, or exclusionary reasons.

As noted earlier, I recognize the difficulties of the alternative, and indeed sometimes the advantages to what Thomas Franck has called 'an idiot rule'.[59] For we may not know in a given instance of flagrant abuses whether we have reached the point of no return. As noted, it is far from clear that any of the secessions tolerated to date—some under Western pressures, like Kosovo and South Sudan—respond to those sorts of abuses or simply a frustration by one side with sharing a state with the other. And Crimea's secession from Ukraine was clearly aided, indeed instigated, by Russia. But the position of international law, with a modest modification, at least provides a framework for navigating the dilemmas inherent in secessions instead of denying them or wishing them away. As Robert Goodin said of utilitarianism generally: 'It tells us what sorts of considerations ought to weigh with us, often while allowing that how heavily each of them actually weighs is legitimately open to dispute.'[60] International law cannot operate with norms whose complexity exceeds the competence of readily available institutions.[61] But we cannot insist on simplicity at the expense of thin justice. The complete denial of separation after post-colonial independence sacrifices that justice.

B. Communitarian and cosmopolitan alternatives

The existing norm has also faced criticism from the opposite direction—for not allowing enough secessions. (The decolonization part of the norm is not generally criticized.) Pressure for a more permissive norm of self-determination has come from a variety of settings. The legal and political case is often made by separatist groups themselves, who insist that their grievances must be addressed through separation. The forum for their claims might be the battlefield, as witnessed in the secession of Bangladesh and Eritrea and the failed attempts of South Ossetia and Chechnya. Others have pursued their claims primarily through political negotiations, such as those that led to the referenda and eventual independence of Montenegro and South Sudan. And rarely, international courts have opined on secession questions, as with the advisory opinions of the International Court of Justice (ICJ) on the status of Western Sahara and the declaration of independence of Kosovo.[62] Some groups making broader claims have joined an NGO, the Unrepresented Nations and Peoples Organization (UNPO); while the organization insists that self-determination

[59] Thomas M. Franck, *The Power of Legitimacy Among Nations* (New York: Oxford University Press, 1990) 67–77.

[60] Goodin, *Utilitarianism as a Public Philosophy, supra* note 29, at 21.

[61] Yet international law has many complex norms implemented by sophisticated international institutions, e.g. in telecommunications, aviation, trade, and transportation.

[62] See *Western Sahara* [1975] ICJ Rep 12 (Advisory Opinion of 16 October); *Kosovo Advisory Opinion, supra* note 20.

encompasses a wide variety of options for its members, it notes that some of those members insist on full independence.[63]

For my purposes here, I want to focus on the claims from philosophical circles both because they are often carefully argued and because they explicitly call for a revision of the state of international law—a position that is quite risky, indeed counterproductive, politically for a group seeking independence under the rules as we have them. Philosophers do not need to worry about the political consequences of revising international law, and, as a result, their approaches to self-determination often begin with a completely different definition of the *problematique* compared to legal approaches.

Consider, for instance, Avishai Margalit and Joseph Raz's framing of the question:

> The core content of the claim to be examined is that there is a right to determine whether a certain territory shall become, or remain, a separate state (and possibly whether it should enjoy autonomy within a larger state). [But] the idea of national self-determination or... the idea of self-government encompasses much more. [Its] value is the value of entrusting the general political power over a group and its members to the group.[64]

By emphasizing separate statehood as the core problem, they shift their focus from the emphasis in international law that peoples should normally enjoy self-determination within existing states. This may simply be a case of the difference between ideal theory and non-ideal theory, or perhaps of scholars identifying the hardest moral question among the issues relevant to self-determination; but the result is that much philosophical discourse downplays the other forms of self-determination, including the alternatives to secession for disaffected peoples within states.

Those philosophical approaches that evince such an openness to secession have serious flaws as a matter of thin justice. These proposals might pass muster under a different standard of justice, but in neglecting to consider the pillars of thin justice, they pose serious dangers compared to the international law rule.

1. *Downplaying the violent consequences of secessions*

In an approach typical of much ethical thinking on self-determination, Margalit and Raz devote considerable attention to the moral grounds for a people to assert control over territory, but then only offhandedly suggest that the ensuing right might be conditional on consequentialist grounds. Thus, in deriving a theory that groups are in the best position to judge whether they need self-government, and that their decisions taken in good faith should be accepted, they simply note that the exercise of the right is conditioned on the group's respect for the basic rights of its inhabitants and that measures should be taken to protect other states

[63] UNPO Principles, 'Unrepresented Nations and Peoples Organization' <http://www.unpo.org>.
[64] Avishai Margalit and Joseph Raz, 'National Self-Determination', *J Phil* 87 (1990): 439, 440.

(by which they have in mind economic cooperation or demilitarization agreements). Such a position's tolerance for secession takes almost no account of the dangers to interstate and internal peace of secession and assumes, with little argument, that they can be rectified after the fact through new regional accords.[65] Margalit and Raz thus open the door to consequentialist considerations, but in the end they seem unwilling to give them their due.

More disconcerting is Michael Walzer's essay from 1985 in which he endorses the completion of the nationalist project through a proliferation of states, each with one nation. He drops a consequentialist claim that vindication of nationalist demands for a state 'does seem to bring, if only locally, something like the peace that the Lockeian argument promises' and that '[s]eparation, secession, partition, liberation—all for the sake of statehood—point the way to a kind of international settlement'.[66] As for the costs of the process, all we get is that '[t]he way itself is bloody enough, and there are probably cases where people from different nations are so radically entangled on the same piece of territory that a 'good border' is virtually inconceivable'.[67] Under a superficial reading of the peace pillar, it might be argued that Walzer's view passes muster insofar as the goal of his proposal is peace through satiation of nationalist desires. And if the time horizon is sufficiently long, this might be acceptable consequentialist reasoning. But a consequentialism that so highly discounts short-term harms ('the way itself is bloody enough') seems flawed methodologically. Perhaps Walzer simply underestimated how 'bloody' the 'way' would be. After the events of the 1990s, it is simply inconceivable to take this position seriously.

In a slightly different vein, David Copp also endorses a broad ex ante right of groups to their own country grounded in the democratic rights of its members. As he puts it, 'all and only societies that are relevantly "territorial" and "political" have the right of self-determination', by which he means the right to their own state.[68] By territorial, he means a society capable of controlling a distinct territory; and by political, he means one with the desire by its members, expressed democratically, to constitute a state.[69] His theory is somewhat consequentialist in considering the feasibility of a society's governance of a territory as a basis for its right to statehood, but it takes no account of the consequences of secession in terms of potential armed conflicts. When Copp proposes transforming this moral right into a legal right through an institutionalized judicial process (more on this later), he recognizes that a legal right to secession could be defeated by other

[65] Ibid., at 459–60. See the response of Horowitz, 'Self-Determination', *supra* note 34, at 444 ('nine times out of ten, the creation of a new set of minority problems [from a secession] is a "risk" that will come to pass').

[66] Michael Walzer, 'The Reform of the International System', in Øyvind Østerud (ed.), *Studies of War and Peace* (Oslo: Norwegian University Press, 1986) 227, 230–1.

[67] Ibid., at 231.

[68] David Copp, 'Democracy and Communal Self-Determination', in Robert McKim and Jeff McMahan (eds.), *The Morality of Nationalism* (New York: Oxford University Press, 1997) 277, 290.

[69] Ibid., at 292–7.

considerations, including how a particular secession might harm human rights.[70] But it still significantly underplays the harms to peace from secessions.

Christopher Wellman has adopted what he calls a hybrid model of secession that attempts to combine a liberty perspective in favor of an individual's choice of a state and a consequentialist consideration that limits the exercise of the liberty when it would produce sufficiently negative consequences. He posits that it is only 'unlimited secession into many minuscule states... which is harmful', and offers the following position:

> [T]he case for liberty is defeated only in those circumstances in which its exercise would lead to harmful conditions. And because harmful conditions would occur in only those cases in which either the seceding region or the remainder state is unable to perform its political function of protecting rights, secession is permissible in any case in which this peril would be avoided. Therefore we can conclude that *any* group may secede as long as it and its remainder state are large, wealthy, cohesive, and geographically contiguous enough to form a government that effectively performs the functions necessary to create a secure political environment.[71]

Like Copp's proposal, Wellman's offers a highly constrained consequentialist calculation, downplaying many if not most of the key costs of secessions: violence during the process, the creation of new barriers to personal and economic discourse, and the other factors noted earlier. The only calculus that seems to matter is whether the new state or the remnant is unable to protect the rights of residents and a 'secure political environment'.

Proposals such as these express an unduly static view of how secession works. It is almost as if Wellman seeks to compare three photos: one of the pre-secession state, one of the state created by the secession, and one of the remnant, and see if people's basic security situation is just as well off in the second two as in the first. But as noted earlier, secessions or attempted secessions (beyond the peaceful dissolutions of the USSR and Czechoslovakia) do not happen this way in most cases. So for a position that starts from a cosmopolitan starting point about enhancing individual rights and autonomy, it ends up countenancing significant disruptions to peace (and human rights). They suffer from the opposite flaw of the no-secession position—whereas that ignored human rights for the sake of peace, their proposals downplay the costs to peace to advance a particular view of individual or group entitlements.

Wellman offers a partial response to this argument in his book with Andrew Altman, where they acknowledge Horowitz's views about the effects of actual secessions. But they regard them as at best an 'educated guess' that does not undercut the basic moral justification for secession.[72] In the end, those possible

[70] David Copp, 'International Law and Morality in the Theory of Secession', *J Ethics* 2 (1998): 219, 237.

[71] Christopher H. Wellman, 'A Defense of Secession and Political Self-Determination', *Phil & Pub Aff* 24 (1995): 142, 161–2.

[72] Andrew Altman and Christopher Heath Wellman, *A Liberal Theory of International Justice* (Oxford: Oxford University Press, 2009) 64.

consequences only cause them to be agnostic about a new international rule justifying secessions. This brings them slightly closer to the international law position, but there is still a significant difference from it. And that difference suffers from two flaws. First, they are wrong to call political science research simply guesses. Second, even if one were to downplay this research, their solution of agnosticism ignores what international lawyers call the Precautionary Principle, namely, that the absence of knowledge about an issue should give a decisionmaker great pause about endorsing options that could make matters worse.[73] The possibility that Horowitz and other scholars are wrong is hardly a reason to move international law away from its currently strong aversion to secession.

David Miller develops a similarly robust theory of self-determination in which he believes that societies can best govern themselves if state borders correspond to national communities, even if this means the breakup of existing states. He posited a general test that would compare an existing state's protection of minority rights with a seceding state's protection of whatever minorities end up in it; he also suggests that a seceding state might have to compensate the remnant state for a taking jointly developed economic assets with it and would not be allowed to secede if the remnant state had no chance of economic survival.[74] Although Miller takes seriously some of the consequences of secession for vulnerable entities, he both ignores a variety of other costs to the erection of new borders discussed earlier and takes no account of the costs of the *process* of secession. Like Wellman, he seems to work on a 'compare the photographs' assumption—that, if only both sides were to accept his theory, the breakup would be efficient and bloodless. Although his theory is, as he says, 'very far from licensing a separatist free-for-all',[75] it sharply discounts the costs from those very secessions that it does countenance.

One exception to this pattern is Allen Buchanan, who advocates what he calls a remedial theory of secession, to distinguish it from the primary right theory of others. Even though, like Copp and Wellman, Buchanan's account is grounded in a theory of the political legitimacy of the state, he considers consequences from the start. These include not only the bloodshed caused by secessions, but the perverse incentives to peaceful integration caused by too permissive a rule.[76] He marshals these consequentialist arguments, along with others, to rebut persuasively the theories of secession that see it as a primary right of nations.

[73] The actual principle is even stronger—namely, that absence of certainty should not delay positive measures. UN Conference on Environment and Development, Rio Declaration on Environment and Development, principle 15, UN Doc. A/CONF.151/26 (1992) ('Where there are threats of serious or irreversible damage, lack of full scientific certainty shall not be used as a reason for postponing cost-effective measures to prevent environmental degradation').

[74] David Miller, *Citizenship and National Identity* (Cambridge: Polity Press, 2000) 118–24.

[75] David Miller, *On Nationality* (Oxford: Oxford University Press, 1995) 115.

[76] See, e.g., Allen Buchanan, *Justice, Legitimacy, and Self-Determination: Moral Foundations for International Law* (Oxford: Oxford University Press, 2004) 376–82.

2. *A human right for a group to its own state?*

The foregoing alternatives to the legal rule come from different moral perspectives—some more communitarian and others more cosmopolitan. Both outlooks do, however, see the need for a right to self-determination as flowing from some sort of right of groups or individuals.[77] In a sense, their vision of justice performs three moves to the standard I have presented: it waters down the peace-based pillar in terms of consideration of those consequences; it reverses the pillars—putting rights first and consequences second; and it beefs up the new rights-based pillar by conditioning justice on granting far more than basic human rights and does so in a strong deontological form.

The contrast between the rights at the core of their vision and those in thin justice is important. They seem to be saying that there is indeed a right not merely to live with others like you, but *to form your own state with them*. I certainly see how there may be a human right to live with certain people—this would be seen in the ICCPR's recognition of the right of persons belonging to minorities 'in community with the other members of their group, to enjoy their own culture, to profess and practice their own religion, or to use their own language'.[78] It might even be the case that that right meets the definition of 'basic' according to the practice of states described in Chapter 3, akin to the freedom to practice one's religion. Certainly the ability to share cultural interactions with those of a similar background is important to many people's identity, as even cultural cosmopolitans will acknowledge.[79] Yet it is a very large step to say that that right extends to political autonomy or even independence. There is no necessary linkage between such a political remedy and the enjoyment of the human right, although there may be a contingent one—the one recognized in the international law rule.

To the extent that those opposed to the international law rule insist that justice requires recognition of a right of individuals or groups who wish to and can live together to form a state, they have clearly staked out a different standard of justice from thin justice. It is one that emphasizes the exit option for disaffected groups. Yet even if we do not look at the peace pillar, and focus, as they do, on the rights for individuals and peoples, it is very hard to say that their alternative is best as a matter of either basic human rights or the full range of human rights. As noted, the creation of a new state may well have seriously negative consequences for the basic human rights of those who did not favor creation of the state. And it is simply impossible to say that the creation of a new state to advance *one right*—the right of minorities to enjoy their culture or perhaps live with whom they choose—will overall advance the enjoyment of the *full range* of human rights. So even if

[77] Compare Margalit and Raz, 'National Self-Determination', *supra* note 64, at 456 ('The right to self-determination derives from the value of membership in encompassing groups', adding that: 'It is a group right, deriving from the value of a collective good'), with Copp, 'Democracy and Communal Self-Determination', *supra* note 68, at 292 ('Democracy requires that the members of the society be given equal authority over the decision [about statehood]').

[78] ICCPR, Art. 27. [79] I appreciate this point from Paolo Carozza.

the human rights pillar is first, and even if that extends to enjoyment of culture, and even if *that* extends to creation of a new state to practice that culture, it seems impossible to justify giving that right such a priority without consideration of the effect on the enjoyment of other human rights.

Buchanan's cosmopolitan focus on democratic legitimacy insulates itself from these criticisms insofar as he does not advocate a primary right to secede by peoples. In the end, he says he does not endorse international law's position. He identifies three grounds for secession: (1) large-scale violations of the human rights of a group; (2) unjust taking of a state's territory; and (3) serious violations of autonomy agreements attributable to the state, where secession is a remedy of last resort.[80] The second of these is part of the mainstream position insofar as the peoples of an occupied territory have a right to re-integration with their state, although ordinarily they have no right to a new state.[81]

The first and third grounds are quite close to the position of international law. The first ground focuses on violations of human rights, rather than denial of representative government. But these typically overlap; when a government systematically discriminates against a particular people, it is certainly doing both. One could, I suppose, imagine a situation where the government denies the basic human rights of a people but does not cross the line by formally denying them a representative government (for example it still allows them to participate in the legislature). One example might be Jews in Iran, who are guaranteed legislative representation but also face serious discrimination.[82] In that case, the current rule would still prevent secessions, whereas Buchanan's rule would permit secessions and be more faithful to the test I propose than international law would be.

Buchanan's third ground also overlaps significantly with international law, insofar as the persistent violation of autonomy agreements may be a marker for an unrepresentative government. Autonomy agreements are not the only way that peoples may participate in the governance of the state,[83] but Buchanan includes the important caveat that no other options short of secession are available. Thus, a state may carry out its duties by granting special rights to the affected people, although it may well prove possible to guarantee effective participation without such special rights. If truly nothing the state offers constitutes a bona fide participation in the life of the state, then Buchanan's option lines up fairly well with the position of international law.

[80] Buchanan, *Justice*, *supra* note 76, at 353–9. On the first two, see Allen Buchanan, *Secession: The Morality of Political Divorce from Fort Sumter to Lithuania and Quebec* (Boulder, CO: Westview Press, 1991).

[81] Indeed, Margalit and Raz think of this issue as outside the scope of self-determination entirely. Margalit and Raz, 'National Self-Determination', *supra* note 64, at 442.

[82] Constitution of the Islamic Republic of Iran, art. 64. However, the Jews of Iran are not territorially concentrated.

[83] See, e.g., OSCE High Commissioner on National Minorities, The Lund Recommendations on the Effective Participation of Minorities in Public Life (1999), <http://www.osce.org/hcnm/32240>.

3. *The role of institutions*

Some of the key proposals for a broader right of self-determination seem to be aware of the institutional consequences of proposing new legal norms. Thus, for instance, when Copp proposes transforming his proposed moral right into a legal right, he proposes that an impartial international body like the ICJ should adjudicate the claims of secessionist groups.[84] Wellman and Altman propose operationalizing it through a standing committee of the UN.[85] It is noteworthy that authors recognize that a legal position requires institutionalization to operate in the system of states we have.

But these and other procedural proposals are based on the idea that some impartial body can apply a philosophical test regarding the merits of the claims of a particular group, including a prediction as to whether a post-secessionist situation is likely to be worse than a presecessionist one. Yet the UN does not work in this way: political bodies make decisions based on politics; and legal bodies, even if we somehow imagine they apply the law without regard to the political origins of the judges, need a legal test. One need only imagine how, for example, the UN Human Rights Council or the ICJ would handle these tests for claims of secession. The Council, like its predecessor, the UN Commission on Human Rights, acts based on the political sympathies of the individual members. Of its forty-seven members, thirty-four are from the developing world, most of whose governments share the 'once and only once' position discussed previously, as a result of which it would almost certainly mean that no secessions would be accepted.

As for the ICJ, it would need a real legal test, not a loose notion of protection of a secure environment. And even if the test were reasonably clear, international tribunals have all sorts of ways to avoid deciding important legal issues. On the one hand, the Canadian Supreme Court was able to apply the international legal test, discussed previously, quite ably to (reject) Quebec's claims. On the other hand, when the ICJ was asked by the General Assembly 'Is the unilateral declaration of independence by the Provisional Institutions of Self-Government of Kosovo in accordance with international law?', it offered an extremely narrow opinion that merely stated that international law did not prohibit groups from issuing declarations of independence, thereby avoiding any question of the entitlement of Kosovo to statehood.[86]

To make the ICJ apply a specific legal test to a proposed secession would require either (a) a request by a political organ or agency of the UN that the Court answer a specific question through the advisory opinion process, or (b) an amendment of the Statute of the International Court of Justice (part of the UN Charter) to allow contentious claims by secessionist groups against their states. The first option would require getting the right sort of question from the same political organs

[84] Copp, 'International Law and Morality', *supra* note 70, at 238 (it is 'not clear...that my proposal is politically unrealistic').

[85] Wellman, 'A Defense of Secession', *supra* note 71, at 170; Altman and Wellman, *A Liberal Theory*, *supra* note 72.

[86] *Kosovo Advisory Opinion*, *supra* note 20.

that are so opposed to secession. The second would require an amendment of the Statute of the Court (which has never been amended), entailing the approval of two-thirds of the members of the UN General Assembly as well as the approval of the Security Council—including its permanent members, two of which, Russia and China, are unalterably opposed to secessionist claims.[87]

Whether these authors see their approaches to self-determination in terms of ideal theory or non-ideal theory, the result is a proposal that is impossible to operationalize, but that impossibility does not seem to affect the content of the proposals for a revised norm. This institutional shortcoming cannot just be wished away; it must be reflected in the content of the underlying rule to govern secessions.[88] In a sense, these proposals suffer from the opposite flaw to that of the 'idiot rule' (in Franck's terms) of banning secession completely. Just as that rule sacrifices thin justice for the sake of simplicity, the alternative rule sacrifices feasibility for the sake of a thicker notion of justice. It relies on institutions that are not equipped to implement the test they propose. This is not, however, merely a case of wishful thinking or a gap between ideals and reality. If secessionist groups seize on these proposals for self-determination at a time when international law still lacks the institutions to apply them as the philosophers would like, we are likely to be far worse off than under the status quo. If there is a horse and cart analogy here, then the institutions are the horse and the norms the cart.

The existing rule (with small modifications) with—or perhaps because of—its open textured criteria, is one that political bodies, whether states or international organizations, can invoke and discuss to evaluate self-determination claims. We cannot expect the decisionmaking process regarding claims for secession to exclude politics or political interest, but we can endorse a norm that channels the discussion toward—even if it does not always achieve—a more objective, nuanced appraisal of the lawfulness of a particular secession.[89]

IV. Self-Determination and Borders

Both international law and ethics recognize that the claims of people for self-determination must be appraised and decided in conjunction with the borders of states. Peoples may have the right of self-determination, and in some cases those rights allow for the creation of new states, but we still need norms that specify the boundaries of the states that result from that process. Although conceptually we might simply think of the resulting territory as whatever in some sense belonged to the people, international law has addressed this question through a separate

[87] ICJ Statute, Art. 69; UN Charter, Art. 108. Russia presumably sees Crimea as falling into a different category.

[88] Buchanan's remedial approach, discussed earlier, is significant in that he acknowledges the institutional dimensions of a theory of self-determination up front. Buchanan, *Justice, supra* note 76, at 346–7.

[89] At the same time, that decisionmaking process will need some basic rules for participation by the relevant actors, an issue discussed in particular in Chapters 6 and 7.

norm. That norm, principally developed through customary international law, is the doctrine of *uti possidetis*.

A. *Uti possidetis* and the retention of colonial boundaries

During the decolonization of Latin America in the early nineteenth century and of Africa and Asia in the mid-twentieth century, the colonial powers and those to whom they ceded power made determinations of boundaries according to the principle of *uti possidetis*—a default rule under which new states inherit their colonial-era borders.[90] This rule applied to borders dividing colonies of different empires—for example the border between Brazil and Colombia was that between the Portuguese and Spanish empires, and that between Ghana and Togo was the UK–French imperial border—as well as those dividing administrative units within one empire—for example Guatemala and El Salvador inherited Spanish imperial internal borders just as Burkina Faso and Mali inherited those within French West Africa. Over time, *uti possidetis* has generally been accepted as a customary law norm that governed the decolonization process wherever it happened.

Effectively, it meant that the colonial people entitled to independence was the people living on a *colonially defined territory*, not a people defined exclusively in terms of ethnic identity, tribal loyalty, or other forms of self-identification. As a result, most new states, whether emerging in the nineteenth or twentieth centuries, inherited their colonial borders without alteration. The doctrine appears in numerous constitutions in Latin America, was subtly endorsed by the UN General Assembly in 1960, and became official policy of the OAU in a famous resolution in 1964.[91] In a dispute between two former French colonies, Burkina Faso and Mali, on the location of their border, the ICJ stated—although only in dicta—that *uti possidetis* is a 'general principle' and a 'rule of general scope' in the case of decolonization.[92] The acceptance of this principle by African governments (or at least most of them) has hardly eliminated disputes among them over borders, but it has represented a starting point for the settlement of many of them.[93]

Nonetheless, the rule is only a default rule, in that in some cases the colonial power(s) or another decisionmaker, such as the UN, determined otherwise, by

[90] The doctrine originated in Roman law, as an edict that, in the case of property disputes, generally granted provisional possession to the possessor during the litigation; it was summarized in the phrase *Uti possidetis, ita possideatis:* 'As you possess, so may you possess'. W.W. Buckland, *A Text-book of Roman Law: from Augustus to Justinian* (Cambridge: Cambridge University Press, 1923; 3rd. ed. as revised by Peter Stein, 1963) 734; John Bassett Moore, *Costa Rica-Panama Arbitration: Memorandum on Uti Possidetis* (Rosslyn, VA: Commonwealth Co., 1913) 5–8.

[91] GA Res. 1514, *supra* note 2, paras. 4, 6; OAU Res. AHG/Res.16(I) (Resolution on Border Disputes) (1964), <http://www.au.int/en/decisions/assembly>; see also Saadia Touval, 'The Organization of African Unity and African Borders', *Intl Org* 21 (1967):102.

[92] *Frontier Dispute* (*Burkina Faso v Mali)* [1986] ICJ Rep 554, 565 (22 December). The statement is only dicta as both parties to the case had agreed to apply the principle to their border dispute.

[93] See Celestine Oyom Bassey, 'Territorial imperatives and border problems in Africa', in Celestine Bassey and Oshita O. Oshita, *Governance and Border Security in Africa* (Lagos: Malthouse Press, 2010) 13.

combining or splitting some territories. Thus, some states emerged from colonial rule with other than their preindependence borders, or single colonies were split at independence; these include India and Pakistan, Togo, Cameroon, and Somalia.[94] Moreover, *uti possidetis* also does not bar post-independence changes in borders or even dissolutions carried out by agreement, as took place with the federations of Mali or Malaysia shortly after independence in the 1960s (leading to the independence of Senegal and Singapore, respectively) and Yugoslavia and the USSR later. Thus, *uti possidetis* is agnostic on whether or not secessions or breakups should occur and is not simply the legal embodiment of a policy condemning them.

Assuming *uti possidetis* is a rule of customary law for the decolonization situation, it is more unsettled legally whether it applies to the borders of entities emerging not from decolonization but through secession or dissolution. On the one hand, in the cases of the separation of Senegal from the Mali Federation, and Singapore from Malaysia, and Eritrea from Ethiopia, the new international border was basically the administrative border within the prior state (in the case of the first two) or the inter-imperial border (in the case of the third).[95]

When Yugoslavia's republics began to declare their independence in 1991, European states and states on the Security Council quickly endorsed the idea that the internal frontiers of the Socialist Federal Republic of Yugoslavia (some of which dated back to Austro-Hungarian times and others of which were set after World War I) could not be altered by the use of force. In essence, they determined that, if Yugoslavia were indeed to dissolve, the only predictable way would be along the lines of the republics.[96] In January 1992, a European Community arbitration commission, created as part of the Yugoslavia peace process, endorsed the applicability of *uti possidetis* to breakups even outside decolonization.[97] Although Serbs sought to enlarge their areas through conquests in Bosnia and Croatia, the final international borders after the war did indeed conform to the inter-republican lines, although Serbs in Bosnia received a quasi-independent republic in the deal. Until Russia's moves on Ukraine in 2014, most of the post-Soviet states also agreed to retain the administrative borders of the USSR, despite their complex history, which was as much about dividing ethnic groups as uniting them.[98] Czechoslovakia split along the lines of the historical

[94] For an account of Britain's line-drawing between India and Pakistan, see Yasmin Khan, *The Great Partition: The Making of India and Pakistan* (New Haven, CT: Yale University Press, 2007) 122–7.

[95] See, e.g., Ian Brownlie, *African Boundaries: A Legal and Diplomatic Encyclopaedia* (London: C. Hurst & Co., 1979) 423; Agreement Between the Government of the Federal Democratic Republic of Ethiopia and the Government of the State of Eritrea, 12 December 2000, Art. 4(2), <http://www.pca-cpa.org>.

[96] See Marc Weller, 'The International Response to the Dissolution of the Socialist Federal Republic of Yugoslavia', *AJIL* 86 (1992): 569, 574–82.

[97] See Opinion No. 3 of the Arbitration Commission of the Peace Conference on Yugoslavia, 11 January 1992, 31 ILM 1499.

[98] Charter of the Commonwealth of Independent States, 22 June 1993, Art. 3, 34 ILM 1279, 1283 (1995).

Moravian-Hungarian border, even though, during World War II, the Germans used this line as an international frontier between the so-called protectorate of Bohemia and Moravia and the 'independent' state of Slovakia.[99]

On the other hand, it is not clear whether such borders were accepted by the parties as a matter of law, policy, or simply inevitability under the circumstances. The opinion of the Yugoslavia commission ignored the significant differences between the decolonization situation and the secession situation; state attitudes are unclear; and the ICJ has yet to rule on this issue.[100] Colonial borders and internal boundaries served very different purposes and their retention after the creation of new states has quite different consequences, all of which counsel against an easy transposition of the norm from one situation to the next. Crimea's separation from Ukraine and integration into Russia suggests that Russia is no longer attached to its 1991 borders.

An appraisal of the thin justice of *uti possidetis* is distinct from, though related to, that of the justice of the basic norms of self-determination. We are no longer asking about the justice of the norms regarding separation per se, but about the justice of a rule that defines the borders of the entities that result from separation—even if those entities are created in violation of the norms regarding separation. Thus, even if the people inhabiting the French colony of Ivory Coast have a clear right to statehood under the norm of self-determination for colonial peoples, it is an open question as a matter of international justice whether the resulting state—Côte d'Ivoire—must conform exactly to the boundaries of the colonial unit. Certainly there would seem to be a claim that some people living just on the other side of the border (for example in Upper Volta, now Burkina Faso) who identify themselves with Côte d'Ivoire ought to be included—along with the land on which they live—in the new state. So *uti possidetis* gets to a deeper question within the norm of self-determination—how do we precisely define the territory associated with a particular colonial people, or, in the case of those seeking secession, with a particular people within a state?

B. The justice of *uti possidetis* during decolonization

Historically, the motivation of states in applying *uti possidetis* to decolonization is fairly clear—although to reiterate a point from Chapter 3, the morality or justice of the rule is a distinct question from the motivation for it. For Latin America, it was to avoid the possibility that uninhabited areas within a colonial unit might be considered *terra nullius*—empty land—that would encourage other imperial powers to occupy them. By making new states with old borders, all land would

[99] Susan Greenberg, 'Borderline Case: Czechoslovakia's Old Internal Frontiers are being Revived', *The Guardian*, 20 October 1992, 21; Jirí Malenovsky, 'Problèmes juridiques liés à la partition de la Tchécoslovaquie', *Ann Fr Droit Intl* 39 (1993): 305, 328.

[100] Compare Steven R. Ratner, 'Drawing a Better Line: *Uti Possidetis* and the Borders of New States'. *AJIL* 90 (1996): 590, with Malcolm N. Shaw, 'The Heritage of States: The Principle of *Uti Possidetis Juris* Today', *BYBIL* 67 (1996): 1.

belong to one or another of the new states. And it lessened the possibility of conflicts among the new Latin American states.

In Africa after World War II, the choice for those seeking independence and those with the power to grant it was clear: either a wholesale restructuring of borders to rectify the boundaries drawn by the European powers with little regard for the wishes of the population, or an acceptance of existing lines as the basis for new states. Pan-Africanists urged the former; but the European states and the indigenous elites opted for maintaining extant lines as the most feasible method for speedy decolonization. Such a policy served an external and an internal purpose: externally, to prevent irredentist tendencies by neighbors from turning into territorial claims and the possible use of force; and internally, to give clear notice to ethnic minorities that secession or adjustment of borders was not an option. Border wars proved the exception, as African states either affirmatively settled their border disputes or simply did not push their claims. Internally, for a generation African leaders firmly rejected secession attempts on the continent.[101]

1. *The peace pillar*

As a matter of preservation of internal and interstate peace, *uti possidetis* represented a clear demonstration by colonial and local elites that decolonization should take place in a manner that would be least likely to lead to armed conflict. That is, even as states were willing to promote human rights over the order of the colonial oppressor by endorsing the creation of new states from empires, they were demonstrating a profound preference for peace during the process. *Uti possidetis* meant that colonial and local elites knew, more or less, what the maps of Africa and Asia would look like before the process began. This agreement on the appropriate territorial unit of self-determination eliminated that aspect of decolonization most likely to lead to continental—or intercontinental—conflict and validates *uti possidetis* under the pillar of peace. In theory, elites in the metropole and colonies could have delayed decolonization to work out some kind of new settlement of borders that better mapped onto the allegiances of different groups within Africa and Asia, but there was no certainty that this would have worked out; indeed, further delay might simply have created more violence than actually took place.

Yet *uti possidetis* did not prevent all conflicts between and within post-colonial states. Latin America experienced a variety of border conflicts in the nineteenth and twentieth centuries. In the years immediately following decolonization, Africa witnessed the attempted secession of Katanga (Congo) and Biafra (Nigeria), as well as interstate conflicts between Ethiopia and Somalia over the Ogaden region of Somalia; with even more secessionist and interstate conflict to follow after the end of the Cold War in Sudan, Ethiopia, Congo, and elsewhere.[102] Empirical

[101] See Ratner, 'Drawing a Better Line', *supra* note 100, at 593–6.

[102] See generally Francis Nguendi Ikome, 'Africa's International Borders as Potential Sources of Conflict and Future Threats to Peace and Security', Institute for Security Studies Paper 223, 30 May 2012.

research has suggested that colonial-era boundaries are more unstable than those not drawn by colonial powers,[103] though these findings do not suggest that matters would have been better had a different path been taken. Yet it remains the case that the bulk of both continents, and Asia as well, did not experience border-related wars or secessionist movements (even though some, like Angola and Mozambique in Africa, were wrought by civil wars fueled by the superpowers).[104] In light of the uncertainty and significant potential for violence in the alternatives, the choice to rely on *uti possidetis* satisfies—with some caveats—the first pillar.

2. *The human rights pillar*

Appraisal of *uti possidetis* under the human rights pillar is more complex. The strongest argument in favor of the norm is that, by making the borders clear and decolonization easier, *uti possidetis* facilitated the end, or at least significant amelioration, of the gross violations of human rights experienced by colonial peoples. It put most African and Asian peoples at least one step closer to full enjoyment of those basic human rights, including that of a minimally representative government. Decolonization through *uti possidetis* thus prevented the perfect from being the enemy of the good. In that sense, it passed the second pillar of global justice insofar as it did not merely respect (not interfere with) basic human rights, but actually promoted them. The doctrine did not grant every individual his or her preference for where to live, but it did not cross the line to violating their fundamental rights. The rule meets a consequentialist version of human rights by promoting a state of affairs in which basic human rights are, in the aggregate, not only not harmed, but are significantly improved.

Yet it is also true that *uti possidetis* certainly meant that some groups and individuals ended up on the 'wrong' side of the border after decolonization, and some of them faced quite severe discrimination after the colonial breakups. Even though relatively few responded with secessionist movements, ethnic groups have faced systematic denial of their basic human rights in places from Nigeria to Kenya. Some groups faced more discrimination as a minority in a new state than they faced from the colonial administration, for example Tutsis in Rwanda (although they certainly were not regarded as equals by their Belgian colonizers).[105] Although

[103] Paul R. Hensel, Michael E. Allison, and Ahmed Khanani, 'The Colonial Legacy and Border Stability: *Uti Possidetis* and Territorial Claims in the Americas', Paper presented at the Annual Meeting of International Studies Association, Montreal, Canada, 17 March 2004, <http://www.paulhensel.org/Research/io05.pdf>.

[104] For the difference between West Africa and the Horn of Africa, see Markus Kornprobst, 'The management of border disputes in African regional sub-systems: comparing West Africa and the Horn of Africa', *Journal of Modern African Studies* 40 (2002): 369.

[105] Elizabeth Neuffer, *The Key to My Neighbor's House: Seeking Justice in Bosnia and Rwanda* (New York: Picador USA, 2001) 86–90.

not all of these violations could be remedied simply by a revision of the border, some of them probably could be. To the extent that *uti possidetis* creates a default rule against such changes, it arguably does not pass the second pillar if one moves beyond a purely consequentialist reading that compares the overall respect for human rights during the colonial period with that afterwards, or that compares the costs in terms of violations of basic human rights to the benefits of lack of armed conflict.

It might be tempting to condemn *uti possidetis* as applied during decolonization as unjust for violating basic human rights, but the rule can be defended on two grounds. First, even though some post-colonial minorities experienced new discrimination, it does not seem that the protection of the human rights of those minorities should play a trumping role vis-à-vis the first pillar if the result is a delay in decolonization. For colonialism itself was so degrading of human rights that there was a moral imperative to end it. Indeed, what we really have here is a clash of two duties—to end the evils of colonialism and to protect the basic human rights of resulting minorities. In this particular case, even if we choose to apply the second pillar in deontological terms, the former duty should prevail. The human rights of the minorities may well provide some exclusionary reasons regarding borders—for example that the wishes of the elites in the new state are not enough alone to justify retention of the border—but they should not go so far as to prevent or delay decolonization.

Yet even this defense has its limits, for at a certain point it may well be that the protection of the human rights of those on the wrong side of the border needs to be a trump: if *uti possidetis* would result in the most serious of violations—for example genocide or crimes against humanity—against those groups, and where a border rectification would avoid such a prospect. In that sense, even in the decolonization context, a norm that automatically presumes inheritance of colonial borders if the clear result would be genocide is deeply problematic as a matter of even thin justice.

A second defense would turn to the values at the time of decolonization. *Uti possidetis* did not ignore the second pillar because the discrimination faced by certain groups in their new state was not part of our sense of harming basic human rights. That might well mean that judged retrospectively, *uti possidetis* failed the second pillar. And it certainly would mean that for the handful of decolonization problems left today, we should be wary of applying *uti possidetis* if the likely result is a violation of the basic human rights of individuals in a group on the wrong side of the border. This defense raises a number of questions about applying contemporary ethical norms, including our views on human rights, retroactively, that are beyond the scope of this book. But it seems plausible in some situations to consider the attitudes at the time a norm develops and is deployed in appraising its justice—although clearly this must be done with care so as not to excuse serious violations of human rights in the name of a sort of historical relativism.

C. *Uti possidetis* during secessions and dissolutions

The extension of *uti possidetis* to internal boundaries raises concerns of thin justice beyond those in the decolonization situation.

1. *Considerations of peace*

With respect to the first pillar, there is a decent argument that *uti possidetis* promotes peace during state breakups for the same reason it does in the decolonization context.[106] In both cases, the certainty of the location of a new border will, it is assumed, prevent actors during secessions and dissolutions from trying to change it forcibly. With the benefit of experience, there is support for this view with respect to some of the borders resulting from recent secessions, in the Czech and Slovak cases, some of the former Yugoslavia cases (for example between Slovenia and Croatia or Serbia and Macedonia), and most of the former Soviet cases. These separations and others took place with clear borders and no little or no armed conflict.

Yet the empirical data is hardly uniform. The decision by elites to define the borders of post-secessionist or post-dissolution states based on *uti possidetis* did not prevent wars over borders between Ethiopia and Eritrea; Sudan and South Sudan; among Bosnia, Serbia, and Croatia; between Armenia and Azerbaijan (and within the latter) over the ethnic Armenian enclave Nagorno-Karabakh in Azerbaijan; between Russia and Moldova over the desire of ethnic Russians in Transdneistria to remain in Russia; and between Russia and Georgia (and within the latter) over the desire of majorities in South Ossetia and Abkhazia to leave Georgia. The 1991 border between Ukraine and Russia, defined based on the USSR's inter-republican border, was not respected in 2014 when self-identified Russians in Crimea saw an opportunity to join Russia. So the extent to which *uti possidetis* promotes international and interstate peace seems at least a bit more questionable in the secession context compared to the decolonization context.

The Yugoslavia case is particularly telling. Although, as stated earlier, both the UN Security Council and the European arbitration commission insisted on transformation of the inter-republican lines into international borders, Serbs (in Bosnia and Croatia) and Croats (in Bosnia) sought new borders that would reflect the distribution of populations within the territories. As David Owen, one of the key European negotiators attempting to manage Yugoslavia's dissolution put it: 'The refusal to make [Yugoslavia's internal] borders negotiable greatly hampered the EC's attempt at crisis management...and subsequently put all peacemaking...within a straitjacket that greatly inhibited compromises'.[107] Although the tactics used by the Serbs and Croats to further their goals of border

[106] See, e.g., Shaw, 'The Heritage of States', *supra* note 100.

[107] David Owen, *Balkan Odyssey* (New York: Harcourt Brace & Co., 1995) 33; Thomas Ambrosio, *Irredentism: Ethnic Conflict and International Politics* (Westport, CT: Praeger Publishers, 2001) 44–6.

revision amounted to ethnic cleansing, war crimes, and crimes against humanity, outsiders' insistence on preserving those borders may well have contributed to the disaster. For example, after ethnic Serbs in the Krajina region of Croatia took control in 1991 of the area from Croatia's government, led by the virulent nationalist Franjo Tuđjman, Croatia eventually responded with an offensive that expelled approximately 200,000 Serbs into Serbia, an outcome that might well have been avoided through earlier border revision.

Defenders of *uti possidetis* have two good responses. First, it may well be the case that these wars would have erupted even if different borders had been adopted, or that *uti possidetis* prevented worse wars from taking place. In Yugoslavia, for instance, perhaps Owen was wrong and the Serbs in Bosnia would have fought just as hard to control territory even if the border question had been officially on the table. This is hard to dispute and may even give the nod to saying that *uti possidetis* passes the first pillar. Second, one could raise the same concerns here as with consequentialist arguments—that the resulting wars were wrongful responses that should not be counted in a consequentialist calculation. Indeed, that point seems particularly compelling insofar as many of the tactics used by those seeking to alter the borders were horrific, including war crimes. But to question the justice of *uti possidetis* under the first pillar on consequentialist grounds is not to endorse the tactics used. Consequentialist thinking requires that we consider the risks from endorsing a particular rule, and history has shown us the risks most vividly.[108]

2. *The pillar of human rights*

The second pillar of thin global justice counsels against endorsement of *uti possidetis* as thinly just in the context of state breakups insofar as the *automatic* transformation of internal boundaries into international ones can itself violate basic human rights. Suppose a group representing the majority of an administrative unit of a state, but a minority within the entire state, intends to split off but, during the disintegration or secession, the nascent state shows that it has no intention of granting the minorities in it a representative government. In this case, that people might receive its basic right to a representative government only by remaining within the remnants of the old state (especially if that minority was part of the majority in the old state). Even more disturbing, suppose it is likely that the group on the wrong side of the border will face severe discrimination, persecution, or worse.

In these circumstances, if we think of respect for basic human rights in consequentialist terms, retention of the internal lines in unaltered form threatens the basic human rights of the new minority, and can only be justified if it is somehow counterbalanced by an improvement in the basic human rights of the majority.

[108] See Horowitz, 'Self-Determination', *supra* note 34, at 436 ('Without further boundary change, warfare is made more likely because kindred minorities... are placed beyond the reach of their cousins across the border').

In the case of colonialism, that improvement was palpable due to the gross violations associated with colonialism; and so, in those situations, the imperative of decolonization *tout court*, with existing borders, may nonetheless enhance overall respect for basic human rights. In the case of secession, although it is possible that secession according to the administrative lines results in such a marked improvement in the basic human rights of the new majority that it outweighs the rights violations against the minority, the reverse seems at least as likely. The people may have seceded without suffering any major human rights violations in the old state; i.e. they may simply have not wanted to live with the other group or wished to assert their cultural identity in a stronger way—for instance, the Slovenes in Yugoslavia, the Trandniestrians in Moldova, and the Russians in Crimea. More importantly, it is not at all evident that, to terminate those violations and create a new state, the new majority needed to take along with it territory occupied by groups opposing the secession and then discriminate against them.

Even if *uti possidetis* passes muster under a consequentialist version of the second pillar, it still raises questions under a more robust version of that pillar. For in the case of state breakups today, in contrast to the 1940s or 1950s, the importance of respect for basic human rights is accepted through the corpus of human rights law; and since the Friendly Relations Declaration in 1970, even the individual's basic human right to some form of representative government is reflected in our understanding of the right of a people to self-determination of peoples. Today, quite simply, violations of basic human rights are less acceptable, and consequentialism is not the only way the second pillar helps us to evaluate justice.

Thus, if we wish to view the tradeoffs in terms of competing duties, in the decolonization struggle we witness a conflict of between the (very strong) duty to grant all colonial peoples a new state and the other (strong but less so) duty to respect the basic human rights of minorities in the new state. But in the case of secessions, we see a conflict between the (rather weak) duty to grant the majority group's wish to form a new state and the (much stronger) duty to protect the basic human rights of the resultant minority in the new state. Viewed in terms of exclusionary reasons, the need to respect human rights provides *more* exclusionary reasons than it did in the past. Because we care more about human rights today, we should no longer be persuaded by the costs of delays to new state formation in the way that we were with respect to decolonization. And, a fortiori, if application of *uti possidetis* leads to the worst sort of violations, for example genocide or crimes against humanity against the minority group, then we should reject *uti possidetis* in secessionist contexts as unjust.

A final concern about *uti possidetis* under the second pillar is that such a rule creates a significant hazard in the name of simplicity—namely, the temptation of ethnic separatists, sometimes with foreign encouragement, to divide the world further along administrative lines.[109] If Georgia's new borders must coincide with those of the former Georgian Soviet Socialist Republic, are not the borders of a

[109] Cf. Hurst Hannum, 'Self-Determination, Yugoslavia, and Europe: Old Wine in New Bottles?', *Transnat'l L & Contemp Probs* 3 (1993): 57, 69.

future Republic of Abkhazia, or South Ossetia, just as clearly those of the former Abkhaz Autonomous Soviet Socialist Republic, or South Ossetian Autonomous Oblast? Would the Quebecois consider secession so readily if the new state had different borders from those established by Canada and the United Kingdom for the purpose of integrating Quebec into the Dominion? Whereas the breakup of empires was a critical goal from the perspective of human rights, it remains subject to significant debate whether the secessions and dissolutions in the former Yugoslavia, the Soviet Union, Czechoslovakia, Eritrea, or South Sudan have created an overall benefit or harm to the basic human rights of the individuals living there. (This is a distinct question from the benefits of the end of the one-party rule of the Communist Party.) As Horowitz has noted, the European arbitration panel's position in favor of clear boundaries for secession units creates a disincentive against domestic devolution schemes along administrative lines—schemes that can greatly improve human rights—as central governments will see them as merely a step toward eventual secession.[110]

3. *Other critiques of post-colonial* uti possidetis

Criticism of the post-colonial application of *uti possidetis* can be made from at least two other ethical perspectives. First, from the communitarian viewpoint, when states are breaking up, the process of forging new national identities in the successor states will give the borders special significance. The international border between Croatia and Serbia, or the Czech Republic and Slovakia, is not merely legally distinct from the previous interrepublican border; the change in its status has clear consequences for the people and governments of those states. These boundaries impart what Walzer has called a 'dimension' of 'physical space' to the rights and 'common life' on each side.[111] When boundary lines assume this new significance, their location becomes even more critical. Some internal lines, especially of the inherited variety, will functionally make optimal international borders because they define a truly distinct community whose unity and identity override other concerns.

But quite often this is not the case. Groups separated by administrative lines within one state may well prove able to protect their interests through influence at the central level, but may not wish to tolerate separation into different states and the loss of that power.[112] Families and other communities separated by administrative borders face special hurdles if they find themselves in two states. Economic efficiencies or codependence taken for granted in areas separated only by internal lines may disappear when the border becomes an international frontier.

[110] Horowitz, 'Self-Determination', *supra* note 34, at 435.

[111] Michael Walzer, *Just and Unjust Wars: A Moral Argument with Historical Illustrations*, 4th ed. (New York: Basic Books, 2006) 55, 57–8.

[112] Lee C. Buchheit, *Secession: The Legitimacy of Self-Determination* (New Haven, CT: Yale University Press, 1978) 29–30.

In response, one might defend *uti possidetis* by asserting that international borders now mean less than ever, and therefore that their precise location is increasingly irrelevant. No doubt in certain parts of the world—in particular, the EU—states are reducing the significance of international borders, with clear benefits. Yet for most of the world they remain one of the defining elements of the polity. Even in Europe, porosity does not equate with irrelevance.[113] States breaking apart seem the least likely to regard the new border as irrelevant—even if secessionists claim that the new state will maintain close economic links with its neighbors.[114]

Second, from a social contract perspective, conversion of administrative lines to international lines disregards the interconnection between the internal borders and the forging or maintenance of national unity. Politicians generally do not draw internal lines with the possibility of secession in mind.[115] (If they foresaw the emergence of separate states, they might well draw the lines differently.) Thus, when the contract among the territorial units (or the people in them) or between those units and the center, or the center's master plan for unity, collapses through disintegration, why assume that one of its core elements—the location of the internal borders—must remain unchanged? Rather, this scenario calls into question the parties' original bargain or scheme premised on the continuity of the whole state. In the case of Quebec, secessionists seemingly sought to have their cake and eat it, too—to secede and take with them land given to Quebec as part of its integration into Canada.[116]

4. *A realistic alternative to* uti possidetis?

In the end, adoption of internal boundaries as the borders of new states may well advance peace without harming basic human rights in a particular situation—certainly a number of post-secessionist borders, particularly within the ex-Soviet Union, have proved stable enough, and whatever problems those states are experiencing are not due to the location of their borders. But the challenge here is to ask about the norms of international law (and not particular outcomes). On that score, it is hard to see how *uti possidetis* should be the rule in those situations where breakups occur, regardless of whether those breakups are lawful under the rules of self-determination. Such a rule might well pass muster under the peace pillar, but its implications for human rights are serious enough that its

[113] See, e.g., Stephen Castle, 'Europe Denies 2 Nations Entry to Travel Zone', *New York Times*, 22 September 2011, A15; Proposal for a Regulation of the European Parliament and of the Council on the establishment of an evaluation mechanism to verify application of the Schengen acquis, 16 November 2010, EU Doc. No. COM (2010) 624.

[114] Draft Bill, An Act Respecting the Future of Quebec, art. 3, 35th Quebec Leg., 1st Sess. (1995) (calling for agreement of economic association between future independent Quebec and Canada).

[115] Owen, *Balkan Odyssey, supra* note 107, at 34–5 (on Yugoslav interrepublican boundaries).

[116] See Grand Council of the Crees, 'Sovereign Injustice: Forcible Inclusion of the James Bay Crees and Cree Territory into a Sovereign Quebec', 207–12, Nemaska, Quebec, 1995.

endorsement, without modification, is quite questionable under the second pillar—whether in terms of promoting a state of affairs characterized by respect of basic human rights, respecting a duty we have to avoid certain gross violations of rights, or passing muster under legitimate, and not excluded reasons, for overriding human rights.

Yet a final argument remains for the defenders of *uti possidetis*, one that I have deployed elsewhere—namely, the absence of a meaningful alternative to it. If not *uti possidetis*, what rule is supposed to guide those groups seeking to separate or those outside the state who must make decisions about the secession? Our project here is to appraise rules, not individual outcomes, and I have remarked elsewhere that the law does need to draw lines (in this case, literally), even when not every outcome is justifiable under the underlying test. So, despite all the problems, it could be argued that *uti possidetis* draws the best line possible for situations of secessions and dissolutions.

But we can easily imagine a feasible alternative rule—a duty upon the parties to negotiate a new border that will both reduce the possibility of conflict and do a decent job of protecting the human rights of all the individuals involved, with no presumption at all in favor of existing administrative lines. Such a negotiation can lay the groundwork for a just separation and protection of vulnerable groups on the wrong side of the new line. As part of that process, a plebiscite may be particularly useful to ascertain the wishes of the individuals.[117] If the parties refuse to negotiate over borders, which might well be the case in the event of a breakup strongly opposed by the original state, outsiders might well insist on a provisional respect for administrative lines until the sides can be persuaded to return to the table, although that position may not be justified if a group of people on the wrong side of that administrative line face a serious threat to their existence from the separation. The result of this alternative process would be a slowing down—and ideally, a cessation—of the process of separation, an outcome that will advance international law's preference that self-determination disputes be worked out within existing states for the sake of peace.

Such a result, with stable borders, should have a great appeal to cosmopolitans. It would be in line with Onora O'Neill's calls for qualitative rather than spatial changes in interstate boundaries, rejecting the assumption that their location is unjust in favor of making them more porous.[118] In a similar vein, Toni Erskine's work on embedded cosmopolitanism emphasizes non-territorial affiliations and an individual's identification with overlapping communities,[119] connections that can be achieved within existing borders through ideas such as dual citizenship.[120]

[117] This position is endorsed in Ratner, 'Drawing a Better Line', *supra* note 100.

[118] Onora O'Neill, *Bounds of Justice* (Cambridge: Cambridge University Press, 2000) 186–202.

[119] See, e.g., Toni Erskine, '"Citizen of Nowhere" or "The Point Where Circles Intersect"? Impartialist and Embedded Cosmopolitanisms', *Rev Intl Stud* 28: (2002) 457; Toni Erskine, *Embedded Cosmopolitanism: Duties to Strangers and Enemies in a World of 'Dislocated Communities'* (Oxford: Oxford University Press, 2008) 169–80

[120] See, e.g., Peter J. Spiro, 'A New International Law of Citizenship', *AJIL* 105 (2011): 694.

V. Conclusion

We have now completed our appraisal of international law's norms of self-determination, including its subsidiary rule of *uti possidetis* on borders. The result is that, generally speaking, the two key norms of self-determination, setting forth the rights of colonial peoples and the rights of peoples within existing states, pass muster under the two pillars of thin justice. Those two rules do not harm, and indeed promote peace—in the decolonization case by endorsing the inevitable transition to independence, and in the secessionist case, by blocking the conflictual and violent consequences of secessionist movements. And those rules do a decent job of respecting basic human rights—in one case by ending the gross violations characterized by colonialism, and in the other by allowing for the possibility that exceptional situations of gross abuses will allow secessions. Yet the fit of the norm concerning secessions with thin justice leaves something to be desired, insofar as (to the extent we can even figure out exactly what it permits) it seems too limited in the sorts of rights violations that might justify secessions. Even so, the alternatives proposed for the norm on secessions fare far worse—a flat-out ban essentially ignores violations of basic human rights in the name of simplicity, and a more permissive rule significantly downplays both the costs to peace and basic human rights and the institutional incapacities of the international system.

With respect to *uti possidetis*, the decolonization form, making the borders of new states generally clear at independence, advanced peace and, by speeding up decolonization, generally improved human rights; yet to the extent that it did not contemplate border adjustments to address the threat or reality of gross violations of human rights being perpetrated against those on the wrong side of the border, it has shortcomings under the second pillar. As for its extension to cover secessions, as advocated by the European arbitration panel on Yugoslavia and some scholars, that proposed norm's contribution to peace is difficult to determine—maybe it helped avoid some armed conflict; maybe it precipitated or exacerbated conflict. But the automatic transformation of administrative boundaries fails under the second pillar for doing nothing for new minorities facing human rights violations in the new state at a time when human rights are now so central to international law.

The examples discussed demonstrate the stakes involved in the thin justice of norms of self-determination. Err too far on the side of peace, or order, and the result is the absence of an important remedy for the evils of colonialism or serious violations of human rights. Err too far on the side of individual or group preferences, whether driven by cosmopolitan or communitarian starting points, and the result is a serious threat of internal conflict and interstate wars. Indeed, in the case of self-determination, the thin justice to which its norms largely *do conform* may well be the only standard of justice to which its norms *should* conform. Unless the case can be made that (a) secessions can be undertaken peacefully; and (b) a world full of seceding states better protects the human rights of individuals compared to the status quo, an alternative rule, based on some thicker standard of justice, is likely to make things significantly worse. Ethno-nationalism has tremendous costs to human welfare, and it remains for the defenders of a norm more tolerant of secession to demonstrate the advantages in the world that we have, with the institutions we have.

6

Norms of Participation: Sovereign Equality of States

States have interests beyond gaining and maintaining sovereignty and independence. They also demand participation as full and equal players in international arenas, including in the process of making, interpreting, and applying international law. International law has responded to the claim for participation through the principle of sovereign equality of states, a bedrock concept that turns out to permeate—some would even say ground—most if not all other international norms as well. This chapter will explain the basics of the norm, appraise its justice under the framework offered in Chapter 3, and then consider proposals to change sovereign equality in key respects. The next chapter will address a crucial practical issue for participation, and one which seemingly challenges much of the idea of sovereign equality—namely, the participation of states in international organizations, and the multitude of possibilities for it envisaged and tolerated by international law and institutions.

I. Prelude to Participation: A Brief Word on the Law of Recognition

Participation, whether in an orchestra, a football league, or international affairs, begins not with the enjoyment of the privileges of membership, but with a decision by the relevant members of the group to admit an applicant. In Chapter 5, I examined the conditions under which international law allows for the *creation* of new states—it turns out they are very few. But the law on that question did not address what should happen when an entity resulting from self-determination actually seeks to play in the legal world like a full player—like a state. The views of the people of the territory that they are entitled to statehood, or that they have actually achieved it, cannot bind other states that must decide whether to treat the entity as a state.

The question of when such an entity achieves statehood—and thus when its claims will be treated as the claims of a state (whether or not they are ultimately accepted under the substantive law) is addressed by international law's rules on statehood and recognition.[1] Traditionally, international law offered a deceptively

[1] This discussion is limited to the *recognition* of an entity as a state as a prerequisite for full

simple answer to these questions. Under the 1933 Montevideo Convention, an entity was a state only if it had 'a) a permanent population; b) a defined territory; c) government; d) capacity to enter into relations with the other states'.[2] In practice, global elites have interpreted these criteria quite flexibly. As for the population, some entities treated by other states as states have very small populations, such as Nauru (9,500) or San Marino (33,000). The requirement of a defined territory has not prevented the international community from regarding as states entities with disputed or even unknown boundaries, such as Israel, the two Koreas, or the states of the Arabian peninsula. New states have emerged even without full capacity to enter into foreign relations with other states. The national defense of Liechtenstein and Monaco is the responsibility of Switzerland and France, respectively. Micronesia, Palau, the Cook Islands, and Niue are termed 'freely associated states', though their defense is controlled by the United States (for the first two) and New Zealand (for the second two).

States have been equally flexible when a state loses one of the traits listed in the Montevideo Convention. During World War II, states did not regard the occupation of most countries in Western Europe as eliminating their legal status as states; rather, such states were regarded as occupied nations.[3] Similarly, Kuwait did not lose its legal status despite Iraq's occupation from August 1990 to April 1991. During much of the Cold War, the states of Eastern Europe effectively lost their ability to conduct foreign and defense relations independent of the USSR and yet continued to be regarded as states. Today, certain states remain under the firm control of neighbors, such as Bhutan vis-à-vis India. And no state has seriously pushed to claim that the collapse of central government control in Somalia since 1991 has deprived it of statehood.

But is satisfaction of the Montevideo criteria, even if not always necessary, sufficient for statehood? In other words, is statehood purely a matter of meeting objective criteria, or does it depend upon the views of other states? Under one approach, the so-called declaratory view of recognition, recognition is a purely political act irrelevant for the legal determination of statehood. An entity that meets the criteria of statehood immediately enjoys all the rights and duties of a state regardless of the views of other states.[4] It creates a duty upon all other states to treat the entity like a state from that point onwards. The contrary position, known as the constitutive view, regards recognition as one of the elements of statehood. Thus, the refusal by states to afford recognition would mean that the entity claiming statehood would not be entitled to the rights of a state. Indeed,

participation in the international legal process. The *admission* of states to international institutions is discussed in Chapter 7. I also do not mean to suggest that participation in the process of international law is limited to states; indeed, as with peoples' claims to self-determination, international law has ways of addressing those claims as well. It also has numerous channels for non-state entities to participate in making and applying the law.

[2] Convention on the Rights and Duties of States, 26 December 1933, 165 LNTS 19.

[3] F.E. Oppenheimer, 'Governments and Authorities in Exile', *AJIL* 36 (1942): 568.

[4] See, e.g., Montevideo Convention, Art. 3 ('The political existence of the state is independent of recognition by the other states').

the fear that powerful states, for political reasons, would refuse to recognize an entity meeting the criteria of statehood and thereby cut it off from interstate relations led the Latin American states to explicitly adopt the declaratory view in the Montevideo Convention. In general, the declaratory view is generally more consistent with the practice of states, which have treated many entities meeting the criteria as states without formally recognizing them. Thus, although most Arab states have not recognized Israel, they have not, for example, ignored rules prohibiting unauthorized overflight by military aircraft.

Yet it is equally clear that the actual determination as to whether a state has met the criteria of statehood is made by other states, not some independent and wholly impartial body. Thus, if states refuse to acknowledge that an entity meets these criteria (even if it clearly does) or ignore the criteria, they might continue to treat the claimant as something less than a state. For example, a state that is unrecognized may find that its passports are not accepted by immigration authorities in other states. This lends some credence to the constitutive view.[5] In 1965, the UN Security Council, following the unilateral declaration of independence from Britain by the white-dominated minority government of Southern Rhodesia (now Zimbabwe), '[c]ondemn[ed] the usurpation of power by a racist settler minority in Southern Rhodesia and regard[ed] the declaration of independence by it as having no legal validity', even though Rhodesia met the Montevideo criteria.[6] As a result, nearly all states refused to conclude treaties with Rhodesia. Certainly Taiwan has difficulties in its international relations as a result of its non-recognition as a state by nearly all states, as does Kosovo with its recognition by only about a third of all states.[7]

On top of this, states making recognition decisions have recently added conditions to the Montevideo criteria. In late 1991, with both Yugoslavia and the Soviet Union falling apart, the European Community (EC) issued two documents expressing its position on whether it would recognize the new entities. With respect to the latter, for example, it insisted that the new states accept the soft law commitments of the Organization for Security and Co-operation in Europe regarding democracy, human rights, and guarantees for minorities; respect one another's existing borders; and accept non-proliferation obligations.[8] Indeed, an EC panel of national judges, discussed in Chapter 5, reviewed the applications of each of the states of the former Yugoslavia under the criteria, finding that most met the criteria.[9] New states such as Kosovo and South Sudan have made

[5] See Robert Jennings and Arthur Watts (eds.), *Oppenheim's International Law*, 9th ed. (Oxford: Oxford University Press, 1992) 133 ('Recognition, while declaratory of an existing fact, is constitutive in nature, at least so far as concerns relations with the recognising state').

[6] SC Res. 217 (20 November 1965).

[7] Some scholars have sought to meld the declaratory and constitutive views, asserting that the existence of a state is determined by recognition, but that outside states have a duty to recognize entities meeting the criteria of statehood. See Hersch Lauterpacht, *Recognition in International Law* (Cambridge: Cambridge University Press, 1947). Yet, as the Rhodesia case and others make clear, states do not seem to have based their recognition policies on such a duty.

[8] Declaration on the 'Guidelines on the Recognition of New States in Eastern Europe and in the Soviet Union', 16 December 1991, 31 ILM 1486–7 (1992).

[9] See the EC Commission opinions in 31 ILM 1488 (1992).

unilateral commitments to respect human rights and other key norms on the understanding that they were needed to receive recognition from outside actors.[10] Many states now seem to expect new states to meet these criteria in addition to those of the Montevideo Convention (even though those continue to be applied somewhat loosely); yet the practice has not reached the point of any kind of norm prohibiting individual states from treating an entity as a state if it does not meet these criteria.[11] Moreover, even for states supportive of the new criteria, they are not applying them retroactively to deny statehood to undemocratic states. A similar trend has also surfaced with respect to the unconstitutional replacement of democratically elected governments within states, where many states and regional organizations like the Organization of American States and the African Union now treat such governments, even if they hold effective power, as illegitimate, although they generally do not treat longstanding undemocratic governments in the same way.[12]

In terms of thin justice, the original Montevideo position, affording entities statehood once they have an effective government controlling a defined population, may have the consequence of advancing peace, but it need not. On the one hand, it ensures that distinct, self-governing territories free of foreign control will enjoy the benefits of statehood, including most importantly territorial integrity, as well as participatory rights, such as engaging in relations with other entities. If we care about interstate peace, then it makes sense to allow entities to take advantage of rules that promote peace among states as soon as they become states, and not wait until they are either recognized by other states or meet some additional criteria for participation (or both).

On the other hand, the consequences of the declaratory view are not always so positive. If we are concerned that secessions create instability and increase the risk of interstate and intrastate violence, as argued in Chapter 5, then treating an entity emerging from secession as a state as soon as its government achieves effective control over territory and population may prevent a restoration of the status quo ante that would actually enhance peace. It would also encourage future secessions elsewhere in the same way as would an extension of *uti possidetis* to these situations—'once you get control, you're a state'. Indeed, observers of the Yugoslavia war have argued that the West prematurely recognized the new states at a time when it was still possible to negotiate a devolution plan or at least a

[10] See, e.g., Kosova Declaration of Independence, 17 February 2008, <http://www.assembly-kosova.org/?cid=2,128,1635>; Transitional Constitution of the Republic of South Sudan, 2011, <http://www.sudantribune.com/IMG/pdf/The_Draft_Transitional_Constitution_of_the_ROSS2-2.pdf>.

[11] See Sean D. Murphy, 'Democratic Legitimacy and the Recognition of States and Governments', in Gregory H. Fox and Brad R. Roth (eds.), *Democratic Governance and International Law* (New York: Cambridge University Press, 2000) 123, 128.

[12] See, e.g., Representative Democracy, OAS AG/Res. 1080 (XXI-O/91) (5 June 1991), para. 1; Constitutive Act of the African Union, Art. 30, 1 July 2000, OAU Doc. CAB/LEG/23.15; Document of the Moscow Meeting of the Conference on the Human Dimension of the CSCE [Conference on Security and Cooperation in Europe], 3 October 1991, paras. 17.1–17.2, <http://www.osce.org/odihr/elections/14310>.

more peaceful dissolution.[13] Nonetheless, in some situations, secessions seem irreversible—where key actors inside the country and out have accepted that a new state will emerge, for example during decolonization, the dissolution of the Soviet Union, and the negotiated separations of Montenegro and South Sudan. In these cases, a norm that requires all states to treat such entities as states immediately upon achievement of the Montevideo criteria advances peace (although clearly the acceptance by the relevant external actors is the most important factor in keeping these secessions peaceful).

Yet the second pillar of thin justice still looms. If the new entity is seriously violating the rights of some of its inhabitants, a rule that demands treating it as a state will advance peace in a way that could undermine their basic human rights. If the prior entity was not violating those rights, then acceptance of the new state clearly makes matters worse for the population. If the prior entity was also violating those rights, the Montevideo rule still results in a sort of seal of approval to continued violations by the new state. In either case, but particularly the former, a rule granting the new entity the benefits of statehood simply by virtue of meeting the four Montevideo criteria is unjust for its failure to pass muster under the second pillar.

This shortcoming of the Montevideo formula provides strong ethical support for—and indeed probably actually explains—the decision of the EC (now the EU) to add additional criteria to its decisions regarding recognition, as well as the move in state expectations regarding the independence of South Sudan, Montenegro, and Kosovo. In other words, as with the example in Chapter 4 regarding the extraterritorial application of criminal law, we witness a *thickening* in the justice of the norms of international law. The law's position of accepting statehood based on effective control alone has adjusted such that it now does a decent job of addressing the human rights pillar, insofar as entities unwilling to commit to certain basic norms of human rights law do not automatically receive the privileges of statehood. I say it does a decent job because the emerging position does not, it seems, require those claimants to statehood to actually *respect* basic human rights, but only to *commit to* doing so up front. (No state has ever reversed its recognition of a state that later breached its pre-recognition human rights commitments.) But it is nonetheless an important change in the law that addresses shortcomings under the second pillar.

The resultant change in the law hews, again decently, to the mitigation strategy set out in Chapter 3—if a norm is unjust under one of the pillars, it must be adjusted so that it can pass muster under that pillar with minimal damage to the other. In this case, the EC criteria take human rights into account without making recognition so hard that the new rule no longer promotes peace. In the case of the former Yugoslavia, the EC panel of judges considering the

[13] Misha Glenny, *The Fall of Yugoslavia: The Third Balkan War* (New York: Penguin Books, 1993) 188–92, 235–8.

applications found that all but Bosnia met the criteria for recognition, in that Bosnia lacked the support of its Serb minority; and the EC recognized all the states of the former Soviet Union as well. (The EC's members went on to recognize Bosnia nonetheless, in the vain hope that recognition would contain the violence; whereas they refused to recognize Macedonia solely due to the political opposition of Greece.)

For cosmopolitans for whom a state's lack of respect for human rights should open it up for military intervention, this emerging expectation on the criteria for statehood might seem as nothing more than an unsatisfactory halfway house, one that privileges existing states and makes only a marginal difference by addressing the handful of new states on the map. For it means that an existing state like China or North Korea can continue to violate the most basic of human rights and still continue to be regarded as a state and thus a full participant in international intercourse. For others, including both states and scholars, these new criteria are a Western-sponsored attempt to deny statehood to entities not meeting their notions of human rights.

I reject both these concerns. On the first, the trend is positive insofar as decisions on whether to treat an entity as a state or formally recognize it represent an entry point to protect human rights that is less harmful to peace than any position that applies such criteria retroactively. To a certain extent, these criteria were applied retroactively when South Africa, a recognized state, was effectively ousted from the General Assembly in 1974 (but not removed from the UN, as that required a Security Council decision).[14] Given that precedent, I would not rule out that it is possible in an individual case that a sort of derecognition might so advance human rights without disrupting peace would be justifiable, but a rule to that effect is still quite disruptive to peace. (If it were applied to a state with an even worse record than that of South Africa, namely North Korea, the consequences for peace in northeast Asia could be catastrophic.) More important, even in those situations that might justify humanitarian intervention—a position I will elaborate on later—it does not serve to advance the human rights of the victims to deny *statehood* to the violating state. Put more starkly, it is one thing to invade Rwanda in 1994 to prevent or stop the genocide and even impose a new government on it; it is quite another to turn it into a *terra nullius* and open it up to a free-for-all by foreign powers.

On the second criticism, the response is brief: although it is certainly possible that adding criteria for statehood to the Montevideo list can be misused, if the norms that are added are generally accepted, or at least become the norm for a particular region, then imposing them on new claimants smacks less of hegemony and more of a creative method of enforcing human rights.

[14] See Official Records of the 2281st Plenary Meeting of the General Assembly, 12 November 1974, UN Doc. A/PV.2281.

II. The Core of Norm of Participation: Sovereign Equality and its Limits

Near the beginning of the UN Charter, just after provisions describing the purpose of the UN but before those banning force and intervention, is paragraph 1 of Article 2, which states: 'The Organization is based on the principle of the sovereign equality of all its Members.'[15] Although sovereign equality did not appear in the Covenant of the League of Nations, it is an old concept, advanced by the great historical scholars of international law and recognized and identified in many important international legal sources. Thus, in the 1922 *Norwegian Shipowners' Case*, the Permanent Court of Arbitration stated: 'International law and justice are based upon the principle of equality between States.'[16] And in the 1943 Moscow Declaration that called for the creation of the UN, the World War II Allies agreed that 'they recognize the necessity of establishing at the earliest practicable date a general international organization, based on the principle of the sovereign equality of all peace-loving states, and open to membership by all such states, large and small, for the maintenance of international peace and security'.[17] It is routinely invoked by states and scholars alike as a bedrock principle of international law.

A. Identifying the ambiguities in sovereign equality

Yet the meaning of sovereign equality remains contested and obscure in many core respects, despite consideration by generations of international lawyers. It is worth briefly highlighting three of these ambiguities to clear some ground for the discussion of its justice. First, scholars disagree on the legal nature of sovereign immunity. Edwin Dickinson crystallized the debate in asking, in 1920, whether state equality is 'an attribute of the state, a right of the state, or a principle of the law of nations'.[18] The answers have not always been clear.[19] Gerry Simpson has usefully called it both 'a principle designed to regulate the interstate system' but also 'the backdrop to a series of rights...and immunities'

[15] The Charter's preamble also refers to 'faith...in the equal rights of...nations large and small'.

[16] *Norwegian Shipowners' Claims (Norway v United States), Award of the Tribunal*, 13 October 1922, <http://www.pca-cpa.org>.

[17] Declaration of Four Nations on General Security, 30 October 1943, *Foreign Relations of the United States, Diplomatic Papers 1943*, Vol. 1 (1963) 755, 756.

[18] Edwin De Witt Dickinson, *The Equality of States in International Law* (Cambridge, MA: Harvard University Press, 1920) 101.

[19] Marcelo G. Kohen, 'Article 2, paragraphe 1', in Jean-Pierre Cot and Alain Pellet (eds.), *La Charte des Nations Unies*, 3rd ed., Vol. 1 (Paris: Economica, 2005) 399, 401 ('un principe structurel (ou plutôt structurant) de la societé internationale' as well as 'une donnée materielle de la societé à laquelle s'applique le droit international'); Juliane Kokott, 'States, Sovereign Equality', in Rüdiger Wolfrum (ed.), *The Max Planck Encyclopedia of Public International Law*, online edition (Oxford: Oxford University Press, 2008–) para. 1, <http://opil.ouplaw.com/home/EPIL>, ('a fundamental axiomatic premise of the international legal order').

of states.[20] Sovereign equality seems to be in some contrast to the international norms discussed elsewhere in this study, which are framed in terms of duties upon global actors.

Second, its relationship to the legal or political notion of sovereignty is contested. Hans Kelsen stated that sovereign equality 'probably means sovereignty *and* equality, two generally recognized characteristics of the State[ ]', adding that state equality 'is explained as a consequence of or as implied by their sovereignty'.[21] This view sees sovereignty as meaning that states cannot be subject to the legal authority of other states, and from that position therefore they are somehow equal.[22] But this close connection just assumes a certain definition of sovereignty that is then used to justify a certain relationship of it to a certain definition of sovereign equality. In fact, one can define sovereignty in multiple ways if one chose to,[23] and, as will be seen later, one can offer many versions of sovereign equality, from a very narrow one to a broad one. If we see sovereignty more narrowly than do these authors, it is easily possible to imagine a world in which states are not equal.[24] Even if we adopt their notion of sovereignty, we can define sovereign equality so broadly (for example to include equality of resources) that such equality is not at all a corollary of sovereignty.

Third, the links between sovereign equality and other norms of international law are not agreed. The 1970 Friendly Relations Declaration, which is as authoritative as international law gets on sovereign equality, states that sovereign equality means that all states 'have equal rights and duties and are equal members of the international community, notwithstanding differences of an economic, social, political or other nature'. It goes on to equate it with six principles and duties—that states are 'judicially equal'; that each state 'enjoys the rights inherent in full sovereignty'; that each state must 'respect the personality of other States'; that 'the territorial integrity and political independence of the State are inviolable'; that each state can freely choose its 'political, social, economic and cultural systems'; and that 'each State has the duty to comply fully and in good faith with its international obligations and to live in peace with other States'.[25] This is an odd list, as

[20] Gerry Simpson, *Great Powers and Outlaw States: Unequal Sovereigns in the International Legal Order* (New York: Cambridge University Press, 2004) 39.

[21] Hans Kelsen, 'The Principle of Sovereign Equality of States as a Basis for International Organization', *Yale LJ* 53 (1944): 207.

[22] Michel Cosnard, 'Sovereign Equality—"the *Wimbledon* sails on"', in Michael Byers and Georg Nolte (eds.), *United States Hegemony and the Foundations of International Law* (New York: Cambridge University Press, 2003) 117, 121 ('Equality is the only answer to the problem of regulating relations between States which are sovereign... equality is a corollary of sovereignty and not of statehood'); see also Kohen, 'Article 2, paragraphe 1', *supra* note 19, at 400 ('ou il n'existe pas de pouvoir superieur aux Etats, il ne peut exister qu'une relation d'egalité').

[23] See, e.g., Stephen D. Krasner, *Sovereignty: Organized Hypocrisy* (Princeton, NJ: Princeton University Press, 1999) (offering several different meanings).

[24] Indeed, Grotius and others long ago talked about the possibility of divided sovereignty, where the state or its rulers did not possess full authorities over governance. Hugo Grotius, *The Law of War and Peace*, Francis W. Kelsey (trans.) (Washington DC: Carnegie Endowment for International Peace, and Oxford: Clarendon Press, 1925), bk 1, ch. 3, paras. XVII–XX.

[25] Friendly Relations Declaration, principle 6.

some of the items seem opaque ('the rights inherent in full sovereignty') and some redundant with other rules (those on territorial integrity and non-intervention). Scholars have made all sorts of lists of norms that flow from sovereign equality as well, including non-intervention, territorial integrity, permanent sovereignty over natural resources, unanimity of states to express the consent of the international community, the territorial scope of jurisdiction, respect for acts of state, reciprocity of treaty obligations, and non-discrimination.[26]

B. The state of sovereign equality today

For purposes of ethical appraisal, I need to identify the reach of sovereign equality. Even though the argument can certainly be made that it is a very broad concept that encompasses many other norms, sovereign equality has a specific content accepted by states that stands apart from those norms. In my view, that content consists of *a right, a duty*, and *an immunity* of all states: (1) the right to participate in the making of international law on a legal footing equal to that of all other states; (2) the duty to comply with legal obligations that bind it on the same legal footing as that of other states; and (3) an immunity from the jurisdiction of other states for certain official acts of the state.

All three of these ideas go to the core of sovereign equality—a *minimal degree of equal respect that states must grant one another in their legal relations*, regardless of size, population, economic wealth, political power, or strategic value. It expresses a sense in which international law must be non-hierarchical in certain important ways—that no state may rise above the others with certain special privileges, and no state may fall below the others with certain special burdens.[27] It is, above all, about making legally irrelevant certain differences for certain purposes in international law. In this sense, sovereign equality is, as Kokott says, 'a device for weak states'.[28]

At the same time, this is far from negating all differences recognized in law. As doctrine clearly recognizes with respect to the three components, sovereign equality is not the same equality of all rights—certainly it is consistent with legal norms that give certain benefits to some states and not others.[29] Both the core and its limits become more clear when we examine each of the three elements more closely.

[26] See, e.g., Kohen, 'Article 2, paragraphe 1', *supra* note 19, at 401; Kokott, 'States, Sovereign Equality', *supra* note 19, paras. 20–54; Nguyen Quoc Dinh, with Patrick Daillier, Mathias Forteau, and Alain Pellet (eds.), *Droit International Public*, 8th ed. (Paris: L.G.D.J., 2009) section 278. But see J.L. Brierly, *The Law of Nations: An Introduction to International Law of Peace*, 6th ed. (New York: Oxford University Press, 1963) 130–3 (rules stem from independence and not sovereign equality).

[27] Simpson, *Great Powers, supra* note 20, at 53–6 ('existential equality'). Simpson's categorization—equality before the courts, equality in lawmaking, and existential equality—overlaps to a certain extent with the view expressed here.

[28] Kokott, 'States, Sovereign Equality', *supra* note 19, para. 11; see also para. 28 ('non-subordination to other States').

[29] Kohen, 'Article 2, paragraphe 1', *supra* note 19, at 408–9; Anne Peters, 'Humanity as the A and Ω of Sovereignty', *EJIL* 20 (2009): 513, 529.

1. Equality in lawmaking

Sovereign equality encompasses core rights of participation for states in the lawmaking process, both absolutely and relative to all other states. With regard to treaties, sovereign equality is reflected in aspects of the treaty-making process now recognized in the Vienna Convention on the Law of Treaties (VCLT). It means that every state has a right to conclude treaties with every other state; that one state or a group of states cannot force another state to conclude or be bound by a treaty; and that two or more states cannot force a treaty obligation on a third state.[30] It does not, however, require that both sides incur equal or reciprocal obligations, let alone that they possess equal bargaining power. Thus, coastal states have different rights from naval states or landlocked states under the United Nations Convention on the Law of the Sea (UNCLOS); states concluding tax treaties or extradition treaties may agree to obligations that are not completely reciprocal.[31] Nor does it prevent some states from having a final say on the treaty commitments of other states (whether that arrangement is originally between two states or part of the independence process of a more recent state), as is the case with U.S. control over some of the treatymaking of Micronesia.[32] It just means that all states must freely consent up front, even if they have unequal bargaining powers and political power to resist, to these disparate forms of treatment.

With respect to customary law, sovereign equality means that, in determining whether state practice and *opinio juris* support the conclusion that a purported norm is now the law, we start this appraisal from the position that all states' views and practices are equally relevant, regardless of the factors listed previously; and that each state has an equal right to opt out of a norm if it chooses to do so.[33] However, this starting point is quickly overshadowed by other parts of the doctrine regarding customary international law: (1) that sovereign equality does not permit the objecting states to prevent a norm from gaining customary law status if the norm has overwhelming support (even if it may not bind the objecting states); (2) that non-objection to an emerging norm may be treated as equivalent to formal assent (a practice that discriminates against states that lack foreign ministries sophisticated enough to protest emerging norms they dislike); (3) that for some norms, some states are 'specially affected', and their views count more than others, for example the positions of coastal states on the breadth of the territorial sea before UNCLOS was concluded; and (4) that states cannot opt out of *jus cogens* norms at all.[34]

[30] VCLT, Arts. 6, 34, 48–52; see also Kelsen, 'The Principle of Sovereign Equality', *supra* note 21, at 209. I leave aside whether states have a duty to participate in the making of treaties or other sorts of international relations.

[31] See, e.g., UNCLOS, Art. 21 (special rights of coastal states to regulate innocent passage); Art. 38 (special rights of naval states in international straits); Art. 125 (rights of land-locked states to access to the sea).

[32] Compact of Free Association, Federated States of Micronesia-United States, as amended, 14 May 2003, section 331, <http://www.uscompact.org>.

[33] *Asylum Case* (*Colombia v Peru*) [1950] ICJ Rep 266, 277–8 (20 November).

[34] *North Sea Continental Shelf Cases* (*Germany v Netherlands and Denmark*) [1969] ICJ 3, para. 74 (20 February); Nuno Sérgio Marques Antunes, 'Acquiescence', in Rüdiger Wolfrum (ed.), *The Max*

Lastly, sovereign equality implies a form of equal participation in the making of law—and policy—in international institutions or at international gatherings. In devising the rules of procedure or adopting texts at conferences, we work from the assumption that each state, no matter its size or power, gets one vote. States might choose to delegate certain responsibilities to smaller groups, but they do so based on a freely expressed choice of all states. At the same time, it is also clear, as discussed in the next chapter, that sovereign equality has not prevented international institutions from providing for special or weighted voting rights to certain states.

2. *Equality in law application*

Sovereign equality also means that, whenever states are bound by a legal rule, however that rule may have originated, it binds all states equally in the sense that each has an obligation to carry it out and incurs international responsibility if it fails to do so, again regardless of any aspect of the state. This concept is the essence of Dickinson's notion of 'equality of capacity for legal rights', or, as he quoted the nineteenth century scholar Pascalo Fiore, 'Whatever is lawful, just, or equitable for one state, should be equally lawful, just and equitable for others.'[35] The UN International Law Commission's (ILC's) authoritative Articles on State Responsibility hold a state responsible for all of its internationally wrongful acts,[36] and the earlier quotation from the Friendly Relations Declaration shows the link between sovereign equality and the duty to follow legal obligations. One narrow way in which this aspect of sovereign equality works is that international tribunals have a duty to treat both parties to a dispute equally.[37]

As with lawmaking, we must be cautious as to the scope of sovereign equality. Sovereign equality does not mean actual equal rights, as shown in the earlier examples; but even if we speak of capacity and not actual equality, it certainly cannot be the case that a landlocked state possesses an equal capacity for the right to a territorial sea as does a coastal state; so both Dickinson's and Fiore's summaries are simplistic. Kelsen thus had a good point when he argued that this second aspect of sovereign equality, in which states are bound when they are bound, but not bound when they are not bound, is 'but a tautological expression of the principle of legality'.[38] Nevertheless, I think sovereign equality does some additional work as a concept by saying that, once a state has become bound to certain rules, it cannot plead any aspects of its status compared to other states to extricate itself

Planck Encyclopedia of Public International Law, online edition (Oxford: Oxford University Press, 2008–) paras. 15–16 <http://opil.ouplaw.com/home/EPIL>; VCLT, Art. 53 (on *jus cogens*).

[35] Dickinson, *The Equality of States, supra* note 18, at 106–8.

[36] ILC Articles on State Responsibility, Art. 1.

[37] Robert Kolb, 'General Principles of Procedural Law', in Andreas Zimmermann, Christian Tomuschat, Karin Oellers-Frahm, and Christian J. Tams (eds.), *The Statute of the International Court of Justice: A Commentary* (Oxford: Oxford University Press, 2012) 871, 877.

[38] Kelsen, 'The Principle of Sovereign Equality', *supra* note 21, at 253.

from them.[39] This idea is implicit in the ILC's Articles in that all the acceptable grounds for precluding wrongfulness of a state's act of violating an international obligation concern the circumstances of the *acts*, and not of the state alone.[40]

3. *Immunity from the jurisdiction of other states*

Sovereign equality lastly captures the idea that, in certain key aspects of interstate interactions, one state may not judge the acts of another state.[41] The immunity within sovereign equality encompasses several specific immunities. The most important of these are (a) immunity of states from lawsuit in the courts of another state—sovereign or state immunity; (b) immunities of diplomatic and other state officials and property from the laws of foreign states—diplomatic, consular, and official immunity; and (c) the requirement under some jurisdictions that a state's court should not judge the legality of foreign acts under the laws of the forum state—the so-called act of state doctrine. These immunities, which date back hundreds of years to immunities that individual sovereigns enjoyed when travelling abroad, are part of the basic notion of respect entailed in sovereign equality. Regardless of the size or power of a state, certain core aspects of its official 'footprint' on the world are to be beyond the scrutiny of other states.

Yet all three of these immunities have significant limitations. None apply in front of international tribunals as a general matter. With respect to the first form, sovereign immunity, international law has confined it for many decades so that it no longer provides a state with immunity for acts taken in a purely commercial capacity (for example a state airline that refuses to honor a ticket), but only covers acts that the state alone can do (for example issue a passport).[42] The second form is sometimes limited by treaty or custom to the *official* acts of the emissary rather than all his or her acts; and former officials or diplomats who may have enjoyed full immunity while in office or at a post enjoy retroactive immunity only for their official acts.[43] And the third form is sometimes overridden by states on compelling domestic public policy grounds, though the practice of states is not uniform.[44]

[39] See Pierre-Marie Dupuy, 'Comments on Chapters 4 and 5', in Michael Byers and Georg Nolte (eds.), *United States Hegemony and the Foundations of International Law* (New York: Cambridge University Press, 2003) 176, 180.

[40] ILC Articles on State Responsibility, Arts. 20–27.

[41] See, e.g., *Jurisdictional Immunities of the State (Germany v Italy, Greece Intervening)* [2012] ICJ Rep 99, para. 57 (3 February). The Latin maxim associated with sovereign immunity is *par in parem imperium non habet* or 'an equal has no power over an equal'.

[42] See, e.g., ibid.; United Nations Convention on Jurisdictional Immunities of States and Their Property, 2 December 2004, Arts. 10–15, UN Doc. A/59/508; European Convention on State Immunity, 16 May 1972, Arts. 5–12, Council of Europe Treaty Series No. 74; Foreign Sovereign Immunities Act, 28 U.S.C. §§ 1601, 1605.

[43] Compare Vienna Convention on Diplomatic Relations, 18 April 1961, Arts. 29–35, 500 UNTS 95 (immunity of diplomats), with ibid., Art. 37(2) (immunity of administrative staff); ibid., Art. 39 (scope of retroactive immunity); *Arrest Warrant of 11 April 2000 (Democratic Republic of the Congo v Belgium)* [2002] ICJ Rep 3 (14 February) (immunity of foreign ministers).

[44] See generally *Oppenheim's International Law, supra* note 5, at 369–70. Because the act of state doctrine practice is so diverse and it is somewhat difficult to discern clear international rules, I will focus on the other two forms of immunity.

Most important, all three forms of immunity can be overridden in some situations if the actions of the state or its agent that another state seeks to judge are contrary to international law. Thus, for instance, the UK House of Lords ruled in 1999 that former Chilean dictator and President Augusto Pinochet was not entitled to the residual immunity of a former head of state from the jurisdiction of British courts (and Spanish courts, which issued the arrest warrant for him). It based the lack of immunity on the UN Convention Against Torture, to which the UK and Chile were parties, which required them to extradite or prosecute alleged torturers, thereby removing any immunity he enjoyed for acts after those states ratified the treaty.[45] And some courts that have found foreign acts to violate international law have refused to give them domestic legal effect.[46]

At the same time, exceptions to individual and state immunity are still more the exception than the rule. In a case brought by Germany against Italy challenging a lawsuit in the latter against Germany for atrocities against Italian POWs during World War II, the International Court of Justice (ICJ) said in 2012 that a state may not deny immunity to foreign *states* from the jurisdiction of domestic courts for official acts—in particular military acts—even if those acts violated *jus cogens* norms.[47] When a Kuwaiti national sued Kuwait in a UK court for torture in Kuwait and the UK's courts refused to waive the state immunity of Kuwait, the European Court of Human Rights refused to find the UK's dismissal of the case a violation of the Kuwaiti's human rights.[48] It reaffirmed that position regarding the immunity of Saudi Arabia and its officials in 2014.[49]

The constrained meaning of sovereign equality makes it, as Nico Krisch has stated, 'an inherently unstable concept, always torn between idealist aspirations and realist concessions'.[50] It constrains certain elements of the lawmaking and law application process by making certain arguments prima facie unacceptable (for example 'we have fewer rights because we are weak; we have more rights because we are rich'), while not preventing the law from recognizing factual inequalities of states in a variety of ways. It is also quite clearly limited to states and does not prevent states from treating non-state entities unequally to states, whether those entities are autonomous substate territories, ethnic groups, indigenous peoples,

[45] *R v Bow Street Metropolitan Stipendiary Magistrate and ors, ex p Pinochet Ugarte (No. 3)* [2000] 1 AC 147 (1999).

[46] *Oppenheim's International Law, supra* note 5, at 375. The key U.S. case to the contrary is *Banco Nacional de Cuba v Sabbatino* 376 U.S. 398 (1964).

[47] *Jurisdictional Immunities* case, *supra* note 41; see also Xiaodong Yang, *State Immunity in International Law* (Cambridge: Cambridge University Press, 2012) 428–40.

[48] *Al-Adsani v United Kingdom* (2002) 34 EHRR 280; for two national cases affirming full immunity, see *Jones v Ministry of Interior Al-Mamlaka Al-Arabiya AS Saudiya (the Kingdom of Saudi Arabia)* [2006] UKHL 26; *Matar v Dichter* 563 F.3d 9 (2d Cir. 2009).

[49] *Jones and Others v United Kingdom* App. Nos. 34356/06 and 40528/06, 14 January 2014.

[50] Nico Krisch, 'More Equal Than the Rest? Hierarchy, Equality and US Predominance in International Law', in Michael Byers and Georg Nolte (eds.), *United States Hegemony and the Foundations of International Law* (New York: Cambridge University Press, 2003) 135, 141. See also Dupuy, 'Comments on Chapters 4 and 5', *supra* note 39, at 176, 179–80 (sovereign equality as both a '*constituent fiction*' and a '*legal institution*').

or quasi-states like Taiwan. In these senses, sovereign equality is as important for what it forbids as for what it requires.[51]

This attempt at encapsulating the *lex lata* on sovereign equality will certainly draw its critics. Indeed, the international legal process is characterized by claims by states and other actors for both a more robust notion of sovereign equality as well as attempts to dilute it even more than it is today. In the sections that follow, I will appraise the three basic elements of sovereign immunity as I view it today as well as the most important challenges to the law, challenges that reflect very different views of sovereign equality.

III. Appraising the Thin Justice of Sovereign Equality

Sovereign equality has been defended as well as attacked from numerous ethical positions. Two of the most famous historical defenses of sovereign equality have proved to have little staying power. Vattel's analogy between states and individuals, building on both Hobbes and Pufendorf, is among the most cited but also reflects a naturalistic, anthropomorphized view of the state.[52] And though Kant did not specifically speak of the equality of nations, he certainly implied such equality in his design for a confederation of states that would ensure perpetual peace; yet that confederation is completely contingent upon each state's adoption of a republican form of government, so it is difficult to see how Kant's position can justify modern notions of sovereign equality in a world with many forms of government.[53]

When seen through the framework of the two pillars, sovereign equality as expressed in current international law turns out to be thinly just in some significant respects but fall short in others.

A. Equality in lawmaking and law application

The first two norms within the principle of sovereign equality concern the equal right of states in lawmaking and the equal duties of states in law application. These equal rights and duties further international peace (though I would not

[51] In ignoring the content, however constrained, of sovereign equality, I think Gabriella Blum goes too far when she calls it 'a legal fiction'. Gabriella Blum, 'The Crime and Punishment of States', *Yale JIL* 38 (2013): 57, 105.

[52] See Emer de Vattel, *The Law of Nations*, Béla Kapossy and Richard Whatmore (eds.) (Indianapolis, IN: Liberty Fund, 2008), section 18 ('Since men are naturally equal, and a perfect equality prevails in their rights and obligations, as equally proceeding from nature—Nations composed of men . . . are naturally equal, and inherit from nature the same obligations and rights. . . . A dwarf is as much a man as a giant; a small republic is not less a sovereign state than the most powerful kingdom').

[53] Immanuel Kant, 'The Perpetual Peace', in Immanuel Kant, *Political Writings*, 2nd ed. H.S. Reiss (ed.) and H.B. Nisbet (trans.) (New York: Cambridge University Press, 1991) 94 (second preliminary article of perpetual peace is that no state may be acquired by another by gift); ibid., at 102–5 (second article of perpetual peace calling for federation of free republics).

claim that they further intrastate peace). Unlike the norms discussed in Chapters 4 and 5, it is, admittedly, hard to come up with relatively simple concepts like deterrence or historical cases to argue that these equal rights and duties can prevent or actually prevented war. So instead I adopt a different tactic and ask us to contemplate a world in which the other norms of statehood that we have discussed still prevailed, but states did not enjoy these components of sovereign equality. The result is a world where large states have more rights than small ones—where they can conclude treaties that bind third states; where they can make customary rules even in the face of objections from numerous weak states; and where they can claim that certain well-accepted (not emerging) rules do not apply to them for the sole reason that they have other compelling interests.

But this image is not, after all, a mere thought experiment. The world lived it; it was characterized by colonialism, a distinction between so-called civilized states and uncivilized ones in terms of their legal rights and obligations, and a hierarchy of statehood in which many entities were states, but not equal to other states. International law even had complex sets of doctrines to explain it all.[54]

The apparent durability of that system, lasting until the middle of the twentieth century, should not belie its profound instability and the extent to which it prevented the possibility of world peace. The conquest of colonial territories brought untold misery to much of the world, and the temptation to use force against uncivilized nations was enormous. The balance of power that may have prevailed among European powers—the domain of 'civilized states' in which sovereign equality was well-accepted—should not obscure large-scale violence beyond that domain, in particular in Africa, but also in Asia as well.[55] Even the laws of war developing in the nineteenth century would not protect the targets of colonial wars, as those rules were not meant to cover 'uncivilized' peoples, who would presumably act in their own barbarous ways.[56] Indeed, the permissibility of hierarchy and violence against unequal entities may well have cast a shadow over all interstate relations and made the prospect of abolishing warfare that much more difficult. I am not suggesting that the absence of sovereign equality was a 'but/for' cause of wars historically, but it would seem that a legal system that worked from a starting point that some states are for most purposes enjoying greater rights and fewer duties by virtue of their power would cause those states to act on that status through ways that will ultimately undermine world peace.

[54] See, e.g., L. Oppenheim, *International Law: A Treatise, Volume I: Peace* (London: Longmans, Green, and Co., 1905) §§ 26–29; Martti Koskenniemi, *The Gentle Civilizer of Nations: The Rise and Fall of International Law 1870–1960* (New York: Cambridge University Press, 2004) 70–88; Antony Anghie, *Imperialism, Sovereignty, and the Making of International Law* (New York: Cambridge University Press, 2004).

[55] See, e.g., Thomas Pakenham, *The Scramble for Africa: White Man's Conquest of the Dark Continent from 1976 to 1912* (New York: Perennial, 1991).

[56] See, e.g., General Order 100: Instructions for the Government of Armies of the United States in the Field, 24 April 1863, art. 24, <http://www.icrc.org/ihl>; Declaration Concerning Expanding Bullets, 29 July 1899, para. 2, <http://www.icrc.org/ihl> (limiting scope of ban on dum-dum bullets to wars between contracting parties).

To move this analogy forward to contemporary times, when one state can be legally superior to another in these ways, the possibilities for tensions and, eventually, war among them inevitably rise. The weak states would find ways to deploy counter-measures against the strong, perhaps withholding cooperation on important matters of global concern or violating other treaties that they have concluded. The odds would also increase of violations of the other norms we have discussed, either by the strong states seeking to enforce their legal superiority—through invasion, the installation of governments, or other coercive interference—or by the weak states seeking to maintain their voices. The result eventually becomes highly deleterious to the preservation of peace. In a legal situation where the politically weak states are also legally inferior, it seems to me highly unlikely that they will simply give up on asserting their claims against the powerful and settle for third-class status.

The essence of the connection between these first two norms of sovereign equality and peace is that they serve to *channel international disputes* into peaceful fora for their resolution. When states work from a starting point of some semblance of equality, even with its limitations—where, for instance, they conclude treaties on an equal basis and are equally bound by the results—the prospects for resolution of disputes through dialogue and institutions seems far greater than in the absence of such a starting point. Jean Cohen suggests this idea when she notes that 'participation in supranational institutions and in the making of international law (on the principle of sovereign equality) makes it possible for autonomous political communities to acknowledge *and* bridge their differences'.[57] And as Kokott writes:

> The concept of sovereign equality is apt to tame the superiority and arrogance of the most powerful States. Against the ideological background of sovereign equality, the most powerful State should act as if it were more *primus inter pares* than king. Sovereign equality enhances a climate of multilateralism and of taking into account the views of other sovereigns before a major power might take and implement decisions which are of interest to all States, large or small.[58]

Sovereign equality is, then, about pluralism,[59] but, in my view, it is not pluralism for its own sake. It is rather that the pluralism advanced by sovereign equality will lessen the prospect of war.[60] In a world in which states are subjected to so

[57] Jean L. Cohen, 'Sovereign Equality vs. Imperial Right: The Battle over the "New World Order"', *Constellations* 13 (2006): 485, 499. See also Jean L. Cohen, 'Whose Sovereignty? Empire vs. International Law', *Ethics & Intl Aff* 18 (2004): 1, 20 ('sovereignty within a community of states *that decides to consider one another as equals* is the political precondition for feasible and effective international law').

[58] Kokott, 'States, Sovereign Equality', *supra* note 19, para. 58; see also Cosnard, 'Sovereign Equality', *supra* note 22, at 121.

[59] Simpson, *Great Powers, supra* note 20, at 55.

[60] Tzvetan Todorov puts it a slightly different way when he writes:

> To attempt to eradicate evil from the surface of the earth... these are projects that resemble the totalitarian utopias in their efforts to perfect mankind... They... require us to be convinced that right is embodied solely and exclusively in ourselves.... In [the] absence [of complete human knowledge], balances of powers, mutual tolerance, and a plurality of centres of decision are more valuable than unity.

many inequalities, sovereign equality represents a sort of firewall (and an imperfect one at that) that has the potential to keep states talking and not simply pushing. There is a certain irony here, in that the very inequalities that are not captured by the concept of sovereign equality—of wealth, power, and even legal obligations—make the kernel of sovereign equality all that much more important.[61]

How does this defense of these two components of sovereign equality take into account the pillar of non-interference with basic human rights? As an initial matter, it does not interfere with them at all. Each state continues to have obligations to respect human rights; and nothing in the equal participation of states in the making of law or the equal force of law for all states violates the basic human rights of individuals within each state. Indeed, the case can be made that sovereign equality advances basic human rights insofar as big states cannot plead their power as an excuse to violate them nor can small states plead their limited capacity to ignore them. At the same time, cosmopolitan scholars have asserted a tension between sovereign equality and human rights, an issue I will address later, in Section IV of this chapter.

B. Jurisdictional immunity

1. *The peace pillar*

Assessing the thin justice of jurisdictional immunity can begin with the same thought experiment as the prior discussion. Consider a world in which states could routinely arrest and prosecute foreign diplomats and other visiting officials, capture foreign military vessels and sell them for auction, and allow lawsuits by their citizens against foreign states for those states' official acts. In such a world, the possibilities for peaceful coexistence among different states quickly lessens. In a remark of a great international lawyer that nonetheless revealed his very realist tendencies, Philip Jessup once stated: 'States have 'feelings,' and the psychological factor cannot be ignored in international politics.'[62] Jurisdictional immunity (and the act of state doctrine that is its first cousin) are precisely about preventing situations in which states feel insulted by another state—so insulted that they are prone to break relations with it and contemplate, if not execute, a forceful response.

The stakes are particularly high when states violate the immunity enjoyed by certain officials. Thus, Iran's seizure of U.S. diplomats in 1979, one of the most flagrant violations of diplomatic immunity in generations, triggered outrage in

Tzvetan Todorov, 'Right to Intervene or Duty to Assist?' in Nicholas Owen (ed.), *Human Rights, Human Wrongs: The Oxford Amnesty Lectures 2001* (New York: Oxford University Press, 2002) 28, 39, 42.

[61] Cf. Benedict Kingsbury, 'Sovereignty and Inequality', *EJIL* 9 (1998): 599, 625 (traditional sovereignty system 'a more realistic system for the management of enduring inequalities... than any of the alternatives on offer').

[62] Philip Jessup, *A Modern Law of Nations: An Introduction* (New York: The Macmillan Company, 1948) 28.

part because of the increased tensions between the two states.[63] In April 1980 the United States used force against Iran in the form of a failed rescue mission, and in the 1980s the two states, now bitter enemies, engaged in naval clashes in the Persian Gulf, during which the United States accidentally shot down an Iranian civilian airliner, killing 290 people.[64] The sorry state of U.S.-Iran relations has wider ramifications for peace, as witnessed in the tensions surrounding Iran's nuclear capability. States have also reacted with outrage to attempts by other states to assert jurisdiction over former foreign officials for international crimes, as occurred a decade ago when Belgium began to investigate foreign officials for crimes against humanity under its universal jurisdiction law.[65]

Deprivation of jurisdictional immunity does not always threaten peace. For example, since 1996, U.S. law has allowed victims of terrorism to sue a small number of states for state-sponsored terrorism despite the normal presumption that states are immune from official acts, even allowing attachment of commercial assets of those states.[66] The law does not threaten individuals overseas, and it is hard to conclude that the limited removal of state immunity has endangered peace (given the already poor relations between the United States and the relevant countries).[67] Yet the law's exemption of diplomatic assets from attachments is a sign that even the U.S. Congress saw the dangers of going too far in removing immunity. The prosecution by Italy of CIA agents, some acting under diplomatic cover, for the kidnaping of a Muslim cleric off the streets of Milan annoyed the United States, but the historically strong relations between the two made force inconceivable.[68] But the norms on sovereign immunity, like other rules of international law, are meant to apply to all states, whatever their relations, and in that sense they clearly promote peace overall.

2. *The human rights pillar*

With jurisdictional immunity, however, the possibility that the rules run afoul of the second pillar of thin justice looms much larger. If, for example, the immunity of a state or its current or former officials in foreign courts for gross abuses of human rights eliminates access by victims to the only forum in which violators might be held responsible criminally or civilly, then immunity might well

[63] See, e.g., SC Res. 457 (4 December 1979) (calling on Iran to release diplomats after noting that 'the dangerous level of tension between Iran and the United States of America...could have grave consequences for international peace and security').

[64] See *Case Concerning Oil Platforms (Iran v United States)* [2003] ICJ Rep 161, para. 78 (6 November) (finding U.S. violation of the ban on the use of force).

[65] See Steven R. Ratner, 'Belgium's War Crimes Statute: A Port-Mortem', *AJIL* 97 (2003): 888.

[66] Foreign Sovereign Immunities Act, 22 U.S.C. § 1605A.

[67] The list, designated by the State Department and dictated very much by U.S. foreign policy, consists of Iran, Cuba, Sudan, and Syria. North Korea, Libya, and Iraq were once on the list but have now been removed.

[68] Rachel Donadio, 'Italy Convicts 23 Americans for C.I.A. Renditions', *New York Times*, 4 November 2009.

be unjust.[69] This tension was recognized by four judges of the ICJ in the *Arrest Warrant* case, where the Court upheld the immunity of the then-sitting foreign minister of the Democratic Republic of Congo from an arrest warrant issued by Belgium for crimes against humanity for his activities during Congo's endless civil war. They wrote:

> On the one scale, we find the interest of the community of mankind to prevent and stop impunity for perpetrators of grave crimes against its members; on the other, there is the interest of the community of States to allow them to act freely on the inter-State level without unwarranted interference. A balance therefore must be struck between two sets of functions which are both valued by the international community. Reflecting these concerns, what is regarded as a permissible jurisdiction and what is regarded as the law on immunity are in constant evolution.[70]

But does impunity—the absence of criminal accountability—interfere with a basic human right? At first glance, if human rights abusers enjoyed immunity from prosecution in the courts of other states, the resultant impact on basic human rights would not be immediately obvious. If the state for whom the official worked tried him, he would not enjoy immunity under international law in any case, so victims would not be adversely affected. If the suspect enjoyed immunity abroad, the result is not the same sort of direct assault on the victim as was the original abuse.

Yet international law has moved toward seeing impunity as interfering with human rights. It has recognized that the right of individuals to a remedy for violations of human rights implies a duty upon states to investigate, prosecute, and punish abusers of human rights. For example, Article 2(3) of the International Covenant on Civil and Political Rights (ICCPR) has been interpreted by the UN Human Rights Committee to require states to investigate all violations of the Covenant and, for gross violations, to bring the alleged perpetrator to justice.[71] In addition, the Convention Against Torture (UNCAT) requires states to investigate and prosecute (or extradite) anyone accused of committing torture. The General Assembly has also interpreted human rights law as including an obligation to investigate;[72] and the Security Council has reiterated the importance of eliminating impunity for serious abuses of human rights.[73]

These trends in the law reflect the understanding of states and civil society that impunity can indeed be a violation of basic human rights for the victims of

[69] The justice of immunity rules is also linked to the rules on universal jurisdiction, namely, the use by a state of its law and courts to address crimes with no connection to its territory and thus prosecute foreigners for acts against other foreigners abroad—a norm to which I turn in Chapter 8.

[70] *Arrest Warrant Case, supra* note 43, para. 75 (sep. op. Higgins, Kooijmans, and Buergenthal).

[71] Human Rights Committee, General Comment No. 31: Nature of the General Legal Obligation Imposed on States Parties to the Covenant, 26 May 2004, paras. 15, 18, UN Doc. CCPR/C/21/Rev.1/Add.13.

[72] Basic Principles and Guidelines on the Right to a Remedy and Reparation for Victims of Gross Violations of International Human Rights Law and Serious Violations of International Humanitarian Law, GA Res. 60/147 (16 December 2005). See also Torture and Other Cruel, Inhuman or Degrading Treatment or Punishment, GA Res. 55/89 (4 December 1989).

[73] SC Res. 1746 (23 March 2007), para. 13; SC Res. 1674 (28 April 2006).

serious abuses. The knowledge that an offender has never been brought to justice can erode and prevent *vindication* of the basic human rights of the victim (though a trial itself cannot bring the much-vaunted 'closure' either). At the same time, victims of human rights abuses or any other crime cannot be generalized—some want only revenge, some reparations from the perpetrator or the state, some an apology, some the ability to testify against their abuser, some a guilty verdict, some prison time, some the death penalty. So even though trials of offenders are neither necessary nor sufficient to address the needs of all victims, it would seem that taking them off the table whenever the accused is a current or former official would undermine basic human rights significantly for some subset of victims.

Looking beyond the victims, we could also see impunity as interfering with basic human rights insofar as it removes a deterrent to future human rights abuses. This argument undergirds much of the support for criminal trials of human rights abusers under universal jurisdiction (as well as at home, or in international tribunals), although it remains quite difficult to know how much officials who commit the sorts of heinous crimes subject to trials in other countries will be deterred by the prospects of punishment there.[74] Beyond the current attitudes of states, deontological theories of criminal law recognize an inherent wrong to the victim or the accused in impunity.[75]

This shortcoming of immunity with respect to human rights is one that international law is now slowly beginning to internalize, with the resultant changes in official immunity discussed previously. However, as noted earlier, at this point, immunity of foreign states for non-commercial acts, including severe human rights violations, is still mandatory; and the lifting of immunity of foreign officials is permissive only (not mandatory) and in any case does not extend to sitting officials.[76] Yet the law is certainly in a state of flux; whereas a generation ago, immunity for states, current officials, and former officials would have been universally regarded as legally required, the picture is changing, although the ICJ's latest ruling seems to cast doubt on any attempts to water down state immunity.

3. *An appraisal and proposal*

The two pillars thus seem to pull in different directions with respect to state and official immunity. On the one hand, immunity itself can easily be justified for its contribution to peace, for the complete absence of immunity would inflame interstate tensions, in particular with respect to officials or former officials being tried in foreign courts. It is somewhat difficult to distinguish among the three forms of immunity, but my sense is that immunity from criminal jurisdiction for

[74] See Nick Grono, 'Negotiating Peace and Justice: Considering Accountability and Deterrence in Peace Processes', 26 June 2007, <http://www.crisisgroup.org>.

[75] Cf. Hugo Adam Bedau and Erin Kelly, 'Punishment', in Edward N. Zalta (ed.), *The Stanford Encyclopedia of Philosophy*, Spring 2010 Edition, <http://plato.stanford.edu/entries/punishment/#3.> I leave aside for now the argument that jurisdictional immunity can also protect the defendant from serious violations of his rights if he faces prosecution in an unfair tribunal.

[76] *Arrest Warrant* Case, *supra* note 43.

current officials—leaders, foreign ministers, and diplomats—is probably the most important for this purpose. Preservation of such immunity permits diplomatic intercourse, a key to avoiding armed conflict; and the absence of such immunity is likely to create very significant interstate tensions.[77] Immunity of *states* and *former officials* seems less pressing, though such immunity does contribute to peace as well. (Certainly a continuous barrage of judgments against a foreign state could aggravate relations with the forum state.) Jessup's point about states having feelings is especially true when they see their own former leaders in the dock in another state.[78]

On the other hand, the harm to basic human rights from impunity does not depend a great deal upon the identity of the actor committing the violation. Certainly from the perspective of the victim, a governmental official who committed abuses and is still in power does not seem very different from one who is no longer in power. And lack of accountability of the state itself, if it is responsible for the official's conduct, can be an affront to basic human rights as much as the lack of accountability of the individuals causing the harm.

Given the tension between the appraisal under the two pillars of at least some forms of immunity, we must ask whether the current norms, in effect, do the least damage to both pillars, and, if they do not, what sort of norms would. This is clearly a consequentialist approach that effectively weighs the harm to interstate peace from immunity against the harm to basic human rights from impunity. Under such an approach, we would see the preservation of immunity for sitting officials as thinly just because their immunity is so important to interstate peace; but insist on a norm allowing or requiring states to deny such immunity for former officials and for states, where the harm to peace from denying immunity is less. I think seeing rights as exclusionary reasons points in the same direction. We would find human rights a good reason to reject some arguments for immunity (such as the inconvenience to former officials) while keeping open the possibility that some arguments might require some impingement on the rights of victims.

Indeed, I think this balancing justifies most of the current positions of international law—full immunity for *sitting officials*; and immunity limited to official acts for *former officials*, with slow acceptance that official acts cannot include international crimes.[79] As for immunity of states, if the ICJ is right, then that form of immunity does not meet the standard of thin justice. In other words, at least for current and former state officials, the *package* of legal norms of immunity preserves that immunity essential to interstate peace while trying to minimize

[77] Immunity from civil jurisdiction is another issue, although a rare one as only one state has a law allowing for suits against foreigners for violations of international law. In the case of the Alien Tort Statute, it seems harder to justify immunity because the risks to peace from a civil lawsuit are quite a bit less than those for a criminal case.

[78] Ratner, 'Belgium's War Crimes Statute', *supra* note 65.

[79] Larry May has offered a moral justification for limiting head of state immunity, but he relies on the *Pinochet* case and does not distinguish between current and former heads of state. See Larry May, *Crimes Against Humanity: A Normative Account* (New York: Cambridge University Press, 2005) 152–4.

the difficulties of the second pillar by at least removing the immunity once a person leaves office. There nonetheless remain shortcomings with respect to the immunity of sitting officials—and of states as well—insofar as that immunity sacrifices respect for (in the sense of vindication of) basic human rights for the sake of advancing peace. If we see basic human rights as trumps, this reconciliation is not acceptable, and immunity would need to give way to the rights of victims.

Yet the current position of international law as far as current officials go may not be that bad (even if one sees human rights as trumps), because there is always the likelihood that they will no longer be sitting officials—that they will eventually retire, be ousted, or lose an election, opening them up to loss of immunity from trial for international crimes they committed while they were in power. I realize that this is not guaranteed in every situation—some leaders, such as Robert Mugabe, Muammar Gadhafi, or Franjo Tudjman, will stay in office until the bitter end. For them, the best way to get around their immunity is through a stronger international judicial mechanism, where immunity does not apply. But many other former leaders who were gross abusers of human rights, from Idi Amin to Hissene Habre to Slobodan Milosevic to Charles Taylor to Augusto Pinochet, did eventually leave office under one circumstance or another.[80]

We are still left with significant deficiencies as a matter of thin justice when it comes to state immunity. The trends in state practice that gave rise to an exception to state immunity for commercial acts have not yet extended to criminal acts for the simple reason that states themselves benefit from the former exception (by giving confidence to their economic partners that they can enforce contracts against them) and see no benefit from the latter exception. But it remains difficult to see the harms to peace from allowing civil suits against states for international crimes, although some kind of statute of limitations seems necessary to prevent the entire history of the modern nation-state from being litigated.[81]

IV. Claims for a Stronger Sovereign Equality

As discussed previously, sovereign equality as a legal notion is consistent with all sorts of ways in which states are not treated equally in international relations and law. Having ended up defending some key norms deriving from the principle of sovereign equality, I now consider the arguments that sovereign equality needs to go further in providing for interstate equality than it currently does and is therefore unjust. The claims fall into two categories—(1) claims that the existing three components of sovereign equality should be adjusted to afford states more equality; and (2) claims that sovereign equality should extend beyond these three

[80] Indeed, full head of state immunity for sitting officials would not have insulated even Hitler had he survived the war, for he would not have been the head of state when he was tried.

[81] See Carlo Focarelli, *International Law as Social Construct: The Struggle for Global Justice* (Oxford: Oxford University Press, 2012) 437.

elements. Although the two categories overlap somewhat, the latter center on demands for more equal participation of states in international organizations (in particular the UN Security Council), concerns about the use of force for humanitarian ends, and demands for a more substantive form of equality in the distribution of resources across the planet.[82] Because these issues are the focus of the next four chapters, they will be considered there.

With respect to sovereign equality in the three respects addressed previously, the core of the criticism of the existing law is that the equality provided to states in lawmaking, law application, and even sovereign immunity is illusory. In order for weak states to be placed on a footing of true equality, those norms need to be enhanced in certain ways.

A. Lawmaking

1. New norms for treatymaking: the Vienna Convention protest

A stronger version of sovereign equality to govern the making of treaties would require guaranteeing states more than just the opportunity to participate in making treaties and the right to choose whether to be bound by them; it would demand more even bargaining power, in particular for weak states, during the negotiation of bilateral or multilateral agreements. In 1969, during the intergovernmental conference to negotiate the VCLT, developing states sought such a version of sovereign equality. They proposed a treaty article that would render treaties void not merely if they resulted from the threat or use of force, as is currently provided in the VCLT, but from any form of economic or political coercion. The proposal threatened to derail the talks on the convention, whose adoption required consensus, because of the strong opposition of the developed world. In the end, their proposal was rejected and thus omitted from the treaty. Instead, the conference adopted a non-binding resolution condemning such pressure in the treatymaking process.[83]

This result was clearly foreordained politically. The developed world exercises many levers of influence over poor states and has used that influence to secure many treaty commitments. Suffice it for our purposes to mention one of the most notable types of treaty in the last decades—the bilateral investment treaty, typically between a rich state and a poor state, that requires both parties to liberalize their treatment of foreign investment, including by granting foreign investors the right to sue states in international arbitral tribunals. Developing states have agreed

[82] For a grouping of claims made by states linked with an expanded notion of sovereign equality, see R.P. Anand, 'Sovereign Equality of States in International Law', *Recueil des Cours* 197 (1986): 9, 118–59.

[83] Declaration on the prohibition of military, political or economic coercion in the conclusion of treaties, in Final Act of the United Nations Conference on the Law of Treaties, 22 May 1969, Annex, UN Doc. A/CONF.39/26 (condemning 'the threat or use of pressure in any form, whether military, political, or economic, by any State in order to coerce another State to perform any act relating to the conclusion of a treaty in violation of the principles of the sovereign equality of States and freedom of consent').

to change their domestic laws because they fear losing Northern investment if they do not do so. So a provision in the VCLT along the lines of that proposed in 1969 would lead these and many other agreements that benefit wealthy states to be called into question legally. From this perspective, the loss by the developing world can be seen as the strong (or rich) prevailing over the weak (or poor).

Yet absence of consensus among states to enhance sovereign equality through a new provision in treaty law is not, in my view, unjust in the sense that the standard of thin global justice does not require such a rule of treaty law. To make such a claim, it would need to be argued initially that the existing rule of sovereign equality with respect to treaty obligations either undermines peace or interferes with basic human rights. The former seems like a stretch; and, as noted, the VCLT already contains a rule that renders void *ab initio* any treaty procured through the threat or use of force.[84] This rule not only penalizes violations of the rules on the use of force but reflects the reality that a party is not truly an equal treaty partner if it has consented after being subjected to or threatened with military force.

As for the idea that sovereign equality in treatymaking as currently understood undermines human rights, that claim is vastly overbroad in two ways. First, one cannot simply assume that human rights are harmed because weak states cannot opt out of treaties with the argument that they were not equal participants in the treaties' negotiation. Indeed, a rule giving them the right to opt out could harm human rights. Think of human rights treaties themselves, where states quite uninterested in respecting some key human rights have sought to question those treaties by claiming Western dominance in human rights lawmaking.[85]

Second, focusing on sovereign equality mislocates the link between human rights and treaty law. Certainly, it is possible that the substantive *content* of certain treaties could interfere with basic human rights, whether those treaties contain limits on the use of force or regulate economic issues. Thin justice might thus demand that the content of treaties should take account of the differing needs of developing states as a way of ensuring that they can continue to guarantee basic economic rights—an idea already reflected in numerous areas of law. Thus, treaties on ozone and climate change capture the idea of 'common but differentiated responsibilities' for rich and poor states; and the International Covenant on Economic, Social and Cultural Rights (ICESCR) says that a state is obligated to act only 'to the maximum of its available resources, with a view to achieving progressively the full realization of the rights' in the treaty.[86] But these provisions,

[84] VCLT, Art. 52. Even if a rule invalidating treaties based on economic coercion also promoted peace—in the sense that treaties resulting from such coercion could cause the weak to resist them, even violently—my purpose here is only to show that the existing rule is permitted, not that it is required.

[85] See Bilahari Kausikan, 'Asia's Different Standard', *Foreign Policy* 92 (1993): 24 (by a Singaporean foreign ministry official).

[86] ICESCR, Art. 2. The UN's monitoring committee has interpreted the ICESCR to nonetheless impose certain minimal obligations upon the states parties such that it cannot simply plead an inability to undertake its responsibilities. Committee on Economic, Social and Cultural Rights, General Comment 3: The Nature of States Parties Obligations (Art. 2, para. 1), 14 December 1990, paras. 9–10, UN Doc. E/1991/23.

some of which might well be required for the relevant norms to survive scrutiny under the second pillar of thin justice, do not represent a change to sovereign equality in lawmaking nor do they require adjusting the principle of sovereign equality when it comes to treaty obligations. In other words, it is not necessary to adjust sovereign equality in order to make any unjust treaty provisions thinly (or even thickly) just. We can handle these concerns through non-reciprocity of obligations in specific treaties.

Moreover, even if we were to somehow accept that sovereign equality in treaty-making is unjust for failing to pass the second pillar, the changes proposed by the developing world at the Vienna Conference raise serious concerns under the fairness and compliance corollaries discussed in Chapter 3 that go to the nature of a legal system. The fairness corollary suggests we refrain from embracing new norms that would be unfair to participants. Certainly a rule permitting states to renege easily on prior legal undertakings entails both significant instability of legal relations as well as a potential for mischievous auto-interpretation (even though we would not want to rule out the possibility of backing out of some agreements, as the VCLT allows). The compliance corollary urges caution in accepting a new rule when that rule might endanger overall observance of legal rules in the international legal system. Were states with less bargaining power able to challenge the validity of all treaties after they are concluded based on this enhanced notion of sovereign equality, all legal arrangements would be called into question and much of the basis for international cooperation would be in danger.

For example, had the coercion formula proposed in 1969 become part of treaty law, perhaps the developing states would begin to deny their free consent to the 1982 UNCLOS. For during the long negotiations over that treaty, the coastal states (overwhelmingly developing nations) accepted a right of innocent passage for foreign warships in their territorial sea and the right of foreign nuclear submarines to stay submerged when sailing through straits off their coasts only after significant political pressure from the major naval powers; the result was a bargain that gave the coastal states vast rights to the continental shelf and exclusive economic zone (EEZ).[87] If they tried to revisit that bargain—perhaps by ignoring their duties to the naval powers on the theory that these duties resulted from coercion—the result would be a disaster for the overall highly effective regulation of the oceans resulting from UNCLOS.[88] Similarly, the ability of a state to walk away from economic agreements would have a major impact on third parties such as transnational investors or traders. Even environmental treaties could be at risk, as poor states discovering the economic burdens of meeting environmental commitments might challenge them as resulting from economic coercion by Northern states.

It is not hard to see such a step as a move closer to the state of nature. I would not rule out the possibility that some treaties could be declared void under some

[87] See UNCLOS, Pts. III, V, VI.

[88] Most states would probably not challenge UNCLOS as a whole, because their gains from access to the continental shelf and EEZ are significant.

circumstances without such a collapse, but I do not think it can be easily avoided. As noted, international law does recognize some situations in which states can renege on treaties, and those measures seem to be ones that both pass the test of thin justice and do not raise serious concerns under the fairness and compliance corollaries.

2. New norms for customary lawmaking: the silence of acceptance

With respect to customary law, a stronger version of sovereign equality could conceivably be achieved through a challenge to the doctrine that the support of 'specially affected states' is required for custom to emerge, since in many cases such states are the powerful states. Thus, for instance, with respect to customary international humanitarian law (IHL), states that have developed particular weapons or deployed force are generally considered specially affected, such that their views are especially important; in most cases these are the powerful and wealthy states. Their views are not dispositive on IHL, but their state practice and *opinio juris* counts for more than that of most other states, at least according to the International Committee of the Red Cross.[89] An alternative would be to count the practices and views of all states equally.

Yet I am not aware of many complaints from states about this doctrine precisely because poor states can benefit from it as well.[90] One obvious example is the law of the sea in the era before UNCLOS, where rules concerning the width of the territorial sea, EEZ, or continental shelf evolved based on giving a special weight to coastal states, which are, as noted, mostly developing states. For example, after Chile, Ecuador, and Peru adopted a 200-mile fishing zone in 1947, states began to accept the idea of special fishing rights for coastal states. Iceland made a move toward a wider zone in 1972, in violation of a 1961 agreement that preserved UK fishing rights in that area; despite losing an ICJ case brought by the UK, Iceland eventually prevailed in a later diplomatic settlement and in the text of UNCLOS. The decision by coastal states to follow the United States after 1945 in declaring sovereign rights over the continental shelf was highly important to the acceptance of such rights in international law.[91]

Similarly, the doctrine that rules can emerge with general, but not unanimous, practice, also can benefit the weak states as much as the strong ones, as the holdouts on the emergence of a new rule might well be the powerful states. One example would be the ban on the death penalty for minors. Courts and observers have declared that norm to be one of customary international law despite the persistent

[89] Jean Marie-Henckaerts, 'Study on Customary International Humanitarian Law: A Contribution to the Understanding and Respect for the Rule of Law in Armed Conflict', *IRRC* 87, No. 857 (2005): 175, 180–1.

[90] See International Law Association Committee on the Formation of Customary (General) International Law, 'Statement of Principles Applicable to the Formation of General Customary International Law' (2000) 26, <http://www.ila-hq.org>.

[91] See *Fisheries Jurisdiction Case (United Kingdom v Iceland)* [1974] ICJ Rep 3, paras. 55–58 (25 July); *North Sea Continental Shelf Cases, supra* note 34.

objection of the United States until the Supreme Court declared the practice a violation of the U.S. Constitution in 2005.[92]

B. Law application

Powerful states are often able to use political pressure to avoid assuming responsibility for some law violations, even though many illegal actions by powerful states do result in serious consequences for the state. They can use leverage to get the states affected by the violations not to press their claims and can withstand formal or informal counter-measures by those states more successfully than can weak states.[93] Whether China's violation of human rights, Japan's flouting of international whaling rules, or uses of force by the United States or Russia that violate the UN Charter, international law has been criticized for centuries for its uneven enforcement that favors the powerful states. Although some of these claims seek to adjust norms beyond the three components of sovereign equality (for example on the use of force or the Security Council veto), they seem to include implicitly the claim that equality in law application is an illusion, resulting in both threats to the peace and violations of human rights.

As an initial matter, it should be pointed out that even so-called weak states can ignore international rules with few consequences, and strong states may face severe penalties for ignoring the rules. Thus, in the Iceland episode mentioned previously, that state managed to flout the existing rules on the law of the sea in blocking British cod-fishing vessels from its waters in the era before UNCLOS, and was eventually rewarded with new rules in its favor, recognizing a state's exclusive economic zone, in the new UN Convention.[94] And the United States cares enough about the integrity of the WTO dispute settlement regime that it often changes its domestic laws and regulations in response to adverse rulings.[95]

In theory, sovereign equality in law application could be adjusted to increase the prospects that both the strong and the weak follow the rules. One possibility might be to alter the rules of state responsibility, the customary law rules that set forth how and when a state's violation of an international law rule becomes a wrongful act (irrespective of what that rule might provide).[96] Thus, we might imagine that a rule of state responsibility would take into account a state's material circumstances and capacity in determining whether the state has committed an international wrong in violating a rule of international law. Just as international

[92] *Domingues v United States* Case 12.285, Report No. 62/02, Inter-Am. C.H.R., 5 December 2002; see also *Roper v Simmons* 543 U.S. 551 (2005) (U.S. death penalty for minors unconstitutional).

[93] For key works on the United States after the Cold War, see Simpson, *Great Powers, supra* note 20; José E. Alvarez, 'Hegemonic International Law Revisited', *AJIL* 97 (2003): 873; Brad R. Roth, *Sovereign Equality and Moral Disagreement: Premises of a Pluralist International Legal Order* (Oxford: Oxford University Press, 2010).

[94] See UNCLOS, Pt. V.

[95] See Bruce Wilson, 'Compliance by WTO Members with Adverse WTO Dispute Settlement Rulings: The Record to Date', *JIEL* 10 (2007): 397, 400.

[96] For these reasons, rules of state responsibility are sometimes called 'secondary' rules that apply to a variety of 'primary rules' of law.

human rights law accepts that the equality of persons nonetheless allows a state to grant special benefits to minority groups to put them on the same general footing as the majority,[97] so we might see sovereign equality as meaning that states would not be responsible for violations of international law if they were incapacitated by poverty, corruption, or other characteristics that may or may not be beyond their control.

Yet states have not made such broad claims for adjusting sovereign equality. Rather, they have worked within the existing framework of state responsibility that excuses certain specific *acts* that violate treaties or custom based on certain *circumstances* but do not excuse *states* based on any of their characteristics, even dire poverty. Thus the ILC's Articles on State Responsibility, which more or less reflect customary law, recognize some notion of necessity as an excuse for some acts by a state that violate treaty or customary rules.[98] Many treaties already recognize that a state of emergency can justify suspension of a state's obligations.[99] International courts and tribunals have offered conflicting interpretations of the ILC rule on necessity, and indeed it is possible that certain interpretations of necessity could so constrain a state's ability to protect human rights that it would not be even thinly just—an issue I will consider in Chapter 11. For now, the important point is that these claims by states for consideration to be given to their economic circumstances in how treaties apply to them are based on specific situations that might lead a state to violate international law. They are not claims that the rules of state responsibility (including the rules on necessity) should not apply equally across states.

If states (or scholars) did make such claims for a rule of sovereign equality permitting selective compliance with the law, the earlier arguments regarding lawmaking would apply here as well—negative consequences for peace with no obvious improvement of human rights. And a major change to the idea of equality of obligations, for example for the benefit of poor states, raises significant concerns as a matter of the rule of law and overall compliance. It seems not only extraordinarily complicated to administer but a major challenge to legal expectations.

C. Sovereign immunity

Calls for greater sovereign immunity are not prevalent among either states or commentators, except to the extent that we witness a certain pushback to the erosion of immunity in cases of international crimes. (The elimination of sovereign immunity for commercial activities of states is now well accepted.) Brad Roth, for instance, defends a robust concept of immunity of officials against the

[97] Minority Schools in Albania, 1935 PCIJ, Series A/B No. 64 (Advisory Opinion of 6 April); International Convention on the Elimination of All Forms of Racial Discrimination, 21 December 1965, Art. 1(4), 660 UNTS 195.

[98] ILC Articles on State Responsibility, Art. 25.

[99] See, e.g., ICCPR, Art. 4; Treaty Between the United States of America and the Argentine Republic Concerning the Reciprocal Encouragement and Protection of Investment, 14 November 1991, Art. XI, 31 ILM 124 (1992).

jurisdiction of foreign courts because he believes that many prosecutions based on universal jurisdiction are based on a false consensus regarding the criminality of the underlying acts, one that undermines the pluralism he finds so essential to global order. He argues that, with the exception of a handful of well-accepted international crimes, the immunity enjoyed by former officials ought to extend to any acts within their official capacity; and that unless the state offers its consent, 'express or tacit, states cannot be said to have authorized such external exercises of power over their agents'.[100] In terms of state practice, most states have not in fact adjusted their state immunity laws through legislation or caselaw to lift immunity of states or former officials for such crimes. As noted, the European Court of Human Rights has said that forum states need not lift the immunity of other states; and the ICJ said that forum states must not do so in the case of sitting senior officials or states outside the commercial context.

Such a move for maintaining a strong concept of immunity could be defended as required under the first pillar of thin global justice (although, as Roth's argument makes clear, it can be defended on other grounds as well). As noted earlier, it is hardly conducive to resolving some of the world's most intractable interstate or civil conflicts for third states to indict and try the officials—maybe even the negotiators—from the warring factions. Yet Roth's view may not be so far from my own, which casts doubt on the justice of immunity for former officials. He seems to acknowledge that immunity should not extend to 'mass persecution or some similarly inadmissible goal',[101] which is quite similar to my sense of an international crime; and he would lift such an immunity if the state consents 'tacit[ly]', which could simply mean through lack of protest when other foreign officials are prosecuted and a norm begins to emerge. So I think even one concerned about the consequences of trials based on universal jurisdiction would acknowledge that, at a certain point, human rights concerns outweigh fears of disrupting peace and argue for lifting immunity.

V. Claims for a Weaker Sovereign Equality

Sovereign equality has received its share of criticism as well. These attacks tend not to be directed at the three individual norms discussed earlier but rather, at the general principle that states are in core senses legally equal and thus that international law should in those respects be non-hierarchical.

A. The realist challenge

The first such challenge comes from apologists for powerful states who see little reason to provide even the minimal respect for weak states inherent in sovereign

[100] Roth, *Sovereign Equality, supra* note 93, at 249; see also at 244–52.
[101] Ibid., at 257.

equality. For these pundits, powerful states should feel no need to respect treaties when their national interests argue otherwise.[102] Sovereign equality becomes not merely about a modicum of respect for other states, but a complete sham that is best rejected. Yet even as one hears such a position, it becomes clear that these views are associated with a broader contempt for international law—about the possibility of rules governing and constraining the behavior of global actors. Both the reality and the advantages of effective international law—questions of ontology and relevance—have been so deeply considered by scholars of both international law and international relations that this volume is not the place to try to overturn the views of those critics.[103]

B. The cosmopolitan critique

A second set of critics are cosmopolitan scholars within both ethics and international law. From the cosmopolitan perspective of global justice, there would seem to be an inherent partiality and indeed injustice in sovereign equality.

1. Sovereign equality and individual equality

The cosmopolitan claim would seem to be that a norm designed to make states equal ends up making individuals unequal and thus does not treat the individual as the fundamental and equal unit of moral concern. It does so in two senses.

First, sovereign equality is unjust in treating *unlike entities alike.* In an almost arithmetical way, the principle ends up favoring the citizens of small states, like San Marino or Tonga, at the expense of those in large states like China, because their state gets the same number of votes at international gatherings, or the same power to object to emerging customary law norms, as do the large states. But sovereign equality is also inimical to cosmopolitanism in that it ends up treating democratic states like undemocratic ones. By granting the same respect to an internally illegitimate state as to a democracy, sovereign equality effectively contributes to the disempowerment of citizens in China and makes them worse off than those in the United States.[104] Under either critique, the problem is in treating *all states* alike.

[102] See, e.g., Charles Krauthammer, 'The Curse of Legalism: International law? It's Purely Advisory', *The New Republic*, 6 November 1989, 44.

[103] Among international lawyers, see Steven R. Ratner, 'Does International Law Matter in Preventing Ethnic Conflict'?' *NYU JIL & Pol* 32 (2000): 59; Abram and Antonia Chayes, *The New Sovereignty: Compliance With International Regulatory Agreements* (Cambridge, MA: Harvard University Press, 1998); Harold H. Koh, 'Bringing International Law Home', *Hous L Rev* 35 (1998): 623, 648–51; Andrew T. Guzman, *How International Law Works: A Rational Choice Theory* (New York: Oxford University Press, 2008). Among international relations scholars, see, e.g., Beth A. Simmons, *Mobilizing for Human Rights: International Law in Domestic Politics* (New York: Cambridge University Press, 2009); Kathryn Sikkink, *The Justice Cascade: How Human Rights Prosecutions are Changing World Politics* (New York: W.W. Norton, 2011).

[104] See David Chandler, 'New Rights for Old: Cosmopolitan Citizenship and the Critique of State Sovereignty', *Political Studies* 51 (2003): 332, 343.

Second, sovereign equality could be said to be unjust in treating *like entities unlike*. Individuals who act through a state are treated better than individuals who act on their own or through non-state groupings like minority groups, secessionist movements, or indigenous peoples. By providing equal legal rights on the international plane to states but not to individuals, sovereign equality does not treat the individual as the fundamental moral unit of concern.[105] Thus, this critique is that sovereign equality unjustly treats *only states* alike.

Though few cosmopolitan philosophers write directly about the legal notion of sovereign equality, Buchanan captures their concerns when he writes:

> Once we abandon the dark fiction that states are moral agents in their own right, entitled to equality as a matter of basic moral principle, it becomes evident that political equality among states is of value *only* so far as it contributes to justice as goal or as process. Political equality among states is not valuable for its own sake, and certainly cannot be regarded as a necessary condition in its own right for system legitimacy.[106]

Stronger cosmopolitans like Barry criticize sovereign equality as an element of a statist morality that seeks to preserve the status quo against all inequalities among individuals.[107]

These claims suggest that sovereign equality is difficult to justify under the sort of impartial ethical reasoning that lies at the root of my (and others') standard of global justice. As an initial matter, they fundamentally challenge the two assumptions I made in Chapter 3 in developing and defending my standard of thin global justice—namely, that state interests need to be taken account of alongside individual interests and that state interests are not simply the sum of human interests. Both of these assumptions, it might be recalled, stem from my sense that the state system is here to stay. To the extent that these attacks on sovereign equality entail a rejection of the state system, I can only respond that they and I are working from very different starting points about a vision of global justice.

2. *Sovereign equality and basic human rights*

Setting that first disconnect aside, we might interpret the argument from cosmopolitanism to say that sovereign equality fails to meet a standard of thin justice (and certainly a standard of thick justice), in particular under the pillar of respect for basic human rights. A number of responses are warranted.

First, with respect to the claim that sovereign equality harms the citizens of large states, whatever perceived indignities people in certain states might suffer from sovereign equality ('Why do we in China have to follow our treaties with

[105] A similar concern is raised in Amy E. Eckert, 'Peoples and Persons: Moral Standing, Power, and the Equality of States', *Intl Stud Q* 50 (2006): 841, 846.

[106] Allen Buchanan, *Justice, Legitimacy, and Self-Determination: Moral Foundations for International Law* (New York: Oxford University Press, 2004) 321.

[107] See, e.g., Brian Barry, 'Statism and Nationalism: A Cosmopolitan Critique', *Nomos* 41 (1999): 12, 26–7.

Tonga?'), they are not violations of basic human rights, but at best a dilution of political power compared to those in other states.[108]

Second, as discussed earlier, sovereign equality does not, in fact, prevent more populous states from having more influence internationally; we have simply precluded certain actions and arguments that they can make by virtue of that size.

Third, it does not seem to me that the modest juridical equality offered by the principle of sovereign equality—the three norms discussed previously—interferes with human rights at all. Rules that ensure that *all states*—even those that are abusers of basic human rights—can enter into international agreements, are bound by them, and are generally immune from each other's laws seem very hard to connect causally to violations of basic human rights (with the exception of the immunity point made earlier). And rules that ensure that *only states* can enjoy the right, duty, and immunity associated with sovereign equality also do not lead to violations of basic human rights. It is certainly the case that other rules of international law discussed in this volume might interfere with human rights. So, as discussed earlier in Chapter 4 and further addressed in Chapter 9, rules on non-intervention and the use of force might protect states abusing rights; and, as addressed in Chapter 5, rules on self-determination might be said to harm the rights of those seeking to secede.

But those are not the rules on sovereign equality. Although historically, sovereign equality implied a broad notion of non-interference, such that a state's human rights practices were immune from international scrutiny,[109] that linkage is not a necessary component of sovereign equality. We can maintain sovereign equality and still have a view of non-intervention under which human rights are a proper subject of international scrutiny. Indeed, if we imagined a world without sovereign equality at all, the unprivileged states abusing human rights would be so insulted that the dialogue needed to improve the status quo would be impossible. It is hard to see that world as any better than today's. As noted, in the colonial era, the European states rejecting the equality of 'uncivilized' states were themselves committing terrible abuses toward their overseas territories.

It is, I suppose, possible to imagine or at least propose a world order with sovereign equality only for states that protect basic human rights or are democratic, a world order that might be most consistent with a strong cosmopolitan vision. Yet this world is not so attractive after all. As discussed earlier, the denial of some minimal level of equal respect to states seems highly (even if not immediately) detrimental to interstate peace. So even if we conceded some shortcomings under the second pillar from sovereign equality, eliminating it fails muster under the

[108] In addition, under the fairness corollary introduced in Chapter 3, it is hard to see how a legal system can be constructed with incremental obligations based on population. At the extreme, it would mean that states with 10 million people would per se have fewer legal obligations than those with 10 million and one. Just as domestic law contains identical obligations for numerous associations of individuals regardless of size, international law should be able to include identical obligations for states regardless of size, even if some obligations might vary based on size (e.g. contributions to international organizations).

[109] Kokott, 'States, Sovereign Equality', *supra* note 19, paras. 50–54.

first pillar. This, I believe, is the proper response to Buchanan's argument that sovereign equality can be justified '*only* so far as it contributes to justice as goal or as process'—for it provides the peace that is essential to justice.

In short, we cannot simply reconstruct the world and pretend that non-democratic states do not exist by denying them the minimal equal treatment inherent in sovereign equality. Democracy and respect for human rights, even the most basic ones, must be sought within the minimally non-hierarchical system created by sovereign equality. In this sense, even Rawls' position in *The Law of Peoples*, which sees both democratic and 'decent' but non-democratic states as part of the society of peoples (and thus is anathema to strong cosmopolitan positions), is disturbing for its apparently dismissive attitude toward so-called outlaw states, those that do not respect basic human rights, are aggressive, or both. Rawls says that 'liberal and decent peoples have the right... not to tolerate outlaw states'.[110] This phrase might simply mean that they have a right to impose sanctions on such states or keep them out of certain treaty regimes, as Rawls suggests later,[111] but it would be highly unfortunate if it were read to mean that those states do not deserve the minimal privileges associated with sovereign equality. Even those states must, in that sense, be tolerated.[112]

Fourth, as Benedict Kingsbury has pointed out, the lack of juridical equality between states and non-state entities, though still significant, has waned in recent decades as non-state actors become increasingly involved in lawmaking and law enforcement. Individuals organized as NGOs, corporations, or other groupings have helped to make soft law that has proved as important a mode of regulating governmental conduct as treaties and custom. They have helped promote compliance in ways more important than traditional interstate enforcement strategies. So the problem of like entities being treated unlike is not as serious as it seems (although certainly non-state actors do not enjoy the same jurisdictional immunities as do states).[113]

Lastly, it seems that many advocates for a cosmopolitan vision of global justice themselves accept that their position need not mean an end to sovereign equality. Rather, many are most concerned about what they view as international law's democratic deficit in terms of the accountability of the norms to popular preferences. Those arguing from within ethics seek a world in which individuals will have a direct role in lawmaking, with proposals for multiple layers of governance.[114] One of their ideas, that of a directly elected global assembly, has

[110] John Rawls, *The Law of Peoples* (Cambridge, MA: Harvard University Press, 1999) 81.

[111] Ibid., at 93.

[112] Going beyond my concern for human rights, scholars such as Brad Roth and Jean Cohen have attacked cosmopolitan visions of this sort for eroding what is most important about sovereign equality—its ability to prevent the strong states (most of which are Western democracies with excellent respect for basic human rights) from dominating the weak. See, e.g., Roth, *Sovereign Equality, supra* note 93; and Cohen, 'Whose Sovereignty?', *supra* note 57.

[113] Kingsbury, 'Sovereignty and Inequality', *supra* note 61, at 610–16.

[114] See, e.g., David Held, *Cosmopolitanism: Ideals and Realities* (Cambridge: Polity Press, 2010) 105–7.

been advanced by legal academics as well.[115] Robert Goodin and I have proposed the use of deliberative democracy fora to validate *jus cogens* norms.[116]

These positions do not seek to eliminate sovereign equality, but rather to supplement it through new forms of lawmaking that are more democratic. None proposes eliminating treaties and custom as forms of law or changing the rules by which all states are responsible for violations. Thus, one proposal endorsed by cosmopolitan scholars calls for a new assembly that would stand next to the General Assembly, not replace it.[117] Richard Falk and Andrew Strauss's 'Global People's Assembly' would be created outside of any treaty framework; this entity would begin as a sort of global NGO (like the International Committee of the Red Cross or the International Olympic Committee) and over time become a locus of decisionmaking, eventually earning and gaining the respect of states. So some of the critiques of sovereign equality for its failure to consider popular opinions can be addressed without replacing any of the three norms associated with sovereign equality.[118]

VI. Conclusion

Sovereign equality is typically described as a central feature of the international legal order. This chapter saw it as entailing a right of equal participation in lawmaking, a duty to comply with rules on an equal basis, and the immunity of states and some officials from the jurisdiction of other states (but not international courts). These three norms leave intact many other inequalities of states and permit states to enter into arrangements that are not fully reciprocal. Yet each generally contributes in an important way to a just world order by advancing peace without interfering with basic human rights. The minimal degree of equal respect that they encapsulate has a far-reaching effect on states to resolve issues through negotiation and not force. That equal respect in and of itself does not interfere with the enjoyment of basic human rights. A world without sovereign equality is far worse in terms of the prospects for violence and harm to human rights than one with it.

[115] Richard Falk and Andrew Strauss, 'On the Creation of a Global Peoples Assembly: Legitimacy and the Power of Popular Sovereignty', *Stan JIL* 36 (2000): 191.

[116] Robert E. Goodin and Steven R. Ratner, 'Democratizing International Law', *Global Policy* 2 (2011): 241.

[117] See Daniele Archibugi, 'From the United Nations to Cosmopolitan Democracy', in Daniele Archibugi and David Held (eds.), *Cosmopolitan Democracy: An Agenda for a New World Order* (Cambridge: Polity Press, 1995) 121, 137–43; Simon Caney, *Justice Beyond Borders: A Global Political Theory* (Oxford: Oxford University Press, 2005) 161–2. For a proposal to replace the General Assembly with a 'World Assembly', see Peter Singer, *One World: The Ethics of Globalization* (New Haven, CT: Yale University Press, 2002) 147–8.

[118] For a rare scholar arguing explicitly for less sovereign equality, see Ulrich Preuss, 'Equality of States—Its Meaning in a Constitutionalized Global Order', *Chicago JIL* 9 (2008): 17 (as international institutions become strong and international law is more constitutionalized, sovereign equality becomes less important as a protection for weak states).

The most troubling aspect of sovereign equality from the perspective of justice turned out to be sovereign immunity and its ancillary norms. The presumption of sovereign immunity contributes to peace, but the norm can prevent the vindication of the basic human rights of victims of human rights atrocities. Immunity does not always interfere with victims' rights, but it can do so where the defendant is called to account for his crimes in a foreign court. At the same time, the hazards to peace from eliminating immunity are real, justifying full immunity for sitting officials from foreign court jurisdiction, but with an exception for states and former officials accused of serious human rights abuses. The law seems to be slowly changing toward one that is thinly just, in particular through treaties on universal jurisdiction and other forms of rejection of immunity of former officials from prosecution for international crimes, but it has not embraced these exceptions fully and still regards states as immune.

Attacks on the current scope of sovereign equality come mostly from those concerned that it is too narrow and harms weak states. This concern, even if valid, does not mean that the current norm of sovereign equality harms human rights; and it does not follow that any proposed alternative would do a better job of protecting human rights, for the interests of weak states and protection of human rights are certainly not coextensive. Even if we assumed the norm were unjust, and that a new norm could be devised, the fairness and compliance corollaries introduced in Chapter 3 play a very significant role here. Notably, if treaty law were changed so that the validity of a treaty could be challenged because of the unequal bargaining power of the parties during their negotiation, much of the certainty in international law, a key component of the idea of the rule of law, would disappear. A similar fate would take place if weak states were to claim that treaties simply did not apply to them. Equally important, these concerns about weak states can be addressed within the bounds of sovereign equality, as treaties themselves provide for different rights and duties of states based on their situations and capacities.

As for cosmopolitan concerns that sovereign equality is too broad in treating large and small states as juridically equal, much of that critique is part of an attack on the state system, rather than any considered view of how the principle really harms human rights. To the extent that cosmopolitans suggest that the law should not afford even minimal respect to states that are not democratic or that violate human rights, they ignore the significant costs to peace from pretending that such states do not exist or treating them as if they have no legal rights of participation. They also ignore the way human rights can be and have been advanced through many channels in a world of juridically equal states. In the end, most recognize the infeasibility of any other starting point and focus instead on supplementary structures of governance to give a greater say to individuals.

Sovereign equality thus turns out to be by and large thinly just—more just than many of its critics, whether from states or the academy, might think. In and of itself it does not do much heavy lifting to eliminate inequalities among states or among individuals, but it promotes peace and does not interfere with human rights. Most important, it lays the basis for cooperation among states that is at the heart of international law.

In Chapter 7, I turn to one final set of norms concerning participation—the rules governing the admission practices and decisionmaking of international organizations. Those institutions, so central to the making, interpretation, and enforcement of international law, make many distinctions among states, distinctions that leave many states as second-class participants and highlight the limits of sovereign equality.

7

Sovereign Equality's Limits: Membership and Decisionmaking Rules in International Organizations

Sovereign equality starts with the rules on lawmaking, law application, and immunity, but we cannot truly understand its contours or its justice without examining the arenas where claims about the equality of states most often arise—international organizations. For the better part of a century, the bilateral venues or ad hoc conferences that characterized lawmaking and law application have been supplemented—indeed overshadowed—by international institutions.[1] There we see organizations seeming to privilege some states over others in terms of membership, special powers in decisionmaking, and outcomes that seem to treat some states better than others.

Indeed, international organizations are important not just for gauging the justice of sovereign equality. They are critical to understanding the justice of the rules on the use of force, because one of those core rules is the authority of the Security Council to both respond to uses of force by states and authorize force by states. But even more fundamentally, they play a key role in understanding the justice of many norms of international law. In the UN, the EU, and countless other lesser known institutions, the principal actors of international law gather to further their claims and make and apply international law in a way that advances them. The justice of the rules themselves cannot be viewed in isolation from the institutions that make, interpret, or apply them. In other words, we cannot settle for a norm that is just if an unjust institution will play a significant role in applying that norm—even if that institution might at times reach a decision we regard as just.

International organizations are also key sites in which international actors, the ones making claims and counter-claims, can jointly *evaluate* existing or proposed rules for their consequences—and thus (assuming we believe justice should be determined in consequentialist terms), the justice of those rules. Whatever observers might think of the justice of rules, institutions are major venues for the

[1] I will use the term international organization and institution interchangeably, consistent with the understanding of lawyers and political scientists in which these terms refer to political structures composed of members of one kind or another. Philosophers tend to see institutions more broadly than organizations, such that law itself is a kind of institution.

decisions that result in just or unjust rules, interpretations of them, or enforcement actions in respect of them. The right kind of institution will do a better job of weighing of consequences so those rules, interpretations, or enforcement measures are just.[2]

In making the move from considering the justice of norms to the justice of institutions, I follow the lead of philosophical literature on justice, which has shown that we can assess not only the justice of rules, but of institutions. I also build on the work that international law and lawyers have achieved with regard to institutions. International lawyers have been arguing over the design and function of global institutions for a century at the very least, a not unsurprising turn of events since lawyers are central to the design and functioning of such organizations. Practicing lawyers, when called upon by policymakers, have attempted to create or reform organizations to match their clients' interests, and academics have evaluated those institutions with regard to their effectiveness and their legitimacy (a term with many meanings).[3]

This chapter, then, seeks to provide a template for assessing the justice of international organizations according to the standard of thin justice. In my view, the justice of an institution turns on the justice of two core structural elements—its membership and its decisionmaking processes. These two features determine more than any other factor whether the institution will provide a venue in which the claims of actors with respect to the issue within the institution's competence are considered in a just manner.

Yet we would be remiss if we stopped our appraisal with the two pillars of justice, for that inquiry may be too limited (particularly for organizations not focused on either peace or human rights). We need also to consider an institution's procedural fairness, a corollary to justice, as discussed in Chapter 3. Institutions characterized by such fairness provide due process to participants, a process that will make it more likely that they will make just (or at least not unjust) rules, interpretations, and enforcement measures. I will thus consider the possibility of a test for the procedural fairness of international organizations.[4]

Before beginning, it is worth noting that international law does not provide a single rule about membership or decisionmaking of international organizations beyond a default position that states can agree upon whatever structures they wish. As a result, this chapter will focus on a small number of leading organizations and examine the justice of their structural provisions. My choices are based on both the importance of the organization to the international legal order—and the core norms discussed elsewhere in this book—as well as the diversity of

[2] See Robert E. Goodin, *Utilitarianism as a Public Philosophy* (Cambridge: Cambridge University Press, 1995) 22–3.

[3] See, e.g., Daniel Bodansky, 'The Legitimacy of International Governance: A Coming Challenge for International Environmental Law?' *AJIL* 93 (1999): 596; Jean-Marc Coicaud and Veijo Heiskanen (eds.), *The Legitimacy of International Organizations* (Tokyo: United Nations University Press, 2001).

[4] Another key factor in the overall effectiveness and legitimacy of an international organization, notably the expertise and independence of its secretariat, is beyond the scope of this study.

approaches exhibited by international organizations. The justice of other institutions can be appraised using the same framework.

I. Membership Rules of International Organizations

The membership rules of an international organization are typically set forth in its constituent instrument—such as Article 4 of the UN Charter—as well as policy documents it develops over time—for example the *acquis communautaire* of the EU. As states set up and operate international organizations, they make choices about whose inclusion will benefit the organization and who will benefit from inclusion in it. In admitting members, the institution agrees to give them special rights vis-à-vis non-members and to create special duties toward members. The organization may, for instance, be bound to give financial advantages to members but not non-members. As a result, non-member states will often seek to become members, as is clear from the history of the EU or the World Trade Organization (WTO).

The centrality of international organizations as loci for discussion and decision-making makes inclusion or exclusion of great importance to states. It may nonetheless be asked whether membership has anything to do with justice at all. Is not a group of states permitted as a matter of justice to pick others with whom to work on a particular issue and keep others out, just like individuals in a private poker or golf club or sorority do? The answer lies in the difference between individual morality and institutional morality discussed in Chapter 2. We do not say that a sorority's membership policy is just; instead, we would say simply (or at least the sorority's defenders would) that it is not morally unacceptable for its members to pick the young women they want as new members, although even there we would recognize some admission policies, for example racially discriminatory ones, as unjust.

But the sorts of institutions at issue here are quite different. First, they enjoy significant power over member states, both in terms of the advantages they bring and the disadvantages they can impose. Second, more generally, they play a critical role in the governance of the planet. Finally, these institutions are often formed through organic instruments and thus founded on *law*, which can and should be appraised for its underlying justice. The sorts of arbitrary preferences that we might be willing to tolerate for some groupings of individuals for a common purpose are thus not sustainable.

The justice of membership rules will now be considered through four examples: the UN, the WTO, and two regional institutions, the Council of Europe and the EU.

A. The United Nations

1. The United Nations' membership criteria

Article 4 of the UN Charter states:

1. Membership in the United Nations is open to all other peace-loving states which accept the obligations contained in the present Charter and, in the judgment of the Organization, are able and willing to carry out these obligations.
2. The admission of any such state to membership in the United Nations will be effected by a decision of the General Assembly upon the recommendation of the Security Council.

As of today, the UN has 193 members—basically all the states in the world. For most of its history, it routinely admitted new states resulting from decolonization, although Cold War politics at times kept other states out (for example a group of Western and Eastern states jointly admitted in 1955, and the two Germanies jointly admitted in 1973).[5] Even when Yugoslavia and the USSR dissolved in the early 1990s, the UN was generally quick to admit the resulting entities. Clearly, the UN members have interpreted the term 'peace-loving' loosely and made scarcely any serious inquiries into whether a candidate is 'able and willing' to carry out the obligations of membership, which include, at a minimum, settling disputes peacefully, carrying out decisions of the Security Council, and paying dues.[6]

Does the UN or its members have a duty to admit all states that meet the criteria of Article 4(1)? A closely related question faced the International Court of Justice in its first advisory opinion in 1946, when the General Assembly asked it whether a state voting on membership in the General Assembly or Security Council is 'juridically entitled to make its consent to the admission dependent on conditions not expressly provided by [Article 4(1)]'.[7] The Court said no, implying that the UN and its members have a duty to all states to admit them to membership if they meet those criteria. It is a general—though clearly contingent—duty. At the same time, the Court noted that states have a great deal of flexibility in applying the criteria,[8] and it remains impossible to know whether states' decisions on admission are actually based on the criteria or on other concerns. When the General Assembly decided in 2012 to allow Palestine to participate as a non-member observer state, upgrading its status from an observing non-state entity, members voting both ways certainly seemed to consider many issues beyond the criteria listed in Article 4.[9]

[5] Although China was an original member of the UN representatives of the Republic of China (Taiwan) occupied the seat until 1971 despite losing control over the mainland in 1949.

[6] Konrad Ginther, 'Article 4', in Bruno Simma, Daniel-Erasmus Khan, Georg Nolte, and Andreas Paulus (eds.), *The Charter of the United Nations: A Commentary*, Vol. I, 3rd ed. (Oxford: Oxford University Press, 2012) 341, 348–50. Indeed, as discussed in Chapter 6, they have also defined the term 'state' somewhat loosely in terms of the Montevideo Convention criteria. Part of the deal to secure Soviet approval for the UN was the admission of the Ukrainian and Byelorussian Soviet Socialist Republics as separate full members.

[7] *Conditions of Admission of a State to Membership in the United Nations (Article 4 of the Charter)* [1948] ICJ Rep 57, paras. 57, 58 (Advisory Opinion of 28 May).

[8] Ibid., paras. 63–64.

[9] See UN GAOR, 67th Sess., 44th Plenary Mtg., 29 November 2012, UN Doc. A/67/PV.44.

2. *A just set of criteria?*

The UN's approach to membership, both the Charter and the practice, seems justifiable under the two pillars of thin justice. An institution whose primary purpose is the maintenance of international peace and security—the advancement of which is the first pillar of thin justice—has good reasons to be open to all the states of the world for several reasons.

First, an inclusive forum has many advantages over a more limited venue as a place to discuss global threats to the peace, take measures to avoid outbreaks of violence, and to halt them once they arise. We need a place for the great issues of war and peace to be discussed in front of all states, and it is no coincidence that nearly all the major crises have appeared on the UN agenda in New York. Although the UN's universal membership is hardly a guarantee that such discussions and actions will serve their purposes, at least one knows that any state involved in an actual or potential armed conflict will participate in the discussions through its permanent mission. Membership encourages minimal participation in the UN's work and some sense among states that they are invested in its decisions. Second, under international law, non-members of the UN are likely not bound by the decisions of the Security Council (though all states are probably bound by Article 2(4)).[10] If we want the UN to be effective, and we see the Security Council as justly acting as its chief decisionmaker with respect to armed conflict (more on this later), then a membership policy that makes as many states as possible bound by the Council's decision passes muster as promoting peace.

Indeed, the imperative of peace justifies not only the legal eligibility of all states to join, but also the very lax way in which the Security Council and General Assembly have applied Article 4 to candidate states. Effectively, since the end of Cold War posturing over membership, no state has been rejected for UN membership by a political organ on the theory that it is not peace-loving and able to carry out the commitments of membership. (Those entities whose admission is rejected are typically ones where there is significant disagreement as to whether it is even a state, such as Taiwan or Kosovo.) In the last twenty years, the UN has admitted two states, Eritrea and South Sudan, though in neither instance was it clear at the time of admission that the state was committed to a peaceful solution to lingering border disputes with the states from which they had split (Ethiopia and Sudan, respectively). And no state, even one labeled an aggressor by the UN, such as Iraq after it invaded Kuwait, has ever been suspended or removed from the UN on any of the grounds permitted in Articles 5 and 6 of the Charter.[11]

[10] Anne Peters, 'Article 25', in Bruno Simma, Daniel-Erasmus Khan, Georg Nolte, and Andreas Paulus (eds.), *The Charter of the United Nations: A Commentary*, Vol. I, 3rd ed. (Oxford: Oxford University Press, 2012) 787, 800.

[11] UN Charter, Art. 5 (suspension against any state subject to Security Council preventive or enforcement action, with the Council's assent); Art. 6 (expulsion of state that 'has persistently violated the Principles' of the Charter, with the Council's assent). The two closest cases are South Africa, whose rights of participation in the General Assembly were suspended in a controversial decision of that body in 1974; and Yugoslavia, whose membership was called into question during its dissolution in the 1990s through a series of decisions of the Security Council and General Assembly.

Though one might argue that the UN's actions deprive Article 4 (as well as Articles 5 and 6) of much meaning—they certainly deprive it of any screening effect—the choice for open membership is just and justifiable on the grounds noted previously. In a world where actual or potential belligerents are loath to appear in the same room, let alone talk to one another, it is vital to continue to have one forum in which they need to hear both sides of the debate and gauge the international reactions to their policies. The proclivity of some states to ignore what they hear at and from the UN is a poor argument for keeping them out in the first place, for it judges effectiveness related to the maintenance of peace based on the measurable failures rather than the harder-to-measure successes.[12] Thin justice does not argue against the utility of smaller organizations focusing on issues of peace. Regional groupings may also contribute to peace, but not as a substitute for the UN.

How do the UN's admission criteria fare regarding respect for basic human rights? As an initial matter, the admission of a state to the UN cannot be said to itself violate, or seriously contribute to the violation of, basic human rights. Although certainly rights-violating states gain some international respect by virtue of the trappings of UN membership, it takes the second pillar too far to suggest that their admission to the organization interferes with basic human rights. The only exception might be the most egregious situation where the horrendous regime of a new state specifically seeks UN membership to bolster its international credibility. Even in that case, it is equally possible that UN admission will improve the human rights situation, as the state feels some need to adjust. This position does not mean that it would be unjust for other institutions to have human rights criteria for admission—which is certainly the case with the two European organizations discussed later—but thin justice does not require an institution dedicated to peace to include them.

Both the American right and some mainstream academics have argued for an organization of democracies as a counterweight or alternative to the UN.[13] This position is different from the proposal discussed in the last chapter for an assembly of peoples, in that it proposes a UN composed of democratic states, not one with a democratically elected organ. Unlike the advocates of such a chamber, who seek a bona fide corrective to the democratic deficit of the UN, those favoring an organization of democracies principally argue that democracies should play a leading, perhaps exclusive, role in matters of international peace and security, suggesting that autocratic regimes have no place at the table.

On the one hand, it seems hard to object to a group of democratic (or autocratic) states that choose to convene to discuss matters of international peace and security if that organization lacks the powers of enforcement that the UN has

[12] A classic defense of the UN in these terms is Thomas M. Franck, *Nation Against Nation: What Happened to the U.N. Dream and What the U.S. Can Do About It* (New York: Oxford University Press, 1985).

[13] See, e.g., Princeton Project on National Security, *Forging a World of Liberty under Law* (Princeton, NJ: Princeton University, 2006) 25–6.

(or if we did not have a UN). Certainly, a talk shop has its advantages. Yet if we consider the proposal as one to alter or replace the UN, with the opportunities it provides for negotiations and the powers it possesses under the Charter, then it raises significant concerns of justice. If states have created an institution as a forum for and powers over matters of international peace and security, then it affirmatively detracts from that goal to exclude from that entity the majority of states that are not democracies. The decisions of such an organization of democratic states are also likely to be viewed with great suspicion by that majority, further reducing the possibility that such an institution can contribute to peace. Such a proposal eliminates the key advantages of universality for the sake of easier agreement among presumably like-minded states, even though that may be an overly optimistic assumption given the differences among democratic states on many core issues of peace.[14] So the current formula is permitted as a matter of thin justice and indeed is required if we had only one international organization dedicated to the advancement of peace.

B. The World Trade Organization

The UN's policies can be usefully contrasted with those of the WTO, the key multilateral organization responsible for the negotiation and implementation of global trade agreements. Under the 1994 Agreement Establishing the WTO: 'Any State . . . may accede to this Agreement, on terms to be agreed between it and the WTO.' The Agreement thus allows any state to apply for membership, but creates no duties on the organization to admit anyone. Instead, each application is treated on a case-by-case basis and typically results in prolonged negotiations among the candidate, the WTO Secretariat, and member states. As stated on the WTO's web page:

> The new member's commitments are to apply equally to all WTO members under normal non-discrimination rules, even though they are negotiated bilaterally [between the WTO and the candidate state]. In other words, the talks determine the benefits (in the form of export opportunities and guarantees) other WTO members can expect when the new member joins. [The talks can be highly complicated. It has been said that in some cases the negotiations are almost as large as an entire round of multilateral trade negotiations.][15]

Thus, the WTO does not specify exactly what obligation it has to any candidate regarding admission. It is possible that, as a de facto matter, the WTO admits

[14] My consequentialist argument about the effects of a selective membership policy on global peace could be supplemented by a deontological argument about a duty to include representatives from all persons affected by the decisions of the organization, or a fear that selectivity would be an excuse for powerful states to exclude the weak. See, e.g., Gerry Simpson, *Great Powers and Outlaw States* (Cambridge: Cambridge University Press, 2004) 276 (defending universality as an abandonment of distinction between civilized and non-civilized peoples).

[15] World Trade Organization, 'Membership, Alliances, and Bureaucracy', <http://www.wto.org/english/thewto_e/whatis_e/tif_e/org3_e.htm>.

members based on clear and uniformly applied criteria, but the constitutive instrument does not provide those criteria.

1. *The justice of the WTO's admission policies*

Unlike the UN, the WTO is not an institution focused on matters of international peace. Yet, as discussed further in Chapter 10, the Bretton Woods institutions were created in the hope, and still are based on the view, that a stable regime of global trade and finance would promote international peace.[16] Other economically-oriented international organizations also ground their purposes in promoting peace.[17] Yet the stated linkage between the missions of these economic organizations and peace is, in my view, insufficient to allow us to appraise the justice of their membership rules under the first pillar.[18] Thus, in the case of the WTO, it is hard to see how the membership criteria stated earlier either promote or detract from interstate or internal peace, even though they certainly affect the institution's decisions on trade, which may ultimately play a role in interstate or internal peace.[19]

As for the effect of membership rules on basic human rights, the WTO, like other organizations, also claims as its mission the promotion of individual economic welfare, and its officials have asserted a link between trade rules and human rights.[20] Yet again, it is difficult to see how the WTO's membership policy either interferes with or promotes human rights.[21] That is not to say that all membership practices would pass muster. If the organization discriminated in its admissions policy based on race or a similar factor, it would fail a deontological form of the second pillar. Moreover, as we will see later, the second pillar may play

[16] See, e.g., World Trade Organization, '10 Benefits of the WTO Trading System', <http://www.wto.org/english/thewto_e/whatis_e/10ben_e/10b01_e.htm> (Benefit 1 is 'The system helps to keep the peace').

[17] See, e.g., Constitution of the International Labor Organization, preamble, para. 2, <http://www.ilo.org/public/english/bureau/leg/download/constitution.pdf> ('whereas conditions of labour exist involving such injustice, hardship and privation to large numbers of people as to produce unrest so great that the peace and harmony of the world are imperiled'); Constitution of the International Telecommunication Union, preamble, para. 1, <http://www.itu.int/net/about/basic-texts/index.aspx> ('having regard to the growing importance of telecommunication for the preservation of peace').

[18] For other institutions whose mission is more clearly connected to preservation of the peace, such as the International Atomic Energy Agency and regional institutions like the Organization of American States (OAS) and the Association of Southeast Asian Nations (ASEAN), the linkages between membership policies and peace would be examined along the lines used for the UN.

[19] See Robert Howse, 'The Legitimacy of the World Trade Organization', in Jean-Marc Coicaud and Veijo Heiskanen (eds.), *The Legitimacy of International Organizations* (Tokyo: United Nations University Press, 2001) 355, 369–70. Certainly some membership criteria, e.g. that an organization is open only to aggressive states, would fail the first pillar.

[20] See, e.g., GATT, preamble, para. 2 ('raising standards of living'); World Trade Organization, 'Lamy: Globalization and Trade Opening can Promote Human Rights', 5 June 2009, <http://www.wto.org/english/news_e/sppl_e/sppl128_e.htm>.

[21] In theory, denial of membership might harm a state's ability to trade and perhaps feed its population, but it is hard to see how non-membership would have this consequence in practice.

an important role in the evaluation of the membership criteria of organizations focused on human rights.

2. WTO admission policies and procedural fairness

In light of the difficulties in connecting these membership policies to the advancement of peace and respect for basic human rights, it is worth considering whether we might yet offer some other sort of ethical appraisal of membership criteria. The best candidate seems to be procedural fairness, in the sense of whether the structures of an institution offer some basic due process to the participants. A standard for procedural fairness could build on Lon Fuller's identification of eight criteria for the internal morality of the law discussed in Chapter 3, i.e. the moral factors that in his view make a rule a legal rule and a system of governance a legal system.[22] Though I need not endorse his opposition to positivism in terms of the formal criteria of a legal rule, I think Fuller seizes on critical attributes of a legal system's fairness to those whom it is meant to govern.[23]

In the case of an organization's admissions criteria and procedures, fairness to those involved in the process suggests the desirability of three baseline conditions: (a) the criteria are publicly stated and generally understandable to applicants, even if they are somewhat open-textured (*the publicity condition*); (b) the criteria bear a rational relation to the goals and functions of the organization (*the functional condition*); and (c) the procedures and criteria are applied, broadly speaking, in good faith, insofar as the organization generally admits states if and only if they meet the criteria, even if it interprets the criteria very broadly (*the good faith condition*).[24] This combination offers some kind of predictability to the process while respecting the discretion of members in admission decisions.

In the case of the WTO, the absence of any admission criteria in the WTO agreements means that each case of new membership is negotiated individually. Although the WTO's members will insist that the applicant change certain domestic laws and policies to put itself in compliance with the WTO agreements, much of the process is still characterized by horse-trading in which politics plays a central role. For instance, the decisions on the admission of Russia and China in the last two decades were tied up with their overall relations with the United States and its allies, including matters unrelated to trade, such as Russia's conflict with Georgia.[25] Perhaps this process is justified from an act-utilitarian perspective—each admission decision is taken in a way to maximize utility according to

[22] Lon Fuller, *The Morality of Law* (New Haven, CT: Yale University Press, 1964) 38–94.

[23] For an argument that Fuller's criteria describe how and why international law shapes behavior and helps build global normative expectations, see Jutta Brunnée and Stephen J. Toope, *Legitimacy and Legality in International Law: An Interactional Account* (Cambridge: Cambridge University Press, 2010).

[24] These do not include all of Fuller's eight ideas, some of which do not arise as a practical matter for international organizations (e.g. non-retroactivity or non-contradiction).

[25] See, e.g., Stephen E. Hanson et al., 'The WTO and Russian Politics', in *Russia and the WTO: A Progress Report*, National Bureau of Asian Research (Seattle, WA: NBR, 2007) 7.

some standard. But it also makes the WTO resemble a club whose members make ad hoc decisions on whom they wish to admit. The absence in an organization that purports to be global (*World* Trade Organization) of any clear criteria for admission creates the potential for that organization to play favorites in its admissions decisions. This procedural unfairness stands in contrast to that of the UN, where the criteria for admission are clearly stated, rationally related to the UN's mission, and applied, for the most part, evenhandedly in the sense that every state is admitted. Certainly the UN did not always follow this practice, notably the deal in the 1950s for the admission of East and West bloc states, but for the most part it has admitted every new state.[26]

Yet the proposed procedural fairness test—indeed *any* non-trivial procedural fairness test for admission—may ask too much of organizations. In the case of the WTO, for instance, it seems impossible to spell out its admission criteria beyond the obvious acceptance of the WTO agreements. Admission is an immensely complex and heavily negotiated process, in which each WTO member first works out bilateral understandings with the candidate state on market access—understandings of which all members will eventually be able to take advantage through the most-favored nation provision of the WTO treaties.[27] Similarly, the UN Human Rights Council has no fixed criteria for membership because each of the proposals for substantive criteria was seen as inadequate to filter out poorly performing states. Instead, the General Assembly resolution creating it states simply that when electing members of the Council: 'Member States shall take into account the contribution of candidates to the promotion and protection of human rights and their voluntary pledges and commitments made thereto.'[28] Rather than substantive admission criteria, advocates for the new Council pushed for processes that they hoped would prevent states with poor records from serving—election of individual states (rather than slates), each requiring a majority of the Assembly's members, with term limits.[29] These examples suggest that fairness should not demand that international organizations do the impossible and have or apply any particular criteria for membership.

A full theory of procedural fairness is not my purpose here. Suffice it to say that, if we need to look beyond the substantive justice of the admission criteria for some test for all organizations to see if they are being fair to applicants, it

[26] The long-delayed admission of the People's Republic of China could be another example, although legally speaking that issue concerned which government would represent China, not the admission of China (an original UN member) per se.

[27] GATT, Art. 1; see also Peter Van den Bossche and Werner Zdouc, *The Law and Policy of the World Trade Organization*, 3rd ed. (Cambridge: Cambridge University Press, 2013) 109–13.

[28] GA Res. 60/251 (3 April 2006), para. 8; see also Philip Alston, 'Reconceiving the UN Human Rights Regime: Challenges Confronting the New UN Human Rights Council', *Melb JIL* 7 (2006): 185.

[29] The hope has not been fully realized, as many states with poor records continue to serve on the Council, although a handful, notably Sudan and North Korea, have never been elected. Indeed, the membership criteria may well be unjust under the second pillar insofar as an institution dedicated to the advancement of human rights rewards states that have violated basic human rights.

will be hard to come up with one beyond the trivial point that the members act with respect for the applicant (for example by reading the relevant application material). Some organizations may well be able to meet the three conditions proposed previously, with a greater chance for principled decisionmaking; but others may justifiably find that so many issues go into membership that the criteria cannot be spelled out in advance. At the same time, institutions can certainly improve their admission processes so that the applicant has a real and not illusory possibility of admission. In the case of the WTO, for instance, the immense financial and institutional burden for the applicant in adjusting all its internal regulations to the highly complex WTO regulatory regime suggests that applicants deserve significant technical assistance to make the accession process a worthwhile exercise.[30]

C. Regional organizations: the Council of Europe and the European Union

To consider the justice of the membership policies of a regional organization, we can turn to two—the Council of Europe (COE), the forty-seven-member organization of European democracies whose most famous treaty is the European Convention on Human Rights, and whose best known organ is the European Court of Human Rights; and the EU, the twenty-eight-member community of European states whose institutions, laws, rules, and policies determine much of the economic and foreign policies of its members.[31]

The 1949 treaty creating the COE states:

> Article 3: Every member of the Council of Europe must accept the principles of the rule of law and of the enjoyment by all persons within its jurisdiction of human rights and fundamental freedoms, and collaborate sincerely and effectively in the realisation of the aim of the Council...
>
> Article 4: Any European State which is deemed to be able and willing to fulfil the provisions of Article 3 may be invited to become a member of the Council of Europe by the Committee of Ministers.[32]

The COE is thus open only to 'European State[s]', and only those who meet the rather general criteria of Article 3. The Treaty on European Union defines EU membership in slightly different terms:

> Article 49: Any European State which respects the values referred to in Article 2 and is committed to promoting them may apply to become a member of the Union.... The

[30] See Igor I. Kavass, 'WTO Accession: Procedure, Requirements and Costs', *Journal of World Trade* 41 (2007): 453.

[31] My choice to focus on the two European institutions, rather than, for example, the African Union or the OAS, is because the latter two have generally admitted all states in their region without controversy, whereas the two from Europe have expanded significantly over the years (and not merely as a result of the emergence of new states due to decolonization).

[32] Statute of the Council of Europe, 5 May 1949, <http://www.conventions.coe.int>.

applicant State shall address its application to the Council, which shall act unanimously after consulting the Commission and after receiving the consent of the European Parliament.... The conditions of eligibility agreed upon by the European Council [the body of ministers from each member state] shall be taken into account.

The conditions of admission and the adjustments to the Treaties on which the Union is founded, which such admission entails, shall be the subject of an agreement between the Member States and the applicant State. This agreement shall be submitted for ratification by all the contracting States.

Article 2, for its part, states:

The Union is founded on the values of respect for human dignity, freedom, democracy, equality, the rule of law and respect for human rights, including the rights of persons belonging to minorities. These values are common to the Member States in a society in which pluralism, non-discrimination, tolerance, justice, solidarity and equality between women and men prevail.[33]

Thus, as with the Council of Europe, the EU is open only to 'European' states, but the process is more complex substantively and procedurally. The applicant must meet conditions of eligibility laid down by the EU Council, known as the Copenhagen criteria,[34] and then agree with the Council on a detailed set of steps to take before or shortly after joining. Procedurally, the application must be approved by the elected European Parliament, the Council, and, ultimately, by all the member states through a separate treaty between the EU's members and the candidate on the terms of membership.[35]

The COE and EU's admissions policies thus extend only to, and create a right of admission only for, European states, a *geographic* criterion; and among those states, there is a criterion of respect for certain human rights, what I will call a *value-based* criterion. Governments and other actors within both institutions have debated the meaning of the term 'European'. Whereas the EU has stayed squarely within generally accepted notions of Europe, the COE has admitted marginally European states—in a geographic sense—like Azerbaijan, Georgia, and Armenia.[36]

33 Consolidated Version of the Treaty on European Union [2010] OJ C83/13.

34 European Commission, 'Conditions for Membership', 4 July 2013, <http://ec.europa.eu/enlargement/policy/conditions-membership/index_en.htm>. The criteria are a stable democracy, with respect for human rights and the rule of law and protection for minorities; a working market economy; and adoption of the *acquis communautaire*.

35 Pascal Fontaine, 'Europe in 12 Lessons' (2010) 17, <http://europa.eu/abc/12lessons/lesson_3/index_en.htm>.

36 This policy contrasts with that of the 57-member Organization for Security and Co-operation in Europe (OSCE), whose original purpose was as a forum for East-West dialogue during the Cold War; it included the USSR (as well as Canada and the United States) and now includes all the ex-Soviet republics, including those in Central Asia (Kazakhstan, Kyrgyzstan, Uzbekistan, and Tajikistan). But it has no organic instrument at all that could specify membership criteria.

1. *The justice of the Council of Europe's and European Union's admissions policies*

As a matter of justice, neither institution's admissions policy clearly promotes or detracts from international or internal peace, and it seems clear that neither policy interferes with basic human rights. It would be harder to say whether they actually promote basic human rights, insofar as we could imagine that admission of states that do not meet these criteria might over time improve their human rights record.

2. *The procedural fairness of the Council of Europe's and European Union's admissions policies*

The geographic and value-based criteria seem fair under the first two conditions of the three-part test mentioned earlier. First, they are publicly stated (condition (a)). Second, as a matter of the functional condition (b), many of the cooperation and coordination problems that international organizations are created to solve can be addressed most efficiently from a regional perspective. Trade, transportation, and the migration of workers are examples, although the solutions to some of these problems do not turn on proximity. And the governance-centered mandates of both organizations make the value-based criterion a rational demand for members insofar as an organization can work better if its members generally agree on certain fundamental principles. Put together, we would thus see, in the case of the COE, a limitation of its membership to European democracies (rather broadly defined, as it includes Russia) might be justified based on the institutional constraints inherent in the enforcement of the European Convention of Human Rights by the European Court. A Council of Europe with too many members would overwhelm the Court with petitions alleging violations (although the Council at its current size already overwhelms the Court with petitions). Similarly, the more stringent value-based criteria of the EU are fair in light of the extremely close relationship among members and the demands placed upon them by membership.

With respect to the good faith condition of procedural fairness (condition (c)), however, the COE has not always acted in accordance with it. It has admitted Russia, a state most of which is east of the Urals and thus not in geographically defined Europe and whose human rights problems have already contributed to a backload of nearly 100,000 petitions in the Court.[37] In the case of the EU, the organization certainly took a risk in admitting Bulgaria and Romania, with their entrenched problems regarding the rule of law, and, as discussed later, it has not admitted Turkey, but its overall record is one of applying the Copenhagen criteria more or less consistently.

[37] European Court of Human Rights, *Annual Report 2013* (2014) 193–5, <http://www.echr.coe.int/Documents/Annual_report_2013_prov_ENG.pdf>.

3. Democratic values or family ties: what is 'European'?'

The ethical problem with these limited membership policies is not so much in the results but in the arguments sometimes used to explain them. Many supporters of limited membership for both the COE and the EU eschew the functional arguments for a very different justification—that a state's status as European creates special links that *alone* permit, or even require, those organizations to limit membership to those states. Christopher Wellman calls these 'associativist' arguments.[38] For their adherents, the critical threshold question for admission is not whether a state is *in Europe*, but whether it is *European*. The debates in Europe about the territorial scope of the EU resemble the debates in ethics about special duties to fellow countrymen noted in Chapter 2 and considered further in Chapter 9.

When politicians argue over whether Turkey is sufficiently 'European' to be in the EU, some are asking whether it is a member of the European family, a group whose members are presumably entitled to be the beneficiaries of special duties. Their notion of the family may hinge on acceptance of the Christian religion, an easy basis on which to exclude Turkey. Yet those focusing on 'European-ness' can argue, in addition or instead, that it encompasses shared values related to individual dignity and the proper role of the state in society. This sort of impartial argument tracks the value-based criterion of membership. Unlike the associativist argument, this argument for limited membership is procedurally fair to applicants because it meets the functionality condition.

Those defending limited membership on associativist grounds have, I suspect, captured the terms of the public debate over expansion. This tendency to argue based on European-ness in the familial sense, rather than European location or democracy, may emanate from the very powers of the Union itself. Because the EU has such strong powers vis-à-vis its members and so many benefits to offer them, public support for its enlargement may well depend on offering up a more accessible justification for inclusion, one that does not seek to reduce European-ness to some impartial geographic or value-based concept. As we know from Bernard Williams, demands for action (for example to save a person from harm) based on impartialist reasoning can demand from us 'one thought too many' compared to demands based on partiality, with its common sense connection to human experience of family and community.[39] Those partialist arguments have a distinct advantage in the Union, which is, after all, still called the 'Community'.

If the regional or value-based criterion for membership *is* actually a proxy for a religious criterion, or applied in a way that it becomes such a proxy, then we have renewed concerns under the *substantive* standard of justice. For at that point, the second pillar is implicated, as the lack of any legitimate reasons to limit

[38] Christopher Heath Wellman, 'Relational Facts in Liberal Political Theory: Is There Magic in the Pronoun "My"?', *Ethics* 100 (2000): 537, 538–40; see also John Rawls, *The Law of Peoples* (Cambridge, MA: Harvard University Press, 1999) 112 ('relations of affinity').

[39] Bernard Williams, 'Persons, Character, and Morality', in *Moral Luck* (Cambridge: Cambridge University Press, 1981) 1, 18.

membership this way suggests invidious discrimination; indeed if the second pillar is seen as a trump, such a policy would clearly be unjust. Given the importance of non-discrimination to the protection of basic human rights, I would then argue that a membership policy or practice that limits the EU to Christian states in Europe would be unjust. [40] If, however, the concept of a European state means one with certain shared beliefs, notably those spelled out in Article 2 of the Treaty on European Union quoted earlier, then even a membership policy defended in terms of European *identity* rather than *location* does not raise these concerns. Whether such a valid identity-based criterion for membership is being properly applied by the EU in the case of Turkey remains in doubt.

Moreover, the decisions of the COE and EU suggest the possibility that the European institutions do not apply the geographic criteria and the value-based criteria independently. One may discover that once COE or EU decisionmakers identify a state as sufficiently European in the sense of common beliefs (or even common religion), they are willing to interpret creatively the value-based membership criteria in a way to allow for admission, and interpret them a different way to deny admission to a state not sufficiently European. This account can explain the willingness of the Council to admit some states with very compromised democracies and guarantees of the rule of law, and of the EU to admit some states with weak or corrupt institutions that cannot carry out EU policies. This strategy raises a broader set of questions about whether these institutions should be so inclusive and whether they should be more demanding of states regarding their human rights practices after admission.

D. Participation of non-state actors

The practice of international organizations with respect to participation by non-state actors has undergone much change in recent decades. On the one hand, international organizations generally exclude non-state actors from full membership.[41] Yet from a time where states completely dominated the agenda of such institutions, many now accord significant rights to non-state entities. The most prominent institution that has long accorded full participatory rights to non-state actors is the International Labor Organization, whose Assembly formally comprises states but with a requirement that each delegation have two delegates from the government, one from industry, and one from organized labor, who can vote independently, and whose smaller Governing Body contains fifty-six individuals based on the same proportions.[42] More recently, in 1996, states in the Arctic

[40] One might ask, in this regard, whether the membership policy of the Organization of the Islamic Conference is unjust for this reason. If the OIC had no real power and were akin to a private fraternity, justice might play no role, but given that the OIC does more, it seems as morally suspect as a Christian EU.

[41] Key exceptions include the WTO (which has admitted Hong Kong) and the Asian Development Bank (which has admitted both Hong Kong and Taiwan (the latter under the name 'Taipei, China')).

[42] Constitution of the ILO, *supra* note 17, Arts. 3, 7.

region created the Arctic Council, giving the status of 'Permanent Participant' to six organizations of indigenous peoples of the Arctic region, who are closely involved in the work of the institution (although their consent is not required for a formal decision of the Council).[43] The International Telecommunication Union provides so-called 'sector membership' to telecommunication companies so they may participate as of right in the important working groups and conferences of the organization, even though they lack a vote in intergovernmental organs.[44]

In addition, international organizations routinely give some kind of observer status to NGOs so that they may attend meetings and circulate documents (at their own expense).[45] NGOs are parties in litigation before regional human rights courts, and even formal state-to-state dispute settlement bodies like that of the WTO increasingly allow for NGOs to present their views.[46] Beyond formal rights of participation, non-state actors often drive the agendas and decisions of international organizations through effective mobilization of governments and even staff governmental delegations.

Although these moves have faced resistance from some governments nervous about voices in international arenas independent of their control (for example China, Russia, and some developing states) as well as academics concerned about the lack of accountability of NGOs,[47] overall the trend for non-governmental participation is laudable. As a matter of procedural fairness, NGO participation serves several important functions. First, it allows for infusion of voices distinct from those of the government, although in some cases they may repeat those views, as, for example, in the case of so-called 'government-organized NGOs' or GONGOs. Second, it permits some representation of constituencies often ignored by governments, such as victims of governmental abuses, or non-human species. And third, it makes possible the incorporation of technical expertise that most governments do not possess. Like other trends we have seen in this volume, they represent a thickening of both the expectations of what is needed for a just and fair international institution and of the response of those institutions to those expectations. Yet the overall practice is still one of flexibility, with each organization taking its own approach to NGO participation.

Is such flexibility just and fair, or must international organizations offer some sort of guaranteed participation to non-state actors? As a matter of procedural fairness, a requirement that organizations grant participatory rights to non-state actors raises enormous problems of administration, in particular if those rights to go all the way to full membership. Whereas the statehood criterion is a relatively

[43] Declaration on the Establishment of the Arctic Council, 19 September 1996, Art. 2, <http://www.arctic-council.org/index.php/en/document-archive/category/4-founding-documents>.

[44] Constitution of the International Telecommunication Union, Art. 3, and Convention of the International Telecommunications Union, Art. 19, <http://www.itu.int>.

[45] See, e.g., the UN website 'UN and Civil Society', <http://www.un.org/en/civilsociety>.

[46] For a useful discussion, see Center for International Environmental Law, 'Transparency and Public Participation in WTO Disputes Settlement' (2009), <http://www.ciel.org/Publications/Transparency_WTO_Dec09.pdf>.

[47] See, e.g., Kenneth Anderson, 'What NGO Accountability Means—And Does Not Mean', *AJIL* 103 (2009): 170.

simple way to limit membership, the determination of criteria for legitimate participation by non-state actors is immensely complex. Unless the participation is extremely pro forma, like the UN's policy on NGOs, the organization will need to make difficult decisions based on the NGO's membership, independence, expertise, and other matters. Although some organizations might be able to derive a set of clear criteria, such as with the Arctic Council's inclusion of certain indigenous peoples, it may be impossible for others to do so, a reality that supports seeing procedural fairness as more a desideratum than a demand.

Beyond these practical impediments to more formal rights of participation, the current practice of international organizations to make decisions regarding participation on a case-by-case basis seems to raise fewer concerns as a matter of thin justice compared to possible alternatives. Flexibility allows an organization the discretion to consider the impact of participation on both peace and basic human rights, each of which can vary depending on the non-state actor and the political context. On the other hand, rules that require or preclude participation raise the possibility of being unjust. A rule that required an organization to give rights of participation to all non-state actors relevant to the organization's mission, perhaps on the belief that such participation promotes dialogue with the government that could help avoid or end civil wars, could run afoul of the second pillar if it covered groups responsible for mass atrocities. Thus, the UN should not be required to allow every rebel movement into Security Council discussions when a civil war is being addressed. And a rule that prohibited participation by all such groups as a matter of principle—perhaps on a deontological view of the second pillar that we simply have a duty not to talk to abusive actors, even if to do so might actually improve their behavior—could run afoul of the first pillar by preventing discussions that would ease conflict. The UN should thus not be precluded from including them as necessary in its deliberations.

We might consider as examples of the need for flexibility the approaches of states at two major negotiations related to major civil conflicts. In the early 1990s, France and Indonesia convened the Paris Conference on Cambodia, a large conference that sought to bring together Cambodia's four warring factions along with their foreign supporters to hammer out a peace agreement. Among the Cambodian groups included in the conference was the Khmer Rouge, which controlled vast territories in the country's west but had committed horrendous crimes against the population (leading to well over a million deaths) when it governed the country from 1975 to 1978. Despite the Khmer Rouge's record, the sponsors of the conference felt their participation was essential to end the war. And although the U.S. government instructed its delegates (I was one of them) not to talk to or even shake hands with Khmer Rouge delegates, it assented to the necessity of including them in the talks. A rule of international law that precluded such participation would have closed off a diplomatic process that eventually ended that civil war and further delegitimated the Khmer Rouge.

In late 2001, however, following the September 11 attacks and the U.S. military invasion of Afghanistan, the UN sponsored peace talks in Bonn on a new government to take over after the Taliban's ouster by U.S. and NATO forces. That meeting did not include the Taliban because of its perceived close connection to Al Qaeda (and it was not clear that the recently defeated regime was interested in power-sharing anyway). Such participation may have been desirable, but waiting for the Taliban to participate and agree might have delayed any transfer of power to an interim government. A rule demanding their participation would not, then, have helped peace or human rights.

In the end, although it is not impossible that justice might constrain international organizations somewhat in their choice of participation options for non-state actors, flexibility seems far preferable to advance peace and human rights, even if it has shortcomings as a matter of procedural fairness. Those institutions need to be able to respond to each non-state actor's agenda in a particular political context rather than being forced to accept or exclude them in all cases.

II. Decisionmaking Processes and Powers of International Organizations

The influence and power of an international organization ultimately turns upon the legal and political effects of its decisions upon member states and others. These effects both *depend upon* and help *determine* the mechanisms it uses for making decisions. The decisionmaking processes used by a number of international institutions have come under great criticism for their perceived injustice insofar as they exhibit favoritism to certain states. As with membership criteria, I cannot appraise all key institutions. Instead, I will examine here two organizations with significant power whose decisionmaking is perceived as flawed or unjust—the UN and the International Monetary Fund (IMF).[48]

A. The United Nations

Decisionmaking within the UN is not centralized in one organ. The two key political organs are the General Assembly and the Security Council, though the Secretary-General has vast powers of his own to determine the policies of the Organization. The General Assembly includes all member states, each of which has the right to one vote. The Assembly passes many resolutions each year, but under the UN Charter the Assembly can legally bind members over only a handful of issues, all of them internal to the operation of the UN, notably the budget and the dues, the admission of new members, the composition of UN bodies, and the election of top UN officials. Resolutions on external issues—an ongoing war, a human rights atrocity, economic injustice—are generally only recommendations,

[48] Aspects of the decisionmaking of the WTO are considered along with the justice of trade law in Chapter 10.

although many internal decisions, like funding a peacekeeping mission, have external effects.[49]

Contrast this with the Security Council, comprising fifteen states, five of them permanent members (the P5) and ten elected for two-year terms from the broader UN membership. Council resolutions require a majority of nine votes, with the additional condition that none of the permanent members opposes the resolution. The decisions of the Council enjoy a special status—automatic binding international law—under Article 25 of the Charter: 'The Members of the United Nations agree to accept and carry out the decisions of the Security Council in accordance with the present Charter.'[50] The Council has repeatedly made such decisions in recent decades, for example to order members to impose economic sanctions or to give states permission to use force that would otherwise be precluded under Article 2(4).

Stated simply, the General Assembly is characterized by equal rights for all states but no binding power over those states beyond internal UN matters; the Security Council is characterized by special rights—for its members vis-à-vis the membership as a whole, and for the P5 on top of that—and vast power over member states. This formula has elicited substantial criticism over the years from the majority of member states, as well as many international lawyers and philosophers, who claim that the Assembly is too weak, the Council too strong, and the Permanent Five too privileged.

The Charter formula is easily traceable historically. The governments preparing the Charter during World War II limited the Assembly's powers precisely because of its universal membership and one-state-one-vote rule, for the strong powers did not want the organization to order them to do anything opposed to their interests. Moreover, they granted the Council vast powers only because of its small membership and the veto, the former essential for rapid decisionmaking and the latter, again, to prevent any decisions against great power interests. And the P5, designated as such in the UN Charter, were the principal World War II victors (with China's membership passing to the PRC upon its replacement of the Taiwan government in 1971). Weaker states, with ideas for a different Council or greater authority for the Assembly, were more or less pushed aside during the negotiations, and they had little choice but to accept the proposal of the victors because they so badly wanted to see the UN come into existence. The status quo is thus the product of a very deliberate process.[51]

[49] Compare UN Charter, Arts. 10, 11, 13, 14, with Arts. 17, 18. The Assembly may adopt a resolution that restates customary international law or offers an authoritative interpretation of the UN Charter, but it is the special content of that resolution as well as near-unanimous passage that makes it binding. See, e.g., Friendly Relations Declaration. For some of the complexities of distinguishing between internal and external decisions, see José Alvarez, *International Organizations as Law-makers* (Oxford: Oxford University Press, 2006) 143–5.

[50] Not all the Council's resolutions are decisions; many are meant to be recommendations. But the decisions are binding under Art. 25 and, moreover, under Art. 103, prevail over any other duties a state may have under other treaties.

[51] See, e.g., Simpson, *Great Powers, supra* note 14, at 165–93; Evan Luard, *A History of the United Nations, Vol. 1: The Years of Western Domination, 1945–1955* (London: Macmillan, 1982) 44–58.

1. The General Assembly's powers

At first glance, the UN Charter's conferral on the Assembly of only limited powers in the area of peace and security might be seen as inconsistent with the principle of sovereign equality. The argument could be made that just as there is a right of all states to vote on the budget, there is or ought to be one to vote on other matters that will bind member states. But to say that states enjoy general (or equal) rights to do some things through the principle of sovereign equality implies nothing at all as to whether they should enjoy general rights to do other things.

As discussed in Chapter 6, sovereign equality does not mean equality for all purposes. It simply means that states are juridical equals, that none of the attributes of a state—size, power, population, etc.—*automatically* endows it with special legal rights over another state. It is a baseline for the future allocation of rights and duties and does not mean states must be treated as equals for all purposes. The General Assembly's makeup and powers flow from sovereign equality, but not directly so. Rather, it originates in a decision by the equally sovereign states ratifying the Charter to create one organ where each state gets one vote—even while they created another organ (the Council) where not every state gets a vote and some get special votes. Simpson has identified the tension well by calling the Charter a 'compromise between the political requirements of hegemony...and the juridical commitment to equality'.[52] Social contract theory also recognizes that equal participants (individuals in that case) may choose to create a system of governance in which they do not in the end enjoy equal rights of participation in decisionmaking.[53]

But even if sovereign equality as currently understood does not undercut the Charter's division of labor between the Council and the Assembly, we still must appraise the justice of that division. Two questions arise: (a) does the voting formula for the issues over which the Assembly has competence pass muster? And (b) does the limitation of the Assembly's binding decisionmaking to the internal workings of the organization and exclusion of that power from matters of international peace and security pass muster? The reply to the first seems to be a rather simple yes, insofar as the equal voting on internal issues certainly does not harm peace—it may even promote it—nor interfere with human rights. But the second question is much more difficult.

One could certainly imagine an Assembly with greater powers, to make the sort of binding decisions that the Security Council now makes. On some issues, given the proclivity of most developing world states to vote together on key issues, it would actually be easier for a majority (ninety-seven states) or even a two-thirds majority of states (129 states)[54] to agree upon a resolution than for all of the P5 to agree not to veto a Security Council resolution. Certainly the General

[52] Simpson, *Great Powers, supra* note 14, at 167.

[53] See John Locke, 'Second Treatise of Government', § 132, in John Locke, *Two Treatises of Government*, Peter Laslett (ed.) (Cambridge: Cambridge University Press, 1988) (choice of people leaving state of nature to create form of government they choose, including democracy, oligarchy, and monarchy).

[54] UN Charter, Art. 18.

Assembly's passage of numerous resolutions condemning South Africa during the apartheid era and Israel since 1967 in the face of far fewer resolutions by the Council is evidence of this possibility.[55] The Assembly also passed a resolution condemning Syria in 2013 when the Council could not because of Russian and Chinese vetoes.[56] We could thus see resolutions passed on issues on which the Council cannot agree, resolutions that generally call for the same action as does the Council, or even resolutions that call for different action.[57] Although such a new state of affairs could lead to new and potentially conflicting resolutions, that is hardly enough to justify the status quo.

At this point, however, it is necessary to take a detour. For the claims regarding greater power for the Assembly are closely intertwined with concerns over the power of the Security Council—indeed they essentially argue that the Assembly should have powers more like those of the Council. Thus, it is important first to assess the justice of the Council's decisionmaking.

2. *The Security Council's decisionmaking processes*

The nub of power to make binding decisions on matters external to the UN lies within the Security Council. To appraise the justice of the UN's decisionmaking we must carefully examine the workings of the Council. This appraisal is also critical to a justification of the substantive rules on the use of force—for at the core of those rules is Chapter VII of the UN Charter, which gives the Council the sole authority to authorize force and is the only other exception to the ban on the use of force beyond self-defense. Those rules are just only if we believe that the Security Council's authority to approve force is just.

The Council is characterized by special rights for (a) its fifteen members, who can participate in UN decisionmaking, and lawmaking in particular, in a way completely precluded to non-members of the Council and (b) the P5 in particular, whose special rights transcend those of the other members.[58]

(a) Limited membership of the Council

As a matter of thin justice, the special rights for the fifteen states need to be appraised in light of the Council's purpose. The Security Council is not just a body responsible for discussion and for making law; it has the 'primary responsibility'

[55] In the 67th session, for example, the GA passed some 17 resolutions about Israeli practices in the occupied territories; during that period, the Security Council passed four, all concerning the extension of UN peacekeeping missions in Lebanon and the Golan Heights.

[56] See GA Res. 67/262 (15 May 2013, passed by vote of 107-12-59).

[57] The Charter's requirement in Article 12 that the Assembly refrain from considering issues on the Council's agenda unless requested has not prevented it from doing so. See Eckart Klein, 'Article 12', in Bruno Simma, Daniel-Erasmus Khan, Georg Nolte, and Andreas Paulus (eds.), *The Charter of the United Nations: A Commentary*, Vol. I, 3rd ed. (Oxford: Oxford University Press, 2012) 507, 513–16.

[58] For an excellent evaluation of the problem from the perspective of international law, see David D. Caron, 'The Legitimacy of the Collective Authority of the Security Council', *AJIL* 87 (1993): 552.

for maintaining international peace and security under the UN Charter.[59] It must make quick and sometimes binding decisions to deal with international crises, a task that seems impossible to fulfill with a large membership. As already noted, it is possible to imagine some speed within the General Assembly given the proclivity of the developing world to vote together, but as a practical matter the modalities of drafting, circulating, and discussing a resolution on a matter of international peace are immensely complicated. If only a third of states were interested in the details, that would still entail the negotiation of a text among over sixty states, which I believe would lead to paralysis on a resolution to promote interstate or internal peace. In that case, a restricted membership is required, not merely permitted, under the first pillar.

As for potential interference with basic human rights, the connection between the Council's size and such an impact is less evident. One example through which to consider this impact is the unanimously passed Resolution 713 of 25 September 1991, which imposed a full arms embargo on the former Yugoslavia as violence was escalating between the Yugoslav republics and ethnic groups within them. At the time, the Council's members were trying to limit that violence, and an arms embargo certainly seemed an important step. Yet Serbia continued to have ample armaments, some of which it used against the new government in Bosnia, or gave to its allies, the Bosnian Serbs, for that purpose.[60] In a suit against Serbia for violations of the Genocide Convention during the Bosnian civil war, Bosnia argued to the International Court of Justice that the Council's embargo deprived it of its right of self-defense; indeed, it may have contributed to the inability of Bosnian forces to prevent the atrocities on Bosnian soil committed by Bosnian Serb forces.[61] This resolution would probably not have passed in the General Assembly, where Bosnia had many allies. So it is certainly possible that the Council could pass a resolution that undermines basic human rights.

Yet ultimately it does not seem that the *size* of the Council and the effect of the resolution on Bosnia's ability to prevent gross human rights violations are connected. In situations other than Bosnia, one could imagine the General Assembly showing as little or less concern about stopping atrocities than the Council. For instance, during the bloody conclusion to Sri Lanka's civil war in the first five months of 2009, neither the Council nor the Assembly passed any resolutions condemning the violations of international humanitarian law committed by the government and the Liberation Tigers of Tamil Eelam. Limited size per se does not, then, seem to interfere with basic human rights. The result, then, under the two pillars is that limited Council membership is just—indeed because of the first pillar it is a necessary, though not sufficient, condition for a just UN. Although it is theoretically possible that states could devise procedures to streamline debate in

[59] UN Charter, Art. 24.

[60] See, e.g., SC Res. 838 (17 April 1993), preamble, para. 8 (condemning arms transfers from Serbia to Bosnian Serbs).

[61] Application of Bosnia-Herzegovina to the International Court of Justice, 20 March 1993, ICJ Press Release 1993/4. See also Erika de Wet, *The Chapter VII Powers of the Security Council* (Oxford: Hart Publishing, 2004) 247–53.

the General Assembly to make it more nimble (perhaps entrusting certain drafting and debating responsibilities to major states within each regional group), the political hurdles to constructing such a system effectively rule it out.[62]

This appraisal of limited membership invites two questions. First, why should the Council have fifteen members, and not a larger (or even a smaller) number? And second, is the current composition of those fifteen just? On the first issue, even if thin justice demands a relatively small Council, it certainly does not require a Council of fifteen members. If a larger Council did a better job of preventing and addressing armed conflict, then it would advance peace more than the status quo. At the same time, states will differ on what a better job would entail. Passage of resolutions would require the approval of more states, which means that the drafters of resolutions would need to take account of the views of the new members.

The frequency, content, and effect of resolutions passed by a larger Council seem hard to predict ex ante. These decisions may be more effective at preventing or ending armed conflict because more states affirmatively back them through their Council vote. Or they may be less effective if, for the sake of consensus or at least passage by the required number of states, the Council's members water them down and fail to grapple with the most difficult aspects of the situation. Similarly, under the second pillar, a larger Council may pass fewer resolutions that further human rights or fewer that interfere with them. In this regard, it is important to consider that most proposals would increase the number of developing states from its current level of only about half of the Council's membership. When the Council decided in 2005 to refer the situation in Darfur to the International Criminal Court, three important developing states—China, Brazil, and Algeria—abstained, while three—Argentina, Benin, and the Philippines, voted yes.[63] With a larger Council, with more developing states, a majority for passage may well have not been found.

As for the choice of non-permanent members (I will turn to the P5 in the next section), the UN Charter specifies that the non-permanent members of the Council should be chosen by the General Assembly based on 'due regard' 'to the[ir] contribution . . . to the maintenance of international peace and security and to the other purposes of the Organization'.[64] The Charter thus implies that the non-permanent members have a special duty to other states to further international peace, textually demonstrating the link between membership in the Council and the prevention and management of armed conflict. This formula itself seems just in that respect.

[62] See Martti Koskenniemi, 'The Police in the Temple: Order, Justice and the UN: A Dialectical View', *EJIL* 6 (1995): 325, 338 (the Assembly's 'composition and working methods would be nonsensical were it for the Assembly to create or maintain the international order'). My conception of justice, however, differs significantly from Koskenniemi's insofar as he sees order and justice as opposed to one another rather than linked.

[63] SC Res. 1593 (31 March 2005) (passed 11-0-4, with the United States also abstaining).

[64] UN Charter, Art. 23.

Yet the practice of the UN since the days of the Cold War under a so-called 'gentleman's agreement' is, in fact, not to pick states based on that criterion. Rather, each of the so-called regional groups in the General Assembly, which differ vastly in membership size and population,[65] is allotted one or two non-permanent members each; each group nominates its own candidates, leading to a final vote in the General Assembly. As a result, Europe, east and west, is overrepresented among the non-permanent members.[66] Moreover, because each region is limited in the number of states from it that will serve, certain very important non-P5 states (for example Japan, India, Indonesia, Brazil, South Africa, Nigeria, and Germany) do not always serve on the Council, although by informal arrangement they do serve more often than most other states in their region.

Although—or better, because—one cannot identify an obvious connection between the current formula and the promotion of peace (or the protection of human rights), it seems at a minimum open to serious debate whether the current allocation is just. In particular, if important global or regional players are excluded from the decisionmaking—a point I develop more later with respect to the P5—Council resolutions may not reflect the views of states that can influence the relevant actors or otherwise contribute to a solution; they may not affect their intended target; or they may not gain the respect they deserve. In that sense, the current membership practice does not advance peace and might even harm it.

For two decades states have been considering alternative compositions to the Council. Under the standard of justice advocated here, the fundamental criterion for determining membership must be its effect on the ability of the Council to respond to interstate and internal armed conflict in a way that does not undermine basic human rights.[67]

(b) Permanent membership on the Council

Under the UN Charter, the P5 enjoy two special rights: permanent membership and veto. The former ensures in principle that those states will always participate in the deliberations of the Security Council, and in practice is the basis for their control of much of the Council's agenda. The veto ensures that the Council will not pass a resolution that any of the P5 oppose, although it does not guarantee that the P5 will convince the other ten members to support their positions, as we

[65] These are: the Africa Group (54 members), the Asia-Pacific Group (53 members), the Latin American Group (33 members), Western European and Other Group (28 members, the 'Others' being the United States, Canada, Australia, New Zealand, and Israel), and the East European Group (23 members). See generally Security Council Report, 'Security Council Elections 2013', 24 September 2013, <http://www.securitycouncilreport.org>.

[66] The Council for 2014 included, in addition to the UK and France, Australia, Lithuania, and Luxembourg.

[67] As for procedural fairness under the three previously-mentioned conditions—publicity, functionality, and good faith—the election of non-permanent members fares somewhat well. The 'gentleman's agreement' on allocation of seats, albeit not in the Charter, is known to all; and the more frequent rotation onto the Council of some states is defensible as a functional matter. Yet the horse-trading and politics in each election seems far from good faith or even-handed application of the criteria.

saw when the United States failed to secure a Council resolution to authorize its 2003 invasion of Iraq. To the critics, this form of partiality smacks of the worst form of favoritism and violation of sovereign equality.[68]

In a world in which different states wield different levers of power, it seems obvious that if the Security Council is to attempt to maintain international peace and security, influential states must be continuously involved in its decision-making. Quite simply, those states have resources not possessed by most other states—information about, political linkages to, contacts with, and, most critically, influence over numerous states and non-state actors, any one of which may be the subject of the Council's deliberations. The Council operates within an institutional setting where it relies on member states to carry out its most important decisions.[69] Some resolutions can be carried out by the Secretariat alone (for example writing a report or setting up a monitoring office), but most key directives—imposing economic sanctions, ordering a cease-fire, assembling of peace operations—require member state cooperation. They are not self-executing. Our moral reasoning about the Council must reflect the way the Charter is set up; we cannot reason as if the Council were like a domestic executive arm that can simply order the police to arrest someone or seize property.

Special participatory arrangements for powerful states where matters of peace and security are being negotiated are routine in international relations. Numerous multilateral peace initiatives involve participation by such states in addition to the belligerents themselves. Recently, these have included the Madrid Conference on the Middle East and its follow-on mechanisms, the Paris Conference on Cambodia, the Minsk Conference on the Nagorno-Karabakh conflict, and other informal 'friends' processes where states with ties to warring parties work behind the scenes to bring them together.[70] These typically include the United States and Russia along with key regional players. This sort of involvement serves not merely to allow powerful states to protect their interests during peace talks, though it certainly includes that goal. Rather, each party to a dispute recognizes that its big-power allies may help to persuade their adversaries' allies of a particular side's position, and that their adversaries' allies may then persuade their adversary of the need to compromise. In the case of Cambodia, China and the Soviet Union played an extraordinarily important role in convincing their allies, the Khmer Rouge and the Cambodian government, respectively, to accept a P5-initiated and brokered peace plan.[71] States also realize that major powers can help to guarantee a resultant agreement in the sense of standing behind it by offering resources for its implementation and by being willing to act against a violating entity.[72]

[68] See, e.g., Simpson, *Great Powers, supra* note 14, at 175–9.

[69] UN Charter, Art. 48.

[70] See, e.g., Teresa Whitfield, *Friends Indeed: The United Nations, Groups of Friends, and the Resolution of Conflict* (Washington DC: United States Institute of Peace, 2007).

[71] See Jin Song, 'The Political Dynamics of the Peacemaking Process in Cambodia', in Michael W. Doyle, Ian Johnstone, and Robert C. Orr (eds.), *Keeping the Peace: Multidimensional UN Operations in Cambodia and El Salvador* (Cambridge: Cambridge University Press, 1997) 53, 68–79.

[72] Steven R. Ratner, 'The Cambodia Settlement Agreements', *AJIL* 87 (1993): 1, 30–1.

Big powers have no legal right to participate in these negotiations, as do the Permanent Five, but the benefits to the process of peace are now well accepted in these diverse situations.

In the Council, which is constantly addressing these sorts of questions, such connections seem to me indispensable to careful deliberations on the best course of action, wherever conflict may be taking place. Although the Charter does not explicitly state that the P5 have a special responsibility regarding international peace, governments have at times reminded them of that unique role.[73] As a result of this essential involvement of powerful states in this particular organ, permanent membership contributes to peace and passes muster under the first pillar.[74] To reject permanent membership on the ground that it demonstrates exceptionalism, i.e. an immunity of those states from international law rules, is far too overbroad an argument. A special privilege for those states in one particular context neither results from overall exceptionalism to the rules nor causes or justifies it.

Yet guaranteed P5 participation is not without costs. José Alvarez, Detlev Vagts, Gerry Simpson, and others have criticized its effect on Council decisionmaking, insofar as the P5 is able to control the agenda of the Council. They point out that as perpetual repeat players in the Council's deliberations, with significant human resources devoted to the Council's work and levers of power to convince the non-P5 to go along, the P5 can produce international law that meets their needs. Thus, Alvarez notes the practice of the Security Council in passing resolutions that respond principally to the concerns of the United States, which he calls an example of (in Vagts's words) 'hegemonic international law'.[75] The results are thus two-fold: limitation of the Council's agenda and too-easy passage of binding resolutions pushed by the P5 or the small 'P3' of the United States, France, and the United Kingdom. Either way, the purpose of the Council under Article 24 is undermined in operation.

One obvious example is the proliferation of sanctions regimes since the 1990s as part of the West's opposition to Saddam Hussein, then the Taliban, then Al Qaeda, and now Iran. These sanctions were initiated by the United States, based primarily on information gathered by the United States, and others acquiesced. And the same power that gives the P5 useful influence over belligerents can also lead them to exert pressure on the non-permanent members. One famous instance concerns an encounter between the U.S. representative to the UN, Thomas Pickering, and the permanent representative of

[73] See, e.g., Statement by Eamon Gilmore, Deputy Prime Minister of Ireland, at the UN General Assembly, 68th Session, General Debate, 28 September 2013, at 6, <http://gadebate.un.org/sites/default/files/gastatements/68/IE_en.pdf>.

[74] This point is not, however, an argument for permanent membership of powerful states in the key decisionmaking bodies of all organizations. Nonetheless, arguments of efficacy and the need for particular expertise may well justify permanent membership of other states in the key decisionmaking bodies of other international organizations. See, e.g., Convention on International Civil Aviation, 7 December 1944, Art. 50(b) (basing membership on ICAO's chief executive body on 'adequate representation' to, inter alia, 'the States of chief importance in air transport' and others that 'make the largest contribution to the provision of facilities for international civil aviation').

[75] José Alvarez, 'Hegemonic International Law Revisited', *AJIL* 97 (2004): 873.

Yemen, just after the latter voted against Resolution 678 in 1990, authorizing force by the United States and its allies to oust the Iraqi army from Kuwait. Reflecting U.S. policy at the time, Pickering told his Yemeni counterpart that his vote 'was the most expensive "no" vote you ever cast', meaning it would cost Yemen $70 million in U.S. aid.[76] The Council ends up advancing the interests of the P5—or even the P3—which may or may not lessen the likelihood of armed conflict.

Such a critique suggests that the presence of the P5 does not prevent or terminate war, but rather, allows them to advance their narrow agendas through the UN's key lawmaking organ. Yet the use by the P5 of the Council for advancing their own interests is not an indictment of *permanent membership of powerful states* per se. It does not show that such participation fails to advance peace or is not necessary to advance peace, though it does show that it is not sufficient to advance peace. Yet Alvarez has a point in showing the shortcomings in the operation of the Council. This means that the Council will need to improve its working methods so that non-permanent members can assume their responsibilities and so that the Council also addresses issues of that matter to them. The P5 will need to be open to that sort of involvement so that the agenda of the Council is not only theirs to decide. Even so, most of the non-permanent members do not have the financial resources to be continuously proactive players in the Council during their two-year stint.

The same concerns can be raised with respect to the second pillar. On the one hand, the permanent presence of powerful states on the Council does not itself mean that the Council will take or not take actions that undermine basic human rights. But it does mean the Council's members will be influenced by the agenda of the P5, with consequences for human rights protection. The clearest example of this possibility is the targeted sanctions on suspected Taliban and Al Qaeda supporters, which have resulted in a freezing of assets and other restrictions on hundreds of individuals and institutions.[77] Two of those listed, a Muslim charity in Sweden that found its assets frozen, and an Italian national banned from traveling to Switzerland, eventually challenged the sanctions, and in particular the absence of any due process for de-listing, in the EU's European Court of Justice and the European Court of Human Rights, respectively, and won.[78] In the case of the charity, even if the sanctions themselves may not have harmed its basic human rights (as I do not think a charity has such rights), they may have prevented it from sending money to protect the basic human rights of others. As for the travel

[76] Robert D. Burrowes, 'The Republic of Yemen: The Politics of Unification and Civil War, 1989–1995', in Michael C. Hudson (ed.), *Middle East Dilemma: The Politics and Economics of Arab Integration* (New York: Columbia University Press, 1999) 187, 191.

[77] For the Al Qaeda list, see the list established and maintained by the 1267 Committee with respect to individuals, groups, undertakings, and other entities associated with Al Qaeda, <http://www.un.org/sc/committees/1267/AQList>.

[78] See C-402/05 P and C-415/05 P *Kadi and Al Barakaat International v Council of the EU and Commission of the EC* [2008] ECR I-6351; *Nada v Switzerland*, ECHR App. No. 10593/08 (2008).

ban, the freedom of movement that the Italian national was denied seems within the range of basic human rights as set forth in Chapter 3.

These examples represent a clear warning sign that permanent membership can at times violate human rights, although the record does not suggest that, in consequentialist terms, permanent membership per se interferes with basic human rights. In the case of these sanctions, the Security Council, prodded by European states that were effectively ordered by these regional courts not to comply, eventually instituted internal reforms of the sanctioning process, including streamlined processes for de-listing and the creation of an ombudsperson to hear complaints from those who believe they should not be on the list.[79]

These concerns under both pillars argue persuasively for reforms within the Council. Yet they do not displace the conclusion that permanent membership for some set of powerful or influential actors in a body whose purpose is the promotion of international peace and security is just. Whatever one's concerns about the agenda, output, and effectiveness of the Council, one need only imagine a Council without permanent members to see the effect on international peace. A random rotation of, for example, three states from each of the five regions, could yield a Council composed of poor, weak states with limited resources in their foreign ministries to either analyze the issues or work to implement the resolutions passed. Some of these concerns could be addressed through a UN fund to provide extra staff and information to poor states serving on the Council. Yet the powerful states with more influence to help implement the resolutions would have still have less incentive to do so if they were not involved in the decisionmaking.

So for all its flaws in operation, some form of permanent membership is justified. I would not say that thin justice *requires* such permanent participation (as I do in the case of limited membership overall), as an alternative could still work to promote peace (for example by involving powerful states continuously without giving them permanent membership), but certainly it is permitted.

(c) The veto

In the case of the veto, we must consider the consequences for peace and respect for basic human rights of mandatory agreement (or at least abstention) by the P5. Criticism of the veto focuses on the effects of such power on the decisionmaking of the Council, notably the impossibility of meaningful action concerning critical issues of peace or human rights even if only one state opposes some aspect of a resolution. Moreover, as Simpson notes, the veto ensures that the P5 'enjoy complete de facto immunity from the enforcement jurisdiction of the Security Council'.[80]

As discussed earlier, under the first pillar of thin justice, peace is promoted when the most powerful states (however we define them) are continuously involved in the decisionmaking of the Council. But that argument, which builds on the institutional reality that the Council decisions are not-self-executing, actually extends

[79] See SC Res. 1904 (17 December 2009), paras. 20–27; SC Res. 1989 (17 June 2011), paras. 21–35; and SC Res. 2083 (17 December 2012), paras 19–35.

[80] Simpson, *Great Powers, supra* note 14, at 188.

further. For peace is also advanced when those states support and stand behind a resolution of the Security Council and is weakened without that endorsement. If they oppose a decision, it is far less likely to be implemented. One could, I suppose, contest the claim that the assent of powerful states is a necessary condition for implementing the decisions of the Council. Perhaps it is not always necessary. But again, if such assent is better for the advancement of peace than the absence of such consent, the rule is justified.[81] Moreover, the veto itself might also have prevented conflict *among* the P5 during the Cold War. Each of the five, but particularly the United States and the Soviet Union, knew the limits of what the UN could do against it, making the organization less of a threat to each and thus encouraging each to participate in its deliberations.[82]

But might not the requirement of consent by the P5 actually harm peace, given that the veto has been used numerous times to block resolutions that could well have advanced the cause of peace, in particular resolutions to condemn or respond to aggression? However useful the assent of the powerful states might be in some instances, if it comes at the cost of non-passage of resolutions in these instances, then the veto cannot be said unambiguously to promote peace.

This scenario seems to me the best criticism of the veto—that in its operation it has paralyzed the Council more often than it has empowered it. Clearly, the P5 have used or threatened the veto over the years in ways that seem to have undercut efforts to bring peace. The Soviets took advantage of the veto frequently in the years when the General Assembly leaned to the West, including to prevent UN action in response to invasions of Hungary, Czechoslovakia, or Afghanistan; the United States made sure that the Council never criticized its actions in Latin America in the 1980s or the invasion of Iraq in 2003 or only rarely Israel's policies in the occupied Palestinian territories; and Britain and France used it in 1956 to prevent the Council from condemning their collaboration with Israel in invading Egypt.[83] The price of the veto for international peace is thus not to be minimized. And these cases reinforce Simpson's critique noted earlier. If the interests of any of the P5 are sufficiently strong and are not addressed in the wording—including the watering down—of a resolution, even when that resolution otherwise enjoys broad support within the Council, the veto will be used.

[81] A second argument, more contractarian in nature, would justify the right of the veto on the responsibilities of the P5. Under this view, the special right of the P5 to veto emanates from their special duties to promote peace (special not in the sense that they are owed only *to* some states, but special in that they are owed only *by* some states). The failure of powerful states to live up to their responsibility might be seen as an indictment of the veto, but it could also suggest that more should be done to get them to assume their responsibilities.

[82] One might even argue that the veto promoted peace insofar as the absence of the veto would have doomed the organization given the views of the victorious powers (in particular the Soviet Union). See Stanley Meisler, *United Nations: The First Fifty Years* (New York: Atlantic Monthly Press, 1995) 10–19; Luard, *A History of the United Nations, supra* note 51, at 27–54.

[83] For a list of vetoed resolutions, see Global Policy Forum, 'Subjects of UN Security Council Vetoes', <http://www.globalpolicy.org/component/content/article/102/40069.html>. A UN peacekeeping force to separate Israeli and Egyptian forces was eventually established by the General Assembly in Res. 1000 (ES-I) of 5 November 1956.

On the other hand, the veto has not prevented the Council from passing well over two thousand resolutions—including resolutions condemning aggression (by Iraq against Kuwait); laying down the terms of peace settlements (in the Middle East, Latin America, and Africa); creating or renewing the mandates of peacekeeping missions (all over the world) and criminal courts (for the former Yugoslavia and Rwanda); imposing sanctions (against Rhodesia, South Africa, Iran, North Korea, and Al Qaeda); and even authorizing force (in Kuwait, Somalia, Bosnia, Haiti, and Libya). Often the strongest advocates and supporters of Council action were outside the P5.

So the veto has not paralyzed the Council overall. In a no-veto world, each of these would have passed as well, and perhaps have reflected the views of the Council majority more—but they would not have had the same political force. The gap between the terms of those resolutions and the behavior of the actors to whom they are directed merely demonstrates the obvious point that the veto is not sufficient to ensure respect for Council resolutions, not that it is not necessary. The veto forces a limited form of consensus on the Council in terms of the views of the key powers. The cases of self-protection notwithstanding, in my view the case has not been made that, overall, the veto harms international peace.

With regard to the second pillar, however, I think objections to the veto are on far stronger ground. The Council has been paralyzed from time to time from acting to rectify gross abuses of human rights directly because of the veto of one or more permanent members. The refusal of the Council's members, in particular the United States and France, to supplement the UN Mission in Rwanda with more troops and more authority after the outbreak of genocide in April 1994 is perhaps the most haunting example of the effect of the veto. As the UN's independent panel investigating the UN response in Rwanda wrote rather laconically: 'The Security Council bears a responsibility for its lack of political will to do more to stop the killing.'[84] Since that time, the veto or threat of a veto by Russia and China has prevented the Council from imposing sanctions on Syria during its brutal attacks on civilians during its civil war.

The veto has precluded the UN from taking action, including requiring its members to impose sanctions or authorizing them to use force, that could prevent or respond to mass atrocities—for without Council approval, force is legally questionable. It is true that a failure to authorize sanctions or force as a result of a veto does not itself violate human rights, and indeed one cannot be certain that the Council's authorization of force would bring about an improvement in the human rights situation, although the Rwanda example certainly suggests otherwise.[85] But the complete preclusion of lawful measures to protect a besieged population as a result of a Council veto renders the veto an interference, even if somewhat indirect, in the basic human rights of the populations of affected states.

[84] See Report of the Independent Inquiry into the actions of the United Nations during the 1994 genocide in Rwanda, 15 December 1999, Annex, 37, UN Doc. S/1999/1257; see also ibid., at 35–9.

[85] Ibid., at 30 ('A force numbering 2,500 should have been able to stop or at least limit massacres').

With respect to the effect of the veto on peace, my response to criticism of the veto relied on the many examples where the veto did not prevent the Council from agreeing on important measures to promote international and internal peace and emphasized the danger to the political force of resolutions that do pass if that passage does not reflect the unanimity of the P5. It is, in my view, harder to deploy that sort of argument regarding the non-interference with basic human rights, for the instances of paralysis exert a larger shadow over the cases of Council consensus in this case. This may be because we can almost count the lives lost for each month during which the Council fails to act due to a veto (even if we know that Council action is no guarantee that that number will go down), whereas it is harder to measure the consequences for peace of Council paralysis. I also think the effect of the veto has been to prevent consensus on, or water down, the human rights components of resolutions to a greater extent than is the case for parts of resolutions aimed at protecting internal or interstate peace. The Council has an easier time achieving consensus on cease-fire, non-proliferation, anti-terrorism issues, piracy, and other issues associated with armed conflict than it does on human rights, although the landscape is changing.[86]

I confess this is not an entirely satisfying argument, for much of the Council's work in the area of internal and international peace also aims to protect the human rights of the victims of armed conflict. But in the end it leaves me less convinced of any advantages of the veto for human rights compared to issues of peace and security, and compared to the disadvantages of the veto. The result is to make the veto highly suspect under the second pillar on consequentialist grounds for eliminating a course of action that may significantly advance the basic rights of populations under siege.

This tension between the appraisal under the first pillar and the second pillar requires that we consider alternatives to the unjust status quo that satisfy both pillars as well as possible. Given the importance of the first pillar, the tension does not argue for simple elimination of the veto. But it does call for an additional duty on the P5—indeed on all the members of the Council—to support resolutions that will directly contribute to an immediate diminution in the worst human rights abuses.

Indeed, in 2012, the so-called 'Small 5' (Switzerland, Costa Rica, Liechtenstein, Jordan, and Singapore) introduced a draft resolution in the General Assembly that would urge the P5 not to veto resolutions so as 'to block Council action aimed at preventing or ending genocide, war crimes and crimes against humanity'.[87] That proposal would also require the P5 to justify any veto in terms of international law and the Charter, a practice that would also address the problems

[86] See Joanna Weschler, 'Human Rights', in David M. Malone (ed.), *The UN Security Council: From the Cold War to the 21st Century* (Boulder, CO: Lynne Rienner Publishers, 2004) 55.

[87] Improving the Working Methods of the Security Council, draft resolution, 28 March 2012, Annex, para. 20, UN Doc. A/66/L/42. The Small 5 withdrew their proposal before a vote in the General Assembly due to strong opposition from the P5 and other states. See also 'Working Methods of the Security Council, Swiss Federation Federal Department of Foreign Affairs', <http://www.eda.admin.ch/eda/en/home/topics/intorg/un/missny/wormet.html>.

of the veto for blocking actions that might advance peace as well.[88] Certainly we can be skeptical that a resolution attempting to limit the P5's discretion will really protect human rights. And as played out in the Security Council regarding Syria since 2012, some states will argue that their veto saves more lives than it costs, and it will sometimes be difficult to know ex ante who is right in this argument.[89] But such a new obligation is a particularly promising way to satisfy the second pillar without undermining the first.

My reluctance to support elimination of the veto, and my position in favor of continued permanent participation of powerful states, are also grounded in the compliance corollary identified in Chapter 3. Relying on Hart's criteria for any legal system, I posited that in considering alternatives to the status quo, we remain aware that for rules to comprise such a system, they must be generally observed. For the Council's special powers under Article 25 of the Charter mean that its binding decisions are part of the international *legal* system, in particular the part governing international peace and security. The guaranteed participation of a core group of states with political power and the non-objection of those states to anything considered legally binding furthers the end of general compliance.[90] Without the compliance of the powerful, the prospects for observance of Council decisions by their many allies are diminished. Moreover, those states also are more likely not merely to refrain from complying, but to block others' compliance as well.

In a world in which the implementation and enforcement of the Council's decisions falls principally to member states, the neutrality or opposition of powerful states decreases the prospects for compliance. The special status of the P5 enhances prospects for their observance because they cannot complain that they were not involved in or opposed the decision. This decisionmaking structure is not a *sufficient* condition for compliance, but it may well be necessary, for in the alternative scenario those states would have to be persuaded to obey something they had opposed. In this sense, the status of permanent membership and the veto are not *just* a case of historical power politics. Rather, they preserve the international law of the collective security system from irrelevance.

One response to this justification for the veto is that it is circular—that it justifies, and not merely assumes, lack of compliance with resolutions that the permanent members oppose. For if the UN Charter gave the Council binding decisionmaking power without veto rights for the P5, those members would still have an obligation to carry out its decisions and should not be able to opt out simply because they were not involved or opposed the resolution. This is a charge that can be leveled at the compliance corollary more broadly, such that Hart's and

[88] Ibid., para. 19.

[89] See, e.g., UN Doc. S/PV.6810, 19 July 2012, p. 13 (in vetoing sanctions resolution, Chinese representative emphasizes 'the interests of the people of Syria'); see also UN Doc. S/PV.6484, 18 February 2011 (in vetoing condemnation of Israel for settlement in the West Bank, U.S. notes importance of 'respect for human rights.... But there simply are no shortcuts').

[90] For a view that the Council has no business enforcing the rules of international law and is merely a 'technician of peace', see Koskenniemi, 'The Police in the Temple', *supra* note 62, at 343–5.

my inclusion of the criteria of general observance can be seen as a justification for violation of rules. But a claim that a legal system can exist only if there is general observance does not do that. It simply flows from a realization that however much we might have legal rules validated by rules of recognition, the existence of a legal system turns upon certain realities about society's attitude toward the rules of recognition.[91] So even if the veto is unjust for failing to satisfy the second pillar, we have good reasons to be extremely reluctant about discarding it.

(d) A stronger General Assembly?

These arguments about the Council's decisionmaking, including permanent membership and the veto, allow us to return to the merits of expanding the General Assembly's powers. For even if we could somehow overcome the core disadvantage of the Assembly with respect to maintaining the peace—its size—we still face squarely both the substantive justice argument in favor of the veto and the compliance corollary. Both essentially turn on the importance of the consent of the powerful, whether for peace or for law. Whereas it may be defensible for states to vote equally on internal UN matters, a binding decision on external matters must carry with it a general expectation of compliance. In the case of the General Assembly, it is not only possible but likely that a coalition of two-thirds of the membership would exclude numerous states with large populations, territory, GDP (both gross and per capita), financial resources, intellectual talent, and military might.

Unless those excluded states felt the need to comply with the majority's view, which is far from the reality we live in today, we can expect significant resistance from many quarters to Assembly-made law. It may not persist across all resolutions, and it may not include all states that did not support the resolution—but it is one of those instances where the compliance corollary rules out this particular alternative to the status quo. The attitudes of enough states, North and South, toward enough General Assembly resolutions would lead to resistance to treating them as law, and the resulting gap between law and behavior would, in my view, threaten the existence of international law. Instead, states would probably treat them like recommendations—which is exactly as is provided in the Charter currently. To treat them as law is simply too at odds with existing state attitudes.

(e) Beyond the status quo

My appraisal of the justice of limited size, permanent membership, and a limited veto do not, however, justify the status quo of the UN Charter and its practical implementation. The number of fifteen is arbitrary as a matter of justice. And the need for a recognition of power within the decisionmaking process of the Council does not translate into a permanent seat, with a veto, for the United States, Russia, the United Kingdom, France, and China. The perpetuation of a leading role for those states based on their status as the leading allies in a war sixty years ago

[91] H.L.A. Hart, *The Concept of Law*, 3rd ed. (Oxford: Oxford University Press, 2012), 103–4, 116–17.

(and even at that, only three really were) seems ridiculously anachronistic. As for political power, for a few decades these arrangements might have made sense as these states had nuclear weapons, colonies, or satellites, and thus a global reach. But today other states have nuclear weapons, colonies are gone, and two or even three of the P5 can hardly be said to be major global powers. Indeed, that lack of congruence suggests that the current membership of the P5 does not advance peace, or at a minimum does not advance it very well. Moreover, the members of the Council, and the P5 in particular, have been quite inconsistent or worse in carrying out their special duty of maintaining international peace. The P5 have shown themselves to be pursuing their own interests just as much as those of other states when they veto resolutions in the Council.

The last twenty years have witnessed hundreds of proposals, from governments and NGOs, for alternative arrangements in the Council that correct these deficiencies. Consider the views of the Secretary-General's High Level Panel on Threats, Challenges, and Change:

> [T]he challenge for any reform is to increase both the effectiveness and the credibility of the Security Council and, most importantly, to enhance its capacity and willingness to act in the face of threats. This requires greater involvement in Security Council decision-making by those who contribute most; greater contributions from those with special decision-making authority; and greater consultation with those who must implement its decisions.
>
> [R]eforms of the Security Council should meet the following principles:
> (a) They should... increase the involvement in decision-making of those who contribute most to the United Nations financially, militarily and diplomatically—specifically in terms of contributions to... assessed budgets, participation in mandated peace operations, contributions to voluntary activities of the United Nations in the areas of security and development, and diplomatic activities in support of United Nations objectives and mandates...;
> (b) They should bring into the decision-making process countries more representative of the broader membership, especially of the developing world;
> (c) They should not impair the effectiveness of the Security Council;
> (d) They should increase the democratic and accountable nature of the body.[92]

Notwithstanding this useful list of criteria for Council membership, including the connection between membership and contribution to peace (as well as development), when states make proposals for expansion, they tend to be based principally on advancing their own interests and those of their friends. It is no coincidence that Indonesia, India, Nigeria, and Brazil have been sympathetic to the (impartial sounding) idea of permanent members from each region of the globe—a quick look at the map reveals who wins under that plan. Every player in

[92] The Secretary-General's High-level Panel Report on Threats, Challenges and Change, 'A More Secure World: Our Shared Responsibility' (2004), paras. 248–249. In addition to changes in the composition of the Council, the Panel and others have made proposals for a greater role of the General Assembly in the Council's work, greater transparency in the Council's deliberations, and increased roles for NGOs.

the debate is suspected by every other player of having self-interested reasons for its proposals.[93]

Thin global justice does not point to any single solution to the reform of the Council. More members are desirable in terms of showing increased support for resolutions, though the risk of deadlock is great; permanent membership and the veto should be calibrated to power, but need not be coextensive. One could have some of the increasingly influential states as permanent members, while limiting the veto to the most powerful—veto for the United States, China, Russia, and the EU (replacing France and the United Kingdom as a permanent member). In making these choices, states need to remember the minimal criteria for justice—prevention of war along with respect for basic human rights. Moreover, if reform of the Council is ever undertaken, it should probably strive for more than thin justice, an issue I leave for the concluding chapter.

Lastly, and looking beyond thin (or thick) justice, reform measures will need to address the importance of procedural fairness discussed in Part I of this chapter. Although procedural fairness in the context of decisionmaking entails different considerations from that in admission and could itself be the subject of a separate book, it must incorporate the basic concept, essential to Fullerian inner morality, of a due process for the *participants in* and *parties affected by* the Council's work. In the case of the Council, this requirement suggests the need for structures and processes that make the non-permanent players active players in the Council's work, even while some are content to be passive. The Council will also need to do a better job on transparency and the imperative of full discussion involving those most affected by decisions, even those outside the Council. The 'Small 5' proposal offers a useful set of suggestions in this regard.[94] The members of the Council have shown some ability to learn from their mistakes, notably in the terrorism sanctions regimes, where individual targets of sanctions now have some minimal procedural protections and an ombudsman to take into account some of their interests.[95] But much remains to be done on matters of procedural fairness.

B. The International Monetary Fund

The Articles of Agreement of the IMF offer a significantly different formula for decisionmaking compared to the UN.[96] The IMF, an organization of 188 states, was created after World War II to foster international financial stability and avoid

[93] For a comprehensive set of documents and reports on Security Council reform, see the website of the Center for UN Reform Education, <http://www.centerforunreform.org>.

[94] See *supra* note 87. For a recent sense of governmental attitudes on the Council's working methods, see Provisional Verbatim Record of the 6672nd Meeting, 30 November 2011, UN Doc. S/PV./6672. For a summary of action already taken by the Council, see Note by the President of the Security Council, 26 July 2010, UN Doc. S/2010/507.

[95] See *supra* note 79; John R. Crook (ed.), 'United States Supports Reform of UN Terrorism Sanctions Procedures', in Contemporary Practice of the United States relating to International Law, *AJIL* 104 (2010): 271, 283.

[96] The formula is also roughly the same for the World Bank, and indeed much of the discussion that follows could be applied to the Bank.

the mistakes that led to the Great Depression; it does so by monitoring states' economic conditions, promulgating international standards and codes for improving national and global financial stability, and offering policy advice and technical assistance to nations rich and poor. Most critically, it serves as a lender of last resort to states experiencing shortfalls of foreign currency, offering a range of different loans subject to repayment conditions. Its views as to a state's creditworthiness are highly influential or even dispositive for other potential public and private lenders. When a state is in financial distress, the IMF exerts tremendous power over it in demands it will make in exchange for access to IMF funds.

The Articles entrust decisionmaking to the full membership of states, but allocate votes based on each state's financial contribution to the IMF, or quota. Quotas are determined based on economic factors about the state, including GDP and foreign exchange reserves. Key decisions—in particular the extension of loans to member states facing shortfalls in foreign exchange reserves—are made by an Executive Board, comprising twenty-four people entitled to cast the votes of all of the states.

The Board has one member from each of the top five quota holders, who casts the vote of that state alone (together they control almost 39 per cent of the votes); and nineteen other members, each representing other groups of countries, with each Director's votes depending on which countries he or she represents. A majority of votes, required for most Board decisions, can be obtained with the votes of as few as eight Directors, representing thirty-six states. The developing world, however, retains more leverage over votes requiring a super-majority (such as adjustments to quotas, which require 85 per cent of votes), where, if they act together, they can block a decision. The total number of votes as of 2014 was 2,519,736. Consider the sample of voting power shown in Table 7.1.

Sovereign equality notwithstanding, the IMF gives special rights to states in proportion to their contribution to the working capital of the Fund. Poor states have little power to influence decisionmaking, and rich states, notably the United States and European states, control the voting; in effect, they enjoy a veto on IMF decisionmaking. As a result, the latter have succeeded in promulgating IMF policy

Table 7.1 Sample of votes per IMF member state

State	Number of votes	Percentage of total
Argentina	21,908	0.87
Botswana	1,615	0.06
China	95,996	3.81
Germany	146,392	5.81
Indonesia	21,530	0.85
Japan	157,022	6.23
Marshall Islands	772	0.03
Russia	60,191	2.39
United States	421,961	16.75*

* See <http://www.imf.org>.

that conditions the IMF's lending to its members on domestic adjustments based on the rich states' views of the role of the state in the economy. These ideas include the 'Washington consensus' on fiscal and monetary policy, as well as concepts of good governance, human rights, and environmental protection.[97] This Western control is exacerbated by the informal arrangement among the leading quota holders that the Managing Director will always be a West European and the Deputy Managing Director a U.S. national, as well as by the hiring of staff—extremely influential in the IMF's oversight responsibilities—whose training makes them sympathetic to these concerns. Many of the developing world complaints about IMF conditionality are actually complaints about how the IMF itself makes decisions, formally and informally. As Marc Williams has said: 'Those in greatest need of the IMF's resources are therefore permanently in a state of subordination.'[98]

The decisionmaking in the IMF has a functional justification and is certainly rationally related to the goals of the organization. In order to increase the overall lending from the bank, help countries experiencing currency shortfalls, and thereby presumably increase overall economic welfare, the IMF needs capital. To get donors to contribute to the IMF's resources, it is fairly sensible that its decisions, like those of any other bank, ought to be made by those who have contributed the money. And the votes afforded are, in fact, in direct proportion to their share in the working capital of the institution. In the case of the IMF, those contributions themselves are determined based on the application of objective economic criteria, criteria that indeed have resulted in adjustments to the quotas over the years as some developing world players have assumed greater prominence. Yet critics of the IMF also point out that the functional justification is not so obvious on its own terms. In fact, a very large part of the expenses of the IMF are paid not by the quota-holders, but by the states receiving IMF assistance, even while the creditors have seen their repayments increase.[99]

When we look beyond the economic or functional sense of the quotas to the justice of the decisionmaking process, the current arrangement raises serious concerns. (I leave aside here the obviously critical issue, the basis of an enormous literature, of whether the IMF is even effective in terms of its stated goals of ensuring global financial stability.) The IMF's policies are driven by the relatively small number of Western states that control the decisionmaking, as well as a leadership and staff sympathetic to their perspectives. This phenomenon translates into particular influence for the United States and the G-7; it also means that potential borrowers can sometimes use their friendship with powerful IMF members to gain better terms when they borrow.[100] Weighted voting, and the other means

[97] Andre Newburg, 'The Changing Roles of the Bretton Woods Institutions: Evolving Concepts of Conditionality', in Mario Giovanoli (ed.), *International Monetary Law: Issues for the New Millennium* (Oxford: Oxford University Press, 2000) 81.

[98] Marc Williams, *International Economic Organizations and the Third World* (Harlow: Harvester Wheatsheaf, 1994) 67.

[99] Ngaire Woods, *The Globalizers: The IMF, the World Bank, and Their Borrowers* (Ithaca, NY: Cornell University Press, 2006) 194–6.

[100] Woods, *The Globalizers, supra* note 99, at 38, 71–2, and 190–3; Axel Dreher, 'IMF Conditionality: Theory and Evidence', *Public Choice* 141 (2009): 233, 251.

of influence by rich states that emanate from it, thus directly determines IMF policies, including, most importantly, the terms for borrowing—conditionality—which has significant impacts on debtor nations.

With respect to the effect of that decisionmaking and the resultant conditionality on international or intrastate peace, the founders of the Bretton Woods Institutions saw a clear connection between economics and peace from their own memories of the Depression and the worldwide financial collapse, the rise of the Nazis, and their consequences for peace in Europe. International financial stability was at the core of their concerns after World War II, and indeed from that perspective it made a great deal of sense to have the leading financial players invest in and be in charge of the IMF.[101] As for results, even the IMF's critics acknowledge that the post-war financial architecture, which the IMF has played a significant role in overseeing, is less prone to the sorts of catastrophes that preceded World War II (though the IMF was powerless to prevent the 2008 crisis). To that extent, the IMF's decisionmaking processes have indeed contributed regularity to the global financial system and thus helped preserve the peace. Certainly the IMF has always emphasized its role in providing that stability.[102]

Yet for purposes of the first pillar of global justice, we should not draw too many conclusions from the lack of a second Depression-like crisis since 1945. Beyond the impossibility of a counterfactual—of a world without the IMF, or a world with different IMF policies—the connection between weighted voting and the lending terms that flow from it, on the one hand, and internal peace or inter-state peace, on the other, still seems rather attenuated. Many factors can cause a state already in economic distress to cross the line to civil conflict or, even more so, for its instability to cross borders; the IMF's policies are only one of them. The recent history of the IMF reveals situations where conditionality imposed by the Bank was not accompanied by violence, notably in Mexico in the 1980s and 1990s, as well as others where domestic unrest broke out, notably in Indonesia during the 1990s Asian financial crisis.[103] Although Stiglitz blames the IMF for Indonesia's riots, the cronyism and incompetence of the Suharto regime were also a major cause of the resultant unrest.[104]

With regard to the second pillar, the impact of the IMF's decisionmaking and decisions on basic human rights is now the subject of a significant literature. Critics of the IMF have made two claims: (a) that the IMF ignores human rights concerns in borrower states by either lending to states with poor human rights practices or not ensuring that the funds lent actually advance human rights;

[101] See generally John Braithwaite and Peter Drahos, *Global Business Regulation* (Cambridge: Cambridge University Press, 2000) 95–101.

[102] See, e.g., International Monetary Fund, 'How the IMF Promotes Global Economic Stability', 23 September 2013, <http://www.imf.org/external/np/exr/facts/globstab.htm>.

[103] See Woods, *The Globalizers, supra* note 99, at 86–103; Joseph E. Stiglitz, *Globalization and its Discontents* (New York: W.W. Norton, 2002) 119–20.

[104] IMF Independent Evaluation Office, 'The IMF and Recent Capital Account Crises: Indonesia, Korea, Brazil' (2003) 15–16, <http://www.imf.org/external/np/ieo/2003/cac/pdf/main.pdf>.

and (b) IMF conditionality actually harms human rights—indeed basic human rights—by hurting the most vulnerable within the borrower state. Thus, on the first point, Human Rights Watch has for many years urged the IMF to take a country's overall human rights practices into account in its lending.[105] And on the second point, the UN' Special Rapporteur on the Right to Food, Jean Ziegler, stated that IMF structural adjustment programs, 'far from improving food security for the most vulnerable populations... have often resulted in a deterioration of food security among the poorest'.[106] One quantitative study claims to demonstrate that the duration of a state's supervision by the IMF is causally related (positively) to the prevalence of torture and summary executions.[107] The IMF has responded to these allegations on numerous fronts, from an unconvincing legal strategy that denied that it was bound by human rights law[108] to a new set of policies that it has claimed aim to protect the very poor within the states where it operates.[109]

My question here is not the legal one of whether the IMF is bound by human rights law, but rather, whether we can say, as a matter of justice, that its decisionmaking causes harm to basic human rights. The most relevant rights here are those of an economic nature, in particular the rights to food and health. On the causal link, the appraisal depends on whether we believe the IMF, its critics, or some other version of the linkages between IMF policies and the borrowing state's ability to respect basic human rights. If IMF policies have the effect of raising some people out of poverty while placing others in it, then a consequentialist version of the second pillar would need to balance the results before assessing the impact on respect for human rights. If, as Ziegler and others more legally oriented suggest, the IMF has a duty to do no harm,[110] i.e. a deontological trump view, then the compensating benefits for human rights of IMF programs are morally irrelevant. In terms of exclusionary reasons, we would need to consider whether there are any possible justifications for policies that can be closely linked to infringing on people's access to food. Although improvement in the state's overall economic welfare or the full repayment of Northern-state creditors might not be

[105] See, e.g., Human Rights Watch, 'Sri Lanka: IMF Should Not Condone Abuses', 22 July 2009, <http://www.hrw.org/news/2009/07/22/sri-lanka-imf-should-not-condone-abuses>; on the World Bank, see Human Rights Watch, 'Abuse-Free Development: How the World Bank Should Safeguard Against Human Rights Violations' (2013), <http://www.hrw.org/sites/default/files/reports/worldbank0713_ForUpload.pdf>.

[106] The Right to Food: Note by the Secretary-General, 12 September 2005, Annex, para. 42, UN Doc. A/60/350; see also Bharati Sadasivam, 'The Impact of Structural Adjustment on Women: A Governance and Human Rights Agenda', *HRQ* 19 (1997): 630.

[107] M. Rodwan Abouharb and David L. Cingranelli, 'IMF Programs and Human Rights, 1981–2003', *Rev Intl Orgs* 4 (2009): 47.

[108] See Andrew Clapham, *Human Rights Obligations of Non-State Actors* (Oxford: Oxford University Press, 2006) 142–52.

[109] See International Monetary Fund, 'The IMF's Role in Helping Protect the Most Vulnerable in the Global Crisis', 30 September 2013, <http://www.imf.org/external/np/exr/facts/protect.htm>. The literature is vast on whether these new policies are effective.

[110] Cf. Clapham, *Human Rights Obligations, supra* note 108, at 151–2 (the IMF has a duty to respect, protect, and fulfill regarding human rights).

an acceptable reason, the meeting of others' basic human rights, assuming IMF policies accomplish this, might justify a rights infringement.

Unless we adopt the rights as trump view, the thin justice standard leaves us with a perhaps frustratingly ambiguous outcome regarding IMF decisionmaking. It does not find IMF decisionmaking unjust simply because it is dominated by Western governments. There are certainly grounds to criticize that domination, whether from the perspective of the efficacy of the institution or a thicker standard of justice that would rely on some deeper sense of responsibility of the rich states for the fate of the poor states. Instead, the justice of the IMF's decisionmaking ultimately turns on whether it harms or does not harm basic human rights, since the first pillar seems too speculative a basis on which to make a conclusion. Under either the consequentialist or exclusionary reasons version of the second pillar, IMF decisionmaking would not be unjust if we can demonstrate affirmative gains to basic human rights from IMF policies. This means that the verdict is out until we can achieve some empirical consensus on conditionality's impact on severe poverty.

Despite this equivocal appraisal, the standard of thin justice still provides a useful framework for improving the workings of the IMF. It suggests that, at a minimum, the IMF's Board needs to ensure that, for each loan it offers, it (a) carefully considers the impact of its loans on the possibility of civil conflict and on the state's ability to protect basic economic rights, such as those to food and health, and (b) seeks to minimize these risks as much as possible.[111] This way of ensuring thin justice might entail new data-gathering that focuses on the very poor as well as the participation of experts on those issues. If the current decisionmaking structure means that the IMF is not able to undertake these two tasks, then that process needs to be reconstructed.

Such a reconstruction need not translate to equal voting power, or even involve a redistribution of votes. Ngaire Woods, for instance, has advocated a 'double-majority' voting formula in which decisions would need to be endorsed not only by a majority of the (weighted) voting power but by a majority of the membership, thus requiring the rich states to build broad-based coalitions with the poorer states; a more transparent process for leadership selection would also help.[112] Joseph Stiglitz has also emphasized the need for greater involvement by the Directors from the poor states, as well as transparency (though he has called for a vastly reduced role for the IMF overall, limiting it to crisis management).[113] The preceding discussion means that the purpose of these proposed reforms must be to ensure that decisionmaking meets the standard of thin global justice first.

The practices of the IMF raise numerous questions about the justice of the decisionmaking of other international economic institutions. The IMF is somewhat

[111] For further proposals in this regard, see Sigrun I. Skogly, 'The Human Rights Obligations of the World Bank and the IMF', in Willem van Genugten, Paul Hunt, and Susan Mathews (eds.), *World Bank, IMF, and Human Rights* (Oisterwijk: Wolf Legal Publishers, 2003) 45, 59–68.

[112] Woods, *The Globalizers, supra* note 99, at 206–11.

[113] Stiglitz, *Globalization, supra* note 103, at 224–33.

unique insofar as its key decisions are generally not part of the enforcement of a set of rules of international law. Certainly, international monetary law, including the Articles of Agreement of the IMF, dictates no particular approach to conditionality.[114] Rather, the IMF has, over the years, devised policies about what recipient states need to do to return to a sound financial footing. For other international economic bodies, however, their decisionmaking needs to be examined along with the underlying law for which the international institution has responsibility. Thus, in Chapters 10 and 11, I will revisit questions of decisionmaking when I consider the thin justice of the core norms of international trade law enforced by the WTO and of international investment law enforced in part by international arbitral bodies.

III. Conclusion: From Institutional Structures to the Justice of Institutional Discretion

The foregoing inquiry into the structures of international organizations suggests that appraisal of their justice needs to move beyond opposition to selectivity or unequal treatment. Instead, it suggests that international organizations may have legitimate reasons to make distinctions in whom they admit. In the case of the UN, the WTO, the Council of Europe, and the EU, those decisions, for the most part, meet a standard of thin justice, although religiously-based discrimination by the EU would not. As for decisionmaking structures, I argued that, even though parts of the exclusivity of the Security Council are thinly just, the unlimited veto currently enjoyed by the P5 seems unjust for its interference with basic human rights. Moreover, other aspects of the Council's decisionmaking need reform so that the P5 does not control the agenda in a way that could harm either peace or human rights. The justice of IMF's weighted voting turns on highly contested views about the impact of IMF lending on states.

Beyond thin justice, two other concerns permeated this chapter. One was the importance of some kind of Fullerian internal morality to admission and decisionmaking, one characterized by fairness or due process for the affected parties. Even though we cannot derive any detailed and mandatory criteria for fairness given the diversity of organizations, organizations can do better in terms of transparency and the involvement of non-powerful states. The second concern was the compliance corollary introduced in Chapter 3. Because a legal system must be characterized by general observance of the rules, I urged great caution in considering alternatives to both permanent membership and the veto within the Council, two of the key targets of cosmopolitan and legal critics of the Council. Unjust institutions need not be tolerated at all costs, but if an institution's structures fail

[114] See IMF Articles of Agreement, Art. V(3), which simply states that the IMF 'shall adopt policies on the use of its general resources'. For the basic policies on conditionality, see International Monetary Fund, 'Guidelines on Conditionality', 25 September 2002, <http://www.imf.org/External/np/pdr/cond/2002/eng/guid/092302.pdf>.

under one of the two pillars, we must be skeptical of proposals that would not elicit the support of powerful actors, particularly when the absence of such cooperation would fundamentally undermine the functioning of the international legal system.

Before wrapping up this chapter, it is worth considering one final point: having examined the justice of institutional *structures* and the fairness of the decisionmaking process, can we not say something more about the *outcomes* of their decisionmaking? For decisionmaking includes not merely following just and fair procedures, but deciding on the substance of real issues. Institutions have enormous discretion on how to dispose of issues that come within their mandates—to ignore claims of states or non-state actors, try to quietly resolve them, condemn actors, or even impose sanctions on them.

To the extent that decisionmaking by international institutions shapes the contours of international rules, those outputs can be appraised under the two pillars. Thus, we consider the justice of the rules on the use of force in part by examining the practice of the UN. This strategy is followed throughout this volume. But beyond the standard of thin justice, I think we can also rely upon the fundamental notion of justice (not global justice) introduced in Chapter 2, in particular Hart's and Hare's conception of justice as treating like cases alike.[115] In the case of judging the trends of decision of international organizations, basic justice or impartiality means that we want to know at a minimum that the organization is *not playing favorites*—whether or not the actual outcomes pass the two pillars. Refraining from playing favorites does not require equal treatment for all states and individuals that are the targets of its actions—just that they be treated as equals.[116] Such consistency is a sort of force field around the two pillars of justice, a critical element of decisionmaking in any institution that *operates under and is constrained by international law.*

Sometimes the organic instruments of international organizations will make this appraisal easier, if, for instance, they require an organization to act under certain circumstances. In the case of the UN, the Security Council 'shall determine' whether there is a threat to the peace and breach of the peace and 'shall make recommendations or decide' what sort of action to take in response to them.[117]

But the charters of organizations are often so open-textured that they leave a huge amount of room for discretion. The Charter's requirement that the UN promote the 'political, economic, social, and educational advancement' of peoples in Trust Territories provides a very amorphous standard on which to judge the UN's actions in different cases.[118] Similarly, the Constitution of the International Labor Organization obligates the ILO to 'further among the nations of the world programmes which will achieve... full employment and the raising of standards

[115] See Chapter 3, Section I.A; see generally Peter Cane, *Responsibility in Law and Morality* (Oxford: Hart Publishing, 2002) 15–28.

[116] Ronald Dworkin, *Taking Rights Seriously* (Cambridge, MA: Harvard University Press, 1977) 227.

[117] UN Charter, Art. 39.

[118] Ibid., Art. 76(b).

of living',[119] not particularly specific a duty to help much in any inquiry into the impartiality of the ILO's actions.

In other cases, the instrument merely authorizes conduct, for example the UN Charter goes on to say that the Council 'may' take non-military measures or military measures, without any requirement that it do so in each case.[120] And the Genocide Convention provides only that: 'Any Contracting Party may call upon the competent organs of the UN to take such action under the Charter of the United Nations as they consider appropriate for the prevention and suppression of acts of genocide.'[121] These permissive provisions do not give us a standard by which to determine whether the UN is acting impartially. That does not make them irrelevant to international organizations, for the law can influence the UN's options by inviting certain actions or channeling it in certain directions. As Rosalyn Higgins long ago observed, the Council's debates and resolutions show 'political operation *within* the law, rather than decision according *to* the law'.[122]

Although international affairs, like life, does not afford any examples of identical or even very like cases, this general principle still forces members and observers of international organizations to inquire continuously whether the disparate treatment the institutions afford different wars, economic crises, health emergencies, human rights atrocities, environmental problems, and other situations are justified by the relevant differences between the cases. As noted earlier, legal scholars have noted the link between the role of the P5 and the Council's failure to treat like cases alike. From philosophy, David Held has offered a list of reforms of the UN—compulsory jurisdiction over all interstate and individual-state disputes, creation of law by a near consensus of the General Assembly—based on the idea that this would end the practice of double-standards, thereby 'establishing and maintaining the "rule of law" and its impartial administration in international affairs'.[123]

International organizations are hardly unaware of these concerns. Thus, for example, the Secretary-General's High-Level Panel stated in 2004:

> The credibility of any system of collective security also depends on how well it promotes security for all its members, without regard to the nature of would-be beneficiaries.... Too often, the United Nations and its Member States have discriminated in responding to

[119] Constitution of the ILO, *supra* note 17, Art. 23(III). [120] UN Charter, Art. 41.

[121] Convention on the Prevention and Punishment of the Crime of Genocide, 9 December 1948, Art. VIII, 78 UNTS 277.

[122] Rosalyn Higgins, 'The Place of International Law in the Settlement of Disputes by the Security Council', *AJIL* 64 (1970): 1, 16 (emphasis in original); see also Robert O. Keohane, *After Hegemony: Cooperation and Discord in the World Political Economy* (Princeton, NJ: Princeton University Press, 1984) 57–9.

[123] David Held, 'Democracy and the New International Order', in Daniele Archibugi and David Held (eds.), *Cosmopolitan Democracy: An Agenda for a New World Order* (Oxford: Polity Press, 1995) 97, 107; see also David Held, 'Cosmopolitanism: Globalisation Tamed?' *Rev Intl Stud* 29 (2003): 465, 475 ('The susceptibility of the UN to the agendas of the most powerful states [is]... indicative of the disjuncture between cosmopolitan aspirations and their partial and one-sided application'). As noted in Chapter 1, I remain skeptical of proposals from Held, Caney, and others that the enhanced power of the ICJ will promote cosmopolitanism.

threats to international security. Contrast the swiftness with which the United Nations responded to the attacks on 11 September 2001 with its actions when confronted with a far more deadly event: from April to mid-July 1994, Rwanda experienced the equivalent of three 11 September 2001 attacks every day for 100 days, all in a country whose population was one thirty-sixth that of the United States.[124]

Vigilance in pointing out double-standards, hoping for what Jon Elster called 'the civilizing force of hypocrisy',[125] remains essential.

Nonetheless, claims about selectivity or bias need to be parsed with care, for they can often be a guilty party's first defense against justifiable measures—the reason courts routinely reject such claims in criminal cases. The Sudanese government's claims that the UN was unfairly singling it out for condemnation over Darfur, or Syria's such claims regarding its civil war, need not be accepted at face value. Each state might be comparing its treatment with that of less grave situations, in which case the government is asking that unlike cases be treated alike (i.e. through non-action). And even if the state is comparing its situation to equally grave or worse violations, we cannot simply say that the most just outcome is inaction in all cases. In other words, some selectivity may advance the purposes of an international organization better than the application of pure evenhandedness, if evenhandedness means perpetual inaction. Moreover, inconsistency is inevitable given that an organization must take into account that it lacks the political, financial, and other resources to make a difference in every similar case before it. International organizations may need to break from past practices even if they appear inconsistent in doing so.

Indeed, inconsistency is not necessarily crippling to an international institution. For example, the Security Council continues to be perceived by states as the most important venue for the consideration of armed conflict despite its flawed membership and decisionmaking and the inconsistent and unprincipled way in which it often acts. In practical terms, it might simply mean that that the Council's resolutions, passed in the context of situation X, will have to be invoked by others—not the Council—in the context of situation Y. This pattern of shifting arenas for the invocation of norms is common in international law. So the sort of impartiality that ought to be followed by international organizations is not a rigid command or dogma. Yet over time, a pattern of grossly inconsistent decisionmaking does constitute a form of playing favorites and thus does and should undermine respect and confidence in the institution.

124 'A More Secure World', *supra* note 92, paras. 40–41.

125 Jon Elster, 'Deliberation and Constitution Making', in Jon Elster (ed.), *Deliberative Democracy* (Cambridge: Cambridge University Press, 1998) 97, 111.

PART III

THE JUSTICE OF TERRITORIALLY-BASED PROTECTIONS OF HUMAN RIGHTS

8

Human Rights for Whom?: Territoriality, Extraterritoriality, and Universal Jurisdiction

When individuals demand recognition and protection of their inherent rights and want to ground that demand in international law, they turn to international human rights law. As discussed in Chapter 2, their claims center on the individual's interest in autonomy and the fulfillment of basic material needs, including protection from forces that can deny these to her, whether states, non-state groups, corporations, or even natural calamities. Human rights law is not alone in this task; international humanitarian law (IHL) plays a critical role during armed conflict, and international criminal law addresses how individuals might be held accountable for violations of human rights and humanitarian law.

The expanse of human rights law is breathtaking in several dimensions. First, individuals have legally recognized rights, and states have corresponding duties, in a wide range of areas, from civil and political rights to economic, social, and cultural rights; to rights of particular importance to vulnerable groups, such as women, children, religious and ethnic minorities, the handicapped, and gays and lesbians. Second, the range of duty-holders now extends beyond states to non-state actors, including armed groups in control of territory and, increasingly, corporations. Third, states and civil society have created an array of mechanisms for addressing violations, from those internal to states to those beyond it, including political and expert bodies at the regional and UN level, regional human rights courts, and countless NGOs. This architecture of enforcement, nearly all a product of the years since World War II, shows both tremendous achievements in terms of acculturating states to protecting human rights, and enormous gaps for which the clearest evidence is the manifold daily abuses of human rights globally.

The role of the state is at the core of human rights law. At the descriptive level, the state is the primary guardian of the rights and welfare of its citizens or residents for the simple reason that it has the most direct political authority over them and the territory in which they live. And states still represent the major, or at least a major, threat to those very rights. Yet reciprocity and other built-in modes of self-restraint that cause states to respect other rules of international law more often than not often will not dissuade states from violating human rights.

More significantly for our purposes, under international law, the state is central because the authority to protect human rights is principally organized on territorial lines. That is, states' duties to individuals are generally limited to those persons on their territory—to the point that states in many senses lack any duty to guarantee rights abroad and even, in most circumstances, the right to do so. The territorial scope of human rights law—which I regard as a fundamental norm of international law—means that states have only limited duties to individuals beyond their borders. And if states have duties only to those on their territory and a highly circumscribed authority to protect those abroad, the justice of international law seems suspect. Even though the substantive content of human rights law is just—under thick or thin standards of justice—its territorial limitation effectively leaves an individual to the mercy of his or her own state. The law plays favorites insofar as states have duties to persons based on the happenstance of the location of a border.

This chapter and the next, then, explore the justice of that core norm of territoriality with respect to human rights law. I begin by examining the starting presumption of international law and then turn to three major exceptions to territoriality—instances where the law has responded to serious claims that states should be required or permitted to protect human rights beyond their borders. They are: (1) the duty of a state to *comply with* human rights law when it takes action abroad; (2) the right or duty of a state to *assert jurisdiction* over, and criminally punish, individuals for their human rights abuses abroad; and (3) the right or duty of a state to *take military action* abroad to defend the human rights of another state's residents, which is the sole subject of the next chapter. The initial presumption and the three exceptions fall into distinct doctrinal boxes and labels for international lawyers—jurisdiction, extraterritorial application of human rights law, and the use of force for humanitarian intervention—but they all concern the same underlying moral question of the justification of a territorial conception of human rights.[1] As with the rest of this volume, my choice of issues is somewhat selective and based on what I regard as the major claims to date.

In focusing on the territorial limits, I recognize that other aspects of human rights are important to ethics and global justice. In particular, the debates about cultural relativity of rights help us understand the extent to which states and individuals share the same conception of human rights. These matters will help us address just how developed and detailed the international law of human rights can become over time. Yet the territorial component remains the starting point for discussion as it represents the most direct challenge to universality.

[1] Thus, for instance, although humanitarian intervention is certainly doctrinally part of the rules on the use of force, it raises distinct ethical issues about the scope of human rights protection compared to those addressed in Chapter 4.

I. International Law's Presumption: Duties Based on State Borders

The basic position of international human rights law is that the duties of states to protect human rights generally extend only to persons under their jurisdiction. The core treaties are worded in slightly different ways—the International Covenant on Civil and Political Rights (ICCPR) requires each state to 'respect and to ensure to all individuals within its territory and subject to its jurisdiction',[2] the International Covenant on Economic, Social and Cultural Rights (ICESCR) is silent but seems to suggest such a limitation,[3] the European Convention on Human Rights (ECHR) obligates states to 'secure to everyone within their jurisdiction',[4] and the American Convention refers to 'all persons subject to their jurisdiction'.[5] Although states still disagree somewhat as to the exact meaning of 'jurisdiction' and in particular whether it can ever extend beyond a state's territory, the more important point is that the basic duties of the treaty are territorial—that any extraterritorial duties or permissions are clearly the exception, not the norm.[6] Thus, State A has a duty to guarantee a fair trial only to all persons accused of crimes living in State A. And it has a duty to ensure certain conditions of labor only to those on its territory. This scope applies to so-called negative rights (to be free of governmental abuse) as much as positive ones (to receive governmental benefits).

The territorial scope is not just about limiting a state's *duty* to guarantee human rights. Rather, it works hand in hand with the statehood norms we have seen in Chapter 4 that protect states from coercion by other states—the bans on the use of force and non-intervention. Were a state to provide a fair trial to those similarly situated in State B without State B's consent, it would violate those other norms. The result is that a state has no *right* to guarantee human rights abroad. In other words, states have a right and a duty to guarantee the human rights of individuals if and only if those persons are on their territory (or under their jurisdiction). In 2001, for example, Hungary passed a law to provide non-Hungarian citizens of ethnic Hungarian origin access to educational and welfare benefits in Hungary, including by giving local Hungarian groups the power to decide on eligibility. This decision elicited criticism from international lawyers in Europe.[7] At the same

2 ICCPR, Art. 2.

3 ICESCR, Art. 14 (requiring each state to devise an implementation plan for free primary education if it has not achieved this 'in its metropolitan territory or other territories under its jurisdiction').

4 European Convention for the Protection of Human Rights and Fundamental Freedoms, 4 November 1950, Art. 1.

5 American Convention on Human Rights, 22 November 1969, Art. 1.

6 See, e.g., *Al Skeini v United Kingdom*, ECHR App. No. 55721/07, 53 EHRR 18, para. 131 (2011) ('A State's jurisdictional competence under Article 1 is primarily territorial').

7 See Act LXII of 2001 on Hungarians Living in Neighboring Countries, 19 June 2001, <http://www.refworld.org/docid/3f460e764.html>; European Commission for Democracy through Law (Venice Commission), Report on the Preferential Treatment of National Minorities by Their Kin-State, 22 October 2001, Council of Europe Doc. CDL-INF-19.

time, as we have seen in Chapter 4, those statehood norms do not preclude one state from *promoting* human rights abroad through foreign assistance, diplomatic protest, or even economic sanctions. Nor do they hinder in any way international organizations and NGOs from monitoring and criticizing states for their compliance with human rights law. So a state may take some actions to stop or prevent human rights abuses abroad; it simply may not guarantee those rights abroad without the other state's consent.

The duties on states thus appear to be special duties in the terms set out in Chapter 2, i.e. the state owes them only to those on its own territory. This observation may well call into question an intuition we have that because human rights are universal, enjoyed by all people, all states owe duties regarding human rights to all people. This tension can be resolved in a number of ways:

- First, the duties flowing from human rights could be both special *and* general duties. They are special in that the state owes them to individuals on its territory, who are the direct beneficiaries of them, but they are general in that the state's obligation is also to all other states. This solution resembles Hart's distinction between beneficiaries and rights-holders[8]—only individuals on the state's territory are beneficiaries, whereas all other states are the rights-holders—though it elevates the individuals insofar as it sees them, consistent with human rights law, as bona fide rights-holders. Thus, by virtue of being bound by customary international human rights law or to a widely ratified human rights treaty like the ICCPR, the state takes on duties to all (or most) other states as well as its own residents.
- Second, we might say that states have certain human rights obligations to all people, wherever situated, such as, for instance, a duty to do no physical harm, but that the global and regional treaties put only some of those obligations in a treaty form as special duties to those under a state's jurisdiction.
- Third, we might see a state's duty to protect certain human rights as a general duty, but one that is overridden by the other international duty mentioned earlier, namely, a duty not to engage in governmental acts on another state's territory without its permission. Under such a view, the duties of states regarding human rights law are special duties that result from the clash of two general duties—to protect human rights generally, flowing from the notion of *human* rights, and to refrain from exercising extraterritorial jurisdiction. Those general duties are similar to what Pettit and Goodin call 'non-conclusive' duties, in that non-fulfillment of them is not itself wrong;[9] the special duties result from the balancing of those general duties.[10] I find this view appealing in that it captures the notion of general duties in the area of human rights while recognizing that the duties actually recognized by the law are special.

[8] See H.L.A. Hart, 'Are There Any Natural Rights?', *Phil Rev* 64 (1955): 175, 181.

[9] Philip Pettit and Robert Goodin, 'The Possibility of Special Duties', *Can J Phil* 16, (1986): 651, 654.

[10] Ibid., at 655. Those special duties themselves might be non-conclusive if they in turn must be balanced against other duties, e.g., a state's duty to preserve domestic public order.

II. The Justice of Territorially-Based Duties

In light of this characterization of a state's duties under human rights law as special duties, I ask whether international law's territorial limitation conforms to thin global justice.

A. The peace pillar

A territorial limitation of human rights law, reflecting international law's ban on coercive intervention in other states, offers a strong measure of prevention of armed conflict, certainly compared to any alternative of general duties. By limiting a state to its own territory, the law keeps it from engaging in precisely those actions that significantly increase the possibility of interstate conflict. If we consider the effects of requiring states to guarantee human rights abroad (even if they were not obligated to guarantee all such rights), we can rather easily imagine the results in terms of increased tensions as states involve themselves coercively in issues that other states consider domestic. When one considers the panoply of human rights for which states have assumed obligations through treaty or custom, a duty to *guarantee* or *secure* rights beyond borders quickly becomes unmanageable.

Even a mere *right* (or privilege in the Hohfeldian sense) to guarantee human rights abroad is likely to promote significant instability and eventual bloodshed. Most states probably lack either the interest or the resources to protect the human rights of people beyond their borders. But some states will see an interest in doing so, in particular a state, even a poor one, that wishes to defend its ethnic kin on the other side of a border that it might find arbitrary. Whether in speaking of Hitler's defense of the rights of ethnic Germans in the Sudetenland, or the Ethiopian conflict with Somalia over the Ogaden, a grant of authority to protect human rights abroad can quickly decay into war. Beyond protection of foreigners, powerful states can easily prey on weaker ones to defend their own citizens abroad if they regard the protection granted by the host state as inadequate. Much of the nineteenth- and early twentieth-century history of Latin America was characterized by interventions by European states and the United States to protect the property rights of their nationals.[11] Russia's intervention in Ukraine, defended as protecting ethnic Russians, is only the latest example. Granted that in some examples the motivation of the intervening state was not to protect human rights, but a rule of law that offered such a lawful authority would open the door to this highly destabilizing conduct.

At the same time, a duty on states to *promote* human rights abroad would pass muster under the first pillar. As it happens, such a duty is very weak—it is not prescribed in the two main human rights treaties but rather listed as one of the purposes

[11] See generally Donald Shea, *The Calvo Clause* (Minneapolis, MN: University of Minnesota Press, 1955).

of some international organizations like the UN and regional organizations.[12] A state is certainly permitted to promote such rights abroad, provided it acts in conformity with the principle of non-intervention discussed in Chapter 4. This scope of the ban on intervention provides the state with significant leeway in this area. So the territorial scope of human rights law is not as complete as one might fear—it is limited to the requirement to guarantee rights.

B. The human rights pillar

The territorial limitation also satisfies the second pillar. Indeed, that limitation does not merely not interfere with basic human rights; it affirmatively enhances global respect for them. This concordance of territorially limited duties and protection of rights receives a cosmopolitan defense in Robert Goodin's argument that states represent a particularly efficient means of allocating general duties among all individuals.[13] They divide up the globe to provide certain benefits (or guarantee certain rights) to individuals. States with effective control over the rights-holders—namely, their residents—rather than some other state, have the duties because they are in the best position to ensure respect for such rights.[14]

This position can also be contested; perhaps effective control over a population does not put the state in the best position to guarantee rights, for example in the case of impoverished states. In these cases, we might want to give other states a right to help the territorial state. Indeed, all three of the exceptions to territoriality explored here are based on the idea that the state on whose territory the individuals reside lacks the ability or willingness to protect basic human rights, so others have a right or duty to step in.[15] But at least as an initial matter, we will place the duties to protect human rights only on the state with control over the relevant people. This approach finds further support in the approach of states in creating the International Criminal Court (ICC), which can hear a case on human rights abuses only if the state that would normally prosecute is unwilling or unable to do so.[16]

Yet the second pillar can cut in the opposite direction as well. If the international law of human rights and non-intervention completely precludes a state from securing or guaranteeing the rights of people beyond its borders and the result is a denial of the basic human rights of those people, then that rule begins to appear quite unjust. At a certain point, the demand of justice that international

[12] See, e.g., UN Charter, Arts. 1, 55.

[13] See Robert E. Goodin, 'What is So Special About Our Fellow Countrymen?', *Ethics* 98 (1988): 663, 665.

[14] This rationale might also justify some of the special duties that international law creates for citizens as well. For instance, regarding immigration, it would say that because states are efficient at granting certain benefits to individuals, a system that permits the state to set the basic rules of participation is ethically acceptable.

[15] The notion that a state's inability or unwillingness to carry out legal responsibilities on its territory triggers a right for other states to do so is also part of the debate over lawful measures of self-defense against terrorist groups operating in another state, as discussed in Chapter 4.

[16] ICC Statute, Art. 17.

law respect basic human rights overrides the imperative of preserving peace. The territorial limitation is unjust if, as a matter of consequences, it tolerates a massive denial of human rights or if, as a matter of deontology, it undercuts a duty we might have to protect vulnerable populations against such abuses. At the same time, if we simply eliminate the law's creation of limited duties and allow or require each state to protect the rights of all people around the planet equally, then we will have violated the first pillar.

As seen from the reference to Goodin, philosophers have offered their own defenses of territorially based duties. In *Spheres of Justice*, Walzer offered a communitarian defense, suggesting that by virtue of an individual's 'right to place', 'the state owes something to inhabitants simply, without reference to their collective or national identity'.[17] While Walzer's defense leaves many details undefined, it offers a justification for the state's special duties to inhabitants, one based on the reality of the territorial state. Walzer also offers an efficiency rationale in noting that 'so many critical issues... can best be resolved within geographic units'.[18]

More common are justifications for special duties that emphasize not ties between the state and its inhabitants, but between the state and its *citizens*. These theories are one strand of a broad group of arguments that seek to find a moral basis for the common sense notion that we have special duties to co-citizens as part of patriotism.[19] In one important theory, Andrew Mason offered a vision based on the idea of citizenship as an intrinsically valuable good, suggesting that this good justified special ties to citizens, but not to nationals (by which he meant members of the same nation) or residents.[20] David Miller argues for the importance of nationality to personal identity, suggesting that such bonds should be strengthened through ties of citizenship if at all possible.[21] Both of these theories argue in terms of a special bond between the state and its citizens that is enough *alone*, and without recourse to other universalist goals like utility or freedom, to justify duties to them only—much like duties to family, friends, or fellow citizens.

This set of arguments may well justify special duties to co-citizens, but it fails as a defense of the special duties in international human rights law because, for the most part, that law does not carve out special rights for or duties to citizens but gives equal rights to all persons on the territory, even tourists or migrants passing through. The key exceptions in the law are that: (1) a state's duty to allow individuals to participate in public affairs and public service is limited to citizens;[22] and

[17] Michael Walzer, *Spheres of Justice* (New York: Basic Books, 1983) 43.

[18] Ibid., at 44.

[19] Most of these theories are interactional in Pogge's sense in that they deal with our individual morality, but they often address or at least imply that they provide a justification for the state's duties as well and are thus part of an institutional morality. Thomas Pogge, 'Cosmopolitanism and Sovereignty', *Ethics* 103 (1992): 48, 50–2

[20] Andrew Mason, 'Special Obligations to Compatriots', *Ethics* 107 (1997): 427.

[21] David Miller, *On Nationality* (Oxford: Oxford University Press, 1995) 65–80. See also Yael Tamir, *Liberal Nationalism* (Princeton, NJ: Princeton University Press, 1993) 124–39. Miller does recognize global duties in his *National Responsibility and Global Justice* (Oxford: Oxford University Press, 2008) 7–8.

[22] ICCPR, Art. 25 ('Every citizen'). See also ibid., Art. 12(4) (right of individual to 'enter his own country'), which has been interpreted by the Human Rights Committee as including some

(2) a state's duties to respect an individual's economic, social and cultural rights allow developing states to opt out of granting such rights to non-nationals.[23] Presumably the response of advocates of special duties to citizens would be to find international human rights law irrationally overinclusive or even immoral. My point is that territorially-based limits are indeed just, even though I recognize that situations may arise in which a blanket territorial rule would be unjust.

Because my goal here is to appraise the rules as they exist and not to construct an ideal theory for the role of the state in protecting the rights of those at home and abroad, I need not provide a comprehensive answer to the question of whom states are morally required to protect. Rather, I will examine the way in which international law has responded to the actual claims made by international actors for recognition of duties by states to protect the rights of those abroad and assess the law under my standard of global justice.

III. Duties on States When Acting Abroad: Extraterritorial Application of Human Rights Law

The first claim for an exception to the territorial scope of human rights law responds to a fairly narrow set of situations—when a state decides to take action abroad in a way that harms foreigners. Such conduct usually takes one of the following forms: (a) use of military force abroad during an armed conflict between two states, and (b) police or intelligence operations to apprehend foreigners abroad, with or without the consent of the host state.[24] The former case is already regulated by a vast corpus of law, IHL, in particular its rules concerning interstate conflict. The latter case, because it does not concern armed conflict, is not governed by IHL, so if a state were not bound by international human rights law, then it would seem to have no duties whatsoever to those abroad. International organizations, expert monitoring bodies, NGOs, and others have argued that that a state should be bound by human rights law in both of these situations.

For my purposes here, I will focus only on the latter situation because, as noted in Chapter 4, I believe that IHL decently protects basic human rights, at least those of non-combatants, during wartime. Moreover, discussion of IHL's possible shortcomings in this regard raises complex questions about the civilian-combatant distinction (some of which are addressed in Chapter 12) that are analytically distinct from the question of territoriality. Much legal scholarship has been devoted

non-nationals. See Human Rights Committee, General Comment 27: Freedom of Movement (Article 12), 1 November 1999, paras. 19–20, UN Doc. CCPR/C/21/Rev.1/Add.9.

[23] ICESCR, Art. 2(3).

[24] There are other examples, for instance where the state operates a diplomatic mission abroad and its officials somehow deny rights of persons abroad. See *Montero v Uruguay*, Human Rights Committee Comm. 106/1981, 31 March 1983, UN Doc. CCPR/C/OP/2, at 136; *X v Federal Republic of Germany*, Eur. Comm'n Human Rts No. 1611/62, *ECHR Yearbook* 8 (1965): 158, 169. In addition, for reasons of space I do not explore here claims that states have duties regarding economic and social rights when their activities have an effect beyond their borders.

to finding some kind of doctrinal answer to the relationship between international human rights law and IHL, but I do not regard it as part of the territorial issue.[25]

I thus turn to the paradigmatic case of extraterritorial conduct not governed by IHL, extraterritorial law enforcement. In Chapter 4, it was pointed out that a state may not, as a general matter, engage in such actions without the consent of the host state. At the same time, we saw a whittling away of that notion when it came to war criminals, where toleration of extraterritorial enforcement seems to be somewhat greater. But the concern for international law here is different: it is not whether the consent of the host state is *necessary* for the act to be legal—we can assume that for most situations it still is—but whether consent is *sufficient* for international legality or whether, on the contrary, the apprehending state is also bound by human rights law when it acts abroad. By way of example, experts of the UN and the Council of Europe as well as NGOs severely criticized the United States for seizing Al Qaeda suspects abroad, abusing them in custody, and then sending them to third countries for the purpose of interrogation that it knew would be inhumane, but the U.S. Secretary of State seemed to rest her case for the legality of this policy on the consent of the host state.[26] Would a rule to this effect be just?

A. The legal norms: areas of consensus and disagreement

The law on the extraterritorial application of human rights law is bounded by two areas of consensus, with a fair degree of difference of opinion in the middle. The areas of consensus are:

(1) A state has at least some duties under human rights law when it acts abroad, and the jurisdictional clauses of human rights treaties do not preclude those duties. This interpretation of the human rights treaties dates back at least to an opinion of the UN Human Rights Committee (set up under the ICCPR to monitor states' compliance with that treaty) that Uruguay had violated the ICCPR when its agents engaged in extraterritorial kidnapping of dissidents in Brazil in the 1970s. The Committee held that it would be 'unconscionable' to interpret the spatial limitation of the duties 'to permit a State party to perpetrate violations of the Covenant on the territory of another state, which violations it could not perpetrate on its own territory'.[27] In the 1990s, the European Court of Human

[25] See, e.g., Orna Ben-Naftali (ed.), *International Humanitarian Law and International Human Rights Law* (Oxford: Oxford University Press, 2011); Monica Hakimi, 'A Functional Approach to Targeting and Detention', *Mich L Rev* 110 (2012): 1365, 1371–3.

[26] Compare Condoleezza Rice, 'Remarks on Departure for Europe', 5 December 2005, <http://2001-2009.state.gov/secretary/rm/2005/57602.htm> ('In those cases the local government can make the sovereign choice to cooperate in a rendition. Such renditions are permissible under international law'), with European Commission for Democracy Through Law, Opinion on the International Legal Obligations of Council of Europe Member States in Respect of Secret Detention Facilities and Inter-State Transport of Prisoners, 17 March 2006, Council of Europe Doc. CDL-AD (2006) 009. The United States denied that it was sending persons to third states for the purpose of torture, but it also maintained that it had no obligations under the UN Convention Against Torture for acts committed abroad.

[27] *Celiberti de Casariego v Uruguay*, Human Rights Committee Comm. 56/1979, 29 July 1981, UN Doc. CCPR/C/OP/1, at 92.

Rights held Turkey responsible for seizures of property in the Turkish Republic of Northern Cyprus based on its effective control of the area.[28] And the International Court of Justice joined in later by holding Israel responsible for violations of the ICCPR in the occupied Palestinian territories.[29] A recent high mark in this area was the 2011 decision in *Al Skeini v United Kingdom*, where the European Court recognized that the phrase in Article 2 of the ECHR quoted earlier requires the state to guarantee rights where the state controls foreign territory as well as where it has effective control of an individual.[30] This interpretation of the jurisdictional clauses of the treaties does not turn the duties into general duties, but rather extends the rights-holders associated with the special duties beyond the borders of the state.

(2) A state does not have the full corpus of duties to all persons in the foreign state in which it is operating. At this point, nobody is seriously claiming that simply by virtue of acting beyond its borders, a state must guarantee all the rights in the human rights treaties to everyone in the target state. In other words, decisionmakers at this point treat the vast majority of persons in the state as legally unaffected by the extraterritorial act.

Between these two points of consensus, the state of the law is contested. With respect to foreign territory under a state's effective control (usually through military occupation), there is certainly a broad trend toward acceptance of a rule that the occupying state's obligations under human rights law extend to all the inhabitants of the territory.[31] The United States remains the outlier on this issue because of its broader concerns that human rights law not displace IHL during an armed conflict, although its views on the exact relationship between the two are now less categorical.[32] In situations short of such control, which characterizes the extraterritorial law enforcement scenario, the most important legal opinion remains that of *Al Skeini*, which held that when a state controls an individual, it must guarantee to him or her all rights 'relevant to the situation of that individual'.[33]

[28] *Loizidou v Turkey* (1996-VI) ECHR 2223.

[29] *Legal Consequences of the Construction of a Wall in the Occupied Palestinian Territory* [2004] ICJ Rep 136 (Advisory Opinion of 9 July); see also *Armando Alejandro Jr and Others v Cuba*, Inter-American Commission on Human Rights (1999), No. 11.589, para. 23 (extraterritorial reach of American Convention on Human Rights concerning Cuban air force shoot-down of civilian aircraft over international waters).

[30] *Al Skeini, supra* note 6, paras. 132–142; see also *Hirsi Jamaa v Italy*, ECHR App. No. 27765/09, paras. 77–82 (2012). For a review of the issue, see generally Nicola Wenzel, 'Human Rights Treaties, Extraterritorial Application and Effects', in Rüdiger Wolfrum (ed.), *The Max Planck Encyclopedia of Public International Law*, online edition (Oxford: Oxford University Press, 2008–) <http://opil.ouplaw.com/home/EPIL>.

[31] *Legal Consequences of the Construction of a Wall, supra* note 29, para. 108; *Al Skeini, supra* note 6, para. 138.

[32] See Fourth Periodic Report of the United States of America to the United Nations Committee on Human Rights Concerning the International Covenant on Civil and Political Rights, 30 December 2011, para. 507, UN Doc. CCPR/C/USA/4 ('Determining the international law rule that applies to a particular action taken by a government in the context of an armed conflict is a fact-specific determination, which cannot be easily generalized').

[33] *Al Skeini, supra* note 6, para. 137. It is uncontested that the host state's obligations do not disappear by virtue of its consent to a foreign state to undertake abuses on its territory.

This holding would presumably protect the individual from torture, summary execution, and denial of due process by the apprehending state, but it might well not grant him the right to free speech or religion. The views of states on this matter are not obvious. Certainly courts in some states normally quite supportive of U.S. policies protested against the United States' renditions for their denial of due process to detainees.[34]

B. The justice of duties to respect human rights while acting abroad

The acceptance of some extraterritorial duties means that the rule offered previously—a state is permitted and required to guarantee the rights of people if and only if they are in its territory—is no longer true. Now a state is permitted and required to guarantee at least some rights to at least some people outside its territory in some (non-war) situations. The result is both a new permission for states and a new duty upon states—the authority to guarantee rights abroad notwithstanding the duty not to intervene in other states' internal affairs, and the duty to guarantee them notwithstanding a strict reading of the jurisdictional clauses of human rights treaties.

Yet this new permission and duty pass muster under the peace pillar for two reasons. First, neither is a new permission or duty *to act abroad* that might interfere with interstate or internal peace; they apply only *once the state acts abroad*, and they apply whether or not the state acts with the consent of the host state. Second, it is not a permission or duty to apply human rights law to the conduct of the host state, but only to that of the extraterritorially acting state; so it does not interfere with how the former state runs its internal affairs. It is thus difficult to imagine how requiring the first state to uphold human rights would erode peaceful interstate or intrastate relations.[35] As for the human rights pillar of the test, a rule of international law that requires states to respect human rights cannot run afoul of a test that is meant to catch rules that have the effect of denying basic human rights. Indeed, this exception to territoriality is not merely just, but is *compelled* by thin justice. For the pure territoriality rule tolerates even the gravest assaults on human rights by a state acting abroad. It means that a state has carte blanche to *itself violate* human rights beyond its territory without any subjection to international human rights law.

[34] See *Abbasi v Secretary of State* (2002) ECWA Civ 1958 (UK); *Canada (Prime Minister) v Khadr* (2010) 1 SCR 44.

[35] One could devise a scenario similar to the 2003 kidnapping by CIA agents of an Egyptian cleric from the streets of Milan, apparently without the knowledge of the Italian law enforcement community (though with the knowledge of at least its intelligence officials), where Italy then prosecuted the kidnapers, who had returned to the United States. If the United States believed it was bound under human rights law to address its own conduct, its investigation might embarrass Italian officials somewhat, but it seems far more likely to contribute to repairing relations between the two states than to eroding peace.

One might respond that the exception to territoriality is not required as a matter of justice because such a result does not leave the conduct in a legal vacuum, insofar as the state where the abuses took place (the 'host state') still has duties to protect all persons on its territory. But relying on that state's duties to protect the human rights of those on its territory is a poor substitute both practically and legally. Practically, the host state (a) may have colluded in the conduct by giving its consent beforehand (as several European states did in the U.S. rendition programs);[36] or (b) be unable either to prevent the conduct or to provide any form of relief to the individual harmed.

Legally, the host state's obligations with respect to the conduct of persons on its soil who are not its agents are not the same as its obligations regarding its own agents' conduct. Under the now well-accepted test first announced by the Inter-American Court of Human Rights regarding the responsibility of a state for actions of third parties, a state has a duty to take 'reasonable' measures and exercise 'due diligence', but it does not have the same absolute duty to prevent abuses as it does with respect to its own actors.[37] The extraterritorially acting state has stronger legal obligations than does the state in which it takes its actions. We thus cannot always rely on the latter state to protect individuals in these situations, but must insist on a rule that obligates the state carrying out the extraterritorial conduct to do so.

This assessment leaves many questions unanswered, including whether a state must grant all the rights to persons affected by its conduct or living in areas under its control. I do not think a standard of thin justice points to one right answer on this question. The *Al Skeini* test certainly offers one approach—all rights when a state exercises territorial control, some rights when it exercises personal control—but we have yet to see how it will work in other situations. At a minimum, to be just under the second pillar, it would seem international law must require the state acting abroad to guarantee the basic human rights of those over whom it exercises control (territorial or personal). A broader position is also appealing. Orna Ben-Naftali and Yuval Shany have suggested that a state should be responsible for whatever rights it violates, wherever it violates them (including during military operations and in occupied territory), and that the nature of its relationship with the individual, including the degree to which it exercises power over him, will determine the rights that it must guarantee.[38] That position would mean that, for instance, CIA agents who kidnapped someone abroad would not merely be

[36] See, e.g., *El-Masri v Macedonia*, ECHR App. No. 39630/09 (2012) (holding Macedonia responsible for its cooperation with the United States in a rendition); *Husayn (Abu Zubaydah) v Poland*, ECHR App. No. 7511/13 (2014) (holding Poland responsible for CIA secret prison there).

[37] *Velásquez Rodriguez v Honduras*, Inter-American Court of Human Rights, Series C No. 4 (1988) paras. 172–177; in the rendition context, see *El Masri, supra* note 36, para. 206 (Macedonia responsible 'for acts performed by foreign officials on its territory with the acquiescence or connivance of its authorities').

[38] Orna Ben-Naftali and Yuval Shany, 'Living in Denial: The Application of Human Rights in the Occupied Territories', *Isr L Rev* 37 (2004): 17, 60–72. For a similar position, see Noam Lubell, *Extraterritorial Use of Force Against Non-State Actors* (Oxford: Oxford University Press, 2010) 227–31.

denying someone their right to due process or security of the person, but rights to free speech or freedom of religion.

IV. State Action to Protect Human Rights Abroad: Universal Jurisdiction

A second set of claims against the territorial limitation of human rights law has been made by those seeking to bring to justice foreigners for abuses of human rights committed abroad. These claimants include governments investigating and prosecuting suspected offenders as well as victims' groups filing criminal complaints against them, as allowed under many civil law systems. The most famous prosecution remains Israel's trial of Adolf Eichmann for his leadership in carrying out the Final Solution, but since the 1990s, other states have begun to bring cases. Austria, Denmark, Germany, Norway, and Switzerland have tried individuals accused of war crimes in the former Yugoslavia. Belgium, the Netherlands, France, and Canada have tried Rwandans (including two nuns tried in Belgium) for atrocities during the 1994 genocide. Spain and Italy have initiated investigations against officials of Argentina, Chile, El Salvador, and Guatemala for human rights abuses associated with their regimes; these have led to both a refusal by the United Kingdom to extradite Augusto Pinochet to Spain in 1999 and a successful prosecution of a former Argentine naval officer, Adolfo Scilingo, in 2007.[39] Beyond Europe, the former Chadian head of state, Hissene Habre, who was living in exile in Senegal, is on trial in a special Senegalese-African Union court for crimes against humanity during his rule in the 1980s, after significant resistance by Senegal and an International Court of Justice (ICJ) judgment that Senegal was required under the Torture Convention to either try him or extradite him to Belgium for trial.[40]

All of these cases challenge the territorial presumption of human rights law because one state is directly enforcing human rights law regarding conduct taking place abroad. The state is not typically taking action abroad in the sense of deploying police beyond its borders (although Israel did so in its hunt for Eichmann), but it is nonetheless using the power of the state through its judicial organs to protect human rights beyond its borders by investigating and prosecuting foreign offenders purely for their acts abroad. Such extraterritorial assertion of jurisdiction over individuals is distinct from economic sanctions against the state. That process is far more passive and does not involve the trial and punishment of individuals—in other words, it is more about promoting rights abroad than guaranteeing them.

[39] See generally Steven R. Ratner, Jason S. Abrams, and James L. Bischoff, *Accountability for Human Rights Atrocities in International Law: Beyond the Nuremberg Legacy*, 3rd ed. (Oxford: Oxford University Press, 2009) 198–203.

[40] See *Questions relating to the Obligation to Prosecute or Extradite (Belgium v Senegal)* [2012] ICJ Rep 422 (20 July).

A. The law's move from territoriality

International law treats the claims of states and victims to prosecute people for offenses committed abroad through rules on jurisdiction. Well-settled doctrine crystallizes the practice and views of states on the authority of states to prescribe, adjudicate, and enforce law. As an initial position, the state has the absolute authority to prescribe law to regulate conduct on its territory, to adjudicate that conduct (or those involved in it), and to enforce the decisions of adjudicative bodies on its own territory.[41] But beyond that fairly obvious starting point, a state's jurisdiction regarding acts abroad is determined by, or perhaps constitutive of, contemporary understandings of the non-intervention norm—namely, that some assertions of jurisdiction over foreign conduct will be regarded as coercive interference in the way the foreign state chooses to regulate its affairs.

The most obvious way in which extraterritorial jurisdiction will violate that norm is the one discussed in Chapter 4, namely, when a state tries to enforce its laws on another state's territory without that state's consent, for example through police action. Short of that extreme, international law allows, or does not prohibit, a state to prescribe law to cover some conduct, and adjudicate some conduct, that takes place beyond its own borders. It may generally do so in five situations: (a) when the conduct takes place abroad but produces significant effects in the state (what international law calls effects-based territoriality); (b) when the conduct takes place abroad but on board an aircraft or ship bearing the nationality of the state (flag jurisdiction); (c) when the conduct is carried out by a national—an individual or corporation—of the state (nationality); (d) when the victim of the conduct is a national of the state (passive personality), although this basis is less accepted; and (e) when it is protecting certain special core interests of the state, for example preventing espionage or counterfeiting of currency (the protective principle).[42]

The scenario in which the state seeks to use its laws and courts to prosecute human rights abuses abroad represents a challenge to the idea that jurisdiction is limited to territoriality and these five other bases (the first two of which are really just an extension of territoriality). For in these situations, the effects are all abroad, the offender is of a foreign nationality, the victims are foreign, and the state cannot be said to be protecting any of its core interests.[43] The claim of these states is that, indeed, international law recognizes yet another basis of jurisdiction—universal jurisdiction. Under that basis, a state would be allowed to prescribe and

[41] Robert Jennings and Arthur Watts (eds.), *Oppenheim's International Law*, Vol. 1, 9th ed. (London: Longman, 1992) 458.

[42] See generally Ilias Bantekas, 'Criminal Jurisdiction of States under International Law', in Rüdiger Wolfrum (ed.), *The Max Planck Encyclopedia of Public International Law*, online edition (Oxford: Oxford University Press, 2008–) <http://opil.ouplaw.com/home/EPIL>. The policy of the United States to tax the worldwide income of American citizens, even if they no longer live in the United States, has aroused the ire of some states.

[43] In some cases where states have sought to prosecute offenders for conduct abroad, the victims are of the nationality of the forum state, as in Spain's attempts to prosecute officials of Latin American military regimes for atrocities in the 1970s and 1980s.

apply its law to conduct and persons having no clear connection to the forum state notwithstanding the norm of non-intervention.[44]

B. International law's approach to assertions of universal jurisdiction

In the case of universal jurisdiction, summarizing the state of the law today is challenging insofar there is not a uniform view among scholars or judges. From my own reading of the practice of states, five key propositions can be made regarding the lawfulness of universal jurisdiction:

(1) States are permitted to prosecute persons found on their territory (or aircraft or ships carrying their flag) for certain offenses regardless of the site of the offenses, nationality of the offender, or nationality of the victim. These offenses include at least piracy, the slave trade, war crimes, crimes against humanity, torture, aircraft hijacking and sabotage, and genocide.[45] The combination of widely ratified treaties that explicitly allow states to prosecute on a universal basis—such as the Geneva Conventions, the Convention Against Torture, and anti-terrorism conventions—combined with the lack of protest when states pass legislation based on universality suggests, as three judges of the ICJ put it, a 'determination by the international community' that people committing those crimes 'should not go unpunished'.[46]

(2) In the absence of a treaty, customary law regards universal jurisdiction as permissive, not mandatory.[47] While customary law only allows states to prescribe and adjudicate based on universality, treaties can contain stronger duties. Most treaties dealing with international offenses require a state to extradite or prosecute an offender found on its soil. If it does not extradite (even if it wants to extradite the person but the state with a stronger jurisdictional link to the acts or person does not want to prosecute), it must prosecute, if necessary based on universality.[48]

[44] Even the definition of universal jurisdiction is somewhat contested. See, e.g., *Arrest Warrant of 11 April 2000* [2002] ICJ Rep 3 (14 February), joint sep. op. Higgins, Kooijmans, and Buergenthal, para. 21; Roger O'Keefe, 'Universal Jurisdiction: Clarifying the Basic Concept', *JICJ* 2 (2004): 735. I will use the term to include investigations and prosecutions where the defendant is already present in the forum state as well as those where he is abroad.

[45] See Ratner, Abrams, and Bischoff, *Accountability, supra* note 39, at 178–83 and sources cited therein; Universal Criminal Jurisdiction with regard to the Crime of Genocide, Crimes against Humanity and War Crimes, Resolution of the Institut de Droit International, 26 August 2005, <http://www.idi-iil.org/idiE/resolutionsE/2005_kra_03_en.pdf>.

[46] See also *Arrest Warrant Case, supra* note 44, joint sep. op. Higgins, Kooijmans, and Buergenthal, para. 51; but see *Arrest Warrant Case*, sep. op. Guillaume, paras. 5–12 (universal jurisdiction limited to piracy).

[47] See Brigitte Stern, 'A propos de la compétence universelle', in Emile Yakpo and Tahar Boumedra (eds.), *Liber Amicorum Judge Mohammed Bedjaoui* (The Hague: Kluwer, 1999) 735, 737–40; Mitsue Inazumi, *Universal Jurisdiction in Modern International Law: Expansion of National Jurisdiction for Prosecuting Serious Crimes under International Law* (Antwerp: Intersentia, 2005) 132–48.

[48] See, e.g., UN Convention Against Torture, Arts. 5, 7; Geneva Convention IV, Art. 146 (grave breaches). The 1956 Slavery Convention and the 1973 Apartheid Convention appear to contemplate mandatory universal jurisdiction without a choice to extradite.

(3) If the person is not on a state's territory, the state can investigate him and request his extradition from another state; but it is more doubtful whether it can proceed to prosecute him in his absence. The question of *in absentia* exercise of universal jurisdiction continues to be a source of disagreement. Investigations by prosecutors or investigating judges have tended to be tolerated, though not all commentators concur in their legality.[49] If a state actually moves to the next stage of trying an individual, this raises doubts as to the possibility of due process for the defendant, although some states allow trials *in absentia*, and international human rights law does not ban the practice.

(4) There is a strong expectation, though probably not a rule, that if the state where the offenses took place wishes to prosecute an offender, other states should refrain from prosecuting based on universal jurisdiction. If that state does not plan to prosecute the person, other states may generally do so. The maxim that justice is best done at home drives the attitude of states with respect to competing claims to jurisdiction. The state asserting territorial-based jurisdiction has the strongest basis of jurisdiction and the best access to the witnesses and evidence related to the crimes. It is hard to find practice or *opinio juris* that other states must defer, but those proposing norms for universal jurisdiction generally argue for such deferral.[50] But if that state does not prosecute—whether by choice (for example through a legal or de facto amnesty), inertia, or incapacity of its courts—or begins a prosecution that is clearly a sham to acquit the defendant, other states may seek the person's extradition; or, if the person is already on their territory, they may proceed to trial. Indeed, under the key international criminal law treaties, a state with custody of an offender must prosecute if it does not extradite.[51] However, the forum state may face protests from the state of territoriality, in particular if it has decided not to prosecute as a matter of national policy during a transition, as happened when Spain tried to prosecute General Pinochet at a time when Chile did not.

(5) If the person on trial in a case of universal jurisdiction is a sitting or former official of a foreign government, the rules regarding immunity of these individuals from the jurisdiction of foreign courts (addressed in Chapter 6) apply as they would in any other prosecution of such officials.[52]

[49] Compare Institut de Droit International, *supra* note 45, para. 3(b); Claus Kress, 'Universal Jurisdiction over International Crimes and the *Institut de Droit International*', *JICJ* 4 (2006): 561, 577–9; and Cedric Ryngaert, *Jurisdiction in International Law* (Oxford: Oxford University Press, 2008) 119–25, with *Arrest Warrant Case, supra* note 44, sep. op. Guillaume, para. 15; and Luc Reydams, *Universal Jurisdiction: International and Municipal Legal Perspectives* (Oxford: Oxford University Press, 2003) 223–54.

[50] See The Princeton Principles on Universal Jurisdiction, principle 8, in Stephen Macedo (ed.), *Universal Jurisdiction: National Courts and the Prosecution of Serious Crimes under International Law* (Philadelphia, PA: University of Pennsylvania Press, 2004) 18, 23; Institut de Droit International, *supra* note 45, para. 3(d); Inazumi, *Universal Jurisdiction, supra* note 47, at 178–95. Cf. ICC Statute, Art. 17.

[51] See, e.g., UN Convention Against Torture, Art. 7.

[52] These five propositions do not encompass the entire law regarding universal jurisdiction, which also addresses issues such as double jeopardy and due process.

C. The thin justice of universal jurisdiction

At first blush, it may seem hard to question the benefits of universal jurisdiction from the perspective of global justice. After all, the entire purpose of the exercise is to bring those accused of international crimes to *justice*. Assuming the territorial state has been given a chance to try the person, as is now expected, how can one possibly argue for the contrary position, in favor of impunity?

Philosophical treatment of universal jurisdiction is generally scant. During the Eichmann trial, Hannah Arendt raised questions about the legitimacy of universal jurisdiction, finding the Israel court's justification for its jurisdiction over crimes against humanity based on an analogy to piracy, the oldest universal jurisdiction crime, to consist of 'elaborate sophisms'.[53] Recent treatments are generally far more supportive. Altman and Wellman argue that states that abuse their people systematically lose the right to object to outsiders' intervening and imposing international law on them. As a result, they endorse what they call 'international jurisdiction' that would cover any widespread and systematic human rights violations, even if the actions did not rise to the level of crimes against humanity or genocide.[54] Their theory would seem to justify trials by both foreign states and international courts, though at times they seem to focus on the latter only.[55] Win-chiat Lee similarly contends that when the state causes serious harms to its citizens, it loses its 'legitimacy as a political authority' and thus its claim to exclusive jurisdiction over acts on its territory.[56] In a different way of grounding universal jurisdiction in cosmopolitan ideas, Alejandro Chehtman asserts that the vindication of the rights of all victims or potential victims of abuses can be achieved only by giving all states the power to prosecute abusers; and Noah Feldman says such prosecutions are indeed required of a morally legitimate state.[57]

Yet all of these defenses act as if universal jurisdiction were just about the legitimacy of generalized outside interest in the crimes; they ignore or downplay the consequences that can arise from *prosecution by other states of individuals* for the crimes. We can grant that in situations where the state has carried out massive atrocities, it has lost some legitimacy, and other states have a right to take an interest, but how does that justify prosecutions by other states? From the standpoint of

[53] Hannah Arendt, *Eichmann in Jerusalem: A Report on the Banality of Evil*, rev. ed. (New York: Viking Press, 1965) 262–3. See also Eugene Kontorovich, 'The Piracy Analogy: Modern Universal Jurisdiction's Hollow Foundation', *Harv ILJ* 45 (2004): 183.

[54] Andrew Altman and Christopher Heath Wellman, 'A Defense of International Criminal Law', *Ethics* 115 (2004): 35. Crimes against humanity are limited to particularly egregious violations as part of a large or systematic attack on a civilian population. See Ratner, Abrams, and Bischoff, *Accountability, supra* note 39, ch. 3.

[55] Altman and Wellman, 'A Defense', *supra* note 54, at 47–51, 49.

[56] Win-chiat Lee, 'International Crimes and Universal Jurisdiction', in Larry May and Zachary Hoskins (eds.), *International Criminal Law and Philosophy* (New York: Cambridge University Press, 2010) 15, 18.

[57] Alejandro Chehtman, *The Philosophical Foundations of Extraterritorial Punishment* (Oxford: Oxford University Press, 2010) 117–21; Noah Feldman, 'Cosmopolitan Law?', *Yale LJ* 116 (2007): 1022, 1056–69.

thin justice, universal jurisdiction is much more complex. For universal jurisdiction, even with extraterritorial apprehension of suspects, represents an exception to the territorial presumption of human rights law that we have already found to be highly justifiable. Indeed, the justice of universal jurisdiction raises harder questions than does the justice of requiring states to follow human rights law when they act abroad, for here the interests and passions of at least two states—the forum state and the territorial state—can directly clash.

1. The peace pillar

In terms of the effect of universal jurisdiction upon the prospects for peace, trials based on universal jurisdiction, even those *in absentia*, do not raise the same concerns for peace as does one state's attempt to enforce its domestic laws on the territory of another. So the justice of the basic holding of the *Lotus* case—affirming the illegality of extraterritorial enforcement—does not simply translate to the case of universal jurisdiction.

One possible threat to peace from universal jurisdiction concerns deterioration of relations between the forum state and the state that would otherwise prosecute and has chosen not to do so. Certainly the case can be made to that effect. When the families of victims of the first Persian Gulf War and of massacres during the Lebanese civil war filed criminal charges in Belgium against U.S. and Israeli officials, respectively (including the sitting prime minister of Israel, Ariel Sharon), at a time when neither the United States nor Israel had any intention of putting its officials on trial, the investigations significantly aggravated relations between the those two states and Belgium.[58] Spain was on the receiving end of diplomatic protests after private plaintiffs tried to bring charges against former U.S. officials involved in counter-terrorism operations, Israelis involved in the Gaza war, and Chinese leaders regarding abuses in Tibet.[59] And its attempt to prosecute General Pinochet was strongly resisted by the Chilean government, first as a violation of its sovereignty and then with promises of a fair trial in Chile.[60] Peter Singer, endorsing the concerns of one of the British judges in the Pinochet case, has noted the possibility of a 'proliferation of charges'[61] by states seeking to score political points against their enemies by investigation and trying the latter's officials, a process exacerbated by the possibility of investigations or prosecutions initiated by victims or their relatives (so-called plaintiff-prosecutions).[62]

[58] Steven R. Ratner, 'Belgium's War Crimes Statute: A Postmortem', *AJIL* 97 (2003): 888.

[59] Máximo Langer, 'The Diplomacy of Universal Jurisdiction: The Political Branches and the Transnational Prosecution of International Crimes', *AJIL* 105 (2011): 1: 37–40.

[60] Naomi Roht-Arriaza, *The Pinochet Effect* (Philadelphia, PA: University of Pennsylvania Press, 2005) 59–66, 80–3; Kathryn Sikkink, *The Justice Cascade: How Human Rights Prosecutions are Changing World Politics* (New York: W.W. Norton, 2011) 129.

[61] Peter Singer, *One World: The Ethics of Globalization* (New Haven, CT: Yale University Press, 2002) 117.

[62] Concerns about the effect of foreign court judgments could prove too much. The trial *in absentia* by Italy of CIA agents who abducted a Muslim cleric from the streets of Milan led to a major protest by the United States, yet no one would deny that Italy had and should have jurisdiction to prosecute kidnapings on its territory.

Yet, as Máximo Langer has concluded after examining contemporary cases based on universal jurisdiction, there is no pattern to suggest that such cases have been brought for the purpose of attacking another state's policy. Only a handful of cases have been brought, all in Western states with judiciaries independent enough to dismiss unwarranted charges; the cases that have made it to trial are strong ones; and most authoritarian states, whose governments can control the courts, will be loath to assert a form of jurisdiction that may come back to haunt them.[63] It seems like a stretch, then, to assert that a rule allowing for universal jurisdiction will undermine peaceful relations between the forum state and the territorial state. This is especially true if propositions (3) and (5) are respected by the state that prosecutes—if it avoids trials *in absentia* and respects the immunity of sitting officials.

A second argument about the dangers of universal jurisdiction centers not on the effects of trials on that bilateral relationship, but their effects on the parties whose representative or official is the defendant in a prosecution in another state. For in most such prosecutions, the defendant is not a lone agent committing an isolated act, but an agent of a party to a larger conflict. Those parties may be states in an international armed conflict or the parties to a civil war or strife; those conflicts may be ongoing, in need of a peaceful solution; or the subject of a peace agreement that ought to be preserved. To illustrate those four possibilities, consider these examples: (a) ongoing international conflict—Israel/Palestine; (b) ongoing internal conflict—Colombian government/FARC; (c) settled international conflict—Eritrea/Ethiopia; and (d) settled internal conflict—Bosnia.

In each of these situations, it is argued, if officials or former officials are brought to justice in a foreign forum against the wishes of one of the two sides, the chances for either creating or preserving interstate or internal peace are reduced. Henry Kissinger, himself the target of plaintiffs' groups in Europe for his activities as U.S. Secretary of State, criticized the Pinochet prosecution precisely for what he regarded as Spain's failure to learn the lessons of its own history—one in which Spain is said to have achieved national reconciliation by not prosecuting the crimes of the civil war or the Franco regime.[64]

These arguments seem much more serious. If a state prosecutes individuals on one side of an ongoing or former conflict, that person's supporters will likely become outraged, defensive, and suspicious of compromise. They will also immediately ask why a representative of one side, but not the other, is being put on trial, unless officials from both sides are charged in the foreign courtroom. The atmosphere necessary to begin peace talks or preserve a peace becomes increasingly difficult to achieve or maintain. If states emerging from internecine conflict have made a decision to avoid prosecutions as part of a transitional justice approach, the second-guessing of that decision by a foreign state could upset some of the deal that was made.

[63] Langer, 'The Diplomacy of Universal Jurisdiction', *supra* note 59, at 41–4.

[64] Henry A. Kissinger, 'The Pitfalls of Universal Jurisdiction', *Foreign Affairs* 80 (July/August 2001): 90, 90–2.

At the same time, one might reject this prediction. Kathryn Sikkink has argued that foreign trials led to accountability at home in Latin American states but not to any increase in conflict.[65] It is certainly possible that the trial of a handful of people, even if just from one side, will not endanger the prospects for or unravel interstate or internal peace. Fears that trials of war criminals by the International Criminal Tribunal for the Former Yugoslavia, which has tried far more people than have been prosecuted under universal jurisdiction, would lead to the end of the fragile peace in Bosnia have proved unwarranted.[66] Indeed, a stronger argument can be made to the effect that such trials can solidify peace, for example, by allowing societies to see the events in question less in terms of collective guilt, to appreciate the perspectives of the victims, or to prepare politically or emotionally for trials at home.[67]

Moreover, those consequentialist arguments against universal jurisdiction have some limits:

- First, if all the relevant states—the forum state and the state(s) where the abuses occurred—are party to a treaty *requiring* the forum state to prosecute an offender found on its soil if the territorial state declines to do so (as with, for example, the Convention Against Torture), then the states should stand by the bargain they have made. For the stability of expectations in a treaty regime is itself a very important goal that promotes interstate peace.
- Second, these arguments against universal jurisdiction do not extend to prosecutions by the ICC. Although claims that trials can undermine potential or actual peace agreements have been made with respect to the ICC, that court can only hear a case (a) if one of the two most affected states (the state where the abuses occurred or the defendant's home state) is a party to the ICC Statute or otherwise consents to the Court's jurisdiction in a particular case; and (b) if neither of those parties is willing or able to prosecute the person.[68] So in this sense, the affected states have already agreed to an arrangement allowing for these prosecutions, and those expectations should not be upset. The only exception to condition (a) is if the Security Council refers the case to the Court over the wishes of the affected state, as has happened with the Court's investigation into atrocities in Darfur and Libya.[69] But here again I see the threat to the peace as diminished because I am willing to defer to the Security Council's judgment that, in that case, prosecutions are necessary to, or at least do not seriously undermine, the prospects for peace.[70]

[65] Sikkink, *The Justice Cascade, supra* note 60, at 153–4.

[66] For an example of such a prediction, see Anthony D'Amato, 'Peace vs. Accountability in Bosnia', *AJIL* 88 (1994): 500. If the Bosnia peace does not last, it will be for other reasons.

[67] See Ratner, Abrams, and Bischoff, *Accountability, supra* note 39, 171–6; Jon Elster, *Closing the Books: Transitional Justice in Historical Perspective* (Cambridge: Cambridge University Press, 2004) 166–87. I will leave aside arguments about the deterrent effect of trials of international crimes, on which the evidence is mixed. See David Wippman, 'Atrocities, Deterrence, and the Limits of International Justice', *Ford ILJ* 23, (1999): 473; Mark A. Drumbl, *Atrocity, Punishment, and International Law* (Cambridge: Cambridge University Press, 2007) 169–73.

[68] ICC Statute, Arts. 12, 17.

[69] ICC Statute, Art. 13(b).

[70] The ICC Statute also recognizes the authority of the Security Council to defer an investigation if it makes a decision to this effect under Chapter VII. See ICC Statute, Art. 16.

On balance, then, in terms of the effect on peace, the past seems to give us some reassurance, and the future carries both risks as well as potential benefits from such trials.

2. *The human rights pillar*

As for the second pillar, we need to ask whether the exception to territoriality entailed in universal jurisdiction interferes with basic human rights. As an initial matter, it seems rather obvious that trials for human rights abusers do not harm basic human rights, with the caveat that they be conducted in a way that respects the defendants' basic rights. But such an argument is not enough to overcome the difficulties of universal jurisdiction with respect to peace. I will instead argue a stronger position—that a rule of territoriality without an exception for universal jurisdiction would not pass the second pillar, i.e. that thin justice requires the norm of universal jurisdiction.

The argument in favor of universal jurisdiction is essentially the same as that already put forth in Chapter 6 against the immunity of certain officials from the criminal jurisdiction of foreign courts. Both universal jurisdiction and the lifting of immunity share a goal of ending impunity of offenders for serious human rights abuses. There I pointed out that, although the absence of a trial of a human rights abuser is not the same sort of direct assault on the victim's human rights as the original abuse, numerous international legal sources now endorse the idea that impunity can indeed interfere with the victim's basic human rights by leaving them completely *unvindicated*. That lack of vindication raises serious concerns about impunity under the second pillar of thin justice. Trials do not satisfy all victims, but eliminating them as an option simply because the state where the abuses took place will not prosecute would undermine human rights for some of them. Another consequentialist argument against impunity—that it interferes with human rights by removing a deterrent to future violations—supports the need for universal jurisdiction. Under those circumstances, something like the current rule of international law that allows for universal jurisdiction is indeed necessary to provide that vindication of rights to victims.[71]

At the same time, the international law position, by authorizing but not requiring states to prosecute based on universal jurisdiction, reflects a consequentialist approach insofar as the protection of human rights does not trump the need to preserve peace. Indeed, even if we were to see basic human rights generally as side-constraints (which I generally do not), a right against impunity—or the vindication of rights that comes from ending impunity—is not the kind of right that should be such a trump on the advancement of peace because impunity does

[71] In contrast to the philosophical discussions noted earlier, my defense of universal jurisdiction is based not on the illegitimacy of the state's crimes or arguments about sovereignty, but about the rights of *victims*. I do not need to assume anything about the relationship between the state and its citizens to argue that, in the case of severe abuses, individuals' rights are interfered with if their abusers cannot be brought to trial somewhere.

not impinge on the autonomy or welfare of the individual in the same way as do violations of some of the other basic rights discussed in this volume (for example the right to life). This permissive rule means that, in some situations, the victim is in fact left with no remedy at all, and the perpetrator achieves full impunity. But given the potential costs to peace noted earlier, a mandatory rule to give the victim a guaranteed remedy would create undue risks. Thus, thin justice permits no more—but also no less—than a permissive rule of international law. States have avoided a rule that would undermine basic human rights—'no universal jurisdiction'—by adopting one that respects it but in a way that is less disruptive to peace than would be the case with a mandatory rule.

The rule permitting but not requiring universal jurisdiction also reflects an additional consequentialist calculation, beyond the promotion of peace. As pointed out by Terry Nardin in the (more costly) case of humanitarian intervention: 'Like an individual person, a state is not obligated to intervene at great cost to itself.'[72] Investigating and prosecuting foreign abuses is not charity work; it entails significant costs for the prosecuting state, both financial and political.[73] Not only would such a duty be excessive morally, but it would also raise concerns under the compliance corollary from Chapter 3. For it seems that states would never agree to expend financial resources and political capital to prosecute every human rights abuser found on their soil for acts abroad.

Yet, even here, we should not take either Nardin's argument or the compliance corollary too far. For the fact is, as noted previously, states have accepted obligations to prosecute offenders on their territory for acts committed abroad in individual treaties on torture, war crimes, enforced disappearances, and other acts. In those treaties, the state agrees to prosecute if it cannot extradite for any reason. The willingness of states to enter into such commitments does not mean that international law should impose an obligation on them as a matter of customary international law to exercise universal jurisdiction. It does show, however, that, at least with respect to certain grave offenses, we are witnessing a thickening of the justice of international law regarding universal jurisdiction. We could with some creativity imagine other institutional mechanisms for a thicker justice, perhaps through a common UN fund to assist states unable to afford universal jurisdiction practices (although this would not eliminate the political tensions associated with such prosecutions).

3. *Enhancing the justice of universal jurisdiction*

If the second pillar of thin justice requires a rule allowing for such trials, then we still need to ensure that the rules governing universal jurisdiction are such that they do the least harm possible to peace. From this perspective, we can re-examine some of the five propositions set out earlier, in Section III.B:[74]

[72] Terry Nardin, 'The Moral Basis of Humanitarian Intervention', *Ethics & Intl Aff* 16 (2002): 57, 69.

[73] See Ratner, 'Belgium's War Crimes Statute', *supra* note 58, at 895–6.

[74] The immunity issue is discussed in Chapter 6.

- The 'right of first refusal' of the territorial state (proposition (4)) is particularly important to trials because it minimizes the possibility of both interstate tensions and tensions among the affected parties to a conflict. If the territorial state makes the choice to prosecute, other states should defer. A harder question arises with the corresponding right of the forum state to proceed even if the territorial state refuses to prosecute. Here my view, consistent with the earlier discussion, is that a just rule under the two pillars would allow the forum state to prosecute in this situation, but only if it represents the only realistic possibility of avoiding full impunity for the alleged perpetrator.[75] If the state of territoriality has some policy in place short of full impunity—perhaps requiring the perpetrator to confess in exchange for an amnesty, as South Africa did, though this strategy may not be enough in other situations—it is much harder to justify a rule that would give foreign states the right to proceed in any event. I realize that victims' groups might applaud the foreign trial, but respect for the basic human rights of the victims does not equate with deferring to their wishes if their state is providing some meaningful vindication of those rights without a trial.
- With regard to the law's disfavoring of trials *in absentia* (proposition (3)), it is hard to know whether this position advances peace. *In absentia* trials may be worse in terms of the peace-related concerns than no trials at all, but they may be better than trials with the defendant present. It is also hard to know whether a rule against them is likely to discourage trials overall by forum states or rather encourage them to apprehend defendants. As for the second pillar of thin justice, in the case of universal jurisdiction, it also demands that the basic human rights of the *defendant* be respected. So the harm to the rights of the defendant from trial *in absentia* needs to be balanced against the vindication of the victims' rights that may come from a trial *in absentia*. The law's presumption against trials *in absentia* certain favors the former's rights, but, if the defendant can somehow defend himself even *in absentia* (through legal representation), then *in absentia* trials do not seem to violate his basic human rights. I think a presumption against *in absentia* trials is a decent compromise between the rights of the defendant and the rights of the victim, though I think it may err too far against the victim's rights.

If universal jurisdiction really takes off, it would be best if the law added other conditions to keep it thinly just. Safeguards, in the form of best practices by forum states, can be built into the process to mitigate the costs to interstate relations as well as avoid abuses of defendants. These would include limiting prosecutions to situations where the evidence is strong, where the forum state has a fair judiciary, and where prosecution will not be perceived as taking sides in an ongoing conflict. It also strongly suggests that the decisions on initiating prosecutions matters should be made by politically accountable prosecutors rather than

[75] This concept is similar to the criterion of last resort in just war theory discussed in Chapter 9; it also raises complicated issues about how states are to judge whether universal jurisdiction is truly the last resort for the vindication of the victims or whether the state where the crimes were committed may yet carry out some form of accountability.

plaintiff-prosecutors, who will not typically be thinking in these terms.[76] The plaintiff-prosecutor system has certain advantages for victims of crimes, but it would undercut the justice of universal jurisdiction as permissive and not mandatory that I have endorsed previously.

The hardest question remaining from the analysis is one where international law still does not offer the clearest of answers—namely, over what offenses should states be entitled to assert universal jurisdiction? The list offered in proposition (1) reflects treaties that allow for universal jurisdiction as well as state practice in the form of domestic legislation, but it is worth asking whether thin global justice requires this list or perhaps another. If universal jurisdiction is justified only to the extent that it protects basic human rights, then it should, as a matter of customary international law, be limited to offenses meeting what Adeno Addis has called the 'heinousness' condition.[77] Certainly crimes against humanity, genocide, slavery, and torture, which are currently on that list, would appear to meet this criterion. It could also cover other heinous crimes, such as enforced disappearances or summary executions.[78] But others on the list are not so heinous, such as aircraft hijacking or sabotage (although if accompanied by massive casualties they can be). Yet as discussed earlier, I do not think it is unjust to allow states to agree by treaty on a list of crimes subject to universal jurisdiction insofar as they have explicitly made the calculation that such prosecutions—usually mandatory in the treaties—will not harm peace. But absent such an explicit calculation, I would be hesitant to expand the list of crimes much further.

V. Conclusion

This chapter began with an apparent tension between the universality of human rights law and international law's insistence that in most situations states can guarantee only the human rights of those within their borders. On close examination, this limitation turned out to be justifiable not only as a matter of thin justice, for its contribution to peace without interfering with basic human rights, but also on a more thickly cosmopolitan conception of justice centered on an optimal regime for the protection of individuals. Yet international law, through the actions of states, has had to respond to actors questioning the territorial paradigm. For those five bases, though defensible as just, still reflect a state-centric approach to international law in which one of the law's key goals is to keep states out of each other's business. As governments, or at least some of them, and civil society

[76] See Ratner, 'Belgium's War Crime Statute', *supra* note 58. The question of whether an investigating judge, who is a government official but independent of the prosecutor, should make these decisions is a difficult question beyond the scope this study.

[77] Adeno Addis, 'Imagining the International Community: The Constitutive Dimension of Universal Jurisdiction', *HRQ* 31 (2009): 129, 138–9.

[78] See Steven R. Ratner, 'The Schizophrenias of International Criminal Law', *Tex ILJ* 33 (1998): 237, 240.

became more aware of violations of human rights abroad, they made inroads into that state-centric system.

As for the justice of the new law developing in response to those claims, extraterritorial protection of human rights by a state when it acts abroad proved not only justifiable under the pillars of thin justice, but, unlike most other norms in this volume, required as well. Universal jurisdiction raised significant questions under the first pillar, but the second pillar, when seen as a requirement for the vindication of basic human rights, pulled in the other direction. In the end, the rule that permits states to exercise universal jurisdiction, coupled with conditions such as deference to accountability mechanisms by the state where the crime occurred, passes muster under both pillars. The law does not represent an embodiment of ideal justice, but it does do an overall decent job of advancing thin justice. These two exceptions to the purely territorial conception preserve the peace central to the justification for territoriality, yet they address the deficiencies of pure territoriality in terms of human rights protection.

The next chapter turns to the third and most normatively controversial exception to the territorial conception of human rights law, humanitarian intervention. At the end of that chapter, I will draw together some of the justice-based implications of all three forms of extraterritoriality discussed in these two chapters.

9

Extraterritorial Protection of Human Rights through Force: From Humanitarian Intervention to the Responsibility to Protect

The most controversial claim to extend human rights protection abroad concerns forcible action by one state on the territory of another to aid the latter's population from assaults by its own government—what has come to be known as humanitarian intervention. Of the three exceptions to the territorial limitation to human rights protection under consideration here, humanitarian intervention has gathered the most scholarly attention in both law and philosophy. The topic poses core questions for applied ethics because it requires an inquiry into the morality of initiating war in the name of the rights of foreigners, an appraisal that demands asking how much we should care about those beyond our borders compared to the costs to ourselves and the preservation of peace. In the view of many scholars, the international law rules are unjust and in need of serious reform. In the discussion that follows, we will see that international law's norms are complex and multifaceted, and that their justice depends a great deal on how one characterizes the state of the law.[1]

I. Thin Justice and the Current Rules on Humanitarian Intervention

A. An attempt to restate the law on humanitarian intervention

A crystallization of the law on humanitarian intervention turns a great deal on the methodology of the appraiser. To some, the issue is as simple as saying that the practice is illegal unless the Security Council approves it; for others, including

[1] For the sake of space I do not address duties to *prevent* human rights abuses abroad, e.g., the obligation to prevent genocide in the Genocide Convention, addressed by the ICJ in holding that Serbia failed to prevent genocide by the Bosnian Serb army. See *Application of the Convention on the Prevention and Punishment of the Crime of Genocide (Bosnia and Herzegovina v Serbia and Montenegro)* [2007] ICJ Rep 43, paras. 425–438 (26 February).

me, a more sensitive approach is necessary to explain the current expectations of states.[2] I would therefore state the law in two broad propositions.

First, as discussed in Chapter 4, *under the text of the UN Charter, states are banned from using force except under two circumstances—self-defense under Article 51 and pursuant to a grant of authority or direction from the Security Council under Chapter VII*. Thus, the only lawful humanitarian intervention is that authorized by the Council and, conceivably, humanitarian action closely tied to action in self-defense.[3] The Council has approved such intervention from time to time since the early 1990s, including in Somalia (1992), Haiti (1994), Bosnia (1992–95), East Timor (1999), Libya (2011), Mali (2012), and Syria (2014, for delivery of humanitarian relief only). All other interventions would be clearly unlawful. I will call this the 'black-letter position'.

Second, notwithstanding this most accepted reading of the UN Charter, *a number of arguments, some better than others, can be made to support the legality of humanitarian intervention outside the Security Council context* (what I will call 'unauthorized humanitarian intervention' or 'UHI'):

(1) One might argue that UHI is simply not covered by Article 2(4), insofar as it could be said to be action not 'against the territorial integrity or political independence' of a state, but only a use of force against the government, on behalf of the people. This argument is often coupled with a broader teleological claim that the revolution in human rights since World War II has so changed the notion of sovereignty that Article 2(4)'s ambit must now be narrowed. Although I agree that human rights norms affect our reading of the Charter and that sovereignty (a term I have generally avoided here) has clearly changed over time, the textual and the broad teleological arguments with respect to UHI lack support in practice and seem to be at odds with the drafters' understanding of Article 2(4).[4]

(2) One might argue that UHI is a legally justifiable action that states may take in extreme situations regardless of the existence of particular rules of law to the contrary. The doctrinal grounding of this position is the customary international law doctrine of necessity, under which a state's action in violation of a rule will not be legally wrongful under very limited circumstances. As recently restated by the International Law Commission (ILC) in its 2001 Articles on State Responsibility, these conditions are if the act 'is the only way for the State

[2] On methodology and its implications for this issue, see Tom J. Farer, 'Humanitarian Intervention before and after 9/11: Legality and Legitimacy', in J.L. Holzgrefe and Robert O. Keohane (eds.), *Humanitarian Intervention: Ethical, Legal, and Political Dilemmas* (Cambridge: Cambridge University Press, 2003) 53.

[3] One example of self-defense that turned into a humanitarian intervention was Vietnam's invasion of Cambodia in December 1978, which led to the ouster of the Khmer Rouge from power in January 1979.

[4] Albrecht Randelzhofer, 'Article 2(4)', in Bruno Simma, Daniel-Erasmus Khan, Georg Nolte, and Andreas Paulus (eds.), *The Charter of the United Nations: A Commentary*, Vol. I, 3rd ed. (Oxford: Oxford University Press, 2012) 200, 215–17. For an exposition of the teleological view, see W. Michael Reisman, 'Sovereignty and Human Rights in Contemporary International Law', *AJIL* 84 (1990): 866. See also Sean Murphy, *Humanitarian Intervention: The United Nations in an Evolving World Order* (Philadelphia, PA: University of Pennsylvania Press, 1996) 358–78.

to safeguard an essential interest against a grave and imminent peril' and 'does not seriously impair an essential interest of the State or States towards which the obligation exists, or of the international community as a whole'.[5] Belgium made such an argument to the International Court of Justice after it was sued by Serbia for participating in NATO's war in Kosovo and sought to legally justify the war.[6] Belgium's argument was flawed, however, for several reasons, including because: (a) the use of force clearly 'impair[ed] an essential interest' of Serbia, and (b) the ILC Articles forbid invocation of necessity to violate a peremptory norm of international law, of which the ban on the use of force is generally considered a prime example.[7]

(3) One might argue that, whatever the words of the Charter, state practice under the Charter points to an obvious tolerance of certain forms of UHI. States have acquiesced, through lack of significant protest or through other actions suggesting support or at least non-opposition, in exceptional situations. These cases have generally been characterized by (1) a grave human rights situation; (2) the failure of other, less coercive methods of improving the situation; (3) a lack of Security Council authorization for force due to the prospect of a veto; (4) a clear (though not exclusively) humanitarian motive by the intervening state(s); (5) ideally participation by a coalition of states; (6) attempts by the intervening state(s) to minimize damage caused and general respect for *jus in bello*, and (7) withdrawal of troops as soon as possible after achievement of the goal.

The overall reactions of states to UHI by Tanzania in Uganda (positive), Vietnam in Cambodia (negative under factor (7) and perhaps (4), in the preceding paragraph), the ECOWAS states in Sierra Leone, and NATO states in Kosovo (both positive) support this view, such that expectations now amount to recognition of the lawfulness of the practice under very limited circumstances.[8] In 2013, the UK government asserted this position quite overtly when it was considering using force against Syria following the Assad regime's use of chemical weapons. It argued that UHI was lawful if the following three conditions were met: (1) 'convincing evidence, generally accepted by the international community as a whole, of extreme humanitarian distress on a large scale, requiring immediate and urgent relief'; (2) 'there is no practicable alternative to the use of force if lives are to be saved'; and (3) 'the proposed use of force must be necessary and proportionate to the aim of relief of humanitarian need and must be strictly limited in time and

[5] ILC Articles on State Responsibility, Art. 25.

[6] Belgium was the only NATO state to make this argument; the other NATO states focused on the Court's jurisdiction to argue that the Court should not grant Yugoslavia's request for provisional measures, a view that prevailed with the Court. See *Case Concerning Legality of Use of Force (Yugoslavia v Belgium)* [1999] ICJ Rep 124 (Order of 2 June).

[7] ILC Articles on State Responsibility, Art. 26.

[8] See Thomas M. Franck, *Recourse to Force* (Cambridge: Cambridge University Press, 2009) 171; Jane Stromseth, 'Rethinking Humanitarian Intervention: the Case for Incremental Change', in J.L. Holzgrefe and Robert O. Keohane (eds.), *Humanitarian Intervention: Ethical, Legal, and Political Dilemmas* (Cambridge: Cambridge University Press, 2003) 232, 248–52.

scope to this aim (i.e. the minimum necessary to achieve that end and for no other purpose)'.[9]

My own interpretive methodology supports such a reading of the UN Charter.[10] Although we lack a 'tidy jurisprudence',[11] we have ample evidence from state practice and attitudes of what counts as illegal UHI and what is legal. My interpretation is not, however, universally shared. Others have read the same practice to simply support the black-letter rule.[12]

(4) Finally, it has been argued that unauthorized humanitarian intervention is illegal still but excusable or otherwise still legitimate. This argument notes the international acceptance under limited circumstances emphasized in the prior view, but refrains from characterizing it as a change in the law, preferring to keep it outside the law. As advanced by some legal scholars, the claim is that law does not and should not provide an ex ante or even ex post justification for such actions because of the importance of Article 2(4); but actors will and should excuse or perhaps forgive such violations from time to time under very limited circumstances because they see them as morally required. Bruno Simma argues that, in the case of Kosovo, NATO gave a good justification for departure from the rule, but warns against 'turn[ing] such an exception into a general policy'.[13] Thomas Franck claims that the law cannot ignore common-sense morality and must find ways 'to bridge any gap between its own institutional commitment to consistent application of formal rules and the public sense that order should not be achieved at too high a cost'.[14] He analogizes the tolerance for UHI to the famous English case in which a court tried sailors who, while in a lifeboat, ate their cabin boy to survive. It found them guilty of murder and sentenced them to death, but urged mercy upon them, whereupon the Home Secretary imposed a mere six-month sentence.[15] The 'illegal but legitimate' position is the international lawyer's vocabulary for ethical inquiry, though without the rigor of the moral philosopher as to what makes the conduct legitimate.

[9] See *Chemical Weapon Use by Syrian Regime—UK Government Legal Position*, 29 August 2013, para. 4, <http://www.gov.uk/government/uploads/system/uploads/attachment_data/file/235098/Chemical-weapon-use-by-Syrian-regime-UK-government-legal-position.pdf>.

[10] One iteration of this view is that customary law has developed alongside the Charter to allow for humanitarian intervention under limited circumstances. J.L. Holzgrefe, 'The Humanitarian Intervention Debate', in J.L. Holzgrefe and Robert O. Keohane (eds.), *Humanitarian Intervention: Ethical, Legal, and Political Dilemmas* (Cambridge: Cambridge University Press, 2003) 15, 44–9.

[11] W. Michael Reisman, 'Why Regime Change is (Almost) Always a Bad Idea', *AJIL* 98 (2004): 516, 517.

[12] See, e.g., Olivier Corten, *The Law Against War: The Prohibition on the Use of Force in Contemporary International Law* (Oxford: Hart Publishing, 2010) 511–49.

[13] Bruno Simma, 'NATO, the UN and the Use of Force: Legal Aspects', *EJIL* 10 (1999): 1, 22.

[14] Franck, *Recourse to Force, supra* note 8, at 177–8.

[15] Ibid., at 181–91. For a slightly different view, one that would require the intervening state to admit the illegality of the act and even pay reparations, see Michael Byers and Simon Chesterman, 'Changing the Rules About Rules?: Unilateral Humanitarian Intervention and the Future of International Law', in J.L. Holzgrefe and Robert O. Keohane (eds.), *Humanitarian Intervention: Ethical, Legal, and Political Dilemmas* (Cambridge: Cambridge University Press, 2003) 177, 198–201.

We thus confront five different arguments about the lawfulness of UHI. As noted, many legal scholars will insist that the alpha and omega of the legal appraisal is the black-letter position that bans the practice. But the last two of the four responses (in paragraphs (3) and (4)) suggest that global expectations, and even the law, may be quite different from that view. We might call these two the 'context-dependent positions' for short. They are important because governments engaging in atrocities, their victims, and the potential intervening parties need to be aware of the extent, however limited, to which important global actors will tolerate such military interventions. Those context-dependent positions do not deny the validity of the black-letter proposition. But they insist that that proposition is only part of a fair description of the state of the law.

B. The thin justice of the rules on humanitarian intervention

Philosophical treatment of humanitarian intervention is by now enormous, dating from the just war theory of Thomas Aquinas through to modern scholars. For many years that scholarship has been characterized by a fairly broad consensus that humanitarian intervention, authorized by the Security Council or not, is at times not only morally permissible but morally required to rescue a besieged population from its own government or another group exercising power over it.

Justifications have varied, from Walzer's defense, in *Just and Unjust Wars*, of intervention as an exception to the principle of non-intervention and self-determination when a community is faced with massacre,[16] to the more extensive claims about the right of outside states to respond to governments violating human rights made by cosmopolitans.[17] Even Nardin, with his preference for a state-centered order, justifies it based on what he calls a 'common morality' that allows us to 'defend the rights of others when those rights are threatened'.[18] I endorse this starting position, and though I do not need to choose a particular rationale, I find Nardin's sense of a duty of beneficence both intuitively appealing and consistent with the basic tenets of cosmopolitan thinking.[19]

Yet the question here is not the permissibility of individual acts of humanitarian intervention, but of a *norm* of international law. Philosophers have noted the difference and, as a result, some who strongly favor humanitarian intervention in particular situations are, at the same time, more cautious about endorsing, or even unwilling to countenance, a change in the law, often adding constraints

[16] (New York: Basic Books, 2006) 101–8; see also Michael Walzer, *Arguing About War* (New Haven, CT: Yale University Press, 2004) 81.

[17] See, e.g., Simon Caney, *Justice Beyond Borders: A Global Political Theory* (Oxford: Oxford University Press, 2005) 226–62; Andrew Altman and Christopher Heath Wellman, *A Liberal Theory of International Justice* (Oxford: Oxford University Press, 2011) 96–115; James Pattison, *Humanitarian Intervention & the Responsibility to Protect: Who Should Intervene?* (Oxford: Oxford University Press, 2010).

[18] Terry Nardin, 'The Moral Basis of Humanitarian Intervention', *Ethics & Intl Aff* 16 (2002): 57, 65.

[19] For a good review of the ethical scholarship, see Holzgrefe, 'The Humanitarian Intervention Debate', *supra* note 10, at 18–36.

to their initial justifications of humanitarian intervention. Substantively, Jerome Slater and Terry Nardin's constraints resemble those from just war theory,[20] while Simon Caney's are more idealistic in hoping to allocate the competence to decide each case to an international institution not controlled by the powerful states.[21] Similarly, Habermas' halting endorsement of the need to respond to abuses is tied to an insistence that the UN and the ICC, and not the great powers, undertake the action.[22]

Whatever their differences about the best or legal position, the philosophical works seem to start from the same assumption—namely, that the law today is encompassed in the black-letter proposition, mentioned previously, that bans humanitarian intervention absent Security Council approval. But as I have suggested, the law is actually more complex than that—in that it *simultaneously* (a) endorses an interpretation of the UN Charter that prohibits such action unless approved by the Security Council;[23] and (b) tolerates and indeed, in my view, renders lawful UHI in exceptional circumstances. This creative ambiguity between the black-letter position and the context-dependent position—what Reisman long ago termed the coexistence of 'myth system' and 'operational code'[24]—makes the ethical inquiry particularly challenging. For we are not merely evaluating the morality of the first rule (as philosophers have done), or even the second rule (which they have not done, even though some of their theories end up quite close to it), but the morality of the *combination* of them.

1. *The peace pillar*

From the perspective of the promotion of peace, in particular interstate peace, the black-letter position stands on a moral high ground. If international law bans individual states from using force against other states that abuse their populations, we have prevented yet another possibility for states to go to war with each other. We have also avoided an increase in internal violence that would be caused by outside involvement in the short run, although such interventions could conceivably also

[20] Jerome Slater and Terry Nardin, 'Nonintervention and Human Rights', *Journal of Politics* 48 (1986): 86, 93–5.

[21] Caney, *Justice Beyond Borders, supra* note 17, at 256; for a similar reliance on multilateral institutions that do not currently have such powers or do not exist, see Daniele Archibugi, 'Cosmopolitan Guidelines for Humanitarian Intervention', *Alternatives* 29 (2004): 1; Gillian Brock, *Global Justice: A Cosmopolitan Account* (Oxford: Oxford University Press, 2009) 177–80.

[22] See Jürgen Habermas, 'Bestiality and Humanity: A War on the Border between Legality and Morality', *Constellations* 6 (1999): 263, 268–9. Buchanan argues that the institutional questions associated with changing the law should affect our moral reasoning about the permissibility of the practice in the first place. Allen Buchanan, *Justice, Legitimacy, and Self-Determination: Moral Foundations for International Law* (Oxford: Oxford University Press, 2004) 22–3; see also Allen Buchanan and Robert O. Keohane, 'The Preventive Use of Force: A Cosmopolitan Institutional Proposal', *Ethics & Intl Aff* 18 (2004): 1.

[23] I will leave aside the self-defense turned humanitarian intervention possibility for the sake of simplicity.

[24] W. Michael Reisman, *Folded Lies: Bribery, Crusades, and Reform* (New York: The Free Press, 1979) 1.

serve to end a civil war decisively. (The 2011 intervention in Libya at first seemed to end the civil conflict between the government and rebels, but war between various armed factions began soon thereafter.) Indeed, this calculation regarding interstate peace explains the practice of most states—the United Kingdom being the notable exception in this regard—to endorse formally only that position and rely on less overt ways to express their sympathies or agreements with the context-dependent positions. For the many legal scholars, and the rare philosopher, who endorse the black-letter rule, it is the threat to international peace that is key. As Jackson writes: 'International order and stability, international peace and security... [are] far more important than minority rights or humanitarian protections in Yugoslavia or any other country.'[25]

The black-letter rule is not, however, a perfect fit under the first pillar insofar as the rule allows the Security Council to approve humanitarian interventions, even when the result will clearly be a new war. Singer seems worried about the power of the Council when he laments its tendency to characterize gross abuses as threats to the peace, noting that these determinations mean that the Council 'has an unconstrained mandate to interfere wherever it sees fit'.[26] Yet the Council needs to determine that some human rights violations are threats to the peace, for only those threats permit the Council to authorize force under the UN Charter.[27] Singer might be complaining that the Council has unfettered discretion to make a determination of a threat to the peace, which is the generally accepted view in international law.[28]

There are two responses to this concern, though they do not completely save the Council's authority to approve humanitarian intervention. First, as a practical matter, the Council has tended to *underact* in response to atrocities. Gaining the approval of nine members, including the P5, is likely to make, and has made, authorization for force overall quite rare, suggesting that the Council's special role can help prevent conflict rather than foment it. But, as discussed in Chapter 8, that very historical reluctance to approve force in the face of major atrocities (like Rwanda) raises serious concerns under the second pillar that the black-letter rule, in giving the Council sole authority to authorize force, is harming human rights.

Second, the Council's plenary authority seems less worrisome if we endorse the idea that it has a special competence to determine threats to the peace and the responses that will best restore the peace with the minimal cost in terms of human lives. The Council's role does not result in simply fewer authorizations for force, but ideally a process in which authorizations for force are done in a way that is the least damaging to peace. Yet, also as discussed in the previous chapter,

[25] Robert Jackson, *The Global Covenant* (Oxford: Oxford University Press, 2000) 291; see also Mark Mazower, *Governing the World: The History of an Idea, 1815 to the Present* (New York: Penguin Books, 2012) 395.

[26] Peter Singer, *One World: The Ethics of Globalization* (New Haven, CT: Yale University Press, 2002) 132.

[27] UN Charter, Art. 39.

[28] See, e.g., *Prosecutor v Tadić*, Case No. IT-94-1-T, Decision on the Defence Motion for Interlocutory Appeal on Jurisdiction (2 October 1995); *Questions of Interpretation and Application of the 1971 Montreal Convention arising from the Aerial Incident at Lockerbie (Libya v United States)* [1992] ICJ Rep 114, paras. 42–43 (Order of 14 April).

the Council's current membership has only some actual competence in this area, with the P5 dominating the agenda. As a result, a rule that empowers the Council to make these decisions could result in a misuse of the power rather than the advancement of peace.[29]

Under the first pillar, the context-dependent positions clearly do less to promote peace than the black-letter rule.[30] They have the added disadvantage, as legal scholars supportive of the black-letter rule have indicated, that the actors deploying them are likely to be powerful states that have the capacity to engage in humanitarian intervention.[31] In particular, the United Kingdom, France, the United States, and Russia seem most eager to take advantage of them in particular situations, whether Kosovo, Libya, Syria, or Russia's 'near abroad'. Those states may take advantage of the flexibility to undertake invasions that do not serve humanitarian purposes.[32]

On the other hand, there is a clear advantage in terms of peace of a rule on UHI that reflects what states actually do and believe, as opposed to one that is not actually observed in practice. As Franck points out: 'When law permits or even requires behavior that is widely held to be unfair, immoral, or unjust, it is not only persons but also the law that suffers.'[33] If states accept certain limits on what is legal or legitimate UHI, their ex ante decisions whether to intervene and our ex post evaluations of its legality or legitimacy will be constrained more than if they were operating in a legal no-man's land following their violation of the black-letter ban.[34] In other words, the black-letter rule, by simply saying 'no', is going to be ignored by states anyway rather than provide true limits to UHI. In that sense, from the perspective of preserving the peace, the context-dependent positions at least clarify the limits of humanitarian intervention in a way that the black-letter rule cannot.

Our willingness to accept this argument may well turn on which of the two context-dependent positions we choose. Recall that the first of the two (argument (3)) deems humanitarian intervention lawful under limited circumstances, whereas the second (argument (4)) deems it unlawful but legitimate, a sort of

[29] One solution is to require the Council to follow the context-dependent criteria itself in setting forth the scope of its authorization, a point explored in Pattison, *Humanitarian Intervention, supra* note 17, at 221–7.

[30] As for the first two alternatives to the black-letter position, reinterpreting 'territorial integrity' twists the Charter language and has no support among states or scholars; relying on a defense of necessity hinges on a finding that UHI does not violate a peremptory norm, and only a new version of that peremptory norm would make UHI not wrongful. So we would still have to redefine the ban on the use of force to be able to take advantage of that strategy.

[31] Nico Krisch, 'Legality, Morality and the Dilemma of Humanitarian Intervention after Kosovo', *EJIL* 13 (2002): 323.

[32] Some recent scholarship on state motivations for starting or avoiding wars questions this claim. See Ryan Goodman, 'Humanitarian Intervention and Pretexts for War', *AJIL* 100 (2006): 107.

[33] Franck, *Recourse to Force, supra* note 8, at 178.

[34] I thus disagree with Chris Brown when he argues that criteria for lawful intervention cannot guide behavior because states, guided by self-interest, will never agree to follow a particular test. See Chris Brown, 'What, Exactly, is the Problem to which the "Five-part Test" is the Solution?', *International Relations* 19 (2005): 225, 228.

excuse concept. The first defense has the advantage of candor and makes very clear to states what they can and cannot do. But, as suggested by scholars who prefer the second approach to the first, the second approach might be preferable under the peace pillar because it seems to offer a greater firewall to war than does the first. By insisting that the practice is unlawful and suggesting that, individually, we might want to tolerate a few illegal acts on a highly exceptional basis, it may well give greater support to the black-letter position and deter states more.[35]

What, then, are the implications for peace of the cohabitation of the two positions? On the one hand, for those favoring the black-letter rule, this combination is just as bad as the context-dependent rule alone. If the black-letter position preserves the peace best, and the context-dependent position does so less, then recognizing the law's toleration for some UHI will undercut the former as states seek to ground and justify their actions based on the context-dependent position. On the other hand, for those, like me, favoring the context-dependent approach, the coexistence of myth system and operational code is not threatening. As long as everyone understands the limits of the black-letter rule, it does not harm the prospects for peace and may indeed serve as a reminder of the costs of UHI.

2. *The human rights pillar*

Once the emphasis shifts from the preservation of peace to non-interference with basic human rights, the black-letter rule's moral high ground seems to be sinking fast. A rule of international law that precludes states from taking the action needed to terminate gross violations of human rights (unless the Security Council approves of the action) is highly suspect. Such a rule essentially requires states to limit their responses to mass atrocities in Cambodia (1.5 to 1.7 million dead between 1975 and 1979), Rwanda (500,000 to 800,000 killed between April and July 1994), or Syria (over 100,000 killed from 2011 to 2014), and elsewhere to protest, diplomacy, or economic sanctions, however ineffective.

A just international law cannot include rules that make it impossible for states to terminate such assaults or, seen deontologically, act on a duty to respect the basic human rights of all on the planet.[36] The numerous rules of human rights law that require the state to cease those abuses and its mechanisms to encourage that cessation are not sufficient in some exceptional situations. There, where the Security Council might refuse to act and non-military measures prove ineffectual, this rule effectively empowers a state to commit heinous abuses against its citizens. Unlike the rules on secession discussed earlier, which strongly discourage the practice but allow it in exceptional situations like decolonization or denial

[35] See, e.g., Byers and Chesterman, 'Changing the Rules About Rules?', *supra* note 15, at 198–9.

[36] This position is not inconsistent with David Miller's notion that a state has a lesser duty to remedy abuses caused by another state than it does to remedy its own abuses. I am rather asserting that a norm of international law nonetheless interferes with basic human rights if it precludes states in the first situation from remedying those abuses. See David Miller, *National Responsibility and Global Justice* (Oxford: Oxford University Press, 2008) 97–107, 272–3.

of basic participatory rights by the state, the black-letter rule regarding humanitarian intervention allows for *no exception*. From this perspective, a move to the context-dependent alternative, or some incorporation of it, is required as a matter of thin (as well as more thickly cosmopolitan) justice.[37]

The only defense of the ban under the second pillar would seem to be a consequentialist argument that UHI harms human rights more than it helps them. As an example, it might be claimed that the U.S. invasion of Iraq overall left the human rights of Iraqis worse off, replacing the brutality of Saddam Hussein with the random violence of a semi-anarchical state. Yet the historical record does not support a blanket ban as a way to respect human rights. In the key cases of UHI, such as the Vietnamese invasion of Cambodia, the Tanzanian invasion of Uganda, and the Indian invasion of East Pakistan, the intervention brought an end to appalling atrocities quite quickly. Even though, in all three cases, the successor regimes violated human rights, the scale was significantly less. Certainly a consequentialist ought to place a premium on the termination of killing that was being carried out by the ousted regimes. The U.S. invasion of Iraq (which the United States did not seek to justify in terms of UHI) further demonstrates the point because it did *not* meet the criteria spelled out earlier. So although that war is certainly an argument against unauthorized force and aggression, it is not an argument against a rule permitting UHI in exceptional circumstances. The argument that the black-letter rule promotes human rights seems to be based on the idea that states cannot observe the criteria in the context-dependent positions.

II. Toward a Just Norm of Unilateral Humanitarian Intervention

A. In defense of the context-dependent positions

In light of the tensions between the pillars of thin justice, the challenge is to propose a rule that passes muster under the second pillar without doing too much damage to the first. Both context-dependent propositions take into account, more or less, that mitigation process.[38] In particular, the seven conditions expressed in legal justification (3), set out in Section I.A, do a decent job of limiting the damages to peace caused by UHI in the real world. Each of the elements seeks in some way to preserve the peace by limiting interventions in terms of the triggers, the parties carrying them out, and the conduct of the operations. Indeed, those elements match up well with those in just war theory—right authority, just cause, right intention, last resort, proportionality, and reasonable hope of success.[39] They also match those

[37] For an endorsement of similar criteria from a cosmopolitan perspective, see Tom Farer, 'Cosmopolitan Humanitarian Intervention: a Five-part Test', *International Relations* 19 (2005): 211.

[38] A related question, which I will address in Chapter 13, is the process by which the law should be changed.

[39] Mona Fixdal and Dan Smith, 'Humanitarian Intervention and Just War', *Mershon International Studies Review* 42 (1998): 283; see also 291 (criteria of open declaration and relative justice are included in the application of the other criteria).

developed by the International Commission on Intervention and State Sovereignty (ICISS), a group of experienced world leaders and thinkers convened by the government of Canada in the aftermath of the Rwandan non-intervention and the Kosovo intervention.[40] Given the costs to peace of UHI, a rule permitting it would be limited to the protection of a subcategory of basic human rights, notably the right to life. Through this incorporation of these criteria, international law, in the form of the two context-dependent positions but not the black-letter, does meet the test of thin global justice.

As between the two context-dependent views, one (argument (3)) permits UHI in exceptional situations by circumscribing conditions within the law on the use of force, whereas the other (argument (4)) does it through incorporating a notion of excuse or extralegal legitimacy. As noted earlier, the former has the advantage of making the law clearer. It takes better account of the rule of law and the fairness corollary introduced in Chapter 3 by providing a greater sense of ex ante transparency and certainty in the planning of operations. At the same time, I acknowledge that the latter has the advantage of preventing the exceptions to the black-letter rule from eating up the rule.[41] It effectively places the burden of proof more strongly on the intervening entity by working from the assumption that such interventions are always illegal but will occasionally be tolerated.

It might be argued that, in the end, the black-letter rule does the best job of passing muster under the two pillars by balancing the costs to peace from UHI against the benefits to human rights from it and finding that the first outweighs the second. This seems to be behind Krisch's defense of the black-letter rule as just.[42] But that position reflects a very subservient view of the role for human rights in appraising the justice of international law. It downplays human rights as much as some cosmopolitan views of UHI downplay UHI's costs to peace.[43] This diversity of viewpoints shows that many of the disagreements among scholars about UHI are ultimately arguments over the priorities of peace versus human rights in the international legal order. Thin justice strikes a balance that I have defended in Chapter 3; alternative positions seem far more skewed in one direction or the other.

Lastly, unlike the approaches of most philosophers who consider the legal rules governing UHI, my defense of the context-dependent positions is not based on finding a morally ideal position that is then limited in its legal incarnation by practical constraints. Rather, my argument is that the legal norm expressed in the context-dependent position is *just, not a second-best alternative*; and part of the reason it is just is because it takes into account all of the institutional constraints,

[40] See 'The Responsibility to Protect: Report of the International Commission on Intervention and State Sovereignty' (December 2001), <http://responsibilitytoprotect.org/ICISS%20Report.pdf>, paras. 4.15–4.43.

[41] See Brad R. Roth, *Sovereign Equality and Moral Disagreement: Premises of a Pluralist International Legal Order* (Oxford: Oxford University Press, 2010) 151–62 (on the need for candid discussion among states so as not to let the powerful act without having to justify their actions).

[42] See, e.g., Krisch, 'Legality, Morality', *supra* note 31, at 331–2.

[43] See Altman and Wellman, *A Liberal Theory*, *supra* note 17, 107–11.

including the possibility of failure by the Security Council to act. In this regard, my approach is particularly different from that of Altman and Wellman. After they offer a broad, deontologically grounded proposal to permit humanitarian intervention against any illegitimate government if the risks to non-combatants is not too great—one that highly discounts the costs to peace—they ultimately conclude that the state of knowledge about possible consequences is so uncertain that they cannot decide whether the law should be changed to incorporate their theory. The audacity of their ethical proposal is thus matched by the modesty of their ambitions about making it a legal rule.[44]

But when we have *unjust* norms like the black-letter rule, then the uncertain consequences of changing a rule should be an invitation to propose new law that best takes account of those uncertainties and mitigates possible harms, subject to respect for the compliance corollary. Maintaining the status quo black-letter rule has the air of giving up too soon. As Andrew Mason and Nick Wheeler respond to arguments that the humanitarian intervention should not be legalized even subject to institutional constraints meant to address consequentialist objections: 'The institutional arrangements [we propose] would minimise the scope for abuse, and create a state of affairs better than the one in which all humanitarian intervention is . . . regarded as a violation of international law.'[45]

B. Subsidiary considerations for a just rule

Once we accept the need to adopt one of the two context-dependent positions, other issues require consideration to achieve the best fit between international law and the two pillars of thin justice. First, we must determine the particular inputs for a consequentialist balancing of the costs to basic human rights versus the costs to peace. One way to formulate the rule would be to allow UHI when the number of people saved from death at the hands of their government (or a rebel group) would clearly exceed the number of troops—from the intervening and the defending government (or rebel group)—killed. Another way might be to broaden the calculation to weigh the lives saved against a fuller range of costs associated with the intervention, including monetary ones, and allow those only where the benefits exceed the costs.[46] Yet even as we devise these possible exceptions, we can see the difficulties with operationalizing them. Is it possible for the intervening states to know the costs of action, or of inaction, so clearly? In light of that difficulty, even a consequentialist might in the end support the black-letter rule, though I regard that position as again somewhat defeatist.

Second, we must determine the scope of 'right authority'. Is it just a set of principles, like human rights law itself, or does it mean the approval of specific

[44] Ibid., at 111–15.

[45] Andrew Mason and Nick Wheeler, 'Realist Objections to Humanitarian Intervention', in Barry Holden (ed.), *The Ethical Dimensions of Global Change* (New York: Palgrave Macmillan, 1996) 94, 106.

[46] See, e.g., Singer, *One World*, *supra* note 26, at 138–9 (endorsing this position).

institutions? The reactions by states to interventions suggest that it means both—that the intervention must be grounded in a need to protect basic human rights (and not just economic interests) and that it must receive some kind of institutional endorsement—but without a consensus on what political institutions must endorse the action (or when).

Here philosophers have had much to say. Cosmopolitan philosophers would entrust such decisions to democratically elected or at least accountable international bodies or perhaps even an international court. They see these bodies as more legitimate than the Security Council. Although my purpose here is not to design such institutions, it is worth pointing out, as I have argued in Chapter 7, that replacing the UN, or the Security Council, with a group of democracies ignores the importance of taking into consideration the views of non-democracies in decisions whether to authorize force. Setting aside what ideal institutions might look like, what if these new bodies become paralyzed by politics just like the Council, or are simply too slow bureaucratically, in the case of an international court? By seeking to ground the morality and legality in another body, these approaches have assumed away the question of *un*authorized intervention. Their solution still leaves the victims defenseless in certain situations. So for a just international law, we need a rule that actually does allow for *unauthorized* humanitarian intervention.

The ICISS, for its part, tackled this difficult question. On the one hand, aware of the difficulties of constructing the sort of new institutions that philosophers might prefer, it favored authority from existing international bodies. It endorsed the Security Council's primary responsibility in this area, with a backup possibility by the General Assembly and regional organizations.[47] On the other hand, and to its credit, it recognized the specter of inaction by all these institutions—indeed, it had happened in Rwanda so it took no stretch of the imagination; in the end, it did not quite rule out action by a single state or group of states if this was truly needed to end large-scale atrocities. In a nuanced and politically astute passage, it wrote:

> If collective organizations will not authorize collective intervention against regimes that flout the most elementary norms of legitimate governmental behaviour, then the pressures for intervention by ad hoc coalitions or individual states will surely intensify. And there is a risk then that such interventions... will not be conducted for the right reasons or with the right commitment to the necessary precautionary principles...
>
> [I]f, following the failure of the Council to act, a military intervention is undertaken by an ad hoc coalition or individual state which *does* fully observe and respect all the criteria we have identified, and if that intervention is carried through successfully—and is seen by world public opinion to have been carried through successfully—then this may have enduringly serious consequences for the stature and credibility of the UN itself.[48]

[47] 'The Responsibility to Protect', *supra* note 40, paras. 6.13–6.35.
[48] Ibid., paras. 6.39–6.40.

Although the risks to the UN's 'stature and credibility' from UHI are real, the risks to the victims from inaction suggest that, if all the established loci of legitimate authority within the UN and regional organizations refuse to act in the face of atrocities meeting the criteria of just cause, and a state or group of states act in a manner that meets the criteria set out previously—whether those that crystallized the expectation of states (i.e. argument (3), set out earlier), or those from just war theory or the ICISS—then international law should regard such action as lawful. In the end, I understand the attachment to the black-letter rule or a variant of it based on a more legitimate institution than the Council. But the position I advocate reflects a different evaluation of the peace-human rights balance and consequently how much international law should be willing to stand in the way of states seeking to terminate large-scale atrocities beyond their borders.

C. A permission or obligation of states?

Lastly, the defense of the context-dependent position faces another possible criticism—if it only *allows* for UHI, then does it not leave the victims defenseless if every state simply chooses to look the other way? Does the human rights pillar not require states to engage in UHI if the conditions of just war theory can be met? The philosophy regarding humanitarian intervention is rich with claims to this effect, often argued in deontological terms of whether humanitarian intervention is a perfect duty (a true obligation) or an imperfect duty (a weaker requirement of beneficence) on states.[49] Some writers argue that any argument in favor of the permissibility of intervention is also an argument in favor of a duty, and that we need only decide under what circumstances the duty is triggered.[50]

International legal scholarship has nonetheless continued to address humanitarian intervention as a right; and, even when it shifts from the descriptive (where nobody seriously argues that it is already a duty) to the prescriptive, the arguments are still in terms of rights (or, in Hohfeldian terms, privileges).[51] The *opinio juris* of states, to the extent it favors UHI at all, is in terms of rights, not duties. The result of these contrasting approaches is that even though the philosophers and lawyers adopting the context-dependent approach might agree on most of the relevant criteria for both moral and legal intervention, they might still disagree on whether that intervention is now a duty or merely an option.

Is this disagreement merely a matter of methodology, where some philosophers' logic—that a right implies (or can imply) a duty—runs up against the lawyer's

[49] See Fixdal and Smith, 'Humanitarian Intervention', *supra* note 39, at 296–9; Terry Nardin, 'Introduction', in Terry Nardin and Melissa S. Williams (eds.), *Humanitarian Intervention: Nomos XLVII* (New York: New York University Press, 2006) 14–18; and, in the same volume, Kok-Chor Tan, 'The Duty to Protect', 84, 95–106; and Carla Bagnoli, 'Humanitarian Intervention as a Perfect Duty: A Kantian Argument', 117.

[50] See Tan, 'The Duty to Protect', *supra* note 49, at 90–6; Pattison, *Humanitarian Intervention, supra* note 17, at 15–20.

[51] Dino Kritsiotis, 'Reappraising Policy Objections to Humanitarian Intervention', *Mich JIL* 19 (1998): 1005, 1027–34.

reliance on sources—that states are not using 'duties-talk' at all? Not completely. In fact, the list that the lawyers compile for lawful UHI leaves out what is probably the most important moral question—to what extent we should respect the insistence by states for the *discretion to decline to intervene* if they choose to expend their resources—including the lives of their soldiers—elsewhere? States have not suggested any limits to that discretion, so international lawyers in essence must characterize unauthorized intervention as merely a right. This concern about the costs to the state also arose in Chapter 8, regarding the costs of a state conducting a trial based on universal jurisdiction. Philosophers seem more willing to ask the difficult questions about the extent of our duties to strangers and how much we should be willing to sacrifice our state's resources and soldiers to help them.[52] Their link between right and duty is conditioned on derivation of a *complete* set of criteria for (both permissible and mandatory) UHI.

On the particular question of whether the law's position—discretionary but not mandatory—is just under my own criteria, the case is very close. On the one hand, if the current permission were transformed into a duty of UHI, it could lead to too many interventions of the wrong kind, thus undermining the first pillar. If I must help my neighbor every time he is in trouble, this new obligation would seem to increase the temptation to help out when it is not necessary or even when it is not permitted. Even if that duty were subject to the listed conditions, such as exhaustion of other remedies and a prior attempt to gain Security Council approval, the recognition of a duty could still lead to a situation worse than the one we have now. Some scholars in favor of humanitarian intervention point out that the solution to this problem is to recognize it as a duty, but one that *must* be discharged through proper international institutions.[53] This is an elegant solution—duties on states, action multilaterally—but it still begs the question of what should happen until we have such institutions, or if they fail to act.

On the other hand, perhaps a duty would not lead to such consequences given the tremendous reluctance of states to respond to human rights abuses abroad right now.[54] And, under a robust interpretation of the second pillar, it may be the case that only a duty would truly protect basic human rights. If everyone has a right to end the atrocities abroad but nobody has an obligation, the law may not be denying the possibility to protect basic human rights, but it is also not doing much to halt the atrocities either. In terms of seeing human rights as exclusionary reasons, we would be saying that a state's own domestic preferences do not allow it to decline to take action to stop human rights abuses if the seven criteria listed

[52] Compare Allen Buchanan, 'The Internal Legitimacy of Humanitarian Intervention', *J Pol Phil* 7 (1999): 71, with Miller, *National Responsibility, supra* note 36, at 270–3. A related question concerns the state's responsibility for its own soldiers who might die in a humanitarian intervention, which limits the scope of any duty. See, e.g., Buchanan, *Justice, supra* note 22, at 468–71.

[53] See, e.g., Tan, 'The Duty to Protect', *supra* note 49, at 102–6; Bagnoli, 'Humanitarian Intervention', *supra* note 49, at 130–5.

[54] See Nicholas J. Wheeler, *Saving Strangers: Humanitarian Intervention in International Society* (Oxford: Oxford University Press, 2000) 295–310.

above are met, i.e. that whereas failure to meet one of the seven criteria would be an acceptable ground for not interfering, mere inclination not to do so would not.

On balance, because the second pillar is directed at ensuring that norms do not interfere with human rights, as opposed to insisting that they guarantee them, the absence of any duty on states seems thinly just, but I still regard it as a close call. Although this volume is not the place for a deep treatment of this complex issue, we still can and should conceive of an international norm that places a general duty on all states in a way that nonetheless takes into account the material circumstances of the state and does not do violence to the first pillar.[55] Under this view, we can maintain the importance of a state's general duty to all persons, including those abroad, while not dismissing the state's special obligations to its citizens and soldiers; and we can respect the need to preserve the peace without giving up on a duty to save strangers. Indeed, developments since 2005 suggest a move in that direction.

III. The Responsibility to Protect: A Step Toward a Just Rule?

In the last decade, policymakers concerned with improving global responses to mass atrocities have shifted the ground of discussion. Lawyers and philosopher may argue over a right or duty of humanitarian intervention, decisionmakers have seen these debates as a dead-end insofar as no consensus among states—beyond formal fidelity to the black-letter rule—is likely to be achieved in the near future. States would rather deal with UHI after the fact than through law before the fact. But this legal impasse does nothing to help the victims of those atrocities. In response, an alternative strategy was developed and advocated, first by the ICISS, then by a high-level panel of UN Secretary-General Kofi Annan, then by Annan himself, culminating in endorsement by the General Assembly in 2005.

The result, as offered by the General Assembly in its authoritative and unanimously passed resolution, is a three-part concept under the rubric of the Responsibility to Protect (R2P): (a) the primary responsibility of the state to protect its own people from 'genocide, war crimes, ethnic cleansing and crimes against humanity'; (b) the responsibility of outside states and institutions to assist the state in meeting its responsibilities through foreign aid and other traditional means; (c) when the state does not fulfill its responsibility, the responsibility of those actors to take measures against it, whether diplomatic, economic, or even military, through the Security Council.[56]

[55] See efforts by Tan, 'The Duty to Protect', *supra* note 49, and Pattison, *Humanitarian Intervention, supra* note 17, at 15–20, 190–9, in this direction.

[56] GA Res. 60/1 (24 October 2005), paras. 138–139. With respect to military action, the resolution states:

> [W]e are prepared to take collective action, in a timely and decisive manner, through the Security Council, in accordance with the Charter, including Chapter VII, on a case-by-case basis and in cooperation with relevant regional organizations as appropriate, should peaceful means be inadequate and national authorities are manifestly failing

These actors thus proposed that states have a political and moral obligation to help out states in distress.[57] The concept is distinguishable from humanitarian intervention in two core respects: first, it advocates a 'responsibility', not a legal right or a duty; and second, it addresses a range of responses beyond military measures. The insight of those behind the idea was to advocate an *increase* in the expectations put upon states—moving from right or discretion to responsibility (but not to a legal duty)—but to make it palatable to states by *broadening* the range of desired responses to include those that states already accept as important, notably parts (a) and (b). Moreover, the move to a new responsibility to protect reflects an appreciation for the perspective of the victim, rather than the prerogatives of states.[58]

R2P has nonetheless made a very halting start since its formal debut in 2005. In terms of state responses to ongoing atrocities, we have not witnessed any dramatic change in action, such as significant sanctions, let alone any interventions, against several states committing or tolerating massacres since 2005, including Sudan, Sri Lanka, and Syria.[59] On the other hand, R2P was mentioned in passing by the Security Council in a resolution expanding the peacekeeping mission in Darfur in 2006 and in two of its core resolutions on Libya in 2011, including the one authorizing a no-fly zone to aid civilians in distress, and was at least invoked by states in other situations.[60] Southern states, who voted for the 2005 resolution, and other critics still profess unease that R2P invites UHI, despite the first two, non-military prongs in the concept and the high substantive and procedural thresholds in the 2005 resolution.[61] Scholars have criticized that high threshold for ignoring the responsibility of the state and the international community to avoid abuses far short of those mentioned,[62] as well as the prospect that the concept will be hijacked by states seeking to impose a Western vision on the world.[63]

to protect their populations from genocide, war crimes, ethnic cleansing and crimes against humanity.

For a useful analysis, see Alex J. Bellamy, 'Whither the Responsibility to Protect? Humanitarian Intervention and the 2005 World Summit', *Ethics & Intl Aff* 20 (2006): 143.

[57] In larger freedom: towards development, security and human rights for all: Report of the Secretary-General, 21 March 2005, paras. 135–136, UN Doc. A/59/2005.

[58] Louise Arbour, 'The Responsibility to Protect as a Duty of Care in International Law and Practice', *Rev Intl Stud* 34 (2008): 445, 448.

[59] For a review of the practice, see Alex J. Bellamy, 'The Responsibility to Protect—Five Years On', *Ethics & Intl Aff* 24 (2010): 143.

[60] SC Res. 1706 (31 August 2006), preamble, para. 2; SC Res. 1970 (26 February 2011), preamble, para. 9; SC Res. 1973 (17 March 2011), preamble para. 4; Bellamy, 'The Responsibility to Protect', *supra* note 59.

[61] See Stanley Foundation, 'Actualizing the Responsibility to Protect' (2008) 24–6 <http://www.stanleyfoundation.org/publications/report/UNND808.pdf>. For a sense of the debate in the General Assembly, see GAOR, 63rd Session, Records of the 97th to 101st plenary meetings, 23–28 July 2009, UN Docs. A/63/PV.97 to A/63/PV.101.

[62] See, e.g., Roth, *Sovereign Equality*, *supra* note 41, at 163–5.

[63] Alvarez goes so far as to say that lawyers should return to the issue of humanitarian intervention, for at least it focused on the core human rights challenge in a way that R2P does not. José E. Alvarez, 'The Schizophrenias of R2P', in Euan MacDonald and Philip Alston (eds.), *Human Rights, Intervention, and the Right to Force* (Oxford: Oxford University Press, 2008) 275.

From the perspective of improving the justice of international law advocated here, R2P's advantages clearly outweigh its disadvantages. To be sure, R2P is, first and foremost, not a legal rule at all—the General Assembly cannot make law; the resolution does not re-state customary international law; and it is not an authoritative interpretation of some provision of the Charter. Moreover, it does not propose a change in the law. The first two prongs of R2P are uncontroversial legally: the first simply restates the truism that a state must fulfill its duties under human rights law, and the second is well within contemporary understandings of the norm of non-intervention (and its limited scope) discussed in Chapter 4.[64] The third part avoids all the hard questions about what international law should prohibit, permit, or require in the event the Security Council is unable to address the state's failure to protect.

But more important, R2P's move from rights, the focus of most academic discussions, to responsibility is a highly significant thickening of the justice of international law. It invites states to see themselves as having duties—not legal duties, but at least moral ones—to those outside their borders in a way that the UN had only hesitantly and indirectly stated in the past.[65] It represents a move by states from rigid, formal adherence to the black-letter rule to endorsement of a new position toward victims of atrocities, but in a way that is more modest than the context-dependent positions insofar as it does not purport to state a legal rule. As Anne Peters writes: 'R2P for the first time clearly states that when the territorial state manifestly fails to fulfil its obligation to protect, it falls on the international community.'[66]

Peters' observation takes us back to the fundamental issue of global justice that is the subject of this part of the book—the justice of the territorial scope of human rights law and of the extraterritorial exceptions to that scope. Just as we have seen that international law obligates the state to observe human rights law in some circumstances when it chooses to act abroad, and allows it to adjudicate the conduct of foreigners under universal jurisdiction, so R2P ends any doubt that states are allowed, indeed encouraged, to extend their responsibilities to protect human rights to those beyond their borders when the state fails to do so. The states' legal rights may be no different from what they were before R2P, but the law regarding human rights now encounters a new set of ideas that can influence dialogue, decision, and conduct over time

64 See Anne Peters, 'The Security Council's Responsibility to Protect', *International Organizations L Rev* 8 (2011): 1, 7–9; Arbour, 'The Responsibility to Protect', *supra* note 58.

65 For a rare example, see GA Res. 46/182 (19 December 1991) (regarding emergency situations, stating that 'humanitarian assistance should be provided with the consent of the affected country and in principle on the basis of an appeal by the affected country'). The use of 'country' rather than 'state' and 'should' rather than 'shall' suggests changing attitudes on this issue.

66 Peters, 'The Security Council's Responsibility', *supra* note 64, at 9–10; see also Anne Orford, *International Authority and the Responsibility to Protect* (Cambridge: Cambridge University Press, 2011) 26–7 (R2P as 'conferring authority and allocating powers', resulting in a new 'distribution of jurisdiction and authority between states and international actors'). Orford links the doctrine to classic political theory as well as earlier operations by the UN.

by states, international organizations, and others—and eventually change our interpretation of the law.

The law may not change with respect to UHI at all, but it could change in other ways. Perhaps R2P will lead to a sense of duty that states must aid other states with limited capacity in the area of the rule of law, or that they must impose sanctions on governments and leaders that are abusing their people, or that the Security Council has a duty to act when those measures fail. Louise Arbour has suggested that R2P can build on duties of bystander states under the Genocide Convention to prevent atrocities and produce a 'protection duty', encompassing a range of required responses by outside actors to mass atrocities.[67] All of these permutations, and others, can shift the conversation away from UHI while changing the broader law on the extraterritorial scope of human rights law as states undertake new duties. In that way, R2P provides an opportunity for a thicker justice than that found in the territorially based law of human rights.

IV. Conclusion

Our discussion of UHI began with a disagreement among international lawyers as to the state of the law—a disagreement that, in my view, stems as much from ethical assumptions about the importance of peace compared to human rights as it does to any methodological disagreements among scholars. If we think the black-letter position forbidding UHI is the international law rule, then that norm is surely unjust—for while that rule protects interstate peace, it seriously interferes with basic human rights. But because my methodology sees international law as offering alternative rules, the context-dependent positions, it is, in the end, quite simplistic to call it unjust. On the contrary, international law reflects, if somewhat messily in doctrinal terms, thin global justice by preserving the peace while allowing for exceptional situations in which we need to protect basic human rights through forcible means. The law does not lay out a transparent codification at this point, but the practice of states shows an acceptance of criteria for legality that map roughly on to principles from just war theory.

Decisionmakers will need to reform the law in a way that assures that both pillars will be respected and do so in a way that is transparent and predictable, as required by the fairness corollary. They will also need to clarify what inputs and outputs of a potential UHI are relevant to its legality, who other than the Security Council ought to be able to approve it, and whether UHI can be seen as a duty and not merely a right. That last question—right versus duty—lies at the core of the significance of R2P. Although R2P does not formally change the law on UHI—it still counts on the Security Council to approve any use of force—it has

[67] Arbour, 'The Responsibility to Protect', *supra* note 58, at 448. We might be witnessing such a trend in the Security Council's decision to authorize aid agencies to deliver supplies to rebel-controlled areas of Syria despite the opposition of the government. SC Res. 2165 (14 July 2014).

the potential at least to shape global expectations about the need to protect the human rights of those facing atrocities abroad. It shifts the discussion in a way that sees a common set of responsibilities.

* * *

When we look at all three cases concerning human rights protections abroad considered in this chapter and in Chapter 8, in each of them the first pillar—the peace pillar—played a different role in our appraisal. It put up no opposition to extraterritorial duties by states when they act abroad; it proved to be somewhat in tension with universal jurisdiction, and it raised a significant barrier to UHI. The second pillar of thin justice meant that any complete ban on a state's power to protect the basic human rights of those beyond its borders would be unjust, with serious ramifications for a complete ban on UHI.

I see international law's development in the face of those claims to protect individuals beyond a state's borders as reflecting decisionmakers' efforts to grapple with the sometimes competing demands of peace and human rights. The result is a spectrum of rules tailored, imperfectly but certainly decently, to the balance between the two imperatives of thin justice. Thus, the law (a) gives us a clear but limited description of duties for states when they act abroad; (b) permits universal jurisdiction subject to some significant conditions; and (c) is of two minds on the issue of UHI through the simultaneous operation of the black-letter and context-dependent positions. In the case of the last two, the law's rejection of a duty in favor of a permission also reflects the compliance corollary, which urges caution in insisting that the law endorse rules too far at odds with existing state capabilities and incentives.

Even while I have argued that both the initial presumption and the three exceptions are thinly just, it is also clear that improvements to the law are possible. I will offer a larger framework for these reforms in Chapter 13, but it is already apparent that each set of rules lacks decent institutions for oversight. Extraterritorially applied human rights rules rely for oversight on the same mechanisms as the underlying treaties. The mechanisms are strong in the case of the European Court of Human Rights, with its caselaw making clearer states' duties when they act abroad, but far weaker for other regions, let alone the global system of the ICCPR. Universal jurisdiction works without any central coordination process other than the possible involvement of the ICC in situations it has decided to investigate. And UHI is itself an option that arises only once the Security Council has decided not to act, with alternative sources of legitimacy or coordination being very limited, NATO's role in Kosovo and Libya notwithstanding.

Lastly, these two chapters raise the question of whether international law will recognize or has recognized other exceptions to the state-centric model of territoriality for the protection of human rights. As discussed in Chapter 4, state foreign policies that serve to *promote* human rights abroad are lawful, even though they would have been regarded as intervention several generations ago. One important emerging debate concerns whether states have a duty to provide foreign assistance as part of their obligations under international human rights law. Claims to this effect have gained significant traction in soft law instruments and some treaty monitoring bodies, yet they raise complex issues about the links between a state's domestic conduct and the rights of those abroad needed to trigger such duties.[68]

A flipside of that issue has arisen with respect to the provision of foreign assistance to victims of natural disasters, where it is increasingly accepted that the host state must allow such assistance, even to the point that other states might be authorized to intervene without it. In a transformative moment of sorts, when Cyclone Nargis hit Burma in May 2008, the Burmese junta initially refused to allow aid into the country, prompting enormous international protest and a suggestion that R2P ought to be invoked as a license for foreign intervention.[69] In that situation, the law may not recognize a duty to provide foreign assistance, but it may be open to a duty to accept it. As states consider rules in this and other areas, the test for the framework of thin justice will be whether its emphasis on an acceptable balance between the preservation of peace and the protection of human rights will provide adequate moral guidance.

[68] For useful treatments, Malcolm Langford, Wouter Vandenhole, Martin Scheinin, and Willem van Genugten (eds.), *Global Justice, State Duties: The Extraterritorial Scope of Economic, Social, and Cultural Rights in International Law* (Cambridge: Cambridge University Press, 2013). Some of these issues are addressed in Part IV of this book.

[69] See International Coalition for the Responsibility to Protect, 'The Crisis in Burma', <http://www.responsibilitytoprotect.org/index.php/crises/crisis-in-burma; Ashley McLachlan-Bent and John Langmore, 'A Crime Against Humanity?: Implications and Prospects of the Responsibility to Protect in the Wake of Cyclone Nargis', *Global Responsibility to Protect* 3 (2011): 37; see also GA Res. 46/182, *supra* note 65; SC Res. 2165, *supra* note 67.

PART IV

THE JUSTICE OF CORE NORMS ON THE GLOBAL ECONOMY

10

Regulating Global Trade

The seven decades since the end of World War II have been marked by a burgeoning of international legal regulation of the global economy. The areas now subject to legal norms include cross-border trade, investment, finance, development assistance, labor, telecommunications, intellectual property, taxation, antitrust, and transportation. International economic law consists of a complex, often dizzying, array of treaties, soft law, and other authoritative documents, along with an alphabet soup of institutions composed of states, with large permanent secretariats, and, in some cases, mechanisms for resolving disputes.

In the scheme of claims offered in Chapter 2, these rules and processes respond primarily to the claims of two major actors for a share in global economic activity and wealth—states and corporations. States have sought to develop rules that will benefit their economic growth. Some rules create uniform treatment of an economic activity; others allow states flexibility to apply diverse regulations. In making new law and institutions, states are often advancing the interests of business entities, usually domestic ones. Those entities participate, directly or indirectly, in fora for the resolution of disputes over whether the rules are being respected. International economic law is also responding to the claims of individuals for economic empowerment, although their involvement in the making and enforcement of international economic law is rarely seen.

The array of economic activities now within the ambit of international law makes imperative an inquiry into the justice of that law. Philosophers have long been focused on the justice of the global economic order. Indeed, the persistent economic inequalities across states and across individuals have made distributive justice, particularly of the Rawlsian variety, the principal focus of philosophers examining global questions. From Peter Singer's *Famine, Affluence, and Morality* to the present day, the plight of the global poor has remained at the center of philosophical inquiry.

This chapter and the following will consider what I regard as the most important aspects of international economic law: trade and investment. In examining these two areas, the discussion, like that in the chapters before it, will address the core norms within each system, as interpreted by the institutions established to help implement them. This analysis will involve a crystallization of complex rules into fairly basic norms. Only such a double limitation—core subjects, and core norms—is feasible in a project such as this one.[1] I will avoid any claims to the effect that all the rules governing one of these three subjects are just or unjust. Lastly, although I will address many critiques of international economic rules, this chapter is not the place to consider broad attacks on the concepts of free trade or open investment as unfair and unjust to the global poor.[2]

I. Prelude to International Economic Law: Permanent Sovereignty over Natural Resources

Before examining the norms of trade and investment, it is worth a short detour to consider a norm that is a cornerstone of contemporary international economic law—the right (privilege in Hohfeldian terms) of the state to dispose of its material wealth as it chooses. This right means that the state is free to choose the extent of its international economic relations—how much it will trade with others, how much it will allow investors to operate on its territory, and how much it will donate to other states that might need its resources. The legal norm that expresses, though not perfectly, this critical privilege is the state's permanent sovereignty over natural resources (PSNR). PSNR has been recognized in numerous legal sources, but the most authoritative statement remains General Assembly Resolution 1803 from 1962, passed with the backing of both developed and developing states. Its key paragraphs state:

1. The right of peoples and nations to permanent sovereignty over their natural wealth and resources must be exercised in the interest of their national development and of the well-being of the people of the State concerned.
2. The exploration, development and disposition of such resources, as well as the import of the foreign capital required for these purposes, should be in conformity with the rules and conditions which the peoples and nations freely consider to be necessary or desirable with regard to the authorization, restriction or prohibition of such activities.

. . .

7. Violation of the rights of peoples and nations to sovereignty over their natural wealth and resources is contrary to the spirit and principles of the Charter of the United Nations and hinders the development of international co-operation and the maintenance of peace.[3]

[1] Although the importance of the IMF is addressed somewhat in Chapter 7, for reasons of length I will not appraise the justice of international financial and monetary rules.

[2] For a small sampling, see Ha-Joon Chang, *Kicking Away the Ladder: Development Strategy in Historical Perspective* (London: Anthem Press, 2002); Dani Rodrick, *One Economics, Many Recipes: Globalization, Institutions, and Economic Growth* (Princeton, NJ: Princeton University Press, 2007); Joseph E. Stiglitz, *Globalization and its Discontents* (New York: W.W. Norton, 2002); and Roberto Mangabeira Unger, *Free Trade Reimagined: The World Division of Labor and the Method of Economics* (Princeton, NJ: Princeton University Press, 2007).

[3] GA Res. 1803 (XVII) (14 December 1962). The resolution was adopted by 87-2-12, with South Africa and France voting no and the East Bloc states abstaining.

Resolution 1803 was very much embedded in the decolonization process, as the newly decolonized states sought to clarify their rights over their natural resources, many of which—whether oil or agricultural lands—had been owned or controlled by Northern states and companies during colonialism. In exchange for this recognition, they agreed to recognize that foreign investment would be governed not only by national law but by international law.[4]

Although invoked by international lawyers as a sort of high-water mark for a consensus position on the state of the law, Resolution 1803 was just one stage in a long-running process of claim and counter-claim about both the extent of the state's control over its resources and the much broader question of North-South redistribution.[5] Thus, the rules in the 1982 UN Convention on the Law of the Sea (UNCLOS) effectively extend the idea of permanent sovereignty over natural resources to the adjacent seas and continental shelf by giving coastal states full control over the wealth in those areas, which proved a great benefit to many coastal states in the developing world (as well as those in the developed world).[6] And the process of negotiating rules for most of international economic law, as well as environmental law norms, has been influenced by the developing world's insistence on respect for permanent sovereignty over their resources and a greater share of the developed world's resources.

A. The thin justice of permanent sovereignty over natural resources

With respect to the two pillars of thin global justice, PSNR generally passes muster under the first pillar for its contributions to peace. By granting each state the right to dispose of its wealth as it chooses, PSNR avoids a sort of free-for-all that could take place were the initial distribution of resources otherwise. Although law and economics discourse might discount initial entitlements and refer to these costs as simply transaction costs, it seems clear that, in the case of independent states, PSNR contributes to world peace. It keeps pressure off violations of the key norms on the use of force and non-intervention. I would not claim that the first pillar requires PSNR insofar as other schemes of ownership over permanent resources could also enhance peace. Certainly customary international law has long recognized that the resources of the high seas are not owned by individual

[4] Ibid., para. 3.

[5] For further background, see Nico Schrijver, 'Natural Resources, Permanent Sovereignty over' in Rüdiger Wolfrum (ed.), *The Max Planck Encyclopedia of Public International Law*, online edition (Oxford: Oxford University Press, 2008–) <http://opil.ouplaw.com/home/EPIL>.

[6] UNCLOS, Art. 56 (coastal state control of the exclusive economic zone), Art. 77 (coastal state control of the continental shelf). The Convention does very little to require those coastal states to share resources. See ibid., Arts. 69–70 (giving landlocked and geographically disadvantaged states the right to share equitably in the resources of the EEZ).

states; and UNCLOS recognizes the deep seabed as 'the common heritage of mankind'.[7]

At the same time, PSNR's benefits to peace are contingent on the acceptance by other states of each state's claim to territory. In situations where territory is disputed, PSNR might be said to encourage interstate conflict because the economic stakes from physical control are so high. Thus, China has engaged in provocative behavior by deploying its military in the South and East China Seas to create 'facts on the ground'—or perhaps the water or air—in order to bolster its claims to islands there (the Spratley and Paracel Islands, claimed by Vietnam and other states and the Senkaku Islands, claimed by Japan). And, in invading Kuwait in 1990, Saddam Hussein's Iraq claimed that Kuwait itself belonged to Iraq, a move meant to gain control over Kuwaiti oil. This risk to peace is exacerbated by both the array of competing principles on title to territory, where administrative authority, physical control, acquiescence, and lines on old maps all play a role; and the absence of any mandatory dispute settlement process for these disputes (though some are settled through negotiation or voluntary submission to the ICJ or arbitration).[8] Some kind of regime of joint exploitation or supranational control over disputed territories might avoid the temptation to use force in order to exploit resources, but it seems quite difficult to come up with an exception to PSNR for disputed territories that will not simply encourage all states to make claims against their neighbors. On balance, because PSNR puts an end to most of those claims, it still seems, as a matter of all the consequences, to advance peace. For in those situations where title is settled, it reduces the risk of confrontation by states that might seek to exploit a neighbor's resources or demand a share of them.

As for the second pillar, PSNR does not seem to interfere with the enjoyment of basic human rights. The basic human rights identified in Chapter 3 are not harmed by giving the state control over its wealth. Indeed, by giving states control over their resources, the rule serves to contribute to the provision of those resources to the people in the state, helping to guarantee their basic economic and social rights. An analogue to Goodin's consequentialist argument discussed in Chapter 8 regarding the justice of the territoriality of human rights law applies here. Namely, a state's control over its resources on its territory and its international economic relations is an efficient way to organize the distribution of global wealth (and our duties regarding its distribution) so as to ensure the enjoyment of basic human rights for all. Again, that is not to say that other methods, including international control, might not also work to secure basic human rights, but PSNR does not seem prima facie to stand in the way of that process.

[7] UNCLOS, *supra* note 6, Art. 89 (high seas), Art. 136 (deep seabed). In the case of the Antarctic, the claims of states are not rejected but not accepted either. Antarctic Treaty, 12 January 1959, Art. IV, 402 UNTS 71.

[8] On the doctrines used by courts, see generally Marcelo G. Kohen, *Possession contestée et souveraineté territoriale* (Paris: Presses Universitaire de France, 1997); on resolution by non-judicial processes, see Steven R. Ratner, 'Land Feuds and Their Solutions: Finding International Law Beyond the Tribunal Chamber', *AJIL* 100 (2006): 808.

B. Two critiques of permanent sovereignty over natural resources

PSNR nonetheless faces challenges from philosophers as to its relationship with justice that might suggest that it does not pass muster under the second pillar of thin global justice.

1. Pogge and the international resource privilege

The first critique of PSNR argues that PSNR can harm basic human rights if the state's resources are used by unscrupulous governments to undermine those rights. This claim is the essence of Thomas Pogge's attack on what he calls the 'international resource privilege'—the legal authority that governments enjoy to enter into agreements with foreign investors. He claims that these deals, which follow from and encourage corruption by state officials, inure to the benefit only of small elites and harm the rest of the population through, for example, income inequality and environmental degradation.[9] From the perspective of international law, this claim concerns not really PSNR alone, but its operation in combination with another norm, i.e. that a government in control of a state has the privilege to conclude agreements on the state's behalf, whether with foreign investors or with other states.[10] This privilege for a government, what we can call the *effective control principle*, flows from the accepted legal criteria for a state discussed in Chapter 6, namely a territory with a population and a government with effective control and a foreign relations capacity.[11] According to Pogge, when we combine PSNR with this privilege, we risk an unjust combination of norms.

Pogge makes an appealing point. If international law regards all agreements concluded by effective governments as presumptively binding upon the populations, then it would seem that little stands legally in the way of agreements that interfere with human rights. Governments in Africa and Asia have indeed concluded agreements with foreign investors and traders that have propped up abusive regimes while denying the benefits of the international intercourse to those who most need them.[12] More broadly, we can say that the land's natural resources and the fruit of the people's labor should belong to the people, not the state.

Four responses are in order. First, the resource privilege may bear little causal connection to violations of human rights. As Mathias Risse writes: 'Authoritarian

[9] Thomas Pogge, *World Poverty and Human Rights: Cosmopolitan Responsibilities and Reforms*, 2nd ed. (Cambridge: Polity Press, 2008) 118–21.

[10] Siegfried Magiera, 'Governments', in Rüdiger Wolfrum and Franke Lachenmann (eds.), *Max Planck Encyclopedia of Public International Law*, online edition (Oxford University Press, 2008–) <http://opil.ouplaw.com/home/EPIL> paras. 30–37. The key legal case is *Great Britain v Costa Rica*, 1 RIAA 369 (1923), in which an arbitrator (U.S. chief justice William Howard Taft) ruled that Costa Rica was bound by contracts concluded by its former president, who had seized power unconstitutionally and whose government was not recognized by Britain, based on that government's effective control.

[11] See the discussion in Chapter 6, Section I.

[12] For an example of one of countless NGO reports on this phenomenon, see 'Transparency and Accountability in Angola', Human Rights Watch, 13 April 2010, <http://www.hrw.org/reports/2010/04/13/transparency-and-accountability-angola>.

predators are *also* thieves, but they are mostly oppressors.'[13] Second, assuming that some violations of basic human rights can be traced to the effective control principle combined with PSNR, international law has begun to adjust to the hazards of the traditional rule. As discussed in Chapter 6, international organizations, including the UN, the African Union, the Organization of American States, and the Organization for Security and Co-operation in Europe, spurred by a sense that governments should be legitimate internally, have adopted policies that de-legitimize governments resulting from unconstitutional changes in power.[14] Leaders in office as a result of coups will find it more difficult to find treaty partners and conclude agreements to the detriment of the population. However, these new policies are prospective only, not targeting existing regimes; and they address only extra-constitutional moves, not the manifold other means by which governments abuse their populations.

Third, international law has developed a set of norms on corruption. These norms, first codified in the United States through the Foreign Corrupt Practices Act and now enshrined in a UN convention and a great many soft law standards, have the potential to make corrupt deals with foreign leaders more difficult. They require states to prevent and punish not merely the receipt of bribes, which those receiving bribes are unlikely to do, but the giving of bribes, where Northern states with more effective justice systems can enforce the rules against their own companies.[15]

Fourth, the effective control principle reaches its limits with respect to *jus cogens*, where treaty law treats as void any agreement concluded in violation of those principles.[16] Although the scope of *jus cogens* is limited, treaty law would seem to render invalid any agreements that directly harm certain basic human rights such as the right to life.

Where do these developments leave the thin justice of PSNR? Certainly, when combined with the effective control principle, if PSNR allows states to conclude agreements that seriously harm their residents, and other rules of international law do not mitigate these effects, it would not pass muster under the second pillar. If, however, other rules are now altering the operation of PSNR such that governments cannot easily conclude agreements with these consequences, then we are witnessing a transition from a rule that is unjust to one that is just. These related norms now make it more difficult for tyrants with no domestic legitimacy to rob their people through the vehicle of foreign trade and investment. Yet the prevalence of trade and investment the benefits of which are confined to elites or not advancing overall welfare (think, for example, of Angola) makes it difficult to be too sanguine.

[13] Mathias Risse, 'Do We Owe the Global Poor Assistance or Rectification?', *Ethics & Intl Aff* 19: (2005): 9, 17.

[14] See Chapter 6, note 12. These organizations have not gone so far as to remove members whose governments are non-democratic but are not the product of unconstitutional coups.

[15] United Nations Convention Against Corruption, 31 October 2003, 2349 UNTS 41. See also ibid., Art. 15.

[16] VCLT, Art. 53.

2. The redistributive critique

PSNR faces a much broader criticism as well, encapsulated in Brian Barry's remark from long ago that 'the principle of national sovereignty over natural resources... is without any rational foundation'.[17] By this, Barry's meant that the distribution of natural resources such that some states with fairly small populations have huge natural wealth while some very large ones have significantly less is morally arbitrary, a point also emphasized by Charles Beitz.[18] Barry and Beitz's point is just the tip of the iceberg of an enormous literature on global distributive justice, discussed in Chapter 1. It has led to major proposals for global redistribution based on a duty of assistance. Whereas the resource privilege critique claims that PSNR is unjust because it gives the state and its government control over resources at the expense of *its own* population, the redistributive critique regards PSNR as unjust because it gives one set of states (rich or resource-rich ones) PSNR over their wealth at the expense of the population of *other* states.

I will have more to say about global redistribution in the conclusion of the book, but for now suffice it to say that neither the attacks on the current distribution of wealth nor calls for a duty of assistance mean that PSNR interferes with basic human rights. First, PSNR may be quite favorable to poor states, and the poor people in them, by making it more likely that they can exploit their natural resources as they choose. It may thus be a factor in favor of redistribution and the guarantee of the economic rights of the poor and not at odds with such benefits. Beitz recognized this point when he called Resolution 1803 'prima facie unjust' but recognized its benefits to developing countries as a remedy for earlier exploitation of their resources.[19] At the same time, PSNR does not always help these states, as we have ample evidence of the so-called resource curse in which some states with abundant resources (Congo is probably the classic case) prove to be failures economically and politically.

Second, PSNR could be said to interfere with the enjoyment of human rights only if it could be shown that a state is unable to guarantee those basic rights because other states have sovereignty over their natural resources. Although it is certainly possible that one state may be so resource-poor that it is unable to secure the basic rights of its population on its own, it seems difficult to trace the lack of enjoyment of basic human rights by one state to the ownership by other states of their natural resources. Moreover, even though PSNR does not include any duty to aid those states unable to guarantee basic human rights, it does not preclude such aid, so it is hard to see how PSNR is standing in the way of proposals for redistribution. In other words, it is not necessary to reject PSNR and completely alter entitlements in order to guarantee the basic human rights of the very poor.

[17] Brian Barry, 'Do Countries Have Moral Obligations? The Case of World Poverty', *The Tanner Lectures on Human Values*, Vol. 2 (Salt Lake City, UT: University of Utah Press, 1981) 25, 36.

[18] Charles R. Beitz, *Political Theory and International Relations* (Princeton, NJ: Princeton University Press, 1979) 138–40.

[19] Ibid., at 142, n.31.

Lastly, we need to take account of the consequences of an alternative norm. In addition to possible concerns about alternatives passing muster under the first pillar (although Beitz argued for alternative entitlements as a way to prevent war),[20] the compliance corollary from Chapter 3 plays a role here insofar as it would seem to be a shock to the state system that it cannot bear to tell states that they no longer have control over their resources. A handful of the very poorest states might welcome the change, but the vast majority would see it as nothing less than a taking of their actual wealth in exchange for some promise of future distribution. A new duty of assistance from the baseline of PSNR, even one as expansive as Pogge's idea of a global resource tax,[21] seems more promising than a set of new entitlements that replaces PSNR.

II. The Role of the Two Pillars in Trade and Investment Law

The appraisal of the core norms of trade and investment under the standard of thin global justice differs in one significant respect from the analysis of other norms in this volume. In prior chapters, the first pillar did a great deal of the heavy lifting in terms of examining the justice of the norms. Norms were defended or rejected as advancing peace; alternatives were considered for their effects on peace. For trade and investment, the first pillar plays a more limited role.

On the one hand, there is little doubt that the drafters of the post-World War II rules on all of international economic law, from the Bretton Woods Agreements to bilateral commercial treaties, were motivated by a desire to prevent another war.[22] Yet today, trade and investment rules, whatever their actual content, are seen as a path toward economic stability and prosperity more than toward peace. The connection between any of the rules of international law and peace is speculative. One can always concoct an argument that a rule of international economic law, for example fair and equitable treatment of foreign investors by host states, promotes peace. These arguments could range from a more Smithian perspective that free trade generally promotes peaceful interstate relations, to arguments that protectionist or anti-foreign regulation provokes certain armed conflicts (with historical examples to support these claims). Yet the same story can be told, just as easily I think, for a different set of rules from the ones that we have; or an opposite set of consequences for peace can be constructed for the rules that we do have.

In light of the seeming indeterminacy of applying the first pillar to international economic law, the analysis that follows will rely exclusively on the second pillar; it will thus ask whether and to what extent the basic norms of trade and investment

[20] Ibid., at 141–2.

[21] See, e.g., Thomas W. Pogge, 'Eradicating Systemic Poverty: Brief for a Global Resource Dividend', *Journal of Human Development* 2 (2001): 59.

[22] John H. Jackson, 'The Evolution of the World Trading System—The Legal and Institutional Context', in Daniel Bethlehem, Donald McRae, Rodney Neufeld, and Isabelle van Damme (eds.), *The Oxford Handbook of International Trade Law* (Oxford: Oxford University Press, 2009) 30, 32.

interfere with basic human rights. The second pillar, acting even without the first, provides a strong normative framework for appraising the core norms of trade and investment. Policymakers within the UN have seized on the importance of reconciling norms of international trade and investment and human rights;[23] and as discussed later, scholars in both philosophy and international law have begun such an examination. Those efforts demonstrate the possibilities of appraising the rules and institutions from the perspective of basic human rights alone. Yet my methodological approach is distinct. I will not offer a doctrinal analysis of the possibilities to reconcile rules in trade or investment treaties with rules in human rights instruments. Although these efforts have value, especially for courts that may have to apply them, my goal is to ask whether the economic norms are just under the standard of thin justice. Legal reconcilability may help answer this question but is not conclusive.

III. International Trade Law's Core Norms and Basic Human Rights

The web of rules governing global trade is the densest of international legal regimes on the transnational economy. Textually and institutionally, it is characterized by a unified set of global treaties with an organization for the negotiation, interpretation, and application of global rules; a set of regional rules with accompanying institutions; and a set of bilateral free trade agreements.

A. The fundamental duty of international trade law and its limits

Despite its enormous complexity, international trade law is organized around one basic duty upon states: the prohibition of discrimination in their treatment of products and services coming across their borders. This basic duty translates into the two core rules originally found in the General Agreement on Tariffs and Trade (GATT): (1) the duty upon a state to impose the same tariffs on products from one state as it does on like products from all other WTO member states—*most-favored-nation treatment* or MFN;[24] and (2) the duty upon a state to treat a foreign product, once imported (with tariffs paid) no worse than a like domestic product—*national treatment*.[25] Non-discrimination does not extend to the elimination of tariffs, but states can only impose tariffs consistent with a complex schedule of tariffs, which result from the commitments states make when they

[23] See, e.g., Office of the High Commissioner for Human Rights, 'Human Rights and Trade', Paper Presented to the Fifth World Trade Organization Ministerial Conference, 10–14 September 2003; Protect, Respect and Remedy: A Framework for Business and Human Rights: Report of the Special Representative of the Secretary-General on the issue of human rights and transnational corporations and other business enterprises, John Ruggie, 7 April 2008, UN Doc. A/HRC/8/5.

[24] GATT, Art. I(1).

[25] GATT, Art. III(4).

join the WTO as well as negotiations by the WTO's members in multilateral rounds of negotiations (over time leading to a reduction in tariffs).[26]

The two non-discrimination rules from the GATT have been extended in three major directions since their original application to products:

- First, under the General Agreement on Trade in Services (GATS), states must provide MFN to foreign services and are constrained through both substantive standards and procedural requirements in their ability to treat domestic and foreign services providers differently.
- Second, under the Agreement on Trade-Related Intellectual Property Rights (TRIPS), states must, as a general matter, provide minimum guarantees of protection to intellectual property and extend these on an MFN and national treatment basis.
- Third, under the Agreement on Trade-Related Investment Measures (TRIMS), states are prohibited from imposing certain conditions on foreign investment, such as requirements to transfer technology or to export a certain amount of their goods.

In a different sort of extension, regional and bilateral agreements often contain even stricter requirements regarding non-discrimination than the WTO accords, for example through 'TRIPs-plus' clauses, upon which the United States insists in its bilateral and regional free trade agreements.

Yet international trade law is also organized around respecting certain prerogatives of the state regarding its trade.[27] As a result, the duty of non-discrimination is far from absolute. Beyond the obvious permission to continue to impose tariffs on foreign goods, the agreements recognize major exceptions that provide states with significant flexibility:

- First, importing states are sometimes allowed, notwithstanding MFN, to give continued preference to goods from some exporting states. Among the most important preferences allowed are those to other members of official customs unions or free trade areas (so-called preferential trade agreements, for instance that of the EU), so that exporting states outside the area are, in effect, not receiving truly MFN;[28] and preferences by developed states for imports from certain developing states under longstanding arrangements between Northern and Southern countries, under the rubric of the Generalized System of Preferences (GSP).[29]

[26] A related obligation is to limit such disparate treatment to tariffs, thus prohibiting most quantitative restrictions on imported goods, GATT, Art. XI. MFN, national treatment, the use of tariffs, and the ban on quantitative restrictions are often called the four pillars of GATT law.

[27] See Gene M. Grossman and Alan O. Sykes, 'A Preference for Development: The Law and Economics of GSP', in George A. Bermann and Petros C. Mavroides (eds.), *WTO Law and Developing Countries* (New York: Cambridge University Press, 2007) 255, 277 (the purpose of trade law is 'to limit the negative international externalities that countries create when they set their trade and industrial policies').

[28] GATT, Art. XXIV.

[29] World Trade Organization, Decision on Differential and More Favourable Treatment, Reciprocity and Fuller Participation of Developing Countries, 28 November 1979, GATT Doc. L/4903.

- Second, the GATT gives developing states the flexibility to implement (as well as exemptions from) numerous commitments, under the mantle of 'special and differential treatment'.[30]
- Third, the GATT contains a series of general carve-outs, such that a state may discriminate if necessary to protect, for example, 'public morals', 'human, animal, or plant life or health', and 'essential security interests' in time of war or national emergency.[31] Some of these state prerogatives are the subject of separate agreements, notably the Agreement on Sanitary and Phyto-Sanitary Standards (SPS) and the Agreement on Technical Barriers to Trade (TBT), both of which start from the presumption that states may regulate entry for legitimate regulatory purposes but not protectionist ones.

The last two categories of limitations on the non-discrimination norm (and numerous less important ones)[32] leave states with what has been termed 'policy space' to formulate and implement economic policies that treat imported goods and services differently from domestic ones, or even those from one state differently from those from other states.

B. Identifying the effects of trade law on human rights

To appraise the thin justice of international trade law, the first step is to identify the ways in which its rules, as applied by its institutions, may interfere with the individual's enjoyment of basic human rights. The trade jurisprudence and opinions about trade law reveal four major intersections between the two.

The first view, represented by a strong current of opinion among policymakers involved in international trade negotiations, argues that the primary relationship between trade law and human rights is one of mutual support.[33] One need look no further than the preamble to the GATT itself to see the vision of the treaty's founders that trade law is aimed at improving economic welfare:

> [R]elations in the field of trade and economic endeavour should be conducted with a view to raising standards of living, ensuring full employment and a large and steadily growing volume of real income and effective demand.[34]

Governmental endorsement of the connection among free trade, individual wealth, and global welfare is pervasive among the industrialized states, still

[30] For a summary, see 'Work on special and differential provisions', <http://www.wto.org/english/tratop_e/devel_e/dev_special_differential_provisions_e.htm>.

[31] GATT, Arts. XX, XXI. See also General Agreement on Trade in Services (GATS), 15 April 1994, Arts. XIV, XIV*bis*, 1869 UNTS 183.

[32] These include measures that allow states to respond to dumping and subsidies by other states as well as to impose temporary measures to protect domestic industries. For a useful overview from an economic perspective, see Alan O. Sykes, 'The Economics of WTO Rules on Subsidies and Countervailing Measures', John M. Olin Law and Economics Working Paper No. 186 (May 2003).

[33] See Susan Ariel Aaronson and Jamie M. Zimmerman, *Trade Imbalance: The Struggle to Weigh Human Rights Concerns in Trade Policymaking* (New York: Cambridge University Press, 2008) 189–90.

[34] GATT, preamble, para. 1.

advancing the so-called Washington Consensus that, until recently, dominated international economic policy after the Cold War.[35]

But the arguments about mutual support are not limited to the idea that trade increases global welfare or the average income of individuals. Rather, supporters seize upon trade law's promotion of individual human rights. Thus, Pascal Lamy, the WTO's former Director-General, has stated:

> [W]hat is the place of international trade law in promoting human rights in practice?... [O]pening international trade creates efficiency for raising standards and conditions of living and in this way can contribute to implementing rights which require more than mere proclamation if they are to be respected.... As an example, I cite Article 11 of the International Covenant on Economic, Social and Cultural Rights, which concerns the right to food and advocates 'taking into account the problems of both food importing and food exporting countries, to ensure an equitable distribution of world food supplies in relation to need'.[36]

Lawyers and philosophers have also defended the positive linkages between free trade and human rights. Some scholars have made broad arguments about free trade as being important to the advancement of human rights—for example that free trade furthers a range of human rights (in particular economic, social, and cultural rights) or is key to eliminating of poverty.[37] Others, critical of aspects of the existing trade law regime, nonetheless argue that free trade enhances individual rights and equality, as well as distributive justice, by allowing for individuals to sell their goods and services without discrimination based on their origin.[38]

[35] See generally Andrew Lang, *World Trade Law after Neoliberalism: Re-imagining the Global Economic Order* (Oxford: Oxford University Press, 2011).

[36] Lamy, 'Globalization and trade opening can promote human rights', World Trade Organization, 5 June 2009, <http://www.wto.org/english/news_e/sppl_e/sppl128_e.htm>. Lamy does not argue that all trade law promotes human rights, but he emphasizes the potential for mutual support:

> [T]he benefit of trade opening for human rights is not automatic. It presupposes rules that are both global and just. Rules of the kind that prompted Lacordaire to say that 'between the weak and the strong, [the] poor and the rich . . ., liberty is the oppressor and the law is freedom'. Negotiating and implementing such rules is the WTO's basic mission.

[37] See, e.g., Ernst-Ulrich Petersmann, 'Time for a United Nations "Global Compact" for Integrating Human Rights into the Law of Worldwide Organizations: Lessons from European Integration', *EJIL* 13 (2002): 621, 636–7; Fernando Tesón and Jonathan Klick, 'Global Justice and Trade', in Chios Carmody, Frank J. Garcia, and John Linarelli (eds.), *Global Justice and International Economic Law: Opportunities and Prospects* (New York: Cambridge University Press, 2012) 217.

[38] See, e.g., Robert Hockett, 'Three (Potential) Pillars of Transnational Economic Justice: The Bretton Woods Institutions as Guarantors of Global Equal Treatment and Market Completion', in Christian Barry and Thomas W. Pogge (eds.), *Global Institutions and Responsibilities: Achieving Global Justice* (Malden, MA: Blackwell Publishing, 2005) 104; John Morijn, *Reframing Human Rights and Trade: Potential and Limits of a Human Rights Perspective of WTO Law on Cultural and Educational Goods and Services* (Portland, OR: Intersentia, 2010) 221–8. See also Andreas R. Ziegler and Betram Boie, 'The Relationship between International Trade Law and International Human Rights Law', in Erika de Wet and Jure Vidmar (eds.), *Hierarchy in International Law* (Oxford: Oxford University Press, 2012) 277 (consistency of free choice for consumers and human rights).

The thrust of these positions is that free trade, and the WTO rules based on non-discrimination that promote free trade, improve human rights. They effectively demand that critics of free trade demonstrate its drawbacks—that they show that the norms of non-discrimination harm human rights—and that the exceptions to non-discrimination that critics advocate will do a better job at promoting those ends.

Yet we cannot apply the human rights prong so simplistically. For whatever the arguments that trade rules easily pass muster under the second pillar, many global actors have advanced serious arguments that WTO rules, in some cases supplemented by regional or bilateral rules, might indeed interfere with basic human rights. Carlo Focarelli has described this in conceptual terms as a clash between the values of wealth and of humanity.[39] So in response to that position of symbiosis between trade and human rights, three critiques emerge: (1) a claim that WTO rules limit the state's *policy space* to protect basic human rights; (2) a claim that WTO *institutions* are incapable of producing rules to account for human rights; and (3) a broad *systemic* claim that WTO rules harm the global poor. Each must be considered in detail to see whether trade rules interfere with basic human rights.

IV. WTO Rules as Limiting a State's Policy Space to Protect Human Rights

The policy space argument, more prevalent in legal than in philosophical literature, claims that, whatever advantages WTO rules might have, some trade rules harm human rights by limiting the state's ability to guarantee them.[40] The generally nuanced critique examines whether specific WTO obligations might render unlawful specific measures by states to fulfill their human rights responsibilities and obligations. Thus, for instance, Robert Howse and Ruti Teitel examine how the rights to work, health, and food may be harmed by WTO obligations that prohibit domestic subsidies, require recognition of intellectual property rights, and limit agricultural export subsidies.[41] Others have attempted to sift through other rights to see how trade law affects a state's ability to guarantee them.[42] The thrust of the scholarship is to consider the arguments for reconciling these duties, in the hope that authorized decisionmakers—in particular the panels and Appellate

[39] Carlo Focarelli, *International Law as Social Construct: The Struggle for Global Justice* (Oxford: Oxford University Press, 2012) 445–56.

[40] On the different duties of states stemming from human rights law, see Chapter 3.

[41] See, e.g., Robert Howse and Ruti G. Teitel, 'Beyond the Divide: The Covenant on Economic, Social, and Cultural Rights and the World Trade Organization', Friedrich Ebert Stiftung Occasional Paper No. 30 (April 2007).

[42] See Lorand Bartels, 'Trade and Human Rights', in Daniel Bethlehem, Donald McRae, Rodney Neufeld, and Isabelle van Damme (eds.), *The Oxford Handbook of International Trade Law* (Oxford: Oxford University Press, 2009) 571; Thomas Cottier, Joost Pauwelyn, and Elisabeth Bürgi Bonanomi (eds.), *Human Rights and International Trade* (Oxford: Oxford University Press, 2005).

Body (AB) established by the WTO (together known as the Dispute Settlement Body or DSB) to rule on members' formal state-to-state disputes—will adopt such harmonization in their decisions rather than solely advance free trade values.

As noted earlier, my approach will not seek a path to *legal* harmonization, but rather examine whether, in practice and as interpreted by authoritative decision-makers, WTO rules have granted or denied states the policy space to respect the basic human rights of their residents. This remains the key inquiry under the second pillar of thin global justice. Because I cannot examine the full range of issues associated with the policy space critique, I will focus on a set of examples that demonstrate, in my view, the approaches of both states and the WTO Appellate Body.[43]

A. The right to life and the Kimberley Process

The most basic human right, the right to life, includes the right of all persons (outside wartime combatants) not to be subject to a violent death.[44] As a matter of international law doctrine, states have duties not only to ensure that they do not violate the right to life, but also to take measures to prevent non-state actors on their territory from violating that right.[45] A rule of trade law that would render unlawful actions by states to protect their citizens from non-state actors intent on violating these rights would clearly interfere with the enjoyment of that right. And if these actors were further committed to waging civil war within a state, the first pillar of thin justice would also demand that trade law allow states to take measures to end the civil war.

Since the mid-1990s, civil wars in parts of Africa have been fueled by armed groups raising funds through the sale of diamonds, mined in areas that they control, on the international market. To bring an end to this fundraising strategy and, it was hoped, to the wars themselves, in 2000 a group of African states, joined by diamond-importing states and diamond companies, created an international certification regime, the Kimberley Process, to keep conflict diamonds out of the international market. Under the scheme, each state involved in the diamond trade must ensure that diamonds that it exports or imports are accompanied by a certificate that the exporting state is supposed to issue only once it has put in place certain safeguards to ensure that it is not exporting conflict diamonds.[46] The UN Security Council endorsed the system in 2003.[47] The system has many gaps and needs improvement, but it is nonetheless an important step in depriving rebel movements of one source of funding.[48]

[43] I leave the question of agriculture, which cuts across the first two critiques, to Section VI of this chapter.

[44] ICCPR, Art. 6.

[45] *Velásquez Rodríguez v Honduras*, Inter-American Court of Human Rights, Series. C No. 4 (1988).

[46] 'About the Kimberley Process Certification Scheme', 1 January 2014, <http://www.kimberleyprocess.com/en/about>.

[47] SC Res. 1459 (28 January 2003).

[48] See, e.g., Jason Miklian, 'Rough Cut', *Foreign Policy*, January/February 2013, 31; 'The Kimberley Process', *Global Witness*, 16 January 2014, <http://www.globalwitness.org/campaigns/conflict/conflict-diamonds/kimberley-process>.

The scheme triggered immediate concerns that it would violate WTO rules, in particular rules prohibiting quantitative restrictions on imports and exports generally and those that require that any quantitative restrictions be imposed on an MFN basis.[49] The latter would seem to require that like products—presumably all diamonds—be treated the same regardless of origin in a Kimberley-compliant state or a Kimberley-violating state. The potential thus existed for a non-Kimberley process state to file an action with the WTO against a Kimberley-participating state. Lawyers had arguments to the contrary—that conflict diamonds and non-conflict diamonds were not 'like products', and that the carve-outs for measures to protect human health and national security, discussed earlier, would permit the Kimberley Process.[50]

In the end, the WTO's members acted to ensure that WTO rules would not stand in the way of the Kimberley Process. In May 2003, the WTO's General Council, the highest level decisionmaking body beneath the trade ministers and composed of the entire membership, issued a formal waiver of the relevant articles of the GATT that might be implicated or violated by the Process. In doing so, it 'recognize[d] the extraordinary humanitarian nature of this issue and the devastating impact of conflicts fuelled by the trade in conflict diamonds on the peace, safety and security of people in affected countries and the systematic and gross human rights violations that have been perpetrated in such conflicts'.[51]

Trade scholars have disagreed on whether the waiver was the best way to reconcile trade and human rights,[52] but the outcome shows that on a core test case about whether WTO rules would be interpreted and applied to deny states policy space to protect basic human rights, the WTO's members decided not to apply them in that way. Those decisionmakers charged with implementing WTO rules demonstrated at least provisionally that some of the core rules on non-discrimination as interpreted and applied do not interfere with the right to life. Reconciliation was not simply a potential, as argued by legal scholars, but a reality. And Kimberley also shows that even the first pillar of thin justice can be relevant in interpreting trade rules, for here the WTO's members ensured that those rules would be interpreted so as to end civil wars and more generally promote peace in Africa.

[49] GATT, Arts. XI(1), XIII(1).

[50] For a review of the arguments, see Krista Nadakavukaren Schefer, 'Stopping Trade in Conflict Diamonds: Exploring the Trade and Human Rights Interface with the WTO Waiver for the Kimberley Process', in Thomas Cottier, Joost Pauwelyn, and Elisabeth Bürgi Bonanomi (eds.), *Human Rights and International Trade* (Oxford: Oxford University Press, 2005) 420–40; Joost Pauwelyn, 'WTO Compassion or Superiority Complex?: What to Make of the WTO Waiver for "Conflict Diamonds"', *Mich JIL* 24 (2003):1177, 1182–98.

[51] WTO General Council, Waiver Concerning Kimberley Process Certification Scheme for Rough Diamonds, Decision of 15 May 2003, WTO Doc. WT/L/518.

[52] Compare Pauwelyn, 'WTO Compassion or Superiority Complex?', *supra* note 50, and Schefer, 'Stopping Trade in Conflict Diamonds', *supra* note 50, at 443–50 (criticizing the waiver as both incomplete for not addressing potential violations of other WTO agreements and giving too much authority to the WTO), with Kevin Gray, 'Conflict Diamonds and the WTO: Not the Best Opportunity to be Missed for the Trade-Human Rights Interface', in Thomas Cottier, Joost Pauwelyn, and Elisabeth Bürgi Bonanomi (eds.), *Human Rights and International Trade* (Oxford: Oxford University Press, 2005) 459–60 (applauding avoidance of litigation).

The lesson from the Kimberley Process waiver might be seen as more limited—that it shows merely a political compromise but without an impact on the law, or that the result is one just *outcome* but not a just *norm* of trade law. On the first point, although a waiver of the rule is legally distinct from an interpretation of it, the result is still the same—the non-discrimination rule in trade law does not invalidate the Kimberley Process. The law as applied by the WTO's members is the governing law. And regarding the basic human right to life, that law withstands scrutiny under the second pillar of thin justice. On the second point, one small victory for the ability of states to protect human rights under trade law does not prove that the law is just under the second pillar. Yet in this case, the one data point we have on the intersection of trade law and policy space on the right to life indicates the absence of other potential conflicts more than it does the presence of them. I am not aware of other serious arguments that WTO rules are undermining a state's right to protect its population against arbitrary deprivation of life. So the just outcome in the case should be seen against a backdrop of the absence of other claims regarding conflicting norms.

Finally, the Kimberley Process offers some reassurance about the possibility for trade measures that guarantee the basic human rights not only of their own citizens, but also of those *abroad*. For the states involved in Kimberley that do not themselves export diamonds are all using trade as a foreign policy measure—seeking to protect *another state's* residents by requiring the certificates as a condition of importation.[53] Most states are still reluctant to use their trade policies for these purposes.[54] But many states, particularly in the North, want to preserve this option; and the treaty body interpreting the International Covenant on Economic, Social and Cultural Rights (ICESCR) as well as NGOs have argued that a state's duties under the ICESCR includes taking action to improve the human rights of those abroad.[55] If the WTO interpreted the law to bar states from imposing sanctions to respond to violations of basic human rights abroad, when those sanctions might help improve the situation of the victims, then the norm would also interfere with basic human rights. Indeed, the injustice would be analogous to that of the black-letter ban on humanitarian intervention, a point argued in Chapter 9.

As of yet, no case has been brought to the WTO Dispute Settlement Body concerning economic sanctions by one state against another related to the latter's human rights practices, suggesting some toleration by states of these practices. Caselaw regarding trade-restrictive measures to protect the environment gives some reason for a belief that, should a case arise, the Appellate Body would allow

[53] See, e.g., Wolfgang Benedek, 'The World Trade Organization and Human Rights', in Wolfgang Benedek, Koen de Feyter, and Fabrizio Marrella (eds.), *Economic Globalization and Human Rights* (New York: Cambridge University Press, 2007) 137, 156–7 (arguing for the legality of a state's ability to prohibit imports based on child labor).

[54] Aaronson and Zimmerman, *Trade Imbalance, supra* note 33, at 190–1.

[55] Committee on Economic, Social and Cultural Rights, General Comment 12: The Right to Adequate Food, 12 May 1999, para. 36, UN Doc. E/C.12/1999/5; Committee on Economic Social and Cultural Rights, General Comment 15: The Right to Water, 20 January 2003, paras. 31–36, UN Doc. E/C.12/2002/11.

such efforts, so trade law will not prevent states from taking measures to protect foreigners.[56] Nonetheless, the doctrine is complex and can be interpreted so as to invalidate some measures.[57] The AB will need to interpret not only the text of the WTO agreements but also decide upon the relevance of non-WTO law regarding human rights. The legal result may hinge on whether indeed states have an obligation, as opposed to a permission, under human rights law, to act abroad.[58]

B. The right to health and the Doha Declaration

A trade norm would also fail to meet the standard of thin justice if it were shown to interfere with basic human rights by preventing the state from guaranteeing or at least improving the physical health of its residents, another basic right.[59] The intersection between that right and trade law has arisen most prominently with respect to HIV/AIDS, whose victims live predominantly in poor countries. Those states and the people in them are generally unable to afford the medicines, developed and patented by Northern pharmaceutical companies, that have prolonged many lives.

To combat the epidemic, a number of states, led by South Africa and Brazil, engaged in two practices. In one, the states allowed the importation of medicines patented in another state without the consent of the patent-holder, a practice known as parallel imports, which can greatly reduce the price of the medicines. In another, the state issued a license allowing domestic producers to make medicines already patented abroad, a practice known as compulsory licensing, which also greatly reduces the costs of the medicines, including to those in third states who may need them. Both practices, however, raise serious questions under TRIPS: in the view of many, TRIPS requires the patent-holder's permission for parallel imports and generally bans compulsory licensing unless the patent-holder is compensated and the product is used predominantly for the domestic market.[60] The outcry from Northern pharmaceutical companies to these plans was overwhelming, as they

[56] The turning point within the DSB on these sorts of external measures was the *Shrimp—Turtle* case, which upheld a state's right under GATT Article XX to condition imports of shrimp on the environmental impact of the method by which it was captured. For a sympathetic analysis, see Robert Howse, 'The Appellate Body Rulings in the Shrimp/Turtle Case: A New Legal Baseline for the Trade and Environment Debate', *Colum J Env L* 27: (2002): 491.

[57] See, e.g., Lorand Bartels, 'Article XX of GATT and the Problem of Extraterritorial Jurisdiction: The Case of Trade Measures for the Protection of Human Rights', *Journal of World Trade* 36 (2002): 353.

[58] Sarah Joseph, *Blame it on the WTO?: A Human Rights Critique* (Oxford: Oxford University Press, 2011) 118 (expressing doubt that the Appellate Body would uphold such measures). This issue is part of a discussion about whether WTO rules permit unilateralism by states to advance global policy concerns such as climate change. See, e.g., Andrew Green, 'Climate Change, Regulatory Policy and the WTO: How Constraining Are Trade Rules?', *JIEL* 8: (2005): 143.

[59] ICESCR, Art. 12 recognizes 'the right of everyone to the enjoyment of the highest attainable standard of physical and mental health', requiring states to take measures needed for the '... prevention, treatment and control of epidemic, endemic, occupational and other diseases'.

[60] Agreement on Trade-Related Aspects of Intellectual Property Rights (TRIPS), 15 April 1994, Art. 31(b), (f), 1869 UNTS 299. TRIPS is quite complex on these issues. For example, with respect to parallel imports, although many states allow them on the theory that a patent-holder's patent is

filed lawsuits in South Africa and their home states threatened to impose sanctions on states implementing them. If trade rules were to prohibit states from taking these measures to save millions of their residents from AIDS and certain death, these rules would seem to fail the tests of justice.[61]

The WTO members' response to the demand for cheap anti-retroviral medicines is a rather complex story, one demonstrating both a certain commitment to interpreting trade rules so as not to interfere with human rights as well as shortcomings on making that commitment meaningful. In November 2001, after intense negotiations, the WTO's members issued the Doha Declaration, which affirmed that TRIPS 'can and should be interpreted and implemented in a manner supportive of WTO members' right to protect public health and, in particular, to promote access to medicines for all'.[62] It further noted the flexibility within TRIPS for this purpose; recognized states' freedom to grant compulsory licenses based on their interpretation of this phrase, among other options; and urged further consideration of the problem that, even with compulsory licensing, developing countries might still lack the capacity to produce generics.[63] Two years later, to address this last concern, the WTO's General Council adopted a formal waiver of the requirement that compulsory licensing be limited to products for the domestic market, thus allowing unlimited exports of generics; a clarification that the patent-holder will be reimbursed only by the state granting the compulsory license and not the importing state; and a waiver allowing poor countries to re-export these drugs to certain other poor states as well.[64] By December 2005, the General Council endorsed this solution as a formal amendment to TRIPS; upon its entry into force it will constitute a permanent change in the legal regime.[65]

Most observers agree that the Doha plan eliminated key legal barriers to the provision of drugs to sufferers of serious diseases. Yet the plan has also fallen short in key ways, and overall few states have taken advantage of it. In particular, (1) developing countries lack the technical capacity to amend their trade laws to reflect the Doha flexibility and then grant the required licenses (or withhold relevant patents); (2) Northern pharmaceutical companies are pressuring developing states not to grant compulsory licenses; and (3) the United States, the home of many such companies, has tried to circumvent the new flexibilities through different strategies,

exhausted after it sells its product in one state, the Article says this allowance may not be a basis for a claim in front of the DSB. See ibid., Art 6.

[61] Issues of the appropriate time horizon are critical here. For an economic argument that, in the long run, strict IP protection of pharmaceuticals saves lives, see Alan O. Sykes, 'TRIPS, Pharmaceuticals, Developing Countries, and the Doha "Solution"', John M. Olin Law and Economics Working Paper No. 140 (February 2002) 16–21.

[62] WTO, Declaration on the TRIPS Agreement and Public Health, 14 November 2001, para. 4, WTO Doc. WT/MIN(01)/DEC/2.

[63] Ibid., paras 4, 5, 6. TRIPS allows the state to waive the normal requirement that it attempt to negotiate for commercial use when there is a 'national emergency or other circumstances of extreme urgency'. TRIPS, *supra* note 60, Art. 31(b).

[64] WTO, Decision of the General Council: Implementation of paragraph 6 of the Doha Declaration on the TRIPs Agreement and Public Health, 30 August 2003. WTO Doc. WT/L/540.

[65] WTO, Amendment of the TRIPS Agreement, 6 December 2005, WTO Doc. WT/L/641.

including by achieving greater IP protections (TRIPS-plus) in regional or bilateral trade accords (for example the Trans-Pacific Partnership Agreement and free trade agreements with Morocco and Korea) and by examining countries for possible countermeasures under U.S. trade law.[66] These gaps suggest that the substance of the Doha solution belies its form in terms of its ability to avoid an interference by trade law with the right to health. If the Doha solution exists merely on paper but, as a practical matter, TRIPs rules still prevent states from getting access to drugs, then the rules cannot be said to be just. So, on the one hand, Doha highlights both the possibility that states will not let trade rules seriously threaten the legality of measures needed to supply anti-retroviral drugs cheaply and, on the other, the possibility that they will, through action or omission, not live up to that commitment.[67]

C. The rights to health and food through WTO caselaw

Beyond the actions of states regarding the Kimberley Process and the Doha compromise, a final set of evidence regarding the policy space critique is in the caselaw of the WTO's panels and Appellate Body. A now-significant body of caselaw has examined government policies aimed at, or at least justified by them as aimed at, the protection of health and, relatedly, food safety.[68] I will briefly summarize six cases that illustrate the AB's approach, though the AB did not itself engage with human rights law (and indeed most complaints brought to the DSB do not implicate human rights). Their results evince a willingness by the AB to uphold the state's power to protect health in principle, but with limitations on a state's policy space.[69] Thus, grouped thematically rather than chronologically:[70]

- In the *EC—Asbestos* case (2001), Canada challenged France's ban on the importation of asbestos products, which France justified based on the need to protect public health. The AB affirmed that asbestos products and non-asbestos substitutes are 'unlike', justifying France's discrimination against the former, and also upheld France's rights under the carve-outs of Article XX of the GATT.[71]

[66] Carlos Correa and Duncan Matthews, 'The Doha Declaration Ten Years on and its Impact on Access to Medicines and the Right to Health', UNDP Discussion Paper, 20 December 2011; Prabhash Ranjan, 'International Trade and Human Rights: Conflicting Obligations', in Thomas Cottier, Joost Pauwelyn, and Elisabeth Bürgi Bonanomi (eds.), *Human Rights and International Trade* (Oxford: Oxford University Press, 2005) 311–21; Mohammed El Said and Amy Kapczynksi, 'Access to Medicines: The Role of Intellectual Property Law and Policy', Global Commission on HIV and the Law Working Paper (2011) 9–13.

[67] See Benedek, 'The World Trade Organization', *supra* note 53, at 156 (on the WTO system showing the 'flexibility necessary to address the human rights problems…if only after widespread criticism').

[68] See ICESCR, *supra* note 59, Art. 11 (right to food).

[69] The policy space sought in these examples does not appear to me to rise in every case to the level of the protection of basic human rights, but these examples nonetheless demonstrate the ways in which WTO caselaw has treated human rights issues.

[70] The cases were brought under the GATT, the TBT agreement, the SPS agreements, or some combination thereof, though the panels and AB often limited their rulings against states to only one of these for reasons of judicial economy.

[71] Appellate Body Report, *European Communities—Measures Affecting Asbestos and Asbestos-Containing Products* (*EC—Asbestos*), 12 March 2001, WT/DS135/AB/R.

- In the *EC—Beef Hormones* case (1998), the United States challenged the EU's ban on the import of beef treated with hormones, which the EU regarded as posing risks to public health. The AB ruled for the United States on the ground that Europe did not engage in the kind of scientific risk assessment required under the SPS Agreement. Specifically, the EU had not backed up its assertion that the use of hormones in violation of standard veterinary practices would cause special cancer risks with scientific studies to that effect.[72]
- Similarly, in the *EC—Biotech* cases (2006 and 2008), the United States, Canada, and Argentina challenged actions and measures of the EU and its members that banned or delayed the import of food containing genetically modified organisms (GMO). The panel found numerous measures to violate the SPS Agreement for showing 'undue delay' in approving imports or for failing to be based on a scientific risk assessment. A later decision by the AB reversed a panel finding that a subsequent EU ban on one GMO was not based on a risk assessment but could not conclude that it actually was based on such an assessment.[73]
- In the *Brazil—Retreaded Tyres* case (2007), the EU challenged Brazil's ban on imported retreaded tires, enacted to reduce the total number of waste tires that would become mosquito breeding grounds. The AB agreed that the measure was 'necessary' to protect human life under Article XX of the GATT, but it found the measure discriminatory because it was underinclusive—it did not apply to Brazil's regional trading partners in MERCOSUR nor to used tires imported as a result of domestic court orders.[74]
- Following a similar kind of reasoning, in the *United States—Clove Cigarettes* case (2012), Indonesia challenged the U.S. ban on clove cigarettes enacted because such cigarettes have a flavor that makes them appealing to young people. The AB found that the ban violated the national treatment and MFN requirement in the TBT Agreement because the ban excluded menthol cigarettes (largely of domestic origin)—a like product because of its similar attraction to young smokers—and was therefore discriminatory.[75]
- Lastly, in the *United States—Country of Origin Labelling Requirements* (2012), Canada complained that U.S. laws and regulations requiring labeling or other provision of information about the origin of pork and beef throughout the

[72] Appellate Body Report, *European Communities—Measures Concerning Meat and Meat Products (EC—Hormones)*, 16 January 1998, WT/DS48/AB/R. The key provision of the SPS Agreement is Article 5.1, which requires states to 'ensure that their sanitary or phytosanitary measures are based on an assessment, as appropriate to the circumstances, of the risks to human, animal or plant life or health'. Agreement on the Application of Sanitary and Phytosanitary Measures (SPS Agreement), 15 April 1994, 1867 UNTS 493.

[73] Panel Report, *European Communities—Approval and Marketing of Biotech Products (Biotech I)*, 29 September 2006, WT/DS291/R, and Appellate Body Report, *United States—Continued Suspension, Canada—Continued Suspension (Biotech II)*, 16 October 2008, WT/DS320/AB/R.

[74] Appellate Body Report, *Brazil—Measures Affecting Import of Retreaded Tyres (Brazil—Tyres)*, 3 December 2007, WT/DS332/AB/R.

[75] Appellate Body Report, *United States—Measures Affecting the Production and Sale of Clove Cigarettes (US—Clove Cigarettes)*, 4 April 2012, WT/DS406/AB/R.

processing chain discriminated against foreign beef and pork. The AB found that the rules violated the TBT Agreement by treating them less favorably than domestic livestock for no legitimate reason, a conclusion that hinged on a finding that the labelling information was often not conveyed to consumers and the rules were so burdensome that they forced many U.S. producers to rely only on U.S. meat.[76]

In all but the first case, the state seeking policy space lost its case in the WTO, rulings that could be interpreted as a defeat for human rights—the state's view of what it wanted to do to protect its residents' health was not given sufficient deference. These losses raise the question of the point at which trade rules make it too difficult for states to have the policy space needed to protect human rights. As a general principle, rules that are interpreted by the DSB or states to impose a small burden on the regulating state in order to make their measures WTO law-compliant would pass muster under the human rights pillar, but rules that, as interpreted, impose a significant burden will fail and are unjust.

Some of the rulings hinged on the question of what restrictions were truly 'necessary' (the key term in Article XX of the GATT) to protect certain values—an issue that comes up in the investment context as well.[77] The Appellate Body recognizes the need to avoid too narrow an interpretation of the term 'necessary' (i.e. one meaning 'absolutely necessary'),[78] but its finding in *Brazil Tyres* that underinclusiveness of a 'necessary' measure can render it illegal discrimination makes it hard for a state to take some piecemeal measures to protect health. Similarly, in *Clove Cigarettes* and *COOL*, the AB found 'less favorable treatment' under the TBT simply because the measures were, respectively, under-inclusive (clove but not menthol cigarettes) or not efficient in their goal (getting information to consumers). And the scrutiny given to state risks assessments under the SPS in the *Hormones* and *Biotech* cases appears to create a significant burden on regulators—a task that would seem even harder for poor states.

The outcomes in these decisions might cause states to abstain from certain regulations for fear of having to defend them, at significant cost, in front of the WTO, especially if the claimant state is prepared to devote enormous resources

[76] Appellate Body Report, *United States—Certain Country of Origin Labelling Requirements (US—COOL)*, 29 June 2012, WT/DS384/AB/R.

[77] See the discussion on the defense of necessity in Chapter 11; see also Andrew D. Mitchell and Caroline Henckels, 'Variations on a Theme: Comparing the Concept of "Necessity" in International Investment Law and WTO Law', *Chicago JIL* 14 (2013): 93.

[78] The key jurisprudence in this area is Appellate Body Report, *Korea—Measures Affecting Imports of Fresh, Chilled and Frozen Beef (Korea—Beef)*, 11 December 2000, WT/DS161/AB/R, para. 161. As summarized in *Brazil—Tyres*, para. 210:

> [T]he fundamental principle is the right that WTO Members have to determine the level of protection that they consider appropriate in a given context. Another key element of the analysis of the necessity of a measure under Article XX(b) is the contribution it brings to the achievement of its objective. A contribution exists when there is a genuine relationship of ends and means between the objective pursued and the measure at issue. To be characterized as necessary, a measure does not have to be indispensable. However, its contribution to the achievement of the objective must be material, not merely marginal or insignificant.

to the case. This chilling effect could extend to a reluctance to pass even those regulations designed to address the concerns of the AB in the earlier cases. The effect on the state's ability to protect the human rights of its residents could be significant, though this would be very hard to measure empirically.

On the other hand, the AB seems to be quite deliberate in reassuring states that it is not in the business of preventing the legitimate protection of public health. For example, in the *Beef Hormones* and *Biotech* cases, it recognized in its opinion that the state has significant flexibility in evaluating scientific evidence to protect public health.[79] Its rhetoric was particularly strong in the *Clove Cigarettes* case:

> We do not consider that the TBT Agreement or any of the covered agreements is to be interpreted as preventing Members from devising and implementing public health policies generally, and tobacco-control policies in particular, through the regulation of the content of tobacco products... [W]e are not saying that a Member cannot adopt measures to pursue legitimate health objectives such as curbing and preventing youth smoking. In particular, we are not saying that the United States cannot ban clove cigarettes: however, if it chooses to do so, this has to be done consistently with the TBT Agreement.[80]

The result for our appraisal of the policy space critique of WTO rules is thus an equivocal and provisional assessment. Certainly, WTO rules can be interpreted in such a way as to avoid interference with human rights, as shown in both the *Asbestos* outcome and the other decisions by the AB to reject arguments by claimants of protectionism, even if the claimant prevailed in the end. And the rhetoric of the AB is certainly one of respect and deference to these goals as well as a recognition that the state should not be forced to bear an 'undue burden' to find less trade-restrictive means to achieve them.[81] But the results have nonetheless been defeats for measures that do or could protect public health and food safety. If losing states are able to enact measures that eventually satisfy claimant states or the AB, the interference with basic human rights may prove negligible, but it is difficult to know.

Much remains to be seen on how the caselaw will turn out in the many other issues of policy space that will end up in the Appellate Body.[82] If states begin to defend their actions as justified or even required by human rights law, the AB will face human rights issues even more directly. Thus far, it has shown what seems to be an institutional aversion on the part of its panel members and secretariat, generally trade experts, to engaging directly with human rights law in its rulings.[83]

[79] *EC—Hormones*, paras. 172, 187, 193–4; *Biotech II*, paras. 522–536. See also *Biotech I*, para. 8.3 (emphasizing what the panel did not examine).

[80] *US—Clove Cigarettes*, paras. 235–236.

[81] The quoted phrase appears in Appellate Body Report, *United States—Measures Affecting the Cross-Border Supply of Gambling and Betting Services (US—Gambling)*, 7 April 2005, WT/DS285/AB/R, para. 308. See also Mitchell and Henckels, 'Variations on a Theme', *supra* note 77, at 132–5.

[82] Another measure concerning cigarettes, a challenge to Australia's plain-packaging of all cigarettes by Honduras, is now working its way through the WTO process.

[83] The insider's perspective is reflected in Gabrielle Marceau, 'WTO Dispute Settlement and Human Rights', *EJIL* 13 (2002):753, 757–79. See also David Kinley, *Civilising Globalisation: Human Rights and the Global Economy* (Cambridge: Cambridge University Press, 2009) 75 (DSB decisions offer 'thin gruel for hopeful human rights advocates to feed on').

One of the key contributions of international lawyers in this regard has been to propose doctrinal solutions to these conflicts that are meant to ensure that WTO rules do not ignore human rights concerns.[84]

D. An assessment of the policy space critique and thin justice

The conclusion to draw from state and DSB practice regarding the thin justice of trade law restrictions on a state's policy space must be nuanced. First, decisionmakers can certainly interpret and apply, or waive and amend, trade rules to avoid forcing states to choose between compliance with them and their responsibility for the basic human rights of their population. Through those strategies or simply a decision by a state not to complain about another state's use of policy space to protect human rights, many conflicts have been avoided.[85] The results to date mean, at a minimum, that it is premature to label trade law rules unjust for interfering with basic human rights by preventing a state from guaranteeing them.

Second, even though decisionmakers state that their interpretations do not deny a state policy space to protect human rights, the burdens on states from trade law are real. Whether in making the Doha solution on TRIPS work or threading the needle of the caselaw on non-discrimination or scientific proof for trade restrictions, trade law has the potential to be unjust under the second pillar. Those seeking to protect policy space for the right reasons—human rights and not protectionism per se—will need to remain vigilant, and the relevant decisionmakers will need to accept the priority of basic human rights in their interpretation of the texts, even if they do not say so explicitly. The rhetoric of states and the AB suggest a desire to allow states to respect basic human rights, but that is not the last word. My sense is the state's right and responsibility to protect human rights will prevail, a view based not on some blind faith in the WTO system, but on a record of practice where self-restraint has been apparent and where decisions of states and the AB reveal an awareness of the consequences for the entire WTO system if they reach the wrong decisions.

Third, my conclusions are provisional in three senses. First, the caselaw is constantly changing, for example between the *EC—Hormones* case discussed previously and a later decision on the same underlying dispute that proved more

[84] See, e.g., Shelly Edwardson, 'Reconciling TRIPS and the Right to Food', in Thomas Cottier, Joost Pauwelyn, and Elisabeth Bürgi Bonanomi (eds.), *Human Rights and International Trade* (Oxford: Oxford University Press, 2005) 382; Kevin R. Gray, 'Right to Food Principles vis à vis Rules Governing International Trade', British Institute of International and Comparative Law (December 2003); Howse and Teitel, 'Beyond the Divide', *supra* note 41; Andrew Lang, 'The GATS and Regulatory Autonomy: A Case Study of Social Regulation of the Water Industry', *JIEL* 7 (2004): 801, 837–8.

[85] See Rob Howse and Makau Matua, 'Protecting Human Rights in a Global Economy: Challenges for the World Trade Organization', *Human Rights Development Yearbook* (1999–2000): 53, 82 ('the trade regime recognizes that human values related to human rights are fundamental and prior to free trade itself, which is merely an instrument of basic human values'); Aaronson and Zimmerman, *Trade Imbalance, supra* note 33, at 191 ('countries have considerable flexibility under WTO rules to protect human rights at home or abroad').

deferential to the regulations.[86] Second, each provision of each agreement is worded differently, and the caselaw is often specific to that provision. So the caselaw on necessity under Article XX of the GATT may differ from that about least restrictive trade restraints under the TBT. In that sense, it is difficult to generalize about trade law as a whole—even more so once one includes regional and bilateral trade agreements that may differ significantly from WTO law. And lastly, my conclusions, like others in this volume, rest on empirical claims, the most important of which concerns the difficulty for a state to comply with trade rules and still respect human rights. If research reveals that some states are truly unable to respect the right to health because of an adverse WTO ruling or the fear of one, this would have obvious implications for the justice of trade law, just as would a finding that states have been able to adjust their domestic policies without too much effort.

V. WTO Institutional Flaws and Basic Human Rights

A second claim that trade law is unjust is that the structure and functioning of the WTO ensures that human rights will be discounted in the process of making and interpreting that law. Chapter 7 considered whether the admission rules of the WTO are procedurally fair and found shortcomings insofar as they did not provide transparency to applicants as to how to attain membership and led to the insertion of extraneous political issues. Critics of the WTO have made a broader institutional critique in two senses.

First, the accession process is not merely procedurally unfair but substantively unjust to developing states in that new members must accept more commitments than incumbents in terms of tariff reductions and other changes to domestic regulations, and that powerful states make these demands of states without the bargaining power to create precedents that will be used in the future.[87] Second, some aspects of WTO decisionmaking are unjust—these include the consensus requirement for trade negotiations that gives undue power to a small number of states; the dominance of experts from the North within the WTO Secretariat; the limited avenues for NGO participation; and the inability of poor states to play a greater role in rulemaking and other processes in Geneva due to the small size of their delegations.[88]

Of particular concern are the onerous costs of litigating a case in the DSB and the limited value to a poor state of a victory. If a state wins a WTO case and the

[86] Michael Ming Du, 'The Rise of National Regulatory Autonomy in the GATT/WTO Regime', *JIEL* 14 (2011): 639, 669–70.

[87] Joseph, *Blame it on the WTO?, supra* note 58, at 156–7; Bernard M. Hoekman and Michel M. Kostecki, *The Political Economy of the World Trading System: The WTO and Beyond*, 2nd ed. (Oxford: Oxford University Press, 2001) 65–8.

[88] See, e.g., Patrick Low, 'WTO Decision-Making for the Future', WTO Economic Research and Statistics Division: Staff Working Paper ERSD-2011-05 (2 May 2011); Mathias Risse, *On Global Justice* (Princeton, NJ: Princeton University Press, 2012) 352–3.

loser refuses to follow the ruling, the winning state can only raise tariffs on products from (or limit intellectual property rights by) the loser, which may amount to very little if the losing state exports few goods (or grants few intellectual property rights) to the winner.[89] These concerns are part of a huge debate about the legitimacy of WTO decisionmaking.[90]

These are persuasive points, and there can be little doubt that these institutional features and others work to the disadvantage of poor and weak states.[91] That problem is not unique to the WTO—the limited resources of poor states affect their participation in many international organizations, which is why they have often worked through coalitions like the G77. Thus, the IMF, controlled by the rich states, can also use its influence to limit poor states' ability to take trade-related measures that might address serious poverty.[92] Developing states pushed for the creation of the United Nations Conference on Trade and Development to provide a forum where development issues would be considered front and center with trade and investment and have envisaged it as a counterweight to the GATT and WTO. But the question with respect to the thin justice of trade law is different: do these institutional shortcomings—with respect to the WTO's accession and decisionmaking—result in rules and decisions that interfere with basic human rights?

One starting point to apprise the justice of the institutional features of the WTO is to judge the specific rules and decisions resulting from them. This appraisal has been conducted earlier with respect to the policy space critique, and we get somewhat ambiguous conclusions. Thus, the paucity of expertise on human rights law within the DSB panels and AB may well explain not only their reluctance to address human rights obligations in their rulings but the restrictions on policy space as well.

At the same time, it is a bit simplistic to judge decisionmaking processes solely in terms of outcomes. For example, certain aspects of the WTO's oversight of trade law, such as the accession process and the regular trade policy reviews to which members submit, may put the human rights practices of states in the

[89] See, e.g., Bernard Hoekman, 'Proposals for WTO Reform: A Synthesis and Assessment', *Minn JIL* 20 (2011): 324, 352–6. This lack of leverage caused West African states to abandon a WTO case against the United States for cotton subsidies despite a WTO ruling against the U.S. in a case brought by Brazil. The U.S. and Brazil entered into a bilateral agreement settling the case, effectively through U.S. subsidies to Brazilian farmers. See John Baffes, 'Cotton Subsidies, the WTO and the "Cotton Problem"', World Bank Policy Research Paper 5663 (May 2011).

[90] In this large literature, see, e.g., Lang, *World Trade Law, supra* note 35, chs. 8–10; Robert Howse, 'The Legitimacy of the World Trade Organization', in Jean-Marc Coicaud and Veijo Heiskanen (eds.), *The Legitimacy of International Organizations* (Tokyo: United Nations University Press, 2001) 375.

[91] Greg Shaffer, 'The Challenges of WTO Law: Strategies for Developing Country Adaptation', *World Trade Review* 5 (2006): 177. For an international relations perspective, see Greg Shaffer, 'Power, Governance, and the WTO: A Comparative Institutional Approach', in Michael Barnett and Raymond Duvall (eds.), *Power in Global Governance* (New York: Cambridge University Press, 2003) 130.

[92] Raymond Saner and Ricardo Guilherme, 'The International Monetary Fund's Influence on Trade Policies of Low-income Countries: A Valid Undertaking?', *Journal of World Trade* 41 (2007): 931.

spotlight in yet another forum.[93] A more careful appraisal, beyond the scope of this book, is needed, probably through case studies, of whether and how specific institutional features of the WTO have led to rules or interpretations that have interfered with basic human rights, notably by disempowering states from taking action needed to guarantee them. Lastly, it bears re-stating that a thicker version of justice, one more deeply distributive that does not focus on basic human rights, would endorse an indictment of the WTO for not putting poverty alleviation at the forefront of the WTO's rules.[94]

VI. The Systemic Critique of International Trade Law

The final and most broad claim that trade law is unjust can be found in assertions that the WTO is systemically skewed to the interests of Northern states and does not sufficiently advance the development of the poorest countries and rectify North–South imbalances.

A. Parsing the critique

In the policy world, debates over a systemic bias of international trade law have dominated the Doha Round of trade negotiations that began in 2001, and in particular the demand by developing countries that WTO agreements be amended to incorporate more the concept of special and differential treatment discussed earlier.[95] Developing states assert the need for greater flexibility to impose protectionist and other currently GATT-prohibited measures in order to move up the economic ladder. These critiques are part of a debate about whether WTO members freely accepted the commitments they made in joining the WTO and whether reciprocity is an acceptable basis for trade relations.[96]

Academic critics of international trade law as systemically unjust are quite varied. Ngaire Woods criticizes the global trading rules for harming developing countries, in particular through high tariffs imposed by Northern countries on goods from developing countries, subsidies by the North on domestic agriculture, the use of non-tariff barriers by Northern states, and limitations on North–South technology transfers as a result of TRIPS and TRIMS.[97] Her criticism seems to

[93] See Susan Ariel Aaronson, 'Seeping in Slowly: How Human Rights Concerns are Penetrating the WTO', *World Trade Review* 6: (2007): 413, 422–7, 434–8.

[94] See, e.g., Frank J. Garcia, *Trade, Inequality, and Justice: Toward a Liberal Theory of Just Trade* (Ardsley, NY: Transnational Publishers, 2003).

[95] See generally Bernard Hoekman, 'Operationalizing the Concept of Policy Space in the WTO: Beyond Special and Differential Treatment', *JIEL* 8 (2005): 405.

[96] See, e.g., Risse, *On Global Justice, supra* note 88, at 351 (the decision to join the WTO is 'a choice between the Scylla of subjection to unwanted and perhaps unreasonable norms and the Charybdis of isolation').

[97] Ngaire Woods, 'Order, Globalization, and Inequality in World Politics', in Andrew Hurrell and Ngaire Woods (eds.), *Inequality, Globalization, and World Politics* (Oxford: Oxford University Press, 1999) 18–20.

combine a dedication to free trade in principle—thus she laments 'barriers to equal treatment'[98] that end up entrenching Northern economic dominance—with some complaints about how far beyond free trade the WTO should go—thus her condemnation of TRIPS and TRIMS. Frank Garcia has criticized the existing trade rules as unjust based on their failure to incorporate a Rawlsian global difference principle. He urges major reforms that would guarantee preferential market access for developing countries, non-reciprocal obligations, and mandatory technical assistance.[99] Margot Salomon has claimed that international trade law fundamentally fails to consider the right to development and leads to violations of basic human rights, and that all states have a legal duty to reform those institutions.[100] In her words, 'world poverty is also attributable to the existing global system, elements of which *by design* cause and/or fail to remedy this widespread deprivation'.[101]

The most influential philosophical critic remains Thomas Pogge, whose broadside on trade rules is part of a larger critique of the international economic law. Thus, in *World Poverty and Human Rights*, he states:

> [O]ur governments, by pressing this WTO Agreement on the rest of the world, have foreseeably taken out millions of poor persons who otherwise would have survived. Most of these deaths would have been avoided had our governments not, for the sake of minor material gains for some of us, insisted on the protectionist exemptions, extraction of monopoly rents for our 'intellectual property' in seeds and drugs, and other onerous commitments by the poorer countries.[102]

Pogge's criticism mirrors that of Woods insofar as the basic claim is that trade rules benefit the North because they contain exceptions to free trade that dull the competitive edge of Southern states for the benefit of Northern industries,[103] and because they go too far in including ideas like intellectual property in the concept of free trade. Pogge's unique argument from the moral perspective is that the creation of these rules is not a violation of a positive duty to make people better off, but of a negative duty of all individuals not to harm others.[104] Pogge has taken particular aim at TRIPS' effects on global health.[105]

The systemic claim, then, is that core rules of the trading system keep the poor very poor. To a certain extent, the argument overlaps with the policy space argument—certainly so with respect to the criticism of TRIPS. And therein

[98] Ibid., at 17. [99] Garcia, *Trade, Inequality, and Justice, supra* note 94.

[100] Margot E. Salomon, *Global Responsibility for Human Rights: World Poverty and the Development of International Law* (Oxford: Oxford University Press, 2007).

[101] Ibid., at 186 (italics in original). [102] Pogge, *World Poverty, supra* note 9, at 22.

[103] See, e.g., ibid., at 232 (concern about quotas, tariffs, anti-dumping duties, etc.).

[104] See generally ibid; Thomas Pogge, 'The Role of International Law in Reproducing Massive Poverty', in Samantha Besson and John Tasioulas (eds.), *The Philosophy of International Law* (Oxford: Oxford University Press, 2010) 417.

[105] See, e.g., Thomas Pogge, 'The Health Impact Fund: Better Pharmaceutical Innovations at much Lower Prices', in Thomas Pogge, Matthew Rimmer, and Kim Rubinstein (eds.), *Incentives for Global Public Health: Patent Law and Access to Essential Medicines* (New York: Cambridge University Press, 2010) 135.

lies one of its shortcomings. If my earlier argument regarding policy space is correct—that the WTO's rules cannot be said at this point to be unjust, even if that could prove to be the case—then the systemic critique is based on hypothetical scenarios rather than actual experiences. The results of that appraisal suggest that the burden should now be on the adherents of the systemic critique to demonstrate, through examples, how trade rules have prevented states from guaranteeing basic (or other) human rights.

Yet the systemic critique is broader than the policy space critique. It essentially argues that international trade law is unjust for two reasons: (1) for having *too many* exceptions to free trade—too many carve-outs that benefit the Northern countries *at the expense of the global poor*; and (2) for having *too few* exceptions to free trade—not enough carve-outs *to benefit the global poor*.

Both concerns arise in numerous agreements, but particularly with regard to agriculture. The WTO Agreement on Agriculture, despite eliminating many barriers to free trade, allows Northern countries to keep export subsidies to protect domestic agriculture and allows them to dump excess products on the international market to the detriment of producers in the South, who face low prices for their commodities. At the same time, developing states can often do little to protect domestic farmers through tariffs, other import-prevention safeguards, and domestic subsidies.[106] In addition, major exporters, such as the United States and the EU, have sought to subsidize more than that permitted by the WTO, hurting Southern farmers—even though the United States and the EU eventually lost one case each (on cotton and sugar, respectively) in the DSB.[107] The overall result is, according to many observers, an absence of food security in developing countries, as they must rely on imported food.

For purposes of thin justice, this critique raises two questions: (1) do the existing carve-outs harm basic human rights in developing states, as claimed by critics; and, (2) does the absence of more exceptions to free trade for those states harm those rights?

B. The problem of causation

Both claims hinge on a very important causal claim—that the global trading rules protecting Northern producers, or the absence of more affirmative measures for the South, themselves interfere with basic human rights. But there is reason

[106] See Christine Breining-Kaufmann, 'The Right to Food and Trade in Agriculture', in Thomas Cottier, Joost Pauwelyn, and Elisabeth Bürgi Bonanomi (eds.), *Human Rights and International Trade* (Oxford: Oxford University Press, 2005) 343–8; Christian Häberli, 'Do WTO Rules Improve or Impair the Right to Food?', in Joseph A. McMahon and Melaku Geboye Desta (eds.), *Research Handbook on the WTO Agricultural Agreement: New and Emerging Issues in International Agricultural Trade Law* (Cheltenham: Edward Elgar Publishing, 2012) 79; and Gray, 'Right to Food Principles', *supra* note 84.

[107] See Baffes, 'Cotton Subsidies', *supra* note 89; Bartels, 'Trade and Human Rights', *supra* note 42, at 575; Wouter Vandenhole, 'Third State Obligations under the ICESCR: A Case Study of EU Sugar Policy', *Nord JIL* 76 (2007): 73, 81; Oxfam International, 'Dumping on the World: How EU Sugar Policies Hurt Poor Countries', Oxfam Briefing Paper 61 (March 2004).

for some doubt on such broad claims. Isolating the effect of trade rules on global poverty—a necessary part of the indictment of them—is an empirically speculative and even morally fraught enterprise. First, a state's domestic policies have by far the greatest influence on its poverty level. This means, as Jeffrey Dunoff has written, that 'access to rich country markets is a necessary but far from sufficient condition for development' and that 'the primary responsibility for the disappointing economic performance of many developing states reflects domestic constraints.[108]

Second, any claim about the WTO as the cause of severe poverty must show that different rules would avoid such poverty. As Howse and Teitel argue, Pogge 'judges the existing order against an imaginary counter-vision of the international economic order', but his claims 'cannot in and of themselves ever establish that alternative rules and institutions *are or were actually available*'.[109] Debra Satz puts her gloss on these points: 'Pogge hasn't really shown that this order *causes* [poor domestic economic institutions] or that reforming our lending and trade policies would necessarily generate better alternatives across the board'.[110]

On the other hand, as Beitz points out, even conceding all this, it remains possible that the global legal and economic order does influence local economic growth.[111] As discussed previously, some evidence regarding causation seems persuasive. The farmers of some crops, like sugar and cotton, in some developing states have been harmed by some trading rules, i.e. the agricultural rules. So even if new rules from the WTO would not lift developing states out of poverty, alternative rules could help some farmers, ensuring consumers get reliable access to affordable food.

C. The systemic claim and basic human rights

Under a consequentialist approach to the human rights pillar, a rule of international law interferes with basic human rights if it leads to a state of affairs characterized by overall decline in respect for such rights. And here the systemic claim faces an additional challenge. Namely, we can accept the critique only if the interferences with the basic rights (principally the rights to food and health) of the global poor caused by trade law exceed the improvement in respect for

108 Jeffrey L. Dunoff, 'Hudec's Methods—and Ours', *Minn JIL* 20 (2011): 437, 471–2. See also Dani Rodrik, Arvind Subramanian, and Francesco Trebbi, 'Institutions Rule: The Primacy of Institutions over Geography and Integration in Economic Development', *Journal of Economic Growth* 9 (2004): 131. For a stronger view from a former WTO Director-General, see Peter Sutherland, 'The Doha Development Agenda: Political Challenges to the World Trading System—A Cosmopolitan Perspective', *JIEL* 8: (2005): 363, 365 ('Whether [developing countries with poor domestic institutions and protectionism] are members of the WTO or not will make little difference').

109 Robert Howse and Ruti Teitel, 'Global Justice, Poverty, and the International Economic Order', in Samantha Besson and John Tasioulas (eds.), *The Philosophy of International Law* (Oxford: Oxford University Press, 2010) 437–8 (emphasis in original).

110 Debra Satz, 'What Do We Owe the Global Poor?', *Ethics & Intl Aff* 19 (2005): 47, 50.

111 Charles R. Beitz, 'Does Global Inequality Matter?', *Metaphilosophy* 32 (2001): 95, 102.

such rights caused by trade law. Thus, even accepting that trade rules interfere with the basic human rights of some groups in developing countries, it is certainly possible that others in the developing world have seen the enjoyment of the basic human right to food improved as a result of international trade rules.[112] So that even if the Agreement on Agriculture entrenches many disadvantages for Southern farmers, the overall regime of free trade may have helped the global poor more than it has hurt them. The answer is highly empirically driven.

A version of the human rights pillars that sees human rights as trumps would not permit such balancing, but instead argue that the harm to basic human rights, assuming it can be proved, is enough to render trade rules unjust.[113] This position has an ethical appeal due to the nature of the right to food, for it is only a degree or two removed from the right to life. Yet the deontological move seems to demand too much. Put in terms of the exclusionary reasons concept, I would not accept as a legitimate reason to interfere with one person's right to food the benefits of trade rules for Northern consumers in terms of lower prices (as those consumers generally already enjoy a standard of living well above that guaranteed by the right to food); but I am willing to consider the benefits to those who actually gain from the rules in terms of enjoyment of their basic human rights. So if a small number of farmers in Zambia are harmed, even in terms of their right to food, by trade rules, but a large number of people in Ghana are guaranteed enough food as a result of them, those rules should not be seen as unjust.

In the end, if we completely reject a causal link between trade rules and the enjoyment of basic human rights, then they cannot be regarded as unjust under the framework of thin justice. If we do see a connection, then indeed it is certainly possible, though empirically contingent, that some trade rules interfere with some people's enjoyment of basic human rights. But whether that interference makes the rules unjust or not turns a great deal on the role for human rights in the standard of thin justice. Although I remain generally committed to a consequentialist approach that looks at the overall effect of the rules on everyone's basic human rights, I see the appeal in the alternative position. And that position may not be unrealistic in practice if we could change trade rules so as to eliminate the harms to the basic human rights of some of the global poor without interfering with the basic rights of others who have benefitted from those rules. But the viability of that project, too, is an intensely empirical question.

[112] See Risse, 'Do We Owe the Global Poor Assistance or Rectification?', *supra* note 13, at 10–12 (on possible benefits from the trading regime).

[113] See Satz, 'What Do We Owe the Global Poor?', *supra* note 110, at 53 ('the fact that a billion people live in conditions of degrading poverty and die of easily preventable diseases while less than 20 percent consume most of the world's resources and live in comparative luxury suffices to condemn that status quo').

D. Evaluating proposals for reform

Despite the problems of causation, many intelligent proposals have been offered to change trade law in a way that *could* help improve the condition of the global poor. The first systemic critique—that trade law has too many carve-outs benefitting powerful states—has been reflected in proposals by trade experts for major changes to the rules. These include: more MFN in areas where developing countries export; an elimination of the rules allowing for subsidies of farmers by Northern states or de facto dumping of food through food aid; limits on avoidance of MFN through preferential trade agreements; and significant reforms to special and differential treatment (including GSP) that make it more narrowly tailored to the development status of the recipients rather than the political interests of key Northern and Southern states.[114] Philosophers have also noted the importance of eliminating WTO-permitted protectionism by Northern states.[115]

The second systemic critique—that trade law needs more carve-outs to benefit the poor—underlines other reform proposals. In the policy world, the Doha Declaration of 2005, issued at the conclusion of the South Summit, includes not only critiques of protectionist measures but a call for greater benefits for the South through the trading rules, including technical assistance and a development-oriented TRIPS.[116] In philosophical circles, Thomas Risse has advocated an adjustment to global trading rules to prevent people in exporting states from being forced into economically exploitative relationships or preventing repressive regimes from benefitting from human rights violations.[117] And Garcia's Rawlsian worldview would use the WTO to instantiate a global difference principle by requiring far more special and differential treatment, along with technical assistance, by the North to Southern states.[118]

If these proposals are aimed at guaranteeing basic human rights—and if we can assume that they will do so, notwithstanding the doubts about causation—then a deontological version of the second pillar would demand them to make the law just; a consequentialist view of it might not, although even such a perspective

[114] See, e.g., Bernard Hoekman, 'Operationalizing the Concept of Policy Space in the WTO: Beyond Special and Differential Treatment', *JIEL* 8 (2005): 405, 408; Alexander Keck and Patrick Low, 'Special and Differential Treatment in the WTO: Why, When and How?', WTO Economic Research and Statistics Division Staff Working Paper ERSD-2004-03 (May 2004); Grossman and Sykes, 'A Preference for Development', *supra* note 27, at 279–80; Häberli, 'Do WTO Rules Improve or Impair the Right to Food?', *supra* note 106. Some of these ideas have already been agreed upon as part of the Doha Round, e.g., a new 'Special Safeguard Mechanism' to allow developing countries to raise tariffs in response to a large influx of agricultural imports.

[115] David Miller, *National Responsibility and Global Justice* (Oxford: Oxford University Press, 2007) 253.

[116] Group of 77, Doha Declaration: Second South Summit, 12–16 June 2005, paras. 15(viii–xiv), G-77/SS/2005/1.

[117] Risse, *On Global Justice, supra* note 88, at 272–5; see also Barnali Choudhury et al., 'A Call for a WTO Ministerial Decision on Trade and Human Rights', in Thomas Cottier and Panagiotis Delimatsis (eds.), *The Prospects of International Trade Regulation: From Fragmentation to Coherence* (Cambridge: Cambridge University Press, 2011) 323, 352–4.

[118] Garcia, *Trade, Inequality, and Justice, supra* note 94, at 168–92.

would require endorsing them if nobody's basic human rights suffered on account of the reforms. The consensus among most trade experts to eliminate agricultural subsidies or non-tariff barriers by the North suggests an agreement that such policies would help poor states, although, as noted, the role of domestic institutions in preventing trade law from helping the ordinary person cannot be underestimated. Yet it is also possible that trade reforms enacted to help the poorest people enjoy their economic rights could undercut efforts to promote other basic human rights. Thus, some of the same U.S. and European trade policies that are criticized by Southern states as discriminatory or imposing a Northern agenda are actually attempts by the rich states—even if often inconsistently applied—to condition preferential treatment on the recipient's respect of human rights, including labor rights. So repealing them would simply deny states an important tool to help improve rights abroad.[119]

On the other hand, proposals that simply call for more favorable—special and differential—treatment for the South as a matter of *right*, without regard for their *actual contribution* to eliminating poverty, do not seem to be premised on any position about the thin justice of the WTO rules. Rather, they work on the assumption, as Patrick Low has stated, 'that the ideal contribution of the WTO to development is to ensure that developing countries are unencumbered by obligations', which he rightly calls 'analysis-free thinking [that] encourages developed countries to dismiss the underlying case for S&D [special and differential treatment]'.[120] Those making such deontological claims are working from a different conception of global justice, but even a deontologically-based redistributive position must be based on concrete connections between trade law and poverty.

But one might still resist the conclusion that these reforms or others to the trading system are required even if they would guarantee the enjoyment of the basic human right to food. For perhaps trade law is not the proper place to fix the problems of global poverty or deprivations of basic human rights of the economic kind. Rather, other measures, for example more development assistance outside the trade context, or sanctions against violators, would be more efficient (economically) or effective (politically). In other words, to argue in favor of these policies as a way to guarantee basic human rights still requires us to assume that trade rules *should* be used for that purpose. In the context of distributive justice, Joel Trachtman has identified the notion of 'justice subsidiarity'. Thus, even as we acknowledge that we must do justice somewhere, we must also choose the best vertical site—within the state or through international cooperation—as well as the best functional areas—the policy vehicle of trade, taxation, development, finance, etc. He argues that 'it is unlikely to be appropriate to effect justice by

[119] See Aaronson, 'Seeping in Slowly', *supra* note 93, at 429, 432–4.

[120] Patrick Low, 'Is the WTO Doing Enough for Developing Countries?', in George A. Bermann and Petros C. Mavroides (eds.), *WTO Law and Developing Countries* (New York: Cambridge University Press, 2007) 334.

every institution or every act... because some vertical or functional areas will be more efficient or effective areas in which to do justice than others'.[121]

Thus we are left with a sense of uncertainty regarding the systemic critique. Even if trade rules can be adjusted to eliminate their possible harm to basic human rights, that option still may be the wrong path to achieve even thin justice. Rather, alternative vehicles, which may not even involve international law at all—for example more development aid, or simply more technical assistance—may be better paths to achieving thin justice. Generalization seems difficult in this area. In some cases, reformed trade rules would be an efficient way to guarantee basic human rights. But in others we may find a better path to that important goal.

VII. Conclusion

This chapter has distilled the hugely complex network of rules governing global trade into two core norms based on non-discrimination, MFN and national treatment. Because of the uncertain link between particular trade rules and the advancement of peace, the analysis has focused on the second pillar of thin justice. Three critiques of trade law for potential interference with human rights framed the analysis. In each case, the actual workings of the law undercut simple conclusions regarding trade law's justice. Trade law can be interpreted to deny a state policy space to protect human rights, but on two core issues—conflict diamonds and HIV medicines—states avoided a direct conflict, although the verdict is still out on the Doha formula's impact on the right to health. As for the numerous Appellate Body rulings, they have insisted that there is no clash of norms but have nonetheless interpreted trade law to constrain states' choices, although it has yet to be shown that it will truly prevent them from protecting basic human rights.

The institutional critique has some greater force insofar as the WTO is organized in both its admission process and decisionmaking to give rich states great power. The decisions of the member states and the AB offer some evidence that the WTO can act in a way that does not interfere with the enjoyment of human rights, but the connection between WTO governance and human rights protection remains highly complex and contested. Further empirical work is needed to judge the persuasiveness of the critique.

Lastly, the systemic critique cuts the broadest swath, condemning trade law itself for violating economic social and cultural rights. This critique had force with respect to agricultural subsidies, but much of the rest of it is based on causal claims that have yet to be proved. In particular, the effect of both actual and reasonably possible alternative trade rules on poverty is subject to significant disagreement, which makes it premature to call the rules on the whole just or unjust.

[121] Joel P. Trachtman, 'Doing Justice: The Economics and Politics of International Distributive Justice', in Chios Carmody, Frank J. Garcia, and John Linarelli (eds.), *Global Justice and International Economic Law: Opportunities and Prospects* (New York: Cambridge University Press, 2012) 273, 276–7.

Some reform might help, but we need to ask whether trade law is an effective vehicle to rectify violations of economic rights.

I now turn to the other major body of international economic law, that regulating foreign investment. In the conclusion of Chapter 11, I will explore some themes common to the appraisal of the justice in the two areas.

11

The International Investment Regime

International investment flows dwarf trade flows. Yet the law of international investment garners less attention in discussions of global justice than does trade law. This shadowy existence likely stems from key differences between the two regimes. Instead of a foundational treaty like the GATT, investment law originated in customary international law. Instead of a set of globally negotiated multilateral treaties, the regime is characterized mostly by some 3,200 bilateral investment treaties (BITs)—along with regional treaties, global accords, and soft law instruments. These accords overlap in coverage but often vary significantly with respect to their obligations on the parties. Instead of an enormous corpus of highly detailed trade rules, annexes, and schedules, investment treaties tend to be relatively brief and at a fairly high level of generality. And instead of a leading institution to develop and interpret rules, the process is highly decentralized, with dispute resolution bodies under diverse institutional arrangements.

I. International Investment Law's Core Norms and Human Rights

A. The fundamental duties of international investment law

Investment law is organized around three core duties for states. First, the state must not *discriminate* in the treatment of foreign investment, a contingent duty in that it is defined in terms of how a state treats investment from another state compared to internal investment and investment from third states. That duty translates into two key obligations in investment treaties: *national treatment* and *most-favored-nation treatment* for all foreign investment. These duties protect investors from measures imposed on them solely by virtue of their nationality.

But because non-discrimination is no guarantee of decent treatment of a foreign investor, investment law includes two other core duties on states that are absolute or non-contingent: *fair and equitable treatment* (FET) of all foreign investment and a *duty to compensate* an investor in the event the state expropriates the investor's assets. States, international organizations, and arbitral tribunals have offered many formulas for these obligations in treaty texts, governmental pronouncements, and arbitral awards. In addition to these two obligations, investment law includes other non-contingent duties, for example to allow investors to repatriate profits freely, to allow them to hire senior personnel, and to refrain from imposing so-called performance requirements on investors (for example local content requirements or technology transfer requirements). Moreover, states generally have a critical duty regarding the enforcement of the rules—to open their courts to foreign investors claiming a breach of the treaty and to accept binding arbitration if an investor brings a claim.[1]

As with trade law, investment law is also meant to preserve the policy options of the state, so both the contingent and non-contingent duties are subject to numerous limitations. Three categories merit mention. First, BITs may explicitly preserve states' prerogatives to screen the entry of investment and thus limit their duties to protect investment only once it is set up in the host state. Second, BITs and similar agreements often exclude or delay from their coverage specific economic sectors. Thus, NAFTA contains a lengthy annex in which each of the three states parties lists industries that are exempt from coverage.[2] Third, BITs contain exceptions for—or interpretations that make clear that the host state will still be able to adopt or maintain—laws, regulations, and other measures to protect national security, the environment, labor rights, or other core national interests.[3] Beyond these explicit carve-outs for the preservation of state policy options, the two core non-contingent obligations, FET and protection against expropriation, give the state significant flexibility to regulate foreign investment.

Two other points deserve mention. First, international investment law creates duties on the state to foreign investors, not domestic investors. So foreign investors can take advantage of any treatment afforded domestic investors through the state's obligation of national treatment, but the reverse is not true. Non-discrimination (in both investment and trade law) is thus not about equality, but about treating foreign investors *no worse* than domestic investors.[4] Though international investment law tolerates special rights for foreign investors compared to domestic investors, it is hard to see how that discrimination interferes with the basic human rights of the state's population. It is not the sort of discrimination, like racial discrimination, linked to human rights. Rather, those special rights are more akin to the guarantees that foreigners generally receive, compared to the domestic population, when they travel or invest abroad—for example rights of consular notification, exemption from the draft, immunity of diplomats, etc.

Second, the law creates only duties on host states toward foreign investors, not on foreign investors toward host states. Investors' duties are limited to fulfilling

[1] For an overview of treaty provisions, see United Nations Conference on Trade and Development, *International Investment Agreements: Key Issues*, 3 Vols. (New York: United Nations, 2004) [hereinafter *UNCTAD IIA Study*].

[2] North American Free Trade Agreement (NAFTA), 17 December 1992, Annexes I–IV, 32 ILM 289 (1993).

[3] See, e.g., Office of the United States Trade Representative, U.S. Model Bilateral Investment Treaty (2012), Arts. 12, 13, 18, <http://www.state.gov/documents/organization/188371.pdf>.

[4] With respect to MFN, nondiscrimination generally amounts to equality between foreign investors, as each investor from a state with an MFN clause in its BIT can take advantage of the best substantive treatment given to another foreign investor, ratcheting all foreign investors up to the same level of protection.

certain procedural requirements in order to make a claim against the host state for a violation of the treaty. This asymmetry of obligations will be considered later in the chapter.

B. Investment law's impact on basic human rights: identifying the faultlines

As with the trade law discussion, the thin justice of international investment law will turn on the second pillar of global justice—the extent to which investment law's rules interfere with basic human rights. Debates over this interaction have permeated both the official and the academic worlds. In an important 2003 report, the UN High Commissioner for Human Rights described possible tensions between investment law and human rights by differentiating between two sets of rights—investment rights, which he considered 'instrumental' insofar as they are meant to protect foreign investment; and human rights, which he considered 'fundamental' insofar as they advance basic human dignity.[5] Although the High Commissioner's terminology is somewhat unsatisfying—both sets of rights are instrumental in the sense of advancing certain goals—the observation nonetheless captures my idea that investment rules should not undermine basic human rights. With respect to the arguments made by public officials, scholars, and advocates regarding the intersection between investment law and human rights, they fall into four categories analogous to those in the trade law discussion.

First, many policymakers and scholars emphasize the positive correlation between investment law rules and human rights. An economic iteration claims that, because investment law provides important guarantees to investors, it increases foreign direct investment, which in turn improves the economic situation of individuals, particularly in the developing world. New employment opportunities pull people out of poverty. This philosophy drives the Washington Consensus and the proliferation of BITs that followed, and a range of economic actors, including many states, have endorsed it.[6]

The legal iteration of this claim is that the rules on investment promote two sets of rights—the rights of all individuals to decent work, food, and other necessities; and equally important, the rights of investors (even in corporate form) to property. A stronger version of this legal iteration is that certain guarantees by

[5] UN Commission on Human Rights, Human rights, trade and investment: Report of the High Commissioner for Human Rights, 2 July 2003, para. 24, UN Doc. E/CN.4/Sub.2/2003/9; see also Bruno Simma and Theodore Kill, 'Harmonizing Investment Protection and International Human Rights: First Steps Towards a Methodology', in Christina Binder et al. (eds.), *International Investment Law for the 21st Century: Essays in Honour of Christoph Schreuer* (New York: Oxford University Press, 2009) 678, 707.

[6] See, e.g., United Nations Conference on Trade and Development, The Doha Mandate, 31 May 2012, para. 58, UN Doc. TD/500/Add.1 ('In order to contribute to development, efforts should be made by all stakeholders to promote FDI in a way so as to complement the development priorities of host countries. FDI requires a stable, predictable and enabling investment climate. It is important to enhance the development impact of foreign investment').

the state for foreign investors are *required* by human rights law.[7] Indeed, the European Convention on Human Rights includes an optional protocol on the right to property, and EU law recognizes a fundamental right to property, both of which have been invoked by investors to challenge domestic regulations.[8] Special rights for foreign investors are also defended as a matter of democratic theory, to protect those affected by regulations of a state in which they cannot vote, though the analogy between a foreign investor and a politically weak minority is strained.[9]

As with those making similar claims regarding trade, these arguments oversimplify the relationship between investment rules and human rights. They neglect to consider serious arguments that the rules of international investment law fail to pass muster under the second pillar of global justice. Three arguments, analogous to those concerning trade law, could undermine claims of the justice of investment law: (1) that the investor protection rules deny states *policy space* for protecting human rights; (2) that *institutions* responsible for investment rules, in particular investment arbitration, are skewed to produce caselaw that will undermine human rights; and (3) that investment law *systemically* hurts poor states. My appraisal of the core rules will be organized around these three concerns.

II. International Investment Law and the Policy Space Critique

The policy space critique of investment law resembles the analogous claim in trade law insofar as it is directed against specific legal rules, as distinguished from a broader critique of investment institutions or the entire legal regime. My response to it will consider three different rules that have been the substance of recent disputes between investors and host states.

A. Fair and equitable treatment and basic human rights

Host states, human rights advocates, and some scholars have argued that the requirement in BITs and customary international law that a host state provide a foreign investor with fair and equitable treatment makes it unlawful for the state to undertake action to protect basic human rights.

[7] See Susan L. Karamanian, 'Human Rights Dimensions of Investment Law', in Erika de Wet and Jure Vidmar (eds.), *Hierarchy in International Law* (Oxford: Oxford University Press, 2012) 236, 240–2.

[8] Steven R. Ratner, 'Regulatory Takings in Institutional Context: Beyond the Fear of Fragmented International Law', *AJIL* 102 (2008): 475, 497–504.

[9] See David Schneiderman, 'Investing in Democracy? Political Process and International Investment Law', *University of Toronto LJ* 60 (2010): 909.

1. Basic contours of fair and equitable treatment

Fair and equitable treatment has two key attributes—it is a *minimum* standard of treatment, regardless of any lower standards provided in national law; but it is also a *broad* standard of treatment, as any matters not addressed in other investor protections are captured by FET. The norm originates in customary international law, but the term, or variations of it, has now been adopted by states in numerous treaties, even though the parties to the treaties may or may not intend the treaty to incorporate the customary law standard.[10] Countless arbitral tribunals interpreting treaties with FET clauses have attempted to define this very open-textured term. One recent tribunal, considering a dispute between a Spanish company, Tecmed, operating a landfill, and the government of Mexico, interpreted FET in a way that seemed to place a significant burden on the state:

> [FET] requires the Contracting Parties to provide to international investments treatment that does not affect the basic expectations that were taken into account by the foreign investor to make the investment. The foreign investor expects the host State to act in a consistent manner, free from ambiguity and totally transparently in its relations with the foreign investor, so that it may know beforehand any and all rules and regulations that will govern its investments.... [and] to act consistently, i.e. without arbitrarily revoking any preexisting decisions or permits... that were relied upon by the investor to assume its commitments.[11]

On the other hand, some tribunals have adopted a far more restrictive meaning, giving the state more leeway. A recent tribunal decision concerning the claims of a Canadian mining company, Glamis Gold, against the United States, stated:

> [A] violation of [FET]... requires an act that is sufficiently egregious and shocking—a gross denial of justice, manifest arbitrariness, blatant unfairness, a complete lack of due process, evident discrimination, or a manifest lack of reasons—so as to fall below accepted international standards.... Such a breach may be exhibited by a 'gross denial of justice or manifest arbitrariness falling below acceptable international standards;' or the creation by the State of objective expectations *in order to induce* investment and the subsequent repudiation of those expectations.[12]

However one sizes up FET, then, it is a norm built on the stability of reasonable or legitimate expectations.[13] It protects foreign investors not from regulation by the state, but from treatment that seems fundamentally unfair—whether conceived in terms of actions beyond any reasonable expectation of the investor (the *Tecmed* view) or in terms of blatantly shocking behavior (the

[10] See, e.g., Rudolf Dolzer and Christoph Schreuer, *Principles of International Investment Law*, 2nd ed. (New York: Oxford University Press, 2012) 130–9.

[11] *Técnicas Medioambientales Tecmed S.A. v Mexico*, ICSID Case No. ARB(AF)/00/2, Award, 29 May 2003, para. 154 [hereinafter *Tecmed*].

[12] *Glamis Gold Ltd v United States*, UNICTRAL Award, 8 June 2009, para. 627.

[13] See Rudolph Dolzer, 'Fair and Equitable Treatment: Today's Contours', *Santa Clara JIL* 12 (2013): 7, 17–29.

Glamis view). In that sense, FET ironically bears some relation to human rights law insofar as it puts absolute limits on what the host state can do to a (foreign) individual or company; indeed, the early arbitral cases relying upon it to hold host states liable for mistreatment of foreigners are forerunners to human rights law.[14]

The potential implications of the FET norm on the host state's ability to protect its residents' human rights—notably economic and social rights—are serious. For the state may decide that one way to guarantee certain rights to its residents is by taking action that investors did not or could not anticipate, that treats them in a way they regard as unfair, and that has a negative impact on the investment's economic return. The range of possible actions is huge: many will be characterized by a sudden alteration in the regulatory environment for a good or service essential to consumers (for example affordable energy, safe food, clean air, or clean water). Others may entail new taxes or royalties to deal with a domestic crisis. If the state regards the matter as sufficiently urgent, its measures can have significant shortcomings as a matter of due process. If the investor cannot negotiate its way out of the new regulatory or fiscal regime (for example through exemptions, grace periods, or grandfathering), it may sue the state for FET violations, either in domestic courts or in international arbitration. And if the state loses, the damages for which it would be liable, merely for taking measures to protect human rights, could be significant.

To argue that there is no conflict between the state's duties under investment law and its duties to protect its residents because the state can simply choose to pay the damages is wrong on two accounts. First, most international law does not rely principally on what Calabresi and Melamed called liability rules, where a state's entitlements are protected only by an external monetary standard that allows a party to pay for its harm to the other. Rather, international law comprises mostly property rules, insofar as the infringement on the victim state's entitlements without its consent makes the other state a law violator.[15] Second, even under a liability model, the choice the state faces may be only a Hobson's choice—to refrain from its duty to protect the rights of its residents or to pay an enormous, potentially crippling, sum to foreign investors who claim that the state's action violated their rights.

[14] See Todd Weiler, *The Interpretation of International Investment Law: Equality, Discrimination and Minimum Standards of Treatment in Historical Context* (Boston, MA: Martinus Nijhoff Publishers, 2013) 170–5.

[15] Compare Guido Calabresi and A. Douglas Melamed, 'Property Rules, Liability Rules, and Inalienability: One View of the Cathedral', *Harv L Rev* 85 (1972): 1089, 1105–6, with ILC Articles on State Responsibility, Art. 2 ('internationally wrongful act' committed whenever a state's conduct breaches its international obligations). On the other hand, Article 20 regards an illegal act as not wrongful if the state to whom the obligation is owed consents to the violation. For more on international law's approach, see Jeffrey L. Dunoff and Joel P. Trachtman, 'Economic Analysis of International Law', *Yale JIL* 24 (1999): 1, 25–7; Joost Pauwelyn, *Optimal Protection of International Law: Navigating between European Absolutism and American Voluntarism* (New York: Cambridge University Press, 2008).

As with trade law, we must dig more deeply into the effect of FET upon a state's ability to protect basic human rights. I thus turn to caselaw from international tribunals that have judged the acts of states against that standard.[16]

2. *Cases on fair and equitable treatment*

To illustrate the potential conflicts between FET and human rights, I examine four arbitral decisions—one about the closure of a landfill in the interest of public health and three in which states took action that they claimed were aimed at protecting a vital water system.[17] Like the trade cases discussed previously, all four implicate basic human rights to health.

- The first case, decided in 2003, is the claim of the Spanish company Tecmed against Mexico, whose opinion was quoted earlier for its expansive view of FET. Tecmed was given a license to operate a landfill in the town of Hermosillo in perpetuity, but after a local election produced a government opposed to the landfill, it agreed with the government to close it and move it to another site. The government assured it that it could continue to operate the existing site and have a smooth transition to the new one. In response to local opposition fueled by local officials, the local and federal government eventually ordered Tecmed to close the first site immediately, based on health concerns. The tribunal ruled for Tecmed on the ground that it had not been told that public attitudes would affect the operation of the landfill and had not been warned of any irregularities in its operation that could be remedied until it was too late for Tecmed to fix them. It pointed out continuous contradictions and lack of transparency by Mexican governmental officials, covering up a political motive for the closure.[18]
- A 2006 arbitral judgment addressed the claim of an American company, Azurix, that obtained a contract for water services for Buenos Aires. (Like most cases against Argentina, these involve public utility sectors opened for privatization during the presidency of Carlos Menem.) After an algae breakout in the water system, the authorities blamed Azurix for it, urging residents not to pay their bills. The parties disagreed over numerous provisions of the concession regarding renegotiation and remedies, leading Azurix to attempt to terminate it, which the provincial authorities refused to accept. Argentina defended its conduct in part based on its responsibility to defend public health, and that it entrusted the claimant with meeting high standards to this effect.[19] The tribunal instead found that the provincial authorities failed to accept their own responsibilities and contributed to

[16] Compared to the trade law cases, my descriptions will be somewhat more elaborate because of the prolonged and fluid relationship between the investor and the host state.

[17] Four other water cases will be mentioned later, in Section II.E, because they concern measures taken during Argentina's fiscal emergency.

[18] *Tecmed*, *supra* note 11, paras. 160–164.

[19] *Azurix Corp. v Argentine Republic*, ICSID Case No. ARB/01/12, Award, 14 July 2006, paras. 129–131.

the crisis. After adopting a high standard for FET,[20] the tribunal rather summarily found that Argentina had violated FET through its politicized approach to the dispute.[21] It briefly touched on the relationship of the BIT to human rights treaties, noting that Argentina had raised the issue but also that it had not been 'fully argued' and that it could not 'understand the incompatibility in the specifics of the instant case',[22] because the services to consumers continued to be provided without interruption.

• The second water case, decided in 2007, concerned the operations of a company owned by the French consortium Vivendi for water services in Tucumán province. A newly elected provincial government vigorously opposed the privatization scheme approved by its predecessor and the new tariffs (which raised prices for consumers), imposing fines on the company and blaming it for not repairing the poorly maintained system that it inherited. When manganese turbidity reappeared in the water, the provincial authorities further mobilized public opinion against the company, urging residents not to pay their bills and enjoining the claimant from collecting payment. The province sought to renegotiate the contract, but talks failed, leading both sides to pull out of the contract and the province eventually to seek additional taxes from the claimant.[23] Argentina argued in part that these actions were justified based on its duty to protect public health.[24] Yet the tribunal found substantial FET violations. Among its key conclusions was that the provincial government's public statements that the water was unsafe, despite clear evidence to the contrary from their own scientific experts, was 'irresponsible'.[25]

• The third water case was a 2008 arbitration between a British company, Biwater Gauff, and Tanzania over a dispute arising from Tanzania's contract to Biwater to operate water and sewage systems in Dar es Salaam. After Biwater did not operate the systems to the government's satisfaction, the government tried to terminate the contract. Again adopting a high standard of FET,[26] the tribunal found that Tanzania had violated FET by inflaming public opinion and falsely announcing prematurely that the contract had been terminated. It also found other treatment, including the withdrawal of a VAT exemption, the seizure of its

[20] Ibid., para. 372 ('To encourage and protect investment is the purpose of the BIT. It would be incoherent with such purpose... to consider that a party to the BIT has breached [FET] only when it has acted in bad faith or its conduct can be qualified as outrageous or egregious').

[21] Ibid., paras. 375–377.

[22] Ibid., para. 261. See also ibid., para. 254 (referring to the Argentine government's expert opinion arguing for the priority of consumer rights over corporate rights, a very weak and overbroad argument as a matter of human rights law).

[23] *Compañía de Aguas del Aconquija S.A. and Vivendi Universal S.A. v Argentina*, ICSID Case No. ARB/97/3, Award, 20 August 2007 [hereinafter *Vivendi*].

[24] Ibid., para. 6.6.6 ('The challenged actions of the Tucumán authorities were simply necessary responses to the inadequate implementation of Claimants' contractual obligations in light of the need to secure accessible supplies of water to the population of Tucumán').

[25] Ibid., paras. 7.4.26–7.4.30.

[26] *Biwater Gauff (Tanzania) Ltd v United Republic of Tanzania*, ICSID Case No. ARB/05/22, Award, 24 July 2008, para. 602.

assets, usurpation of control and deportation of the claimant's staff, to be 'unreasonable' or a denial of 'constant protection and security' (under a different clause of the BIT).[27] However, the company could not link any of the government's actions to economic harm, so no damages were awarded.

3. *Tentative conclusions about the justice of fair and equitable treatment*

In each of the four cases, the arbitral tribunals ruled that the government had breached the duty of FET—rulings that seem to limit the policy space of states to protect the right to health.[28] The tribunals set the FET bar at a high level for the state, rejected the public health justification in each case, and left it (with the exception of Tanzania) liable for millions of dollars in damages. This sort of outcome lay behind a broad indictment of international investment arbitration by more than fifty academics in a 2010 statement. They criticized arbitral awards that privilege corporate interests over 'the right to regulate of states', noting that FET and other duties 'have been given unduly pro-investor interpretations at the expense of states, their governments, and those on whose behalf they act'.[29]

Yet when read closely, these cases are not just about denial of policy space. First, tribunals acknowledge the state's legitimate policy space. Thus the *Vivendi* tribunal wrote:

> [W]hile it would have been entirely proper for a new government with a different policy perspective on privatisation to seek to renegotiate a concession agreement in a transparent non-coercive manner, it is clearly wrong (and unfair and inequitable in terms of the BIT) to seek to bring a concessionaire to the renegotiation table through threats of rescission based on colourable allegations after having wrongly deprived the concessionaire's billings of formal legitimacy.[30]

And in *Biwater*, despite the finding of an FET violation, the tribunal refused to question the reasons for the city's decision to terminate the contract. Moreover, it interpreted the renegotiation process in a way that generally gave the benefit of the doubt to Tanzania, finding that it acted in good faith in the negotiations to revise the contract.[31]

Second, and more significantly, the common thread among the four cases is that the words and deeds by the state appear so attenuated from the merits of its dispute with the claimant that they suggested a political agenda rather than

[27] Ibid., paras. 626–628, 696, 698, 707, 709.

[28] See Andreas Kulick, *Global Public Interest in International Investment Law* (New York: Cambridge University Press, 2012) 294 (adopting this interpretation for *Vivendi*).

[29] Public Statement on the International Investment Regime, 31 August 2010, para. 5, <http://www.osgoode.yorku.ca/public-statement/documents/Public_Statement_(final)_(Dec_2013).pdf>.

[30] *Vivendi, supra* note 23, para. 7.4.31; see also *Azurix, supra* note 19, para. 144 ('governments have to be vigilant and protect the public health of their citizens'); *Biwater, supra* note 26, para. 654.

[31] *Biwater, supra* note 26, para. 674; see also ibid., para. 654 ('[T]he financial situation at both City Water [the claimant] and DAWASA [the city's water authority] demanded immediate action. At least in theory, and viewed at that time, this crisis could have threatened a vital public service and the situation therefore had to be resolved one way or the other in the near future').

a legitimate concern for public health. In that sense, the authorities engaged in a gratuitous and thus unfair action against each company. Thus, for instance, in *Tecmed*, the tribunal repeatedly points out that the Mexican government's own environmental quality office had concluded that the landfill was not dangerous to public health and that the motives were thus purely political.[32]

In light of these facts, FET does not seem to interfere with the enjoyment of basic human rights so much as it requires the state to follow certain basic processes fair to the defendant, for example adhere to the renegotiation procedures specified in the contract. In the *Glamis* case noted earlier (in which the policy space concerned environmental protection rather than basic human rights), the respondent's adherence to procedural fairness—as well as the tribunal's adoption of a much lower standard for FET—yielded a loss for the claimant.[33] Thus, it seems premature to suggest that the FET obligation forced the governments to choose between honoring the investment contract to the detriment of its people and protecting the people but at the cost of a significant damage award.[34] At this point, it cannot be said that FET, as interpreted, interferes with the enjoyment of basic human rights. Indeed, even though FET does not command the incorporation of human rights concerns, it certainly permits it.

Yet even though FET seems to pass the test of thin justice so far, it does constrain regulatory space somewhat, and it is certainly not some embodiment of an ideal balance between the need for stability and change.[35] As with trade law, we could see a chilling effect on states, as they are reluctant to take action to protect residents' right to life or health for fear of an expensive case brought against them in an arbitral tribunal. It is very difficult to know whether states will refrain from guaranteeing key economic rights of their residents for this reason, but the losses suffered in the above cases are likely in the minds of government lawyers contemplating the risk of suits by foreign investors.

In the end, the key test of the justice of FET will be whether arbitral tribunals go so far as to define and apply FET in a way that makes it significantly difficult for a state to meet its responsibilities to guarantee basic human rights. One

[32] *Tecmed, supra* note 11, paras. 124, 129–130, 162–163.

[33] In *Glamis*, the claimant challenged measures by the U.S. federal government and California that made its mining operations economically infeasible. The tribunal found that the U.S. government acted in good faith in its reviews of the mining operation and that a California law was not targeted at Glamis' investment. Central to its conclusions was that the investor had never received any inducements or commitments by the United States or California that it would be permitted to mine. *Glamis, supra* note 12, paras. 766–767, 801, 811. A Native American tribe asserted that human rights law required denial of a permit, but the tribunal never addressed these issues. *Glamis, supra* note 12, Non-Party Supplemental Submission of the Quechan Indian Nation, Submission of Non-Disputing Party, 16 October 2006, <http://www.state.gov/s/l/c10986.htm>.

[34] See Andrew Newcombe, 'A Brief Comment on the "Public Statement on the International Investment Regime"', *Kluwer Arbitration Blog*, 3 September 2010, <http://kluwerarbitrationblog.com>.

[35] See Roland Kläger, *'Fair and Equitable Treatment' in International Investment Law* (New York: Cambridge University Press, 2011) 153 (FET as 'an embodiment of justice'); Ioana Knoll-Tudor, 'The Fair and Equitable Treatment Standard and Human Rights Norms', in P.M. Dupuy, F. Francioni, and E.U. Petersmann (eds.), *Human Rights in International Investment Law and Arbitration* (New York: Oxford University Press, 2009) 310, 342–3.

upcoming test will take place as an arbitral tribunal deals with Philip Morris's claim against Australia that Australia's packaging rules violate the FET provisions of the Hong Kong-Australia BIT.[36] But to pass muster under the second pillar of thin justice, FET does not have to give the state an automatic win in cases where its conduct is undertaken in order to secure the basic human rights of its people. A tribunal could interpret FET flexibly to take into account the state's needs to protect those rights while also considering whether the investor should bear the full burden of those measures in light of the previous commitments made to it and the commitments by the state in the BIT. Just as FET does not interfere with the enjoyment of basic human rights if it requires the state to be procedurally fair to the foreign investor, it does not do so if it requires the state to shoulder some of the costs.

We cannot generalize as to when those procedural regularities or costs are too much to expect of the host state, but the notion of an *undue burden* from the trade law cases expresses the idea.[37] Unfortunately, although trade law already contains some textual hooks—like Article XX of the GATT—allowing for states to protect human rights, FET clauses do not. And, as discussed in Section III of this chapter, we can be skeptical about the willingness of arbitral tribunals to consider human rights in their understanding of FET, even if the state argues that it was obligated to act under human rights law. If they insist on excluding it even in cases where the government claims it is protecting basic human rights,[38] then the norm, as interpreted, could yet prove unjust.

B. Rules on expropriation and basic human rights

A second policy space concern is that the requirement for a state to provide (in most cases) full compensation to a foreign investor whose property it takes will put the state in a bind when it needs to take control of foreign property in order to guarantee basic human rights. If a state has to compensate the investor for the taking—which might be defined to include a mere loss in value due to regulatory measures—then it will not have the funds it needs to take care of its people.

1. Contours of the rules on expropriation

Customary international law has long recognized a state's sovereign prerogative to expropriate both domestic and foreign property for a public purpose.[39] At the

[36] See *Philip Morris Asia Ltd, Written Notification of Claim*, 22 June 2011, <http://www.italaw.com/sites/default/files/case-documents/ita0664.pdf>.

[37] See Ch. 10, Section III.C.

[38] For an endorsement of this exclusion and consideration of human rights concerns only at the damages phase, see Knoll-Tudor, 'The Fair and Equitable Treatment Standard', *supra* note 35, at 343.

[39] On the possibility of expropriations that are unlawful even if a state compensates for them, compare Giorgio Sacerdoti, 'Bilateral treaties and multilateral instruments on investment protection', *Recueil des Cours* 269 (1997): 251, 389, with Jan Paulsson, 'Ghosts of Chorzów: *Maha Nuñez-Schultz* v. *Republic of the Americas*', in Todd Weiler (ed.), *International Investment Law and Arbitration* (London: Cameron May, 2005) 777, 789.

same time, states have differed significantly, mostly along North–South lines, about the amount of compensation due in the event of a taking. Capital exporting states have urged something close to full value nearly always; capital importing states have sought more discretion in the amount to pay. Investment treaties codify certain generally accepted understandings of when a state may expropriate and often specify a formula for compensation. Thus, they typically require that any expropriation be (a) for a public purpose; (b) non-discriminatory insofar as the identity of the target is not chosen based on nationality or invidious considerations; (c) in accordance with due process of law; and (d) accompanied by payment of compensation—which is typically elaborated, for example, as 'appropriate', 'just', 'prompt, adequate and effective', or 'full value'.[40] Arbitral tribunals have devoted countless pages to interpreting and applying the terms on compensation, where the practice is to award the investor the economic value of the expropriated investment.[41]

The duty to pay foreign investors the value of their investments when property is expropriated could have serious implications for the state's treasury and its ability to protect residents' basic human rights. To test the implications for thin justice, I focus on two questions: (1) Which governmental action does the law regard as an expropriation to begin with? If it is broad enough to cover numerous state policies with a deleterious economic impact on investors, then a requirement to compensate is a severe constraint on policy space to protect human rights. (2) If the state does expropriate, must it always pay the investors full compensation? If the law is inflexible on this question, the implications for policy space can be quite serious, as the state may need to expropriate significant foreign property in the name of human rights protection.

2. *What is an expropriation?*

The classic expropriation is a taking or nationalization of private property, where the government, typically through a formal act of state, assumes ownership and control of land, an industry, facilities, or assets. This so-called 'direct expropriation' is indeed the easiest case both legally and morally. As an initial position, setting aside whether the investor achieved his gains through dubious dealings or has been enriched at the expense of the local community, it seems prima facie wrong not to compensate him for his loss—though we will still need to ask whether thin justice demands non-compensation in any event (the second question, to be addressed next). But governments take numerous actions with harmful economic impacts on foreign investors—think of taxation or environmental regulations—well short of this direct expropriation. Where then, is the line between those actions that we can call 'indirect' or 'regulatory' expropriations—takings by other

[40] *UNCTAD IIA Study*, *supra* note 1, Vol. I, at 238–51.

[41] See, e.g., World Bank, Guidelines on the Treatment of Foreign Direct Investment, Art. IV, 31 ILM 1379 (1992) (offering different formulas for determining full value).

means that still trigger a duty to compensate—and all those other actions that are not expropriations?

International law has developed some basic doctrine on these questions.[42] States and parties are free to define a compensable taking in whatever way they choose (for example in a BIT, an agreement between an investor and a host state, or an insurance contract between an investor and an insurance company). But where the term 'expropriation' is not specifically defined, those trying to decide whether governmental regulation is an indirect expropriation focus on the substance of the measure and not its form. Decisionmakers have generally considered three factors under both treaties and custom: (a) the impact of the measures on the investment, so that regulatory action is an indirect expropriation when it deprives the investor for a significant period of control of the investment in a manner akin to a direct expropriation; (b) the extent to which the investor had vested property rights in the investment, as contrasted with some less entrenched form of possession or expectations; and (c) the context of the governmental measure, including its purpose and the proportionality of the harm to the investor to the benefit to the public.[43]

As for specific controversies, we discover that, as a general matter, close cases tend to be resolved in favor of the government.[44] That is, even in arbitrations where the government is found to have violated FET, tribunals have typically not found an expropriation. In a series of cases against Argentina regarding its emergency measures during the 2001–03 financial crisis that harmed foreign investors, discussed further later, although most of the tribunals found a violation of FET, only a handful found that Argentina had expropriated the investors. In the many NAFTA cases, a tribunal has found an expropriation in only one case, *Metalclad v Mexico*, a case that has been significantly criticized for setting too low a threshold on expropriations. In 2012, an arbitral panel found that even Ecuador's 99 percent tax on oil revenue was not an indirect expropriation because the company was still able to generate a commercial return with only diminished profits.[45]

Yet indirect expropriation claims sometimes prevail. In *Tecmed*, the tribunal ruled that because the harm to the claimant was disproportionate to the public interest, the act was an expropriation.[46] In *Vivendi*, the tribunal found that the claimants had been 'radically deprived of the economic use and enjoyment of their investment';[47]

[42] For further elaboration, see Ratner, 'Regulatory Takings', *supra* note 8.

[43] For another endorsement of these three factors, see Andrew Newcombe, 'The Boundaries of Regulatory Expropriation in International Law', *ICSID Rev: Foreign Inv LJ* 20 (2005): 1, 40–9.

[44] Beyond investment tribunals, the ECHR's inclusion of protection of private property in Protocol I has meant that the European Court of Human Rights has compensated private investors for governmental conduct. And the European Court of Justice has developed a caselaw tailored to the integration goals of the EU. See generally Ratner, 'Regulatory Takings', *supra* note 8, at 496–505.

[45] *Burlington Resources Inc. v Republic of Ecuador*, ICSID Case No. ARB/08/5, 14 December 2012, paras. 450–457.

[46] *Tecmed, supra* note 11, paras. 122–139.

[47] *Vivendi, supra* note 23, para. 7.5.34.

and in *Biwater* it found that the harm there was a 'substantial deprivation of rights' of the investor so as to constitute an expropriation.[48]

Most indirect expropriation claims will fail for the first two factors—because the impact on the investor is simply not severe enough to neutralize the investment or deprive the investors of the operation of the investment, or because it did not sufficiently conflict with the investors' vested property rights or similar expectations. So if the government needs to protect basic human rights by imposing certain regulations—even higher taxes—on the investor, a significant economic impact will not, under the existing caselaw, constitute an expropriation.

In addition, the third factor above, i.e. the legitimate interests of the government and the proportionality of the measures, helps distinguish bona fide regulations from indirect expropriations. Sometimes, this factor is explicit in treaties. Thus, the U.S. Model BIT, which is presented to states interested in such a treaty with the United States (in a more or less 'take it or leave it' mode) provides that the 'character of the government action' is relevant to the existence of an indirect expropriation and that '[e]xcept in rare circumstances, non-discriminatory regulatory actions...designed and applied to protect legitimate public welfare objectives, such as public health, safety, and the environment, do not constitute indirect expropriations'.[49] Many similar clauses were added in reaction to the now-discredited *Metalclad* arbitral ruling that had found Mexico's closure of a municipal landfill operated by a U.S. investor to be expropriatory. Arbitral panels have noted this factor as well.[50] The state's police powers—the government's authority to protect the public from crime, hazardous situations (natural or man-made), and other serious threats to public order—are also mentioned by tribunals as giving the state ample discretion before its actions are compensable.[51] Andrew Newcombe has argued that this power could give the state latitude to protect many important interests (such as those recognized in Article XX of the GATT), such as closing a factory that was emitting poisonous fumes.[52] So a

[48] *Biwater, supra* note 26, paras. 463–465, 519.

[49] U.S. Model BIT, *supra* note 3, Annex B, Arts. 4(a)(iii), (b). For other examples, see Agreement Between the Government of Canada and the Government of the People's Republic of China for the Promotion and Reciprocal Protection of Investments, 9 September 2012, Annex B.10, Art. 3, <http://www.international.gc.ca/trade-agreements-accords-commerciaux/agr-acc/fipa-apie/china-text-chine.aspx>; South African Development Community, 'SADC Model Bilateral Investment Treaty Template with Commentary' (2012), Art. 6, Art. 6 comment, <http://www.iisd.org>.

[50] See, e.g., *Fireman's Fund Insurance Co. v Mexico*, ICSID Case No. ARB(AF)/02/01, Award, 17 July 2006, para. 176 (listing as factors 'whether the measure is within the recognized police powers of the host State; the (public) purpose and effect of the measure; whether the measure is discriminatory; the proportionality between the means employed and the aim sought to be realized; and the bona fide nature of the measure'); but see *Tecmed, supra* note 11, para. 122 (relying on European Court of Human Rights cases for the idea of proportionality but still ruling for the claimant).

[51] See *Burlington Resources, supra* note 45, paras. 507–529 (finding a direct expropriation of two oil fields, though recognizing that had Ecuador acted under its police powers, it would not have been an expropriation); *Tecmed, supra* note 11, para. 119; *Chemtura Corp. v Canada*, UNCITRAL Award, 2 August 2010, para. 266.

[52] Newcombe, 'The Boundaries of Regulatory Expropriation', *supra* note 43, at 25–40.

tribunal could interpret the idea of a legitimate purpose, and the police power in particular, to include measures to protect basic human rights.[53]

3. Non-compensable expropriations?

But what if, in the name of assuming its responsibilities for the basic human rights of its people, the state takes action that is clearly expropriatory—for instance, outright confiscation of foreign property—and in circumstances hard to justify under the police power? One example would be large-scale expropriation of land from wealthy foreign investors to redistribute to the local population, an action taken by Mexico against U.S. landowners in the 1930s. This action might be seen by the government as part of its duty to provide food to the population. Or suppose a foreign-owned mine is run such that few of its profits remain in the host state, and that state decides that it needs to take it over in order to provide enough revenue to build schools for its population?[54] If international investment law required every such expropriation to be compensated, these measures directed at ensuring the basic human rights of the population might be impossible.

This possibility has led to some recognition of at least one exception to the requirement of compensation—expropriatory measures taken by a state as part of a large-scale restructuring of the economy. Thus, the World Bank Guidelines for the Treatment of Foreign Investment, adopted by the Bank in 1992 after a long study of state and arbitral practice, state:

> In case of comprehensive non-discriminatory nationalizations effected in the process of large scale social reforms under exceptional circumstances of revolution, war and similar exigencies, the compensation may be determined through negotiations between the host State and the investors' home State and failing this, through international arbitration.[55]

Yet the implications of this exception for the protection of basic human rights remain uncertain. The Guidelines are not binding treaty or customary law, and I am not aware of any provisions in BITs allowing for such exceptions. Perhaps an arbitral tribunal could interpret vague terms like 'just' or 'appropriate' compensation to reflect the different situation of a large-scale nationalization, but recent arbitral practice has focused on the economic value of the nationalized asset, not

[53] For a strategy to use proportionality to consider a state's human rights obligations, see Jasper Krommendijk and John Morijn, '"Proportional" by What Measure(s)? Balancing Investor Interests and Human Rights by Way of Applying the Proportionality Principle in Investor-State Arbitration', in P.M. Dupuy, F. Francioni, and E.U. Petersmann (eds.), *Human Rights in International Investment Law and Arbitration* (New York: Oxford University Press, 2009) 432.

[54] I recognize that neither action may accomplish the goal set out and that indeed governments may clearly nationalize in order to control the proceeds for selfish ends.

[55] World Bank Guidelines, *supra* note 41, art. IV.10. Note that these measures must be non-discriminatory, so actions against foreign investors based solely on their nationality (as opposed a more neutral criterion such as possession of economic assets) would be barred. Ibid., art. IV.1.

the ability to pay of the host state.[56] In what could have been a test of this provision, in 2006, a group of Italian nationals sued South Africa alleging that its law transferring ownership of certain mines to black South Africans was an illegal expropriation. However, the two sides settled the case before any tribunal ruling, and South Africa's early pleadings suggested that its defense would assert that the action was either not an expropriation or that compensation had been given, rather than the sort of defense contemplated by the World Bank Guidelines.[57]

4. *Tentative conclusions about the justice of the expropriation rules*

Investment law's rules on expropriation, even more than its rules on FET, have, thus far as interpreted by tribunals, not generally forced a state to pay compensation for regulatory measures that might be aimed at protecting the residents' basic human rights. In that sense, they can be said, at least provisionally, to pass muster as a matter of thin justice. The outlier cases have been overtaken by a string of defeats for claimants and revisions of BITs confirming the narrow meaning of an expropriation. Most scenarios where a state actually needs to take alien property to protect human rights would fall under the police power and thus prove non-expropriatory, though one can imagine closer cases where tribunals might insist on compensation. As with FET, thin justice does not demand that expropriation rules always and completely insulate the state from liability if it takes private property to protect human rights. It is certainly possible that a more textured doctrine would pass the test of thin justice while at times demanding some limited compensation.

C. The necessity defense as a safety valve for thin justice?

A final policy space critique of investment law is that, whatever the rules on FET or expropriation, the law should, but does not, excuse measures by states against foreign investors if they are truly needed to carry out its responsibilities to protect the rights of its people. The closest inquiry within international investment law regarding a conflict between substantive investment obligations of the state and true necessity concerns a series of cases in the last decade against Argentina.

1. *The cases on Argentina's emergency measures*

In the early 2000s, when Argentina faced a severe shortfall of foreign currency and a resulting economic emergency, the state took a series of measures against

[56] UN Conference on Trade and Development, 'Expropriation' (UNCTAD Series on Issues in International Investment Agreements II, 2012) 115 (suggesting a decisionmaker could take into account 'broader equitable considerations'), <http://unctad.org/en/docs/unctaddiaeia2011d7_en.pdf>.

[57] *Piero Foresti et al. v Republic of South Africa*, ICSID Case No. ARB(AF)/07/1, Award, 4 August 2010 (discontinuing proceedings after settlement).

foreign companies in recently privatized sectors. The government enacted a new foreign exchange convertibility law that meant the investors were paid income on their investment in highly depreciated pesos rather than in pesos convertible to dollars at a highly favorable exchange rate of one dollar per peso. The facts are immensely complicated in each of the arbitrations brought against Argentina under its BITs with the United States, France, Italy, and the United Kingdom. In each, Argentina was found to have violated FET or similar provisions. The cases diverged, however, on whether the measures were nonetheless permissible under (a) an emergency clause in the U.S.-Argentina BIT permitting a state to take 'measures necessary for the maintenance of public order... or the protection of its own essential security interests'[58] or (b) the customary international law defense of necessity. The latter is now more or less codified in Article 25 of the International Law Commission's Articles on State Responsibility, which effectively excuses a state's breach of a legal obligation under very limited circumstances.[59]

International lawyers have analyzed the approaches of the arbitral tribunals and the annulment committees—panels of arbitrators with the authority to conduct a limited review of rulings of tribunals created under the 1965 Convention on the Settlement of Disputes Between States and Nationals of Other States—to the legal relationship between (a) and (b). I will avoid these doctrinal thickets to focus on the question for thin justice: do arbitral rulings that interpret international investment law reveal any clues as to whether a bona fide emergency where the state must take action to protect basic human rights will excuse a violation of investment rules?

In these cases, Argentina argued that its legislative and regulatory responses to the emergency were needed to protect its people, and at points specifically invoked human rights norms.[60] Nine cases concerned the energy sector. In *CMS Gas*, the tribunal rejected the grounds of necessity under the BIT and custom.[61]

[58] Treaty Between United States of America and the Argentine Republic Concerning the Reciprocal Encouragement and Protection of Investment, 14 November 1991, Art. XI, 31 ILM 124 (1992).

[59] In the words of Article 25:

1. Necessity may not be invoked by a State as a ground for precluding the wrongfulness of an act not in conformity with [its] international obligation... unless the act:
   (a) is the only way for the State to safeguard an essential interest against a grave and imminent peril; and
   (b) does not seriously impair an essential interest of the State or States towards which the obligation exists, or of the international community as a whole.
2. In any case, necessity may not be invoked by a State as a ground for precluding wrongfulness if:
   (a) the international obligation... excludes the possibility of invoking necessity; or
   (b) the State has contributed to the situation of necessity.

[60] See, e.g., *LG&E v Argentina*, ICSID Case No. ARB/02/1, Decision on Liability, 3 October 2006, paras. 215–219; *SAUR v Argentina*, ICSID Case No. ARB/04/4, Award, 6 June 2012, para. 328; *Continental Casualty Co. v Argentina*, ICSID Case No. ARB/03/9, Award, 5 September 2008, para. 172; *EDF International et al. v Argentina*, ICSID Case No. ARB/03/23, Award, 11 June 2012, paras. 191–195 [hereinafter *EDFI*].

[61] *CMS Gas Transmission Co. v Argentina*, ICSID Case No. ARB/01/8, Award, 12 May 2005, paras. 331, 355; Annulment Decision, 25 September 2007 (criticizing the tribunal for conflating BIT and customary standard but not annulling the award).

But in *LG&E*, the tribunal accepted Argentina's necessity defenses and exempted Argentina from liability for a seventeen-month period.[62] In *Enron*, the tribunal rejected the grounds of necessity, but the annulment committee annulled the decision for faulty reasoning.[63] In *Sempra*, the tribunal again rejected the necessity defenses, but the annulment committee again annulled the award.[64] And in *El Paso*, the tribunal rejected the necessity defense under the BIT.[65] In four energy cases under non-U.S. BITs (which lacked similar emergency clauses)—*BG, National Grid, Total*, and *EDFI*—the tribunal rejected the customary law necessity defense.[66] Four cases—*AWG, InterAgua, Impregilo*, and *SAUR*—concerned emergency measures against foreign companies involved in the recently privatized water and sewage sector, and in all four the tribunals again rejected the customary law necessity defense.[67] One case concerned the insurance sector—*Continental Casualty*—where the tribunal upheld the claim of necessity to dismiss most of the investor's claims.[68]

The results send quite an uncertain signal: Argentina's necessity defense prevailed in two cases (*LG&E* and *Continental Casualty*) and failed in ten (*CMS, El Paso, BG, National Grid, Total, EDFI, AWG, InterAgua, Impregilo*, and *SAUR*), with two cases (*Enron* and *Sempra*) a blank slate, insofar as the annulment committee overturned the original panel's rejection of the necessity defense but did not reach its own conclusion. In the cases where the tribunals rejected necessity, the rejection was generally based on a finding, typically after considering expert testimony, that Argentina had policy tools at its disposal (other than the measures against the investors) to address the crisis, or that Argentina had contributed to the economic situation through its policies. Either of these findings essentially meant that its measures were not 'necessary' to handle the crisis under the treaty or customary law. Numerous subsidiary issues were considered, notably the point at which a state can be said to contribute to the emergency and at which it cannot take advantage of the defense.

[62] *LG&E, supra* note 60, para. 266.

[63] *Enron Corp. v Argentina*, ICSID Case No. ARB/01/3, Award, 22 May 2007, paras. 313, 339; Annulment Decision, 30 July 2010, paras. 355–395, 400–405.

[64] *Sempra Energy v Argentina*, ICSID Case No. ARB/02/16, Award, 28 September 2007; Annulment Decision, 29 June 2010, paras. 186–222 (annulled because the tribunal applied customary law but not the BIT).

[65] *El Paso Energy International Co. v Argentina*, ICSID Case No. ARB/03/15, Award, 31 October 2011.

[66] *BG Group v Argentina*, UNCITRAL, Award, 24 December 2007, paras. 407–412; *National Grid v Argentina*, UNCITRAL, Award, 3 November 2008, paras. 260–262; *Total v Argentina*, ICSID Case No. ARB/04/1, Decision on Liability, 27 December 2010, paras. 482–484; *EDFI, supra* note 60, paras. 1171–1181.

[67] *Suez, Vivendi, and AWG v Argentina*, ICSID Case No. ARB/03/19, Decision on Liability, 30 July 2010, paras. 257–265 [hereinafter *AWG*]; *Suez and InterAgua v Argentina*, ICSID Case No. ARB/03/17, Decision on Liability, 30 July 2010, paras. 236–243; *Impregilo v Argentina*, ICSID Case No. ARB/07/17, Award, 21 June 2011, paras. 344–359; *SAUR, supra* note 60, paras. 458–463.

[68] *Continental Casualty, supra* note 60, paras. 192–236; Annulment Decision, 16 September 2011 (declining to annul).

Several panels noted human rights issues. The *CMS* panel seemed to reject the relevance of fundamental human rights when it wrote that the Constitution and BIT obligations were compatible 'because the Constitution carefully protects the right to property, just as the treaties on human rights do, and secondly because there is no question of affecting fundamental human rights when considering the issues presented by the parties'.[69] The tribunal in *SAUR* recognized the right to safe water as a fundamental human right, but then placed it on the same plane as the rights of investors:

> En réalité, les droits de l'homme en général, et le droit à l'eau en particulier, constituent l'une des diverses sources que le Tribunal devra prendre en compte pour résoudre le différend.... L'accès à l'eau potable constitue, du point de vue de l'État, un service public de première nécessité et, du point de vue du citoyen, un droit fondamental.... Pour ce motif... l'ordre juridique peut et doit réserver à l'Autorité publique des fonctions légitimes de planification, de supervision, de police, de sanction, [et] d'intervention...
>
> Le droit fondamental à l'eau et le droit de l'investisseur à bénéficier de la protection offerte par l'APRI opèrent sur des plans différents:... l'administration publique... dispose de pouvoirs spéciaux pour en garantir la jouissance en raison de la souveraineté du droit fondamental à l'eau; mais l'exercice de ces pouvoirs ne se fait pas de façon absolue et doit, au contraire, être conjugué avec le respect des droits et des garanties octroyés à l'investisseur étranger en vertu de l'APRI. Si les pouvoirs publics décident... de traiter l'investisseur injustement .... en violant l'APRI, l'investisseur aura le droit d'être indemnisé.[70]

But these tribunals, to the extent they discussed human rights at all, summarily found no conflict between the two obligations and concluded that Argentina could have complied with both.[71]

[69] *CMS Gas* Award, *supra* note 61, para. 121.

[70] *SAUR, supra* note 60, paras. 330–331:

> In reality, human rights in general, and the right to water in particular, represent one of the various sources that the Tribunal will have to take into account to resolve the case.... Access to potable water represents, from the state's point of view, a public service of the first order, and, from the point of view of the citizen, a fundamental right.... For this reason... the legal order can and must reserve to the public authorities the legitimate functions of planning, supervising, policing, sanctioning, and intervening...
>
> The fundamental right to water and the right of the investor to benefit from the protection offered by the BIT operate on different planes:... the public administration disposes of special powers to guarantee the enjoyment [of the former] by reason of the supremacy of the fundamental right to water; but the exercise of these powers cannot be done in an absolute way and must, on the contrary, be combined with respect for the rights and guarantees provided to the foreign investor under the BIT. If the public authorities decide... to treat the investor unjustly... in violation of the BIT, the investor will have the right to be compensated.

[71] See, e.g., *AWG, supra* note 67, para. 262 ('Argentina is subject to both... human rights *and* treaty obligation[s], and must respect both of them equally. Under the circumstances of these cases, Argentina's human rights obligations and its investment treaty obligations are not inconsistent, contradictory, or mutually exclusive'); *EDFI, supra* note 60, para. 912 ('[N]o showing has been made that Argentina was not able to comply with the relevant [human rights] treaty provisions later, through a rectification of the economic equilibrium which had been disrupted by the Emergency

2. *Tentative conclusions about the justice of the necessity defense*

The Argentine cases should give us pause about the ability of investment law to preserve a state's policy space to protect human rights, although the diverse outcomes also militate against concluding that those rules are unjust. Moreover, given that the customary international law rule regarding necessity offers the possibility of exculpating violations of other rules of international law (for example trade law) during emergencies, our concerns over thin justice extend beyond investment law to that customary law rule as well. That is, if the investment cases suggest that the defense of necessity is so narrow that it prevents states from protecting basic human rights when they need to—or effectively does so by making it so expensive that they will not wish to—then at least *that* rule does not pass the test of thin justice. Four trends from the investment cases should give us cause for worry.

- First, if tribunals insist on a very high standard to demonstrate a state of emergency under a BIT (or 'grave and imminent peril' under custom), such an interpretation might preclude the state from taking measures where basic human rights are at stake. Thus, the tribunal in *CMS* said that in the absence of 'total economic and social collapse',[72] a state may not invoke necessity.[73] But we can imagine numerous scenarios short of such collapse, for example natural disasters, where the government may need to violate FET or the ban on uncompensated takings. Thus, the nature of a crisis and the interests to be protected during it must take into account basic human rights.[74]
- Second, if a tribunal subjects a state's decisions as to what is necessary to a very high threshold—for example did the state take the least FET-inconsistent means to protect human rights under the circumstances—as seems to have been done in the *Sempra*, *CMS*, and *AWG* cases[75]—the state could be cut off from reasonable actions needed to protect its citizens from harm. (The *LG&E* tribunal managed to apply this standard and conclude that Argentina's actions were the only ones possible.)[76] Article 25 of the ILC Articles on State Responsibility requires that the BIT-inconsistent measures be the 'only way' to safeguard an essential interest. In the key ICJ case concerning that issue, between Hungary and Slovakia, the Court rejected Hungary's claims that it needed to suspend construction on a dam over the Danube by noting that other methods, though

Measures.'). Despite the statement of principle in *SAUR* quoted earlier, the tribunal never discussed human rights again in its opinion.

[72] *CMS Gas* Award, *supra* note 61, paras. 354–355.

[73] See also *Sempra* Award, *supra* note 64, para. 348 (a situation involves essential state interest when it 'compromise[s] the very existence of the State and its independence').

[74] Francisco Orrego Vicuña, 'Softening Necessity', in Mahnoush H. Arsanjani et al. (eds.), *Looking to the Future: Essays on International Law in Honor of W. Michael Reisman* (Boston, MA: Martinus Nijhoff Publishers, 2011) 741, 747–8.

[75] *Sempra* Award, *supra* note 64, para. 350 ('whether the measures taken under the Emergency Law were the "only way" to achieve this result, and whether no other alternative was available'); *CMS Gas* Award, *supra* note 61, para. 324; *AWG, supra* note 67, paras. 235, 237, 260.

[76] *LG&E, supra* note 60, para. 257.

'more costly', were 'available' to avoid environmental harm and supply drinking water.[77]

But how much more costly? Certainly feasibility must play a role. The *Continental Casualty* tribunal interpreted necessity under the BIT with reference to WTO caselaw and found it far more deferential to states—asking only 'whether the Measures were apt to and did make such a material or a decisive contribution' to protecting the state's essential interests and whether alternative measures 'would not have been reasonably available or would have been impracticable or speculative as to their effects'.[78] Thus, analogous to trade law, if investment law and the necessity defense impose an undue burden on host states in terms of alternatives to the BIT-violating action, it can interfere with the enjoyment of basic human rights.

- Third, if even a small contribution by the state to the crisis situation cuts off the possibility of overriding its FET duty, then it would again seem that the law is seriously constraining a state's ability to protect basic human rights. Thus, in *El Paso*, the tribunal considered it enough that the state has 'significantly' or 'substantial[ly]' so contributed, although the panel split 2–1 as to whether that had been proved.[79]
- Fourth, just as tribunals have been reluctant to bring human rights into their FET considerations, they have not given them ample discussion in their necessity jurisprudence. We see an acknowledgment of the importance of human rights, but in the end those rights do not seem to give the host state any margin of maneuver under the necessity defense. In the end, the tribunals seem to regard the gravity of the human rights at issue as legally irrelevant, and only the availability of other tools is significant.

Two points cut against these concerns about the justice of investment law. First, the tribunals may be correct that Argentina could have, without much difficulty, responded to the crisis without violating the BIT. After all, almost all the tribunals reached this conclusion, which suggests that the Argentine emergency cases may not be the right ones to demonstrate the potential injustice of investment law and the necessity defense. Second, as with trade law, even if a state should be allowed to invoke necessity, thin justice does not demand that it be completely exempt from paying investors. It is not unjust for the state to pay something, though in the limiting—and probably hypothetical—case, it would be unjust if payment were to undermine the enjoyment of basic human rights. This issue raises complex questions about what the state should be required to do in such

[77] *Case Concerning the Gabcikovo-Nagymaros Project (Hungary/Slovakia)* [1997] ICJ Rep 7, para. 55 (25 September).

[78] *Continental Casualty, supra* note 60, paras. 196, 198.

[79] *El Paso, supra* note 65, paras. 615–624, 665–670; *EDFI, supra* note 60, para. 1173 ('Argentina's contribution to its economic situation is clear or was far from negligible.'); but see *LG&E, supra* note 60, para. 256 (relevance of Argentina's 'desire to slow down by all means available' the crisis). See also Orrego Vicuña, 'Softening Necessity', *supra* note 74, at 748 (criticizing approval of 'retrospective repentance').

emergencies, for example cut its military expenditures in order to keep its promise to investors. But thin justice does not demand that necessity should preclude all payments by the host state.[80]

The necessity defense can thus be analogized to a door providing the state with a means to protect human rights notwithstanding the protections that investment law provides for foreign investors. If the norms of FET or compensation for expropriation do not provide the state with the policy space it needs to protect rights, then treaty or customary law-based defenses of necessity can, if interpreted in a human rights-oriented manner, help preserve the thin justice of investment law norms. But the trend in the caselaw is to keep this door closed. Thin justice requires that investment law (and customary law norms on necessity) not prevent the state from protecting human rights. Perhaps we are just waiting for the case with the right facts to show whether the law is thinly just in this manner.

III. Institutional Impediments to a Just Investment Law

No single institution assumes the kind of prescriptive, interpretive, or enforcement role in investment law that the WTO does for trade. BITs are negotiated in pairs, not through any centralized process. When disputes between foreign investors and host states arise, if renegotiation of an investment is not possible and the investor does not swallow its losses or settle for payment from an insurance company, it may institute legal proceedings in either domestic courts or international arbitral fora. In addition, investor-state claims can end up before regional courts, whether the European Court of Justice or the European Court of Human Rights.

Of all these arenas, arbitral bodies addressing investor-state disputes have assumed a special importance in the interpretation of investment law. States and investors follow and rely upon their interpretations, and those addressing future disputes will cite, consider, or even adopt the reasoning of earlier tribunals. Most are ad hoc tribunals resolving a single dispute between an investor and a state under a BIT or regional agreement (like NAFTA). Our judgments about investment rules' compatibility with the second pillar of thin justice and, equally important, about the possibility that those rules might achieve a higher standard of justice, will depend in part on the capacity of these tribunals to take human rights into account. States are certainly free to contract around or override the interpretations of arbitral panels through new BITs,[81] so they remain, as it were, the master of future investment law, but the influence of tribunals is quite significant.

[80] Nor does customary international law. See ILC Articles on State Responsibility, Art. 27 (necessity and other rules precluding wrongfulness do not cover the question of compensation).

[81] The three NAFTA parties effectively overruled one tribunal's interpretation of FET in a Note of Interpretation issued in 2001. See NAFTA Free Trade Commission, 'Notes of Interpretation of Certain Chapter 11 Provisions' (31 July 2001), <http://www.international.gc.ca/trade-agreements-accords-commerciaux/topics-domaines/disp-diff/NAFTA-Interpr.aspx?lang=eng>.

Arbitral tribunals have their own accepted practices—what Thomas Carbonneau calls 'the arbitral legal culture'.[82] Arbitrators who treat their profession seriously will do certain obvious things to further that end—notably decide only matters within the scope of the arbitration, utilize rules that treat each party equally and fairly, and write opinions that rely on persuasive legal reasoning.[83] That culture includes several additional components: (a) repeat players, notably the arbitrators and counsel who appear in many cases, as well as secretariat officials from institutions like ICSID or the International Chamber of Commerce; (b) ethical constraints on arbitrators, for example concerning their relationship with the parties that appoint them;[84] (c) a desire by arbitrators to get reappointed to future arbitrations, as a result of which their opinions will stay within the mainstream of legal opinion; and (d) an awareness by arbitrators of the constraints on the enforceability of awards both legally and practically.[85]

It also seems clear from the caselaw that that arbitral culture does *not* include a proclivity to focus on human rights issues in arbitral awards. The rulings rather suggest an aversion to addressing most non-investment norms, including human rights.[86] (States too have been reluctant to defend their actions on human rights grounds.) Most arbitrators are investment law specialists. Human rights law is not only beyond their expertise, but probably seen by them as not particularly relevant to an arbitration and an issue that, if discussed, might hurt the arbitrator's chance for reappointment. Some of the ideas proposed earlier for ensuring the thin justice of investment law would be at odds with the commercial orientation of the arbitral culture. Although arbitrators faced with a state claiming directly that its duties to human rights justify its conduct to a foreign investor would need to address such a claim or risk annulment, it is difficult to be confident that they would give it much weight. The tribunals' reluctance to address human rights concerns are part of a much larger set of concerns on the part of host states that the arbitral process is now skewed against them. These worries have led Ecuador, Bolivia, and Venezuela to withdraw from the ICSID Convention entirely and

[82] See Thomas E. Carbonneau, 'Arbitral Law-Making', *Mich JIL* 25 (2004): 1183, 1199.

[83] Failure to do so opens up the possibility of nullification or non-enforcement of the award under treaties or domestic laws. Convention on the Settlement of Investment Disputes Between States and Nationals of Other States, 18 March 1965, Art. 52, 575 UNTS 159; Convention on the Recognition and Enforcement of Foreign Arbitral Awards, 10 June 1958, Art. 5, 330 UNTS 38. See generally W. Michael Reisman, *Systems of Control in International Adjudication and Arbitration: Breakdown and Repair* (Durham, NC: Duke University Press, 1992).

[84] See, e.g., International Bar Association, 'IBA Guidelines on Party Representation in International Arbitration' (2013), <http://www.ibanet.org>.

[85] On the repeat players in the arbitration process, see Sergio Puig, 'Social Capital in the Arbitration Market', *EJIL* 25 (2014): 387; on enforceability, see Günther J. Horvath, 'The Duty of the Tribunal to Render an Enforceable Award', *J Intl Arb* 18 (2001): 135.

[86] See Moshe Hirsch, 'Interactions between Investment and Non-investment Obligations', in Peter Muchlinski, Federico Ortino, and Christoph Schreuer (eds.), *The Oxford Handbook of International Investment Law* (New York: Oxford University Press, 2008) 154; Moshe Hirsch, 'Investment Tribunals and Human Rights: Divergent Paths', in P.M. Dupuy, F. Francioni, and E.U. Petersmann (eds.), *Human Rights in International Investment Law and Arbitration* (New York: Oxford University Press, 2009) 97.

Australia to issue a policy refusing to accept any investor-state arbitration clauses in new investment treaties.[87]

This state of affairs cannot be blamed on international law doctrine. International law has a variety of methodologies by which human rights law can be discussed even when the arbitral body's task seems to be focused on the interpretation of a BIT.[88] Beyond the arbitral awards discussed previously, that at least pay lip service to human rights, one other case is worth mention. In the 2009 arbitration between an Israeli company and the Czech Republic, brought under the Israel-Czech BIT, the tribunal dismissed the case based on its view that the claimant did not have a bona fide investment in the Czech Republic and thus that the tribunal lacked jurisdiction under the ICSID Convention. It nonetheless added that protection could not be 'granted to investments made in violation of the most fundamental rules of protection of human rights, like investments made in pursuance of torture or genocide or in support of slavery or trafficking of human organs'.[89] But these little occasional paragraphs aside, the landscape is still fairly barren when it comes to the incorporation of even basic human rights into investment arbitration.

Other tribunals that have addressed claims by investors against states have far more willingly considered the responsibility of governments to protect human rights. Thus, the European Court of Justice considered a claim by a German company importing mature-themed videos that a German government order to cease mail-order operations violated the company's rights under EU law to move goods freely across borders. It rejected the claim based on Germany's argument that it had a duty to protect German children under human rights law.[90] It recognized 'the Member States' right to take the measures necessary for reasons relating to the protection of young persons'.[91] Moreover, as we might expect, the European Court of Human Rights, when addressing claims that governments have violated property rights, have readily integrated the state's responsibilities to protect human rights into its reasoning.[92]

[87] See Jürgen Kurtz, 'Australia's Rejection of Investor-State Arbitration: Causation, Omission and Implication', *ICSID Rev: Foreign Inv LJ* 27 (2012): 65; Malcolm Langford, 'Cosmopolitan Competition: The Case of International Investment', in Cecilia M. Bailliet and Katja Franko Aas (eds.), *Cosmopolitan Justice and its Discontents* (Milton Park: Routledge, 2011), 178, 185–9.

[88] For one approach, see Simma and Kill, 'Harmonizing Investment Protection', *supra* note 5.

[89] *Phoenix Action, Ltd v Czech Republic*, ICSID Case No. ARB/06/5, Award, 15 April 2009, para. 78. See also *World Duty Free Company Ltd v Republic of Kenya*, ICSID Case No. ARB/00/7, Award, 4 October 2006, para. 157 (bribes paid by a British company operating duty-free stores at the Nairobi airport to the Kenyan President violated international public policy as well as Kenyan law, thereby rendering the contract unenforceable). For more on this issue, see generally Hilmar Raeschke-Kessler and Dorothee Gottwald, 'Corruption', in Peter Muchlinski, Federico Ortino, and Christoph Schreuer (eds.), *The Oxford Handbook of International Investment Law* (New York: Oxford University Press, 2008) 584.

[90] Case C-244/06 *Dynamic Medien Vertriebs GmbH v Avides Media AG* [2008] ECR I-505.

[91] Ibid., para. 41. See generally Bruno De Witte, 'Balancing of Economic Law and Human Rights by the European Court of Justice', in P.M. Dupuy, F. Francioni, and E.U. Petersmann (eds.), *Human Rights in International Investment Law and Arbitration* (New York: Oxford University Press, 2009) 197.

[92] See, e.g., *Velikovi and ors v Bulgaria*, ECHR App. No. 43278/98, 48 EHRR 27 (2007), para. 172 (considering whether Bulgarian law returning land to victims of communist-era nationalizations

There are some signs of change on the horizon within investor-state arbitration. A number of investment panels or the states signing investment agreements agreed to allow for the submission of *amicus curiae* briefs from interested third parties. Some of these filings, like that by a Native American advocacy group in the *Glamis* case and five NGOs in the *AWG* case, have argued human rights concerns.[93] A range of other reforms has been proposed to make investment arbitration more transparent, and some have been adopted in BITs.[94] These proposals seek to move investment arbitration away from its party-controlled approach closer to what Gus Van Harten has called a public law system of adjudication.[95] The success of these reforms will help determine whether investment law will pass muster under the standard of thin justice. At the same time, much remains in the hands of states, and if they make the decision to incorporate human rights concerns more explicitly into investment treaties, arbitrators will have little choice but to take these norms into account.

IV. The Systemic Critique of International Investment Law

The final and broadest critique of international investment law claims that its flaws are not limited to its constraining effect on a state's policy space or the institutions that enforce it, but include overall harmful effects caused by foreign investment. For critics, foreign investment, while in theory important for development, has in practice contributed to corruption, environmental degradation, and severe income inequality within developing states. Investment law promotes the interests of—and gives rights only to—corporations, principally from the North, while burdening developing states in ways that they did not expect. Moreover, investment law does not place obligations on foreign investors or on their home states to address these problems, thereby contributing to these harms. The formally reciprocal nature of BITs is thus undermined by their utility only to one party to the treaty—the capital exporting state—and by the asymmetry of duties between investors and host states. Observers from both South and North criticize the lopsided nature of BITs and the harms caused by the duties placed

violated the property rights of later owners who had obtained property based on abuse of official positions, and concluding that: 'The underlying public interest in such cases is to restore justice and respect for the rule of law').

[93] See NAFTA Free Trade Commission, 'Statement of the Free Trade Commission on non-disputing party participation' (7 October 2003), <http://www.state.gov/documents/organization/38791.pdf>. See also James Harrison, 'Human Rights Arguments in *Amicus Curiae* Submissions: Promoting Social Justice?', in P.M. Dupuy, F. Francioni, and E.U. Petersmann (eds.), *Human Rights in International Investment Law and Arbitration* (New York: Oxford University Press, 2009) 396.

[94] See, e.g., U.S. Model BIT, *supra* note 3, Art. 29.

[95] Gus Van Harten, *Investment Treaty Arbitration and Public Law* (New York: Oxford University Press, 2007); see also José E. Alvarez and Karl P. Sauvant (eds.), *The Evolving International Investment Regime: Expectations, Realities, Options* (New York: Oxford University Press, 2011).

on host states in them, attacks that build on and overlap with the policy space critique.[96]

A. Causal challenges

The relationship between FDI and the welfare of poor people in developing countries is extraordinarily complex and turns a great deal on the host country's policies, the industry concerned, and the structure of the investment. Certain foreign investment flows have been shown to be helpful to developing countries and others less helpful or even harmful.[97] As for the effect of investment law on developing states, international relations scholars have hypothesized that BITs signal to foreign investors that the state will be a safe place in which to invest and serve to lock in host states on their promises to investors by making it more costly to their reputations to violate them. But the empirical studies have reached differing conclusions on whether states that conclude BITs receive greater inward foreign investment.[98] Moreover, the possible effects of BITs and investment law on foreign investment are quite distinct from the effect of those rules on the basic human rights—notably the rights to life, health, and food—of those in developing states. The causal questions discussed in Chapter 10 with respect to trade rules apply in equal force to investment rules.

To illustrate the causal challenges, we can consider the series of horrific accidents in the Bangladesh apparel industry in recent years, notably the fire in November 2012 that killed 112 people and the building collapse in April 2013 that killed over 1,100 workers. The factories, owned and operated by Bangladeshi companies, produced apparel under contract for large multinational companies, including Benetton, Bon Marché, H&M, and Walmart.[99] The dangerous conditions in

[96] See, e.g., M. Sornarajah, *The International Law on Foreign Investment*, 3rd ed. (New York: Cambridge University Press, 2010) 172–233; Joseph E. Stiglitz, 'Regulating Multinational Corporations: Towards Principles of Cross-Border Legal Frameworks in a Globalized World Balancing Rights with Responsibilities', *Am U Intl L Rev* 23 (2007): 451, 506–29. Pogge's criticism of the resource privilege can also be considered as part of the systemic critique of foreign investment law.

[97] See generally Theodore H. Moran, Edward M. Graham, and Magnus Blomstrom (eds.), *Does Foreign Direct Investment Promote Development?* (Washington DC: Institute for International Economics, 2005). Compare Joseph E. Stiglitz, *Globalization and its Discontents* (New York: W.W. Norton, 2002) 67–73, with Michael Klein, Carl Aaron, and Bita Hadjimichael, 'Foreign Direct Investment and Poverty Reduction', Briefing Paper, OECD Global Forum on International Investment, 26 March 2001, <http://www.oecd.org/daf/inv/investmentstatisticsandanalysis/2422017.pdf>.

[98] See, e.g., the studies in Karl P. Sauvant and Lisa E. Sachs (eds.), *The Effect of Treaties on Foreign Direct Investment: Bilateral Investment Treaties, Double Taxation Treaties, and Investment Flows* (New York: Oxford University Press, 2009); UNCTAD, 'The Role of International Investment Agreements in Attracting Foreign Direct Investment to Developing Countries' (2009), UNCTAD/DIAE/IA/2009/5, <http://www.unctad.org/en/Docs/diaeia20095_en.pdf>; Todd Allee and Clint Peinhardt, 'Contingent Credibility: The Impact of Investment Treaty Violations on Foreign Direct Investment', *Intl Org* 65 (2011): 401, 404–6.

[99] See Steven Greenhouse, 'Clothiers Act to Inspect Bangladeshi Factories', *New York Times*, 7 July 2013, <http://www.nytimes.com>.

these factories led to the violation of the rights to life and health of these workers. But the foreign companies' purchases of apparel were probably not governed by international investment law because purchases are not investments.[100]

Even if a factory in Bangladesh were set up by a foreign company and thus constituted an investment, we would still need to know if the investment was done pursuant to an investment treaty and whether that treaty's provisions gave the investor guarantees that may have contributed to the accident. As with trade, our appraisal as to the justice or injustice of investment law would turn a great deal on whether we adopt a consequentialist position, one that would balance the advantages to the enjoyment of basic human rights from existing investment law with the disadvantages; or a deontological position that would regard the deaths in Bangladesh as violations of basic human rights that cannot be balanced. In the case of the deaths at the factories, the trumping position is more appealing intuitively, though even the consequentialist position would regard the situation as unjust if the rules that presumably led to the fire had no countervailing benefits.[101] But, as with trade, if we cannot find causal connections between investor protections and violations of basic human rights, then we cannot regard those rules as unjust.

B. Toward new duties on investors

Yet there is still a version of the systemic critique of investment law that remains persuasive, namely that the law is unjust because it lacks affirmative obligations on investors, either to host states or to individuals in them. For if it could be shown that the absence of such duties contributes to violations of basic human rights (at least without overriding benefits to them), the current law does not pass muster under the second pillar. Although the Bangladesh case shows that harms to workers in a multinational supply chain need not arise from a foreign investment, some workers do work for companies that are foreign investments. And to the extent that the investor has significant power over workers, any resultant violations of their basic human rights might be linked to the lack of investor duties under investment law.

In thinking about whether and how to change international investment law, we should recall Trachtman's concerns regarding trade law and consider whether investment law is a useful vehicle for improving worker safety.[102] The most direct avenue for the protection of worker rights might well be to help the state improve its capacity to enforce its own laws and place additional responsibilities on the purchasers of the clothing. As the state has the primary duty to protect the rights

[100] On the structure of the Bangladeshi apparel industry, see Sarah Labowitz and Dorothée Bauman-Pauly, *Business as Usual is Not an Option: Supply Chains and Sourcing After Rana Plaza* (New York University Stern School Center for Business and Human Rights, April 2014).

[101] If the provision were common to most BITs, we could speak about international investment law as a whole being unjust due to such provisions as opposed to one treaty.

[102] See Chapter 10, note 121.

of its residents, this path may be more efficient. European companies that buy from Bangladeshi factories, in response to the disasters in Bangladesh (including the effect on their image and profits) signed on to a code of conduct in 2013 to do just that. It sets up a new inspection regime, funded by the companies, meant to be transparent and credible, requiring purchasers to sever contact with factories that do not participate in inspections.[103] American companies opposed to certain parts of the European scheme set up their own inspection regime, leading to accusations by each that the other regime is too weak.[104] Even with the disagreements between the two monitoring groups, this direct route to improving worker safety would appear to be (it is premature to know its effects) more efficient than a process of getting Bangladesh to sign new BITs with worker protections or amend its BITs to include such provisions.

If we move beyond the clothing industry, since the mid-2000s, prodded by NGOs and civil society, both states and corporations have begun to accept the important role that corporations play in both the violation and improvement of human rights. As a result, they have engaged in an impressive array of lawmaking to place responsibilities on corporations and even their states of origin—not just host states—for the protection of human rights.[105] One avenue to this end might be to amend BITs to include investor or home state duties.[106] Yet the route taken thus far has been not to focus on BITs. Rather, states and industries have prepared soft law instruments and codes for particular industries—like the extractive or apparel industries—with some home states of investors passing regulations as well.[107] In 2011, the UN's special expert on this issue, John Ruggie, issued the so-called Guiding Principles on Business and Human Rights, which set forth the legal duties of the host state and the responsibilities of business enterprises and now serve as a highly significant marker for what is expected of investors, purchasers, contractors, and other businesses.[108]

[103] See 'Accord on Fire and Building Safety in Bangladesh', 13 May 2013, <http://www.industriall-union.org/sites/default/files/uploads/documents/2013-05-13_-_accord_on_fire_and_building_safety_in_bangladesh_0.pdf>.

[104] See 'Alliance for Bangladesh Worker Safety, Bangladesh Worker Safety Initiative', <http://www.bangladeshworkersafety.org/files/Alliance-Action-Plan-Package-FINAL.pdf>; Steven Greenhouse and Elizabeth A. Harris, 'Battling for a Safer Bangladesh', *New York Times*, 21 April 2014.

[105] For a theoretical grounding of this need, see Steven R. Ratner, 'Corporations and Human Rights: A Theory of Responsibility', *Yale LJ* 111: 443 (2001); see also Sornarajah, *The International Law on Foreign Investment, supra* note 96, 144–71.

[106] See International Institute for Sustainable Development, 'IISD Model International Agreement on Investment for Sustainable Development' (2005) 9–11, 16–17, <http://www.iisd.org/pdf/2005/investment_model_int_agreement.pdf>.

[107] For an example of non-binding industry codes, see, e.g., Extractive Industries Transparency Initiative Standard, <http://eiti.org>; Fair Labor Association Workplace Code of Conduct, <http://www.fairlabor.org/our-work/labor-standards>; for a domestic statute, see Dodd-Frank Wall Street Reform and Consumer Protection Act, P.L. 111–203, § 1502 (disclosure requirements related to trade in conflict minerals).

[108] See UN Human Rights Council, Guiding Principles on Business and Human Rights: Implementing the United Nations 'Protect, Respect and Remedy' Framework, 21 March 2011, UN Doc. A/HRC/17/31; see also United Kingdom Foreign & Commonwealth Office, 'Good Business: Implementing the UN Guiding Principles on Business and Human Rights' (September 2013), <https://www.gov.uk/government/publications/bhr-action-plan>.

We might see these developments as proof of Trachtman's point of seeking justice in multiple areas of the law. Insofar as these initiatives cover all sorts of corporate conduct, not just investment, they show the importance of finding the right site for justice. But I think they also show that international investment law itself is expanding in its legal sources beyond investment treaties and customary rules and also deepening in its appreciation of human rights. Investors and their home states are now seen as not only having the rights given them by investment treaties, but also duties. By gradually accepting these responsibilities, decision-makers prescribing international law are closing a gap in the protection of human rights in traditional investment law.

V. Conclusion

International investment law's two core norms of fair and equitable treatment and the duty to compensate turn out to yield quite a complex landscape of state and arbitral decisionmaking. As with trade, the justice of these norms in terms of their interference with basic human rights was assessed from the perspective of three major critiques. The policy space critique required an inquiry into caselaw concerning those two norms as well as the ancillary norm excusing a state's conduct based on necessity. The caselaw is generally too undeveloped to show that investment law has been authoritatively interpreted in a way that prevents states from protecting basic human rights, but some of the signs, particularly in some of the Argentina cases, are discouraging in the way that tribunals consistently downplay human rights concerns.

The institutional critique also leaves us with cause for unease, as the arbitral culture does not yet seemed to be attuned to the possibility that the law may have this effect nor how investment law and human rights responsibilities can be reconciled. Serious reforms will be needed to ensure that the institutions interpreting investment law do not ignore those responsibilities of host states. As for the systemic critique, like the similar critique in trade law, it hinges on certain causal claims that are not yet proved. Certainly foreign investment has caused harms in some situations, with the death toll in Bangladesh among the most obscene, but it is not clear that any of these harms are associated with international *law* on foreign investment. As for the law's lack of affirmative duties on investors, some limited progress is being made to create new responsibilities on corporations through industry-specific regulations or codes of conduct.

* * *

With respect to both trade and investment (covered in this chapter and Chapter 10), despite their differing rules and the institutions to implement them, several common themes emerged. First, the core norms of trade and investment provisionally pass muster as thinly just, insofar as they neither explicitly prevent the state from protecting basic human rights nor have they generally been interpreted (with the key exception being the necessity defense in investment cases) thus far to do so. A more conservative way of stating this appraisal is that, at a minimum, when we consider the three main critiques—policy space, institutional, and systemic—of each body of law, we cannot say that any of those critiques has demonstrated that either body is unjust under the standard of thin justice.

Second, states, the World Trade Organization's Dispute Settlement Body, and investment tribunals have interpreted these norms in ways that could yet end up constraining the state enough that they would interfere with basic human rights by forcing a state to choose between compliance and the protection of its inhabitants (or foreigners') human rights. In the cases and crises they have faced, decisionmakers have recognized the human rights responsibilities or even the obligations of the state, but they also demonstrated first and foremost a commitment to advancing the policy goals of trade and investment law—to which, after all, states agreed in the relevant treaties. The overall mood of the decisions, even when they show some deference to host state interests, is decidedly *not* about the priority of human rights, so we cannot assume that the norms will remain thinly just as applied. Moreover, the existing decisions could have a chilling effect on states' attempt to protect human rights through measures affecting trade or investment.

Third, trade and investment, more than the other subjects in this book, implicate numerous rules that flow from the core norms, as well as ancillary norms, like the rules on necessity. Thus, categorical appraisals are both simplistic and unwise. Instead, we are likely to find currents where the law is clearly not interfering with basic human rights and others where dangers lie due to interpretations by authorized decisionmakers. So the interpretation of the SPS Agreement might be more sensitive to the state's human rights responsibilities than the interpretation of the GATT, just as the interpretation of the rules on expropriation might be more deferential to the state than that of the rules on FET and necessity.

Fourth, trade and investment raise special problems of causation compared to some of the other norms considered in this volume. Although consequentialist reasoning demands a degree of educated prediction as to the impact of a norm on respect for basic human rights, in responding to the systemic critiques of trade and investment law we find ourselves ensnared in competing economic theories about economic development and the role of international regulation in that process. My conclusions are provisional, then, in part because I have been unwilling (as I am unable) to take a firm position in those debates. If we could be confident of the causal connection between trade or investment law and the enjoyment of basic human rights—a confidence that seems more justified in limited areas like Northern agricultural subsidies or the lack of duties on investors for worker safety—the systemic critique would have a great deal more persuasive force. We could then say that the rules are unjust for leaving so many people without the right to food or health. For those who are confident of the effect of all trade and investment rules on respect for basic human rights, these sorts of less nuanced conclusions will be easier.

Lastly, both trade and investment have implicated basic rights of the economic variety—the sort of subsistence rights to which Henry Shue referred—whereas the other norms have been largely about civil and political rights. As a result, more than in the earlier chapters in this book, the norms of international economic law are overshadowed by debates about global distributive justice. This shadow is particularly large because many of the suggested cures to North-South inequalities involve changes to the rules of international economic law, not only for trade and investment, but in other areas like international monetary and financial law. My conclusion that it has not been proved that the core norms of either trade or investment are unjust, even while the dangers of interference with basic human rights are real, may not satisfy those for whom the project of justice with respect to international economic relations must be about major redistribution. But my appraisal of international economic law hardly precludes redistribution of a more robust sort. It should, however, force us to consider very carefully whether that project should be undertaken by amending trade and investment law or by taking other, parallel approaches to economic development.

PART V

LIMITATIONS AND ASPIRATIONS

12

The Limits of Thin Justice: International Humanitarian, Criminal, and Environmental Law

The framework of thin justice has offered a valuable heuristic for understanding the purpose and contours of the core norms of international law as well as a critical evaluative lens for assessing their moral stature. Yet like other frameworks of justice, thin justice has its limits as a tool of understanding and ethical evaluation. In particular, certain core norms of international law do not fit within the framework easily, as their links to peace and basic human rights are elusive or seemingly unimportant for appraising their justice. Thin justice, then, may not pose the right sorts of questions for helping us think about and determine the justice of all of international law.

It is essential to be frank about these limitations rather than claim that the standard can be applied to all norms or contort it into a standard that loses the key attributes of thin justice. At the same time, the very inability of the framework to 'fit' with certain norms tells us something very important about the underlying purposes of those norms and about the modalities by which they can be improved without damaging the thin justice in the system. My discussion of the limits of thin justice focuses on three sets of norms not discussed thus far that merit the qualification as core to international law—those within international humanitarian law (IHL, or the law of armed conflict), international criminal law (ICL), and international environmental law.

I. International Humanitarian Law and the Distinctiveness of Wartime Norms

International humanitarian law or *jus in bello*—the law governing the conduct of armed conflict—is one of the most ancient areas of international law, far older than the norms of *jus ad bellum* discussed in Chapter 4. Its rules on the treatment of prisoners, civilians, and methods of warfare date back to ancient civilizations in India, Greece, and China. The modern law developed beginning in the mid-nineteenth century, accelerating with the drafting of key treaties before and after World Wars I and II—notably the Hague Conventions of 1907, the

Geneva Conventions of 1949, the first two Additional Protocols to the Geneva Conventions of 1977, and treaties on weapons (chemical, bacteriological, and others). Today, the norms apply not only to interstate wars, but civil wars and anti-colonial wars.[1] And IHL places obligations on both states and organized armed groups.[2] It is the subject of exhaustive ethical scrutiny, including the scholarship that has emerged in the generation since Michael Walzer's *Just and Unjust Wars*. It will not be my purpose to revisit most of this ethical analysis, but rather, to see whether the core norms of IHL are consistent with the standard of thin justice.

A. Two levels of norms

For all its complexity in terms of treaty and customary law, IHL can be envisaged as composed of two levels of norms: a *meta-norm* and three distinct *core norms*. The meta-norm is international law's fairly sharp distinction between the obligations upon states with respect to the conduct of a war and their duties when they employ state power during peacetime. This division—what I will call the *separation meta-norm*—was traditionally recognized through the so-called Law of War/ Law of Peace distinction, where the great international law treatises of generations past and present would elaborate upon the two sets of norms in separate volumes.[3] The most critical ramification of the meta-norm today is that, as a general matter, international law gives the state a far freer reign with respect to the treatment of individuals in wartime than in peacetime. Whether with respect to life or death, freedom or detention, free speech or assembly, or the content of criminal law, the individual can generally expect more protections from the law in peacetime than in wartime.

As international law's protections of individuals in peacetime is the ambit of international human rights law, the separation meta-norm means, generally speaking, that international human rights law affords far more protections to the individual than does IHL. Indeed, although IHL developed long before human rights law, today the protections granted by human rights law are considered the default standard for the state's duties to individuals; IHL is today the exceptional regime that applies only in the context of armed conflict. Human rights law is, as Orna Ben-Naftali and Yuval

[1] States and other global actors are currently debating and assessing whether IHL should also apply to sustained military action against non-state actors across borders, as practiced by states against certain terrorist groups. For one useful study, see International Committee of the Red Cross, 'International Humanitarian Law and the Challenges of Contemporary Armed Conflicts', 31 October 2011, International Conference of the Red Cross and Red Crescent Doc. 31IC/11/5.1.2.

[2] Protocol Additional to the Geneva Conventions of 12 August 1949, and Relating to the Protection of Victims of International Armed Conflicts (Protocol I), 8 June 1977, Art. 1(4), 1125 UNTS 4; Protocol Additional to the Geneva Conventions of 12 August 1949, and Relating to the Protection of Victims of Non-International Armed Conflicts (Protocol II), 8 June 1977, Art. 1, 1125 UNTS 609.

[3] See, e.g., L. Oppenheim, *International Law, Volume I: Peace* (New York: Longmans, Green and Co., 1905); L. Oppenheim, *International Law, Volume II: War and Neutrality* (New York: Longmans, Green and Co., 1906).

Shany write, 'the normal order of things'.[4] In essence, then, international law recognizes a sort of temporal limitation on the scope of human rights law, analogous to the territorial limitation on the scope of human rights law discussed in Chapter 8. Just as the duties of states with respect to conduct outside their territory are far more limited than their duties for conduct on their own territory, so their duties are limited once they cross the threshold to war, either with another state or with a domestic insurgency. International human rights law does allow states to derogate from some of their duties to individuals in the event of a 'public emergency which threatens the life of the nation',[5] which would include many wars, but it generally contains a list of protections for individuals that are absent from IHL.[6]

That very emphasis on human rights law as the normal law to govern the state's duties to individuals has resulted in a doctrinal shift in the law that seems to have been generally accepted by states—namely, notwithstanding the different layers of protections in wartime and peacetime, states recognize that human rights law applies *in principle* even during armed conflict.[7] However, coupled with that acceptance is the insistence that the meaning of the particular human rights law protections will be quite distinct during war—in formal terms, that IHL is a kind of *lex specialis* that informs our interpretation of, and effectively limits the protections provided by, international human rights law.[8]

The three core norms of IHL reflect this meta-norm insofar as they prescribe very different conduct for the state regarding harm to individuals than does human rights law:

- First, under the principle of *necessity*, states may use only that force against enemy forces needed to remove them as a threat, and thus must avoid inflicting any unnecessary suffering upon the enemy. This prohibition has been operationalized through bans on certain weapons, such as dum-dum bullets, poison gas, and laser-blinding weapons.
- Second, under the principle of *distinction*, states may not target either civilians or military personnel who have been rendered *hors de combat* (outside of combat) as a result of surrender or wounds—those deemed non-combatants and

[4] Orna Ben-Naftali and Yuval Shany, 'Living in Denial: The Application of Human Rights in the Occupied Territories', *Isr L Rev* 37 (2003): 17, 41–2; see also Orna Ben-Naftali, 'Introduction: International Humanitarian Law and International Human Rights Law—Pas de Deux', in Orna Ben Naftali (ed.), *International Humanitarian Law and International Human Rights Law: Pas de Deux* (Oxford: Oxford University Press, 2011) 3, 4 ('paradigmatic shift').

[5] ICCPR, Art. 4.

[6] In some instances IHL provides for greater protections, e.g. on property rights, where the law of occupation provides greater rights than does human rights law. See Sylvain Vité, 'The Interrelation of the Law of Occupation and Economic, Social and Cultural Rights: the Examples of Food, Health and Property', *IRRC* 90, No. 871 (2008): 629, 642–50.

[7] See the discussion of both state practice and the practice of UN Charter bodies to this effect in Louise Doswald-Beck, *Human Rights in Times of Conflict and Terrorism* (Oxford: Oxford University Press, 2011) 6–9.

[8] *Legality of the Threat or Use of Nuclear Weapons* [1996] ICJ Rep 226, para. 25 (Advisory Opinion of 8 July); *Legal Consequences of the Construction of a Wall in the Occupied Palestinian Territory: Advisory Opinion* [2004] ICJ Rep 136, paras 105–106 (Advisory Opinion of 9 July).

thus protected persons—or engage in so-called indiscriminate attacks, where the attack cannot distinguish between civilians and combatants. This prohibition underlies critical bans or limitations on methods of warfare and weapons (such as carpet bombing or cluster munitions) as well as protections of prisoners of war from torture and other ill treatment. It bans the targeting of civilians unless they are directly participating in hostilities.[9]

• Third, under the principle of *proportionality*, states may not take action against military objects or combatants that will cause even incidental, unintended harm to protected persons unless that harm will be outweighed by the military advantage of the operation against the target.[10] Although it is difficult to enforce, this principle has led at least some armies to take potential civilian casualties into account before initiating an attack. In 1999, the office of the Prosecutor of the International Criminal Tribunal for the Former Yugoslavia analyzed NATO's conduct in the Kosovo war and found insufficient evidence to conclude that the resultant civilian casualties violated either the principle of distinction or the principle of proportionality.[11]

IHL has many, many other rules, from special rules on the detention of prisoners and civilians to those on occupied territory to detailed bans on certain weapons systems.[12]

The content of the three norms highlights the fundamental role of the meta-norm. Thus, international human rights law generally forbids the state from killing an individual in peacetime without due process (i.e. following a lawfully authorized conviction) except in the immediate defense of self or others—normally a policeman engaged in self-defense. IHL affirmatively allows the state to kill combatants (and civilians directly participating in hostilities) on the other side and prohibits actions that will lead to civilian deaths only when those actions are intentionally directed against civilians or the harm to civilians is disproportionate to the military advantage.[13] Similarly, whereas international human rights law has a strong bias against (though not a ban on) detention without trial, IHL authorizes it for both prisoners of war and for some civilian security risks. Formally human rights law applies in both situations, but the ban on arbitrary killing or arbitrary deprivation of liberty means something quite different during wartime as compared to peacetime—i.e. that the special rules of IHL inform the meaning of arbitrary during wartime.

[9] Protocol I, *supra* note 2, Art. 51(1)–(3). For the many complexities in interpreting this norm, including who may be targeted and for how long, see International Committee of the Red Cross, *Interpretive Guidance on the Notion of Direct Participation in Hostilities under International Humanitarian Law* (February 2009), <http://www.icrc.org/eng/assets/files/other/icrc-002-0990.pdf>.

[10] Protocol I, *supra* note 2, Art. 51(5)(b).

[11] Final Report to the Prosecutor by the Committee Established to Review the NATO Bombing Campaign Against the Federal Republic of Yugoslavia, 39 ILM 1257, 1272–73 (2000), <http://www.icty.org/sid/10052>.

[12] For a useful summary of the principles, see Gabriella Blum, 'The Fog of Victory', *EJIL* 24 (2013): 391, 415–20.

[13] Civilians directly participating in hostilities are not immune as targets in the first place.

B. Thin justice of international humanitarian law?

Both the meta-norm and three core norms are international law's way of setting apart war from peace and creating a separate regime to regulate combatants during wars. Yet as important as all four are to international law, the standard of thin justice is one that seems to bounce off, rather than analytically cut into, them.

1. *International humanitarian law and the advancement of peace*

In appraising these rules' conformity with the first pillar of thin justice, how can we say whether norms to regulate armed conflict advance or hinder interstate or internal peace? Defenders and detractors of IHL have made claims in either direction. One can start with the International Committee of the Red Cross (ICRC), responsible for both developing and monitoring warring parties' compliance with IHL. It has emphasized that the key purpose of IHL is to 'limit the effects of armed conflict',[14] by which it means that IHL is about limiting human suffering *during* a war. Normally the ever-cautious ICRC does not suggest a linkage between IHL and peace, because it wants to preserve a clear distinction between *jus ad bellum* and *jus in bello*.[15]

Yet at times the ICRC has defended IHL with reference to the rules' effects on war generally. One ICRC publication noted that such rules do not, in fact, prolong wars, although this claim does not address whether IHL actually reduces the incidence of war.[16] Olivier Bangerter, a former ICRC official who has investigated why parties might comply with IHL, went further, pointing out that respect for IHL promotes a more durable peace after civil wars:

> The conclusion and subsequent maintenance of peace are rendered more complex by the memory of atrocities carried out by the parties. First, the negotiators have often been victims themselves through targeting of their family or of their ethnic group; second, they are often under pressure from their constituency not to forget the violations and therefore to be seen to be 'firm' with the enemy. The more equally matched the two sides are, the more heavily the atrocities committed by them will weigh against the conclusion of peace.[17]

14 International Committee of the Red Cross Advisory Service on International Humanitarian Law, 'What is International Humanitarian Law?' (July 2004) 1, <http://www.icrc.org/eng/assets/files/other/what_is_ihl.pdf>.

15 This caution is not driven by logic. For the separation of IHL from *jus ad bellum*, which makes sense in order to convince parties to comply with IHL regardless of the legality of their positions in starting the conflict, does not require arguing that IHL compliance has no effect on the prospect or intensity of wars.

16 Frits Kalshoven and Liesbeth Zegveld, *Constraints on the Waging of War: An Introduction to International Humanitarian Law* (Geneva: International Committee of the Red Cross, 2001) 12–15.

17 Olivier Bangerter, 'Reasons Why Armed Groups Choose to Respect International Humanitarian Law or Not', *IRRC* 93, No. 882 (2011): 353, 366; see also Elizabeth G. Salmon, 'Reflections on International Humanitarian Law and Transitional Justice: Lessons to be Learnt from the Latin American Experience', *IRRC* 88, No. 862 (2006): 327, 329–30.

On the other side are those, like the Prussian General Helmut von Moltke, who have argued, though seemingly without evidence, that the rules of war merely prolong conflict and that decisive victory through recourse to all means to defeat the enemy will bring the war to a speedy conclusion.[18]

The evolution of IHL since von Moltke's time suggests a willingness by states to develop such norms, but that willingness could reflect a variety of calculations, for example (a) that states reject any tradeoff between the development of IHL rules and *peace*—that they accept that protecting some individuals in wartime, in some circumstances, does not undermine peace; (b) that states reject any tradeoff between IHL and *victory*; or (c) that states accept the idea of a tradeoff between IHL and either peace or victory but have decided that the development of IHL norms is worth the costs. As for empirical research, nobody has demonstrated that the presence or absence of IHL norms, or respect for them, causes or inhibits a speedy end to a war, the durability of the subsequent peace, or war avoidance generally.[19]

So whether there really is a trade off is a matter of speculation. I am willing to assume, in the absence of evidence to the contrary, that there is no inherent tradeoff insofar as respect for the core norms of IHL does not cause, prolong, or reignite wars. If Bangerter is correct, then respect for core IHL norms actually promotes peace in an important way. The idea that reconciliation is easier without a history of atrocities seems sensible, although this claim does not address whether IHL actually serves to prevent new wars from breaking out.

Yet even if we assumed that the core norms of IHL promote peace in some way, we have not held the separation meta-norm itself up to scrutiny. For the meta-norm is fundamentally a *comparative* one—that states owe individuals fewer protections in wartime than in peacetime. It is not just about what IHL requires of states, but about what it permits compared to the duties of human rights law. And to argue that the meta-norm either promotes or does not undermine peace seems a much harder hill to conquer. Does a norm allowing the state or non-state armed group to kill civilians incidentally but not deliberately advance or undermine peace compared to one that the state may kill civilians only in self-defense or after a capital trial? It is neither conceptually nor empirically clear which way that core separation cuts in terms of the promotion of peace. Those who find IHL insufficiently protective of individual rights might well argue that more protections would also promote peace; those who want to give states some greater room for maneuver under IHL with respect to civilian casualties might argue that these adjustments might deter or conclude wars more effectively and promote peace.

[18] Von Moltke wrote: 'The greatest kindness in war is to bring it to a speedy conclusion. It should be allowable, with that view, to employ all means save those that are absolutely objectionable.' Translated and quoted in Michael Walzer, *Just and Unjust Wars*, 3rd ed. (New York: Basic Books, 2006) 47.

[19] International relations scholars have shown that the longer wars are characterized by greater IHL violations against civilians, but their research focuses on IHL violations as the dependent rather than independent variable. See, e.g., Alexander B. Downes, *Targeting Civilians in War* (Ithaca, NY: Cornell University Press, 2008).

Richard Brandt's criticism of the principle of distinction on utilitarian grounds seemed close to the latter view, although Brandt's focus was more on the promotion of victory than of peace.[20] In the end, the status of IHL's meta-norm under the first pillar is quite speculative. Allowing certain harms to combatants but limiting them through the principle of necessity, or allowing certain harms to civilians but limiting them through the principles of distinction and proportionality, may or may not promote peace.

2. *International humanitarian law and basic human rights*

Do these basic elements of IHL survive scrutiny under the second pillar? On the one hand, the three core norms do not at first glance interfere with basic human rights. Insofar as they attempt, as the ICRC put it, to 'limit the effects of armed conflict' and thereby protect those caught up in war, they certainly seem connected with the idea of preserving the most basic rights of soldiers and civilians. Yet, as with the first pillar, it is the separation meta-norm and the comparison with human rights law that raises the most serious questions. Can we say that allowing the deliberate killing of soldiers and tolerating some incidental killing of civilians does not interfere with their basic human rights? The law's answer to this question is a simple yes—through the bootstrapping technique of redefining the state's duties regarding human rights in wartime with reference to those very permissions of IHL.[21]

But to ask whether the law is just, we need to engage with another set of debates—about whether individuals do or should enjoy *different* basic human rights in times of war compared to times of peace. For example, does the individual have less of a right to life, freedom of religion, or right to food in wartime than in peacetime (even if some rights, for example the right not to be tortured, apply in both situations)?

The compatibility of the norms of *jus in bello* with thin justice thus turns on what it means to enjoy basic human rights in wartime, in particular as compared to peacetime. The two main strands of contemporary ethical theories of IHL do not directly address *jus in bello* in quite these terms, though one may draw some inferences from their views. Walzer's defense of the basic IHL rules in *Just and Unjust Wars* turns on the notion that war makes combatants and civilians different, giving the former a license to kill and the latter an immunity from deliberate killing. Thus the principle of distinction is defended on the theory that 'no one can be forced to fight or to risk his life, no one can be threatened with war or warred against, unless through some act of his own he has *surrendered or lost his*

[20] R.B. Brandt, 'Utilitarianism and the Rules of War', in Marshall Cohen, Thomas Nagel, and Thomas Scanlon (eds.), *War and Moral Responsibility* (Princeton, NJ: Princeton University Press, 1974) 25.

[21] See *Nuclear Weapons Advisory Opinion, supra* note 8, paras. 74–84. For criticism, see Marko Milanovic, 'Norm Conflicts, International Humanitarian Law, and Human Rights Law', in Orna Ben Naftali (ed.), *International Humanitarian Law and International Human Rights Law: Pas de Deux* (Oxford: Oxford University Press, 2011) 95, 113–16.

rights'; and that soldiers 'as a class are set apart from the world of peaceful activity . . . and this fact radically distinguishes the individual soldier from the civilians he leaves behind. . . . [T]he soldier has already been forced to fight'.[22] Walzer seems to suggest that soldiers in wartime, by virtue of their status that turns each into what Walzer calls 'a dangerous man',[23] have a different set of basic human rights, one that does not include a protection against extrajudicial killing by the enemy state.

On the other hand, Jeff McMahan criticizes the principle of distinction because he sees civilians who support or bear some responsibility for a war of aggression by his state as morally culpable and thus possibly a legitimate target of attack from the wronged side of a conflict, just as the soldier defending his state against an unjust war is an illegitimate target of attack.[24] McMahan reaches this conclusion from a starting point that 'the justifications for killing of people in war are of the same forms as the justifications for the killing of persons in other contexts'.[25] War itself does not change the fundamental rights of individuals, and a person loses his or her protections from attack because, and only because, of 'his having *forfeited* his right not to be attacked . . . in relation to certain persons acting for certain reasons in a particular context'.[26]

Both Walzer's and McMahan's approaches are about distinguishing between the legitimate target and the truly innocent, but do so in fundamentally different ways. They give us a sense of the sorts of question we need to consider to decide to what extent the norms of IHL interfere with basic human rights. Walzer sees the person's *status* as a potential threat as defining the scope of his or her human rights; McMahan sees the morality of one's *actions*, including one's choices about which side to support and how, as doing so. Ultimately, it would seem that we need to take a position (within these debates or others) about whether and how the state of armed conflict changes the content of the basic human rights enjoyed by individuals—and of which individuals, civilians or warriors.

As I have defined basic human rights in Chapter 3, those rights do not change because individuals are involved, as combatants or civilians, in an armed conflict. These are fundamental rights to security, subsistence, and protection against the most major threats to the individual. From this perspective of basic human rights, neither Walzer nor McMahan offers a convincing argument for how IHL does or should respect those rights. Walzer's defense of the war convention leaps over any concerns about a soldier's basic human rights by consigning him to be killed by the other side as an inevitable part of how we conduct wars. This might represent

[22] Walzer, *Just and Unjust Wars, supra* note 18, at 135, 144–5 (emphasis added). See also Thomas Nagel, 'War and Massacre', in Marshall Cohen, Thomas Nagel, and Thomas Scanlon (eds.), *War and Moral Responsibility* (Princeton, NJ: Princeton University Press, 1974) 3, 20 ('we must distinguish combatants from noncombatants on the basis of their immediate threat or harmfulness'); Blum, 'The Fog of Victory', *supra* note 12, at 416–19.

[23] Walzer, *Just and Unjust Wars, supra* note 18, at 145.

[24] See generally Jeff McMahan, *Killing in War* (Oxford: Oxford University Press, 2009). This is a simplification of a highly nuanced argument about the liability of soldiers and civilians to attacks.

[25] Ibid., at 156.

[26] Ibid., at 10.

an acceptable moral argument for IHL, but it is not based on respect for basic human rights.

McMahan's attack on current IHL builds on a concern about individual rights insofar as only the morally guilty are liable to attack. But we are not really respecting the rights of civilians if they can so readily be forfeited—if the possibility remains that they can be attacked by the just side in a way that we would not permit a policeman to kill them in peacetime.[27] Moreover, McMahan's idea for respecting the human rights of combatants demands institutions far removed from present-day constraints. For no institution, certainly not the Security Council, can authoritatively determine which side is just and which is unjust in its war participation, a prerequisite under his view to ascertaining each side's rights and duties under a revised IHL. Indeed, this institutional gap causes McMahan to offer begrudging support of the legal principle of distinction even if he finds it morally suspect.[28] My difference with him is that the moral reasoning itself should take account of the institutional realities rather than just use them to justify a second-best position.[29]

If neither Walzer's defense of IHL nor McMahan's alternative demonstrates the law's respect for basic human rights, we might consider an alternative position under which IHL would pass muster under the second pillar only if it treats basic human rights the same in wartime as peacetime. But such an alternative to the status quo requires us to consider the compliance corollary introduced in Chapter 3—namely that, even if *jus in bello* is provisionally unjust for failing to respect the second pillar, in considering alternatives to it we must take into account the prospects for compliance by actors who wage war. In this case, states will not be willing to conduct wars under such rules, just as they are equally unwilling to give up war altogether, wars that international law recognizes their right to conduct in some cases.

The shift to such a norm, on such an important issue, combined with the likelihood that it would be so flagrantly ignored by states undertaking wars, argues against an affirmative endorsement of it. I would not completely rule out the possibility of humanizing war in this direction, but at this point it seems so at odds with state behavior that it must be relegated to ideal theory. Walzer makes a similar point when he writes that 'these are rules of war, rules for war. They have to accommodate the necessities of warfare; they have to make fighting and winning possible. They are not, or they should not be, pacifist rules'.[30]

[27] See ibid., 221–31, specifically at 230, where McMahan states, 'individual civilians may be liable to attack if they bear a significant degree of responsibility for an unjust war'. McMahan nonetheless draws many distinctions to limit the permissibility of such attacks.

[28] See Jeff McMahan, 'The Ethics of Killing in War', *Ethics* 114 (2004): 693, 729–33; Jeff McMahan, 'Laws of War', in Samantha Besson and John Tasioulas (eds.), *The Philosophy of International Law* (Oxford: Oxford University Press, 2010) 493, 506 ('it is more important to deny this legal permission to the unjust, and to prevent its being abused by the just, than it is to offer it to the just on those rare occasions when they would be morally justified in acting on it').

[29] McMahan proposes addressing this institutional shortcoming through the creation of an international court. See Jeff McMahan, 'The Prevention of Unjust Wars', in Yitzhak Benbaji and Naomi Sussman (eds.), *Reading Walzer* (New York: Routledge, 2014) 233, 241–9.

[30] Michael Walzer, 'Coda: Can the Good Guys Win?', *EJIL* 24 (2013): 433, 439.

The result of this analysis is that it is difficult either to defend IHL for respecting basic human rights or to offer a realistic alternative to IHL that does so. I would not wish to preclude some good theory that does either of those, though Walzer's and McMahan's non-human rights-based treatments may be better ways of understanding the justice or injustice of IHL.

Yet these difficulties of assessing IHL under the second pillar of thin justice do not preclude options for reform in order to increase the extent to which IHL protects innocent individuals. In particular, the notion of proportionality could merit significant reform without sacrificing operational needs or the safety of attacking troops.[31] For example, in 2013, U.S. President Obama announced new policies for the use of targeted killing against terrorists that included a requirement that operations take place only with '[n]ear certainty that non-combatants will not be injured or killed'.[32] If other states are willing to apply proportionality on such a near-zero casualty basis, then the principles of distinction and proportionality will come closer to the norms against arbitrary killing in human rights law. Regardless of the current justice or injustice of the meta-norm separating the law of war from the law of peace, this sort of reform would be a welcome thickening of the justice of *jus in bello.*

II. International Criminal Law and the Two Tracks of State and Individual Responsibility

International criminal law is the body of rules and processes that provide for individual criminal responsibility for certain violations of international law. It overlaps with IHL, international human rights law, and other areas of international law insofar as violations of some of the rules in those areas engender the responsibility of individuals and not merely states.[33] Individual criminal responsibility's modern incarnation began after World War I, with some trials for war crimes committed during that conflict as well as treaties on slavery, prostitution, and counter-terrorism providing for individual penalties. The law emerged more dramatically after World War II, with the Allies' decision to try Nazis and Japanese war criminals at tribunals in Nuremberg and Tokyo as well as in numerous military trials, often quite summary, in formerly occupied lands.

[31] Ibid., at 438–44.

[32] White House, Fact Sheet: U.S. Policy Standards and Procedures for the Use of Force in Counterterrorism Operations Outside the United States and Areas of Active Hostilities, 23 May 2013, <http://www.whitehouse.gov/the-press-office/2013/05/23/fact-sheet-us-policy-standards-and-procedures-use-force-counterterrorism>. A footnote defined non-combatants 'as individuals who may not be made the object of attack under applicable international law', and the U.S. Administration has a narrow view of who is included in this category.

[33] For an introduction, see Steven R. Ratner, Jason S. Abrams, and James L. Bischoff, *Accountability for Human Rights Atrocities in International Law: Beyond the Nuremberg Legacy*, 3rd ed. (Oxford: Oxford University Press, 2009) ch. 1.

Its contemporary form took shape in the 1990s with the Security Council's creation of ad hoc courts for the former Yugoslavia and Rwanda; the establishment of hybrid domestic-international courts for Sierra Leone, Cambodia, and Lebanon; and the conclusion of the Statute for the International Criminal Court. Each development had both a substantive law dimension, as those creating these courts codified certain abuses as engendering individual responsibility, and a procedural one as international courts were set up. In addition, since the 1960s, states have completed treaties effectively identifying certain international crimes by authorizing or requiring trials by domestic courts—for human rights abuses (for example torture and enforced disappearances), terrorism-related offenses (for example actions against civilian aircraft), drug trafficking, and corruption.[34] ICL has also become the subject of ethical scrutiny, though far less than international humanitarian law.

A. Two levels of international criminal law

As with IHL, ICL essentially comprises a meta-norm and core norms. The meta-norm is the law's distinction between state responsibility and individual responsibility, what I will call the *differentiated responsibility meta-norm*. The law has mostly responded to the claims of states by putting duties on states, and the failure to comply with those duties makes the state responsible, in terms we might think of as civil responsibility. States found liable for violations of the law have to restore a situation to the status quo before their violation or pay damages. But in the areas covered by ICL, those competing claims have led to a recognition of duties on the individual as well, with criminal responsibility and susceptibility to trial by a domestic or international court.[35] The norms are enforced against individuals in part on the assumption that individual responsibility will be an additional deterrent to the conduct.[36]

Yet individual criminal responsibility remains the exception in international law. When we think about most duties of international law, the state alone is liable if they are breached; the law does not make an individual official of a

[34] I regard an act as internationally criminal even if states have merely required, or even authorized, domestic courts to prosecute the act. See ibid., at 11–13. For a view that limits international crimes to those crimes for which an international court is given jurisdiction, see Bruno Simma and Andreas L. Paulus, 'The Responsibility of Individuals for Human Rights Abuses in Internal Conflicts: A Positivist View', *AJIL* 93 (1999): 302, 308.

[35] International law also provides for group responsibility insofar as IHL norms bind organized armed groups, though it is unclear whether that responsibility is civil or criminal. It also accepts individual civil responsibility insofar as it does not prevent states from providing for such liability (e.g. in the U.S. Alien Tort Statute and Torture Victim Protection Act). The possibility of state criminal responsibility has been discussed, though it was rejected in the important 2001 International Law Commission Articles on State Responsibility. See ILC Articles on State Responsibility, Arts 40–41 and accompanying commentary.

[36] In some cases of individual responsibility, notably piracy, the perpetrators are not agents of the state, so individual liability may be the only way to deter such conduct.

government liable. If, for instance, a state conducts military maneuvers just off the coast of another state without the latter's permission, in violation of innocent passage rules in the law of the sea, international law does not put any legal responsibility on the prime minister or admiral who ordered the maneuvers.[37] So just as we might think of IHL as an exceptional (wartime) regime compared to the (peacetime) norms of international human rights law, ICL is an exceptional (personal) regime compared to the (state-focused) norms governed by state responsibility.

In practice, the operation of the differentiated responsibility meta-norm results in a rather odd relationship between ICL and the other areas of international law. In some instances, ICL recognizes terrible wrongs as crimes—for instance, genocide, crimes against humanity, slavery, and torture. But many terrible wrongs are not international crimes. For example, if a state arbitrarily executes a political opponent in peacetime, an egregious violation of the ICCPR, the action is not an international crime under either treaty or customary international law unless it can be demonstrated that it is part of a campaign of wrongdoing, constituting a crime against humanity or genocide.[38] An act only reaches those levels if it meets certain contextual requirements in the definition of those crimes (part of an attack on a civilian population in the former case, or with an intent to destroy certain groups in the latter case).[39] On the other hand, a single act of governmentally approved torture or enforced disappearance, or the killing of a POW, is an international crime.[40]

To further muddy the waters, many crimes under ICL are not terrible wrongs. For example, the United States regards any violation of the laws of war as a war crime;[41] this would presumably include something as minor as not providing a POW with the opportunity for recreational sports to which he is entitled under the Geneva Conventions.[42] Aircraft hijacking, even if it does not result in any deaths or injuries, is an international crime as well.[43] I once called these divisions examples of the 'schizophrenias' of ICL.[44] Indeed, an additional schizophrenia is that ICL still recognizes that certain violations of IHL in interstate wars are war crimes whereas the exact same violations in civil wars are not.[45] This meta-norm,

[37] For the rules of innocent passage see, UNCLOS, Arts. 18–19.

[38] ICCPR, *supra* note 5, Art. 6. States do have a duty to provide a remedy for such conduct. ICCPR, Art. 2.

[39] See Ratner, Abrams, and Bischoff, *Accountability, supra* note 33, at 37–40, 59–63.

[40] See, e.g., UN Convention Against Torture, Art. 4; International Convention for the Protection of All Persons from Enforced Disappearance, 20 December 2006, Art. 4, UN Doc. A/61/448; Geneva Convention III, Art. 130.

[41] United States Department of the Army, *The Law of Land Warfare: Field Manual 27–10* (1956) section 499.

[42] Geneva Convention III, Art. 38.

[43] Convention for the Suppression of Unlawful Seizure of Aircraft, 16 December 1970, Arts. 1, 2, 860 UNTS 105.

[44] Steven R. Ratner, 'The Schizophrenias of International Criminal Law', *Texas ILJ* 33 (1998): 237.

[45] See ICC Statute, Art. 8(2)(a) and (b) (defining war crimes in international wars) and Art. 8(2)(c) and (e) (defining war crimes in non-international wars).

then, is not just about a division between state responsibility and individual responsibility and an exceptional regime for the latter, but about a division that is at times very hard to justify.

As for the substantive norms of ICL, the number of crimes, albeit small in proportion to the number of duties on states that trigger state responsibility alone, makes it difficult to identify any as core. Certainly the 'big three' listed in the statutes of the ad hoc tribunals for the former Yugoslavia and Rwanda and of the ICC—genocide, crimes against humanity, and war crimes—are major for their historical connection to Nuremberg and the idea of human rights-related atrocities.[46] But the other human rights-related crimes that do not fall within the jurisdiction of an international court—for example torture, slavery, and enforced disappearances—are also significant. And many states would regard the terrorism-related crimes as most important both historically (as they were among the first acts made crimes) and as a response to current realities.[47] Certainly the Security Council's decision in 2001 to require all states to criminalize the financing of acts of international terrorism, regardless of whether those states were a party to a 1999 treaty that required them to do so, was an audacious legislative act by the Council.[48]

Beyond specific crimes, one might identify other norms as core, such as those in what lawyers call the 'general part' of ICL, because they apply to all crimes. These include *nullum crimen sine lege*, the responsibility of non-direct participants through notions of complicity and vicarious responsibility, the rejection of official acts as a defense, or the severe limitation of the 'following orders' defense.[49] Appraisal of the thin justice of all these norms may help us understand something about them, depending on their connection to war and human rights. But because of the large number of norms involved, I will limit my focus to the thin justice of the meta-norm of separation between state (civil) and individual (criminal) responsibility.

B. Thin justice of international criminal law's meta-norm?

The meta-norm of ICL that makes individual criminal responsibility an exceptional regime is not easily amenable to scrutiny under the two pillars of thin justice.

[46] See ICC Statute, Arts. 6–8. The ICC also formally has jurisdiction over aggression, although the amendments to the ICC Statute giving it the ability to exercise such jurisdiction have not yet entered into force. See International Criminal Court Assembly of States Parties, Amendments to the Rome Statute of the International Criminal Court on the Crime of Aggression, Resolution RC/Res.6, 11 June 2010, Annex I (containing proposed amendments to the ICC Statute).

[47] For a list of such treaties, see United Nations Action to Counter Terrorism, 'International Legal Instruments', <http://www.un.org/en/terrorism/instruments.shtml>.

[48] See SC Res. 1373 (28 September 2001), paras. 1(b), 3(d). See also Paul Szasz, 'The Security Council Starts Legislating', *AJIL* 96 (2002): 901, 901.

[49] See generally Ratner, Abrams, and Bischoff, *Accountability, supra* note 33, ch. 6.

1. *The international criminal law meta-norm and the advancement of peace*

Does the limitation of individual criminal responsibility to only a small set of unlawful acts promote or detract from interstate and internal peace? At first blush, it does not seem as if peace is implicated in this limitation. The decision by states to make only a handful of human rights violations international crimes, or to make bribery of a foreign official but not dumping of toxic materials a crime,[50] does not seem to affect peace either way. In one sense, the *enforcement* of ICL might have consequences for peace. As discussed in Chapter 4, if one state seizes a person suspected of an international (or domestic) crime from the territory of another state without the latter's permission, in violation of the norm against non-intervention, this can raise tensions between the two, leading to armed conflict. Or as discussed in Chapter 6, if it seeks to try a sitting or former official of another state for a crime and ignores that person's immunity, this can equally raise tensions.

Yet even in those two situations, the norms that preserve peace are the norms concerning non-intervention and immunity, *not* the meta-norm that makes only some violations of international law crimes. If states decided to enforce ICL without recourse to those particular methods, in ways that did not bring those additional norms into the picture, it would be very difficult to see why a short list of crimes is better or worse for peace than a longer list of crimes.

2. *The international criminal law meta-norm and basic human rights*

The inquiry into the second pillar is also somewhat indeterminate. On the one hand, it might be the case that limiting individual responsibility to relatively few illegal acts interferes with basic human rights in one of two senses: (1) it could be said that such a limit encourages future violations of basic human rights that are subject only to state responsibility and thereby leads to an overall decrease in respect for those rights; or (2) as respect for basic human rights includes some sense of vindicating rights by acknowledging the victim's experience through a criminal trial of her abuser, then if international law provides only for state responsibility, it removes that possibility and undercuts respect for the human rights of particular victims.

On the first of these, it seems quite speculative to link the lack of international criminalization with the increased prevalence of human rights violations. Such a connection puts a great deal of emphasis on international criminality as a causal factor in the prevention of abuses. Although such criminality might deter violations, scholarship is significantly divided on this question, and the data available are subject to multiple interpretations.[51] Moreover, if an act is not an international

[50] The London Dumping Convention requires states to 'prevent and punish' illegal dumping but does not expressly criminalize it. Convention on the Prevention of Marine Pollution by Dumping of Wastes and Other Matter, 29 December 1972, Art. VII(2), 1046 UNTS 137.

[51] For useful commentary, though with respect to the ICC as an institution rather than criminalization generally, see Christopher W. Mullins and Dawn L. Rothe, 'The Ability of the International

crime but it is a domestic crime, the additional deterrent effect of international criminalization is hard to gauge.

On the second possible interference, it appears similarly difficult to know whether limited criminalization per se interferes with vindication of victims' rights. International criminalization can vindicate rights by lessening the possibility of impunity—by encouraging or requiring states to criminalize that act in domestic law, or requiring them to prosecute. But many serious abuses are already international crimes, and the meta-norm does not preclude additional international criminalization. On the other hand, some victims may well not feel vindicated unless all violations of basic human rights engender both state and individual responsibility. As noted in Chapters 6 and 8, where I considered state immunity and universal jurisdiction, respectively, and their effects on the vindication of victims' rights, victims of atrocities have multiple reactions and seek different forms of redress.[52] The thin justice framework thus does not fit easily with the ICL meta-norm.

Yet setting thin justice aside, we can still say that the differentiated responsibility meta-norm remains ethically dissatisfying in one sense—in the haphazard way in which states have recognized some acts but not others as international crimes. One can understand that the institutional constraints of the international legal system limit the scope of acts we would wish to designate as international crimes. International courts cannot be given jurisdiction over more crimes than they can prosecute; and domestic courts cannot be required to prosecute too many violations of international law when they too are stretched for resources. But those acts that do fall within the limits should be determined based on some clear, ethically compelling rationale. Criminal law theory is full of these ideas, and debate is intense about where to draw the line between civil wrongs and crimes.[53]

But international law has simply responded to the political exigencies of the moment. Sometimes, as with terrorism, states initiate the process of criminalization, often in response to dramatic events. Both the spate of airline hijackings in the 1960s and the September 11 attacks led states to draft new treaties in fairly short order. Sometimes, as with torture, it is NGOs and victims' groups that push states to act—Amnesty International and other groups helped mobilize support for the 1984 Convention Against Torture and still use their membership and other 'name and shame' tactics to pressure states to comply with it.

Criminal Court to Deter Violations of International Criminal Law: A Theoretical Assessment', *Intl Crim L Rev* 10 (2010): 771; Patrick Wegner, 'International Criminal Law and Deterrence—A Pointless Endeavour?', *Justice in Conflict Blog*, 25 October 2011, <http://justiceinconflict.org>.

[52] For examples of the multiplicity of reactions, see Elizabeth Neuffer, *The Key to My Neighbor's House: Seeking Justice in Bosnia and Rwanda* (New York: Picador, 2001); Jon Elster, *Closing the Books: Transitional Justice in Historical Perspective* (Cambridge: Cambridge University Press, 2004).

[53] See, e.g., Larry Alexander, 'The Philosophy of Criminal Law', in Jules Coleman and Scott Shapiro (eds.), *The Oxford Handbook of Jurisprudence and Philosophy of Law* (Oxford: Oxford University Press, 2002) 815, 851–64.

Sometimes, as with war crimes, it is a special institution, like the ICRC, that pushes states to criminalize some violations.

The schisms created when identically severe acts are treated differently in terms of their criminalization still casts a shadow over international law. It is hard to find any rationale, for example, for the criminalization of individual acts of torture but not of summary executions. If we see justice as most fundamentally about not picking favorites, about treating like cases alike, then however ICL fares under the two pillars of thin justice, we would seem to have found a core injustice in the law as it stands.

And yet, such a principled justification for the meta-norm may be asking too much. For we can certainly say that states have agreed to criminalize some very serious acts—the process is certainly not random. More important, we can find ethical justifications for the criminalization of individual atrocities, such as crimes against humanity or genocide.[54] ICL may score no better than domestic criminal law here, where the enactment of new crimes is very often a response to the passions of the moment. Although this issue extends beyond the scope of this volume, we might well conclude that, if we can find an ethical justification for *each* crime, without an overarching theory for the meta-norm, then ICL—more in its parts than in its sum—is at least not unjust. So though the corpus of proscribed acts may reflect political expediency, the particular proscriptions are ethically justified.

III. International Environmental Law: Intergenerational and Non-Human Complications

Lastly, we see some limitations of the framework of thin justice in seeking to apply it to the norms of international environmental law. Since the UN's 1972 Stockholm conference on the environment, the corpus of international environmental law has grown vastly. Its coverage includes the regulation of transborder pollution; the protection of common spaces, such as the oceans, atmosphere, and Antarctica; and the preservation of species of flora and fauna. The law's vast array of treaties and customary international law places duties on states and non-state actors like corporations. Many of the treaties are accompanied by complex implementation mechanisms under UN or regional auspices. International environmental law has become part of the decisions of international courts, regional courts, and domestic courts.

[54] See, e.g., David Luban, 'A Theory of Crimes Against Humanity', *Yale JIL* 29 (2004): 85; Larry May, *Crimes Against Humanity: A Normative Account* (Cambridge: Cambridge University Press, 2005) 80–90; Steven R. Ratner, 'Can We Compare Evils?: The Enduring Debate on Genocide and Crimes Against Humanity', *Wash U Global Studies L Rev* (2007): 583.

A. Seven core norms

Within the thick web of treaties and customary law are a set of core norms. Some of these have driven lawmaking efforts; others have been distilled from commonalities within the treaties. States and scholars often refer to these norms as principles rather than rules because of their open-textured nature. On their own they may provide significant flexibility to states, but treaties often spell out in more precise terms the specific conduct required of states or corporations. I rely on Philippe Sands' identification of seven core principles:

(1) the duty of a state not to undertake activities within its own jurisdiction that cause environmental harm beyond that jurisdiction;[55]
(2) the duty to prevent damage to the environment generally;
(3) the principle of interstate cooperation in solving environmental problems;
(4) the principle of sustainable development, whereby economic development must be pursued in a manner that does not exhaust natural resources or the environment in a way harmful to future generations;
(5) the Precautionary Principle, whereby lack of scientific knowledge of the environmental consequences of an activity cannot be used as an excuse to postpone environmental mitigation measures;
(6) the polluter-pays principle, which seeks to apportion the costs of pollution firstly on those entities responsible for it; and
(7) the principle of common but differentiated responsibilities, which requires all states to cooperate but takes into account different levels of responsibility based on economic, historical, and other factors.[56]

Whereas the other norms discussed in this book respond to the competing claims of the actors discussed in Chapter 2—states, peoples, individuals, and corporations—international environmental law addresses not merely their claims but the unspoken interests of non-human species. Although it is possible to appraise our duties regarding the environment solely by examining our obligations to other peoples (living now or in the future)—anthropocentric frameworks—a fuller environmental ethics demands embracing the claims of non-human interests and even recognizing duties toward them.[57] This possibility of addressing the interests of non-humans through legal norms affects the suitability of the thin justice framework for appraising international environmental law.

[55] A concomitant right, to permanent sovereignty over natural resources, is addressed in Ch. 10's discussion of international economic law.

[56] Philippe Sands, *Principles of International Environmental Law*, 2nd ed. (Cambridge: Cambridge University Press, 2003) 232–90.

[57] See Christopher D. Stone, 'Ethics and International Environmental Law', in Daniel Bodansky, Jutta Brunnée, and Ellen Hey (eds.), *The Oxford Handbook of International Environmental Law* (Oxford: Oxford University Press, 2007) 291, 292–5.

B. Thin justice of core international environmental law norms?

1. International environmental law and the advancement of peace

The seven core norms may contribute to peace in the general sense that a healthier planet in terms of the sanctity of common spaces and the preservation of non-human species reduces some tensions between states. The most direct connection between those norms and the promotion of peace concerns the first three duties just described—not to cause transboundary harm, to prevent harm, and to cooperate in addressing environmental harms. If a state engages in significantly harmful environmental activity vis-à-vis its neighbors, it certainly risks an eventual armed conflict with them (or at least force by the neighbors to terminate the pollution). A leading arbitral award concerning a U.S. complaint over Canadian pollution recognized that a state cannot allow its territory to be used to pollute another 'when the case is of serious consequence'[58] (although in that case there was no danger that the United States and Canada would fight over Canada's pollution).

States, international organizations, and scholars have linked the ban on transboundary harm to the duty in the UN Charter and customary international law that states bordering one another must act as 'good neighbors', a principle linked to the Charter's emphasis on peace.[59] As one arbitral tribunal put it, 'neighbourliness . . . in the legal sense characterizes situations of proximity at risk of creating continuous frictions that call for a continuous collaboration . . . of two or several states whose activities interpenetrate in the same geographic space'.[60] Even though states on the receiving end of such harm would not have a lawful right of self-defense to such measures (as self-defense is still triggered only by an armed attack), imposing a duty up-front not to cause such harm could prevent interstate war as well as civil conflict.

Academic research is now recognizing the links between environmental harm and war.[61] In the case of civil strife, the effect of environmental harm on the prospect for violence turns on its interaction with political and social factors in the state. States, international organizations, NGOs, and scholars are also considering scenarios in which climate change could lead to state failure and eventually armed conflict.[62] Yet the literature emphasizes the complexity of the linkages.

[58] *Trail Smelter Case (United States v Canada)*, 3 RIAA 1907, 1965 (1941).

[59] UN Charter, Art. 74. See generally Laurence Boisson de Chazournes and Danio Campanelli, 'Neighbour States', in Rüdiger Wolfrum (ed.), *The Max Planck Encyclopedia of Public International Law*, online edition (Oxford: Oxford University Press, 2008–) <http://opil.ouplaw.com/home/EPIL>.

[60] *Affaire concernant le filetage à l'intérieur du Golfe du Saint-Laurent entre le Canada et la France*, 17 July 1986, 19 RIAA 225 (1986), para. 27.

[61] For key treatments, see generally, e.g., Thomas F. Homer-Dixon, *Environment, Scarcity, and Violence* (Princeton, NJ: Princeton University Press, 1999); Colin Kahl, *States, Scarcity, and Civil Strife in the Developing World* (Princeton, NJ: Princeton University Press, 2006).

[62] See, e.g., Jeffrey Mazo, *Climate Conflict: How Global Warming Threatens Security and What to Do About It* (Abingdon: Routledge, 2009); Jon Barnett and W. Neil Adger, 'Climate Change, Human Security and Violent Conflict', *Political Geography* 26 (2007): 639.

Thus, it would be going too far to say that environmental disputes between states or between governments and their citizens are a leading cause of armed conflict.[63] Nonetheless, the first three general norms set out earlier—with accompanying specific rules for states on greenhouse gases, ocean pollutants, and other arms, for instance—would seem to contribute to both interstate and internal peace.

2. *International environmental law and basic human rights*

At first glance it appears that none of the seven norms per se interferes with the enjoyment of basic human rights, whether seen in consequentialist or deontological terms. That is, if a state carries out its obligations under these norms, it need not and does not even seem to be tempted to violate basic human rights. Indeed, the opposite case can be made—that carrying out the core duties of international environmental law promotes basic human rights, in particular the rights to food and health. Thus, if states comply with the first five norms, the result can be reductions in pollution that enable individuals to earn a decent living and avoid the worst consequences for health of a polluted environment. These positive relationships between a clean environment and human rights have long been recognized by states, international organizations, and other global actors.[64]

Indeed, many states recognize in their constitutions a right to a clean environment and have advocated for an international human right to this effect. The Philippines Supreme Court went so far as to declare the Philippines constitution's right to 'a balanced and healthful ecology' not merely basic as a matter of constitutional law but seemingly more, as one that 'predate[s] all governments and constitutions' and can be 'assumed to exist from the inception of humankind'.[65] If such a right were a basic human right, then clearly international environmental law norms do not interfere with that basic human right. Nonetheless, as recognized by the UN Human Rights Council's special expert on human rights and the environment, the practice of states—my touchstone for the existence of rights, as discussed in Chapter 3—does not yet extend to the acceptance of such a human right, let alone as a basic one.[66] Yet even without a basic human right to a clean environment, we might stick with the prior sense that international

[63] Even the most serious environmental harms, such as nuclear testing by France in the 1960s and 1970s in the general neighborhood of New Zealand and Australia, did not create any serious risk of war between those states.

[64] For the linkages, see UN Human Rights Council, Report of the Independent Expert on the issue of human rights obligations relating to the enjoyment of a safe, clean, healthy and sustainable environment, John H. Knox, 24 December 2012, paras. 18–24, UN Doc. A/HRC/22/43. See generally UN Human Rights Council, Analytical study on the relationship between human rights and the environment: Report of the United Nations High Commissioner for Human Rights, 16 December 2011, UN Doc. A/HRC/19/34.

[65] *Minors Oposa v Secretary of the Department of Environment and Natural Resources (DENR)* [1993] (Phil. Sup. Ct.), 33 ILM 173, 175, 187 (1994).

[66] See Report of the Independent Expert, *supra* note 64, paras. 14–16. On the philosophical hazards to recognizing environmental rights of the moral kind, see John G. Merrills, 'Environmental Rights', in Daniel Bodansky, Jutta Brunnée, and Ellen Hey (eds.), *The Oxford Handbook of International Environmental Law* (Oxford: Oxford University Press, 2007) 663, 667–76.

environmental law does not interfere with basic human rights. Yet two issues show some difficulties with this conclusion.

(a) Intergenerational concerns

Consider first the principle of sustainable development (principle (4)). As originally defined in 1987 by the Brundtland Commission, it is meant to ensure that the basic economic needs of both present and future generations are met, although it does not contain guidance to states in the event of a possible tradeoff between generations. Thus, in terms of the second pillar, does the norm allow a state to exploit a natural resource in order to feed its population if doing so means depleting that resource for future generations and depriving them of their right to food? A state seeking to protect the basic human rights of one generation might do so at the expense of a future generation.[67] This potential conflict also arises with respect to indigenous peoples, where environmental conservation measures may conflict with their unique rights to the land as well as basic rights to food. International law has not grappled adequately with these conflicts between norms of environmental law requiring certain state regulatory action and protection of human rights.[68] And advocates for environmental improvement often downplay the risk of harm to human rights from new environmental regulation.[69]

This quandary resembles that faced with respect to IHL. In that situation, the extent to which the separation meta-norm or the core norms respected or violated human rights and thus were or were not thinly just required a sort of *renvoi* to a different theoretical framework, one that asked what it means to have human rights in time of war. With respect international environmental law, the second pillar requires us to answer fundamental questions about *whose* basic human rights are part of the pillar. In previous examples, I have assumed that we are considering the basic human rights of those alive at the present moment. But international environmental law, more than any other areas of law, forces us to shed that assumption.

Consider two versions of the human rights pillar. First, we might hold that justice demands or permits that we consider only the interests of the present generation. In that case, a norm like sustainable development or a more specific rule based on it, which *requires* us to consider future generations, will pass scrutiny only if compliance with it does not harm the basic human rights of the present

[67] See Stone, 'Ethics', *supra* note 57, at 308–11; Edith Brown Weiss, *In Fairness to Future Generations: International Law, Common Patrimony, and Intergenerational Equity* (Dobbs Ferry, NY: Transnational Publishers, 1989) 95–7 (future generations have group rights, though defining them in terms of 'rights to planetary conditions of diversity and quality comparable to those enjoyed by previous generations', rather than in terms of human rights).

[68] See the impressive study by Ellen Desmet, *Indigenous Rights Entwined with Nature Conservation* (Cambridge: Intersentia, 2011) in particular ch. 4.

[69] See Naomi Roht-Arriaza, '"First, Do No Harm": Human Rights and Efforts to Combat Climate Change', *Georgia J Int'l & Comp L* 38 (2010): 593, 610 (linking the reluctance of the climate change regime to consider human rights concerns to the 'anthropocentric nature of human rights [and] the idea that rights constitute threshold or minimum requirements that constrain action independently of the economic or scientific tradeoffs').

generation. If consideration of future generations means states will interfere with the enjoyment of the basic human rights of the present generation, then the norm is unjust. Second, we might believe that justice allows or requires us to consider the interests of both the present and future generations (let us assume equally for the moment). In that case, the norm of sustainable development would be just only if compliance with it does not harm the basic human rights of *both* generations.

The best defense of the principle of sustainable development as it stands with respect to basic human rights is to interpret it as not requiring or permitting states to make any choice between generations. Rather, it requires them to respect the rights of both generations. In that sense, the norm as described by the Brundtland Commission would be just under either version of the second pillar. Yet it does not address the dilemma where the state *cannot* guarantee the rights of both generations. Perhaps any tradeoffs are more theoretical than real, and states can act upon the principle of sustainable development in a way that respects the basic human rights of those in present and future generations, even if it cannot respect a larger set of their rights (such as a right to inherit the planet in the same condition as did the prior generation).

The possibility of such tradeoffs between generations is already visible with respect to rules on the trading of emissions of greenhouse gases. The idea of linking the allocation of emissions gases that each state will receive to its inhabitants' basic human rights to health, food, and other essentials is now part of philosophical debates on climate change.[70] Simon Caney recognizes in his argument that any just scheme should respond to the 'basic needs of all persons current and future and throughout the world'; yet he adds that we can only make proposals that the natural world, with its limited resources, will permit—i.e. that 'principles of justice have environmental preconditions'.[71] As he describes the ethical dilemma: '[T]he practices permitted by one component of a proposed theory of justice (for example, its account of what those currently alive are entitled to) may have environmental effects which entail that another component of that theory (most notably its account of what those currently alive owe to future generations) simply cannot be attained.'[72] If it cannot, then a theory must reconsider what is owed contemporaries initially, what is owed future generations, or both.[73]

Put in terms of the second pillar of global justice, Caney's insight means that if a proposed set of norms on greenhouse gas emissions trading is to respect basic human rights (i.e. if we fix that aspect of justice as a minimum beneath which any just distribution may not go), it may well have to make choices between current and future generations. A trading scheme that distributed allocations evenly over current and future generations but did so in such a way that it did not provide the

[70] See, e.g., Narasimha Rao and Paul Baer, '"Decent Living" Emissions: A Conceptual Framework', *Sustainability* 4 (2012): 656, 658–62 (identification of 'basic goods' in terms defined by Henry Shue); Simon Caney, 'Just Emissions', *Phil & Pub Aff* 40 (2012): 255, 291–3.

[71] Caney, 'Just Emissions', *supra* note 70, at 293–4.

[72] Ibid., at 294.

[73] Ibid., at 295.

minimal level of respect for either group's basic human right to subsistence would not be thinly just.

The reality of climate change law seems to take account of this concern somewhat. The UN's 1992 Framework Convention on Climate Change (FCCC), the basic treaty meant to govern all future emissions schemes, recognizes the need to avoid such an outcome when it requires the stabilization of greenhouse gases to 'ensure that food production is not threatened and to enable economic development to proceed in a sustainable manner'.[74] It comes quite close to permitting only trading schemes that would not interfere with basic human rights, at least of the economic variety, even if it is not specific on the intergenerational issue.

In summary, the norm of sustainable development itself seems to pass muster under the second pillar. And there is certainly a commitment in such a direction in the FCCC. Yet we are left in a bit of a state of limbo as to the justice of more specific rules that purport to further sustainable development. If they end up making tradeoffs between generations (even though sustainable development is supposed to avoid such tradeoffs in theory), then we need to make a choice, based on other theories of intergenerational justice, of how much we want to count the interests of future generations. In addition, we still lack much of a sense of the effect of compliance with environmental law on the basic human rights of each generation. Nonetheless, the framework of thin justice points us to a set of important inquiries regarding rules claiming to flow from the norm of sustainable development. In particular, we will need to ask whose basic human rights are relevant and how the rules under consideration might interfere with them.

(b) Intragenerational equity

Sustainable development encompasses an element of intragenerational equity as well, so that, for instance, environmental rules provide for the right sharing of the burdens between rich and poor states.[75] Here again, the rules on climate change suggest a tension between sustainable development and respect for basic human rights. As Naomi Roht-Arriaza has pointed out, the Kyoto Protocol's incentives for rich states parties to fund projects in the developing world that reduce greenhouse gases (the 'Clean Development Mechanism') could encourage projects that lead to forced displacement and impinge on the right to food; similar concerns can be raised about incentives for biofuel production.[76] Although states have downplayed these tensions, the UN expert committee responsible for overseeing compliance with the International Covenant on Economic, Social and Cultural Rights has warned states not to tackle climate change in a way that affects the right to food (at this point more of a hypothetical warning in light of the absence of much concerted action at all).[77]

[74] United Nations Framework Convention on Climate Change, 9 May 1992, Art. 2, 1771 UNTS 107.

[75] Sands, *Principles*, *supra* note 56, at 262–3. I would also reiterate the general point from Chapter 3 about thin justice as not focusing on broad distributive questions. These are certainly central to questions of environmental justice, but beyond the scope of my inquiry here.

[76] Roht-Arriaza, 'First, Do No Harm', *supra* note 69, at 596–9.

[77] Committee on Economic, Social and Cultural Rights, The World Food Crisis: Statement, 20 May 2008, para. 13, UN Doc. E/C.12/2008/1.

The committee is likely to be speaking in deontological terms; it may well turn out that the overall consequences for the observance of basic human rights as a result of some mechanisms under the Kyoto Protocol are positive. Thus, the norm of sustainable development does not prima facie fall short under the second pillar, but more detailed rules developed from it could interfere with basic human rights.

3. *Excluded stakeholders*

Thin justice has one last gap in its ability to ask and answer the right questions about all of international environmental law, namely, its omission of the impact of the norms on non-human interests and claimants. Both peace and human rights fit within an anthropocentric view of international law, whereas international environmental law is also ecocentric—about responding to the interests of other entities, certainly living (like plants and animals) and perhaps even not (like waterfalls, rivers, and rock formations). Our determination that a norm meets the two-pillar standard might well be seen as morally vacuous to those who believe in ecocentric ethics. And a contrary determination would be equally morally irrelevant for such an audience, for the norm might well be just once non-human interests are considered. So it is not even the case that calling a norm thinly just is necessary but not sufficient for ecocentric ethical perspectives; it is, rather, the philosophical equivalent to barking up the wrong tree.

It is tempting to respond to a gap in a theoretical framework by gap-filling, but I will not do so here. As stated earlier in this volume, I do not claim that the standard of thin justice works as a heuristic or evaluative lens for all norms of international law—it has little to say, for instance, about norms of coordination typical of much international law. Rather, environmental law needs to be appraised ethically through an additional lens. That framework could build on the idea of thin justice by adopting a second revised pillar that combines the basic human rights of humans with, perhaps, the basic rights of survival of some or all non-human species. But one can see how quickly determining which species count, and how they count compared to humans, becomes immensely complex.[78] And at a certain point, we may well be better off analytically, under Occam's razor at least, starting from different first principles.

IV. Conclusion

The three subject areas appraised in this chapter all have very different pedigrees and purposes. IHL, one of the oldest subjects of international law, developed to regulate one of the oldest activities of human kind. ICL, with the exception of the crime of piracy, is for the most part a product of twentieth-century attempts

[78] See, e.g., David Schmidtz, 'Are All Species Equal?', in David Schmidtz and Elizabeth Willott (eds.), *Environmental Ethics: What Really Matters, What Really Works*, 2nd ed. (Oxford: Oxford University Press, 2012) 114.

to enforce existing interstate obligations, with new penalties on individuals as a way of strengthening the fabric of international law. And international environmental law grew only with the global consciousness of the effects of pollution that began in the 1960s and 1970s, with the aim of regulating an enormous array of activities of states and companies previously subject only, and at best, to national law.

Yet all three subject areas highlight some limitations to the framework of thin justice. IHL, with its rules for war, cannot easily be said to promote or detract from peace. Its meta-norm giving states permission to carry out acts that in peacetime would be clear violations of human rights forces us to consider whether we have different basic human rights in wartime. ICL's meta-norm of differentiated responsibility seems fairly attenuated from promoting or detracting from peace, interstate or internal, and its effect upon respect for basic human rights is fairly speculative. Its ethical shortcoming lies in the rather haphazard form of criminalization. International environmental law seems somewhat attenuated from promoting peace, and its implications for human rights depend in part on one's understandings about intergenerational obligations and intragenerational equity. Moreover, the protection of non-human interests is not captured in either pillar. In each case, thin justice can be a lens for appraisal, but important questions about justice slip through—what is special about war? What is the principled basis for making an international wrong into an international crime? And how do we balance the interests of living humans against those of future humans and non-humans?

These unanswered questions reinforce a point made in Chapters 2 and 3, that there are not only many subjects of justice (what I called levels of justice), but also many kinds of justice. Although all kinds of global justice share some common idea of being about relations among global actors, they focus on very different concerns. So distributive justice, intergenerational justice, interspecies justice, the justice involved in just war theory (or theories), and thin justice all pose different questions. I think that thin justice answers many important questions insofar as those norms that pass scrutiny under its pillars respond to key ethical imperatives in the world today and are, generally speaking, deserving of respect.

But these examples show something deeper. Some norms that do *not* meet the standard of thin justice, or at least for which we need to make many moral or factual assumptions to say that they meet the standard—norms that we can at best say are *not unjust*—can also be deserving of respect. All three sets of norms fit this description. IHL's meta-norm might violate the basic human rights of both combatants and civilians in times of war; but the institutional hurdles and political obstacles to the alternatives, whether in McMahan's direction or for adoption of the incorporation of full human rights into IHL, render it worthy of our respect. ICL's meta-norm may not vindicate the basic human rights of victims, and the corresponding list of criminal acts is not principled; but the norms criminalizing some acts deserve our respect as reflecting a decent notion of particularly serious acts. And international environmental law's seven principles at least reflect, though they do not resolve, the claims of living and non-living global actors and are worded at such a level of generality that it is hard to think of a good reason to oppose them. At the same time, some specific rules derived from the seven principles may end up not deserving our respect, for example if they sacrifice the protection of the basic human rights of some individuals—with the caveat that disrespect of norms arrived at through processes that states regard as acceptable has a significant cost for the rule of law.

These three examples also demonstrate something important about ways to improve international law. As discussed further in Chapter 13, the challenge to reform efforts is to rectify those norms currently deficient as a matter of thin justice and to improve those norms that meet the standard but ought to do better, but to do so in a way that does not endanger their thin justice. I will leave aside for now what it means for a norm to do better. But certainly with respect to the norms in this chapter, reform runs less of a risk of undercutting the norm's thin justice for the simple reason that these norms do not connect so well with thin justice in the first place. If we want to add protections for civilians to IHL, or criminalize more human rights atrocities, or protect the planet with tighter regulation of greenhouse gases, these actions are unlikely to upset the critically important first pillar of peace. This possibility gives us significantly greater space for improvement in international law without as many risks. At the same time, reform could implicate and violate basic human rights in a way that the existing norms currently do not. To give just one obvious example, if ICL criminalizes more acts in the name of punishing international terrorism, we risk the development of norms that will harm people's basic human rights to freedom of conscience, religion, speech, and privacy.

Having foreshadowed here and in other chapters the possibilities for reforms to international law, I now address more thoroughly what it means for international law to move beyond thin justice.

13

Beyond Thin Justice

On 10 April 1953, upon his election as the UN's second—and, it would turn out, most influential and far-sighted—Secretary-General, Dag Hammarskjöld told the delegates of the General Assembly: 'Ours is a work of reconciliation and realistic construction. This work must be based on respect for the laws by which human civilization has been built.'[1] In laying out his vision for the UN, Hammarskjöld was also, I think, capturing the task of international law, which he knew how to deploy skillfully, in international affairs. For international law is very much about reconciling contrasting visions of governance across national and other communities and about constructing an improved world order in a realistic way. Hammarskjöld sought to ground progress for the UN and international cooperation on respect for the only sort of 'laws' that could be said to be the foundation for human civilization—namely a moral code. That compass should also be the one guiding international law, and thus we ought to be able to assess international law's respect for moral law and its contribution to a just world.

That assessment has been the task of this volume. Its starting point was one of non-ideal theory—inherent in Hammarskjöld's 'realistic construction'—for I believe that that approach, one reflecting and not wishing away certain realities of the international system, provides the better path toward actually improving the world we live in. Thus, I accepted the continued centrality of states in the global system, the importance of global institutions and in particular the limitations of some of them, and the inevitability of power differentials among global actors. I then developed a standard of global justice that sees international law norms as just to the extent that they advance peace and do not interfere with basic human rights—the two pillars. Although the values underlying those two pillars came from a logic of discovery, namely my observations of the overall normative structure of international affairs, I defended my particular standard as one worthy of the term justice. Yet it is also a standard that is 'thin' compared to both traditional conceptions of domestic justice and other accounts of global justice.

The two-pillar standard reflected an overall consequentialist approach to deciding what norms are just, so inevitably the justice of norms depends upon their contribution to certain states of affairs, namely those characterized by the promotion

[1] Dag Hammarskjöld, 'Statement before the Plenary Session of the General Assembly', in Wilder Foote (ed.), *Servant of Peace: A Selection of the Speeches and Statements of Dag Hammarskjöld* (New York:, Harper & Row, 1962) 28, 29.

of peace and non-interference with human rights. Yet I also embraced the need for deontological thinking when it comes to the second pillar. Because human rights are rights, international law rules allowing for infringements of those rights require very special reasons to be just, and some potential rules (like toleration of torture) are never just. I also defended my account against other versions of global justice, which I saw as either incomplete or as reflecting ideal theory.

I proceeded to hold the core norms up to scrutiny in the subsequent eight chapters. In each case, after attempting to crystallize the content of each norm, as interpreted and applied by relevant institutions, I appraised it under the two pillars. I asked whether the standard of thin justice permitted each norm, although at times it turned out that a norm we have is actually required as a matter of thin justice. When a norm proved unjust for failing the tests of one of the pillars, I proposed reforms to it. I also considered whether alternatives to the existing norms offered by governments, scholars, and others would pass muster under both pillars. At times in the analysis, we needed to consider the implications of either the existing rules or the alternatives for their procedural fairness, because we are evaluating rules within a legal system that must have a certain internal morality—the idea behind the rule of law—vis-à-vis its participants. At times, we needed to bring into the analysis the prospects for compliance with existing rules, for non-ideal theory in general and an analysis of a legal system rejects the idea of demanding the impossible, or even the extremely difficult, of international actors.

Rather than some movie-review sort of 'thumbs up' or 'thumbs down' answer, the norms proved to be ethically complex and nuanced. If justice rolls on like a river (Amos 5:24), thin global justice has open waters and well as rocks and eddies. They reflected manifold ways in which the law can take into account, or not, the imperative of peace and the demand of respecting human rights. As a result, depending on how they mediated the requirements of the two pillars, some norms were overall thinly just, some were more than thinly just, and some were not even thinly just, with the differences more along a sliding scale than characterized by hard lines. My degree of confidence in these assessments varied across norms, because lawyers might disagree as to the content of the norm in the first place, because the norm might be undergoing change, or because the norm might be embedded with other norms. And some core norms seemed impossible to judge based on this standard.

At each step along the way, I attempted to respond to critiques of the norms from within law and ethics. Much of the legal critique reflected a contrasting vision of the importance of peace as compared to human rights; much of the philosophical critique was grounded in a conception of global justice quite different from mine. In the end, I hope to have demonstrated the significant and decent conformity between many of the core norms of international law and the standard of thin justice; the shortcomings of others, in particular for their interference with the enjoyment of basic human rights; and the imperative for those global actors contemplating the reform of international legal rules to consider the ethical implications of those proposals under the pillars of peace and human rights.

This concluding chapter will attempt to bring these assessments together and point the way toward an international law whose norms are more than thinly just. I will begin with a recapitulation of the essential judgments I have reached regarding the core norms. Then I will offer what has been hinted at throughout the volume—a thicker sort of justice to which international law can aspire as well as a path for decisionmakers to get there.

I. The Thin Justice of the Basic Norms

The norms examined here were those by which international law responds to the most important claims by states, peoples, individuals, and, to a certain extent, business entities. I grouped them thematically rather than according to any doctrine of international law, and can summarize the basic assessments as follows:

- The norms on the *use of force*, in terms of the ban on force in Article 2(4) of the UN Charter and the exception for self-defense in Article 51, met, indeed exceeded, the standard. Both norms are central to the preservation of interstate peace without interfering with, in fact usually advancing, the protection of human rights (with the caveat of the ban on humanitarian intervention, discussed in Chapter 9). Self-defense can be justly extended to cover attacks by non-state actors because of the threats they represent to both peace and human rights, although procedural safeguards are needed to prevent abuses of self-defense by powerful states. As a temporal matter, an extension of self-defense beyond anticipatory self-defense to preventive self-defense would generally run afoul of the first pillar.
- The norms on *non-intervention* were also thinly just insofar as the ban on intervention, as it is currently construed, promotes peace among states while leaving room for them to promote human rights across borders in a non-forceful way. Expanding the ban so as to prohibit sanctions or aid cuts by one state linked to another state's human rights practices could prevent states from addressing serious human rights violations. But limiting the ban to allow states to offer military aid to rebel movements abroad also seems very dangerous, though conceivably just if this is needed to terminate atrocities. The recent move in the law to allow states to impose economic sanctions against human rights abusers while trying to limit their harm to innocent parties was welcomed. I also endorsed the law's tacit toleration of states' arresting human rights abusers abroad, as long as the accused's basic rights are respected. I see both moves as a sort of thickening of the law in terms of its underlying justice.
- The norms on *self-determination*, really a set of rules whose corresponding rights and duties depended on the unit seeking self-determination, generally passed muster under the two pillars. The contrast between the right of colonial peoples to independence and the strong presumption against secession from existing states balanced in an overall decent way the tremendous costs to interstate and internal peace from secession with the possibility that that remedy might be

needed in cases of exceptional repression. *Uti possidetis*, the default position under which new states inherit the borders they had in their pre-independence incarnation, proved more easily defensible in the colonial context than in the secession context. As for alternatives, a complete ban on secession would violate the second pillar. And even though the law has shortcomings in the disconnect between some serious rights abuses and the remedy of secession, I found cosmopolitan critiques of the law unpersuasive for failing to treat the first pillar seriously enough.

• The norms on *sovereign equality* proved quite a mixed bag in terms of their justice. The rules on the recognition of states have improved insofar as they now take into account, up to a point, the human rights practices of states seeking recognition. As for the rather limited core of sovereign equality, the right of states to participate as formal equals in both lawmaking and law application survives scrutiny under the two pillars. Neither a more robust equality nor a lesser form is required under the pillar of human rights. Some alternatives have significant shortcomings, and many of the goals of those seeking a different form of sovereign equality can be addressed by changes to other norms. However, the norm of immunity of one state from another's jurisdiction raised significant concerns. It insulated key actors from accountability for violations, and therefore interfered with the vindication, of basic human rights. Whereas immunity for sitting heads of state and government is needed for the sake of interstate peace, other forms of immunity proved to be unjust in key aspects.

• With respect to *admission to and decisionmaking in international organizations*, I reviewed the admissions policies of the UN, the Council of Europe, the EU, and the World Trade Organization (WTO). The policies of the four passed the test for thin justice, but it also proved important to consider the fairness of the process to applicants in terms of publicly stated admissions criteria, functionally relevant criteria, and good faith application of the criteria. On this score, the WTO's policies lacked procedural fairness to applicants. As for decisionmaking, I defended the UN Charter's allocation of authority to make legally binding decisions to the Security Council. The special role for a small group of permanent members also survives scrutiny, though the status quo of the current P5 does not. And the veto power of a small group of powerful states turns out to serve important functions for peace and contributes to the existence of the international legal system as a whole. Yet to the extent that the veto can prevent, and has prevented, the Council from responding strongly to human rights atrocities, it does not meet the test of the second pillar; it needs certain procedural reforms. And as for the International Monetary Fund (IMF), although the weighted voting power has a clear functional rationale, if it causes the Bank to take action that undermines basic human rights—an empirically contested claim at this point—that decisionmaking mechanism is also flawed.

• International law's presumption of a *territorially limited scope of human rights protection* advanced peace, but potentially failed muster under the second pillar insofar as it could prohibit states from protecting basic human rights beyond their borders. States have recognized three exceptions to that presumption, each with its own moral valence. First, international law's recognition of some *duties on states to respect rights when they act abroad* was compelled by the second pillar of global justice. Without such duties, states would be free to violate rights whenever they undertook extraterritorial conduct like a police operation. Second, the *permission of a state to exercise universal jurisdiction* over some crimes was thinly just insofar as it took into account, in an overall decent way, the risks to peace and the need to vindicate the basic human rights of victims. Essential to that justice are certain procedural mechanisms, such as the right of the state where the crimes took place to exercise jurisdiction first.

• In the case of *humanitarian intervention* without Security Council approval, the black-letter rule banning it is unjust for its interference with the protection of basic human rights. Yet I argued that state expectations actually conform better to a more context-dependent position that tolerates interventions in situations largely consistent with key criteria from just war theory. That position is just under the two pillars. In the case of both universal jurisdiction and humanitarian intervention, the law's posture of permitting but not requiring states to act generally reflects a balancing of the two pillars, although it does not fully respond to the claims of victims of atrocities.

• *International economic law* proved to be particularly complex in terms of gauging the effect of the norms on respect for basic human rights (notably economic rights), a task essential to consequentialist analysis. Economic law's foundational norm of *permanent sovereignty over natural resources* generally survives scrutiny under the two pillars; but it needs to be supplemented by other norms of international law to prevent corrupt governments from making deals with foreigners that violate the basic human rights of the population.

• In the case of *international trade law*, we saw possibilities for those norms as applied to interfere with basic human rights by denying states policy space to protect their citizens' economic and social rights. The decisions of states and cases in the WTO Dispute Settlement Body (DSB) show some attempts to accommodate human rights concerns. Trade rules have been interpreted to allow a conflict diamond sanctioning system, some possibilities for low-cost manufacturing of antiretroviral drugs, and various domestic protections for health. But the Appellate Body has struck down other schemes that might have been needed by the state to respect the right to health. Moreover, the DSB has institutional features that lead it to downplay human rights in its rulings. In response to systemic critiques that assert that trade law is unjust for harming the global poor, I argued that most of them turn on claims of causation that are not yet proved. As a result, it is premature in most cases (agricultural subsidies seem to be an exception) to conclude that they undermine basic human rights. Because the consequences of the rules and decisions present a muddy enough picture, we should be very cautious in any assessment of the thin justice of trade law.

• These conclusions held in many respects with regard to *international investment law*. Investment tribunals have avoided finding that key investment rules on fair and equitable treatment or compensation for expropriation override human rights concerns, but they have also generally rejected defenses by host states that their actions against foreign investors were necessary to protect their populations from serious peril. The arbitral culture at the core of investment-state dispute settlement has many of the same barriers to incorporation of human rights concern as does the WTO. The systemic critique of investment law is, however, persuasive only if we can find causation between investment law and global poverty. In this context, the absence of firm legal duties on foreign investors may well contribute to violations of basic human rights. States and companies have slowly begun to respond to this gap through codes and soft law recognizing corporate responsibilities toward those in host states affected by their investments. Proposals to alter trade and investment law must ask whether those two sets of rules are the right sites for addressing the human rights consequences of global commerce.

- Lastly, *international humanitarian, criminal, and environmental law* demonstrated the limits of the approach of thin justice. *International humanitarian law* is characterized by a meta-norm that generally grants individuals fewer protections during armed conflict than in times of peace. To evaluate that meta-norm under the second pillar requires that we tackle a distinct set of questions about what it means to enjoy human rights in peacetime versus wartime. And that is a huge issue on which there is a vast range of disagreement, and where I am not prepared to stake a position. *International criminal law* has its own meta-norm, making crimes of only a small handful of international law violations. That list turns out not to be based on any coherent notion of the gravity of the crimes in terms of peace, human rights, or any other values. That meta-norm proved difficult to evaluate under the two pillars because the possible effects on peace and human rights of a limited set of crimes are quite speculative. *International environmental law*'s core norms were also not closely associated with, and thus hard to evaluate with respect to their impact upon, peace. As for their impact on human rights, that assessment brings up a distinct set of ethically complex issues regarding intergenerational and intragenerational equity. Decisionmakers do not share one interpretation of the law regarding these issues, and the moral considerations of both are again subject to huge disagreement. Moreover, the pillar of human rights does not help us appraise norms meant to benefit non-human species.

My overall consequentialist approach to both pillars of thin justice means that the justice of international law's core norms is *contingent on facts and predictions about the effect of the norms*—namely their effect, assuming compliance with them by the actors to whom they are directed, on the promotion of peace and respect for human rights.[2] The analysis occasionally invoked human rights as trumps that would render some norms unjust regardless of their overall effects on human rights or peace. And the consequentialist analysis included the possibility that the rights pillar would exclude certain reasons from a balancing exercise without ruling out an examination of consequences. I recognize that one's view of the justice

[2] Cf. Russell Hardin, *Morality within the Limits of Reason* (Chicago, IL: University of Chicago Press, 1988) 3 ('the utilitarian dictates for action are contingent, not a priori').

of a particular norm might depend on whether one viewed the second pillar in terms of trumps or balancing. But on the whole, the result is a very fact-specific set of appraisals.

These moral assessments may lack the elegance of conclusions based on deontological or social contractarian approaches. Although those sorts of theories may contribute to our understanding of the justice of international law, I think, given the diversity of norms and the state of the international system, we need to focus on what international law actually does or is likely to do in terms of affecting the behavior of global actors. Even if others make predictions regarding the effect of certain rules on the advancement of peace and respect for basic human rights that are different from mine—and thus end up with contrasting appraisals of the justice of certain norms—the two-pillar consequentialist approach still offers a valuable framework for the moral reckoning of international law.

The diversity in the norms' moral valences should disabuse us of the simple verdict that international law, as a whole, or the international legal system, is just or unjust. Rather, we can say that (1) most of the core norms of international law meet a standard of thin justice; (2) some very important ones do not; and (3) other norms are not amenable to this type conclusion, whether for reasons specific to the norms or because the framework itself is not comprehensive enough. We might represent this complexity through the idea of a regression line or curve. If the norms of international law are data points, then the standard of thin justice is one that at least decently fits the pattern of dots. Some points have been shown to be on the line, as thinly just; but others will be below the line, as still unjust; and others are above it, meeting a higher standard of justice. Well above my line would be another line, that of a standard of justice that is not yet achieved but may well be achievable—the subject of Section II of this chapter.

Such a conclusion crystallizes the point that international law has indeed played a significant role in creating a more just world, and that, regardless of its origin in power politics or historical contingencies, a large set of its norms have significant moral stature. Those norms that are at least thinly just are not only victories of the strong over the weak or pragmatic compromises among groups of states, but also morally justifiable rules for addressing globally significant claims.

Beyond different predictions about the effect of rules on peace and basic human rights, criticisms of the norms that I regard as thinly just seem to reflect three fundamental disagreements with my approach. One concerns the *content and weight of the two pillars*. For example, those working from a strong cosmopolitan perspective would urge a more robust second pillar, or human rights or equality as a first pillar, and overall less emphasis on peace. Other critics, often from the developing world, put more emphasis on peace for fear that a human rights focus will harm Southern interests.

The second disagreement centers on the extent to which moral evaluation should be affected by *institutional constraints*. As an international lawyer, I have insisted throughout that institutional constraints should affect our moral reasoning. Many criticisms of international law consider institutions last, rather than first. As a result, my defense of norms as critical to the advancement of peace, given the limited institutional architecture to guarantee such peace, will ring hollow for some.

Third, disagreements between my assessments and those of the critics lie with significantly contrasting perspectives on the inevitability or desirability of the *state system* as a whole. Certainly those with no commitment to the state system, who are working much closer to ideal theory, will ask very different questions about the norms of international law. But I would argue those are not the right questions. For law is meant to apply to existing agents, and states certainly are agents. As long as those agents exist and make law, we should focus on the justice of that law, whatever standard one might adopt. We cannot criticize the law by simply arguing that it can be just only if it governs the relations of fictitious or imagined agents. My analysis has rejected such an approach at numerous points, whether in the assumptions made in Chapter 3 or in the occasional invocation of the compliance corollary to criticize some alternatives to existing rules.

These three clashes may originate from pre-theoretical positions about global justice. Certainly they may reflect distinctions between a lawyer's approach and a philosopher's, although one should not ignore the many perspectives within each field. My own perspective has reflected my own legal lens and particular experiences. In the end, the framework, with its two pillars grounded in the two most basic values permeating international law and then refined to offer a rubric for normative appraisal, allows us to appraise in a rigorous way the justice of international law.

II. A Thicker Justice for International Law

It is now time to take the final step in the ethical evaluation of international law—to move beyond a standard of thin justice and propose a standard of thicker justice which international law *can* and *should* strive to meet. Scholarship within ethics has offered many conceptions of global justice over the past generation, but, consistent with my focus on international law's contribution to a just world order, I will offer a standard tailored to the subject and project at hand. I will thus refrain from offering any sort of ideal standard of justice even here.

A. Criteria for a higher standard of global justice

The new standard of global justice needs to reflect both the *capacities and the limitations* of international law as a vehicle for achieving global justice. On the capacities side, we should recognize that law is not merely a vessel into which moral theories are poured. Rather, law can change and should change our moral outlook. It need not always trail morality, but at times can push it forward.[3] As most

[3] Leslie Greene, 'Should Law Improve Morality?', University of Oxford Legal Research Paper No. 73/2013, 16 July 2013, 11–24, <http://http://www.ssrn.com>; H.L.A. Hart, *The Concept of Law*, 3rd ed. (Oxford: Clarendon Press, 2012) 176–7.

international lawyers and international relations scholars now take for granted, the change in the law on the use of force resulting from the UN had a huge effect on state attitudes regarding the legitimacy of war.[4] As a result, the makers of international law have an opportunity to shape our views of a just world order and not merely react to it. Moreover, international law does not just shape the content of international morality, but of the polity to which it applies. It is thus constitutive of a community at the international level. In Jean Cohen's terms, the development of international law 'can thicken commonalities and consensus'.[5]

On the limitations side, it should also be clear that international law cannot be the only site for the realization of global justice. This limitation can be justified morally, whether through Walzer's distinction between thick domestic morality and thin international morality; Rawls' unwillingness to adopt a global difference principle in *The Law of Peoples*; or David Miller's argument for apportioning responsibility over global justice between inward-focused state action and outward-focused joint action. But my argument for the right apportionment between domestic and international law is essentially pragmatic, one that accepts from experience and observation the limited capacity of international law. To put too many new duties on states (or other actors) as a matter of international law when it is so difficult to construct new institutions to interpret, implement, and enforce that law is a recipe for pretended law, not effective law.

Although new international institutions have been built from originally audacious ideas (as with the international criminal tribunals), overall we still must not ask international law to provide the very thick network of rights and duties that we expect of domestic law.[6] We still need strong states. As a result, the standard of thicker justice against which to measure international law will not rise to the level of the standard against which to judge domestic law (unless one has a very low standard for the latter).

This capacity constraint about international law not only argues for the right balance between domestic and international law, but between international law and what we might just call non-law. For surely not every aspect of justice needs to be reflected in legal rules. Justice will often be reflected in social norms that do not need a legal form or enforcement. As Hart pointed out, social morality is often enforced by moral pressure, which is quite different from legal sanction.[7] So it would be a mistake not only to put all our eggs in the basket of international

[4] Mark W. Zacher, 'The Territorial Integrity Norm: International Boundaries and the Use of Force', *Intl Org* 55 (2001): 215.

[5] Jean L. Cohen, 'Whose Sovereignty? Empire vs. International Law', in Christian Barry and Thomas W. Pogge (eds.), *Global Institutions and Responsibilities: Achieving Global Justice* (Malden, MA: Blackwell Publishing, 2005) 159, 181.

[6] This difference should not, however, be equated with seeing international law as primitive or minimalist. Given what we know about what international law has already regulated, Robert Jackson's statement that international law is 'universally recognized and accepted because its norms are minimal in what they demand of sovereign states' seems wrong both descriptively and normatively. Robert Jackson, *The Global Covenant: Human Conduct in a World of States* (Oxford: Oxford University Press, 2000) 417.

[7] Hart, *The Concept of Law, supra* note 3, at 178–80.

law, but to put them in any basket called law. For instance, certain expectations we have about mutual respect and decency across national lines—whether avoiding stereotypes or hurtful comments toward foreign states or peoples, or the need for some forbearance in intelligence-gathering on foreigners—may be part of a conception of global justice not yet amenable to legal regulation. In the end, I do not know for certain how thickly just international law can be, but I propose a formulation that strives to balance these capacities and limitations judged from observation of how the law works.

My approach in identifying a thicker standard of global justice might be called one of aspirational theory, a sort of bridge or weigh station between the non-ideal theory I have employed and ideal theory.[8] It retains the core assumptions of my non-ideal theory regarding international law—the durability of states, the capacities and incapacities of institutions, and the uneven distribution of global power—while loosening their constraints in terms of thinking about proposals for change. Aspirational theory builds on existing achievements, legal and institutional, rather than jettisoning them for a grand new scheme dictated by ideal theory. It seeks to move the law in a direction that is not attainable in the near term, but that I think is possible for the medium to long term without crossing the line to the fantasy of ideal theory.

B. Justice based on a new arrangement of the two pillars

A thicker standard of global justice to which international law should strive would, then, be one where *the norms are just if and only if they advance the enjoyment of human rights without interfering with interstate or internal peace.* This standard is based on the pillars of peace and human rights, but it makes three significant moves from the standard of thin justice.

- First, the pillars have been reversed, such that human rights are now at the core of the first and primary criterion. In this respect, it moves closer to the cosmopolitan position that might have rejected putting peace first. It forces us to ask, when we appraise international law, first and foremost, what the norms are doing for human rights.
- Second, the human rights whose protection is critical extend beyond basic human rights, to the full range of human rights accepted as a matter of international practice. That range is large, though limited; it can be found in the same practice used to identify the basic human rights in Chapter 3. For simplicity's sake, we might think of it as the content of the most widely accepted human rights treaties, although global actors will still argue over the interpretation of the rights and the scope of state and non-state duties.
- Third, a just norm is one that does not merely interfere with the enjoyment of rights, but actually promotes or advances it. Consequently, a norm of

[8] I appreciate this insight from Elizabeth Anderson.

international law would not be just if it did not make this positive contribution. In this critical way, the task for all of international law is not merely to do no harm to the enjoyment of human rights, but to *fill in gaps* in the protection of human rights. In other words, whereas before we were putting the onus of protection of human rights on human rights law, under the new standard we expect all of the core norms to contribute to that cause.[9]

The new standard maintains a human rights-based standard for global justice. This move is not uncommon; Rawls, Miller, and others give a central role to human rights in their important works on global justice, though those two limit their concern to basic human rights.[10] It is certainly the case that we could measure justice, in particular distributive justice, against other criteria. But my choice of advancement of human rights as a criterion for thick justice, like my choice in Chapter 3 of non-interference with basic human rights as a criterion for thin justice, considers the role that human rights plays in the world today. Those rights are the most widely accepted standards for the treatment of the individual by those with power over him or her (not just states), and they represent a readily accessible baseline against which to appraise the justice of international law. For all the open-textured nature of human rights law, and all the diverse cultural perspectives as to its meaning, it seems better than the obvious alternatives (for example dignity, security, needs, or utility) in terms of both definitiveness and global acceptability. International law can certainly treat individuals better than that required to guarantee human rights, but my standard does not require it to do so to be just.

By taking human rights as its core criterion, the standard is vulnerable to the criticism that it does not give us guidance for lawmaking in many areas where human rights are not the point of the law, whether in technical areas like aviation security, economic issues like antitrust, or those environmental issues that cannot be seen in terms of individual welfare (for example the welfare of other species). I accept this limitation, for I think that much of international lawmaking can and should be about issues that are not fundamentally about advancing global justice (except in the limited sense that the rule of law can be a just endeavor). States should not shirk from using international law to regulate numerous areas of planetary interest, but that does not mean that all of the resultant regulation is either just or unjust in terms of consequences for human rights or peace.[11] Certainly some of the project of expanding state duties may improve human rights—global

[9] My new standard does not suggest that just norms of international law should ignore the interests already recognized in international human rights law by which governments can limit the enjoyment of certain human rights. In this sense, norms of international law, to be just under this higher standard, need not (indeed probably should not) seek to provide greater protections to human rights than those recognized in human rights law today.

[10] See John Rawls, *The Law of Peoples* (Cambridge, MA: Harvard University Press, 1999) 78–81; David Miller, *National Responsibility and Global Justice* (Oxford: Oxford University Press, 2007) 163–200.

[11] For a proposal to orient international law toward turning states into trustees for planetary interests and not merely those of their own citizens, see Eyal Benvenisti, 'Sovereigns as Trustees of Humanity: On the Accountability of States to Foreign Stakeholders', *AJIL* 107 (2013): 295.

hunger is, for instance, a planetary interest—but other new duties for states may not improve human rights and yet be no less important. Advancement of those other interests should not require stretching the notion of human rights beyond that accepted by states. Rather, we should acknowledge that some international lawmaking serves the ends of global justice, as measured in terms of human rights, whereas other international lawmaking serves other purposes.

C. Alternative criteria for thicker global justice

Several concepts associated with other visions of global justice are not in the standard just offered. Each, the subject of its own vast literature, raises numerous issues about the construction of world order beyond the scope of this book. In this conclusion I sketch only briefly my choice not to incorporate them in thicker global justice.

First, thicker justice does not require *robust equality*, whether of individuals or states, across the planet. Some type of equality of persons, captured in the notion of equality of status, is essential. It is already recognized in both human rights law's bans on invidious discrimination and its rule of equality before the law, and in the cosmopolitan position of the individual as the fundamental unit of moral concern. Yet distributive equality is not part of thicker justice. This exclusion is based on a stronger version of the argument presented in Chapter 3 for excluding distributive equality from the pillars of *thin* justice. There, in response to Charles Beitz's argument that inequality causes significant harm to individuals—deprivation of what is needed to flourish, personal humiliation, and loss of control over one's future—I argued that a norm meeting the second pillar of thin justice goes a long way to addressing those harms. A fortiori, the more robust first pillar of thicker justice offered here sets a standard such that legal rules that meet it would, if respected by states, produce conduct that would eradicate many of these harms. In particular, positive action to secure respect for economic and social rights would be a major contribution to addressing harms caused by vast disparities in wealth across the planet.

But in the end my focus on human rights and not equality is mostly pragmatic, although it resonates with the philosophical dictum that 'ought' implies 'can'. International law lacks the capacity to guarantee the equality of individuals, beyond addressing some legal inequalities through the ban on invidious discrimination or equality before the law. A respect for the range of human rights will help to eliminate some of the more serious distributional inequalities, but I do not think it can do more than that. Even as a matter of aspirational theory, I will not, then, insist upon as an indicium for a just international law an end that international law and its institutions are incapable of carrying out.

As for equality of states, some type of equality of states—sovereign equality—is important to preserve the peace, as discussed in Chapter 6. A stronger version of sovereign equality may be a bulwark against hegemony,[12] but the ultimate aim

[12] Cohen, 'Whose Sovereignty?', *supra* note 5, at 180.

of greater equality of states must be advancing the full range of human rights. Some more robust equality, perhaps with respect to participation in international organizations, may increase the likelihood that the law is developed and interpreted to protect human rights. But this is hardly guaranteed, as many states that would benefit from such equality have autocratic governments and poor human rights records. The goal should be respect for human rights and not greater state equality.

Second, thicker justice does not demand *democracy* within states.[13] Without discounting international law's progress from a human rights perspective in endorsing democracy and condemning the overthrow of democratic regimes,[14] democracy in the sense of a required form of government centered on free elections should not be a top priority or standard for the achievement of thicker global justice.[15] Here Rawls has offered a defense of toleration of non-democratic states through the notion of so-called decent states.[16]

But, as with equality, my reasons are fundamentally pragmatic. International law must start with an acceptance of and respect for some diversity across states and work with the standards to which they have agreed, which are those of human rights and not democracy. If we could get a world with universal respect for human rights under international law, I at least would be prepared to call that a remarkable achievement. Democracy might well follow, but the goal should remain respect for human rights. As for arguments that democracy is necessary to the enjoyment of human rights, even if it is true (certainly democratic regimes generally have better human rights records), the task of transforming states into democracies seems beyond the capacity of international law, even if it may be valid for governments to encourage such change through non-coercive means.[17] International law can do a better job in getting non-democracies to protect human rights than in remaking all states into democracies. And we should not forget that democracies can violate human rights, whether political or economic.

Lastly, thicker justice does not require *constitutionalism*. Global constitutionalism is the subject of many debates about international law, and some scholars see it as the next logical step to building a world where international law constrains power and popular preferences, for that is what constitutions do domestically.[18] But as with democracy, I do not see global constitutionalism as a priority for

[13] Nor do I place a priority on democracy across states, as discussed earlier regarding the issue of state equality.

[14] See generally Gregory H. Fox and Brad R. Roth (eds.), *Democratic Governance and International Law* (Cambridge: Cambridge University Press, 2000).

[15] Here democracy is distinct from the representativeness of the government, which is essential to preserving internal peace, as recognized in the law regarding self-determination.

[16] Rawls, *The Law of Peoples, supra* note 10, at 62–78.

[17] For an argument that only democracies can reliably protect human rights, see Thomas Christiano, 'An Instrumental Argument for a Human Right to Democracy', *Phil & Pub Aff* 39 (2011): 142.

[18] See the contrasting views in Jeffrey L. Dunoff and Joel P. Trachtman (eds.), *Ruling the World?: Constitutionalism, International Law, and Global Governance* (Cambridge: Cambridge University Press, 2009).

international law. If we can develop just norms with robust and just institutions, we might decide at some point to call that a constitutional order.[19] But justice will be achieved through those norms and institutions, rather than some constitutional features of them. Most notably, constitutions are deliberately drafted to be difficult to change, and it is not at all obvious that the project of global justice would benefit from such rigidity.

III. The Path to a More Just International Law

How, then, do we get from a set of norms that are thinly just to those meeting this higher standard? This seems to me the critical question, one to be answered in a way that takes account of the institutional constraints in international law. For even an aspirational approach to global justice does not permit simply inventing institutions to match up to a particular vision of justice.

A. The process of legal reform

I propose four moves toward a more just international law that participants in the making of international law, as well as theorists of global justice, should consider. I will refrain from referring to them as steps, which sounds more like a cookbook or instruction manual, or as phases, as these moves may be undertaken simultaneously or sequentially depending upon the norm at issue.[20]

1. Ensure the thin justice of international law

Thickly just norms must be built on a foundation of thinly just norms. Thus, the first task of states, international organizations, and other actors must be to rectify those norms discussed here, as well as others, that do not or might not meet the test of thin justice, to ensure that they do. States, tribunals, and other institutions making and interpreting international trade and investment law must ensure that those norms do not interfere with basic human rights, a goal that we cannot say they have yet achieved. If pressures arise to adjust norms that are already thinly just in a way that might undermine that feature, such pressures should be resisted. For example, states should continue to reject calls by some states for a norm permitting recourse to preventive self-defense (as explicitly advanced by the United States during the Bush years), or aid to any insurgent group that claims to be fighting for democracy.

[19] For an appealing and more moderate use of constitutional principles to reforming the global order, see Jean L. Cohen, *Globalization and Sovereignty: Rethinking Legality, Legitimacy, and Constitutionalism* (Cambridge: Cambridge University Press, 2012).

[20] I will also not offer a roadmap for how international law doctrine should adjust to this new standard. One possibility is for some type of supremacy of international human rights norms over other norms, though again such supremacy should not undermine peace.

2. *Explore and develop avenues to revise those norms that are thinly just in order to meet the thicker standard, without risk of sacrificing their thin justice*

This move requires us to envision and work toward rules of international law that are more just than the status quo without giving up the thin justice that they already have. More specifically, the new standard requires that we revise the norms to do more to *improve all human rights* without losing their important role in the preservation of peace. This transformation is not a monolithic process, where decisionmakers should follow one path for all norms. Some norms can and should be changed, for the risk that reforming them would undermine their benefits to peace is small. For others, the balance they strike between advancing peace and non-interference with human rights would mean that altering them so that they positively advance human rights may undercut their contribution to the preservation of interstate and internal peace. Moreover, this process needs to keep in mind the two corollaries from Chapter 3, namely, the need to respect the rule of law through fairness to the participants—in particular, predictability of legal rules—and the need to maintain a minimum level of compliance with new rules.

For instance, the rules on trade and investment should be revised to enable them to play a more positive role in eliminating the economic rights violations caused by deep poverty, even though we may disagree on just how significant that role can be. We can revise these norms without threatening peace, in large part because, as discussed in Chapter 10, the substance of those norms does not have a major effect on peace in the first place. On the other hand, the rules on self-defense in the UN Charter should not be changed by, for instance, taking Rawls' suggestion of eliminating a right of self-defense for outlaw states. A middle case might be the norms of self-determination, where it might be possible to revise the strong presumption against secession in a way not too destabilizing to interstate and internal peace. We have already witnessed a significant move in this direction, as states have now afforded forms of recognition to non-state groups (such as national minorities or indigenous peoples) in a way that advances the range of their human rights without undermining peace.[21] But to revise the norm to allow secession by any ethnic group seeking its own state would clearly go too far.

3. *In exploring avenues to improve the justice of international norms, serious consideration should be given to developing norms that expand the range of duty-holders or at least bearers of responsibility*

Joseph Raz pointed out many years ago that 'one may know of the existence of a right... without knowing who is bound by duties based on it or what precisely are those duties'.[22] More positively, Miller has argued in the context of global

[21] See generally Emannuelle Jouannet, *Qu'est-ce qu'une societé juste?: Le droit international entre développement et reconnaissance* (Paris: A. Pedone, 2011) 194–258.

[22] Joseph Raz, *The Morality of Freedom* (Oxford: Oxford University Press, 1986) 184.

responsibilities that the denial of basic human rights means that 'any agent, individual or collective, who is able to help protect them may in principle bear remedial responsibilities'.[23] International law is familiar with the idea of expanding the number of duty-holders associated with certain rights. International criminal law recognizes duties on individuals, international humanitarian law places duties on non-state armed groups, and human rights law increasingly recognizes duties (at least soft and sometimes hard ones) on business enterprises.[24]

This expansion can and should continue in two dimensions. First, international law should continue to develop responsibilities or duties for *non-state actors* regarding human rights. Just as the Convention on the Elimination of all Forms of Discrimination against Women recognizes that cultural institutions and the family should prevent discrimination against women,[25] we can imagine new duty-holders for other rights.[26]

Second, even within the more traditional construct of duties on states, we can see the need for more responsibilities or duties of an *extraterritorial* nature. As discussed in Chapter 9, R2P is an obvious move in this direction insofar as it places a responsibility on states to aid, and, if needed, interfere through the UN Security Council, in situations of mass atrocities. International environmental law treaties place duties on rich states that export hazardous materials and not merely on poor states that import them.[27] But international law needs to move more in this direction with respect to economic and social rights. States need to think more affirmatively about their responsibilities for those violations beyond their borders and prescribe international law, whether hard or soft, to guarantee the economic rights of those suffering from violations associated with severe poverty.[28] An increase in duty-holders will also require international organizations to develop the capacity to enforce those new rights and duties, which leads to the final required move.

4. *Improve the capacities of international institutions to effect compliance by all actors*

For these reforms of the law to truly influence behavior, they will need to be accompanied by significant innovations within institutions. International organizations, both formal and informal, will need to bolster their capacity to promote

[23] Miller, *National Responsibility, supra* note 10, at 164.

[24] See Steven R. Ratner, 'Corporations and Human Rights: A Theory of Responsibility', *Yale LJ* 111 (2001): 443.

[25] Convention on the Elimination of All forms of Discrimination against Women, 18 December 1979, Art. 5, 1249 UNTS 13.

[26] For a skeptical view of such new duties and duty-holders, see John H. Knox, 'Horizontal Human Rights Law', *AJIL* 102 (2008): 1.

[27] See, e.g., Basel Convention on the Control of Transboundary Movements of Hazardous Wastes and Their Disposal, 22 March 1989, 1673 UNTS 57.

[28] See generally Margot E. Salomon, 'Deprivation, Causation and the Law of International Cooperation', in Malcolm Langford et al. (eds.), *Global Justice, State Duties: The Extraterritorial Scope of Economic, Social, and Cultural Rights in International Law* (Cambridge: Cambridge University Press, 2012) 259.

compliance with the new human rights-centered norms. They will need to develop—and adequately fund—new procedures to monitor state action and to induce the right behavior, such as mediation or the use of carrots and sticks. They will need to create a new culture among staff and governments of the importance of human rights in their work. Innovation of institutions could take place at the global level—within the UN, WTO, or IMF—but institutions at the regional level, like the EU or the African Union, can also play a role in developing and enforcing core norms so that they benefit human rights.

This change will not be easy. Many institutions consider human rights to be outside their mandate, and many governments, particularly from the developing world, are wary of giving new human rights mandates to existing institutions for fear that such a move will merely solidify Western dominance. Judging from the fate of existing institutions with respect to human rights, one cannot underestimate the obstacles to adequate funding. But without such empowerment of these bodies, the reform of international law can only exist on paper.

B. The core norms revised

In what way, then, would the norms discussed in this book need to change to meet the thicker standard of global justice? I offer here only an outline of this process, but clearly some norms would be quite different:

- The basic norms on the *use of force* in Articles 2(4) and 51 of the UN Charter should, in my view, remain unchanged. With the exception of humanitarian intervention (which, as noted, I already regard as lawful), to carve out new limitations in the name of promoting human rights would risk a loss of their critical role in the preservation of peace. The norms on *non-intervention* also seem to fit in the same category. They already allow for significant action to promote human rights, and to change them so as to allow for coercive efforts to advance human rights would undercut their main peace-preservation advantage.
- As for *self-determination*, it seems both possible and desirable to recognize a greater set of rights for peoples organized along subnational or transnational lines without undermining peace. In particular, we can consider the possibility of a right to autonomy of certain groups within states. Autonomy could be organized along territorial lines, as with the Basque region of Spain, or along functional lines, as with the Sami people in Finland and Sweden.[29] A legal right to autonomy would help advance the human rights of minority groups in a more significant way than the status quo, where states have the full option of whether or not to grant autonomy. At the same time, we would need to be careful in deciding which sorts of groups deserve autonomy so as to avoid creating new cleavages within the state that could ultimately lead to internal armed conflict.[30]

[29] For a review of key examples, see Hurst Hannum, *Autonomy, Sovereignty, and Self-Determination*, rev. ed. (Philadelphia, PA: University of Pennsylvania, 1996) Part II.

[30] See the careful treatment of this issue in Will Kymlicka, *Multicultural Citizenship* (Oxford: Clarendon Press, 1995) 176–92.

• Regarding *sovereign equality*, one obvious move would be the creation of mechanisms to give poor states the resources to participate more as equals in international lawmaking and law interpretation. Although some states in the WTO set up a small program to assist developing states in bringing cases in the DSB,[31] a more ambitious program would provide expertise to poor states in all sorts of venues that make or interpret international law. In addition, the rules on the immunity of states and former officials need to change so as to allow for more accountability against state actors for human rights atrocities. It might even be possible to construct a limited removal of immunity for sitting heads of government without giving up the thin justice of the existing immunity.

• The *admissions and decisionmaking processes of international organizations* can also be reconsidered under this higher standard of global justice. International institutions should consider more serious participatory rights for non-state actors whose input might result in decisions that better incorporate and advance respect for human rights. Just as the Nordic Council's acceptance of indigenous groups serves to inform states of the implications for their rights of the Council's decisions, we can see other possibilities, in particular for financial institutions such as the World Bank, the IMF, or even the Basel Committee. As for decisionmaking, even if the existing processes pass the test of thin justice, some institutions can do better. The UN could adopt new procedures to integrate human rights concerns into Security Council decisionmaking. We can revisit the procedures of the IMF in order to improve the prospect that Fund decisions will actually advance some human rights. This improvement need not involve a change to weighted voting but rather, the insertion of other checks on the lending process.

• The *territorial scope of human rights protection* also has room for improvement as well. One might entail a move, probably through a treaty, toward making *universal jurisdiction* over certain gross violations of human rights mandatory rather than permissive, a process that would advance human rights without obvious disruptions to peace. International law comes close to this goal for some offenses, like torture, war crimes, and enforced disappearances, where treaties require states to extradite or prosecute all offenders. With respect to *humanitarian intervention*, the black-letter law should embrace formally the context-dependent position that incorporates just war theory. Beyond that, we might also envisage humanitarian intervention in exceptional cases as a duty, though one should not understate the dangers of entrusting it to states without strong oversight and accountability by international institutions. And, more ambitiously, the territorial scope of human rights protection can also be extended in a completely different direction, to encompass a duty to assist states and individuals when there are serious violations of economic and social rights, a process that might be undertaken without disrupting interstate peace. This possibility leads to the next set of core norms.

• A large area of reform remains *international economic law*. For even as we must be careful in choosing the right sites for advancing global distributive

[31] See the website of the Advisory Centre on WTO Law, <http://http://www.acwl.ch>.

justice, two points seem clear: First, some aspects of *international trade law* can be reformed to make them a more positive force for the advancement of economic and social rights. These changes are already a major topic of international discussion in the Doha Round, most notably regarding agricultural subsidies. And similarly for *international investment law*, the law needs to include new duties on foreign investors and their home states to transform that area of law into a regime that advances human rights and not just investor interests. Second, even outside of trade and investment law, other programs can be devised to transfer expertise and resources to, or otherwise adjust the terms of cooperation with, those states whose capacity makes it impossible for them to guarantee economic and social rights.[32] This is not fantasy thinking for international law in that we have already witnessed significant normative movement through the Millennium Development Goals. Though not binding, these goals, adopted unanimously by the world's states at the General Assembly in 2000, include a call for improvement in the situation of the world's poorest people as well as improvements in global public health.[33]

• Even though we encountered challenges to appraising the three bodies of law in Chapter 11 under the two pillars of thin justice, we can sketch out a few areas of improvement toward a more just norm. *International humanitarian law* could evolve to provide greater protections for civilians. These could include changes in the proportionality rule to reduce risks to the innocent from military operations, as well as increased protections for those in occupied territories where the overall balance of power is still strongly in favor of the occupier's military needs.

• On the other hand, *international criminal law* seems to be at too early a stage to expect it to do much more to promote human rights. We would not, for instance, want to dismantle the meta-norm that places most duties under human rights law on states by either shifting them to individuals or by duplicating them through individual responsibility, for we lack global (and even national) institutions that can be counted on to try individuals for human rights abuses.

Lastly, a more just *international environmental law* would be one that does more to improve human rights. For example, in light of the impact of climate change on the rights to life and health of those in poor states through weather-related disasters and sea levels rising, we should be able to develop international environmental law to advance the rights to life and health. This might even include accountability regimes for payments by states contributing to climate change to those suffering most from it, part of current debates over so-called climate justice. Yet, as stated in Chapter 12, I am not convinced that human rights-oriented justice should be the major mission of international environmental law. So many of

[32] Cf. Miller, *National Responsibility, supra* note 10, at 253 (need for fairer terms of cooperation to help those most vulnerable).

[33] GA Res. 55/2, para. 19, 18 September 2000. Their implementation, on the other hand, remains a very mixed bag. See United Nations, Millennium Development Goals: 2013 Progress Report, <http://http://www.un.org/millenniumgoals/pdf/report-2013/2013_progress_english.pdf>.

it goals, notably protection of non-human species or mitigation of climate change more generally, are distinct from the advancement of human rights.

This review of the norms in this volume is merely a glimpse at what reform might entail. Certainly other areas of law not considered here, such as the law of the sea or financial regulation, could be more thickly just as well. And as noted, we should not assume that the thick justice standard offered earlier is all that international law can do, for much of its potential lies in important regulation that cannot be put in the human rights framework.

C. Procedural fairness

The process of making international law norms more just cannot be divorced from improving its procedural aspects as well. As first introduced in Chapter 3, the rule of law in general, and procedural fairness in particular, is an important complement to substantive justice, and indeed for many simply part of it. Legal rules, whatever their content, must be promulgated, interpreted, enforced, or changed in an ethically acceptable manner in order to gain the respect of those to whom they are directed. I have discussed fairness only selectively in this volume, when I saw it as most linked to substantive justice, in particular regarding the rules of membership and decision-making of international organizations addressed in Chapter 7. In this conclusion, I would emphasize the importance of three general and well-known principles of fairness for institutional venues, whether in lawmaking, law interpretation, or law enforcement. (Other key elements of the rule of law, such as those identified by Fuller in his conception of an internal morality of law, must be respected in all these processes as well.) Decisionmakers in these venues will need to flesh them out into more detailed rules of procedure.

First, fairness demands *inclusiveness of participation* in these venues, such that those most affected by decisions generally have a chance, at a minimum, to set forth their views to decisionmakers. They need not be full and equal participants in the decisionmaking process, however, for that process to be procedurally fair. (The target of economic sanctions for human rights abuses should not get to vote in the institution, like the Security Council, applying them, nor must the WTO Appellate Body include judges appointed by the disputing parties, even if the ICJ does.) Inclusivity in participation suggests the need for many reforms within international organizations to improve access by poor states as well, although these procedural reforms must not undercut the substantive goal of promoting human rights. For example, the change between the membership of the UN Human Rights Council and that of its predecessor, the Human Rights Commission, though undertaken in the name of greater participation by the developing world, seems to have done nothing to eliminate, and may indeed have worsened, that body's politicized selectivity in picking situations to discuss.[34]

[34] See, e.g., Human Rights Watch, 'Curing the Selectivity Syndrome', 24 June 2010, <http://www.hrw.org/sites/default/files/reports/hrc0610webwcover.pdf>. Nonetheless, the Council engages in a Universal Periodic Review procedure in which every state's record is at least assessed by the full Council on a regular basis.

Second, fairness demands in many instances *transparency*, to inform interested constituencies of the process and, equally important, put some pressure on those in the decisionmaking process to act according to accepted modes of reasoning, discourse, or persuasion.[35] Like inclusive participation, transparency also increases the likelihood that norms will be accepted by their targets, whether those who are on the receiving end of new duties or those who will gain new rights. At the same time, secrecy has its role, whether in crafting compromises within a political body like the Security Council or crafting judgments within a court.[36]

Third, fairness demands *accountability*, broadly conceived as the process by which participants in lawmaking, interpretation, and enforcement have their actions reviewed by others with a legitimate claim to such review according to accepted standards, with consequences for failure to meet them. Domestic accountability permits citizens, legislatures, or domestic courts to review the actions of governments in the making and enforcement of international law. As for international accountability, the legal literature is replete, in fact overly replete, with proposals for increased recourse to judicial or non-political settlement of international disputes.

Even though we should not fall prey to 'a judicial romanticism in which we imagine that merely by creating entities we call "courts" we have solved major problems',[37] the judicialization of some international disputes today is an indication that state and individual accountability can be strengthened. We have witnessed these trends with respect to human rights law in the European and Latin American regional courts; trade law through the work of the WTO DSB; investment law through resort to arbitral tribunals; certain aspects of the law of the sea under the dispute settlement provisions of UN Convention on the Law of the Sea; and a huge range of issues that one jurisdiction, the EU, has entrusted to the European Court of Justice.[38] And the ICTY, ICTR, and ICC have enhanced (the last of these very modestly) the accountability of individuals.[39] Courts also have the benefit of enhancing sovereign equality by putting states with different resources or political power (or nationals of those states in the case of criminal courts) on a more equal footing.[40]

[35] See generally Ian Johnstone, *The Power of Deliberation: International Law, Politics and Organizations* (Oxford: Oxford University Press, 2011) (on argumentation within the UN).

[36] See Steven R. Ratner, 'Behind the Flag of Dunant: Secrecy and the Compliance Mission of the International Committee of the Red Cross', in Andrea Bianchi and Anne Peters (eds.), *Transparency in International Law* (Cambridge: Cambridge University Press, 2013) 297.

[37] W. Michael Reisman, 'Institutions and Practices for Restoring and Maintaining Public Order', *Duke J Comp & Int'l L* 6 (1995): 175.

[38] As for the ICJ, only 70 states have accepted its compulsory jurisdiction; among the more powerful states, only Germany, India, and the United Kingdom accept it, the first two subject to significant limitations.

[39] At the same time, the ICC Statute denies the Court jurisdiction over offenses by nationals of a non-state party committed on that state's own territory, unless the Security Council refers the case; ICC Statute, Art. 12.

[40] Steven C. Roach, 'Rawls's Law of Peoples and the International Criminal Court', in Roland Pierik and Wouter Werner (eds.), *Cosmopolitanism in Context: Perspectives from International Law and Political Theory* (Cambridge: Cambridge University Press, 2010), 179, 193. During the drafting of the UN Charter, Hans Kelsen, echoing earlier scholars and diplomats, suggested that the only

Accountability should also extend to international organizations and the officials within them. Through internal and external review procedures by administrative bodies or courts, we can imagine greater oversight over the institutions entrusted with the enforcement of much of international law.[41] And as philosophers have recognized, accountability may require new structures of governance allowing individuals most affected by the decisions of international officials to judge their work in some way. Though beyond the scope of this study, the number of possible modalities is enormous, from increased NGO involvement to more direct connections between individuals and international organizations. Whether or not we choose to conceptualize those structures as a sort of global or cosmopolitan democracy, the important point is that those involved in lawmaking, interpretation, and enforcement need to respect relevant legal standards as well as answer to, in some way, the individuals whose fate they influence.[42]

D. A word on the modalities of reform

The four moves toward a more substantively just international law, and the three aspects of procedural fairness that must accompany them, will come about through the usual modalities by which international law has changed over time. These methods are claim and counter-claim, state practice that may lead to new custom, the development of soft law by state and non-state actors, binding and non-binding decisions of international organizations and expert bodies, rulings of international courts, and round after round of negotiations of new treaties. Each of these modalities of lawmaking writ large is now the subject of significant scholarship as to the implications for changes in the law over time, and especially whether certain modes privilege strong states over weak actors.[43]

For my purposes here, I will bracket these debates but simply note that I remain to be convinced that the modalities of international lawmaking require some

way to ensure that the UN would accomplish its goals of preventing war while respecting the sovereign equality of states was by subjecting all states to the compulsory jurisdiction of an international court. Hans Kelsen, 'The Principle of Sovereign Equality of States as a Basis for International Organization', *Yale LJ* 53 (1944): 207, 214–20.

[41] See, e.g., Jan Klabbers, 'International Institutions', in James Crawford and Martti Koskenniemi (eds.), *The Cambridge Companion to International Law* (Cambridge: Cambridge University Press, 2012) 228, 238–42.

[42] For important contributions, see David Held, *Democracy and the Global Order: From the Modern State to Cosmopolitan Governance* (Stanford, CA: Stanford University Press, 1995) 231–7; Gillian Brock, *Global Justice: A Cosmopolitan Account* (Oxford: Oxford University Press, 2009) 84–110.

[43] In the legal literature, some discussion addresses whether states should be able to take counter-measures—tit-for-tat violations of treaties or custom—and their implications for lawmaking. See, e.g., Monica Hakimi, 'Unfriendly Unilateralism', *Harv ILJ* 55 (2014): 105. In philosophy, Allen Buchanan has argued that a new norm in favor of humanitarian intervention must come about through 'illegal law reform'. Allen Buchanan, *Justice, Legitimacy, and Self-Determination: Moral Foundations for International Law* (Oxford: Oxford University Press, 2004) 456–9. Cf. Jane Stromseth, 'Rethinking Humanitarian Intervention: the Case for Incremental Change', in J.L. Holzgrefe and Robert Keohane (eds.), *Humanitarian Intervention: Ethical, Legal, and Political Dilemmas* (Cambridge: Cambridge University Press, 2003) 232, 248–52.

fundamental reconstruction to accomplish the task of creating more just and fairer norms and institutions. Rather, based on the results thus far, in particular impressive codification of rules regarding human rights, the environment, and other areas, the processes just mentioned are flexible enough to get us much further than we have currently achieved. With respect to custom, international law doctrine allows for adaptation. It respects the need for stability of expectations central to the idea of the rule of law and fairness, while implicitly allowing for deviations from rules that states might find unjust. As Rosalyn Higgins has written, 'if…norms no longer serve[ ] community interests, then those norms can properly be subjected to processes for change. The normal processes for change will include non-compliance'.[44]

A revolutionary break from past practices of lawmaking risks undermining whatever respect international law already enjoys, and the thin justice associated with such respect; moreover, I doubt it can be accomplished anyway.[45] Within the existing lawmaking processes, I think it essential that the three procedural elements of fairness inform and secrete themselves into all the modalities of lawmaking. These three values serve as guideposts for the necessary reform project without insisting on an entirely new set of lawmaking modalities.

IV. The Human Factor in Global Justice

If international law moves from at best thinly just to a set of norms and institutions that can truly advance human rights, with procedural fairness for its participants, it can offer a more significant contribution to the project of global justice. It cannot codify ideal theories of global justice, but it can move the debate forward. And its framework or skeleton can over time bear more weight through additional duties, duty-holders, and norms of procedural fairness. But regardless of the plan to move toward a more just international law and just world order—mine or others'—a final question remains: Who precisely can make this happen? The lawyer's obsession with institutions includes a professional requirement to identify those decisionmakers and venues ready and willing to effect legal change.

One set of individuals will be critical to advancing global justice, whether of the thin or thick variety. These 'moral entrepreneurs', as aptly called by international relations scholars, are people with a demonstrated capacity to change international expectations on key global norms.[46] Many are quite well known: Henri Dunant in regulation of warfare, Fridtjof Nansen in refugee protection, René Cassin and

[44] Rosalyn Higgins, *Problems and Process: International Law and How We Use It* (Oxford: Clarendon Press, 1994) 252.

[45] See Andrew Hurrell, *On Global Order: Power, Values, and the Constitution of International Society* (Oxford: Oxford University Press, 2007) 312–13.

[46] See Ethan Nadelmann, 'Global Prohibition Regimes: The Evolution of Norms in International Society', *Intl Org* 44 (1990): 479, 524–5. See also Margaret E. Keck and Kathryn Sikkink, *Activists beyond Borders: Advocacy Networks in International Politics* (Ithaca, NY: Cornell University Press, 1998) 14.

Eleanor Roosevelt in an architecture to guarantee human rights, Rachel Carson in environmental protection, John Maynard Keynes for international economic cooperation, Raphael Lemkin in international criminal justice, Dag Hammarskjöld on the role of the UN, and Jean Monnet on the construction of a European Community.

Most of these were not lawyers, but beneath or alongside or after them were lawyers serving as advisers, judges, negotiators, and scholars who designed, pushed, or enforced a set of legal norms and institutions to advance global justice. These include Hersch Lauterpacht and Navanethem Pillay (human rights), Oscar Schachter (the UN Charter), Antonio Cassese (criminal law), Tommy Koh (law of the sea), Eric Stein (EU law), and Max van der Stoel (minority rights). Each brought plans and skills to transform the big ideas of norm entrepreneurs into international law. Lawyers can bring to bear their imagination and technical prowess to identify the best arenas for progress; draft and negotiate documents, both binding and non-binding; and design institutions. Together with norm entrepreneurs, they can locate and navigate through venues with effective power to turn the ideas of global justice into a web of rights, duties, and responsibilities, as well interpretive and enforcement processes. Along the way, the norm entrepreneurs and lawyers will need to compromise to achieve reform in the law. Such political deal-making should not be seen as anathema to the construction of a better international law but as an essential part of it.

At the same time, the process described in this chapter is one to which all participants in international lawmaking, interpretation, and enforcement, across multiple communities, state and non-state alike, can contribute. There are roles for strong and weak states, international organizations, NGOs both domestic and transnational, and individuals across the planet.[47] Thus, unlike Rawls, I do not see this project as laying the groundwork solely for the foreign policy of liberal peoples or states.[48]

V. The Role for Theory in Advancing Global Justice

Theoretical work on global justice may precede, follow, or develop simultaneously with international legal reform. Either way, it should incorporate the insights of both international law and ethics. International lawyers can gain from moral and political philosophy a carefully derived set of ideas for evaluating the existing state of the law, promoting changes in it, and developing institutions to implement it. For instance, one of the most significant advances in our understanding of human rights law took place when the UN Committee on Economic, Social and Cultural Rights endorsed the concept of a state's duties to respect, protect, and promote

[47] An important question, though one beyond the scope of this volume, is what specific moral duties individuals might have to effectuate a more thickly just international law.

[48] Rawls, *The Law of Peoples*, *supra* note 10, at 10.

rights, first developed by Henry Shue.[49] But the benefits are not one-way. The norms accepted by states through international law have become an important part of the moral universe that the philosopher considers. The more philosophers of global justice know about international law and institutions, the more relevant can be their prescriptions to work with—or, if needed, supplant—those laws and institutions.

These complementary roles call for a more integrated approach to global justice. I hope that this study will encourage philosophical scholarship to move beyond the assumption that international law lacks a moral basis as well as to consider the advantages and disadvantages of ideal theory when it comes to global justice—where, after all, we are talking about changing the world. Engagement with international law implies a move beyond ideal theory. Philosophers should be willing to engage with the ethical significance of norms whose status as law suggests an acceptance by key actors of a *moral*, and not merely a political, position. As Habermas has said of cosmopolitanism, it 'remains an empty, even deceptive, promise without a realistic assessment of the totality of accommodating trends in which it is embedded'.[50]

But legal scholars should also move beyond any assumption that ethical inquiry is irrelevant or *ultra vires*. As with the philosophers, I hope this volume will encourage them to look behind their interpretive methods for hidden ethical assumptions and claims. For lawyers must recognize that when they engage in normative and even descriptive scholarship, they often, if not inevitably, *are already taking an ethical and not just a pragmatic position* on issues of global justice. For all but the most mundane analysis, legal scholars are assuming something about key global values. Indeed, as argued throughout this volume, many of the disagreements among lawyers are about the relative value of peace compared to human rights. Moreover, as Martti Koskenniemi has pointed out, we cannot avoid issues of morality by focusing on the broader, and somewhat vaguer, concept of legitimacy.[51]

International law and ethics can then discover and build upon their common agendas. Two priorities seem to represent the most fertile ground for such joint consideration. First is the allocation of global responsibilities, a concept central to my third step of legal reform. Although one discipline may talk in terms of Hohfeldian correlatives and the other in terms of right behavior, they ask about, in the most general sense, who is to blame or to praise, as well as be punished or rewarded, for a state of affairs; and who deserves in some sense, or is in the best position, to fix it.[52] What distinguishes a focus on responsibilities from one on

[49] Economic, Social, and Cultural Rights Committee, General Comment 12: The right to adequate food, 12 May 1999, para. 15, UN Doc. E/C.12/1999/5; Henry Shue, *Basic Rights: Subsistence, Affluence, and U.S. Foreign Policy*, 2nd ed. (Princeton, NJ: Princeton University Press, 1996) 52.

[50] Jürgen Habermas, *The Divided West* (Cambridge: Polity Press, 2006) 144.

[51] Martti Koskenniemi, 'Legitimacy, Rights, and Ideology: Notes towards a Critique of the New Moral Internationalism', *Associations: Journal for Legal and Social Theory* 7 (2003): 349, 371. See also Rosalyn Higgins, 'Ethics and International Law', *LJIL* 23 (2010): 277, 279.

[52] Compare, e.g., Peter Cane, *Responsibility in Law and Morality* (Portland, OR: Hart Publishing, 2002) 29–43, with Miller, *National Responsibility, supra* note 10, at 81–109; Robert E. Goodin, *Protecting the Vulnerable: A Reanalysis of our Social Responsibilities* (Chicago, IL: University of Chicago Press, 1985) 113–14.

duties is the idea of *multiplicity* and *allocation*: that in a world where numerous entities might well have duties, or indeed might have failed to carry out those duties, we must choose how to allocate among them in order to improve the state of affairs. It is about selecting who should do what when there are multiple plausible candidates.[53]

The legal approaches to global responsibilities include forays into the meaning of obligations *erga omnes*, the environmental law concept of common but differentiated responsibilities among states, especially as it affects climate change; and the Responsibility to Protect. And, as noted, the law has also looked beyond states, by addressing the accountability of other actors. Philosophers have moved from basic questions such as whether artificial entities, such as states, even have responsibilities as compared to individuals, to flesh out ideas of group and institutional responsibility.[54] Many of the key philosophical contributions to global justice literature are ultimately about responsibility.

Second, both legal and ethical inquiries into global justice sooner or later also face the question of the proper role of international institutions. Each recognizes that at a certain point states need to and will cooperate to undertake common goals, and will do so through institutions. In legal scholarship, it is inconceivable to discuss the state of the law or prescribe future courses for it without significant attention to these bodies. In ethics, the previously barren landscape is changing in a way promising for consideration of institutions.[55] The potential for collaboration is enhanced by the fluid nature of international organizations today. That is, whereas the state system evinces a certain level of stability, the reach of global and regional institutions is up for grabs. From the EU to the WTO, states and non-state actors are grappling with how much authority to delegate to these bodies. Philosophers are thus confronted with a set of promising arenas to realize new approaches to justice, but their very legalized nature—their constitutive instruments and procedures—demands some engagement with international law.

Breaching the barriers of inquiry of two major disciplines is not easy. Philosophy will always be more abstract in some sense than law, with its grounding in practice and institutions. But these differences also invite each to learn from the other. International law has shown itself to be generally open to the insights of other disciplines, whether political science, economics, or even literary theory. Ethics need not represent any greater a challenge. As for philosophy, the effort might be greater, but philosophers have invoked domestic law in their arguments, and some have appraised international law or even used it as a building block in their

[53] My emphasis on the allocation of responsibilities in this context does not equate with viewing justice as concerned only with allocations, a point made in Chapter 2.

[54] See, e.g., Toni Erskine, 'Assigning Responsibilities to Institutional Moral Agents: The Case of States and Quasi-States', *Ethics & Intl Aff* 15 (2001): 67; Goodin, *Protecting the Vulnerable, supra* note 52, at 134–67; Henry Shue, 'Mediating Duties', *Ethics* 98 (1998): 687.

[55] See, e.g., Allen Buchanan and Robert O. Keohane, 'The Legitimacy of Global Governance Institutions', *Ethics & Intl Aff* 20 (2006): 405; Pierik and Werner, *Cosmopolitanism in Context, supra* note 40; and the works by Thomas Pogge cited in Chapter 10.

arguments. Clearly, part of this process will involve a sort of division of labor—dare I say responsibilities—for the global justice project.

The move from the thin justice reflected in much of international law to a thicker justice aimed at advancing human rights is a project that will require the collected efforts of multiple fields. Theory will continue to emerge from international relations with its descriptive strengths, philosophy with its deep normative inquiries, and law with its institutional bent and problem-solving orientation. But, depending upon the issue for which we wish to devise just international norms, that community of expertise extends further, to other social sciences as well as natural sciences. In the end, scholars, decisionmakers, and the public should harness them all to design and construct a just international law based on peace between and within states and respect for everyone's human rights.

Bibliography

Secondary sources only. Official documents of governments and international organizations not included. In the case of multiple chapters in an edited collection, only the collection is listed.

Aaronson, Susan Ariel. 'Seeping In Slowly: How Human Rights Concerns are Penetrating the WTO'. *World Trade Review* 6: (2007): p. 413.

Aaronson, Susan Ariel, and Jamie M. Zimmerman. *Trade Imbalance: The Struggle to Weigh Human Rights Concerns in Trade Policymaking* (New York: Cambridge University Press, 2008).

Abi-Saab, Georges. 'Cours général de droit international public'. *Recueil des Cours de l'Académie de Droit International* 207 (1987): p. 9.

Abouharb, M. Rodwan, and David L. Cingranelli. 'IMF Programs and Human Rights, 1981–2003'. *Review of International Organizations* 4 (2009): p. 47.

Addis, Adeno. 'Imagining the International Community: The Constitutive Dimension of Universal Jurisdiction'. *Human Rights Quarterly* 31 (2009): p. 129.

Allee, Todd, and Clint Peinhardt. 'Contingent Credibility: The Impact of Investment Treaty Violations on Foreign Direct Investment'. *International Organization* 65 (2011): p. 401.

Allott, Philip. 'Power Sharing in the Law of the Sea'. *American Journal of International Law* 77 (1983): p. 1.

Allott, Philip. *Eunomia: A New Order for a New World* (New York: Oxford University Press, 1990).

Alston, Philip. 'Reconceiving the UN Human Rights Regime: Challenges Confronting the New UN Human Rights Council'. *Melbourne Journal of International Law* 7 (2006): 185.

Altman, Andrew, and Christopher Heath Wellman. 'A Defense of International Criminal Law'. *Ethics* 115 (2004): p. 35.

Altman, Andrew, and Christopher Heath Wellman. *A Liberal Theory of International Justice* (Oxford: Oxford University Press, 2011).

Alvarez, José E. 'Hegemonic International Law Revisited'. *American Journal of International Law* 97 (2003): p. 873.

Alvarez, José E. *International Organizations as Law-makers* (Oxford: Oxford University Press, 2006).

Alvarez, José E. 'The Schizophrenias of R2P'. In Euan MacDonald and Philip Alston (eds.), *Human Rights, Intervention, and the Right to Force* (Oxford: Oxford University Press, 2008), p. 275.

Alvarez, José E., and Karl P. Sauvant (eds.). *The Evolving International Investment Regime: Expectations, Realities, Options* (New York: Oxford University Press, 2011).

Ambrosio, Thomas. *Irredentism: Ethnic Conflict and International Politics* (Westport, CT: Praeger Publishers, 2001).

Anand, R.P. 'Sovereign Equality of States in International Law'. *Recueil des Cours de l'Académie de Droit International* 197 (1986): p. 9.

Anderson, Elizabeth. 'What is the Point of Equality?'. *Ethics* 109 (1999): p. 287.

Anderson, Kenneth. 'What NGO Accountability Means—And Does Not Mean'. *American Journal of International Law* 103 (2009): p. 170.

Anghie, Antony. *Imperialism, Sovereignty, and the Making of International Law* (New York: Cambridge University Press, 2004).

Anghie, Antony, and B.S. Chimni. 'Third World Approaches to International Law and Individual Responsibility in International Conflict'. In Steven R. Ratner and Anne-Marie Slaughter (eds.), *The Methods of International Law* (Washington DC: American Society of International Law, 2004), p. 185.

An-Na'im, Abdullahi. *Islam and Human Rights: Selected Essays of Abdullahi An-Na'im.* Mashood Baderin (ed.) (Burlington, VT: Ashgate Publishing, 2010).

Arbour, Louise. 'The Responsibility to Protect as a Duty of Care in International Law And Practice'. *Review of International Studies* 34 (2008): p. 445.

Archibugi, Daniele. 'Cosmopolitan Guidelines for Humanitarian Intervention', *Alternatives* 29 (2004): p. 1

Archibugi, Daniele. 'Cosmopolitan Humanitarian Intervention is Never Unilateral'. *International Relations* 19 (2005): p. 220.

Archibugi, Daniele, and David Held (eds.). *Cosmopolitan Democracy: An Agenda for a New World Order* (Cambridge: Polity Press, 1995).

Archibugi, Daniele, David Held, and Martin Köhler (eds.), *Re-imagining Political Community: Studies in Cosmopolitan Democracy* (Cambridge: Polity Press, 1998).

Arendt, Hannah. *Eichmann in Jerusalem: A Report on the Banality of Evil*, rev. ed. (New York City: Viking Press, 1965).

Atack, Iain. *The Ethics of Peace and War: From State Security to Human Community* (New York: Palgrave MacMillan, 2005).

Baffes, John. 'Cotton Subsidies, the WTO and the "Cotton Problem"'. World Bank Policy Research Paper 5663 (May 2011).

Bailliet, Cecilia M., and Katja Franko Aas. *Cosmopolitan Justice and its Discontents* (Milton Park: Routledge, 2011).

Bangerter, Olivier. 'Reasons Why Armed Groups Choose to Respect International Humanitarian Law or Not'. *International Review of the Red Cross* 93, No. 882 (2011): p. 353.

Barnett, Jon, and W. Neil Adger. 'Climate Change, Human Security and Violent Conflict'. *Political Geography* 26 (2007): p. 639.

Baron, Marcia. 'Impartiality and Friendship'. *Ethics* 101 (1991): p. 836.

Barry, Brian. 'Do Countries Have Moral Obligations? The Case of World Poverty'. *The Tanner Lectures on Human Values*, Vol. 2 (Salt Lake City, UT: University of Utah Press, 1981): p. 25.

Barry, Brian. *Theories of Justice* (Berkeley, CA: University of California Press, 1989).

Barry, Brian. *Justice as Impartiality* (New York: Oxford University Press, 1995).

Barry, Brian. 'Statism and Nationalism: A Cosmopolitan Critique'. *Nomos* 41 (1999): p. 12.

Barry, Christian, and Thomas W. Pogge (eds.). *Global Institutions and Responsibilities: Achieving Global Justice* (Malden, MA: Blackwell Publishing, 2005).

Bartels, Lorand. 'Article XX of GATT and the Problem of Extraterritorial Jurisdiction: The Case of Trade Measures for the Protection of Human Rights'. *Journal of World Trade* 36 (2002): p. 353.

Bassey, Celestine Oyom. 'Territorial Imperatives and Border Problems in Africa'. In Celestine Bassey and Oshita O. Oshita, *Governance and Border Security in Africa* (Lagos: Malthouse Press, 2010), p. 13.

Bedau, Hugo Adam, and Erin Kelly. 'Punishment'. In Edward N. Zalta (ed.), *The Stanford Encyclopedia of Philosophy* (Spring 2010). <http://plato.stanford.edu/entries/punishment/#3>.

Beitz, Charles R. *Political Theory and International Relations* (Princeton, NJ: Princeton University Press, 1979).

Beitz, Charles R. 'Cosmopolitan Ideals and National Sentiment'. *Journal of Philosophy* 80 (1983): p. 591.
Beitz, Charles R. 'International Liberalism and Distributive Justice'. *World Politics* 51 (1999): p. 269.
Beitz, Charles R. 'Social and Cosmopolitan Liberalism'. *International Affairs* 75 (1999): p. 515.
Beitz, Charles R. 'Does Global Inequality Matter?'. *Metaphilosophy* 32 (2001): p. 95.
Beitz, Charles R. 'Cosmopolitanism and Global Justice'. *Journal of Ethics* 9 (2005): p. 11.
Beitz, Charles R. *The Idea of Human Rights* (Oxford: Oxford University Press, 2009).
Beitz, Charles R. 'The Moral Standing of States Revisited'. *Ethics & International Affairs* 23 (2009): p. 325.
Bellamy, Alex J. *Just Wars: From Cicero to Iraq* (Cambridge: Polity Books, 2006).
Bellamy, Alex J. 'Whither the Responsibility to Protect? Humanitarian Intervention and the 2005 World Summit'. *Ethics & International Affairs* 20 (2006): p. 143.
Bellamy, Alex J. 'The Responsibility to Protect—Five Years On'. *Ethics & International Affairs* 24 (2010): p. 143.
Benedek, Wolfgang. 'The World Trade Organization and Human Rights'. In Wolfgang Benedek, Koen de Feyter, and Fabrizio Marrella (eds.), *Economic Globalization and Human Rights* (New York: Cambridge University Press, 2007), p. 137.
Ben-Naftali, Orna (ed.). *International Humanitarian Law and International Human Rights Law: Pas de Deux* (Oxford: Oxford University Press, 2011).
Ben-Naftali, Orna, and Yuval Shany. 'Living in Denial: The Application of Human Rights in the Occupied Territories'. *Israel Law Review* 37 (2003–04): p. 17.
Ben-Naftali, Orna, Aeyal M. Gross, and Keren Michaeli. 'Illegal Occupation: Framing the Occupied Palestinian Territory'. *Berkeley Journal of International Law* 23 (2005): p. 551.
Bentham, Jeremy. 'Principles of International Law'. In John Bowring (ed.), *The Works of Jeremy Bentham* (Edinburgh: William Tait, 1843), p. 537.
Benvenisti, Eyal. 'Sovereigns as Trustees of Humanity: On the Accountability of States to Foreign Stakeholders'. *American Journal of International Law* 107 (2013): p. 295.
Bermann, George A., and Petros C. Mavroides (eds.). *WTO Law and Developing Countries* (New York: Cambridge University Press, 2007).
Besson, Samantha, and John Tasioulas (eds.), *The Philosophy of International Law* (Oxford: Oxford University Press, 2010).
Bianchi, Andrea. 'Human Rights and the Magic of Jus Cogens'. *European Journal of International Law* 19 (2008): p. 491.
Blake, Michael. 'Distributive Justice, State Coercion, and Autonomy'. *Philosophy & Public Affairs* 30 (2001): p. 257.
Blum, Gabriella. 'The Crime and Punishment of States'. *Yale Journal of International Law* 38 (2013): p. 57.
Blum, Gabriella. 'The Fog of Victory'. *European Journal of International Law* 24 (2013): p. 391.
Bobbitt, Philip. *The Shield of Achilles: War, Peace, and the Course of History* (New York: Knopf, 2002).
Bodansky, Daniel. 'The Legitimacy of International Governance: A Coming Challenge for International Environmental Law?'. *American Journal of International Law* 93 (1999): p. 596.
Bodansky, Daniel. *The Art and Craft of International Environmental Law* (Cambridge, MA: Harvard University Press, 2011).

Bodansky, Daniel, Jutta Brunnée, and Ellen Hey (eds.). *The Oxford Handbook of International Environmental Law* (Oxford: Oxford University Press, 2007).

Boyle, Alan, and Christine Chinkin. *The Making of International Law* (Oxford: Oxford University Press, 2007).

Braithwaite, John, and Peter Drahos. *Global Business Regulation* (Cambridge: Cambridge University Press, 2000).

Brandt, R.B. 'Utilitarianism and the Rules of War'. In Marshall Cohen, Thomas Nagel, and Thomas Scanlon (eds.), *War and Moral Responsibility* (Princeton, NJ: Princeton University Press, 1974), p. 25.

Brandt, Willy. 'Speech on the occasion of the 100th anniversary of the J.H.W. Dietz Publishers, Nov. 3, 1981'. In Karl Rudolf (ed.), *Willy Brandt: Berliner Ausgabe, vol. 5: Die Partei der Freiheit. Willy Brandt und die SPD 1972–1992* (Bonn: Verlag J.H.W. Dietz Nachfolger, 2002), p. 363.

Brierly, James Leslie. 'The Rule of Law in International Society'. In Hersch Lauterpacht and C.H.M. Waldock (eds.), *The Basis of Obligation in International Law and Other Papers by the Late James Leslie Brierly* (Oxford: Clarendon Press, 1958), p. 250.

Brierly, J.L. *The Law of Nations: An Introduction to International Law of Peace*, 6th ed. (Oxford: Oxford University Press, 1963).

Brilmayer, Lea. 'International Justice and International Law'. *West Virginia Law Review* 98 (1996): p. 611.

Brock, Gillian. *Global Justice: A Cosmopolitan Account* (Oxford: Oxford University Press, 2009).

Brown, Chris. 'What, Exactly, is the Problem to which the 'Five-Part Test' is the Solution?'. *International Relations* 19 (2005): p. 225.

Brown, Chris. 'After "*Caroline*": NSS 2002, Practical Judgment, and the Politics and Ethics of Preemption'. In Deen K. Chatterjee (ed.), *The Ethics of Preventive War* (Cambridge: Cambridge University Press, 2013), p. 27.

Brownlie, Ian. *African Boundaries: A Legal and Diplomatic Encyclopaedia* (London: C. Hurst & Co., 1979).

Brunnée, Jutta, and Stephen J. Toope. *Legitimacy and Legality in International Law: An Interactional Account* (Cambridge: Cambridge University Press, 2010).

Buchanan, Allen. *Secession: The Morality of Political Divorce from Fort Sumter to Lithuania and Quebec* (Boulder, CO: Westview Press, 1991).

Buchanan, Allen. 'Liberalism and Group Rights'. In Jules L. Coleman and Allen Buchanan (eds.), *In Harm's Way: Essays in Honor of Joel Feinberg* (Cambridge: Cambridge University Press, 1994), p. 1.

Buchanan, Allen. 'The Internal Legitimacy of Humanitarian Intervention'. *Journal of Political Philosophy* 7 (1999): p. 71.

Buchanan, Allen. 'Rawls's Law of Peoples: Rules for a Vanished Westphalian World'. *Ethics* 110 (2000): p. 697.

Buchanan, Allen. *Justice, Legitimacy, and Self-Determination: Moral Foundations for International Law* (Oxford: Oxford University Press, 2004).

Buchanan, Allen, and Robert O. Keohane. 'The Preventive Use of Force: A Cosmopolitan Institutional Proposal'. *Ethics & International Affairs* 18 (2004): p. 1.

Buchanan, Allen, and Robert O. Keohane. 'The Legitimacy of Global Governance Institutions'. *Ethics & International Affairs* 10 (2006): p. 405.

Buchanan, Allen, and Robert O. Keohane. 'Precommitment Regimes for Intervention: Supplementing the Security Council'. *Ethics & International Affairs* 25 (2011): p. 41.

Buchheit, Lee C. *Secession: The Legitimacy of Self-Determination* (New Haven, CT: Yale University Press, 1978).

Buckland, W.W. *A Text-book of Roman Law: from Augustus to Justinian*, 3rd. ed. as revised by Peter Stein (Cambridge: Cambridge University Press, 1963).

Bull, Hedley. *The Anarchical Society: A Study of Order in World Politics*, 3rd ed. (New York: Columbia University Press, 2002).

Burke, Anthony. 'Just War or Ethical Peace? Moral Discourses of Strategic Violence after 9/11'. *International Affairs* 80 (2004): p. 329.

Burrowes, Robert D. 'The Republic of Yemen: The Politics of Unification and Civil War, 1989–1995'. In Michael C. Hudson (ed.), *Middle East Dilemma: The Politics and Economics of Arab Integration* (New York: Columbia University Press, 1999), p. 187.

Byers, Michael, and Georg Nolte (eds.). *United States Hegemony and the Foundations of International Law* (Cambridge: Cambridge University Press, 2003).

Calabresi, Guido, and A. Douglas Melamed. 'Property Rules, Liability Rules, and Inalienability: One View of the Cathedral'. *Harvard Law Review* 85 (1972): p. 1089.

Cane, Peter. *Responsibility in Law and Morality* (Oxford: Hart Publishing, 2002).

Cane, Peter. 'Morality, Law and Conflicting Reasons for Action'. *Cambridge Law Journal* 71 (2012): p. 59.

Caney, Simon. *Justice Beyond Borders: A Global Political Theory* (Oxford: Oxford University Press, 2005).

Caney, Simon. 'Just Emissions'. *Philosophy & Public Affairs* 40 (2012): p. 255.

Caron, David D. 'The Legitimacy of the Collective Authority of the Security Council'. *American Journal of International Law* 87 (1993): p. 552.

Carbonneau, Thomas E. 'Arbitral Law-Making'. *Michigan Journal of International Law* 25 (2004): p. 1183.

Carmody, Chios, Frank J. Garcia, and John Linarelli (eds.). *Global Justice and International Economic Law: Opportunities and Prospects* (Cambridge: Cambridge University Press, 2012).

Carr, Edward H. *The Twenty Years Crisis, 1919–1939: An Introduction to the Study of International Relations*, rev. ed. (London: Palgrave Macmillan, 2001).

Carrasco, Enrique R., and Alison K. Guernsey. 'The World Bank's Inspection Panel: Promoting True Accountability through Arbitration'. *Cornell International Law Journal* 41 (2008): p. 577.

Cashman, Greg, and Leonard C. Robinson. *An Introduction to the Causes of War: Patterns of Interstate Conflict from World War I to Iraq* (Lanham, MD: Rowman & Littlefield Publishers, 2007).

Cassese, Antonio. *Self-Determination of Peoples: A Legal Reappraisal* (Cambridge: Cambridge University Press, 1995).

Cassese, Antonio. 'Soliloquy'. In P. Gaeta and S. Zappalà (eds.), *The Human Dimension of International Law: Selected Papers* (New York: Oxford University Press, 2008), p. lix.

Castle, Stephen. 'Europe Denies 2 Nations Entry to Travel Zone'. *New York Times*, 22 September 2011: p. A15.

Center for International Environmental Law. 'Transparency and Public Participation in WTO Disputes Settlement' (2009). <http://www.ciel.org/Publications/Transparency_WTO_Dec09.pdf>.

Chandler, David. 'New Rights for Old: Cosmopolitan Citizenship and the Critique of State Sovereignty'. *Political Studies* 51 (2003): p. 332.

Chang, Ha-Joon. *Kicking Away the Ladder: Development Strategy in Historical Perspective* (London: Anthem Press, 2002).

Charlesworth, Hilary, and Christine Chinkin. *The Boundaries of International Law: A Feminist Analysis* (Huntington, NY: Juris Publishing, 2000).

Chayes, Abram, and Antonia Chayes. *The New Sovereignty: Compliance With International Regulatory Agreements* (Cambridge, MA: Harvard University Press, 1998).

Chehtman, Alejandro. *The Philosophical Foundations of Extraterritorial Punishment* (Oxford: Oxford University Press, 2010).

Choudhury, Barnali, Katja Gehne, Simone Heri, Franziska Humbert, Christine Kaufmann, and Krista Nadakavukaren Schefer. 'A Call For A WTO Ministerial Decision On Trade And Human Rights'. In Thomas Cottier and Panagiotis Delimatsis (eds.), *The Prospects of International Trade Regulation: From Fragmentation to Coherence* (Cambridge: Cambridge University Press, 2011), p. 323.

Christiano, Thomas. 'An Instrumental Argument for a Human Right to Democracy'. *Philosophy & Public Affairs* 39 (2011): p. 142.

Clapham, Andrew. *Human Rights Obligations of Non-State Actors* (Oxford: Oxford University Press, 2006).

Coggins, Bridget L. 'The History of Secession: An Overview'. In Aleksandar Pavković and Peter Radan (eds.), *The Ashgate Research Companion to Secession* (Surrey: Ashgate, 2011), p. 23.

Cohen, G.A. *Rescuing Justice and Equality* (Cambridge, MA: Harvard University Press, 2008).

Cohen, Jean L. 'Whose Sovereignty? Empire vs. International Law'. *Ethics & International Affairs* 18 (2004): p. 1.

Cohen, Jean L. 'Sovereign Equality vs. Imperial Right: The Battle over the 'New World Order''. *Constellations* 13 (2006): p. 485.

Cohen, Jean L. *Globalization and Sovereignty: Rethinking Legality, Legitimacy, and Constitutionalism* (Cambridge: Cambridge University Press, 2012).

Cohen, Joshua. 'Minimalism About Human Rights: The Most We Can Hope For?'. *Journal of Political Philosophy* 12 (2004): p. 190.

Cohen, Joshua, and Charles Sabel. 'Extra Rempublicam Nulla Justitia?'. *Philosophy & Public Affairs* 34 (2006): p. 147.

Coicaud, Jean-Marc, and Veijo Heiskanen (eds.). *The Legitimacy of International Organizations* (Tokyo: United Nations University Press, 2001).

Coleman, Jules, and Scott Shapiro (eds.). *The Oxford Handbook of Jurisprudence and Philosophy of Law* (Oxford: Oxford University Press, 2002).

Copp, David. 'International Law and Morality in the Theory of Secession'. *Journal of Ethics* 2 (1998): p. 219.

Correa, Carlos, and Duncan Matthews. 'The Doha Declaration Ten Years on and its Impact on Access to Medicines and the Right to Health', UNDP Discussion Paper. 20 December 2011.

Corten, Olivier. *The Law Against War: The Prohibition on the Use of Force in Contemporary International Law* (Oxford: Hart Publishing, 2010).

Corten, Olivier. 'Regulating Resort to Force: A Response to Matthew Waxman from a "Bright-Liner"'. *European Journal of International Law* 24 (2013): p. 191.

Cottier, Thomas, Joost Pauwelyn, and Elisabeth Bürgi Bonanomi (eds.). *Human Rights and International Trade* (Oxford: Oxford University Press, 2005).

Crawford, James. *The Creation of States in International Law*, 2nd ed. (Oxford: Oxford University Press, 2006).

Crawford, James, and Martti Koskenniemi (eds.). *The Cambridge Companion to International Law* (Cambridge: Cambridge University Press, 2012).

Crawford, Neta C. 'The Slippery Slope to Preventive War'. *Ethics & International Affairs* 17 (2003): p. 1.

Criddle, Evan J. 'Humanitarian Financial Intervention'. *European Journal of International Law* 24 (2013): p. 583.

Crook, John R. (ed.). 'Contemporary Practice of the United States relating to International Law'. *American Journal of International Law* 104 (2010): p. 271.

D'Amato, Anthony. 'Peace vs. Accountability in Bosnia'. *American Journal of International Law* 88 (1994): p. 500.

Darwall, Stephen L. 'Theories of Ethics'. In R.G. Frey and Christopher Heath Wellman (eds.), *A Companion to Applied Ethics* (Malden, MA: Blackwell Publishing, 2005), p. 17.

d'Aspremont, Jean. 'The Foundations of the International Legal Order'. *Finnish Yearbook of International Law* 18 (2007): p. 219.

de Vattel, Emer. *The Law of Nations*. Béla Kapossy and Richard Whatmore (eds.) (Indianapolis, IN: Liberty Fund, 2008).

de Visscher, Charles. *Théories et réalités en droit international public*, 2nd ed. (Paris: A. Pedone, 1955).

de Wet, Erika. *The Chapter VII Powers of the Security Council* (Oxford: Hart Publishing, 2004).

de Wet, Erika. 'From *Kadi* to *Nada*: Judicial Techniques Favouring Human Rights over United Nations Security Council Sanctions'. *Chinese Journal of International Law* 12 (2013): p. 787.

de Wet, Erika, and Jure Vidmar (eds.). *Hierarchy in International Law* (Oxford: Oxford University Press, 2012).

Desmet, Ellen. *Indigenous Rights Entwined with Nature Conservation* (Cambridge: Intersentia, 2011).

Dickinson, Edwin De Witt. *The Equality of States in International Law* (Cambridge, MA: Harvard University Press, 1920).

Dinh, Nguyen Quoc, Patrick Daillier, Mathias Forteau, and Alain Pellet (eds.), *Droit international public*, 8th ed. (Paris: L.G.D.J., 2009).

Dolzer, Rudolph. 'Fair and Equitable Treatment: Today's Contours'. *Santa Clara Journal of International Law* 12 (2013): p. 7.

Dolzer, Rudolf, and Christoph Schreuer. *Principles of International Investment Law*, 2nd ed. (New York: Oxford University Press, 2012).

Donadio, Rachel. 'Italy Convicts 23 Americans for C.I.A. Renditions'. *New York Times*. 4 November 2009.

Donnelly, Jack. *Universal Human Rights in Theory and Practice*, 2nd ed. (Ithaca, NY: Cornell University Press, 2003).

Doswald-Beck, Louise. *Human Rights in Times of Conflict and Terrorism* (Oxford: Oxford University Press, 2011).

Dower, Nigel. *The Ethics of War and Peace* (Cambridge: Polity Press, 2009).

Downes, Alexander B. *Targeting Civilians in War* (Ithaca, NY: Cornell University Press, 2008).

Dreher, Axel. 'IMF Conditionality: Theory and Evidence'. *Public Choice* 141 (2009): p. 233.

Drumbl, Mark A. *Atrocity, Punishment, and International Law* (Cambridge: Cambridge University Press, 2007).

Dunoff, Jeffrey L. 'Hudec's Methods—and Ours'. *Minnesota Journal of International Law* 20 (2011): p. 437.

Dunoff, Jeffrey L., and Mark A. Pollack (eds.). *Interdisciplinary Perspectives on International Law and International Relations* (Cambridge: Cambridge University Press, 2013).

Dunoff, Jeffrey L., and Joel P. Trachtman. 'Economic Analysis of International Law'. *Yale Journal of International Law* 24 (1999): p. 1.

Dunoff, Jeffrey L., and Joel P. Trachtman (eds.), *Ruling the World?: Constitutionalism, International Law, and Global Governance* (Cambridge: Cambridge University Press, 2009).

Dupuy, René-Jean. 'Communauté internationale et disparités de développement'. *Recueil des Cours de l'Académie de Droit International* 165 (1979): p. 9.

Dupuy, P.M., F. Francioni, and E.U. Petersmann (eds.). *Human Rights in International Investment Law and Arbitration* (New York: Oxford University Press, 2009).

Dworkin, Ronald. *Taking Rights Seriously* (Cambridge, MA: Harvard University Press, 1977).

Dworkin, Ronald. *Justice for Hedgehogs* (Cambridge, MA: Harvard University Press, 2011).

Dworkin, Ronald. 'A New Philosophy for International Law'. *Philosophy & Public Affairs* 41 (2013): p. 2.

Eckert, Amy E. 'Peoples and Persons: Moral Standing, Power, and the Equality of States'. *International Studies Quarterly* 50 (2006): p. 841.

El Said, Mohammed, and Amy Kapczynksi. 'Access to Medicines: The Role of Intellectual Property Law and Policy'. Global Commission on HIV and the Law Working Paper (2011).

Elster, Jon. 'Deliberation and Constitution Making'. In Jon Elster (ed.), *Deliberative Democracy* (Cambridge: Cambridge University Press, 1998), p. 97.

Elster, Jon. *Closing the Books: Transitional Justice in Historical Perspective* (Cambridge: Cambridge University Press, 2004).

Entous, Adam. 'U.S. Legal Grounds for Backing Syrian Rebels'. *Wall Street Journal.* 14 July 2013.

Erskine, Toni. 'Assigning Responsibilities to Institutional Moral Agents: The Case of States and Quasi-States'. *Ethics & International Affairs* 15 (2001): p. 67.

Erskine, Toni. '"Citizen of Nowhere" or "The Point where Circles Intersect"? Impartialist and Embedded Cosmopolitanisms'. *Review of International Studies* 28 (2002): p. 457.

Erskine, Toni. *Embedded Cosmopolitanism: Duties to Strangers and Enemies in a World of 'Dislocated Communities'* (Oxford: Oxford University Press, 2008).

Estlund, David M. *Democratic Authority: A Philosophical Framework* (Princeton, NJ: Princeton University Press, 2008).

Falk, Richard, and Andrew Strauss. 'On the Creation of a Global Peoples Assembly: Legitimacy and the Power of Popular Sovereignty'. *Stanford Journal of International Law* 36 (2000): p. 191.

Farer, Tom. 'Cosmopolitan Humanitarian Intervention: A Five-Part Test'. *International Relations* 19 (2005): p. 211.

Feinberg, Joel. 'Noncomparative Justice'. *Philosophical Review* 83 (1974): p. 297.

Feldman, Noah. 'Cosmopolitan Law?'. *Yale Law Journal* 116 (2007): p. 1022.

Ferguson, Niall. *The War of the World: Twentieth-Century Conflict and the Descent of the West* (London: Allen Lane, 2006).

Fisse, Brent, and John Braithwaite. 'The Allocation of Responsibility for Corporate Crime: Individualism, Collectivism and Accountability'. *Sydney Law Review* 11 (1988): p. 468.

Fixdal, Mona, and Dan Smith. 'Humanitarian Intervention and Just War'. *Mershon International Studies Review* 42 (1998): p. 283.

Focarelli, Carlo. *International Law as Social Construct: The Struggle for Global Justice* (Oxford: Oxford University Press, 2012).

Follesdal, Andreas. 'The Distributive Justice of a Global Basic Structure: A Category Mistake?'. *Politics, Philosophy, & Economics* 10 (2011): p. 46.

Forst, Rainer. 'Towards a Critical Theory of Transnational Justice'. *Metaphilosophy* 32 (2001): p. 160.

Fox, Gregory H., and Brad R. Roth (eds.). *Democratic Governance and International Law* (Cambridge: Cambridge University Press, 2000).

Franck, Thomas M. *Nation Against Nation: What Happened to the U.N. Dream and What the U.S. Can Do About It* (New York: Oxford University Press, 1985).

Franck, Thomas M. 'Some Observations on the ICJ's Procedural and Substantive Innovations'. *American Journal of International Law* 81 (1987): p. 116.

Franck, Thomas M. *The Power of Legitimacy Among Nations* (New York: Oxford University Press, 1990).

Franck, Thomas M. 'The "Powers of Appreciation": Who Is the Ultimate Guardian of UN Legality?'. *American Journal of International Law* 86 (1992): p. 519.

Franck, Thomas M. *Fairness in International Law and Institutions* (Oxford: Oxford University Press, 1995).

Franck, Thomas M. *Recourse to Force* (Cambridge: Cambridge University Press, 2002).

Frost, Mervyn. *Ethics in International Relations: A Constitutive Theory* (Cambridge: Cambridge University Press, 1996).

Fuller, Lon. *The Morality of Law* (New Haven, CT: Yale University Press, 1964).

Gallie, W.B. 'Essentially Contested Concepts'. *Proceedings of the Aristotelian Society* 56 (1956): p. 167.

Galtung, Johan. 'Violence, Peace, and Peace Research'. *Journal of Peace Research* 6 (1969): p. 167.

Garcia, Frank J. *Trade, Inequality, and Justice: Toward a Liberal Theory of Just Trade* (Ardsley, NY: Transnational Publishers, 2003).

Garcia, Frank J. 'Global Justice and the Bretton Woods Institutions'. *Journal of International Economic Law* 10 (2007): p. 461.

Gardner, John. 'What is Tort Law for? Part I. The Place of Corrective Justice'. *Law & Philosophy* 30 (2011): p. 1.

Gathii, James Thuo. 'TWAIL: A Brief History of its Origins, its Decentralized Network, and a Tentative Bibliography'. *Trade, Law, and Development* 3 (2011): p. 26.

Gibbard, Allen. 'Constructing Justice'. *Philosophy & Public Affairs* 20 (1991): p. 264.

Glenny, Misha. *The Fall of Yugoslavia: The Third Balkan War* (New York: Penguin Books, 1993).

Global Policy Forum. 'Subjects of UN Security Council Vetoes'. 31 October 2013. <http://www.globalpolicy.org/component/content/article/102/40069.html>.

Global Witness. 'The Kimberley Process'. 16 January 2014. <http://www.globalwitness.org/campaigns/conflict/conflict-diamonds/kimberley-process>.

Glover, Jonathan. *Humanity: A Moral History of the Twentieth Century* (London: Jonathan Cape, 1999).

Goodin, Robert E. *Protecting the Vulnerable: A Reanalysis of our Social Responsibilities* (Chicago, IL: University of Chicago Press, 1985).

Goodin, Robert E. 'What is So Special About Our Fellow Countrymen?'. *Ethics* 98 (1988): p. 663.

Goodin, Robert E. *Utilitarianism as a Public Philosophy* (New York: Cambridge University Press, 1995).

Goodin, Robert E., and Steven R. Ratner. 'Democratizing International Law'. *Global Policy* 2 (2011): p. 241.

Goodman, Ryan. 'Humanitarian Intervention and Pretexts for War'. *American Journal of International Law* 100 (2006): p. 107.

Grand Council of the Crees. *Sovereign Injustice: Forcible Inclusion of the James Bay Crees and Cree Territory into a Sovereign Quebec* (Nemaska: Grand Council of the Crees, 1995).

Gray, Christine. *International Law and the Use of Force*, 3rd ed. (Oxford: Oxford University Press, 2008).

Gray, Kevin R. 'Right to Food Principles vis à vis Rules Governing International Trade'. *British Institute of International and Comparative Law* (December 2003).

Green, Andrew. 'Climate Change, Regulatory Policy and the WTO: How Constraining Are Trade Rules?'. *Journal of International Economic Law* 8 (2005): p. 143.

Greenberg, Susan. 'Borderline Case: Czechoslovakia's Old Internal Frontiers are being Revived'. *The Guardian*, 20 October 1992.

Greene, Leslie. 'Should Law Improve Morality?'. University of Oxford Legal Research Paper No. 73/2013. 16 July 2013. <http://www.ssrn.com>.

Greenhouse, Steven. 'Clothiers Act to Inspect Bangladeshi Factories'. *New York Times*. 7 July 2013.

Greenhouse, Steven, and Elizabeth A. Harris. 'Battling for a Safer Bangladesh'. *New York Times*. 21 April 2014.

Grono, Nick. 'Negotiating Peace and Justice: Considering Accountability and Deterrence in Peace Processes'. 26 June 2007. <http://www.crisisgroup.org/en/publication-type/speeches/2007/grono-negotiating-peace-and-justice-considering-accountability-and-deterrence-in-peace-processes.aspx>.

Grotius, Hugo. *The Law of War and Peace*. Francis W. Kelsey (ed.) (Oxford: Clarendon Press, 1925).

Guzman, Andrew T. *How International Law Works: A Rational Choice Theory* (New York: Oxford University Press, 2008).

Guzman, Andrew T. 'International Organizations and the Frankenstein Problem'. *European Journal of International Law* 24 (2013): p. 999.

Häberli, Christian. 'Do WTO Rules Improve or Impair the Right to Food?'. In Joseph A. McMahon and Melaku Geboye Desta (eds.), *Research Handbook on the WTO Agricultural Agreement: New and Emerging Issues in International Agricultural Trade Law* (Cheltenham: Edward Elgar Publishing, 2012), p. 79.

Habermas, Jürgen. 'Bestiality and Humanity: A War on the Border between Legality and Morality'. *Constellations* 6 (1999): p. 263.

Habermas, Jürgen. *The Divided West* (Frankfurt: Suhrkamp Verlag, 2006).

Hakimi, Monica. 'A Functional Approach to Targeting and Detention'. *Michigan Law Review* 110 (2012): p. 1365.

Hakimi, Monica. 'Unfriendly Unilateralism'. *Harvard International Law Journal* 55 (2014): p. 105.

Hammarskjöld, Dag. 'Statement before the Plenary Session of the General Assembly'. In Wilder Foote (ed)., *Servant of Peace: A Selection of the Speeches and Statements of Dag Hammarskjöld* (New York: Harper & Row, 1962), p. 28.

Hannum, Hurst. 'Self-Determination, Yugoslavia, and Europe: Old Wine in New Bottles?'. *Transnational Law and Contemporary Problems* 3 (1993): p. 57.

Hannum, Hurst. *Autonomy, Sovereignty, and Self-Determination*, rev. ed. (Philadelphia, PA: University of Pennsylvania, 1996).

Hanson, Stephen E. et al. 'The WTO and Russian Politics'. In *Russia and the WTO: A Progress Report* (Seattle, WA: National Bureau of Asian Research, 2007), p. 7.

Hardin, Garrett. 'The Tragedy of the Commons'. *Science* 162 (1968): p. 243.

Hardin, Russell. *Morality within the Limits of Reason* (Chicago, IL: University of Chicago Press, 1988).

Hare, R.M. *Moral Thinking: Its Levels, Method, and Point* (Oxford: Clarendon Press, 1981).

Hargrove, John Lawrence. 'The *Nicaragua* Judgment and the Future of the Law of Force and Self-Defense'. *American Journal of International Law* 81 (1987): p. 135.

Harris, David, Michael O'Boyle, Ed Bates, and Carla Buckley, *Law of the European Convention on Human Rights*, 2nd ed. (Oxford: Oxford University Press, 2009).

Harsch, Ernest. 'Africa Defends Democratic Rule: 'Zero Tolerance' for Coups, Constitutional Violations'. *Africa Renewal Online* (April 2010). <http://www.un.org/africarenewal/magazine/april-2010/africa-defends-democratic-rule>.

Hart, H.L.A. 'Are There Any Natural Rights?'. *Philosophical Review* 64 (1955): p. 175.

Hart, H.L.A. *The Concept of Law*, 3rd ed. (Oxford: Oxford University Press, 2012).

Hedges, Chris. *War is a Force that Gives Us Meaning* (New York: Public Affairs, 2002).

Held, David. *Democracy and the Global Order: From the Modern State to Cosmopolitan Governance* (Stanford, CA: Stanford University Press, 1995).

Held, David. 'Law of States, Law of Peoples: Three Models of Sovereignty'. *Legal Theory* 8 (2002): p. 1.

Held, David. 'Cosmopolitanism: Globalisation Tamed?'. *Review of International Studies* 29 (2003): p. 465.

Held, David. *Cosmopolitanism: Ideals and Realities* (Malden, MA: Polity Press, 2010).

Hellman, Gunther. *Justice and Peace: Interdisciplinary Perspectives on a Contested Relationship* (Frankfurt: Campus Verlag, 2013).

Henckaerts, Jean-Marie. 'Study on Customary International Humanitarian Law: A Contribution to the Understanding and Respect for the Rule of Law in Armed Conflict'. *International Review of the Red Cross* 87, No. 857 (2005): p. 175.

Henkin, Louis. *International Law: Politics and Values* (Boston, MA: Martinus Nijhoff Publishers, 1995).

Hensel, Paul R., Michael E. Allison, and Ahmed Khanani. 'The Colonial Legacy and Border Stability: *Uti Possidetis* and Territorial Claims in the Americas'. Paper presented at the Annual Meeting of International Studies Association. 17 March 2004. <http://www.paulhensel.org/Research/io05.pdf>.

Higgins, Rosalyn. 'The Place of International Law in the Settlement of Disputes by the Security Council'. *American Journal of International Law* 64 (1970): p. 1.

Higgins, Rosalyn. *Problems and Process: International Law and How We Use It* (Oxford: Clarendon Press, 1994).

Higgins, Rosalyn. 'Ethics and International Law'. *Leiden Journal of International Law* 23 (2010): p. 277.

Hobbes, Thomas. *Leviathan* (New York: Penguin Books, 1985).

Hoekman, Bernard. 'Operationalizing the Concept of Policy Space in the WTO: Beyond Special and Differential Treatment'. *Journal of International Economic Law* 8 (2005): p. 405.

Hoekman, Bernard. 'Proposals for WTO Reform: A Synthesis and Assessment'. *Minnesota Journal of International Law* 20 (2011): p. 324.

Hoekman, Bernard M., and Michel M. Kostecki. *The Political Economy of the World Trading System: The WTO and Beyond*, 2nd ed. (Oxford: Oxford University Press, 2001).

Holzgrefe, J.L., and Robert O. Keohane (eds.). *Humanitarian Intervention: Ethical, Legal, and Political Dilemmas* (Cambridge: Cambridge University Press, 2003).

Homer-Dixon, Thomas F. *Environment, Scarcity, and Violence* (Princeton, NJ: Princeton University Press, 1999).

Hooker, Brad. *Ideal Code, Real World* (Oxford: Oxford University Press, 2000).

Horvath, Günther J. 'The Duty of the Tribunal to Render an Enforceable Award'. *Journal of International Arbitration* 18 (2001): p. 135.

Horowitz, Donald L. 'Self-Determination: Politics, Philosophy, and Law'. In Ian Shapiro and Will Kymlicka (eds.), *Ethnicity and Group Rights* (New York: New York University Press, 1997), p. 421.

Howse, Robert. 'The Appellate Body Rulings in the Shrimp/Turtle Case: A New Legal Baseline for the Trade and Environment Debate'. *Columbia Journal of Environmental Law* 27 (2002): p. 491.

Howse, Rob, and Makau Matua. 'Protecting Human Rights in a Global Economy: Challenges for the World Trade Organization'. *Human Rights Development Yearbook* (1999–2000): p. 53.

Howse, Robert, and Ruti G. Teitel. 'Beyond the Divide: The Covenant on Economic, Social, and Cultural Rights and the World Trade Organization'. Friedrich Ebert Stiftung Occasional Paper No. 30 (April 2007).

Human Rights Watch. 'Sri Lanka: IMF Should Not Condone Abuses'. 22 July 2009. <http://www.hrw.org/news/2009/07/22/sri-lanka-imf-should-not-condone-abuses>.

Human Rights Watch. 'Transparency and Accountability in Angola'. 13 April 2010. <http://www.hrw.org/reports/2010/04/13/transparency-and-accountability-angola>.

Human Rights Watch. 'Curing the Selectivity Syndrome'. 24 June 2010. <http://www.hrw.org/sites/default/files/reports/hrc0610webwcover.pdf>.

Human Rights Watch. 'Abuse-Free Development: How the World Bank Should Safeguard Against Human Rights Violations'. 2013. <http://www.hrw.org/sites/default/files/reports/worldbank0713_ForUpload.pdf>.

Huntley, Todd C. 'Controlling the Use of Force in Cyberspace: The Application of the Law of Armed Conflict During a Time of Fundamental Change in the Nature of Warfare'. *Naval Law Review* 60 (2010): p. 167.

Hurd, Ian. 'Legitimacy and Authority in International Politics'. *International Organization* 53 (1999): p. 379.

Hurrell, Andrew. 'Norms and Ethics in International Relations'. In Walter Carlsnaes, Thomas Risse, and Beth A. Simmons (eds.), *Handbook of International Relations* (New York: Sage Publications, 2002), p. 137.

Hurrell, Andrew. 'International Law and the Making and Unmaking of Boundaries'. In Allen Buchanan and Margaret Moore (eds.), *States, Nations, and Borders: The Ethics of Making Boundaries* (Cambridge: Cambridge University Press, 2003), p. 275.

Hurrell, Andrew. *On Global Order: Power, Values, and the Constitution of International Society* (Oxford: Oxford University Press, 2007).

Ignatieff, Michael. *The Lesser Evil: Political Ethics in an Age of Terror* (Princeton, NJ: Princeton University Press, 2004).

Ikome, Francis Nguendi. 'Africa's International Borders as Potential Sources of Conflict And Future Threats to Peace And Security'. Institute for Security Studies Paper 223. 30 May 2012.

Inazumi, Mitsue. *Universal Jurisdiction in Modern International Law: Expansion of National Jurisdiction for Prosecuting Serious Crimes under International Law* (Antwerp: Intersentia, 2005).

Independent International Fact-Finding Mission on the Conflict in Georgia. Report of the Independent International Fact-Finding Mission on the Conflict in Georgia, Vol. 2 (September 2009). <http://www.ceiig.ch/pdf/IIFFMCG_Volume_II.pdf>.

Institute of International Law. 'Universal Criminal Jurisdiction with regard to the Crime of Genocide, Crimes against Humanity and War Crimes: Resolution'. 26 August 2005. <http://www.idi-iil.org/idiE/resolutionsE/2005_kra_03_en.pdf>.

International Bar Association. 'IBA Guidelines on Party Representation in International Arbitration'. 2013. <http://www.ibanet.org>.

International Coalition for the Responsibility to Protect. 'The Crisis in Burma'. <http://www.responsibilitytoprotect.org/index.php/crises/crisis-in-burma>.

International Commission on Intervention and State Sovereignty. *The Responsibility to Protect: Report of the International Commission on Intervention and State Sovereignty*. December 2001, <http://responsibilitytoprotect.org/ICISS%20Report.pdf>.

International Committee of the Red Cross Advisory Service on International Humanitarian Law. 'What is International Humanitarian Law?'. July 2004. <http://www.icrc.org/eng/assets/files/other/what_is_ihl.pdf>.

International Committee of the Red Cross. *Customary International Humanitarian Law*. Jean-Marie Henckaerts and Louise Doswald Beck (eds.) (Cambridge: Cambridge University Press, 2005).

International Committee of the Red Cross. *Interpretive Guidance on the Notion of Direct Participation in Hostilities under International Humanitarian Law*. February 2009. <http://www.icrc.org/eng/assets/files/other/icrc-002-0990.pdf>.

International Committee of the Red Cross. 'International Humanitarian Law and the Challenges of Contemporary Armed Conflicts'. 31 October 2011. ICRC Doc. 31IC/11/5.1.2.

International Institute for Sustainable Development. 'IISD Model International Agreement on Investment for Sustainable Development' (2005). <http://www.iisd.org/pdf/2005/investment_model_int_agreement.pdf>.

International Law Association Committee on the Formation of Customary (General) International Law. 'Statement of Principles Applicable to the Formation of General Customary International Law' (2000). <http://www.ila-hq.org>.

Interview by Wolf Blitzer with Dr Condoleezza Rice, Assistant to the President for National Security Affairs. 7 September 2002. <http://www.cnn.com/2003/US/01/10/wbr.smoking.gun/>.

Jackson, John H. 'The Evolution of the World Trading System—The Legal and Institutional Context'. In Daniel Bethlehem, Donald McRae, Rodney Neufeld, and Isabelle van Damme (eds.), *The Oxford Handbook of International Trade Law* (Oxford: Oxford University Press, 2009), p. 30.

Jackson, Robert. *The Global Covenant: Human Conduct in a World of States* (Oxford: Oxford University Press, 2000).

Jennings, R.Y. 'The Caroline and McLeod Cases'. *American Journal of International Law* 32 (1938): p. 82.

Jennings, Robert, and Arthur Watts (eds.), *Oppenheim's International Law*, 9th ed. (Oxford: Oxford University Press, 1992).

Jessup, Philip. *A Modern Law of Nations: An Introduction* (New York: The Macmillan Co., 1948).

Johnstone, Ian. *The Power of Deliberation: International Law, Politics and Organizations* (Oxford: Oxford University Press 2011).

Joseph, Sarah. *Blame it on the WTO?: A Human Rights Critique* (Oxford: Oxford University Press, 2011).

Jouannet, Emannuelle. *Qu'est-ce qu'une societé juste?: Le droit international entre développement et reconnaissance* (Paris: A. Pedone, 2011).

Judt, Tony. 'Edge People'. *New York Review of Books*. 25 March 2010.

Julius, A.J. 'Nagel's Atlas'. *Philosophy & Public Affairs* 34 (2006): p. 176.

Justino, Patricia. 'War and Poverty'. Microcon Research Paper No. 32 (2010). <http://papers.ssrn.com/>.

Kahl, Colin. *States, Scarcity, and Civil Strife in the Developing World* (Princeton, NJ: Princeton University Press, 2006).

Kalshoven, Frits, and Liesbeth Zegveld. *Constraints on the Waging of War: An Introduction to International Humanitarian Law* (Geneva: International Committee of the Red Cross, 2001).

Kant, Immanuel. *Kant: Political Writings*, Hans Reiss (ed.) and H.B. Nisbet (trans.) 2nd ed. (New York: Cambridge University Press, 1991).

Kant, Immanuel. *Groundwork of the Metaphysics of Morals*, Mary Gregor and Jens Timmermann (ed. and trans.) rev. ed. (Cambridge: Cambridge University Press, 2012).

Kausikan, Bilahari. 'Asia's Different Standard'. *Foreign Policy* 92 (1993): p. 24.

Kavass, Igor I. 'WTO Accession: Procedure, Requirements and Costs'. *Journal of World Trade* 41 (2007): p. 453.

Keck, Alexander, and Patrick Low. 'Special and Differential Treatment in the WTO: Why, When and How?'. WTO Economic Research and Statistics Division: Staff Working Paper ERSD-2004-03 (May 2004).

Keck, Margaret E., and Kathryn Sikkink. *Activists beyond Borders: Advocacy Networks in International Politics* (Ithaca, NY: Cornell University Press, 1998).

Kelsen, Hans. 'The Principle of Sovereign Equality of States as a Basis for International Organization'. *Yale Law Journal* 53 (1944): p. 207.

Kennedy, David. 'When Renewal Repeats: Thinking Against the Box'. *New York University Journal of International Law and Politics* 32 (2000): p. 355.

Kennedy, David. *The Dark Sides of Virtue: Reassessing International Humanitarianism* (Princeton, NJ: Princeton University Press, 2004).

Keohane, Robert O. *After Hegemony: Cooperation and Discord in the World Political Economy* (Princeton, NJ: Princeton University Press, 1984).

Keynes, John Maynard. *The Economic Consequences of the Peace* (London: Macmillan and Co., 1920).

Khan, Yasmin. *The Great Partition: The Making of India and Pakistan* (New Haven, CT: Yale University Press, 2007).

Kimberley Process. 'About the Kimberley Process Certification Scheme'. 1 January 2014. <http://www.kimberleyprocess.com/en/about>.

Kingsbury, Benedict. 'Sovereignty and Inequality'. *European Journal of International Law* 9 (1998): p. 599.

Kinley, David. *Civilising Globalisation: Human Rights and the Global Economy* (Cambridge: Cambridge University Press, 2009).

Kissinger, Henry A. 'The Pitfalls of Universal Jurisdiction'. *Foreign Affairs* 80 (2001): p. 90.

Kläger, Roland. *'Fair and Equitable Treatment' in International Investment Law* (New York: Cambridge University Press, 2011).

Klein, Michael, Carl Aaron, and Bita Hadjimichael. 'Foreign Direct Investment and Poverty Reduction'. Briefing Paper, OECD Global Forum on International Investment (26 March 2001). <http://www.oecd.org/daf/inv/investmentstatisticsandanalysis/2422017.pdf>.

Knox, John H. 'Horizontal Human Rights Law'. *American Journal of International Law* 102 (2008): p. 1.

Koh, Harold H. 'Bringing International Law Home'. *Houston Law Review* 35 (1998): p. 623.

Kohen, Marcelo G. *Possession contestée et souveraineté territoriale* (Paris: Presses Universitaire de France, 1997).

Kohen, Marcelo G. 'Article 2, paragraphe 1'. In Jean-Pierre Cot and Alain Pellet (eds.), *La Charte des Nations Unies*, 3rd ed., Vol. 1 (Paris: Economica, 2005), p. 399.

Kohen, Marcelo. 'The Principle of Non-Intervention 25 Years after the *Nicaragua* Judgment'. *Leiden Journal of International Law* 25 (2012): p. 157.

Kolb, Robert. 'General Principles of Procedural Law'. In Andreas Zimmermann, Christian Tomuschat, Karin Oellers-Frahm, and Christian J. Tams (eds.), *The Statute of the International Court of Justice: A Commentary* (Oxford: Oxford University Press, 2012), p. 871.

Kontorovich, Eugene. 'The Piracy Analogy: Modern Universal Jurisdiction's Hollow Foundation'. *Harvard International Law Journal* 45 (2004): p. 183.

Kornprobst, Markus. 'The Management of Border Disputes in African Regional Sub-Systems: Comparing West Africa and the Horn of Africa'. *Journal of Modern African Studies* 40 (2002): p. 369.

Koskenniemi, Martti. *From Apology to Utopia: The Structure of International Legal Argument* (Helsinki: Finnish Lawyers Publishing Co., 1989).

Koskenniemi, Martti. 'The Police in the Temple: Order, Justice, and the UN: A Dialectical View'. *European Journal of International Law* 6 (1995): p. 325.

Koskenniemi, Martti. 'Carl Schmitt, Hans Morgenthau, and the Image of Law in International Relations'. In Michael Byers (ed.), *The Role of Law in International Politics* (Oxford: Oxford University Press, 2000), p. 17.

Koskenniemi, Martti. *The Gentle Civilizer of Nations: The Rise and Fall of International Law 1870–1960* (Cambridge: Cambridge University Press, 2001).

Koskenniemi, Martti. 'Legitimacy, Rights, and Ideology: Notes towards a Critique of the New Moral Internationalism'. *Associations: Journal for Legal and Social Theory* 7 (2003): p. 349.

Koskenniemi, Martti. 'Global Governance and Public International Law'. *Kritische Justiz* 37 (2004): p. 241.

Krasner, Stephen D. *Sovereignty: Organized Hypocrisy* (Princeton, NJ: Princeton University Press, 1999).

Krauthammer, Charles. 'The Curse of Legalism: International law? It's Purely Advisory'. *The New Republic*, 6 November 1989: p. 44.

Kress, Claus. 'Universal Jurisdiction over International Crimes and the *Institut de Droit International*'. *Journal of International Criminal Justice* 4 (2006): p. 561.

Krisch, Nico. 'Legality, Morality and the Dilemma of Humanitarian Intervention after Kosovo'. *European Journal of International Law* 13 (2002): p. 323.

Kritsiotis, Dino. 'Reappraising Policy Objections to Humanitarian Intervention'. *Michigan Journal of International Law* 19 (1998): p. 1005.

Kritsiotis, Dino. 'Imagining the International Community'. *European Journal of International Law* 12 (2002): p. 961.

Kulick, Andreas. *Global Public Interest in International Investment Law* (New York: Cambridge University Press, 2012).

Kupchan, Charles A. *How Enemies Become Friends: The Sources of Stable Peace* (Princeton, NJ: Princeton University Press, 2010).

Kurtz, Jürgen. 'Australia's Rejection of Investor-State Arbitration: Causation, Omission and Implication'. *ICSID Review* 27 (2012): p. 65.

Kymlicka, Will. *Multicultural Citizenship* (Oxford: Clarendon Press, 1995).

Labowitz, Sarah, and Dorothée Bauman-Pauly. *Business as Usual is Not an Option: Supply Chains and Sourcing After Rana Plaza* (New York: New York University Stern School Center for Business and Human Rights, April 2014).

Lachs, Manfred. 'Quelques réflexions sur la communauté internationale'. In *Le droit international au service de la paix, de la justice et du développement* (Paris: A. Pedone, 1991), p. 349.

Lang, Andrew. 'The GATS and Regulatory Autonomy: A Case Study of Social Regulation of the Water Industry'. *Journal of International Economic Law* 7 (2004): p. 801.

Lang, Andrew. *World Trade Law after Neoliberalism: Re-imagining the Global Economic Order* (Oxford: Oxford University Press, 2011).

Lang, Andrew, and Joanne Scott. 'The Hidden World of WTO Governance'. *European Journal of International Law* 20 (2009): p. 575.

Langford, Malcolm, Wouter Vandenhole, Martin Scheinin, and Willem van Genugten (eds.), *Global Justice, State Duties: The Extraterritorial Scope of Economic, Social, and Cultural Rights in International Law* (Cambridge: Cambridge University Press, 2013).

Langer, Máximo. 'The Diplomacy of Universal Jurisdiction: The Political Branches and the Transnational Prosecution of International Crimes'. *American Journal of International Law* 105 (2011): p. 1.

Lauterpacht, Hersch. *The Function of Law in the International Community* (Oxford: Clarendon Press, 1933).

Lauterpacht, Hersch. *Recognition in International Law* (Cambridge: Cambridge University Press, 1947).

Lauterpacht, Hersch. 'Professor Carr on International Morality'. In E. Lauterpacht (ed.), *International Law: Being the Collected Papers of Hersch Lauterpacht* (New York: Cambridge University Press, 1975), p. 67.

Lee, Win-chiat. 'International Crimes and Universal Jurisdiction'. In Larry May and Zachary Hoskins (eds.), *International Criminal Law and Philosophy* (New York: Cambridge University Press, 2010), p. 15.

Lieblich, Eliav. *International Law and Civil Wars: Intervention and Consent* (New York: Routledge, 2013).

Locke, John. 'Second Treatise of Government'. In John Locke, *Two Treatises of Government*, Peter Laslett (ed.) (Cambridge: Cambridge University Press, 1988).

Lopez, Theresa, Jennifer Zamzow, Michael Gill, and Shaun Nichols. 'Side Constraints and the Structure of Commonsense Ethics'. *Philosophical Perspectives* 23 (2009): p. 305.

Low, Patrick. 'WTO Decision-Making for the Future'. WTO Economic Research and Statistics Division: Staff Working Paper ERSD-2011-05 (2 May 2011).

Luard, Evan. *A History of the United Nations, Volume 1: The Years of Western Domination, 1945–1955* (London: Macmillan, 1982).

Luban, David. 'Just War and Human Rights'. *Philosophy & Public Affairs* 9 (1980): p. 160.

Luban, David. 'A Theory of Crimes Against Humanity'. *Yale Journal of International Law* 29 (2004): p. 85.

Lubell, Noam. *Extraterritorial Use of Force Against Non-State Actors* (Oxford: Oxford University Press, 2010).

Lutz, Ellen L., and Kathryn Sikkink. 'International Human Rights Law in Practice: The Justice Cascade: The Evolution and Impact of Foreign Human Rights Trials in Latin America'. *Chicago Journal of International Law* 2 (2001): p. 1.

MacCormick, Neil. 'Natural Law and the Separation of Law and Morals'. In Robert P. George (ed.), *Natural Law Theory: Contemporary Essays* (Oxford: Oxford University Press, 1992), p. 105.
MacCormick, Neil. *Practical Reason in Law and Morality* (New York: Oxford University Press, 2008).
Madison, James. 'Political Observations, 20 April 1795'. In *Letters and Other Writings of James Madison*, Vol. 4 (Philadelphia, PA: J.B. Lippincott, 1867), p. 491.
Madison, James. 'Number X'. In James Madison, Alexander Hamilton, and John Jay, *The Federalist Papers*, Isaac Kramnick (ed.) (Hardmondsworth: Penguin, 1987), p. 127.
Malenovsky, Jirí. 'Problèmes juridiques liés à la partition de la Tchécoslovaquie'. *Annuaire français de droit international* 39 (1993): p. 305.
Mapel, David R., and Terry Nardin (eds.), *International Society: Diverse Ethical Perspectives* (Princeton, NJ: Princeton University Press, 1999).
Marceau, Gabrielle. 'WTO Dispute Settlement and Human Rights'. *European Journal of International Law* 13 (2002): p. 753.
Margalit, Avishai, and Joseph Raz. 'National Self-Determination'. *Journal of Philosophy* 87 (1990): p. 439.
Mason, Andrew. 'Special Obligations to Compatriots'. *Ethics* 107 (1997): p. 427.
Mason, Andrew, and Nick Wheeler. 'Realist Objections to Humanitarian Intervention'. In Barry Holden (ed.), *The Ethical Dimensions of Global Change* (New York: Palgrave MacMillan, 1996), p. 94.
May, Larry. *Crimes Against Humanity: A Normative Account* (Cambridge: Cambridge University Press, 2005).
May, Larry. *Aggression and Crimes against Peace* (Cambridge: Cambridge University Press, 2008).
Mayer, Jane. 'The Predator War'. *The New Yorker*. 26 October 2009.
Mazo, Jeffrey. *Climate Conflict: How Global Warming Threatens Security and What to Do About It* (Abingdon: Routledge, 2009).
Mazower, Mark. *Governing the World: The History of an Idea, 1815 to the Present* (New York: Penguin Books, 2012).
Mazzetti, Mark, C.J. Chivers, and Eric Schmitt. 'Taking Outsize Role in Syria, Qatar Funnels Arms to Rebels'. *New York Times*. 29 June 2013: p. A1.
McCrudden, Christopher. 'Human Dignity and Judicial Interpretation of Human Rights'. *European Journal International Law* 19 (2008): p. 655.
McCrudden, Christopher (ed.). *Understanding Human Dignity* (Oxford: Oxford University Press, 2013).
McCrudden, Christopher, and Brendan O'Leary. *Courts and Consociations: Human Rights versus Power-Sharing* (Oxford: Oxford University Press, 2013).
McDougal, Myres S., Harold D. Lasswell, and Lung-chu Chen. *Human Rights and World Public Order: The Basic Policies of an International Law of Human Dignity* (New Haven, CT: Yale University Press, 1980).
McDougal, Myres S., and W. Michael Reisman (eds.), *International Law Essays* (Mineola, NY: Foundation Press, 1981).
McKim, Robert, and Jeff McMahan (eds.), *The Morality of Nationalism* (New York: Oxford University Press, 1997).
McLachlan-Bent, Ashley, and John Langmore. 'A Crime Against Humanity?: Implications and Prospects of the Responsibility to Protect in the Wake of Cyclone Nargis'. *Global Responsibility to Protect* 3 (2011): p. 37.

McMahan, Jeff. 'The Ethics of Killing in War'. *Ethics* 114 (2004): p. 693.

McMahan, Jeff. *Killing in War* (Oxford: Clarendon Press, 2009).

McMahan, Jeff, 'The Prevention of Unjust Wars'. In Yitzhak Benbaji and Naomi Sussman (eds.), *Reading Walzer* (New York: Routledge, 2014), p. 233.

Meckled-Garcia, Saladin. 'On the Very Idea of Cosmopolitan Justice: Constructivism and International Agency'. *Journal of Political Philosophy* 16 (2008): p. 245.

Meisler, Stanley. *United Nations: The First Fifty Years* (New York: Atlantic Monthly Press, 1995).

Mendus, Susan. *Impartiality in Moral and Political Philosophy* (Oxford: Oxford University Press, 2002).

Meron, Theodor. 'On a Hierarchy of International Human Rights'. *American Journal of International Law* 80 (1986): p. 1.

Mertens, Thomas. 'Defending the Rawlsian League of Peoples: A Critical Comment on Tan'. *Leiden Journal of International Law* 18 (2005): p. 711.

Miklian, Jason. 'Rough Cut'. *Foreign Policy* (January/February 2013): p. 31.

Milanovic, Marko. 'Self-Defense and Non-State Actors: Indeterminacy and the Jus Ad Bellum'. *EJILTalk! Blog.* 21 February 2010. <http://www.ejiltalk.org>.

Miller, David. *On Nationality* (Oxford: Clarendon Press, 1995).

Miller, David. *Citizenship and National Identity* (Cambridge: Polity Press, 2000).

Miller, David. 'Distributing Responsibilities'. *Journal of Political Philosophy* 9 (2001): p. 453.

Miller, David. *National Responsibility and Global Justice* (Oxford: Oxford University Press, 2007).

Ming Du, Michael. 'The Rise of National Regulatory Autonomy in the GATT/WTO Regime'. *Journal of International Economic Law* 14 (2011): p. 639.

Mitchell, Andrew D., and Caroline Henckels. 'Variations on a Theme: Comparing the Concept of "Necessity" in International Investment Law and WTO Law'. *Chicago Journal of International Law* 14 (2013): p. 93.

Moore, John Bassett. *Costa Rica-Panama Arbitration: Memorandum on Uti Possidetis* (Rosslyn, VA: Commonwealth Co., 1913).

Moran, Theodore H., Edward M. Graham, and Magnus Blomstrom (eds.), *Does Foreign Direct Investment Promote Development?* (Washington DC: Institute for International Economics, 2005).

Morgan-Foster, Jason. 'The Relationship of IMF Structural Adjustment Programs to Economic, Social, and Cultural Rights: The Argentine Case Revisited'. *Michigan Journal of International Law* 24 (2003): p. 577.

Morgenthau, Hans J. *Politics Among Nations: The Struggle for Power and Peace*, 7th ed. Kenneth W. Thompson and W. David Clinton (eds.) (Boston, MA: McGraw-Hill Higher Education, 2006).

Morijn, John. *Reframing Human Rights and Trade: Potential and Limits of a Human Rights Perspective of WTO Law on Cultural and Educational Goods and Services* (Portland, OR: Intersentia, 2010).

Moyle, J.B. *The Institutes of Justinian*, 5th ed. (Oxford: Clarendon Press, 1913).

Muchlinski, Peter, Federico Ortino, and Christoph Schreuer (eds.). *The Oxford Handbook of International Investment Law* (New York: Oxford University Press, 2008).

Mullins, Christopher W., and Dawn L. Rothe. 'The Ability of the International Criminal Court to Deter Violations of International Criminal Law: A Theoretical Assessment'. *International Criminal Law Review* 10 (2010): p. 771.

Murphy, Sean. *Humanitarian Intervention: The United Nations in an Evolving World Order* (Philadelphia, PA: University of Pennsylvania Press, 1996).
Musgrave, Thomas D. *Self-Determination and National Minorities* (Oxford: Clarendon Press, 1997).
Nadelmann, Ethan. 'Global Prohibition Regimes: The Evolution of Norms in International Society'. *International Organization* 44 (1990): p. 479.
Nagel, Thomas. 'The Problem of Global Justice'. *Philosophy & Public Affairs* 33 (2005): p. 113.
Nardin, Terry. *Law, Morality, and the Relations of States* (Princeton, NJ: Princeton University Press, 1983).
Nardin, Terry. 'The Moral Basis of Humanitarian Intervention'. *Ethics & International Affairs* 16 (2002): p. 57.
Nardin, Terry, and Melissa S. Williams (eds.), *Humanitarian Intervention: Nomos XLVII* (New York: New York University Press, 2006).
Neuffer, Elizabeth. *The Key to My Neighbor's House: Seeking Justice in Bosnia and Rwanda* (New York: Picador, 2001).
Newburg, Andre. 'The Changing Roles of the Bretton Woods Institutions: Evolving Concepts of Conditionality'. In Mario Giovanoli (ed.), *International Monetary Law: Issues for the New Millennium* (Oxford: Oxford University Press, 2000), p. 81.
Newcombe, Andrew. 'The Boundaries of Regulatory Expropriation in International Law'. *ICSID Review: Foreign Investment Law Journal* 20 (2005): p. 1.
Newcombe, Andrew. 'A Brief Comment on the Public Statement on the International Investment Regime'. *Kluwer Arbitration Blog*. 3 September 2010. <http://kluwerarbitrationblog.com>.
Nickel, James W. *Making Sense of Human Rights*, 2nd ed. (Malden, MA: Blackwell Publishing, 2006).
Nozick, Robert. *Anarchy, State, and Utopia* (New York: Basic Books, 1974).
O'Keefe, Roger. 'Universal Jurisdiction: Clarifying the Basic Concept'. *Journal of International Criminal Justice* 2 (2004): p. 735.
O'Neill, Onora. *Bounds of Justice* (Cambridge: Cambridge University Press, 2000).
Oppenheim, L. *International Law: A Treatise, Volume I: Peace* (New York: Longmans, Green, and Co., 1905).
Oppenheim, L. *International Law: A Treatise, Volume II: War and Neutrality* (New York: Longmans, Green, and Co., 1906).
Oppenheimer, F.E. 'Governments and Authorities in Exile'. *American Journal of International Law* 36 (1942): p. 568.
Orford, Anne. *International Authority and the Responsibility to Protect* (Cambridge: Cambridge University Press, 2011).
Østerud, Øyvind (ed.). *Studies of War and Peace* (Oslo: Norwegian University Press, 1986).
Owen, David. *Balkan Odyssey* (New York: Harcourt Brace & Co., 1995).
Oxfam International. 'Dumping on the World: How EU Sugar Policies Hurt Poor Countries'. Oxfam Briefing Paper 61 (March 2004).
Page, Edward A. 'Cosmopolitanism, Climate Change, and Greenhouse Emissions Trading'. *International Theory* 3 (2011): p. 37.
Pahuja, Sundhya. *Decolonising International Law: Development, Economic Growth and the Politics of Universality* (Cambridge: Cambridge University Press, 2011).
Pakenham, Thomas. *The Scramble for Africa: White Man's Conquest of the Dark Continent from 1976 to 1912* (New York: Perennial, 1991).

Pattison, James. *Humanitarian Intervention & the Responsibility to Protect: Who Should Intervene?* (Oxford: Oxford University Press, 2010).

Paulsson, Jan. 'Ghosts of Chorzów: *Maha Nuñez-Schultz* v. *Republic of the Americas*'. In Todd Weiler, *International Investment Law and Arbitration* (London: Cameron May, 2005), p. 777.

Pauwelyn, Joost. 'WTO Compassion or Superiority Complex?: What to Make of the WTO Waiver for 'Conflict Diamonds''. *Michigan Journal of International Law* 24 (2003): p. 1177.

Pauwelyn, Joost. *Optimal Protection of International Law: Navigating between European Absolutism and American Voluntarism* (New York: Cambridge University Press, 2008).

Peters, Anne. 'Humanity as the A and Ω of Sovereignty'. *European Journal of International Law* 20 (2009): p. 513.

Peters, Anne. 'The Security Council's Responsibility to Protect'. *International Organizations Law Review* 8 (2011): p. 1.

Petersmann, Ernst-Ulrich. 'Time for a United Nations "Global Compact" for Integrating Human Rights into the Law of Worldwide Organizations: Lessons from European Integration'. *European Journal of International Law* 13 (2002): p. 621.

Pettit, Philip, and Robert Goodin. 'The Possibility of Special Duties'. *Canadian Journal of Philosophy* 16 (1986): p. 651.

Philpott, Daniel. 'In Defense of Self-Determination'. *Ethics* 105 (1995): p. 352.

Philpott, Daniel. 'Should Self-Determination be Legalized?'. *Terrorism and Political Violence* 12 (2000): p. 106.

Philpott, Daniel. *Just and Unjust Peace: An Ethic of Political Reconciliation* (Oxford: Oxford University Press, 2012).

Pierek, Roland, and Wouter Werner (eds.). *Cosmopolitanism in Context: Perspectives from International Law and Political Theory* (Cambridge: Cambridge University Press, 2010).

Pildes, Richard H. 'Why Rights are not Trumps: Social Meanings, Expressive Harms, and Constitutionalism'. *Journal of Legal Studies* 27 (1998): p. 725.

Pinker, Steven. *The Better Angels of Our Nature: Why Violence Has Declined* (New York: Viking Press, 2011).

Pogge, Thomas W. *Realizing Rawls* (Ithaca, NY: Cornell University Press, 1989).

Pogge, Thomas W. 'Cosmopolitanism and Sovereignty'. *Ethics* 103 (1992): p. 48.

Pogge, Thomas W. 'Eradicating Systemic Poverty: Brief for a Global Resource Dividend'. *Journal of Human Development* 2 (2001): p. 59.

Pogge, Thomas W. 'Recognized and Violated by International Law: The Human Rights of the Global Poor'. *Leiden Journal of International Law* 18 (2005): p. 717.

Pogge, Thomas. *World Poverty and Human Rights: Cosmopolitan Responsibilities and Reforms* 2nd ed. (Cambridge: Polity Press, 2008).

Pogge, Thomas. 'The Health Impact Fund: Better Pharmaceutical Innovations at Much Lower Prices'. In Thomas Pogge, Matthew Rimmer, and Kim Rubinstein (eds.), *Incentives for Global Public Health: Patent Law and Access to Essential Medicines* (New York: Cambridge University Press, 2010), p. 135.

Preuss, Ulrich K. 'Equality of States—Its Meaning in a Constitutionalized Global Order'. *Chicago Journal of International Law* 9 (2008): p. 17.

'Princeton Principles on Universal Jurisdiction'. In Stephen Macedo (ed.), *Universal Jurisdiction: National Courts and the Prosecution of Serious Crimes under International Law* (Philadelphia, PA: University of Pennsylvania Press, 2004), p. 18.

Princeton Project on National Security. *Forging a World of Liberty under Law* (Princeton, NJ: Princeton University, 2006).

Puig, Sergio. 'Social Capital in the Arbitration Market'. *European Journal of International Law* 25 (2014): 387.

Quigley, John. *The Six-Day War and Israeli Self-Defense: Questioning the Legal Basis for Preventive War* (New York: Cambridge University Press, 2013).

Railton, Peter. 'Alienation, Consequentialism, and the Demands of Morality'. *Philosophy & Public Affairs* 13 (1984): p. 134.

Rao, Narasimha, and Paul Baer. '"Decent Living" Emissions: A Conceptual Framework'. *Sustainability* 4 (2012): p. 656.

Ratner, Steven R. 'The Cambodia Settlement Agreements'. *American Journal of International Law* 87 (1993): p. 1.

Ratner, Steven R. 'Drawing a Better Line: *Uti Possidetis* and the Borders of New States'. *American Journal of International Law* 90 (1996): p. 590.

Ratner, Steven R. 'The Schizophrenias of International Criminal Law'. *Texas International Law Journal* 33 (1998): p. 237.

Ratner, Steven R. 'Does International Law Matter in Preventing Ethnic Conflict?'. *New York University Journal of International Law and Politics* 32 (2000): 591.

Ratner, Steven R. 'Corporations and Human Rights: A Theory of Legal Responsibility'. *Yale Law Journal* 111 (2001): p. 443.

Ratner, Steven R. 'Belgium's War Crimes Statute: A Postmortem'. *American Journal of International Law* 97 (2003): 888.

Ratner, Steven R. 'Is International Law Impartial?'. *Legal Theory* 11 (2005): p. 39.

Ratner, Steven R. 'Land Feuds and Their Solutions: Finding International Law Beyond the Tribunal Chamber'. *American Journal of International Law* 100 (2006): p. 808.

Ratner, Steven R. 'Can We Compare Evils?: The Enduring Debate on Genocide and Crimes Against Humanity'. *Washington University Global Studies Law Review* 6 (2007): p. 583.

Ratner, Steven R. 'Regulatory Takings in Institutional Context: Beyond the Fear of Fragmented International Law'. *American Journal of International Law* 102 (2008): p. 475.

Ratner, Steven R. 'Law Promotion beyond Law Talk: The Red Cross, Persuasion, and the Laws of War'. *European Journal of International Law* 22 (2011): p. 459.

Ratner, Steven R. 'Behind the Flag of Dunant: Secrecy and the Compliance Mission of the International Committee of the Red Cross'. In Andrea Bianchi and Anne Peters (eds.), *Transparency in International Law* (Cambridge: Cambridge University Press, 2013), p. 297.

Ratner, Steven R., 'Persuading to Comply: On the Deployment and Avoidance of Legal Argumentation'. In Jeffrey L. Dunoff and Mark A. Pollack (eds.), *Interdisciplinary Perspectives on International Law and International Relations* (Cambridge: Cambridge University Press, 2013), p. 568.

Ratner, Steven R., Jason S. Abrams, and James L. Bischoff, *Accountability for Human Rights Atrocities in International Law: Beyond the Nuremberg Legacy*, 3rd ed. (Oxford: Oxford University Press, 2009).

Ratner, Steven R., and Gerald Helman. 'Saving Failed States'. *Foreign Policy* 89 (1992): p. 3.

Ratner, Steven R., and Anne-Marie Slaughter (eds.). *The Methods of International Law* (Washington DC: American Society of International Law, 2004).

Rawls, John. *The Law of Peoples* (Cambridge, MA: Harvard University Press, 1999).

Rawls, John. *A Theory of Justice*, rev. ed. (Cambridge, MA: Harvard University Press, 1999).

Rawls, John. *Justice as Fairness: A Restatement* (Cambridge, MA: Harvard University Press, 2001).

Rawls, John. *Political Liberalism*, expanded ed. (New York: Columbia University Press, 2005).

Raz, Joseph. *The Morality of Freedom* (Oxford: Clarendon Press, 1986).

Raz, Joseph. *Practical Reasons and Norms*, rev. ed. (Oxford: Oxford University Press, 1999).

Reinold, Theresa. 'State Weakness, Irregular Warfare, and the Right of Self-Defense Post-9/11'. *American Journal of International Law* 105 (2011): p. 244.

Reisman, W. Michael. 'Humanitarian Intervention to Protect the Ibos'. In Richard B. Lillich (ed.), *Humanitarian Intervention and the United Nations* (Charlottesville, VA: University of Virginia Press, 1973), p. 167.

Reisman, W. Michael. *Folded Lies: Bribery, Crusades, and Reform* (New York: The Free Press, 1979).

Reisman, W. Michael. 'Sovereignty and Human Rights in Contemporary International Law'. *American Journal of International Law* 84 (1990): p. 866.

Reisman, W. Michael. 'The Concept and Functions of Soft Law in International Politics'. In Emmanuel G. Bello and Bola A. Ajibola (eds.), *Essays in Honour of Judge Taslim Olawale Elias* Vol. 1 (Leiden: Martinus Nijhoff Publishers, 1992), p. 135.

Reisman, W. Michael. *Systems of Control in International Adjudication and Arbitration: Breakdown and Repair* (Durham, NC: Duke University Press, 1992).

Reisman, W. Michael. 'Remarks by W. Michael Reisman'. *American Society of International Law Procedure* 87 (1993), p. 258.

Reisman, W. Michael. 'Institutions and Practices for Restoring and Maintaining Public Order'. *Duke Journal of Comparative & International Law* 6 (1995): p. 175.

Reisman, W. Michael. 'Why Regime Change is (Almost) Always a Bad Idea'. *American Journal of International Law* 98 (2004): p. 516.

Reisman, W. Michael, and James E. Baker. *Regulating Covert Action* (New Haven, CT: Yale University Press, 1992).

Reus-Smit, Christian. 'Imagining society: constructivism and the English School'. *British Journal of Political & International Relations* 4 (2002): p. 487.

Reus-Smit, Christian and Duncan Snidal (eds.). *The Oxford Handbook of International Relations* (Oxford: Oxford University Press, 2008).

Reydams, Luc. *Universal Jurisdiction: International and Municipal Legal Perspectives* (Oxford: Oxford University Press, 2003).

Risse, Mathias. 'Do We Owe the Global Poor Assistance or Rectification?'. *Ethics & International Affairs* 19 (2005): p. 9.

Risse, Mathias. *On Global Justice* (Princeton, NJ: Princeton University Press, 2012).

Rodin, David. *War and Self-Defense* (Oxford: Clarendon Press, 2002).

Rodrick, Dani. *One Economics, Many Recipes: Globalization, Institutions, and Economic Growth* (Princeton, NJ: Princeton University Press, 2007).

Rodrik, Dani, Arvind Subramanian, and Francesco Trebbi. 'Institutions Rule: The Primacy of Institutions over Geography and Integration in Economic Development'. *Journal of Economic Growth* 9 (2004): p. 131.

Roht-Arriaza, Naomi. *The Pinochet Effect* (Philadelphia, PA: University of Pennsylvania Press, 2005).

Roht-Arriaza, Naomi. '"First, Do No Harm": Human Rights and Efforts to Combat Climate Change'. *Georgia Journal of International and Comparative Law* 38 (2010): p. 593.

Roth, Brad R. *Sovereign Equality and Moral Disagreement: Premises of a Pluralist International Legal Order* (New York: Oxford University Press, 2011).

Ruys, Tom. *'Armed Attack' and Article 51 of the UN Charter: Evolutions in Customary Law and Practice* (New York: Cambridge University Press, 2010).

Ruys, Tom. 'Of Arms, Funding and "Non-lethal Assistance"—Issues Surrounding Third-State Intervention in the Syrian Civil War'. *Chinese Journal of International Law* 13 (2014): 13.

Ryngaert, Cedric. *Jurisdiction in International Law* (Oxford: Oxford University Press, 2008).

Sacerdoti, Giorgio. 'Bilateral treaties and multilateral instruments on investment protection'. *Recueil des Cours de l'Académie de Droit International* 269 (1997): p. 251.

Sadasivam, Bharati. 'The Impact of Structural Adjustment on Women: A Governance and Human Rights Agenda'. *Human Rights Quarterly* 19 (1997): p. 630.

Salmon, Elizabeth G. 'Reflections on International Humanitarian Law and Transitional Justice: Lessons To Be Learnt From The Latin American experience'. *International Review of the Red Cross* 88, No. 862 (2006): p. 327.

Salomon, Margot E. *Global Responsibility for Human Rights: World Poverty and the Development of International Law* (Oxford: Oxford University Press, 2007).

Sandel, Michael J. *Justice* (New York: Farrar, Straus and Giroux, 2009).

Sands, Philippe. *Principles of International Environmental Law*, 2nd ed. (Cambridge: Cambridge University Press, 2003).

Saner, Raymond, and Ricardo Guilherme. 'The International Monetary Fund's Influence on Trade Policies of Low-income Countries: A Valid Undertaking?'. *Journal of World Trade* 41 (2007): p. 931.

Sangiovanni, Andrea. 'Global Justice, Reciprocity, and the State'. *Philosophy & Public Affairs* 35 (2007): p. 3.

Satz, Debra. 'What Do We Owe the Global Poor?'. *Ethics & International Affairs* 19 (2005): p. 47.

Sauvant, Karl P., and Lisa E. Sachs (eds.). *The Effect of Treaties on Foreign Direct Investment: Bilateral Investment Treaties, Double Taxation Treaties, and Investment Flows* (New York: Oxford University Press, 2009).

Sceats, Sonya, and Shaun Breslin. *China and the International Human Rights System* (London: Chatham House, 2012).

Schachter, Oscar. 'In Defense of International Rules on the Use of Force'. *Chicago Law Review* 53 (1986): p. 113.

Scheffler, Samuel. *Boundaries and Allegiances: Problems of Justice and Responsibility in Liberal Thought* (New York: Oxford University Press, 2001).

Schmidtz, David. 'Are All Species Equal?'. In David Schmidtz and Elizabeth Willott (eds.), *Environmental Ethics: What Really Matters, What Really Works*, 2nd ed. (Oxford: Oxford University Press, 2012), p. 114.

Schmitt, Michael N. (ed.). *The Tallinn Manual on the International Law Applicable to Cyber Warfare* (Cambridge: Cambridge University Press, 2013).

Schneiderman, David. 'Investing in Democracy? Political Process and International Investment Law'. *University of Toronto Law Journal* 60 (2010): p. 909.

Shaffer, Greg. 'Power, Governance, and the WTO: A Comparative Institutional Approach'. In Michael Barnett and Raymond Duvall (eds.), *Power in Global Governance* (New York: Cambridge University Press, 2003), p. 130.

Shaffer, Greg. 'The Challenges of WTO Law: Strategies for Developing Country Adaptation'. *World Trade Review* 5 (2006): p. 177.

Shapiro, Scott J. 'The "Hart-Dworkin" Debate: A Short Guide for the Perplexed'. In Arthur Ripstein (ed.), *Ronald Dworkin* (Cambridge: Cambridge University Press, 2007), p. 22.

Shavit, Ari. *My Promised Land: The Triumph and Tragedy of Israel* (New York: Spiegel and Grau, 2013).

Shaw, Malcolm N. 'The Heritage of States: The Principle of *Uti Possidetis Juris* Today'. *British Yearbook of International Law* 67 (1996): p. 1.

Shea, Donald. *The Calvo Clause* (Minneapolis, MN: University of Minnesota Press, 1955).

Shue, Henry. *Basic Rights: Subsistence, Affluence, and U.S. Foreign Policy*, 2nd ed. (Princeton, NJ: Princeton University Press, 1996).

Shue, Henry, and David Wippman. 'Limiting Attacks on Dual-Use Facilities Performing Indispensable Civilian Functions'. *Cornell International Law Journal* 35 (2002): p. 559.

Sikkink, Kathryn. *The Justice Cascade: How Human Rights Prosecutions are Changing World Politics* (New York: W.W. Norton, 2011).

Simma, Bruno. 'From Bilateralism to Community Interest in International Law'. *Recueil des Cours de l'Académie de Droit International* 250 (1994): p. 217.

Simma, Bruno. 'NATO, the UN, and the Use of Force: Legal Aspects'. *European Journal of International Law* 10 (1999): p. 1.

Simma, Bruno, and Andreas Paulus. 'The "International Community": Facing the Challenge of Globalization'. *European Journal of International Law* 9 (1998): p. 266.

Simma, Bruno, and Andreas L. Paulus. 'The Responsibility of Individuals for Human Rights Abuses in Internal Conflicts: A Positivist View'. *American Journal of International Law* 93 (1999): p. 302.

Simma, Bruno, Daniel-Erasmus Khan, Georg Nolte, and Andreas Paulus (eds.). *The Charter of the United Nations: A Commentary*, 2 vols., 3rd ed. (Oxford: Oxford University Press, 2012).

Simmons, Beth A. *Mobilizing for Human Rights: International Law in Domestic Politics* (Cambridge: Cambridge University Press, 2009).

Simpson, A.W. Brian. *Human Rights and the End of Empire: Britain and the Genesis of the European Convention* (Oxford: Oxford University Press, 2001).

Simpson, Gerry J. 'Is International Law Fair?'. *Michigan Journal of International Law* 17 (1996): p. 615.

Simpson, Gerry. *Great Powers and Outlaw States: Unequal Sovereigns in the International Legal Order* (Cambridge: Cambridge University Press, 2004).

Singer, Peter. 'Famine, Affluence, and Morality'. *Philosophy & Public Affairs* 1 (1972): p. 229.

Singer, Peter (ed.). *A Companion to Ethics* (Malden, MA: Blackwell Publishing, 1993).

Singer, Peter. *One World: The Ethics of Globalization* (New Haven, CT: Yale University Press, 2002).

Singer, Peter. 'Ethics and Institutions'. *Journal of Ethics* 9 (2005): p. 331.

Skogly, Sigrun I. 'The Human Rights Obligations of the World Bank and the IMF'. In Willem van Genugten, Paul Hunt, and Susan Mathews (eds.), *World Bank, IMF, and Human Rights* (Oisterwijk: Wolf Legal Publishers, 2003), p. 45.

Slater, Jerome, and Terry Nardin. 'Nonintervention and Human Rights'. *Journal of Politics* 48 (1986): p. 86.

Slaughter, Anne-Marie. *A New World Order* (Princeton, NJ: Princeton University Press, 2004).

Snyder, Timothy. *Bloodlands: Europe between Hitler and Stalin* (New York: Basic Books, 2010).

Song, Jin. 'The Political Dynamics of the Peacemaking Process in Cambodia'. In Michael W. Doyle, Ian Johnstone, and Robert C. Orr (eds.), *Keeping the Peace: Multidimensional UN Operations in Cambodia and El Salvador* (Cambridge: Cambridge University Press, 1997), p. 53.

Sørenson, Max (ed.). *Manual of Public International Law* (New York: St Martin's Press, 1968).

Sornarajah, M. *The International Law on Foreign Investment*, 3rd ed. (New York: Cambridge University Press, 2010).

South African Development Community. 'SADC Model Bilateral Investment Treaty Template with Commentary' (2012). <http://www.iisd.org>.

Spiro, Peter J. 'A New International Law of Citizenship'. *American Journal of International Law* 105 (2011): p. 694.

Stanley Foundation. 'Actualizing the Responsibility to Protect' (2008). <http://www.stanleyfoundation.org/publications/report/UNND808.pdf>.

Stern, Brigitte. 'À propos de la compétence universelle'. In Emile Yakpo and Tahar Boumedra (eds.), *Liber Amicorum Judge Mohammed Bedjaoui* (The Hague: Kluwer, 1999), p. 735.

Stiglitz, Joseph E. *Globalization and its Discontents* (New York: W.W. Norton, 2002).

Stiglitz, Joseph E. 'Regulating Multinational Corporations: Towards Principles of Cross-Border Legal Frameworks in a Globalized World Balancing Rights with Responsibilities'. *American University International Law Review* 23 (2007): p. 451.

Stilz, Anna. 'Nations, States, and Territory'. *Ethics* 121 (2011): p. 572.

Stone, Julius. 'Approaches to the Notion of International Justice'. In Cyril E. Black and Richard A. Falk (eds.), *The Future of the International Legal Order*, Vol. 1 (Princeton, NJ: Princeton University Press, 1969), p. 372.

Strange, Susan. *The Retreat of the State: The Diffusion of Power in the World Economy* (Cambridge: Cambridge University Press, 1996).

Sutherland, Peter. 'The Doha Development Agenda: Political Challenges to the World Trading System—A Cosmopolitan Perspective'. *Journal of International Economic Law* 8 (2005): p. 363.

Sykes, Alan O. 'TRIPS, Pharmaceuticals, Developing Countries, and the Doha "Solution"'. John M. Olin Law and Economics Working Paper No. 140 (February 2002).

Sykes, Alan O. 'The Economics of WTO Rules on Subsidies and Countervailing Measures'. John M. Olin Law and Economics Working Paper No. 186 (May 2003).

Synder, Timothy. *Bloodlands: Europe between Hitler and Stalin* (New York: Basic Books, 2010).

Szasz, Paul. 'The Security Council Starts Legislating'. *American Journal of International Law* 96 (2002): p. 901.

Talbot, William J. *Which Rights Should be Universal?* (Oxford: Oxford University Press, 2005).

Talmon, Stefan. 'Recognition of the Libyan National Transitional Council'. *ASIL Insight* 15 (2011).

Tamir, Yael. *Liberal Nationalism* (Princeton, NJ: Princeton University Press, 1993).

Tams, Christian J. 'The Use of Force Against Terrorists'. *European Journal of International Law* 20 (2009): p. 359.

Tams, Christian J. 'Individual States as Guardians of Community Interests'. In Ulrich Fasternath et al. (eds.), *From Bilateralism to Community Interest: Essays in Honor of Judge Bruno Simma* (Oxford: Oxford University Press, 2011), p. 379.

Tan, Kok-Chor. *Justice Without Borders: Cosmopolitanism, Nationalism, and Patriotism* (Cambridge: Cambridge University Press, 2004).

Tan, Kok-Chor. 'International Toleration: Rawlsian versus Cosmopolitan'. *Leiden Journal of International Law* 18 (2005): p. 685.

Tasioulas, John. 'International Law and the Limits of Fairness'. *European Journal of International Law* 13 (2002): p. 993.

Tasioulas, John. 'Customary International Law and the Quest for Global Justice'. In Amanda Perreau-Saussine and James Bernard Murphy (eds.), *The Nature of Customary Law: Legal, Historical and Philosophical Perspectives* (Cambridge: Cambridge University Press, 2007), p. 307.

Tesón, Fernando R. 'The Kantian Theory of International Law'. *Columbia Law Review* 92 (1992): p. 53.

Tesón, Fernando R. *A Philosophy of International Law* (Boulder, CO: Westview Press, 1998).

Tesón, Fernando R. 'Ending Tyranny in Iraq'. *Ethics & International Affairs* 19 (2005): p. 1.

Tesón, Fernando R. *Humanitarian Intervention: An Inquiry into Law and Morality* (Ardsley, NY: Transnational Publishers, 2005).

Todorov, Tzvetan. 'Right to Intervene or Duty to Assist?'. In Nicholas Owen (ed.), *Human Rights, Human Wrongs: The Oxford Amnesty Lectures 2001* (New York: Oxford University Press, 2002), p. 28.

Touval, Saadia. 'The Organization of African Unity and African Borders'. *International Organization* 21 (1967): p. 102.

Unger, Roberto Mangabeira. *Free Trade Reimagined: The World Division of Labor and the Method of Economics* (Princeton, NJ: Princeton University Press, 2007).

Unrepresented Nations and Peoples Organization. 'UNPO Principles'. 22 August 2013. <http://www.unpo.org>.

Valentini, Laura. 'Ideal vs. Non-ideal Theory: A Conceptual Map'. *Philosophy Compass* 7 (2012): p. 654.

Van Boven, Theo. 'Distinguishing Criteria of Human Rights'. In Karel Vasak and Philip Alston (eds.), *The International Dimensions of Human Rights*, Vol. 1, rev. ed. (Portsmouth, NH: Greenwood Press, 1982), p. 43.

Van den Bossche, Peter, and Werner Zdouc. *The Law and Policy of the World Trade Organization*, 3rd ed. (Cambridge: Cambridge University Press, 2013).

van den Herik, Larissa, and Nico Schrijver (eds.). *Counter-Terrorism Strategies in a Fragmented International Legal Order: Meeting the Challenges* (Cambridge: Cambridge University Press, 2013).

Van Harten, Gus. *Investment Treaty Arbitration and Public Law* (New York: Oxford University Press, 2007).

Van Harten, Gus et al. 'Public Statement on the International Investment Regime'. 31 August 2010. <http://www.osgoode.yorku.ca/public_statement/>.

Vandenhole, Wouter. 'Third State Obligations under the ICESCR: A Case Study of EU Sugar Policy'. *Nordic Journal of International Law* 76: (2007): p. 73.

Vicuña, Francisco Orrego. 'Softening Necessity'. In Mahnoush H. Arsanjani, Jacob Katz Cogan, Robert D. Sloane, and Siegfried Wiessner (eds.), *Looking to the Future: Essays on International Law in Honor of W. Michael Reisman* (Boston, MA: Martinus Nijhoff Publishers, 2011), p. 741.

Vilmer, Jean-Baptiste Jeangène, and Ryoa Chung (eds.). *Éthique des relations internationales: Problématiques contemporaines* (Paris: Presses Universitaires de France, 2013).

Vincent, John R. *Nonintervention and International Order* (Princeton, NJ: Princeton University Press, 1974).

Vincent, R.J. *Human Rights and International Relations* (Cambridge: Cambridge University Press, 1986).

Vité, Sylvain. 'The Interrelation of the Law of Occupation and Economic, Social and Cultural Rights: The Examples of Food, Health and Property'. *International Review of the Red Cross* 90, No. 871 (2008): p. 629.

Voice of Russia Radio. 'We View US Statement on NGO's Inspections as Interference in Russian Internal Affairs—Foreign Ministry'. 30 March 2013. <http://english.ruvr.ru/2013_03_30/We-view-US-statement-on-NGOs-inspections-as-interference-in-Russian-internal-affairs-Foreign-Ministry-207>.

Waldron, Jeremy. 'Taking Group Rights Carefully'. In Grant Huscroft and Paul Rishworth (eds.), *Litigating Rights: Perspectives from Domestic and International Law* (Oxford: Hart Publishing, 2002), p. 203.

Waldron, Jeremy. 'Cosmopolitan Norms'. In Seyla Benhabib (ed.), *Another Cosmopolitanism* (New York: Oxford University Press, 2006), p. 83.

Waldron, Jeremy. 'The Concept and the Rule of Law'. *Georgia Law Review* 43 (2008): p. 1.

Waldron, Jeremy. 'Are Sovereigns Entitled to the Benefit of the International Rule of Law?'. *European Journal of International Law* 22 (2011): p. 315.

Waldron, Jeremy. 'How Law Protects Dignity'. *Cambridge Law Journal* 71 (2012): p. 200.

Walzer, Michael. *Spheres of Justice* (New York: Basic Books, 1983).

Walzer, Michael. *Thick and Thin: Moral Argument at Home and Abroad* (Notre Dame, IN: University of Notre Dame Press, 1994).

Walzer, Michael. *Arguing About War* (New Haven, CT: Yale University Press, 2004).

Walzer, Michael. *Just and Unjust Wars: A Moral Argument with Historical Illustrations*, 4th ed. (New York: Basic Books, 2006).

Walzer, Michael. 'Coda: Can the Good Guys Win?'. *European Journal of International Law* 24 (2013): p. 433.

Walzer, Michael. 'The Political Theory License'. *Annual Review of Political Science* 16 (2013): p. 1.

Wegner, Patrick. 'International Criminal Law and Deterrence—A Pointless Endeavour?'. *Justice in Conflict Blog*. 25 October 2011. <http://justiceinconflict.org>.

Weiler, Todd. *The Interpretation of International Investment Law: Equality, Discrimination and Minimum Standards of Treatment in Historical Context* (Boston, MA: Martinus Nijhoff Publishers, 2013).

Weiss Brown, Edith. *In Fairness to Future Generations: International Law, Common Patrimony, and Intergenerational Equity* (Dobbs Ferry, NY: Transnational Publishers, 1989).

Weller, Marc. 'The International Response to the Dissolution of the Socialist Federal Republic of Yugoslavia'. *American Journal of International Law* 86 (1992): p. 569.

Wellman, Christopher H. 'A Defense of Secession and Political Self-Determination'. *Philosophy & Public Affairs* 24 (1995): p. 142.

Wellman, Christopher Heath. 'Relational Facts in Liberal Political Theory: Is There Magic in the Pronoun "My"?'. *Ethics* 100 (2000): p. 537.

Weschler, Joanna. 'Human Rights'. In David M. Malone (ed.), *The UN Security Council: From the Cold War to the 21st Century* (Boulder, CO: Lynne Rienner Publishers, 2004), p. 55.

Wheeler, Nicholas J. *Saving Strangers: Humanitarian Intervention in International Society* (Oxford: Oxford University Press, 2000).

Whitfield, Teresa. *Friends Indeed: The United Nations, Groups of Friends, and the Resolution of Conflict* (Washington DC: United States Institute of Peace, 2007).

Wight, Martin. 'Western Values in International Relations'. In Herbert Butterfield and Martin Wight (eds.), *Diplomatic Investigations: Essays in the Theory of International Politics* (Cambridge, MA: Harvard University Press, 1966), p. 89.

Williams, Bernard. 'Persons, Character, and Morality'. In *Moral Luck* (Cambridge: Cambridge University Press, 1981), p. 1.

Williams, Bernard. 'Consequentialism and Integrity'. In Samuel Scheffler (ed.), *Consequentialism and its Critics* (Oxford: Oxford University Press, 1988), p. 20.

Williams, Marc. *International Economic Organizations and the Third World* (Harlow: Harvester Wheatsheaf, 1994).

Williams, Paul D. 'From Non-Intervention to Non-Indifference: The Origins and Development of the African Union's Security Culture'. *African Affairs* 106 (2007): p. 253.

Wilmshurst, Elizabeth. 'The Chatham House Principles of International Law on the Use of Force in Self-Defence'. *International and Comparative Law Quarterly* 55 (2006): p. 963.

Wilson, Bruce. 'Compliance by WTO Members with Adverse WTO Dispute Settlement Rulings: The Record to Date'. *Journal of International Economic Law* 10 (2007): p. 397.

Wippman, David. 'Treaty-Based Intervention: Who Can Say No?'. *Chicago Law Review* 62 (1995): p. 607.

Wippman, David. 'Atrocities, Deterrence, and the Limits of International Justice'. *Fordham International Law Journal* 23, (1999): p. 473.

Wolfrum, Rüdiger (ed.). *The Max Planck Encyclopedia of Public International Law*, online edition (Oxford: Oxford University Press, 2008–) <http://opil.ouplaw.com/home/EPIL>.

Woods, Ngaire. 'Order, Globalization, and Inequality in World Politics'. In Andrew Hurrell and Ngaire Woods (eds.), *Inequality, Globalization, and World Politics* (Oxford: Oxford University Press, 1999).

Woods, Ngaire. *The Globalizers: The IMF, the World Bank, and Their Borrowers* (Ithaca, NY: Cornell University Press, 2006).

Yang, Xiaodong. *State Immunity in International Law* (Cambridge: Cambridge University Press, 2012).

Young, Iris Marion. *Global Challenges: War, Self-Determination and Responsibility for Justice* (Malden, MA: Polity Press, 2007).

Ypi, Lea, Robert E. Goodin, and Christian Barry. 'Associative Duties, Global Justice, and the Colonies'. *Philosophy & Public Affairs* 37 (2009): p. 103.

Zacher, Mark W. 'The Territorial Integrity Norm: International Boundaries and the Use of Force'. *International Organization* 55 (2001): p. 215.

Index

Aaland Islands 92, 132
Abkhazia 150, 176, 179
Afghanistan 107, 112–13, 236–7
African Union 128, 160, 187, 279
Agreement on Trade-Related Investment Measures (1994) (TRIMS) 324, 340–1
Al Qaeda 112–14, 236–7, 246, 275
***Al Skeini v United Kingdom* (2011)** 276, 278
Allot, Philip. 26
Altman, Andrew 164, 168, 283, 303
Alvarez, José 245
American Convention on Human Rights 1969 269
Amnesty International 397
Anderson, Elizabeth 95
Annan, Kofi 307
Antarctic Treaty 1995 318
Anticipatory self-defense 115–19
Aouzou Strip 122
Aquinas, Thomas 296
Arctic Council 235
Arendt, Hannah 283
Argentina 137–8, 255, 361, 364–70
Armenia 176
Arrest of war criminals 137–41
***Arrest Warrant of 11 April 2000* (Democratic Republic of the Congo v Belgium) (2002)** 195, 202
***Attorney-General of the Government of Israel v Eichmann* (1961)** 138
Austria 279

Ban on force
basic contours of norm 103–7
claims for expanded ban 111–19
claims for contracted ban 119–26
thin justice of the ban 107–11
Bangladesh 148, 150, 161, 374–6
Barry, Brian 29, 36, 43–5, 55–7, 96, 214, 321
Beitz, Charles 30, 32, 73–4, 95–6, 158, 321–2, 343
Belgium 284, 294
Ben-Naftali, Orna 384–5
Bentham, Jeremy 62
Biafra 150, 173
Bilateral investment treaties 206–7, 349–77 *passim*
***Biwater Gauff (Tanzania) Ltd v United Republic of Tanzania* (2008)** 361–2
Bobbit, Philip 92
Bolivia 371
Borders
plebiscites 181
self-determination 169–81, 411
uti possidetis
decolonization 170–5
secessions and dissolutions 176–81
Bosnia 92–3, 120, 148, 171, 176, 189, 241, 286
Bougainville 150
Brandt Commission 28
Brandt, R.B. 389
Brandt, Willy 67
Brazil 243, 253, 331
***Brazil-Retreaded Tyres* (2007)** 334–6
Brezhnev Doctrine 142
Brierly, J.L. 33
Brown, Chris 299
Brundtland Commission 402–3
Buchanan, Allen 5, 31, 36, 57, 61, 118, 165, 167, 169, 214, 216, 297, 429
Bulgaria 232
Bull, Hedley 39
Burma 312

Calabresi, Guido 354
Cambodia 236, 244, 293, 294, 300, 301, 393
Canada 116, 146, 147, 150, 153, 179, 180, 231
Cane, Peter 6, 7, 46
Caney, Simon 86, 91, 97, 123–4, 403
Carbonneau, Thomas 371
***Caroline* Doctrine** 116, 118
Carr, E.H. 38, 119, 123, 125
Carson, Rachel 431
Cassese, Antonio 148, 431
Cassin, René 430
Chad 122
Chechnya 150, 161
Chehtman, Alejandro 283
Chile 196, 209, 279, 282, 284
China 130–1, 169, 189, 210, 213–14, 223, 228, 229, 238,244, 249, 284, 318; *see also* **United Nations,** Security Council
***CMS Gas Transmission Co. v Argentina* (2005)** 365, 365–69
Cohen, G.A. 34
Cohen, Joshua 32, 58
Cohen, Jean 97, 199, 216, 416
***Compañía de Aguas del Aconquija S.A. and Vivendi Universal S.A. v Argentina* (2007)** 356–7
Compliance with legal rules
corollary to thin justice pillars 88–9, 131, 208–9, 251–2, 260, 288, 311, 322, 391, 415
role in global justice 10, 14, 88–9, 401–4, 409, 442–4

Congo 113, 202, 321
Consequentialist reasoning
humanitarian intervention 301, 303
international investment law 375, 378
international organizations 250, 258–9
international trade law 344–5
non-intervention 135, 138
self-determination 151–2, 163–4, 174–8
sovereign immunity 204
thin justice framework 62–6, 69–70, 73, 79–84, 93, 94, 96, 413–4
use of force 109, 119–21, 124
Constructivism 39
***Continental Casualty Co. v Argentina* (2008)** 365–9
Convention Against Torture 1984 196, 202, 275, 276, 282, 286, 397
Convention on the Settlement of Disputes Between States and Nationals of Other States (1965) 365, 371–2
Copp, David 163–4, 165, 168
Cosmopolitanism
approaches to global justice 30–41, 58–61
emphasis on human rights 91, 414
humanitarian intervention 296–7, 301–4
recognition of states 189
self-defense 120, 123–6
self-determination 161, 164–8, 181
sovereign equality 213–8, 260
territorially limited duties and human rights 272
thicker global justice 417, 419
thin justice as cosmopolitan justice 69, 95–8, 411, 414
universal jurisdiction 283
see also **Global justice**
Costa Rica 250
Côte d'Ivoire 160, 172
Council of Europe 230–4
Covenant of the League of Nations 1920 104, 132, 190
Crawford, Neta 118
Crimea 150, 161, 169, 172, 176, 271
Critical approaches to international law 24–5
Croatia 148, 176, 177, 179
Cuba 105, 201
Customary international law
human rights 270
international investment law 353, 359, 363
necessity defense 293–4, 365–70
permanent sovereignty over natural resources 317
sovereign equality 193, 198, 209–10, 213
thicker global justice 430
universal jurisdiction 281, 288, 290
use of force 103, 106
uti possidetis 170
Cyprus 93, 150, 276
Czechoslovakia 55, 105, 122–3, 125, 150, 171, 176, 179
Darfur 242, 263, 286, 308
De Vattel, Emer 197
Decolonization *see* **Self-determination; *Uti possidetis***
Democracy
cosmopolitan democracy 32
Europe 233
self-determination 145, 157
thicker justice and 420
see also **Sovereign equality**
Deontological reasoning
humanitarian intervention 273, 300, 303, 305
international environmental law 405
international investment law 375
international organizations decisionmaking 236, 258
international trade law 345–6
non-intervention 137
selective membership policies 226
self-determination 166, 175
sovereign immunity 203
territorially-based duties 275
thin justice framework and 57–62, 80–3, 414
use of force 123
Dickinson, Edwin 194
Discrimination *see* **Non-discrimination**
Distributive justice
forms of justice 42–5
global justice debates 27–8, 31, 35, 58
thin justice and 90, 94–5
see also **International investment law; International trade law; Permanent sovereignty over natural resources**
Doha Declaration (2001) 331–3
Dokmanović, Slavko 138
Dower, Nigel 97
Dunant, Henri 430
Dworkin, Ronald 94

East Timor 293
***EC-Asbestos* (2001)** 334–6
***EC-Beef Hormones* (1998)** 334–6
***EC-Biotech* (2006 & 2008)** 334–6
Economic sanctions
extraterritorial assertion of jurisdiction 279
international trade 330
non-intervention 128–30, 136–41, 410
Responsibility to Protect 310
Security Council 238, 244–7, 249
Ecuador 361, 371
***EDF International et al. v Argentina* (2012)** 365–9
Egypt 116, 248
Eichmann, Adolf 137–8, 279, 283
***El Paso Energy International Co. v Argentina* (2011)** 365–9
El Salvador 108, 112
Elster, Jon 263

English School 38–40
Enlightened positivism 22
Enron Corp. v Argentina (2007) 365–9
Equality
thicker global justice and 419–20
thin justice and 94–5, 414
see also **Sovereign equality**
Eritrea 148, 150, 161, 171, 176, 224
Erskine, Toni 181
Estlund, David 89
Ethiopia 173, 271; *see also* **Eritrea**
European Convention on Human Rights 1950 (ECHR) 82, 230, 232, 269, 276, 352, 361
European Court of Human Rights 82, 136, 139, 196, 212, 246, 275–6, 311, 372
European Court of Justice (ECJ) 136, 246, 372
European Union (EU) 254
international trade 334–6, 342
membership rules 230–4
see also **European Court of Justice**
Exclusionary reasons
humanitarian intervention 306
human rights as 81–2, 84
international organizations decisionmaking 259
international trade law 344
non-intervention 135
self-determination 156, 161, 175, 178
sovereign equality 204, 258
use of force 109
Expropriation 359–64, 412
Extraterritoriality *see* **Human rights,** extraterritorial application

Fair and equitable treatment 352–59, 412
Fairness
corollary to thin justice pillars 87–8, 208–9, 215, 302, 310
role in global justice 26, 56, 221, 228–30, 232, 235–7, 243, 254, 409, 411, 422, 427–8, 430
Falk, Richard 217
Feinberg, Joel 44–5
Feldman, Noah 283
Ferguson, Niall 67
Finland 92, 132
Fiore, Pascalo 194
Fisse, Brent 46
Focarelli, Carlo 327
Force *see* **Use of force**
Foreign Corrupt Practices Act 1977 320
Forst, Rainer 56, 73
Framework Convention on Climate Change 1992 404
France 111, 147, 236, 279, 299, 333; *see also* **United Nations,** Security Council
Franck, Thomas 26, 35, 53, 59, 161, 295, 299
Friendly Relations Declaration 1970 104, 111, 127, 130, 133, 144–9, 156, 158–60, 178, 191, 194
Frost, Mervyn 30
Fuller, Lon 87–8, 228, 254, 260, 427

Gabcikovo-Nagymaros Project **(Hungary/ Slovakia) (1997)** 368–9
Galtung, Johan 66, 71
Garcia, Frank 341
General Agreement on Tariffs and Trade 1994 (GATT) *see* **International trade**
General Agreement on Trade in Services 1994 *see* **International trade**
General Assembly *see* **United Nations,** General Assembly
Geneva Conventions 1948 281, 384, 394
Genocide Convention 1948 241, 262, 292, 310
Georgia 116, 117, 160, 176, 178–9, 231
Germany 55, 105, 113, 122, 125, 196, 271, 372, 428
Glamis Gold Ltd v United States **(2009)** 353–4, 358, 373
Global justice
compared to distributive justice 43–4
compared to domestic justice 44–6
international relations approaches 38–40
legal approaches 19–28
philosophical approaches 29–37
thicker global justice 415–30
thin justice 65–99
alternatives to 91–5
cosmopolitanism and 95–8
two pillars 64–85
see also **Human rights; Justice; Peace**
Glover, Jonathan 67
Goodin, Robert 32, 53, 80–1, 83, 86, 161, 217, 270, 272, 318
Great Britain v Costa Rica **(1923)** 319
Greece 189
Griffin, James 73
Grotius, Hugo 39, 191
Guinea 160
Guinea-Bissau 160

Habermas, Jürgen 30, 297, 432
Hague Convention 1907 383
Hague, William 133
Haiti 107, 125, 160, 293
Hammarskjöld, Dag 408, 431
Hare, R.M. 43, 57, 261
Hart, H.L.A. 8, 43, 52–3, 88, 251, 261, 270, 416
Hedges, Chris 68
Held, David 30, 32, 36, 49, 56, 60, 262
Hezbollah 115
Higgins, Rosalyn 262, 430
Hill, Thomas 56
Hobbes, Thomas 39, 55–6, 65, 98, 197

Honduras 160, 336
Hooker, Brad 13, 83
Horowitz, Donald 153, 164, 179
Howse, Robert 327, 343
Human dignity
founding value of EU 231
impact of investment law 351
New Haven School 23
thin justice 78
see also **Human rights**
Human rights
basic human rights and thin justice 73–8
extraterritorial application 274–9; *see also* **Humanitarian intervention; Universal jurisdiction;**
functions for thin justice 79–83
notion of respect 78–9
territorial scope of 269–74
thicker global justice 417–21
see also **Global justice; individual norms under consideration; Territorial scope of human rights law**
Human Rights Watch 258
Human security 78
Humanitarian intervention
basic contours of law 292–6
philosophical approaches to 296–7
Responsibility to Protect 307–10
thin justice of norms of 296–307, 412
Hungary 269
Hurrell, Andrew 7

Iceland 209–10
Ideal vs. non-ideal theory 4–10
approach to international community 61
self-determination 152, 162, 169
thin justice 64–5, 77, 79, 88, 98, 408
thicker global justice 417
Ignatieff, Michael 82
Immunity *see* **Jurisdictional immunity**
Impartiality
decisionmaking by international institutions 261–3
ethical frameworks based on 57–63
justice as 43–4, 55–6
***Impregilo v Argentina* (2010)** 365–9
India 185, 253, 301, 428
Indonesia 236, 253
Inter-American Court of Human Rights 278
International Atomic Energy Agency 227
International Chamber of Commerce 371
International Civil Aviation Organization 61
International Commission on Intervention and State Sovereignty 302, 304–05, 307
International Committee of the Red Cross 209, 387, 389, 398
International community
global basic structure and 58–63
legal conception 59–60
International Convention on the Elimination of All Forms of Racial Discrimination 1965 145, 147
International Court of Justice (ICJ)
compulsory jurisdiction 428
distributive justice 28
human rights 270, 276, 279, 281, 292
international organizations membership policies 223
law of the sea 28, 209
necessity 294, 368–9
non-intervention 127, 132
proposals for recourse to 31, 33, 121, 125, 168
self-determination 147–8, 161, 168, 170
sovereign immunity 195–6, 202
universal jurisdiction 279, 281
use of force 105, 108, 112–13, 117, 121, 241, 294
International Covenant on Civil and Political Rights 1966 (ICCPR) 74–6, 152–3, 166, 202, 269, 275–6, 311, 394
International Covenant on Economic, Social and Cultural Rights 1966 (ICESCR) 74, 136, 207, 269, 330
International Criminal Court (ICC) Statute 33, 105, 242, 272, 286, 297, 311, 393, 395, 428
International criminal law 392–8, 413
International Criminal Tribunal for Rwanda (ICTR) 428
International Criminal Tribunal for the Former Yugoslavia (ICTY) 49, 138–9, 386, 428
International economic law *see* **International investment law; International Monetary Fund; International trade law**
International environmental law 398–405, 413
International humanitarian law 383–92, 413
International institutions *see* **International organizations**
International investment law
arbitral tribunals 371–3, 413
expropriation 359–64
fair and equitable treatment 352–9
fundamental duties 349–51
impact on human rights 351–2
necessity defense 364–70
policy space critique 352–70
systemic critique 373–7
International Labor Organization (ILO) 58, 234, 261–2
International law
actors 46–50
duties 50–54
general and special duties distinguished 52–4
global justice and 1–2, 6–8
institutions as key to 7
limits of 416–17

see also **individual norms under consideration; Compliance; Fairness; Global justice,** legal approaches
International Law Commission Articles on State Responsibility 211, 293–4, 365, 368, 393; *see also* **Necessity defense**
International Military Tribunal Charter 1945 105
International Monetary Fund (IMF) 137, 339, 424, 425
decisionmaking processes 254–60, 411
International organizations
actors in international law 49–50
decisionmaking processes
International Monetary Fund 254–60
United Nations 237–54, 411
institutional discretion 260–3
membership rules
Council of Europe and EU 230–4, 411
overview 222
participation of non-state actors 234–7
United Nations 223–6, 411
World Trade Organization 226–30, 411
role in theories of global justice 28, 168–9
see also **individual organizations**
International relations approaches to global justice 38–40
International trade law
Dispute Settlement Body cases 333–8, 412
Doha Declaration 331–3
effects on human rights 325–7
fundamental duties 323–5
Kimberley Process 328–31
policy space critique 327–38
role of two pillars of thin justice 322–3
systemic critique 340–7
TRIPS agreement 324, 331–3
World Trade Organization 338–40
Iran 167, 200–1, 245
Iraq 104, 107, 116–118, 136, 185, 224, 246, 248, 301, 318
Israel 68, 111, 113, 115, 116–18, 137–8, 240, 248, 276, 279, 284
Italy 196, 201, 277, 279, 284

Jackson, Robert 60, 298, 416
Jessup, Philip 200
Judt, Tony 67
Jurisdiction
basic rules 269–70
thin justice of norms on 271–4
see also **Humanitarian intervention; Human rights; Universal jurisdiction**
Jurisdictional immunity
forms of 195–97
thin justice of 200–05, 211–12
Jus ad bellum *see* **Use of force**
Jus in bello *see* **International humanitarian law**
Justice
definitions 42–3
distributive vs. other forms 43–44
global vs. domestic 44–5
see also **Global justice; Thin justice; individual norms under consideration**

Kant, Immanuel 4, 57, 65, 88, 95, 197
Kashmir 150
Katanga 150, 173
Kellogg-Briand Pact 1928 104
Kelsen, Hans 191, 194, 428–9
Kenya 139, 372
Keohane, Robert 38, 118
Keynes, John Maynard 107, 431
Khmer Rouge 236, 244, 293
Kimberley Process 328–31
Kingsbury, Benedict 216
Kissinger, Henry 285
Koh, Tommy 431
Kokott, Juliane 192, 199
Koskenniemi, Martti 25, 242, 432
Korea-Beef **(2000)** 335–6
Kosovo 33, 121, 147, 154, 156, 168, 186, 188, 294–5, 299, 302
Krajina 177
Krisch, Nico 93, 196, 302
Kritsiotis, Dino 59
Kurdistan 150
Kuwait 104, 107, 136, 185, 196, 224, 246, 318
Kyoto Protocol (2002) 404–5

Lamy, Pascal 326
Langer, Máximo 285
Lasswell, Harold 23
Latvia 129, 154
Lauterpacht, Hersch 66, 431
Law of the sea *see* **United Nations,** Convention on the Law of the Sea
League of Nations *see* **Covenant of the League of Nations 1920**
Lebanon 115, 240, 393
Legal approaches to global justice 19–28
Lemkin, Raphael 431
LG&E v Argentina **(2006)** 365–369
Libya 107, 122, 134, 201, 286, 293, 298
Low, Patrick 346
Luban, David 123–5

MacCormick, Neil 22, 55
Macedonia 189
Madison, J. 69, 154
Malaysia 113
Mali 293
Margalit, Avishai 162–3, 166–7
Mason, Andrew 273, 303
May, Larry 119–20, 122–3, 204
McDougal, Myres 23
McMahan, Jeff 390–2, 406

Melamed, Douglas 354
Mertens, Thomas 32
Mexico 139, 257, 353, 355, 362, 363
Miller, David 76–7, 96, 165, 273, 300, 416, 418, 422
Minorities 48, 146–7, 153–4, 165–7, 211, 214, 424; *see also* **Self-determination; *Uti possidetis***
Moldava 176, 178
Monnet, Jean 431
Montenegro 150, 161
Montevideo Convention 1933 185–9, 223
Morgenthau, Hans 38
Most-favored nation treatment
  international investment law 349
  international trade law 323–5, 329, 334, 345
Munich Agreement 1938 55, 105, 119–20, 125
Murphy, Liam 86

Nagel, Thomas 58
Nagorno-Karabakh 150, 176, 244
Nansen, Fridtjof 430
Nardin, Terry 31, 56, 288, 296–7
***National Grid v Argentina* (2008)** 365–9
National treatment
  international investment law 349, 350
  international trade law 323–4, 334
Necessity defense 211, 293–4, 364–70
Neuffer, Elizabeth 68
New Haven School 22–4
New Zealand 147
Nicaragua 108, 112; *see also* **Use of force; Non-intervention**
Nickel, James 73, 74
Nigeria 24
Non-discrimination
  European Union 231, 234
  human rights 76, 93, 95, 154–7, 419; *see also* **Self-determination; *Uti possidetis***
  international investment law 349–50, 360, 362–3
  international trade law 323–7, 330, 333–5
Non-governmental organizations 50, 234–6, 252, 338, 397, 429
  see also **Amnesty International; Human Rights Watch**
Non-intervention
  ban on use of force distinguished 126–9
  push for more robust norms 129–32
  push for weaker norms
    aid to rebel movements 132–6
    arrest of war criminals 137–41
    economic sanctions 136–7
  thin justice of 141–2, 410
North American Free Trade Agreement 1992 (NAFTA) 350, 361
North Atlantic Treaty 1949 106
North Atlantic Treaty Organization (NATO) 33, 106, 121, 138, 294, 295, 386
North Korea 107, 201, 229
Northern Ireland 92–3
Nozick, Robert 80

Obama, Barack 392
Ocalan, Abdullah 139
Ogaden 173
O'Neill, Onora 51, 181
Organization for Security and Co-operation in Europe (OSCE) 69, 186, 231, 320
Organization of African Unity (OAU) 122, 159; *see also* **African Union**
Organization of American States (OAS) 160, 187, 320
Organization of the Islamic Conference (OIC) 234
Owen, David 176–7

Pacifism 119–23, 391
Pakistan 114, 115, 154, 171, 301
Palestine 68, 147, 223, 248, 276, 285; *see also* **Israel**
Palme Commission 28
Papua New Guinea 150
Peace
  defined 65–6
  pillar of thin justice 65–73
  role in thicker justice 417
  see also **individual norms under consideration; Thin justice**
Peoples *see* **Self-determination**
Permanent Court of Arbitration (PCA) 190
Permanent Court of International Justice (PCIJ) 51, 126, 137
Permanent Five (P5)
  Security Council membership 243–7, 252–3
  veto power 247–52
Permanent sovereignty over natural resources 316–22, 412
Peru 209
Peters, Anne 22, 309
Pettit, Philip 53, 270
Philippines 401
Philosophical approaches to global justice 29–37, 58
  ideal vs. non-ideal theory 4–6
  see also **individual norms under consideration**
Philpott, Daniel 71, 157–8
Pildes, Richard 81
Pillay, Navanathem 431
Pinker, Steven 72
Pinochet, Augusto 141, 196, 279, 282, 284, 285
Pogge, Thomas 31, 34, 36, 57, 90, 273, 319–22, 341, 343, 374
Preuss, Ulrich 127
Preventive self-defense 115–19, 421

Quebec 146, 150, 153, 168, 179–80

Rawls, John 1, 2–3, 6
difference principle 26, 27, 31, 57, 341, 345, 416
global justice scholarship and 23, 26, 27, 30–3, 35, 55–7, 60–5, 216
justice definitions and conceptions 42–4
self-determination 155, 422
sovereign equality 216
thicker global justice and 418, 420, 431
thin justice and 55–7, 60–5, 71–2, 74–5, 88, 90
use of force and non-intervention 124–5, 130
Raz, Joseph 4, 51, 74, 81, 162–3, 166–7, 422
Reagan Doctrine 142
Recognition of states 184–9
Reinold, Theresa 114
Reisman, W. Michael 24, 88, 297
Responsibility to Protect 307–10; *see also* **United Nations,** Security Council
Rhodesia 107, 136, 186
Risse, Mathias 86, 319–20
Risse, Thomas 345
Rodin, David 106, 119–22, 124
Roht-Arriaza, Naomi 404
Romania 232
Roosevelt, Eleanor 431
Roth, Brad 27, 130, 211–12, 216
Ruggie, John 376
Rule of law 14, 262, 310, 407
Council of Europe 232, 234
see also **Fairness**
Russia 47, 92, 116, 127, 129, 154, 160, 161, 169, 171–2, 176, 178, 228, 232, 271, 299
see also **Soviet Union, United Nations,** Security Council
Rwanda 68,189, 249, 263, 300, 302, 304, 395

Sabel, Charles 58
Saloman, Margot 341
Satz, Debra 343
Saudi Arabia 196
SAUR v Argentina **(2012)** 365–9
Schachter, Oscar 431
Scheffler, Samuel 95–6
Secession; *see* **Self-determination;** ***Uti possidetis***
Security Council *see* **United Nations,** Security Council
Self-defense
basic contours and justice of 103–11, 410
broad right of
anticipatory self-defense 115–119
non-state actors 111–115
preventive self-defense 115–119, 421
narrow right of
human rights abusers 123–6
pacifist challenge 119–23
Self-determination
basic contours of norm 143–9
communitarian and cosmopolitan approaches 161–9
decolonization 145–6, 151, 154–5, 158–9
minority rights 146–7, 152–4, 165
secession 146–9, 150–57, 160–69
thin justice of norms 410–11
human rights pillar 152–7
other rationales 157–8
peace pillar 150–2
see also ***Uti possidetis***
Sempra Energy v Argentina **(2007)** 365–9
Sen, Amartya 73
Senegal 279
Serbia 120–21, 148, 150, 154, 156, 171, 177, 241, 294
Shany, Yuval 278, 384–5
Shue, Henry 74–6, 78, 80, 378, 432
Sierra Leone 294
Sikkink, Kathryn 286
Simma, Bruno 22, 59, 295
Simpson, Gerry 190–1, 239, 245, 247
Singapore 150
Singer, Peter 32, 61, 69, 124, 284, 298, 315
Slater, Jerome 297
Snyder, Timothy 67
Somalia 107, 125, 173, 185, 271, 293
South Africa 127, 136, 145, 189, 224, 240, 289, 331–2, 364
South Korea 107
South Ossetia 150, 161, 176, 179
South Sudan 148, 150, 161, 176, 179, 186, 188, 224
Sovereign equality
basic components of 192–7
cosmopolitan approaches to 213–17
definitional disagreements 190–2
stronger sovereign equality 205–12
thin justice of 197–205, 411
weaker sovereign equality 212–17
see also **Jurisdictional immunity**
Sovereign immunity *see* **Jurisdictional immunity**
Soviet Union 67, 107, 111, 150, 154, 171, 176, 186, 188, 189, 223, 231
see also **Russia; United Nations,** Security Council
Spain 127, 170, 279, 280, 282, 284–5, 424
Sri Lanka 150, 241, 308
S.S. 'Lotus' **(France v Turkey) (1927)** 51–2, 284
State system 4, 85–87, 97, 123–4, 149, 214, 218, 415
Stein, Eric 431
Stiglitz, Joseph 257
Stilz, Anna 157

Strauss, Andrew 217
Sudan 148, 150, 176, 229, 263, 308
Sudetenland 105, 122–3, 271
***Suez, Vivendi, and AWG v Argentina* (2010)** 365–9
Sweden 92, 132, 424
Switzerland 246, 279
Syria 112, 133–6, 240, 249, 251, 263, 293, 294, 300, 308

Taiwan 46, 186, 197, 223–4, 238
Taliban 112, 236–7, 245, 246
Tamil Tigers 241
Tan, Kok-Chor 32
Tanzania 294, 301, 356
Tasioulas, John 26
***Técnicas Medioambientales Tecmed S.A. v Mexico* (2003)** 353–5, 358, 361
Teitel, Ruti 327, 343
Territorial scope of human rights law
  basic rules 269–70
  extraterritorial application 274–9
  thin justice of 271–4, 411–12
  universal jurisdiction 279–90
  see also **Humanitarian intervention**
Tesón, Fernando 26–7
Thicker global justice
  definition and pillars of 415–21
  process to achieve 421–30
  see also **Thin justice**
Thin justice
  additional components of framework 85–9
  compared to other visions of global justice 91–5
  cosmopolitanism and 95–8
  definition 89–90
  pillars of 64–85, 414
  review of core norms of international law 410–15
  see also **individual norms under consideration; Global justice; Thicker global justice**
Third World Approaches to International Law (TWAIL) 28
Thürer, Daniel 151
Tibet 150, 284
Todorov, Tzvetan 199
***Total v Argentina* (2010)** 365–9
Trachtman, Joel 346, 375, 376
Trade-Related Aspects of Intellectual Property Rights 1994 (TRIPS) 324, 331–3, 340–1, 345
Transdneistria 176
Treaties 53–54
  human rights 74, 269–70
  sovereign equality 199–200, 206–09
  see also **Customary international law; Territorial scope of human rights law**
Turkey 139, 147, 150, 232–4, 276

Uganda 122, 294, 301
Ukraine 150, 161, 171–2, 176
United Kingdom 133, 196, 209, 248, 279, 294, 298–9; *see also* **United Nations,** Security Council
United Nations
  admission and membership 223–6
  Charter
    basic principles of peace and human rights 65
    humanitarian intervention 293–6
    membership rules 222–6
    principle of self-determination 143, 144
    sovereign equality 190
    use of force and
      self-defense 103–11, 119–23
    see also **Friendly Relations Declaration**
  Commission on Human Security 78
  Convention Against Corruption 2003 320
  Convention Against Torture 1985 196, 202, 279, 281, 397
  Convention on the Law of Sea 1982 (UNCLOS) 51, 193, 208, 209, 317, 318
  decisionmaking processes
    General Assembly and Security Council contrasted 237–8
    General Assembly powers 239–40, 252
    reform proposals 252–4
    Security Council 240–52
  Economic, Social and Cultural Rights Committee 79, 136, 330, 404, 431–2
  Framework Convention on Climate Change (1992) 404
  General Assembly
    decisionmaking contrasted with Security Council 237–8
    powers 239–40, 252
    sovereign equality 217
  Human Rights Committee 152–3, 202, 273, 275
  Human Rights Council and Commission 159, 229, 427
  Security Council
    decisionmaking processes 240–54
    humanitarian intervention 293, 298–9
    membership 240–7
    Permanent Five (P5) 243–52
    proposed reforms to 252–4
    relation to General
      Assembly 239–40, 252
    Responsibility to Protect 307–10
    veto 247–52
United States 147, 154, 200–1, 271, 280, 284, 362, 393, 421
  customary international law 209–10
  extraterritorial application of human rights law 275, 276–8
  humanitarian intervention 299, 301
  international humanitarian law 392, 394
  International Monetary Fund 255–6

international trade 320, 332–4, 339, 342
see also **Non-intervention; United Nations, Security Council; Use of force**
Universal jurisdiction
basic rules 279–82
thin justice of norms on 283–90, 412
Unrepresented Nations and Peoples Organization (UNPO) 161–2
***US-Clove Cigarettes* (2012)** 334–6
***US-Country of Origin Labelling Requirements* (2012)** 334–6
***US-Gambling* (2005)** 336
Use of force
anticipatory self-defense 115–19
ban on intervention distinguished 126–9
basic contours of norm 103–7
preventive self-defense 115–19, 421
self-defense
pressures for broad right 111–19
pressures for narrow right 119–126
thin justice of the ban 107–11, 410
see also **Humanitarian intervention; Non-intervention; United Nations,** Security Council
Uti possidetis
basic contours of norm 170–72
thin justice regarding decolonization 172–5
thin justice regarding secessions and dissolutions 176–81

Van der Stoel, Max 431
Venezuela 371
Versailles Treaty 1919 125
Veto *see* **United Nations,** Security Council
Vienna Convention on the Law of Treaties 1969 (VCLT) 54, 105, 193, 206–8, 320
Vietnam 122, 293, 294, 301
Vincent, J.R. 97, 130
Von Moltke, Helmut 388
Pufendorf, Samuel 197

Wai, Robert 46
Waldron, Jeremy 45–6, 87, 158
Walzer, Michael 8, 29, 90, 108, 120–1, 158, 163, 179, 273, 296, 389–92
Washington Consensus 351
Webster, Daniel 116
Wellman, Christopher 164–5, 168, 233, 283, 303
Wheeler, Nicholas 303
Wight, Martin 39
Williams, Bernard 233
Woods, Ngaire 259, 340
World Bank 137, 254, 363-4
World Trade Organization (WTO) 58, 210, 235, 412, 425, 427
Dispute Settlement Body cases 333–8
Doha Declaration 331–3
institutional flaws and human rights 338–40
membership rules 228–30, 411
see also **International trade law**

Young, Iris 48
Yugoslavia 68, 69, 120, 186–9, 223, 224, 241, 279, 294, 393, 395; *see also* **Self-determination**

Zambia 344
Ziegler, Jean 258
Zimbabwe 186